FLEETWOOD MAC

ALL THE
SONGS

The Story Behind Every Track

OLIVIER ROUBIN AND ROMUALD OLLIVIER

FLEETWOOD MAC
ALL THE
SONGS

The Story Behind Every Track

BLACK DOG
& LEVENTHAL
PUBLISHERS
NEW YORK

CONTENTS

30

70

102

140

156

198

224

242

264

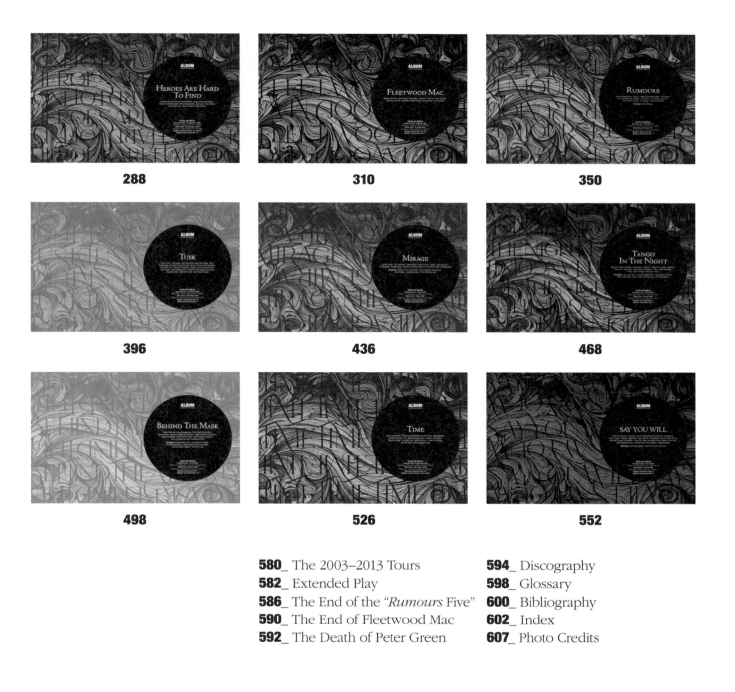

THE FIFTEEN LIVES
OF FLEETWOOD MAC

The echoes of a rough blues, with swaggering bottleneck blows on screaming guitars, escape from the fashionable clubs of Swinging London: the Ram Jam, the Marquee, the Nag's Head...This music, imported from the United States, which thrilled the British youth of the sixties, was the prodrome of a cultural revolution called the British blues boom. One of the main architects of that movement was Peter Green, the co-founder and first leader of Fleetwood Mac. As early as the mid-1960s, the walls of London were adorned with inscriptions glorifying Peter, the "Green God," drawn by hero worshippers wishing to dethrone Eric Clapton. These celebrate the mystical power of this virtuoso guitarist to whom we owe the albums *Black Magic Woman* and *Green Manalishi*. In addition to his virtuosity on the guitar, Green also seems to have been a visionary. Indeed, when he left John Mayall's Bluesbreakers in 1967 to set up his new project, he gave it the names of his two playing partners, drummer Mick Fleetwood and bassist John McVie: Fleetwood...Mac. These are the same people who would remain, for more than 50 years, the same members of a very successful band troubled by the repeated defections of its musicians.

The chronic instability that should have caused Fleetwood Mac to falter has, on the contrary, pushed it to reinvent itself and develop an admirable resilience. Over the course of the fifteen lineups, each member has contributed not only to the survival of Fleetwood Mac but also to its renewal, by bringing to it various musical inspirations. That includes, in addition to the idealist Peter Green and the indestructible Mick Fleetwood, the monolithic John McVie, the mischievous Jeremy Spencer, the sunny Christine McVie, the tormented Danny Kirwan, the innovators Bob Welch and Lindsey Buckingham, the sorceress Stevie Nicks, the energetic Billy Burnette, the skillful Rick Vito, or the more ephemeral but essential Bob Brunning, Bob Weston, Dave Walker, Bekka Bramlett, Dave Mason, Mike Campbell, and Neil Finn.

Beyond the names and faces, it is the evolution of the group that fascinates. Fleetwood Mac became an American pop hit machine in only ten years, reached the peak of its artistry by sublimating its music with a consummate science of melody and stunning vocal harmonies, and changed the course of pop history by driving its eleventh opus, *Rumours*, to rise up among the ten best-selling albums of all time.

It is their extraordinary journey that this book retraces through 320 songs, each of which contains a fragment of history of this group of ever-changing geometry, and which made its creations the expression of its internal torments and its achievements, its loves, and its resentments.

FIFTEEN LINEUPS OF FLEETWOOD MAC

Fleetwood Mac Version 1

Period: 1967 / **Members:** Peter Green / Mick Fleetwood / Jeremy Spencer / Bob Brunning

Brief History: In the summer of 1967 guitarist Peter Green and drummer Mick Fleetwood left John Mayall's band, John Mayall and the Bluesbreakers, and decided to form their own group. They asked bassist John McVie to join them, but McVie was reluctant to give up the stability afforded by the Bluesbreakers. Bob Brunning joined in his place. Guitarist Jeremy Spencer completed Fleetwood Mac's original lineup. Peter Green was confident that John McVie would soon join them…

Fleetwood Mac Version 2

Period: 1967–1968 / **Members:** Peter Green / Mick Fleetwood / Jeremy Spencer / John McVie

Brief History: Peter Green was right, and John McVie quickly replaced Bob Brunning. Meanwhile, Fleetwood Mac moved toward a kind of blues sound that was inspired by genre pioneers Elmore James and Robert Johnson, and which the band took up under the impetus of its Peter Green–Jeremy Spencer guitar partnership. With this configuration in place, the band recorded the first milestones of its discography—*Fleetwood Mac* and *Mr. Wonderful*.

Fleetwood Mac Version 3

Period: 1968–1970 / **Members:** Peter Green / Mick Fleetwood / Jeremy Spencer / John McVie / Danny Kirwan

Brief History: At the end of 1968, Peter Green invited Danny Kirwan, a guitarist and composer who pulled the public's attention away from Green himself, to join the group. This changed the face of the band. Now with five members, and still devoted to the blues, this new iteration of the band appealed to a wider audience, with more pop-rock-sounding songs like "Man of the World." Unfortunately, the album *Then Play On* and the single "The Green Manalishi (with the Two Prong Crown)," was Peter Green's swan song with the group.

Fleetwood Mac Version 4

Period: 1970–1971 / **Members:** Mick Fleetwood / Jeremy Spencer / John McVie / Danny Kirwan / Christine McVie

Brief History: After the loss of their front man, Mac managed to reinvent themselves, and on *Kiln House* they welcomed Christine McVie on piano and backing vocals. Though she was not credited on the album, she officially joined the band after its release. Then, in early 1971, Jeremy Spencer disappeared just as he was due to appear on stage for a Fleetwood Mac show. He joined a religious group called the Children of God. The band had to replace him…with Peter Green, who played the rest of the tour. But Green didn't officially return to the fold.

Fleetwood Mac Version 5

Period: 1971–1972 / **Members:** Mick Fleetwood / John McVie / Danny Kirwan / Christine McVie / Bob Welch

Brief History: The brain drain finally stopped with the arrival of Californian guitarist Bob Welch, who offered new and more melodic perspectives. Welch was already highly experienced, having previously worked with bands including the Seven Souls and Head West. Two new albums were released during this period: *Future Games* in 1971 and *Bare Trees* in 1972.

Fleetwood Mac Version 6

Period: 1972–1973 / **Members:** Mick Fleetwood / John McVie / Christine McVie / Bob Welch / Dave Walker / Bob Weston

Brief History: Danny Kirwan and Bob Welch were never to go on vacation together. By the time Kirwan was kicked out of the band in 1972, he had become so isolated from the rest of the group that he was communicating only with Mick Fleetwood. Bob Weston then joined the band as guitarist, while Dave Walker made a fleeting appearance as a singer—just long enough to be credited on two songs off the *Penguin* album.

Fleetwood Mac Version 7

Period: 1973 / **Members:** Mick Fleetwood / John McVie / Christine McVie / Bob Welch / Bob Weston

Brief History: The group re-formed as a quintet for the 1973 album *Mystery to Me*. The songwriting duo of Christine McVie and Bob Welch managed to find their feet, but the balance was upset when Bob Weston had an affair with Mick Fleetwood's wife. When Fleetwood found out, Weston was out of the band. As if that wasn't enough, the band's manager decided to appropriate the Fleetwood Mac brand and let other musicians play under its name—a grim chapter in the band's history that would later end up in court.

Fleetwood Mac Version 8

Period: 1973–1974 / **Members:** Mick Fleetwood / John McVie / Christine McVie / Bob Welch

Brief History: With Bob Weston abruptly out of the band, Mick Fleetwood asserted himself as captain of the ship. Fleetwood Mac settled in California and recorded the album *Heroes Are Hard to Find*, which climbed the US charts all the way to number thirty-four. Unfortunately, touring was a punishing experience, and that, coupled with the still unresolved imbroglio surrounding the "fake" Fleetwood Mac, proved to be too much for Bob Welch, who eventually left the band.

Fleetwood Mac Version 9
Period: 1975–1987 / **Members:** Mick Fleetwood / John McVie / Christine McVie / Lindsey Buckingham / Stevie Nicks

Brief History: Following Welch's departure, the band started looking for new blood. Mick Fleetwood remembered hearing the song "Frozen Love"—performed by the Buckingham Nicks duo in early 1974—and he was particularly taken by the guitarist's deft touch. He invited Buckingham to join Fleetwood Mac, but Lindsey insisted that his girlfriend, Stevie Nicks, be part of the adventure. Charmed by her aura, Mick Fleetwood agreed. The band went on to become extremely popular, releasing a string of successful albums: *Fleetwood Mac*, *Rumours*, and *Tusk*.

Fleetwood Mac Version 10
Period: 1987–1991 / **Members:** Mick Fleetwood / John McVie / Christine McVie / Stevie Nicks / Billy Burnette / Rick Vito

Brief History: Some members of the band, including Stevie Nicks, Lindsey Buckingham, and Christine McVie, tried their hand at solo careers. Meanwhile, Mick Fleetwood was officially declared bankrupt. Tensions that had accumulated over more than a decade took their toll on the band's unity, and Lindsey Buckingham left with a bang after his rescue of *Tango in the Night*. Two new guitarists were needed to compensate for this loss: Billy Burnette and Rick Vito, with whom the Mac recorded *Behind the Mask* in 1990.

Fleetwood Mac Version 11
Period: 1991–1995 / **Members:** Mick Fleetwood / John McVie / Christine McVie / Billy Burnette / Bekka Bramlett / Dave Mason

Brief History: Rick Vito bowed out of the group in 1991, but the departure of Stevie Nicks left the biggest mark on the band and plunged them into disarray. How could they recover? With the arrival of a new singer, Bekka Bramlett (daughter of American blues musicians Delaney & Bonnie), and a renowned guitarist, Dave Mason (Traffic). This new configuration resulted in the 1995 album *Time*, which was a resounding commercial failure. Following this setback, Bramlett, Mason, and Burnette left Fleetwood Mac.

Fleetwood Mac Version 12
Period: 1997–1998 / **Members:** Mick Fleetwood / John McVie / Christine McVie / Lindsey Buckingham / Stevie Nicks

Brief History: The departures of Bramlett, Mason, and Burnette could've spelled the end for the Mac, but instead they provided the opportunity for a long-awaited reunion. For the first time since 1982, Lindsey Buckingham, Stevie Nicks, John McVie, Mick Fleetwood, and Christine McVie reunited onstage at Bill Clinton's presidential inauguration gala on January 19, 1993. The reunion resulted in the live album *The Dance*, which was released on May 23, 1997, and became the first Fleetwood Mac album since 1982's *Mirage* to go to the top of the US charts. But after the forty-four-date tour that followed the band's reunion, Christine McVie announced her retirement in 1998.

Fleetwood Mac Version 13
Period: 1998–2013 / **Members:** Mick Fleetwood / John McVie / Lindsey Buckingham / Stevie Nicks

Brief History: With Christine McVie out of the music business, Lindsey Buckingham assumed the responsibility of composing the bulk of Fleetwood Mac's next album, which was going to be based, in part, on his solo opus *Gift of Screws*. That album was originally scheduled for release in 2001, but it didn't actually come out until 2008. In the meantime, a number of other tracks were "salvaged" for *Say You Will*, the group's 2003 album, which also featured compositions from Stevie Nicks. A commercial success, the album was a landmark event in that it was Fleetwood Mac's first album released without Christine McVie since 1970. After the release of *Say You Will*, the band put its discography on hold for a decade, until the *Extended Play* EP was released in 2013.

Fleetwood Mac Version 14
Period: 2014–2017 / **Members:** Mick Fleetwood / John McVie / Lindsey Buckingham / Stevie Nicks / Christine McVie

Brief History: In September 2013, Christine McVie finally reappeared onstage alongside her fellow bandmates during a concert in London before making her official, full-time return to the group in 2014. The band began working on new material, but hopes of a new Mac album never came to fruition.

Fleetwood Mac Version 15
Period: 2018–2022 / **Members:** Mick Fleetwood / John McVie / Stevie Nicks / Christine McVie / Mike Campbell / Neil Finn

Brief History: Hopes for a new Mac album waned as the years passed, and fans had to content themselves with seeing the band on tour. In the meantime, the relationship between Stevie Nicks and Lindsey Buckingham, which had been stormy for so many years, once again pushed the guitarist toward the exit. Before setting out on their next tour, the band replaced Buckingham with Mike Campbell, the former guitarist for Tom Petty and the Heartbreakers, and Crowded House front man Neil Finn. From then on, niceties were occasionally exchanged via the press, but otherwise Buckingham and the rest of the band went their separate ways. Difficult times in the years ahead—including Lindsey Buckingham's health problems and Christine McVie's death on November 30, 2022—spelled the end of the road for fans, who undoubtedly would have loved to see more new work from the group.

MICK FLEETWOOD, ENFANT TERRIBLE

By family tradition, the Fleetwoods have always served their country. Mick Fleetwood's grandfather, who was killed in Italy during the First World War, never knew his son John, who was born in Liverpool in 1915. Raised by his mother in Ireland, John joined the Royal Air Force in 1936 and was decorated during the Second World War, climbing as high as the rank of major. It was not far from the St. Devel airfield in Redruth, Cornwall—where his father John had been posted—that Michael John Kells Fleetwood, known as Mick, was born on June 24, 1947. He was welcomed by his parents and his two sisters, Susan and Sally.

A Chaotic Education

Three years later, the Fleetwood family moved to Egypt, where John had been transferred for work. Although he has often described his childhood as a happy one, Mick experienced terrible growing pains during his younger years, and he was forced to wear braces on his legs at night. This suffering continued when the family moved to Norway, where Mick's father took up his new post at a NATO base. Mick's schooling followed the dictates of his father's postings, and like most sons of English families serving abroad, Mick was sent to boarding school in England to help prepare him for his first major school exams. Far from his family, in an old manor house somewhere in the middle of Sussex, England, young Mick was inevitably overcome by feelings of melancholy, which were compounded by the difficulties he experienced with his schoolwork. His teachers failed to understand Mick's problem, and he became fatally allergic to all forms of learning. A diagnosis was made much later in his life: Mick was dyslexic. Fortunately, Mick's relationship with the other kids at school was good, and he managed to save face in sports, where he showed real aptitude. When his parents, who had relocated back to England after his father's retirement, moved Mick to another school to save him from having to repeat a year of classwork, he decided to take off. Picked up by a motorcyclist, the young runaway was dropped off at the nearest road station before eventually returning to his parents. They took Mick back to school, but he left for good a year later after failing his exams.

An Obsession with the Drums

All of this happened by the time Mick was thirteen years old, and at this point he was really only interested in one thing: music in general, and drums in particular. That year, Mick's father, who also played the drums, gave him his first kit. This drum set enabled Mick to play along with the hits he heard broadcast on the radio, and he spent a lot of time focusing on tracks by the Everly Brothers and the Shadows, whose drummer was Tony Meehan. Mick was not finished with his studies, however. In 1961, he enrolled at the King's School in Sherborne. There, his obsession with drums continued to take precedence over everything else in his life, and while his repeated exam failures inevitably dented his self-esteem, he vowed to become a professional drummer within the next two years. Mick's parents were worried about his future following his latest academic setback. If their now fifteen-year-old son didn't succeed at school, how would he ever get into a university? Eventually, John and Bridget Fleetwood accepted the situation. Their eldest daughter, Sally, was married to an art dealer and studying in London. She had a room where Mick could live, so the decision was made to send Mick to stay with her so he could pursue his dream of becoming a drummer. (Mick's other sister, Susan, was away at drama school and studying to become an actress, so therefore unable to host her brother). With no job and no real education, Mick left for London with a brand-new Rogers drum kit that his father had just given him and moved into his sister's attic.

Jumping in the Deep End of Swinging London

If Mick was going to succeed in the music business, he had to learn to support himself. He got a job at Liberty's, a chic West End department store, from which he was quickly fired. Without really knowing what tomorrow would bring, but with the firm conviction that something positive would eventually happen, Mick devoted himself entirely to the drums. One day, while playing in his sister's garage, the door opened and a boy his own age popped his head in to listen. Mick recognized him: It was Peter Bardens, who lived in the neighborhood. Peter was an organist with a trio that had already played a few gigs at the Marquee and other London clubs. Bardens had a plan for Mick: The Senders, another local band, were looking for a drummer to play a gig at a Catholic youth club. Thus, it came to be that Mick played his first date as a member of a real band. And he would get paid for it! In addition to all this excitement, Mick

Already a charismatic figure, Mick Fleetwood (circa 1965) did not excel at school and set out, at the age of 15, to become a professional musician.

also learned that Peter was planning to set up a pop band to try and capitalize on the popularity of bands like the Beatles and the Rolling Stones.

In July 1963, the Cheynes took their first steps with Peter Bardens on organ and vocals, Peter Hollis on bass, Eddie Lynch on guitar and vocals, and Mick Fleetwood on drums. Their gigging partners included up-and-coming bands such as the Yardbirds, the Animals, the Spencer Davis Group, and Manfred Mann. Of course, their repertoire included very few original songs, and they mostly played classics by Bo Diddley, Buddy Holly, and Little Richard. No matter because Mick was exactly where he had always dreamed of being: playing music in clubs that he was too young to get into. Luckily his tall stature was an asset, and nobody ever asked him about his age. The Cheynes were doing very well, and they kept booking one concert after another. They even played in Liverpool at the legendary Cavern Club, home of the Beatles at the beginning of Beatlemania.

From Dream to Reality

Eventually, Mick managed to save enough money to move out of his sister's attic. He moved in with a singer named Roger Peacock, who joined the Cheynes in April 1964. Peacock took up with a young girl named Jenny Boyd, the sister of Pattie Boyd, who was then the girlfriend of Beatles

guitarist George Harrison. Mick stared to have feelings for Jenny, but he managed not to act on his feelings...for a time.

The band recorded three singles in 1964, but none of them became hits. As the Cheynes slowly but surely headed for oblivion, Mick made the acquaintance of John McVie, then a bassist playing with the prestigious Bluesbreakers, another blues powerhouse group playing on the London circuit. Their acquaintanceship gradually developed into a friendship as the two men spent time together, talked about girls, drank many pints, and talked about music—but they did not actually play together. In the spring of 1965, the Cheynes split up. Peter Bardens joined Van Morrison's band, Them, and Mick was hired by the Bo Street Runners. At the same time, Jenny Boyd left Roger Peacock for Mick. Peacock was furious, and he went so far as to threaten Mick with a knife in front of the Marquee Club in London.

Mick did not stay with the Bo Street Runners for long. After a recording session that resulted in a single titled "Baby Never Say Goodbye," Peter Bardens asked him to join a new instrumental group with him on organ, Mick on drums, Dave Ambrose on bass, and Mick Parker on guitar. Parker left the band shortly thereafter, and an audition was held to choose his successor. This was when a young guitarist from Putney, Peter Green, appeared on the scene.

PETER GREEN, THE BLUES ORIGINS OF FLEETWOOD MAC

Peter Allen Greenbaum was born on October 29, 1946, in the London borough of Tower Hamlets, in the neighborhood of Bethnal Green, where the famous Tower of London hovers over the surrounding area. Like the precious crown jewels that are housed inside the Tower of London, young Peter—who was a self-taught guitarist with a virtuosity comparable to that of Eric Clapton—was metaphorically viewed as a precious jewel in his own right. Unfortunately, his career was short lived, but his artistry had a decisive impact on British blues and on the destiny of Fleetwood Mac, which he formed with Mick Fleetwood in 1967.

A Self-Taught Genius

Fame and fortune were not preordained for Peter, born the youngest of four siblings in a working-class Jewish family from London's East End. In the early 1950s, the Greenbaums moved to Putney, a quieter, residential neighborhood where the young boy would spend his formative years. His parents could not afford to send him to one of the capital's posh schools, but this mattered little, since young Peter disliked studying and never dreamed of becoming a lawyer or a doctor. His only passion, which helped him manage the boredom of his schooling, was music. He was about ten years old when one of his brothers taught him a few guitar chords, and from then on nothing else was as important to Peter as music. The pupil soon outstripped the teacher, and Peter learned more on his own by listening to the blues records he found lying around his house. His parents, of course, would have preferred to see him studying rather than spending his time strumming his guitar or dismantling and reassembling the family record player to figure out how it worked, but in 1961 the realities of the Greenbaum family's economic situation caught up with him. To help support his family, Peter was forced to take work as a laborer and then as a butcher's apprentice. Still, he never abandoned his dream of becoming a musician, and he devoted all his free time to his ambition.

Peter Greenbaum's Transformation

Although his first musical influences were Muddy Waters, Howlin' Wolf, Freddie King, John Lee Hooker, B. B. King, and Sister Rosetta Tharpe, Green took his first steps as a professional musician not with a guitar, or by playing blues, but with a bass and a pop-inflected sound. At the age of fifteen, the young amateur musician became the bassist for Bobby Dennis and the Dominoes, a local band that played a mix of current hits and rock'n'roll standards, including covers of the Shadows, whose lead guitarist, Hank Marvin, was a major influence on young Greenbaum. It was also around this time that he decided to shorten his name to Peter Green.

The discovery of Eric Clapton, who had joined the Yardbirds in 1963 and whose reputation was growing in London, confirmed to Peter that the blues were where his true passions lay. The young man became a major fan of the guitarist. Whenever he had the chance, Peter went to see Clapton play live at the Crawdaddy Club, a musical venue where another influential band called the Grebbels opened for the Yardbirds. The Grebbels' guitarist Roger Pearce also made a lasting impression on Peter. So when he heard that the band was breaking up in early 1965, Peter went to Pearce's house to suggest forming a new group. This would eventually lead to the formation of a band called the Muskrats, with Dave Bidwell on drums (Bidwell would later join Christine McVie's first band, Chicken Shack). "Even though Peter was playing bass at the time," Roger Pearce later recalled, "he could already play Eric's lead break from The Yardbirds' 'I Ain't Got You.' Nobody except Peter had worked out what Eric was doing. When The Muskrats did the song live, we did the solo twice, I'd take the first one and cock it up and then Peter would do it faultlessly on bass. He was a very, very good bass player; but he obviously came to the realization that he could play guitar just as well as anybody else."[1]

Self-taught Peter Green (here circa 1968) cultivated a guitar style as rigorous as it was instinctive, in the manner of his idol Eric Clapton.

On the Blues Trail

After repeated listenings to the work of Eric Clapton and the Yardbirds, Peter realized that the blues spoke to him like no other form of music ever had. Just like his role model, he began to study the great blues pioneers with a fervor that bordered on fanaticism. He even ended up buying himself a Gibson Les Paul guitar that was identical to Clapton's.

In March 1965, when Clapton decided to leave the Yardbirds to join John Mayall's Bluesbreakers, Peter applauded his decision. He knew that with the Bluesbreakers and their focus on honoring the genre's traditions, Clapton would be able to indulge his blues obsession, which Peter now shared.

In the meantime, Peter himself joined the Tridents, a band that had just lost a talented young guitarist by the name of Jeff Beck, who left the group to replace Eric Clapton in the Yardbirds. Still, Peter followed the Bluesbreakers assiduously and by the summer of 1965, the name John Mayall and the Bluesbreakers was changed to John Mayall and the Bluesbreakers Featuring Eric Clapton—a clear indication of the guitarist's importance on the British rhythm'n'blues scene.

In the autumn of 1965, Peter Green was presented with an unexpected opportunity. Clapton escaped to Greece with a band he had created from scratch: the Acorns. This was Green's big chance! Green answered John Mayall's ad in *Melody Maker* for a temporary replacement for Clapton. With his back to the wall, Mayall was ready to do anything to keep the band's commitments in the absence of their regular guitarist. Mayall called Peter, whom he had never heard of, and arranged for a sit-down. The meeting was a success, and Mayall hired him to play a few dates with the group.

But Clapton soon returned from his romantic but unsuccessful musical escapade and resumed his post, leaving Peter Green in the lurch. Although he was disappointed by his brief stint with the Bluesbreakers, Green knew one thing: He had a future as a blues guitarist. A few months later, he auditioned for a guitar position with Peter B's Looners, a band with a young drummer named Mick Fleetwood. Peter Green did not know it at the time, but this encounter was going to change his life.

Mick Fleetwood (circa 1968) was skeptical at first about Peter Green's integration into the Looners.

THE ROOTS OF FLEETWOOD MAC

However casual and innocuous they might have seemed at first, the meetings that took place between John Lennon and Paul McCartney at St. Peter's Church, and between Mick Jagger and Keith Richards on the platform of Dartford Station, belong to the annals of rock history. The meeting between Peter Green and Mick Fleetwood is another fateful example of a chance encounter, and it would prove to be the first step toward Fleetwood Mac's unimaginably fascinating rock'n'roll destiny.

The Decisive Audition

On Christmas Eve, 1965, Peter B's Looners were scheduled to open for Georgie Fame and The Blue Flames. But earlier that day, the band's musicians were preoccupied with recruiting a new guitarist. They auditioned a shaggy young musician named Peter Green. When Green entered the audition space, Mick Fleetwood and Dave Ambrose, who formed the rhythm section of the band, exchanged skeptical looks. Peter Bardens, the organist and leader of the band, could not take his eyes off the young player's hands, which were frantically navigating the neck of his guitar as he painstakingly reproduced the sounds of one of his favorite bluesmen, Freddie King. After he finished, Green then improvised a solo working from a traditional blues scale. During the postaudition group discussion, opinions were divided. Mick, the drummer, and Dave, the bassist, saw Green, who had declared at the start of his audition that he had only limited experience as a guitarist, as a first-rate blusterer. And despite their limited guitar knowledge, they were not impressed by his audition. On the other hand, Green had made a strong impression on Peter Bardens, who perceived something great in his playing: "He pulled me aside and said: 'You're wrong, this guy's special,'"[1] recalled Mick Fleetwood. In time he would come to appreciate the extent of his error. Admittedly, Green's talent was still a little…green. He had not developed all the subtleties of his instinctive playing, but the seeds of greatness were there. "I can say without hesitation that Peter Green was the most brilliant musician I have ever played with," Mick Fleetwood affirmed in 2014. "When he was well, he was on a par with a genius like Miles Davis. Like Miles, Peter said things about music that as a young man I didn't understand but never forgot and now, after a lifetime of playing, make complete sense. He was my mentor, he was my teacher, my captain, and for a time, my best friend."[2]

First Steps with the Looners

Peter Green was finally recruited, and his talent was honed during the band's first period, when it played exclusively instrumental tracks, as well as during the band's second,

John Mayall, Hughie Flint, Eric Clapton, and John McVie: the dream team at work on the seminal album *Blues Breakers*.

more mature period, during which it adopted the new name of Shotgun Express and brought in two singers named Beryl Marsden and Rod Stewart, who was a close friend of Peter's. Despite the presence of this impressive duo at the microphone, the public was mostly fascinated by the guitarist, whose coolness was in direct proportion to his virtuosity on the guitar. He exuded an aura, a rare charisma that was not lost on Beryl Marsden.

Beryl and Peter soon got together and spent most of their time in the company of Mick Fleetwood and Jenny Boyd. A strong bond of friendship developed between the two musicians, and Mick and Peter eventually became inseparable. "As young men we had an incredible friendship," said Mick. "I was basically...in love with him. We roomed together. When it was cold we slept together. I knew this man."[1]

Peter's and Beryl's feelings for each other did not develop along the same lines. The guitarist, who took their budding romance very seriously, considered proposing to the singer. Beryl, for her part, was very attached to her freedom and preferred to steer clear of any kind of formal commitment. With the two lovebirds not flying in the same direction, their relationship soon deteriorated, with inevitable repercussions for the band. The situation became so untenable that Peter decided to retire from Shotgun Express in July 1966.

The Bluesbreakers: Fleetwood Mac's Incubator

Green did not stay on the sidelines for long. In July 1966, John Mayall offered him Eric Clapton's spot in the band. Clapton had just definitively distanced himself from the Bluesbreakers after dropping them for the first time in 1965. It was only logical that the spot should go to the man who had saved the Bluesbreakers previously when he replaced Clapton on short notice for a short series of concerts. The ex–Shotgun Express guitarist accepted enthusiastically, and was more modest than when he auditioned for the Looners: "John Mayall said, 'Eric Clapton's going to form The Cream, with Ginger [Baker] and Jack [Bruce], do you want to come with me and get some experience? And be a blues band again instead of Booker T. & The MGs and soul sections?' I said, 'Yes I would very much like it.' But I was only just starting. I wasn't a blues guitarist. I could play Hank Marvin stuff, 'Teen Scene' by The Hunters, those old instrumentals. I could play all those fine. Semi-pro I was. But I chucked in my job..."[1]

The public—at least, some of them—was quickly won over when they discovered Green for the first time onstage with the Bluesbreakers on July 24, 1966, at the Britannia Rowing Club in Nottingham, a week after he joined the group. There was a real split among Bluesbreakers fans between those who remained loyal to Clapton—many

Peter Bardens (here circa 1965) was the leader of Peter B's Looners and Shotgun Express, two breeding grounds for future talents such as Rod Stewart, Peter Green, and Mick Fleetwood.

walls in the British capital bore the inscription "Clapton is God"—and those who claimed that Green was better.

After the missed appointment in 1965—when Peter Green acted as a stand-in while John McVie was replaced by Jack Bruce—Green finally got to know McVie, his future Fleetwood Mac bandmate, though they didn't play together in the band until 1966. Their complementary styles first shined through on the album *A Hard Road*, which was recorded over five days in October and November 1966 and released on February 17, 1967. On an album filled with covers by Freddie King, Willie Cobbs, and Elmore James, alongside compositions by John Mayall, two tracks by Peter Green appear: "The Same Way" and "The Supernatural."

Green's Growing Influence

Decca producer Mike Vernon made his debut on the Bluesbreakers' first album, teaming with sound engineer Gus Dudgeon. Unaware of the band's latest personnel changes, Vernon was late to the realization that Eric Clapton was no longer in the picture. "I am reasonably sure that I had not met Peter [Green] prior to his arrival at West Hampstead. Me and Gus were looking at him and thinking, 'Who the hell is this? Where's Eric?' John Mayall just said, 'Oh, he's Eric's replacement.' I hadn't even heard that Eric

had left The Bluesbreakers. John said Peter was as good as Eric, which was a bit hard to believe until he actually plugged in and then we thought, 'Ummm, he can play a bit!' Initially, Peter seemed like a very quiet and somewhat reserved kind of guy...not outspoken or aggressive in any way. He must have felt somewhat awkward, though, following in Clapton's footsteps. As the sessions progressed, Peter became a little more certain of his role as a Bluesbreaker...especially when he was given the chance to exercise his vocal cords. He certainly was not as reluctant to sing as his predecessor had been...he seemed to really enjoy that role and he was very good. When I heard Peter sing 'The Same Way' for the first time, I thought 'Wow! Here is a great blues singer, no inhibitions about singing with an English accent, expressive and individual.' I had a feeling that Peter was destined to make his mark in the music business."[3]

While Peter was building a national reputation, Mick was still the drummer with Shotgun Express, and he was suffering in Peter's absence. To make matters worse, his love affair with Jenny Boyd came to an abrupt end. After two years together, Boyd dumped him unceremoniously. As for Shotgun Express, Rod Stewart's departure from the Jeff Beck Group in February 1967 signaled the band's demise. But there was renewed hope for Mick when, in April 1967, John

Above left: Eric Clapton (circa 1967) and his 1964 Gibson SG, which was nicknamed *The Fool* in reference to the collective of artists who created the psychedelic mural covering it.

Above right: Mike Vernon (in 1979), in-house producer at Decca Studios, played a key role in the rise of Fleetwood Mac.

Mayall and the rest of his band invited Fleetwood to join the Bluesbreakers—at the instigation of Peter Green, of course.

The stage was officially set for a future version of Fleetwood Mac. Its three founding members—Peter Green, Mick Fleetwood, and John McVie—were finally playing together. As the rhythm section of the Bluesbreakers, Fleetwood and McVie would soon discover an irresistible affinity for each other, both personally and professionally. This affinity was a double-edged sword, however. In addition to their love of music, the two men shared a passion for booze that started around this time, and they embarked on a devastating downward spiral together.

A Story of Music and Friendship

John Mayall, who already took a dim view of his bassist's immoderate penchant for the bottle, could not see himself dealing with such a new and disruptive element in the form of Mick Fleetwood. Especially given that the new drummer was not as warmly received by fans as Peter Green. Fleetwood's predecessor, Aynsley Dunbar, left his mark on the Bluesbreakers with his technique and versatility. Once considered for a spot in the Jimi Hendrix

Experience, Dunbar went on to build up an impressive résumé by playing with the likes of Frank Zappa, David Bowie, Lou Reed, Journey, and UFO. Mick Fleetwood's more romantic and nuanced style of playing left Mayall unconvinced. But John McVie stood up for Fleetwood from his very first concert, when some of the audience started calling for Dunbar's return. He picked up the microphone and asked the audience to shut up and listen. Mick Fleetwood saw this as a moment of true solidarity. The moment marked the beginning of a long friendship as well as another milestone on the road to the formation of Fleetwood Mac. The next milestone was set by John Mayall, quite unwittingly, and without fully realizing the consequences of his own actions.

On Peter Green's twentieth birthday, in October 1966, Mayall offered him a recording session at Decca Studios. When the guitarist wanted to take advantage of this opportunity, a few months later, he chose to go along with Mick Fleetwood and John McVie. The trio enjoyed playing a cover of Howlin' Wolf's "No Place to Go," and they worked on three new compositions: "First Train Home," "Looking for Somebody," and an instrumental track which Peter

The nineteenth-century former factory at 165 Broadhurst Gardens (left of the large, gable-roofed building in the center) was converted into a recording studio by Crystalate Gramophone Records in 1928. Throughout the 1960s, as the home of Decca, it shone in London's blues microcosm.

Green, the composer, affectionately named "Fleetwood Mac," a title he got by combining the surnames of his two friends and collaborators.

Toward a New Horizon

John Mayall broke up this loosely formed trio when he fired Mick Fleetwood from the Bluesbreakers in May 1967. Without their drummer, the band no longer held the same appeal for Peter Green. Additionally, Green's new preference for a more jazz-inflected type of sound over the Bluesbreakers' pure blues sound further dented his faith in the project. He continued with the group for another month, working with new bassist Keef Hartley before handing over guitar duties to Mick Taylor, the future guitarist for the Rolling Stones.

Bluesbreakers producer Mike Vernon, who no longer knew what kind of band he was dealing with, jumped at the chance to sign Peter Green to his fledgling Blue Horizon label. He also introduced Green to future Fleetwood Mac guitarist Jeremy Spencer, then an eighteen-year-old with an impish streak. Green saw Spencer play when his band, Levi Set, was working at Decca Studios. A light in the middle of a sonic disaster, Spencer's passion for Elmore James and his slide guitar playing convinced Peter Green to take him on

board for a new project he was creating: Peter Green's Fleetwood Mac. Mick Fleetwood was obviously on board, so the only thing missing was the "Mac." The bassist was still committed to Mayall, but Green was convinced that he would soon be joining them. In the meantime, the band placed an ad in *Melody Maker*: "Bass player wanted for Chicago-type blues band."[4] Bob Brunning responded to the ad, and he was helped along by the fickle hand of fate: The telephone number in the ad was wrong. More persistent than the other applicants, Brunning succeeded in obtaining Peter's address. When they met for the first time and Green introduced himself, Brunning could think of nothing better than to ask him if he knew the Peter Green who played with John Mayall. Luckily, the guitarist did not hold this against Brunning. Green was aware that the newcomer did not have the same melodic and rhythmic qualities as McVie, but he was determined to make it work, and as a former bassist, he was able to tell Brunning exactly what to play. Green's eagerness can be explained by the fact that an important upcoming gig had already been booked. The band had a month in which to put together a solid set for the Jazz and Blues Festival to be held in Windsor, England, on August 13, 1967. This date was to mark the official birth of Peter Green's Fleetwood Mac.

JEREMY SPENCER, THE GUITARIST WITH TWO FACES

Peter Green was not a man to seek the limelight. When he launched Fleetwood Mac in June 1967, he immediately set out to find a second guitarist with whom he could share the stage. In addition to looking for someone with a certain amount of charisma, this new band member would also need to help flesh out the group's sound and bring it closer to Peter's musical ideal of mimicking the Chicago blues. The band needed a slide guitar specialist to make the melodies twirl, someone who ideally possessed a good knowledge of American blues and all its wide and varied influence. Jeremy Spencer, who was also a keyboardist and a singer in addition to playing the guitar, fit the bill nicely.

An Ideal Recruit

Born in Hartlepool, England, on July 4, 1948, Jeremy began playing the piano at the age of nine. Although he switched to the guitar in his teens—after discovering blues singers and guitarists like Son House and Homesick James—he retained a solid grasp of the instrument. Jeremy set the keyboard aside while he studied art, during which time he also developed his guitar playing and formed his own band, the Levi Set Blues Band. This was an insubstantial outfit that he had no trouble abandoning when the time came.

Mike Vernon, the producer who supervised one of the band's early recording sessions at Decca Studios, suggested Spencer as a possibility while Green was searching for a new guitarist. On June 11, 1967, Vernon arranged for the Levi Set Blues Band to play for an hour and a half between two John Mayall gigs at Le Metro, a music venue in Birmingham, England. Peter wanted to see Spencer play, and the two musicians hit it off first by talking about their shared passion for B. B. King and Elmore James, and then by talking guitar and the missing pickup on Green's Gibson Les Paul. After a short demonstration of his skills, Jeremy received the highest of compliments from Green, who told him that he was the first guitarist to make him smile since Jimi Hendrix.

Jeremy Spencer later recalled that he did not feel intimidated when he joined Fleetwood Mac, even though he was playing alongside musicians who were well established on the British blues scene. "It all just fell into place musically. I did feel a lack of confidence, however, playing without a slide to do riffs to back Pete. That's why I didn't, and he ended up having to recruit Danny [Kirwan] to do that!"[8]

Dr. Jekyll and Mr. Hyde

With his mischievous look and his five-foot-five stature, Jeremy created an almost comical contrast whenever he stood next to Mick Fleetwood, who was almost six foot two. However, the audience took him seriously from the moment the apparently calm musician leapt onto the stage and plugged in his instrument. There, Spencer became a different man, strumming his semi-acoustic guitar with its wide F-shaped gills, which he later swapped for a Flying V. He also played the slide guitar in the style of the master of the discipline and his role model, Elmore James. This did not escape Peter Green, who also worshiped him. As soon as he finished playing and raised his head, Jeremy turned his laughing eyes on the audience and improvised an imitation of Elvis Presley, Cliff Richard, Little Richard, Buddy Holly, and others. Often, during performances he would slip in a saucy joke to get the crowd laughing. This earned him a few reprimands from his bandmates, who paid the price when his suggestive behavior onstage provoked the

wrath of promoters and even led to a temporary ban from London's famous Marquee Club: "I had—and still have to some extent—a silly streak and a penchant for liking to shock people, especially in those days with the staid British. It certainly wasn't all in good taste, and I'm not proud of a lot of those antics. But we were a bunch of silly kids, really—boys in the band acting up."[8]

It's true that Spencer was only nineteen when he joined Fleetwood Mac, but Peter Green found it hard to come to terms with Jeremy's excesses, especially since he tended to take up a lot of space musically as well as emotionally. Green frequently backgrounded himself in the service of Spencer's compositions, taking care not to overshadow his partner. The reverse was not always true.

In an intimate context, Spencer's behavior was light-years away from the persona he took on as soon as he got his hands on a guitar. Far from the fury of certain rock stars who vent their nerves on hotel room furniture, Jeremy usually spent his time reading and rereading the Bible. This was the first manifestation of a spiritual journey that would eventually cause him to leave Fleetwood Mac in 1971 and turn to a religious movement, the Children of God. "I believed in God and was searching the Bible and other spiritual books for the answers. I didn't understand it myself, really, why I was such an irreverent little so-and-so onstage and off, yet had those religious inclinations. I realized later that it was true what Jesus said, that the whole need not a physician, but those that are sick. I was just sick, period."[8]

Marquee Club founders
Harold and Barbara Pendleton
in 1983, in front of the stage
at this 1960s mecca of UK
jazz and blues.

PENDLETON, FESTIVAL FOUNDER

As secretary of the National Federation of Jazz, Harold Pendleton was a major devotee of the genre when he opened the Marquee Club in 1958. In 1961, he founded the National Jazz and Blues Festival to provide a better platform for the next generation of performers. From its first location in Richmond, the festival moved on to Windsor, then Sunbury, before settling in Reading in 1971 and laying the foundations for a rock festival of the same name, which was formalized in 1976.

AUGUST 13, 1967:
FLEETWOOD'S FIRST CONCERT AT THE WINDSOR NATIONAL JAZZ & BLUES FESTIVAL

A Baptism by Fire for Peter Green's Fleetwood Mac

At the end of his audition for Peter Green's Fleetwood Mac, Bob Brunning innocently asked when the group's first concert was scheduled. He was expecting a gig at a small club—something to ease the new group into being. Peter replied without batting an eyelid: "Windsor Jazz and Blues Festival, in a month's time."[5] The bassist thought he was going to pass out! The festival, which became a national institution when it was launched in 1961 by Marquee Club founder Harold Pendleton, attracted some forty thousand blues fans over the course of a weekend. The cream of the British blues boom would be there. By coincidence, Peter Green's Fleetwood Mac was scheduled to perform a twenty-minute set at 7:30 p.m., just after a band named Chicken Shack, featuring Christine Perfect—the future Christine McVie. "I also remember a big commotion over a hot new blues band from Birmingham called Chicken Shack," Mick Fleetwood recalled, "word having gotten around that the singer and keyboard player was a beautiful blonde named Christine Perfect. We all went to see Chicken Shack's set at this blues event, and everyone in Fleetwood Mac immediately fell in love with Christine."[4] Three hours later, on the very same stage, John Mayall and the Bluesbreakers were also expected to play. And to round off the evening's reunion-like atmosphere, Cream would also be there, led by Eric Clapton.

In preparation for the fateful date of Sunday, August 13, 1967, the band rehearsed intensively at the Black Bull, a pub located on London's Fulham Road. They worked under the guidance of Peter Green, who structured the set list and played the role of leader to the hilt, encouraging his troops when he felt even a slight dip in morale. The band's first songs took shape, including "Long Grey Mare," "Rambling Pony," and "I Believe My Time Ain't Long."

Heading for Windsor

At eleven o'clock on the morning of August 13, the band loaded its equipment into a pale blue Ford Transit and set out for the so-called Balloon Meadow on Maidenhead Road in Windsor. This was the location where the festival, now in its second year, was set to take place. "There was an uncharacteristic silence on board," Bob Brunning remembered later. "Usually the van was full of laughter and ribald jokes as the band members traveled to rehearsals together. But today was different. The four musicians looked pale and nervous. Jokes fell flat and conversations died."[5]

The group's eventual appearance onstage was greeted with tentative applause. The audience was curious to see this new combo, whose members were familiar from their

Nestled in the giant origami stage of Windsor National Jazz & Blues Festival, Peter Green's Fleetwood Mac (with Bob Brunning on bass), performing their very first set.

appearances in various other notable groups in the UK blues scene. But the band took their time winning over the crowd—Peter Green launched into a pentatonic blues scale while Bob Brunning, who was about to announce the title of the first track, forgot the name due to the stress of the event. Apart from this slight faux pas and an inadequate sound system (only one thousand watts), the rest of the set went perfectly. The musicians played seven songs total. They opened with "Talk to Me Baby," a twelve-bar blues track borrowed from Elmore James, that hypnotized the audience with an extended intro that slowly developed into a decibel deluge. Then, they moved on to the haunting "I'm Going Home" (a precursor to "I Loved Another Woman") on which Peter Green sang while knitting his scales over Bob Brunning's deep, languorous bass line. The buildup to "I Need You" was slightly imperfect, but everyone quickly found their footing before delivering an intense moment with "Fleetwood Mac," an instrumental song played at an unusually high tempo. The musicians' all-consuming passion for Elmore James resurfaced on "Fine Little Mama," which they served up with a suitably large sound achieved after a little necessary retuning. "The World Keep on Turning" was a testament to the musicians' songwriting talents. Though he had been tense from the start of the set, Jeremy Spencer eventually put his nervousness to good use on the upbeat "Shake Your

Moneymaker," raising his voice as if his life depended on it. As part of its review of the festival, the monthly magazine *Music Maker* named the festival's musical sensations: Clapton, Ten Years After, Tomorrow, Pat Arnold and the Nice, John Mayall, Donovan, Denny Laine, and…Peter Green.

John McVie didn't miss a single beat of the band's first show. He was captivated by the sense of enjoyment and fun that Peter, Jeremy, Bob, and Mick all seemed to share onstage. These feelings were compounded by the fact that he found it hard to be satisfied with the jazzy turn Mayall's band had taken since Green's departure. McVie stayed on only for the financial security, and his former bandmates, Peter and Mick, spent the evening teasing him and repeatedly asked him to join their group. Amused, McVie still resisted their advances, but in the back of his mind an idea began to take root.

On this 1967 *Raw Blues* compilation, two generations and two nations (United States and England) unite for a joint session of electric blues.

Alexis Korner, revered as the "father of British blues," welcomed the cream of the R&B scene, from Jack Bruce to Charlie Watts and Long John Baldry, into his band, Blues Incorporated.

THE BRITISH BLUES BOOM, AN ANGLO-AMERICAN IDYLL

Driven by a youth eager to discover new things, the 1960s saw an unprecedented tectonic shift in the musical landscape: England and the United States suddenly drew closer together. The cultural flow worked in both directions. Young English musicians fell in love with the original blues of their American cousins, giving rise to a new movement, the British blues boom. In return, the Americans fell in love with young, clean-cut Brits like the Beatles and the Rolling Stones, who had digested the blues classics to feed their fresh, sophisticated rock. We refer to this phenomenon as the "British invasion." A very peaceful annexation.

The British blues boom gave new vigor to traditional blues. Far from being a matter of cultural appropriation, the movement, a veritable groundswell, spawned a generation of gifted musicians throughout England: the Yardbirds, Georgie Fame, the Pretty Things, Them, the Animals, Long John Baldry and the Hoochie Coochie Men, and so on. Enamored of the American blues of the first part of the century, they became deeply immersed in this culture, swapping LPs and spending hours reproducing the melodies on their instruments until they mastered them to perfection, reciting their chord progressions with devotion, setting them ablaze with their youthful ardor.

While they were passionate about Delta blues (the original blues of Blind Lemon Jefferson, Robert Johnson, or Blind Blake), which absorbed slave work songs and Black spirituals to nourish their tales of freedom-loving outcasts, young British bluesmen also paid close attention to the electric blues from the northern United States: Chicago blues. Led by musicians such as Elmore James, Freddie King, Howlin' Wolf, and J. B. Lenoir, it was another major source of inspiration for English bluesmen.

John Mayall's Bluesbreakers, or the Making of British Blues

The Bluesbreakers established themselves as the main catalysts of the British blues boom, and John Mayall as the movement's charismatic guru. Mayall was one of the first to bring Chicago blues to Britain. Son of Murray Mayall (a guitarist and jazz fanatic), John extended his passion from jazz to blues, with the firm intention of one day blending the two currents. In 1962, he began to build up a solid stage reputation in Manchester, where he played regularly with his band at the time, the Powerhouse Four, at the Bodega and the Twisted Wheel Club. But in the eyes of Alexis Korner, another pioneer of British blues, the industrial city in the north of England was no match for Mayall's talent, and he recommended that Mayall move to London if he wished to shine and reign over British blues. On the strength of this advice, the gaunt guitarist packed his bags

Peter Green observes one of his mentors, B. B. King, during a 1971 recording session at Olympic Studios.

and set about finding musicians to create a new project blending blues and jazz. This was to be the Bluesbreakers.

The group soon took up residence at the Marquee Club, a venue on Oxford Street that until then had specialized in jazz and R&B, but was now opening up to the blues and burgeoning rock'n'roll scene. Although small, it was no less influential, attracting a number of young bands. It offered them regular residencies and attracted the cream of the music press, eager for new discoveries. From 1962 onward, the heart of the hall reverberated to the rhythm of the blues. Brian Auger, Alexis Korner, Cyril Davies, and Manfred Mann (who played 102 times between 1962 and 1976!) made it their landmark. From the Marquee Club, the Bluesbreakers gradually extended their influence. They began to play wherever they could, in any club however small, cranking out an increasingly wide-ranging set nourished by a host of cover versions. The band's mastery of the blues was such that whenever an American blues luminary came to London in need of local musicians, the Bluesbreakers were called in. On March 26, 1965, the group's first album was released, a live recording of a concert at Klooks Kleek, a famous London club, entitled *John Mayall Plays John Mayall*.

Eric Clapton and Peter Green: Two Greats in the Cause of the Blues

On April 9, 1965, the Bluesbreakers got their hands on the gem that the whole British blues microcosm had been coveting since his departure from the Yardbirds a fortnight earlier: Eric Clapton. The arrival of the twenty-year-old guitarist, already elevated to the status of six-string deity, catapulted the Bluesbreakers into the limelight. But the honeymoon quickly turned sour. In October 1965, Clapton bailed on them by setting off with the Acorns, a band hastily formed with a few friends who had the ambition of touring the world in a double-decker bus. Faced with this incomprehensible decision, the Bluesbreakers had to act quickly to find a new guitarist. John Mayall placed a classified ad in *Melody Maker* and auditioned a large number of candidates. In the end, the young Peter Green won.

The future members of Fleetwood Mac are at the heart of this effervescence, playing an active part in the advent of the British blues boom. Peter Green, of course, but also John McVie and Mick Fleetwood, who also got their first taste of the blues alongside John Mayall, while Jeremy Spencer played with the Levi Set Blues Band and Christine Perfect with Chicken Shack. This lineage was the foundation of Fleetwood Mac's blues origins.

The Ten Albums That Triggered the Explosion

During this period of musical ferment, a number of essential albums were released. This is a selection of the ten considered to be essential.

ALEXIS KORNER'S BLUES INCORPORATED
R&B from the Marquee
UK Release Date: November 16, 1962

Alexis Korner founded Blues Incorporated in 1962 alongside fellow American blues enthusiast Cyril Davies. The first lineup also included guitarist Art Wood, drummer Charlie Watts, singer Keith Scott, and bassist Andy Hoogenboom, though this is not the exact configuration that would eventually appear on the album. The group went on to become a lively laboratory where Long John Baldry, Ginger Baker, and Duffy Power came together. They performed regularly at the Marquee Club, then signed a recording contract with Decca Records. The album, which includes reworkings of songs by Muddy Waters, Jimmy Witherspoon, and Leroy Carr, was recorded in June 1962 and released in November of the same year. The recording took place in Decca's West Hampstead studios, and would go on to become one of the most influential of the movement.

GEORGIE FAME & THE BLUE FLAMES
Rhythm and Blues at the Flamingo
UK Release Date: February 21, 1964

Georgie Fame and the Blue Flames were resident at the Flamingo Club in London's Soho district when they recorded *Rhythm and Blues at the Flamingo* live in September 1963. The album, released by Columbia Records, perfectly captures the combo's fiery spirit. You can hear Johnny Gunnell struggling to raise his voice above the noisy crowd to announce the songs. Glyn Johns, a future legendary sound engineer who would go on to distinguish himself in the service of the Rolling Stones and the Beatles, cut his teeth on this album, alongside producer Ian Samwell (who produced, among others, John Mayall and the Small Faces). Despite the strong presence of the single "Do the Dog," the album initially failed to chart. Other tracks include covers of Louis Jordan's legendary "Let the Good Times Roll," the Miracles' "Shop Around," and "Baby, Please Don't Go" by Sonny Boy Williamson.

THE ROLLING STONES
The Rolling Stones
UK Release Date: April 16, 1964

The Rolling Stones' first offering to the world, its eponymous album, released under the sales title *England's Newest Hit Makers* in the United States, contains just three original compositions. But it was no less exciting. There was "Route 66," Bobby Troup's twelve-bar blues classic. Then we leave the asphalt for Mississippi with Willie Dixon and his "I Just Want to Make Love to You," Jimmy Reed and his "Honest I Do," Bo Diddley and "Mona (I Need You Baby)," or Rufus Thomas and "Walking the Dog," after taking a detour of a few miles to Slim Harpo's Louisiana, where the band covers "I'm a King Bee." The bottleneck makes one of its earliest appearances on an English rock, thanks to Brian Jones, who uses it on this album.

LONG JOHN BALDRY & THE HOOCHIE COOCHIE MEN
Long John's Blues
UK Release Date: December 1964

Despite a few short-lived hits, Long John Baldry never achieved lasting success. He did, however, exert a major influence on the British music scene in the 1960s. After collaborating with Alexis Korner's Blues Incorporated and Cyril Davies's All Stars, the man who later boasted a young keyboardist by the name of Reginald Dwight (the future Elton John) put together a crack team of musicians he had worked with. He brought together Cliff Barton on bass, Billy Law on drums, Geoff Bradford on guitar and harmonica, and Ian Armit on piano to form the Hoochie Coochie Men. The only member missing from the *Long John's Blues* album is Rod Stewart, absent for contractual reasons. He does, however, appear on the 1971 US reissue of the album. The band's covers include such standards as Muddy Waters's "Got My Mojo Workin'," Willie Dixon's "Hoochie Coochie," John Lee Hooker's "Dimples," and Eddie Boyd's "Five Long Years."

THE YARDBIRDS
Five Live Yardbirds
UK Release Date: December 4, 1964

A new live recording was made, better able to capture the club atmosphere, the fervor of the audience, and the musicians' ability to improvise, a quality that characterized blues players of the era. *Five Live Yardbirds* documents the Yardbirds' appearance on March 20, 1964, at the Marquee Club, a landmark of London rock. Covers of songs by British blues boomers such as Slim Harpo, Howlin' Wolf, Bo Diddley, and John Lee Hooker are featured on the program, with "I Got Love If You Want It," "Smokestack Lightnin'," "Pretty Girl," and "Louise," respectively. The band, which benefits from the blossoming of Eric Clapton (on his way to becoming the guitar "God," as he would be nicknamed), established its name among the most worthy heirs of the blues with this first discographic milestone. Clapton's departure from the blues path marked out by this first opus would eventually lead to his next album.

THE PRETTY THINGS
The Pretty Things
UK Release Date: March 12, 1965

The Pretty Things struck a blow with their first eponymous album, which reached number six in the UK Albums Chart. A blow too powerful for producer Jack Baverstock, who resigned early in the sessions, unable to stand the musicians playing so loudly. Drummer Bobby Graham stepped in to fill his shoes. The Pretty Things were brought up on the same records as their colleagues, and took on classics by Bo Diddley ("Road Runner," "Mama, Keep Your Big Mouth Shut," and "She's Fine, She's Mine"), Jimmy Reed ("The Moon Is Rising"), and Willie Dixon ("Pretty Thing").

THEM
The "Angry" Young Them!
UK Release Date: June 18, 1965

The blues tidal wave also splashed over Ireland and one of its flagship bands, Them, in which the immense Van Morrison made his debut. By the time they recorded their first album, *The "Angry" Young Them!* (known as *Them* in North America), the band had already established its name with the hits "Baby, Please Don't Go" (number ten in the UK in 1964) and "Here Comes the Night" (number two in 1965). But they also lost a few feathers during a grueling tour. Despite the nervous atmosphere, the musicians produced an essential work, punctuated by future classics such as "Gloria" and "Mystic Eyes." Straddling garage rock, rhythm'n'blues, and blues rock, the album was striking in its maturity and cohesion. Jimmy Page, a future Led Zeppelin member, put his divine touch on "Gloria" and "Mystic Eyes."

JOHN MAYALL WITH ERIC CLAPTON
Blues Breakers: John Mayall with Eric Clapton
UK Release Date: July 22, 1966

John Mayall picked up the defector of the year in April 1965, just a fortnight after leaving the Yardbirds. Here again, Eric Clapton would not stay long (barely a year), but long enough to make a lasting mark on the repertoire and contribute a pivotal album for the British blues boom. If we had to choose just one album to represent the English blues boom, "the Beano album," as it is nicknamed, would be the best candidate. A first recording attempt was made at the Flamingo Club, as a live recording seemed to be the best way of capturing Eric Clapton's dazzling solos. Jack Bruce, who would go on to form Cream with Clapton after this album, appeared on bass. But the recording was of poor quality, and a slot was reserved at Decca Studios in May 1966. This time, a certain John McVie officiated on four-string. American electric blues permeates this work, with tributes to Otis Rush and Freddie King, but Clapton also delivered one of his first homages to his idol, Robert Johnson, with a burst of talent on "Ramblin' on My Mind." John Mayall, meanwhile, launched into a cluster of essential compositions, with "Little Girl," "Another Man," and "Double Crossing Timing," which he co-wrote with Clapton.

CHICKEN SHACK
O.K. Ken?
UK Release Date: February 1969

A comet in the tail of the British blues boom, Chicken Shack established itself as one of the genre's leading figures. Formed in 1965 by Stan Webb on vocals and guitar, Andy Sylvester on bass, and Alan Morley on drums (he would later be replaced by Dave Bidwell), the band was joined in 1967 by Christine Perfect, who more than fulfilled their need for a keyboard player. Hosted by Blue Horizon, Fleetwood Mac's record label, the band's second album, *O.K. Ken?* was a success, reaching number nine on the UK Albums Chart. Stan Webb was responsible for the songwriting, although he co-wrote two tracks with Christine Perfect: "Get Like You Used to Be," and "A Woman Is the Blues." Covers remained marginal—songs by Howlin' Wolf, T-Bone Walker, and B. B. King were featured—and Chicken Shack imposed its own identity. It successfully synthesized boogie blues and pop, between tradition and modernity, as evidenced by the original use of brass instruments.

THE ANIMALS WITH ERIC BURDON
In the Beginning
US Release Date: 1970

The Animals were among the first importers of Black American rhythm'n'blues. Released only in 1970, *In the Beginning* takes us back to December 30, 1963, at Newcastle's Club A'Gogo, in the early days of the British blues boom. That evening, Eric Burdon's band opened for Sonny Boy Williamson, the legendary American harmonica player for Chess Records who had played with Robert Johnson and who was then touring Europe. Blessed with a completely inappropriate psychedelic cover, the opus captured a boisterous set totally steeped in American blues. The standards are accompanied by a flurry of Chuck Berry covers ("Let It Rock," "Gotta Find My Baby," "I'm Almost Grown"). Next, we are immersed in Mississippi, with songs from the cradle of the blues: Bo Diddley's "Pretty Thing" and two John Lee Hooker covers, "Dimples" and "Boom Boom." To conclude, the Animals welcome Sonny Boy Williamson on drums for a jam session in the key of *C*, totally improvised.

I Believe My Time Ain't Long / Rambling Pony

UK Release Date: November 3, 1967 / Reference: Blue Horizon / CBS (45 rpm ref.: 3051) / Best UK Chart Ranking: Did Not Chart

Several versions of this single were released in 1967. The first version that was released features a blue-and-white photographic montage of the four musicians on the sleeve.

FOR MAC-ADDICTS

The 1969 reissue of this single was released under the same reference number, but it has one difference: The song is credited to Jeremy Spencer (as "G. Spence") and not to Elmore James or Robert Johnson.

Side A

Fleetwood Mac's first single was a tribute to Elmore James, an artist the band would cover many times.

I BELIEVE MY TIME AIN'T LONG

Elmore James / 2:55

Musicians: Jeremy Spencer: vocals, guitar / Peter Green: harmonica / Bob Brunning: bass / Mick Fleetwood: drums / **Recorded:** CBS Studios, London, September 9, 1967 / **Technical Team:** Producer: Mike Vernon

Genesis and Lyrics

From the outset, American guitarist Elmore James was the link that brought Peter Green and Jeremy Spencer together, and both men worshipped the Mississippi native. So, it was only natural that a rendition of one of his songs was chosen as the A side to their first single. Originally released by Elmore James in 1951 under the title "Dust My Broom (I Believe My Time Ain't Long)," the song pays homage to Robert Johnson's classic "Dust My Broom." The famous Delta blues guitarist laid down this rare track at San Antonio's Gunter Hotel in 1936. If we go even *further* back in the song's history, Johnson's recording was, in turn, an interpretation of the Sparks Brothers' "I Believe I'll Make a Change," which was engraved in wax four years before Johnson's version. Johnson had not clearly set down the song's lyrics, and they tended to vary from concert to concert. Nevertheless, a clear theme emerged: the bitterness of a betrayed man.

Jeremy Spencer made a few marginal adjustments to James's 1951 version: the words "Man, she's a no good doney" became "She's a no good little darling." Like James, Spencer also omitted a verse about the young woman's travels abroad, and he retained the image of the man "dusting off [his] broom," a biblical metaphor referring to Matthew chapter 10, according to which "shaking off the dust from your feet" when returning from a pagan land means "not letting yourself be contaminated by other religions." In the context of this song, the gesture of shaking the dust "off my broom" shows the contempt the singer feels for his "best gal," who has been stepping out with other men. Additionally, Jeremy Spencer also modified the song's title, retaining only "I Believe My Time Ain't Long"; this phrase had been added to the lyrics of another version of this track performed by Arthur Crudup in 1949.

Production

Musically, Fleetwood Mac chose an intermediate path between the Johnson and James versions of this song. The harmonica, played by Peter Green, maintains a traditional Delta blues feel that's more closely associated with the Johnson version, while the amplified slide guitar is clearly inspired by the James version. The harmonica was certainly also present in James's version—it was played by Sonny Boy Williamson II—but it took on a minor role and was rendered barely audible by the quality of the recording. In the Mac version, Green's harmonica follows the slide guitar, producing simultaneous tremolos (trembling effects) and high notes. Following a traditional twelve-bar blues arrangement, Fleetwood Mac's two guitarists retain the rapid triplet bursts that make the song so special.

The Muddy Waters Band: (L to R) Muddy Waters, Henry Armstrong, Otis Spann, Henry Strong, Elga Edmonds, and Jimmy Rogers at a rehearsal in Chicago in 1953.

RAMBLING PONY
Peter Green / 2:37

Musicians: Peter Green: vocals, guitar, harmonica, backing vocals / Jeremy Spencer: guitar, backing vocals / Mick Fleetwood: drums, backing vocals / Bob Brunning: backing vocals / Mike Vernon: backing vocals / **Recorded:** CBS Studios, London, September 9, 1967 / **Technical Team:** Producer: Mike Vernon

Genesis and Lyrics
Reserving the band's previously unreleased song for the B side denotes a slight reticence among the group. If there was one thing for the band to fear with this track, it was, more than the song's failure, the risk of getting caught by the owners of Decca Studios, where producer Mike Vernon worked. Technically, the four Fleetwood Mac musicians and Vernon had secretly recorded their first demos and this single. One evening, after a concert at the Railway Pub in London, Green, Fleetwood, Spencer, and Brunning walked the five hundred feet from the venue to 165 Broadhurst Gardens, where Decca Studios was located, carrying their equipment under their arms. Vernon was waiting for them in front of the unoccupied redbrick building with his keys in hand. In a way, the producer saw this as fair compensation for the inertia of the record company, which had not lifted a finger to recover the distribution of the Blue Horizon label with which Peter Green had signed. Having snubbed the Beatles in 1962, Decca had just made a second blunder by letting Green go as well.

FOR MAC-ADDICTS

Could "Rambling Pony" be an unintentional cover? The song bears many similarities to the standard "Roll and Tumble Blues" (also known as "Rollin' and Tumblin'") composed by Hambone Willie Newbern in 1929 and popularized by Robert Johnson and Muddy Waters. Beyond the riff, the entire vocal melody is matched note for note. This practice was very common in the blues, which fed off its own heritage without necessarily bothering to provide credit to a song's originator.

Production
A popular recording spot for symphony orchestras, the fine parquet flooring at Decca Studios provided excellent acoustics. It is this aspect that is most striking when listening to "Rambling Pony." Behind the crackle of the vinyl, the dull sound of Mick Fleetwood's bass drum is surprisingly sharp as it sets the tempo from the opening moments of the track. The voices of Peter Green and Jeremy Spencer, rising above the primal drumbeat, sound like otherworldly incantations. The strings of Spencer's guitar clatter, giving the impression that the instrument is attempting to mingle with the singers' voices. The bottleneck then makes the guitar vibrate, simulating a tremolo effect that adds to the ambient psychedelia. The arrival of the harmonica adds a completely different color, transporting the listener to the heart of the bayou. The backing vocals resonate in a different way, taking the listener back to the origins of traditional blues music, a genre that was formed in communities of formerly enslaved Black Americans as a means of expressing melancholy and pursuing creative escape.

The lyrics are in keeping with this tradition: They tell the story of a man searching for a life of simplicity, whose dream is to find a kind woman who lets him fish to his heart's content.

ALBUM

FLEETWOOD MAC

My Heart Beat Like a Hammer . Merry Go Round . Long Grey Mare .
Hellhound on My Trail . Shake Your Moneymaker . Looking for Somebody .
No Place to Go . My Baby's Good to Me . I Loved Another Woman .
Cold Black Night . The World Keep on Turning . Got to Move .
Outtakes: I'm Coming Home to Stay .
Be-I-Bicky-Bop Blue Jean Honey Babe Meets High School
Hound Dog Hot Rod Man . Something Inside of Me

RELEASE DATES
United Kingdom: February 24, 1968
Reference: Blue Horizon—7-63200
Best UK Chart Ranking: 4
United States: February 24, 1968
Reference: Epic—BN 26402
Best US Chart Ranking: 198

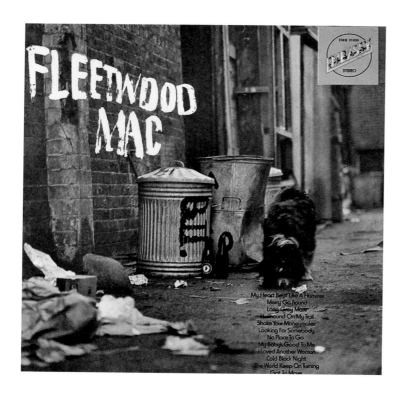

The pessimistic cover of Fleetwood Mac's first album in 1968. To distinguish it from the 1975 album of the same name, the first one is often referred to as the Dog and Dustbin Album.

BLUES EXPRESS

While John McVie dithered and prevaricated, hesitating about whether to leave the Bluesbreakers so he could join the band that already bore his name, Fleetwood Mac was fulfilling its destiny. After a series of concerts given in London clubs in September 1967, Rik and John Gunnell (the band's agents/managers) planned a tour that would run from October 4 through December 8. The tour would take the musicians out of the capital and across the English countryside from south to north, from Southampton to Manchester. However, the group still found time to record their first 45 rpm single ("I Believe My Time Ain't Long" / "Rambling Pony"), which was released in November 1967. Unfortunately, the public's enthusiasm on the tour was not reflected in the chart rankings, where the single didn't even register.

The Formation of a Winning Quartet

As time went by, John McVie seemingly convinced himself that he had made the wisest decision—economically speaking, at any rate—by continuing to stay with the Bluesbreakers. But during a rehearsal in early September 1967, a remark from Mayall changed all that. "At the time, John [Mayall] had horn players in the band and we were rehearsing at some club when John turned to one of them and said, 'Okay, just play it free-form there.' I said, with typical blues snobbishness, 'I thought this was a blues band, not a jazz band!'" The usually even-tempered McVie suddenly saw red. "I immediately went across the street, called Peter, and asked if he still wanted me to join up."[9] Peter, who was always certain that John would eventually give in to his advances, found himself

with two musicians gunning for the same job. Bob Brunning, the band's current guitar player, was neither surprised nor offended by McVie's arrival, although he was immediately ousted from the group. Brunning knew from the start that he had been recruited by default, and that his days with the band were always numbered. Fleetwood Mac's "Mac" had finally come home!

Mick Fleetwood, for his part, made no secret of his delight over the arrival of his colleague: "He makes my form of expression effortless and I do the same for him. If you can imagine doing whatever you feel comes most naturally to you and then finding a partner that accompanies you so perfectly that neither of you need to even talk about it, then you're close. Imagine doing that together year after year; [John] the only constant in a life that has shown you all manner of ups and downs. [...] Once we had John McVie we were a tight musical juggernaut, off and running. We'd record late-night sessions in studios after playing for hours in seedy blues clubs and in doing so we quickly became a well-oiled machine. I can't say it enough—John taught me everything, his playing freed me up, and he made me a better drummer. With such a strong backbone, Peter and Jeremy were able to get out there and lay it down like they never had before."[2]

The split between Brunning and Fleetwood Mac went smoothly. Bob soon found a job with Savoy Brown, where he stayed for a year before leaving the music business entirely to become a primary school teacher. Despite the shuffling of the lineup, Brunning maintained excellent

The Spring Thing is on **APRIL 25th** at Reading Football Stadium Elm Park, Norfolk Rd., Reading **MID-DAY—7 p.m.** with

fleetwood mac

CHICKEN SHACK **JON HISEMANS** **MIKE COOPER**

VIV STANSHALLS **BIG GRUNT** **COLOSSEUM** **CHRISTINE PERFECT**

COMPERE MIKE RAVEN

LIVERPOOL SCENE

TICKETS **£1** AVAILABLE FROM ALL BRANCHES OF HARLEQUIN RECORD SHOPS, XPLOR, READING AND OXFORD, OR READING FOOTBALL CLUB.

To Reading Football Club, Elm Park, Norfolk Road, Reading. Please send me .... tickets for the Spring Thing. I enclose £...................... (cheques, P.O.'s payable to Reading Football Club Ltd.) and stamped, addressed envelope.
Name ....
Address ....

Flyer from 1970. On this evening, Christine Perfect performed solo and with Chicken Shack while rubbing shoulders with Fleetwood Mac, her future band.

relations with his former partners, so much so that he was at their side during some of the recording sessions for their first opus. He later had this to say about one of those early recording sessions: "It stretched from an early evening start until late at night, when John McVie fell asleep after a couple of glasses of wine. And so I played bass for a couple more tracks, unreleased for very good reasons, I'm sure."[5] Only one song was kept in the final track listing: "Long Grey Mare," dated September 9, 1967.

The precise date when Bob Brunning was actually replaced by John McVie remains uncertain. The versions of the story vary somewhat from one account to another. Mick Fleetwood himself has offered several versions over the years. In his autobiography, *My Twenty-Five Years in Fleetwood Mac*, published in 1992, he wrote that McVie joined three weeks after the Jazz and Blues Festival in Windsor, at the beginning of September 1967. But in another book written by Mick Fleetwood and published in 2014, *Play On: Now, Then, and Fleetwood Mac: The Autobiography*, he claims that McVie left the Bluesbreakers and joined the Mac in December 1967. Bob Brunning adds to the confusion in his own autobiography, *The Fleetwood Mac Story: Rumours and Lies*, which was released in 2004. Brunning cites the October and December concert dates that he had written down on a sheet of paper at the time, without specifying whether he actually played the dates, or whether he should have played had he not been ousted. In his 2007 book, *Strange Brew*, author Christopher Hjort shed some much-needed light on the matter, claiming that John McVie's departure was noted in John Mayall's diary dated September 3, 1967. This version of events was contemporaneously corroborated by the Bluesbreakers fan club newsletter, which mentioned the change in its September issue, and also in *Melody Maker*, which reported the news on September 9, 1967.

A Rapid, Fragmented Recording

Peter Green wanted to record a live album, although not necessarily in public, just in concert-like conditions. Green wanted a live album without the constraints of a track-by-track recording, and without overdubbing or mixing, something that would protect the band's sound from any kind of overprocessing that was too superfluous for his taste. "I've always wanted to play straight through the LP—no stopping for mixing and reductions etc.,"[10] he explained in 1968. Far from the new trend set by the Beatles with *Sgt. Pepper's Lonely Hearts Club Band* and its six-month gestation period in the studio, and notwithstanding the reticence of producer Mike Vernon, this first album was completed, more or less, in just three days. Mick Fleetwood alludes to this in an interview with Dick Weindling: "We recorded the one with the dog and the dustbin on the front at Decca's studio off Regent Street, and it was probably done in about three days, all live. We set our PA up in the studio and played it like a gig."[11] But memories can be fickle. If the album was indeed completed in three days (apart from the recording of "Long Grey Mare" on September 9), it was not done in three consecutive days, but rather on three separate dates that were spread across several months, between April and December 1967. The recording sessions would also have taken place in different UK recording venues: Decca Studios in West Hampstead, and CBS Studios on New Bond Street.

The earliest recordings go back to the famous session that took place on April 19, which was given to Peter Green by John Mayall as a birthday present, and during which Mick Fleetwood, John McVie, and Peter Green were united as a group for the first time. Of the tracks recorded on that day, two were chosen for the album: "No Place to Go" and "Looking for Somebody," and both are credited as such,

though it is not certain if they were subsequently rerecorded. Two additional tracks are said to have been recorded during a session at Decca Studios that took place in August 1967, "Fleetwood Mac," and "First Train Home." However, these two tracks were not included in the album's track list.

In September, "Long Grey Mare" was put to bed with Bob Brunning on bass. Five other tracks from the LP were recorded in a session on November 22, 1967. Those tracks were "Merry Go Round," "I Loved Another Woman," "The World Keep on Turning," "Cold Black Night," and "Hellhound on My Trail." Two more songs were recorded on December 11, "My Heart Beat Like a Hammer" and "Shake Your Moneymaker." The dates of the recordings of "My Baby's Good to Me" and "Got to Move" remain unknown, and we cannot rely on the memories of the protagonists themselves, which have become hazy.

When it came to choosing a name for the album, Green and the record company clashed. Mike Vernon wanted to call the first LP *Peter Green's Fleetwood Mac*. But Green did not want his name mentioned before the band's. According to Mick, he was very opposed to the cult of the guitar hero, and he didn't want to be placed on a pedestal. But Vernon insisted, and against Peter's will, the words "Peter Green's Fleetwood Mac" appeared on the back cover of the British

editions of the album, as well as on the vinyl itself. Green won the battle for the American edition of the album, which bore only the words "Fleetwood Mac."

An Album of Two Minds

Fleetwood Mac's debut album hit record stores on February 24, 1968. It featured a well-balanced mix of blues covers and original compositions from Spencer and Green.

Although the band wanted the album to reflect their founding motivation, which was derived from a devotion to the blues, they nonetheless showed a certain originality in their approach that surprised the public. *Fleetwood Mac* exuded an innovative musical assurance and ardor that neophytes in the audience somewhat hastily described as rock. This was incorrect because the Mac's first LP was indeed a blues album, but it was a new kind of blues that was played with an almost rock'n'roll style of impetuosity.

This first album also served as a testament to the evolution in Peter Green's playing. While retaining (for the most part) the classic twelve-bar blues structure for the guitar accompaniment, he developed his own language on his guitar solos, where he was more concerned with conveying emotion rather than creating a certain kind of sound. Just listen to "I Loved Another Woman" if you want to hear an example of

Fleetwood Mac on stage at the Falkoner Center in Copenhagen, Denmark, on November 17, 1968.

this evolution at work. More generally, a kind of melancholy emerges in Green's solos, which, like Eric Clapton, favor slowness, precision, and emotion over speed of execution. Jeremy Spencer's much edgier playing was the perfect counterbalance to his partner's romantic inflections, as evidenced by the adrenaline rush of the tracks where he takes over, such as on "My Heart Beat Like a Hammer," which is intense from the very first moment and almost verges on punk. On "Shake Your Moneymaker," Spencer even becomes slightly unbearable, subjecting his guitar strings to the worst possible abuse on his slide sections. And although he takes all the limelight in the song, that suits Green just fine.

The precision and solidity of the John McVie–Mick Fleetwood duo provide the foundation and groove that enable Spencer to indulge without the risk of falling into an indigestible magma of sound…something that was lacking in his previous band, the Levi Set. McVie and Fleetwood managed to create a slightly floating rhythm that still had a singular feel, largely due to the fact that the two were not quite aligned. The drummer (Fleetwood) played very slightly behind the beat with a laid-back feel, while the bassist (McVie) played slightly ahead of the beat. Together, they found a way to land on their feet quite naturally.

In addition to sharing guitar duties on this album, Spencer and Green also share the microphone and prove themselves to be excellent singers. Spencer's vocals are raspy, powerful, and throaty. Green, on the other hand, is not only an exceptionally talented guitarist with fluid phrasing and undeniable melodic ability, but also a true blues singer with a voice that B. B. King once said gave him "the cold sweats," according to an October 2022 article in *Far Out* magazine.

Fleetwood Mac's first album featured two visions of the blues as offered by its two guitarists, Spencer and Green, and

their playing naturally meshed to create something new. At the beginning of March 1968, barely two weeks after the album's release, Peter Green expressed a few reservations about the record in the pages of the *Record Mirror* weekly newspaper: "Our own LP I'm not fully satisfied with, but I don't think I'd ever be satisfied with our records."[10]

A Quick and Unexpected Success

The reaction to *Fleetwood Mac* was unexpected, to say the least. The band's debut album struck a chord with the public and established them at the forefront of the British blues scene. The album went to number four on the UK album charts, and it stayed on the charts for forty weeks! *Fleetwood Mac* would remain on the charts until it eventually sold over a million copies. The news from the US was just as good: The record broke into the Billboard 200 chart, landing at number 198. The clubs in which the band played soon became too small to accommodate the ever-growing number of fans who were coming out to discover this new phenomenon. The music press had seized upon the band, talking about the group as frequently as the Beatles and the Stones.

Peter Green told the *Record Mirror* that he hoped for good sales, but the commercial dimension of the music business never really interested him. Otherwise, he almost certainly would have chosen a cliché other than that of a roaming dog scavenging through dustbins in a filthy alleyway for the cover of the band's first album. This cover earned the album the nickname of the Dog and Dustbin Album. The lonely stray dog on the album cover is seen as a metaphor for the blues, both for the low regard in which it is held by the general public—a fact belied by the album's sales—and for the album's often miserabilist lyrics. With this notable debut, Fleetwood Mac conquered the public and established themselves as the pack leaders of the British blues boom.

Before Peter Green and John McVie were part of Fleetwood Mac, they were studio musicians for American blues singer and musician Eddie Boyd.

FOR MAC-ADDICTS

At the end of July 1967, while Fleetwood Mac was preparing for the Windsor Festival, Peter Green found himself joining a short-lived supergroup. Mike Vernon had taken the initiative of bringing together old acquaintances in the studio: Aynsley Dunbar, Jack Bruce, Rod Stewart, and Peter Green. During this one-off session, the musicians recorded covers of Buddy Guy's "Stone Crazy" and "Stick Around," as well as Lonnie Johnson's "Fly Right, Baby."

In 2000, the British trade magazine *Guitarist* included *Fleetwood Mac* in its ranking of "101 Essential Guitar Albums."

FLEETWOOD MAC, RECORDING WITH EDDIE BOYD

The only thing that mattered to Peter Green was the pleasure of playing music. This was the motivation behind his participation—along with Mick Fleetwood and John McVie—in blues pianist Eddie Boyd's London recording sessions, which took place in January 1968. This was a recreational interlude of sorts before the verdict came in on their own album, which was due to be released shortly.

The Incarnation of the Blues

American Eddie Boyd was inducted into the Blues Hall of Fame in 2020. In the eyes of the members of Fleetwood Mac, Boyd embodied the quintessence of the artform. Born on a Mississippi plantation, Boyd spent his youth in Memphis and then moved to Chicago. He played with such greats as Muddy Waters (who also happened to be his cousin), Sonny Boy Williamson II, and Buddy Guy. Eddie Boyd recorded a series of singles during the 1950s, including the remarkable "Five Long Years" in 1952, but he did not record his first studio LP (also called *Five Long Years*) until 1966.

For the recording of his 1968 opus, *7936 South Rhodes*, Boyd opted to work with Peter Green and John McVie after

the three recorded a handful of earlier tracks on March 14, 1967, as part of the Bluesbreakers. The Bluesbreakers, the group that was formed by John Mayall, were known as the ideal session band for visiting American artists to work with if they wanted to make the most of London's recording studios.

7936 South Rhodes features twelve tracks recorded by producer Mike Vernon and sound engineer Mike Ross on the Blue Horizon label: "You Got to Reap," "Just the Blues," "She Is Real," "Backslap," "Be Careful," "Ten to One," "The Blues Is Here to Stay," "You Are My Love," "Third Degree," "Thank You Baby," "She's Gone," and "I'll Never Stop (I Can't Stop Loving You)."

In the CBS studios located on London's New Bond Street, Peter Green was finally able to enjoy the recording conditions that he'd wanted to achieve on his own album: including a live recording done without overdubbing or mixing. In the live recording session, all the elements were played and performed simultaneously, including Eddie Boyd's vocals and Peter Green's solos. The album was completed in a single day, on January 25, and it was released in March 1968, one month after Fleetwood Mac's own album was released, to avoid disrupting its promotion.

JOHN MCVIE,
A QUIET STRENGTH

John Graham McVie had a relatively quiet and idyllic child-hood. The son of Reg and Dorothy McVie, he was born on November 26, 1945, in Ealing, West London. He grew up much loved by his parents, who had sadly lost his sister at a very young age. In his youth he developed a passion for music, which was a constant presence in the McVie house-hold, and he began learning to play the trumpet at the age of fourteen.

The Rock Bug

At the end of the 1950s, McVie had a revelation during a visit to his cousins, with whom he'd listened to Buddy Holly's "Rave On" until they wore out their 45 rpm single. He had just caught the rock bug. His neighbor, Cliff Barton (who would join Cyril Davies and His R&B All Stars as bass-ist in June 1963), introduced him to other pioneers of the genre like Chuck Berry, Little Richard, and Jerry Lee Lewis. Like many young people at the time, John took up the gui-tar, and he eventually formed his first real band—the Krewsaders—with a few of his neighbors. The band mainly covered songs by the Shadows, whose guitarist Hank Marvin was an inspiration to all the kids of that era, and they performed mostly at parties and weddings. This was more than enough for John, who had no larger plans to pursue a career in music. McVie was an inherently shy young man, and rock stardom didn't seem like a natural fit.

A Place in the Shade

Noting that the position of bassist did not seem to appeal to his contemporaries, who preferred to compete on guitar, McVie decided to devote himself to the lower frequencies. The only problem was that John was a novice bassist… without a bass. So, he did what many people had done before him, and he removed the two high strings from his guitar, a Framus acoustic, to create a makeshift bass. The result was hardly convincing, but it enabled him to experi-ment. Without taking lessons, he learned by trying to

reproduce the lines he heard on records. This was in keep-ing with his hard-working but modest nature. His only aim was to have fun. Even though his parents were concerned about what kind of professional future music could offer their son, they supported him from day one. John's level-headed, rational nature reassured them. So, they were enthusiastic when they saw him play in concert and blossom onstage. They were unaware, however, that a fire was smoldering inside their son. John's involvement with the Krewsaders had given John an appetite for music, and this passion was about to become his top priority.

Under Mayall's Wing

In 1961, John Mayall was looking for a new bassist for his band, the Powerhouse Four, and he wanted to hire the McVies' neighbor, Cliff Barton. At that time, Barton was the guitarist with Ricky Wade and the Crossfires. Cliff declined Mayall's offer, but he suggested that Mayall audition John, who was not yet sixteen. Owing to his youth, McVie was not selected by Mayall, who nevertheless took a liking to the promising youngster. Mayall wanted to see him con-tinue down the virtuous path of the blues, and he advised McVie to listen to records by B. B. King and Willie Dixon so that he could learn from the masters. Self-disciplined as always, John listened, deciphered, and played, all the while continuing his journey with the Krewsaders as they played weddings and small local gigs. Two years later, in 1963, John McVie was out of school, seventeen years old, and about to take his first steps in professional life working as a tax collector. In itself, this job was already quite an achieve-ment for the son of a metalworker, as it meant John was able to get away from factory work, and it would allow him to keep music as a main pillar of his personal life. "The tax inspector bit. I don't know how that came about," he later explained. "One minute I was in school and the next I was in an office doing something I had no talent for and even less desire to do."[6]

Denied the status of being a founding member of Fleetwood Mac in favor of Bob Brunning, John McVie made up for it by establishing himself as a pillar of the band.

The Perfect Link

When the Krewsaders split up in early 1963, John Mayall was left to pick up the pieces. He asked John McVie to join him in his new band, the Bluesbreakers. The usually cautious, level-headed McVie did not hesitate before plunging into the uncertainty of a musical career. He worked well with Mayall, who had already recruited guitarist Bernie Watson and drummer Peter Ward. Thus, the Bluesbreakers were born. McVie felt safe with the mentoring and reassuring figure of Mayall, the "Godfather of British Blues," as he continued to develop his talent.

Although he was determined to seize his chance, John was, as always, very pragmatic, and he did not give up his day job: "The best part was that the first day at the office was also my first gig with John Mayall. That's how it went for the next 9 months. Office in the day and gigs in the evening. Until something had to go. […] Fortunately, John was becoming better known and the gigs were coming in. There really wasn't any choice."[6] Concert after concert, John McVie grew in confidence, and although the first lineup of the Bluesbreakers did not produce any recordings, the second iteration of the band (which saw Martin Hart replace Peter Ward behind the drums) recorded the single "Crawling Up a Hill" in 1964. This was the very first recording on which John McVie, then aged eighteen, can be heard playing bass with John Mayall and the Bluesbreakers.

A Slippery Slope

Around this time, April 1964, two more band members were also replaced. Hughie Flint was the third drummer to join the band in less than a year, and Roger Dean also replaced guitarist Bernie Watson. At this point, John McVie and John Mayall were the only original members of the Bluesbreakers. Despite these personnel changes, the band went on to play more and more concerts, and in March 1965 they produced a live album called *John Mayall Plays John Mayall*, which was recorded at a London club known as Klooks Kleek. McVie's bass playing on the album demonstrates a growing ease with being onstage. Just a few days after the album's release, Eric Clapton joined the band to record the single "I'm Your Witchdoctor." Devoted to the blues, Clapton took John Mayall and the Bluesbreakers into another dimension. Yet it was precisely at this point that John McVie gradually began to lose his footing. "When I joined Mayall the drinking was part of the scene," McVie said later. "I met a lot of people who drank, and it snowballed until I'd be drinking half a bottle of spirits a gig."[7] In 1965 McVie was sidelined by John Mayall in favor of Jack Bruce (Eric Clapton's future bandmate in Cream) and he wasn't reinstated until a month later. Fascinatingly, this was all the time it took to torpedo what could have been the first meeting between two future members of Fleetwood Mac. During McVie's brief absence from the group, Peter Green briefly replaced Eric Clapton on guitar. Clapton returned to the Bluesbreakers, ousting Peter Green in the process, at the same time that John was also brought back into the fold.

MIKE VERNON, THE MAN WHO BROADENED EVERYONE'S HORIZONS

Mike Vernon was just nineteen years old when, in 1963, he joined the prestigious Decca Records label. A few months before his arrival, Decca had failed to sign the Beatles, but they made up for it by signing the Rolling Stones and the Who, among others. Mike had already decided that his future lay in the world of music, but he did not yet know that he would become one of the essential components in the blossoming success of Fleetwood Mac.

A Fanzine and a Label

A native of Harrow, England, Vernon was born on November 20, 1944, and he was passionate about rhythm'n'blues and rock'n'roll since childhood. At Decca, Vernon started out as a jack-of-all-trades. He made tea and worked as a courier, but he didn't mind performing these seemingly menial tasks. He knew his future was in music, and he was ready to work his way up the proverbial ladder. In the evenings, Mike spent his time in London clubs, soaking up the blues. Having become a connoisseur of the genre, in January 1964 he launched a monthly fanzine called *R&B Monthly* with his childhood friend Neil Slaven. Together, the two men pursued their passion, writing articles for the magazine, spotting new trends, and becoming true tastemakers in the process. Mike's position at Decca put him at the epicenter of the British blues boom, and he quickly realized that many blues albums were simply not being distributed by British labels.

The Creation of Blue Horizon

To fill this gap, in February 1965 Mike Vernon and Neil Slaven decided to sell a 45 rpm single by Hubert Sumlin along with the thirteenth issue of their magazine. At the time, Sumlin was a guitarist known for his work with blues legend Howlin' Wolf. The single was entitled "Across the Board" and it was recorded at Vernon's parents' house in the residential suburb of Kenley. This marked the beginning of the independent blues label known as Blue Horizon, even though production runs remained very limited, with fewer than one thousand copies sold per run. Vernon's aim was to offer his enthusiastic public reissues of rare singles from American blues musicians like J. B. Lenoir and "Champion" Jack Dupree.

Later in 1965, Blue Horizon took another step forward when it released its first full-length album, which featured the Harmonica Boss, Mississippi bluesman Doctor Ross. To make this happen, Vernon took advantage of Doctor Ross's visit to Europe during the American Folk Blues Festival tour to stop by his hotel room in London and offer him this recording.

The Success of Fleetwood Mac

In 1966, Vernon's activities at Decca led him to produce the famous collaboration between John Mayall and Eric Clapton, *Blues Breakers*. While he loved showcasing great blues musicians, Vernon's greatest dream was to champion the voices of British blues artists, and Clapton and Mayall were just the tip of the iceberg.

When Peter Green permanently replaced Eric Clapton in the Bluesbreakers, Mike Vernon was immediately dazzled by his talent, and he followed Green's meteoric rise attentively. Meanwhile, he produced David Bowie's first album for Deram Records, a division of Decca, in 1967. Vernon also spent time cutting his teeth in the British blues market; Blue Horizon released Chicken Shack's early albums and singles, including "It's Okay with Me Baby" written by Christine Perfect.

Green left the Bluesbreakers in 1967, but Vernon managed to dissuade him from giving up music and setting off on an uncertain road trip to Morocco, as he had originally intended. He convinced Green to stay in England and launch his own project. It wasn't long before guitarist Jeremy Spencer got in on the act and Fleetwood Mac was (almost) born.

At the end of 1967, Mike Vernon signed a deal with CBS to distribute Blue Horizon releases worldwide. At the same time, the Fleetwood Mac "family" was taking its place on the label; Peter Green, Mick Fleetwood, and John McVie were sometimes brought together in the studio to assist other artists, as happened with Eddie Boyd in January 1968.

Thus, when Fleetwood Mac took off, the group capitalized fully on the promising partnership between CBS and Blue Horizon. It released *Fleetwood Mac*, also known as *Peter Green's Fleetwood Mac*, on February 24, 1968, and thus enabled Blue Horizon not only to achieve its first major success, but also to seal its role in Mac history.

Blue Horizon: Promoter of the Blues

The Blue Horizon label's catalog continued to grow in the years that followed, with the release of more than seventy

Mike Vernon poses dramatically with a guitar that has no strings or fittings. He shines brightly behind a mixing console.

singles and a hundred albums by artists from both sides of the Atlantic. The American side of the business was represented by artists like Otis Rush, Lightnin' Hopkins, Sonny Boy Williamson II, B. B. King, Lightnin' Slim, Bukka White, and Mississippi Joe Callicott. Some of these musicians, such as Otis Spann and Champion Jack Dupree, were backed on some of their recordings by British musicians like Paul Kossoff, Stan Webb, Pete Wingfield, Irishman Rory Gallagher, and, of course, Peter Green.

British artists that signed to Blue Horizon include Chicken Shack, Duster Bennett, Key Largo, Gordon Smith, Jellybread, and Christine Perfect (who was soon to become Christine McVie).

Over the years, the label managed to place numerous singles onto the charts, including songs by Chicken Shack ("I'd Rather Go Blind" in 1969) and Fleetwood Mac ("Need Your Love So Bad," "Black Magic Woman," and the number one song "Albatross," which were all released in 1968).

Before signing with Reprise Records for *Then Play On* in 1969, Fleetwood Mac released its first two albums, *Fleetwood Mac* (number four in the UK) and *Mr. Wonderful* (number ten), with Blue Horizon. In late 1969, the label also released *Blues Jam at Chess*, which included Fleetwood Mac with some of the bluesmen who inspired them and which was reissued in the US in 1971 as *Fleetwood Mac in*

Chicago. Thirty years later, in 1999, the boxed set *The Complete Blue Horizon Sessions 1967–1969* was released by Columbia / Blue Horizon.

Blue Horizon ceased operations in 1972 as the flame of the British blues boom gradually started to die out, but it was resurrected in the early 2010s by music executives Seymour Stein and Richard Gottehrer, although they had no access to the label's historic catalog. Today, the label is distributed in North America by Fat Possum Records.

A Life in the Service of Music

Mike Vernon released his own solo album entitled *Moment of Madness* in 1973 and continued his work as a musician and producer. He played in various projects, including working with the Olympic Runners from 1974 to 1979, and Rocky Sharpe and the Replays, for whom he played bass between 1979 and 1983 under the pseudonym Eric Rondo. Vernon went on to set up two new labels—Indigo and Code Blue—in the 1990s, before re-donning his musician's hat and releasing the album *Beyond the Blue Horizon* in 2018, which supported a European tour with his band the Mighty Combo.

For his lifetime of service to music, he was made a Member of the Order of the British Empire (MBE) in 2020. Throughout Fleetwood Mac's storied career, Mick Fleetwood never forgot the key role that Mike Vernon played in the band's early days.

Fleetwood Mac's first album opens with a blues boogie borrowed from Buster Brown, but it was played in the style of the inimitable Elmore James (pictured here).

MY HEART BEAT LIKE A HAMMER

Jeremy Spencer / 2:55

Musicians: Jeremy Spencer: vocals, slide guitar / Peter Green: electric guitar / John McVie: bass / Mick Fleetwood: drums / **Recorded:** CBS Studios, London, December 11, 1967 / **Technical Team:** Producer: Mike Vernon / Sound Engineer: Mike Ross / Assistant Sound Engineer: Richard Vernon

Genesis and Lyrics

The conditions for recording live in the studio were just as stressful for Peter Green, who would have preferred live recording onstage, as they were for Mike Vernon and Mike Ross, who would have preferred the comfort of instrument-by-instrument recording on the four-track at their disposal at CBS Studios. But their earlier November 22, 1967, recording session proved fruitful and reassured everyone that they were on the right track. So, it was with confidence and relaxation that the musicians embarked on their December 11 session, with two choice tracks still to be finalized: "My Heart Beat Like a Hammer" and "Shake Your Moneymaker." Both afforded the group the opportunity to really go for it, and to prioritize intention over technique. Their more raw, instinctive playing also lent itself to a dirtier sound, which did not displease Peter Green.

Green watched with a satisfied eye as Jeremy Spencer took the reins on "My Heart Beat Like a Hammer." He would like to have pushed Spencer toward writing new songs, but Jeremy had a natural affinity for playing covers. Ever since his early days on the guitar, he had been regurgitating—with flair—the repertoire of his role models, with Elmore James at the top of the list. But Spencer felt so strongly that perfection had already been achieved by his predecessor that he saw himself more as an apostle than a prophet. "Peter had asked me on the band's onset if I ever wrote my own material and I had told him that I didn't. The problem was that I was uninspired with getting anything new."[3] This sentiment was confirmed on "My Heart Beat Like a Hammer." The first composition is credited to Spencer but it is, in fact, a crudely concealed borrowing from "Don't Dog Your Woman" (the dog on the album cover is perhaps a nod in that direction). Buster Brown, an American bluesman famous for his hit "Fannie Mae," recorded "Don't Dog Your Woman" seven years earlier, in 1959. Jeremy simply changed the placement of the song's second verse, which now comes before the chorus—a clever way of securing the songwriter's credits.

This practice was common and far from disreputable at the time. Buster Brown himself did not pull the song out of his hat. His version of "Don't Dog Your Woman" was an update of an even earlier rendition of "When My Heart

Jeremy Spencer (here in 1968) shows his reverence for pre-war American blues in *Fleetwood Mac*'s opening track.

Beats Like a Hammer," which B. B. King recorded with his band in 1954. King, in turn, modeled his song on "Million Years Blues," by Sonny Boy Williamson I, who had given birth to the melody in 1941. Who knows where Williamson found *his* inspiration for the track!

In any case, compared with Buster Brown's version, Jeremy Spencer's new arrangement did not alter the original meaning of the lyrics except that it provided an explanation for the singer's grief. He wakes up at dawn and his first thoughts are of his partner, who left home earlier in the morning. The repentance he expresses in the lyrics—he regrets not treating her as well as he should have—suggests that she left the house following an argument. The lament is intended both for the object of his love, and for the listener, in the form of a moral lesson to be learned. The lyrics include this following piece of advice: "Don't ever dog your woman / You know you're gonna ruin yourself." This song offers a notable counterpoint to the machismo that was so common in pre-war blues lyrics.

Production

Nevertheless, it would be unfair to reduce the reworking of this song to a simple shell game played with the order of the verses. Jeremy Spencer breathes new life into the track with his bubbly playing and spirited, almost rock-like interpretation. While John McVie and Mick Fleetwood strive to restore the song's original swagger, Spencer indulges in musical pyrotechnics from the very first bars (even before the other instruments come in), making his strings roar under the effect of the bottleneck slide. The staggered entrance of the rhythm section makes for a punchy intro, which is ideal for an album's opening track. The metallic sound of Spencer's guitar strings flirts with distortion, but it is his voice that really sets the track alight. Highly controlled, his unbridled vocals (he wails and shouts like Mick Jagger), including mocking accents (on "risin' sun" at 0:31 you can almost hear him let out a forced laugh), exude an alluring spontaneity. At times, you can almost visualize Spencer's movements during the take, as at the 2:27 mark when he lets out an "oh yeaaah": You can hear that he is moving away from the microphone as he positions himself for his final moments on the guitar.

With this sparkling blues boogie, Fleetwood Mac provided an emblematic and programmatic opening track for what was to come: a record of pure blues magic. The album pays unbridled tribute to a past, a culture, and a musical religion, but it also proclaims that blues is written in the future as well.

MERRY GO ROUND

Peter Green / 4:05

Musicians
Peter Green: vocals, guitar
John McVie: bass
Mick Fleetwood: drums

Recorded
CBS Studios, London: November 22, 1967

Technical Team
Producer: Mike Vernon
Sound Engineer: Mike Ross
Assistant Sound Engineer: Richard Vernon

Peter Green and his Gibson on the set of a Danish TV show, May 4, 1968.

Genesis and Lyrics

As with any self-respecting blues song, the self-pitying lamentations in this track are hammered home to help elevate the drama: "When I first met you baby, I didn't even know your name / Yes, when I first met you baby, I didn't even know your name." Beyond the fact that it is not uncommon to meet someone for the first time without knowing their name, it is easy to sense that the lyrics of this song are secondary to the sound of the music itself. This is the case even though Peter Green sings weepily about a past love that led him to a feeling of despair, concluding the song with a beautiful and naïve declaration to his beloved: "Yes, I never realized, people, just how sweet and kind one woman can be / Yes, but when I looked in your eyes / Yeah, I knew true love had come to me."

Production

Peter Green's creativity was put to the test on November 22, 1967, when the band recorded several tracks in quick succession, including "Merry Go Round." For this slow blues number, Jeremy Spencer did not see the need to contribute his guitar, much to the dismay of Green, who would later remark that Spencer often shied away from playing on songs that Green wrote. Here, the only rhythmic presence is provided by John McVie on his low-frequency bass, and Mick Fleetwood's scraggily drums. To make up for Spencer's absence, Mick sometimes emphasizes his cymbals, and he also plays with his hi-hat (the pair of cymbals on a drum kit operated by a foot pedal) open for practically the whole song. This supporting instrumentation is ideal for Peter Green's inspired playing and the deep guitar sound he produces. His approach on this track is probably one of the clearest indications of his admiration for B. B. King, whose influence is strongly felt throughout the song. As for his vocals, which are gentle and moving, they occasionally become husky following a technique popularized by most blues pioneers. "Merry Go Round," underneath its "tired end-of-rehearsal" jam-session feel, is in fact very revealing of Peter Green's magnetism. The song is a harbinger of the reverence he would soon command among guitar fans.

LONG GREY MARE

Peter Green / 2:15

Musicians: Peter Green: vocals, electric guitar, harmonica / Bob Brunning: bass / Mick Fleetwood: drums and washboard / **Recorded:** CBS Studios, London, September 9, 1967 / **Technical Team:** Producer: Mike Vernon / Sound Engineer: Mike Ross / Assistant Sound Engineer: Richard Vernon / **Single:** Side A: Black Magic Woman / Side B: Long Grey Mare / **US Release Date:** June 7, 1968 / **Reference:** Epic (ref.: 5-10351) / Best US Chart Ranking: Did Not Chart

Genesis and Lyrics

Forced out of the band in favor of John McVie, Bob Brunning left three meager testimonies to his time in the studio with Fleetwood Mac. On September 9, 1967, at CBS Studios, the bassist laid down his lines for "I Believe My Time Ain't Long," "Rambling Pony," and "Long Grey Mare." The first two songs formed both sides of the single that was released on November 3, 1967, while "Long Grey Mare" was eventually included on the band's first album. In his 2004 book *The Fleetwood Mac Story: Rumours and Lies*, Bob Brunning confirmed his involvement on these tracks: "Three tracks on which I played were eventually released: 'Long Grey Mare,' 'Ramblin' Pony' and 'I Believe My Time Ain't Long.'"[5] He was surprised, however, that his version of "Long Grey Mare" was later chosen as the B side for the US version of the "Black Magic Woman" 45, even though he had already been out of the band for some time: "It curiously featured [me] on bass, rather than John McVie."[5] His role is eminently important on this track composed by Peter Green.

There is something childlike about this track, and perhaps this is no coincidence since it shares similarities with the traditional folk song "The Old Gray Mare," which has become a children's standard thanks to its basic lyrics and endearing story of a mare with a broken leg. Beyond the closeness of the names, the structure of these songs, their lyrics, and themes are also very similar. However, in "Long Grey Mare," a more salacious reading can be made of the text, due to the use of the feminine "she" instead of "it," which causes ambiguity: "She makes me brush her in the morning / And put her to bed every night." The same applies to the verb "ride," which can be understood in the context of a horseback ride, or in the context of making love. But the most ambiguous phrase is: "When I dig you with my spur / You turn around the other way."

Production

Peter Green does not bother with a convoluted structure. Once he's past the introductory double stop, in which two notes are played simultaneously on adjacent strings, the guitarist moves on to a "galloping" section that remains unchanged throughout the song. It is impossible to ignore the song's close resemblance to "Killing Floor" by Howlin' Wolf, whose repertoire was more than familiar to Peter Green. The riff is built on a succession of string jumps, and its apparent simplicity works in favor of the track's effectiveness and bonhomie. The right-hand playing, however, requires rigorous rhythmic control, especially as the bass simultaneously reproduces the same phrase. It is this parallel running theme that makes the song so enjoyable. In the mix, the guitar is placed on the left and the bass on the right, both framing the central voice of Peter Green, who displays all his great qualities as a singer. Unlike his idol, Eric Clapton, who was slow to step out of his musician's role, Green seems delighted to be behind the microphone. His vocals come across as powerful, assured, and pure, with a few well-judged vibratos.

FOR MAC-ADDICTS

On Gary Moore's Peter Green tribute album, *Blues for Greeny*, Moore included a cover of "Long Grey Mare" with numerous added effects and a frenzied guitar solo played on Green's original, and very famous, Greeny guitar.

HELLHOUND ON MY TRAIL

Robert Johnson / 2:00

Musicians
Jeremy Spencer: piano, vocals

Recorded
CBS Studios, London: November 22, 1967

Technical Team
Producer: Mike Vernon
Sound Engineer: Mike Ross
Assistant Sound Engineer: Richard Vernon

The intersection of Highways 61 and 49 in Clarksdale, Mississippi, is the spot where, according to legend, Robert Johnson sold his soul to the devil.

Genesis and Lyrics

Long before he experienced the divine revelation that sealed his departure from Fleetwood Mac, Jeremy Spencer was already fully steeped in Christianity through his religious upbringing. Yet his love for the blues led him down the path of a man who, legend has it, signed a pact with the devil and traded his soul for exceptional guitar skills: Robert Johnson. Spencer set his sights on Johnson's most mystical and best-known work, "Hellhound on My Trail," which has become a classic blues standard. The legendary Delta bluesman recorded it in 1937, thirty years before Fleetwood Mac's version was laid down in 1967. The song's lyrics are among the darkest Robert Johnson ever wrote. In the track, wherever the protagonist goes, he feels spied upon, pursued by a "hellhound" who forces him to keep moving so he can avoid falling into the hellhound's clutches. This vision of Cerberus—the mythological figure of a typically three-headed dog who is charged with guarding the entrance to the underworld—was widespread in Southern churches at the time to keep believers away from sin. But the vision of a hellhound was also present in the collective blues imagination, as traces of it can be found in Sylvester Weaver's aptly named "Devil Blues" from 1927: "Hellhounds start to chase me man / I was a running fool."

The threat hanging over the narrator in these songs is not merely spiritual: Many twentieth-century African Americans feared for their lives in the United States, when Black men and women were hunted, terrorized, and killed by angry white mobs, often with dogs in tow. The natural elements described in this song's lyrics relay the terror of this threat, creating an almost paranormal atmosphere: "Every old place I go, every old place I go / I can tell the wind is risin', the leaves tremblin' on the tree." The narrator tries to protect himself by spreading "hot foot powder" on the threshold of his house, a kind of magic powder whose recipe—based on sulfur, chili pepper, and essential oil—is supposed to ward off evil spirits and prowlers.

One of the only authenticated photos of Robert Leroy Johnson, the tutelary figure of Mississippi blues.

Production

Robert Johnson's original version of this song is literally bloodcurdling, thanks to Johnson's seemingly possessed vocals, and his oppressive, deep guitar playing. But Fleetwood Mac takes this masterpiece in a slightly lighter direction. Far from the rough, sandy tracks of the American South, where only a well-traveled, dented guitar can transcribe your state of mind, Jeremy Spencer retreated behind a piano at CBS Studios in London. The instrument, which removes much of the tension contained in the original song, is a surprising choice until one considers the possibility that Fleetwood's two guitarists, Jeremy Spencer and Peter Green, did not want to take on the master, Robert Johnson, for fear of being found wanting. Behind his piano, Spencer has fun punctuating the melody with a few "yeahs" while invoking slippery notes that ease the tempo. But his spontaneity is what makes this reinterpretation so appealing. In fact, the band chose to use the first take they recorded on the final album because they felt it was the most natural and authentic.

Simultaneously subdued and almost bouncy in places, this reinterpretation sounds like it belongs in an old-time saloon, and it is not without charm. Spencer's impeccable vocal performance is also quite admirable. The lesson here is that if you want to avoid being crushed by a monumental song, you should maneuver around it carefully. During the same session in which he recorded "Hellhound on My Trail," Spencer also recorded "You're So Evil," which was an improvisation around the theme of "Hellhound on My Trail," but with a change of lyrics. This time, the song's threat comes from a demon-possessed woman.

SHAKE YOUR MONEYMAKER

Elmore James / 2:55

Musicians
Jeremy Spencer: vocals, slide guitar
Peter Green: electric guitar
John McVie: bass
Mick Fleetwood: drums

Recorded
CBS Studios, London: December 11, 1967

Technical Team
Producer: Mike Vernon
Sound Engineer: Mike Ross
Assistant Sound Engineer: Richard Vernon

Elmore James's song was also the subject of a tribute by the Black Crowes, who named their first studio album *Shake Your Money Maker* (1990). While the band often performs the song live, it was not included on the album.

Chris Robinson is shown here in 2022, leader of Atlanta-based rock band the Black Crowes.

Genesis and Lyrics

As the composer of "Shake Your Moneymaker" in 1961, was the Elmore James version of the song the starting point of a story that would eventually end with his inclusion on the 2014 list of the Rock and Roll Hall of Fame's "500 Songs That Shaped Rock'n'Roll"? Or was he one of many links in a chain that began in 1929 with Charlie Patton's "Shake It and Break It" and then transformed into Bukka White's "Shake 'Em on Down" in 1937 before turning into Shakey Jake Harris's "Roll Your Money Maker" in 1958? Whatever the case, Elmore James set the definitive contours of this track, crafting it into a blues classic and imbuing it with a rock'n'roll approach. This was what won over Paul Butterfield, who revisited the song in 1965 before Fleetwood Mac got hold of it in 1967. Spencer and Green were both fans of the song, and it was only logical that it would appear on the track list of the band's first album. "Shake Your Moneymaker" served as an opportunity for the musicians to let off some steam, with its fast tempo and pleasingly repetitive lyrics. The song's story is indeed a succinct one, centering around the narrator's infatuation with a woman who is not of the same social standing. She lives "up on the hill," and he is well aware that she will not stoop to his level.

Production

John McVie and Mick Fleetwood do not hide their pleasure while playing this song, and they both clearly give it their all during the recording session. This is reflected in the unintentional acceleration of the song's tempo, although the musicians continued to play as one cohesive unit. For his part, Mick displayed his concentration and pleasure in the song by working like hell on his snare drum while his foot pounds the hi-hat pedal frantically. Aside from a few cymbal strikes, Mick's playing remains deliberately rudimentary throughout, and he never loses himself in unnecessary rolls.

Mick said, "My ineptness to do separate things at speed became my style of drumming. When it got to a certain speed in the early days, the only way I could hang in there was if all my hands and feet were doing the same thing on the same beat. 'Shake Your Moneymaker' is one where everything is going flat out and doing the same thing, so it kind of defines my style, the ultimate blues shuffle. Onstage

The four musicians (posing for a group photo in 1968) develop an almost rock'n'roll approach to the blues with a blistering version of "Shake Your Moneymaker."

it often ended up three times faster than the album version, and that's already fast enough. As a song, it's what the original Fleetwood Mac was all about. Elmore James was top of the list. 'Dust My Broom' and so forth, endless funky, chunky shuffles and, in retrospect, I must say we were darn good at doing them. At that time, though, we didn't actually know what we were doing, we were just doing it."[14]

John McVie, on the other hand, shows more finesse. With the thumb of his right hand resting on the low *E* string, he strikes the strings with metronomic rigor and the swing of a double bass player. Despite his long fingernails, which had been specially manicured for fingerpicking,

Peter Green still played his guitar with a pick. He sets up this twelve-bar blues chord progression, whose originality lies in the question-and-answer game that's played against Jeremy Spencer's slide guitar, and which sounds like a scratch every time it appears. Spencer exploits the full range of his playing here, alternating with bottleneck-free parts that double up on Peter Green's own guitar playing. His voice, which is naturally husky, sounds as though it's on the verge of breaking up. This fits perfectly with a jubilant song that must have warmed up the cockles of the musicians' hearts when the song was recorded on a cold December evening.

LOOKING FOR SOMEBODY

Peter Green / 2:50

Musicians
Peter Green: vocals, harmonica
John McVie: bass
Mick Fleetwood: drums

Recorded
Decca Studios, London: April 19, 1967 (?)

Technical Team
Producer: Mike Vernon
Sound Engineer: Mike Ross
Assistant Sound Engineer: Richard Vernon

FOR MAC-ADDICTS

Before their first album was released, Fleetwood Mac unveiled its contents on November 7, 1967, when they played "Looking for Somebody" on a new radio program that had been launched on the BBC a few weeks earlier, on September 21. The "Peel sessions" were presented by the legendary John Peel until his death in 2004.

Radio host John Peel is named Best Disc Jockey at the Melody Maker Music Awards ceremony on September 18, 1969.

Genesis and Lyrics

Peter Green's twentieth-birthday recording session at Decca Studios in April 1967—a gift from John Mayall and also from destiny—was put to good use when he invited his Bluesbreakers bandmates Mick Fleetwood and John McVie to join him in the studio. During this early recording session a new composition was laid down and given the name "Looking for Somebody." A few months later, the song was included on the band's first album. Behind its apparent simplicity and sparse lyrics, the song actually has a lot to say. First, it proclaims Peter Green's love of the blues in the most naïve and sincere way possible: "I got a feeling, blues gonna be my only way." With this sentence, Green takes a vow and joins the fellowship of blues lovers. Second, the song also tells us, through its double meaning, how Green sees the blues: It is cast in a dark hue, with a certain amount of despondency and constant suffering. Embracing the blues means showing a willingness to carry the cross and live with despair. Linked to the lack of love ("I'm looking for somebody") and the vain search for physical pleasure, the blues symbolizes a state of permanent suffering. Paradoxically, as Green invokes the spirit of the blues, the sound that emerges on this track is both spiritual and intense, but no longer entirely blues. "Looking for Somebody" is equal parts soul as well as blues in that it juxtaposes the sacred and the profane.

Production

In the absence of love, there is still friendship for Peter Green in the form of his playing partners. "Looking for Somebody" is the foundational act (and track) from the trio that started it all. The three musicians appear here as tightly knit as ever, all focused on a single goal: producing emotion. The best proof of this collegial working relationship is the central place Peter Green reserves for his fellow musicians. The whole track rests on John McVie's deep, haunting bass and Mick Fleetwood's airy playing, which is concentrated on the hi-hat and a few tom strokes. Jeremy Spencer wasn't yet in the picture when this track was conceived and recorded, and the other notable absence of this track is Greeny, Peter Green's famous guitar. Green was temporarily unfaithful to his guitar, dropping it in favor of playing the harmonica on this track. Between breaks and solos, Green even develops his own melody. His breath is contained and controlled, and his musical interventions are concise and clean, even as he constantly alternates between vocals, featuring his warm, melancholy voice, and the harmonica.

Chester Arthur Burnett at San Francisco's Fillmore in 1968. His exceptional voice projection earned him the nickname Howlin' Wolf.

Peter Green was honored in a showcase concert organized by Mick Fleetwood and held on February 25, 2020, at the London Palladium theater. The concert was held just five months before the guitarist's death. A host of guests included Kirk Hammett, Billy Gibbons, Pete Townshend, and David Gilmour. Noel Gallagher, guitarist and composer with Oasis, chose to cover "No Place to Go," accompanied by Rick Vito, who had replaced Lindsey Buckingham in the Mac between 1987 and 1991.

NO PLACE TO GO

Chester Burnett / 3:20

Musicians: Peter Green: vocals, guitar, harmonica / John McVie: bass / Mick Fleetwood: drums / **Recorded:** Decca Studios, London, April 19, 1967 / **Technical Team:** Producer: Mike Vernon / Sound Engineer: Mike Ross / Assistant Sound Engineer: Richard Vernon

Genesis and Lyrics

Had his name not been incorporated into the plot of *Die Hard 3*, Chester A. Arthur, the twenty-first president of the United States, would surely have been consigned to the obscurity of history. Not so for Chester Arthur Burnett's family, who must have thought that giving their son the first and last name of a noted statesman would predestine him to achieve great things. They were not mistaken, for Burnett, who also answered to the evocative stage name of Howlin' Wolf, left his lupine mark on American blues both in Mississippi and Chicago. Burnett eventually left his home state of Mississippi and headed north to Illinois, where he made his career on the Chess Records label.

The blues, Mississippi, Chicago, Chess Records…there are so many shared points of interest that make up the map of Peter Green's musical heart, and that led him to adore Howlin' Wolf. "No Place to Go" was one of the first songs on which the future Fleetwood Mac cut its teeth as a band. This happened during a recording session on April 19, 1967, which took place before Jeremy Spencer joined the group.

"No Place to Go" is the only cover that Peter Green submitted for inclusion on the band's first album; the other covers would be introduced by Spencer later in the recording process. This shows Green's determination to establish himself first and foremost as a composer and to blaze new trails as a means of preventing the blues from becoming too inwardly focused. This was done at the risk of not offering anything new as Howlin' Wolf had done in the 1930s. Although Chester Burnett went by the nickname Howlin' Wolf, he also had the nicknames Big Foot and Bull Cow. These names emanated from his size as well as from the primal power that he was able to access, and which enabled him to project his voice with force, his throaty cries sustained by incredible breath capacity while also producing a vibrato reminiscent of a wolf's howl.

"No Place to Go" is played in a single chord, and it synthesizes the blues into its simplest form. The story told in the song itself is simple and heartbreaking: A man, bending under the weight of the years ("Now I'm old and gray"), addresses his wife and asks how much longer their relationship will last, when it will stop ruining his life both literally and figuratively: "How many more years / Have you got to wreck my life? / Well, the way you done me / Gonna wreck my life").

Production

Despite its expressive vocals and respectful approach, this cover feels a little academic, and at the very least more neutral than Howlin' Wolf's original interpretation, which truly embodied the character of the track. However, Fleetwood Mac's version is worthy of note because of the singer's harmonica playing, which occupies a central place on the track. The guitar, on the other hand, evokes the regular rhythm of train wheels—the rhythm of the narrator's life as he watches it pass him by, unable to slow it down. Green's vocals are deeper and raspier than usual, lending realism to the text and accurately portraying a middle-aged man.

Mick Fleetwood's previously primitive playing expanded under the influence of his partners.

MY BABY'S GOOD TO ME

Jeremy Spencer / 2:50

Musicians: Jeremy Spencer: vocals, guitar / Peter Green: guitar / John McVie: bass / Mick Fleetwood: drums / **Recorded:** CBS Studios, London (?) / **Technical Team:** Producer: Mike Vernon / Sound Engineer: Mike Ross / Assistant Sound Engineer: Richard Vernon

Genesis and Lyrics

Written and composed by Jeremy Spencer, this track makes no attempt to emancipate itself from the influence of Elmore James, and more specifically his interpretation of "Dust My Broom." "My Baby's Good to Me" has little depth to offer in the way of lyrics. The song tells the story of a man who falls in love with a charming young woman: "She got a fine pair of legs / Mm, her figure is a sight to see."

Production

The rhythm section, led by Mick Fleetwood and John McVie, plays a supporting role on this track. The song's main interest lies in Jeremy Spencer's slide guitar playing. He delivers an inventive, unbridled performance, including vocals that are influenced by Elmore James.

McVie and Fleetwood lay down a solid, if slightly jerky, foundation on bass and drums while Peter Green's guitar provides an effective and less academic-sounding rhythm.

The slightly muddled impression that's created by "My Baby's Good to Me" is reinforced by Mick Fleetwood's drumming, where he routinely opens his hi-hat on the song's instrumental sections. Mike Ross and Richard Vernon have often spoken about the headache of recording songs live because they were forced to test numerous combinations and orientations of microphones and amps.

In 1987, Rick Vito, formerly with Todd Rundgren, had the onerous task of replacing Lindsey Buckingham as guitarist with Fleetwood Mac.

I LOVED ANOTHER WOMAN

Peter Green / 2:55

Musicians: Peter Green: vocals, guitar / John McVie: bass / Mick Fleetwood: drums / **Recorded:** CBS Studios, London: November 22, 1967 / **Technical Team:** Producer: Mike Vernon / Sound Engineer: Mike Ross / Assistant Sound Engineer: Richard Vernon / **Singles:** Side A: Save Me / Side B: I Loved Another Woman (Live) / **UK Release Date:** April 23, 1990 / **Reference:** Warner Bros. Records (45 rpm ref.: 5439-19866-7) / Best UK Chart Ranking: 53 / **Single:** Side A: Hold Me / Side B: No Questions Asked; I Loved Another Woman (Live) / **UK Release Date:** June 1989 / **Reference:** Warner Bros. Records (45 rpm ref.: W7528T) / Best UK Chart Ranking: 94

Genesis and Lyrics

This Peter Green composition is probably one of the most mature songs on the album. Not only does it foreshadow "Black Magic Woman" musically—so much so that one wonders if it served as a rough draft—but its lyrics hint at a more complex approach to songwriting. Not everything is black and white in this love story. The narrator readily admits that he sealed his own fate by betraying his beloved. Guilty of cheating on her and allowing himself a moment's distraction, he acknowledges the role he has played, but still hopes for a happy ending: "She wouldn't do me no harm / But I loved another woman [...] / Well, come back baby / I know I treated you wrong."

Production

With a rhythm inspired by the sounds of Cuba, Mick Fleetwood's drumming is astonishingly restrained, merely marking the beat by tapping his sticks on the rim of his snare drum while John McVie plays his bass with velvet fingers. Jeremy Spencer doesn't appear on this recording, so all guitar duties fell to Peter Green, which was just as well since "I Loved Another Woman" requires restraint and finesse. His exceptional playing is modified by an icy reverb, and Green transfers the narrator's adulterous guilt directly into his guitar. His deep, heart-rending vocals also mark sincere regrets as expressed in the song's lyrics. As for the heartbreaking final "who-ooh" sung by Green, it contains all the nostalgia and pain felt by an unhappy man who longs to find happiness again.

COLD BLACK NIGHT

Jeremy Spencer / 3:15

Musicians: Jeremy Spencer: vocals, guitar / Peter Green: guitar / John McVie: bass / Mick Fleetwood: drums / **Recorded:** CBS Studios, London, November 22, 1967 / **Technical Team:** Producer: Mike Vernon / Sound Engineer: Mike Ross / Assistant Sound Engineer: Richard Vernon

Genesis and Lyrics

This song is another shameless appropriation by Jeremy Spencer. He uses the melody from Elmore James's "The Sun Is Shining." When he is confronted with the exercise of composition, Spencer seemingly takes spiritual refuge in his musical inspirations. Here, he begins the song by playing notes in slide; John McVie hesitates and joins in. Mick Fleetwood, for his part, seems unsure about when to enter the song. The musicians stop and the drummer asks the guitarist why he has not started singing. Then he says that he wanted to create an instrumental intro, also inspired by Elmore James's "The Sky Is Crying." Unfortunately, later listeners would miss out on hearing the famous intro, which was eventually abandoned. Recorded in 1959 during an improvised recording session in Chicago, "The Sky Is Crying" has established itself as one of the centerpieces of Elmore James's repertoire. At the tender age of nineteen, Jeremy Spencer shamelessly took these two tracks and invented new lyrics. But he never strayed too far from the "paternal bosom," and he retained the original theme: that of a narrator who has been abandoned by his girlfriend. This topic is a classic blues theme, and the song only has one element of suspense: Who is responsible for the breakdown of the relationship? The way the singer has been treated, and the way he treats his partner, marks a key narrative milestone in this musical genre. "She used to treat me real good / And I wonder why I didn't treat her right."

A kind of youthful insouciance on the part of Fleetwood Mac's troublemaker runs through this track, and it does not sit well with the original songs written by James, who had more experience than Spencer, since he was forty-one at the time he composed these songs. Spencer does not shy away from clichés, for example when he sets the scene: "It was a cold black night / And the rain was falling down." Similarly, the many sentences beginning with "And" are another example of repeated clumsiness.

Production

These facts should not detract from the feeling and fervor that Jeremy Spencer manages to instill in the song. His vocals, while not the best for such a lament, do provide a few shining moments, such as the slight vocal break when he climbs into a higher register. Spencer masters the blues traditions to perfection, and he slips in a few vocal punctuations and onomatopoeia to further breathe life into the track, like the "Yessss…mmmmh" that can be heard at 2:30. Moreover, the languor induced by the track's slower tempo enables listeners to observe another facet of Spencer's playing, which is that he can be more restrained when he wishes. More precise than usual, Spencer plays with economy, knowing that he is backed up by Peter Green, who spins elegant chord progressions that are set off by a delicate reverb.

"The World Keep on Turning" served as the basis for the song "World Turning," which appeared on *Fleetwood Mac* in 1975. However, Christine McVie and Lindsey Buckingham changed the song so much that the credits do not refer to the original track, or to Peter Green.

Preacher-turned-bluesman Son House elevated the bottleneck guitar technique to an art form.

THE WORLD KEEP ON TURNING

Peter Green / 2:30

Musicians: Peter Green: vocals, guitar / **Recorded:** CBS Studios, London, November 22, 1967 / **Technical Team:** Producer: Mike Vernon / Sound Engineer: Mike Ross / Assistant Sound Engineer: Richard Vernon

Genesis and Lyrics

With "The World Keep on Turning" Peter Green created one of the most dazzling songs on Fleetwood Mac's debut album. A pure blues number that draws from the sources of pioneers like Robert Johnson, Howlin' Wolf, Johnny Shines, Honeyboy Edwards, Robert Lockwood Jr., and Son House, this minimalist track was one of the songs that convinced the British media that Peter Green had perfectly infused his illustrious influences into his new band. A favorite theme of bluesmen, women are at the heart of Green's lyrics. Here a woman is seen as a source of problems ("Don't look for no worries / Worries and troubles come around"), and of sorrows ("Nobody saw me cryin' /

Nobody knows the way I feel" and "I need the woman so bad / I need her like the sky needs the sun"). A fatalist, here the narrator knows he cannot change the woman he loves, and he resigns himself to carrying on with his life as best he can ("The world keep on turning / I got to keep my feet on the ground").

Production

Peter Green's particularly moving voice follows the throbbing rhythm of his guitar, revealing a discreet vibrato to great effect. Mike Ross's work on microphone positioning is particularly evident on this track. The sound of the pick hitting against Peter Green's hollow body guitar is clearly audible. Meanwhile, Spencer's absence is surprising, but he apparently preferred acoustic guitar to electric. According to Richard J. Orlando's *A Love That Burns*, fear of playing badly, or of weighing the song down, kept Spencer from stepping in.

GOT TO MOVE

Homesick James, Marshall Sehorn / 3:20

Musicians
Jeremy Spencer: vocals, guitar
Peter Green: guitar
John McVie: bass
Mick Fleetwood: drums
Recorded
CBS Studios, London (?)
Technical Team
Producer: Mike Vernon
Sound Engineer: Mike Ross
Assistant Sound Engineer: Richard Vernon

Harmonica player Sonny Boy Williamson II on the British music show *Ready, Steady, Go*, on January 8, 1965.

Production

Starting with a cover song that's propelled by Jeremy Spencer's swaggering vocals, this album closes in much the same way, albeit with less nuance. "Got to Move" does not have the same stakes as "My Heart Beat Like a Hammer," but this final track satisfies an artistic need that Peter Green expressed to Mike Vernon. Green wanted to produce a live recording that sounded as close as possible to a live concert performance. By placing fades into the intro and outro of this song, Mike Vernon cleverly underlined the "jam session" feel of the track. The stretched and repetitive structure, the floating setup, the musicians' interjections, and the whistling sounds heard in the distance all help to set the live mood of the recording. This track seems to show the band members as they let off steam and enjoy themselves.

Genesis and Lyrics

Jeremy Spencer gives full rein to his swaggering style of play on this track. Homesick James composed the original version of the song and Marshall Sehorn wrote the lyrics, both on behalf of none other than Elmore James. Homesick James presented himself as Elmore's cousin and claimed to have given him his first guitar. However, Homesick James was known to make dubious claims. Nevertheless, Elmore immortalized this song in 1960. A master of the classic version, Jeremy Spencer puts on quite a show. From the very first seconds, he urges an imaginary woman to dance for him: "Yes, uh, oh baby, mm, you got to move your legs, baby." Whether intentionally or not, he creates ambivalence in relation to the verb *move*, which recurs throughout the track as it later takes on the meaning of "move away" when the narrator asks his wife to leave the house. The lyrics play with paradox, multiplying declarations of love that are invariably followed by requests for someone to leave the premises. The listener logically expects a declaration of love to conclude these fine promises, but the song ends with a harsh "Still you've got to go away from here, yeah."

Although Jeremy Spencer usually used his Gibson
Jazz Box in the studio, he preferred the Flying V
model whenever he played this song onstage.

Is the narrator trying to protect her from himself by asking
her to leave?

The musicians clearly enjoy playing this unpretentious
ditty, which could have been the occasion for some very
freeform solos. But, apart from a few punctuations that
Jeremy Spencer performs, he does not take the reins. The
band remains focused on their overall performance rather
than on individual moments. This spirit of togetherness is
at its height when Jeremy exclaims in the finale, this time
addressing his bandmates directly: "Let's play it out now
boys, yeah, yes."

The Gibson Flying V, a guitar popularized by Hendrix, was a favorite of
Fleetwood Mac's Jeremy Spencer.

I'M COMING HOME TO STAY

Jeremy Spencer / 2:29

Musicians: Jeremy Spencer: vocals, guitar, piano / Peter Green: guitar / John McVie: bass / Mick Fleetwood: drums / **Recorded:** 1967 / **Technical Team:** Producer: Mike Vernon / Sound Engineer: Mike Ross / Assistant Sound Engineer: Richard Vernon

Genesis and Lyrics

Although this composition is credited to Jeremy Spencer, the slide-stroked melody is instantly recognizable from "Dust My Broom," the Robert Johnson 1936 song that was inspired by a sketch from Leroy Carr in 1934. The version that caught Jeremy Spencer's attention was (unsurprisingly) Elmore James's rendition. Spencer seems to have set himself the challenge of reproducing James's entire repertoire, like a monomaniacal Alan Lomax (the famous blues ethnomusicologist). Spencer has already fashioned "I Believe My Time Ain't Long" from the same melodic skeleton, and he will use "Dust My Broom" again on Fleetwood Mac's second opus, *Mr. Wonderful*, but with entirely different lyrics. This time, the roles are reversed. In "Dust My Broom," the narrator lamented his girlfriend's departure, whereas in "I'm Coming Home to Stay," the narrator is the one who has run off, only to later return by train. He assures his companion that he will not be caught leaving her again, and that if he does return, it will be for good. It is worth noting that in this very egocentric vision, the narrator does not even consider that

the young woman may not forgive him for running away, and that she may not want him back. On the contrary, feeling confident that she will welcome him back with open arms, the narrator promises: "I'm going to give you a no good mother every night and every day." The sexual innuendo is unambiguous, and it matches Jeremy Spencer's juvenile persona.

Production

"I'm Coming Home to Stay" was dropped from the first album's track list. This was an understandable decision given that its twin, "I Believe My Time Ain't Long," had already been released as a single. Musically, however, this track has a few extra assets. It is missing the harmonica that Spencer's voice seemed to struggle against in "I Believe My Time Ain't Long." It also boasts sharper guitar attacks and a slightly better sound recording, as the proximity and dynamics of the sound seem to have been handled more carefully. This track remained unreleased until it was included in the 1999 compilation *The Complete Blue Horizon Sessions 1967–1969*. It also appeared on the Japanese reissue of *Fleetwood Mac* in 2000 and on the 2004 European reissue. The track had been languishing in the masters archives of Sony, the parent company of Columbia and Epic, but there was no record of a recording date when the master recording was unearthed.

The four members of Fleetwood Mac fixed their eyes on the British charts, which ranked their first album at number four.

BEE-I-BICKY-BOP BLUE JEAN HONEY BABE MEETS HIGH SCHOOL HOUND DOG HOT ROD MAN

Jeremy Spencer / 3:22

Musicians: Jeremy Spencer: vocals, piano / Peter Green: guitar, backing vocals / John McVie: bass / Mick Fleetwood: drums / **Recorded:** Aeolian Hall Studio 2, London, January 16, 1968 / **Technical Team:** (?)

Available on various bootlegs, including *Peter Green's Fleetwood Mac Original Live Broadcasts 1968* (2019), this song's long-winded title is indicative of its improvised and parodic nature. It's a delicacy from a session at the BBC recorded on January 16, 1968, and broadcast on the *Top Gear* radio show on the twenty-first. A little doo-wop gem, it sounds like a neurasthenic Elvis song accompanied by the not-quite-right Jordanaires. This song is worth listening to for its falsetto backing vocals and a healthy dose of self-mockery.

SOMETHING INSIDE OF ME

Elmore James / 3:54

Musicians: Jeremy Spencer: vocals, guitar / Peter Green: vocals, guitar / John McVie: bass / Mick Fleetwood: drums / **Recorded:** The Middle Earth Club, London, February 15, 1968 / **Technical Team:** Producer: Mike Vernon / Sound Engineer: Mike Ross

Although Jeremy Spencer's fascination with Elmore James often borders on obsession and caricature, it would be unfair to dismiss the guitarist and singer as a vulgar blues bellower, incapable of subtlety. In territory usually reserved for Peter Green, Jeremy Spencer is more than credible. A case in point is "Something Inside of Me," inexplicably left by the wayside. Intense, flamboyant, with a crackling lo-fi sound that adds to its charm, this track is a total success. And even if it lacks the intensity of the Elmore James original (1960), which featured two guitarists and two saxophonists, it deserves better than languishing on bootlegs like a soul in pain.

Black Magic Woman / The Sun Is Shining

UK Release Date: March 29, 1968
Reference: Blue Horizon (45 rpm ref.: 57-3138)
Best UK Chart Ranking: 37

Black Magic Woman / Long Grey Mare

US Release Date: June 7, 1968
Reference: Epic (45 rpm ref.: 5-10351)
Best US Chart Ranking: Did Not Chart

Bob Welch, who sang "Black Magic Woman" on stage during his time with Fleetwood Mac, released his own recording of the song on *His Fleetwood Mac Years and Beyond, Vol. 2* in 2006.

FOR MAC-ADDICTS

"Black Magic Woman" remained in Fleetwood Mac's live repertoire until 1974. Later, John McVie vetoed placing it in the set list, feeling that Santana's version had become too overpowering. It was reintroduced in 2018 in a slightly rewritten version with Stevie Nicks on vocals.

Side A

BLACK MAGIC WOMAN

Peter Green / 2:57

Musicians: Peter Green: vocals, guitar / John McVie: bass / Mick Fleetwood: drums / **Recorded:** CBS Studios, London, February 22, 1968 / **Technical Team:** Producer: Mike Vernon / Sound Engineer: Mike Ross

Mac's First Hit

The surprise success of the *Fleetwood Mac* album, which had critics raving about it—one called it "the best English blues record ever"—generated high expectations in the media and the public. But expectations are synonymous with pressure, a concept that clashed with Peter Green's increasingly fragile psychology.

He struggled to understand and rationalize the flurry of "good news" that descended on Fleetwood Mac: The public was starting to fight to get into the concert halls where the band was playing, the blues was becoming more popular thanks in part to their band, and other bands like Savoy Brown and Ten Years After were now following in Fleetwood's footsteps. And Fleetwood Mac was now being treated as the equal of the Beatles or the Rolling Stones by the music media, which was a lot to handle.

The Gunnell brothers, who had been the band's managers since 1967, were determined to make the most of this opportunity, and they succeeded in getting the band an appearance on the BBC. Fleetwood Mac played in front of the entire country…without a major hit under their belts. It was precisely to remedy this state of affairs that the Gunnell brothers commissioned a hit single from the band—to keep the media and public waiting for a second album while also demonstrating that the success of the first was no fluke. But

no one orders a hit from Peter Green! At least not on such terms. Predictably, Green was moved by a sort of self-defense reflex, and he composed the furthest thing from a hit that was designed to top the charts. And so, unwittingly, he gave Fleetwood Mac its first hit.

Genesis and Lyrics

"Black Magic Woman" has its origins on the other side of the Atlantic, between Chicago and the Mississippi Delta. In 1957, a Chicago blues guitarist by the name of Jody Williams released the song "You May," whose B side, the instrumental "Lucky You," was undoubtedly the starting point for Peter Green's hit. Jody Williams was no stranger to the limelight, having written the sumptuous solo for his mentor Bo Diddley's hit "Who Do You Love?" But he also played alongside other American blues figures of the time, such as Memphis Minnie and the inescapable Elmore James. Listening to "Lucky You," it is impossible not to hear the groove that would eventually run through "Black Magic Woman" eleven years later.

In the interim, Otis Rush, another blues guitarist from Chicago, seized on the riff and the general mood of the song, and used it to give birth to his 1958 song "All Your Love (I Miss Loving)," which was produced by Willie Dixon. Rush was notably accompanied by Ike Turner on rhythm guitar. He innovated by adding a vocal melody to the original instrumental track. Now one of the most iconic tracks in Otis Rush's repertoire, the song was covered in 1966 by John Mayall and his Bluesbreakers on *Blues Breakers*. Green had, of course, heard about Clapton's cover of the

Overshadowed by Santana's memorable 1970 single, Peter Green's version of "Black Magic Woman" contained its trademark bridging of jazz, blues, and Latin music.

Otis Rush hit, and he decided to follow John Mayall's oft-repeated advice: The best thing to do when you like a song is draw heavily on the opening bars to create a new rendition.

But before giving birth to "Black Magic Woman," Peter Green composed a rough draft of sorts with "I Loved Another Woman," another blues-inflected song with slightly different lyrics that is included on Fleetwood's first album. In "I Loved Another Woman," the narrator mourns a love lost because he "loved another woman." But in the mystical "Black Magic Woman," the narrator finds himself almost bewitched, and in the thrall of a woman. For the latter track Green drew inspiration from his former girlfriend, Sandra Elsdon, whom he nicknamed "Magic Mamma": "Yes, I've got a black magic woman / She's got me so blind I can't see / But she's a black magic woman / And she's tryin' to make a devil out of me." Later in the song, Peter Green confirms

that this woman has cast a spell on him and takes the opportunity to assure her of his fidelity. Again, this seems to be in reaction to the song "I Loved Another Woman" which saw the narrator bitterly regretting his adultery: "Yes, you got your spell on me, baby / You're turning my heart into stone / I need you so bad, magic woman, I can't leave you alone."

Production

On February 22, 1968, Peter Green, flanked by John McVie and Mick Fleetwood, went into the studio to record his latest composition, which had been chosen to feature on the A side of the single requested by their managers. Jeremy Spencer, who was responsible for the B-side track, was also present, but he did not contribute to the recording.

While Peter Green's sound on the first album might sometimes have seemed rudimentary due to the live

"Black Magic Woman" appears on Santana's second album, *Abraxas*, and skillfully blends Fleetwood Mac's standard with Gábor Szabó's "Gypsy Queen." It climbed to number four on the Billboard Hot 100.

Fleetwood Mac's induction into the Rock and Roll Hall of Fame in 1998 was an opportunity for uniting Peter Green and Santana onstage for a joint rendition of "Black Magic Woman." It took some bitter discussions and all Mick Fleetwood's negotiating skills to convince Green, who did not see any point in celebrating a song that had become almost alien to him.

recording, the recording of "Black Magic Woman" is exquisitely sophisticated, whether on the vibrant opening chord or on the slightly crunchy rhythm guitar, which gives space to the reverb-laden lead guitar.

Without belittling the role of the slippery, venomous rhythm section conceived by the John McVie–Mick Fleetwood duo, it is Peter Green's guitar leads and his vivacious vocals that are the real assets on this track. His touch, sharp and precise, is truly unique. So is his sense of placement and his ability to hold notes that seem unattainable for the average guitarist. His playing has a dexterity that impressed and influenced another king of sustained notes: Carlos Santana.

With two exceptional solos performed in under three minutes, Green took his band far beyond blues territory. One simply has to listen to Mick Fleetwood's tom playing to be convinced of this new sound, with its languorous, swaying rhythm. The final coda brings back a racy blues flavor that enables Peter Green to create a musical synthesis unheard of at the time, with an irresistibly spellbinding effect that's reinforced by lyrics evoking old New Orleans blues and Cajun music traditions. In the end, "Black Magic Woman" stands out as a piece that is as much influenced by blues as it is by rock and mixed with Caribbean nuances.

Completed in a single session, the single was released in the UK on March 29, 1968. It was not released in the United States until June, and it appeared in the States with another track on the B side. Success, even if it did not live up to their expectations, had officially come for Fleetwood Mac. Radio stations picked up the song, and it became the band's first Top 40 hit. Even though the group's managers had hoped for better, this kept the musicians in good spirits as they headed into recording of their second album.

"Black Magic Woman" would go down in history two years later when it was rerecorded by Carlos Santana and his eponymous band. Its reworking, sung by keyboardist Gregg Rolie, was included on the Santana band's *Abraxas* album, and the single reached number four on the US Billboard Hot 100 chart. The updated rendition followed the same musical structure as the original, using the same lyrics and melody, but its chord grid is modified, enabling Santana to add a jazzlike touch while reinforcing Latin musical traditions through the addition of congas and timbales. This musical formula often characterizes Santana's hybrid universe, which lies between rock and world music.

Black Magic Woman / The Sun Is Shining

UK Release Date: March 29, 1968
Reference: Blue Horizon (45 rpm ref.: 57-3138)
Best UK Chart Ranking: 37

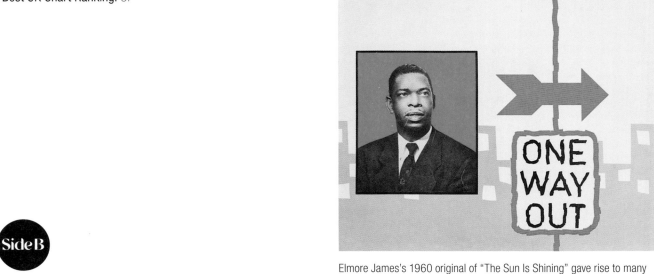

Elmore James's 1960 original of "The Sun Is Shining" gave rise to many cover versions, including those by Barry Melton in 1970, the Oscar Benton Blues Band in 1971, and Wilson Diesel in 1996.

Side B

THE SUN IS SHINING

Elmore James / 3:12

Musicians: Jeremy Spencer: vocals, electric guitar, piano / John McVie: bass / Mick Fleetwood: drums / **Recorded:** CBS Studios, London, February 22, 1968 / **Technical Team:** Producer: Mike Vernon / Sound Engineer: Mike Ross

Genesis and Lyrics

"My earliest influences came from Buddy Holly, Elvis, the Everly Brothers, Fabian, and Cliff Richard!" Jeremy Spencer recalled. "Primarily I'm a rocker rather than a bluesman. But I heard a record in 1964, a blues LP with a track on it called 'The Sun Is Shining.' That was the first time I heard Elmore James. I was never a blues fan, but that particular sound and the vocal as well started it all."[5] He went on to explain the link between his first musical love and rock, and how it pertains to this track in particular: "As a kid, plaintive ballads such as 'Unchained Melody,' 'It's Only Make Believe,' and 'Young Love' got to me the most, especially when I would hear a solitary guitar in the distance echoing the emotion. That's what got me about Elmore James when I heard 'The Sun Is Shining'—that extension of the voice through the guitar."[15] This track triggered the big bang in Jeremy's life as a musician. So, it was only logical for him to cover it for the B side of "Black Magic Woman." He does his best to re-create the emotion he perceived in Elmore James's original interpretation, and it all comes down to what he conveys through his vocals rather than through his lyrics, which are a bland collection of clichés about breaking up. There is a clumsy attempt in the use of

antonyms: "The sun is shining / But it's rainin' in my heart" and "I'm in love with my baby / And I hate to see us part." The lyrics express distress in the most prosaic way: "My baby left me this mornin' / No, she didn't even say good-bye." They feed the cliché of the bluesman who loses his wife, and his dog, and laments on his guitar while sipping bad bourbon.

Production

The simplicity of this song's story does have one advantage: It enables Jeremy Spencer, who had an annoying tendency of forgetting the original lyrics and filling in the gaps with his own words midtake, letting him concentrate on his performance. From this point of view, "The Sun Is Shining" is a complete success. Spencer has never sung so viscerally, so primally. He does not spare his voice, opening the song in a guttural register. The emotion he conveys with his vocals is transmitted right through to his playing: He smashes the piano keys, hammers the chords, and performs multiple upward and downward pitch changes. Without thinking about it, he reproduces exactly what he frequently did on the slide guitar. In fact, he is equally at home on the piano as he is on the guitar, alternating between fingerpicking and slide, with the bottleneck on his finger. On his six-string, more than on the piano, where his fingers are everywhere, he plays sparingly, following the laid-back rhythm of the bass-drums combination.

Need Your Love So Bad / Stop Messin' Round
UK Release Date: July 5, 1968
Reference: Blue Horizon (45 rpm ref.: 57-3139)
Best UK Chart Ranking: 31

Christine Perfect at the keyboard with her Chicken Shack partners in 1968.

Side A

NEED YOUR LOVE SO BAD

Little Willie John / 3:36

Musicians: Peter Green: vocals, guitar / John McVie: bass / Christine Perfect: clavier / Mick Fleetwood: drums / Mickey Baker: arrangements and direction / Orchestra: (?) / **Recorded:** CBS Studios, London, April 11, 1968 / **Technical Team:** Producer: Mike Vernon / Sound Engineer: Mike Ross

In April 2021, a few months after Peter Green's death, David Gilmour laid down his crystalline guitar on a new version of "Need Your Love So Bad," released to promote the book *Peter Green: The Albatross Man*. His version takes the form of an unexpected posthumous duet. The Pink Floyd guitarist used the vocal track that Peter Green recorded in his mother's attic in 1968. This cover version was begun while Green was alive, and it was approved by Green himself.

Genesis and Lyrics

The commercial success of *Fleetwood Mac* did not pull along "Black Magic Woman" in its wake, much to the chagrin of Peter Green, who had high hopes for the single. However, the number did help to establish in the public mind the image of Fleetwood Mac as an innovative band. It reinforced the guitarist's determination to offer new perspectives to the blues. "Need Your Love So Bad" would finally put to rest the prejudices of the less charitable mentalities of the time, who alternately sought to dismiss Fleetwood Mac as a vulgar substitute for Elmore James, or as an outrageous live band that was fun to go see but not worth taking seriously. To dispel this image, Peter Green thought of covering "Need Your Love So Bad," a sumptuous ballad immortalized by Little Willie John in 1955.

According to Christopher Hjort in *Strange Brew* (2007), John Mayall himself suggested this cover to Peter Green. Green recorded it on a small tape recorder in his mother's attic, then left the tape to gather dust.

This was by no means the first time the song had been covered. The song was originally recorded by Little Willie John, and it went to number five on the US R&B charts in 1955. The song was also covered by Dakota Staton in 1960, Irma Thomas in 1965, and Sonny Knight in 1966. Then, in 1968, the spotlight shone more brightly when the song attracted the interest of Solomon Burke, James Brown, B. B. King, and Fleetwood Mac…

The similarity of the British band's version with B. B. King's would suggest that Peter Green was inspired by King's version, which was released on his *Lucille* album in 1968. Though B. B. King toured Europe in early 1968, he

did not stop in the UK. Peter Green was therefore unlikely to have heard him live before creating his own version of this song, unless he heard a radio broadcast of one of King's concerts.

Through the narrator's search for physical contact, the lyrics of "Need Your Love So Bad" evoke a fragility that's unlike any other composition or cover version in Fleetwood Mac's repertoire up to this point: "Need someone's hand to lead me through the night / I need someone's arms to hold and squeeze me tight […] / I need some lips to feel next to mine." Peter Green allows himself just one deviation from the original lyrics: In the third line, he replaces "The dew remains" with the less lyrical "I'm at an end."

Production

Until now, Fleetwood Mac's approach, reverent as it was, consisted of modernizing old blues music by awakening its primal rock dimensions. The approach to "Need Your Love So Bad" is fundamentally different. In its original form, the song was already a hybrid, fusing blues, gospel, rhythm'n'blues, and soul. Sumptuous in its first version, it should not, in Peter Green's eyes, be defanged, but rather sublimated by an inspired interpretation in which the guitar is the main emotional medium.

The recording of this track took place on April 11, 1968, with a musician at the piano whose name and face would soon become familiar to Fleetwood Mac fans: Christine Perfect, the future Mrs. McVie. Jeremy Spencer could have taken on this task, but a mixture of disinterest and, according to Orlando's *A Love That Burns*, fear of doing the wrong thing held him back. Mike Vernon suggested Chicken Shack's keyboardist as a fill-in replacement. The musicians did not know Christine personally, but they knew of her musical capabilities, and the proposal was unanimously accepted. Several takes were required to get the song right. The first included a false start by Mick Fleetwood, who thought he had to place a drum roll. Then Christine Perfect

was caught off guard on the finale when Peter Green launched into ascending scales, and her part suddenly sounded off-key.

But Mike Vernon was still left wanting more. In his opinion, there was something not quite right with Christine Perfect's playing. He suggested that she switch to a Hammond B3 organ, whose warm, organic sound was more in keeping with the rhythm'n'blues spirit that the producer wanted to infuse into the track. This choice seems to have had a liberating effect on Peter Green's vocals, whose voice and vocals took center stage. Peter Green emphasized his choice of feeling over musical velocity. "I like to play slowly, and feel every note," he explained in a 1967 interview. "It comes from every part of my body and my heart and into my fingers, I have to really feel it. I make the guitar sing the blues—if you don't have a vocalist then the guitar must sing."[18] And if one is lucky enough to have a singer of Peter Green's caliber, then a listener's enjoyment is doubled.

With this track, Green takes a decisive step forward, revealing an extraordinary voice that's warm, velvety, and endowed with a certain soul quality that the tracks on the first Fleetwood Mac album only hinted at.

Although satisfying in many respects, this new effort still lacked a certain sparkle, in the eyes of Mike Vernon. He and Green decided to add a backing orchestra, a move that was the antithesis of Fleetwood Mac. The proposal seemed so improbable that it somehow won over the musicians. This improbable feeling was amplified when they came up with the idea of calling on Mickey Baker, the guitarist who worked on the very first version of this song with Little Willie John. Baker was asked to compose the string arrangement and to conduct the orchestra during the overdubbing session on May 15.

Unveiled on July 5, 1968, with "Stop Messin' Round" on the B side, "Need Your Love So Bad" performed fairly well on the UK charts, landing at number thirty-one. (Incidentally, it also reached number seven in the Netherlands.) Released independently of any album, "Need Your Love So Bad" found its way onto the Fleetwood Mac compilation album *The Pious Bird of Good Omen*. Released on August 15, 1969, that album was a motley assemblage of singles that included songs from *Mr. Wonderful* and two tracks recorded with Eddie Boyd. Another, unedited version of "Need Your Love So Bad" that clocked in at 6:55 was unveiled in 1999 on the album *Fleetwood Mac: The Complete Blue Horizon Sessions 1967–1969*. That album also includes a version of the song that was originally intended for the American market, where the band had considered releasing the track as a single before abandoning the idea. The 1999 release features vocal overdubs by Peter Green and an additional guitar.

Designed in 1959, Peter Green's Les Paul Gibson became an inseparable part of the guitarist's life.

GREENY, PETER GREEN'S LEGENDARY GUITAR

Peter Green's career took a serious turn in the summer of 1966, when he joined John Mayall's Bluesbreakers. When he was asked to join the band, his challenge was to replace Eric Clapton, who was considered a guitar god by many. It was impossible to accept the job without being totally up to the task. So, wanting to follow in Clapton's footsteps, Peter decided to buy the same guitar that Clapton used: a Gibson Les Paul Standard with a sunburst finish. Green bought the 1959 model, which cost him around £60. The result was a unique sound that became his trademark, so much so that the instrument, which was affectionately nicknamed "Greeny," was said to have magical powers!

A Guitar with a Unique Sound

With his new instrument, Peter Green created an atypical, out-of-phase sound that produced a nasal tone which was otherwise absent from the usual Les Paul repertoire. "I never had a magic one," he would declare with amusement many years later. He modestly admitted that he had simply tried to copy Eric Clapton: "Mine wasn't magical. [...] The pickups were strong, but I took one of them off. I copied Eric [Clapton]. I heard him play one night, and he was on the treble pickup all night long. It sounded so good, I thought I'd take my bass pickup off altogether. Try and wait for the same luck. As if it was luck! It takes a lot of genuine practice and worry to get a sound like that."[12]

For those who aren't well versed in electric guitars, a pickup is a small device that's embedded into the body of the guitar directly beneath the strings, and it converts string vibrations into electrical signals that are then sent to an amplifier. When Green decided to put his neck pickup back on, he accidentally reversed the magnetic polarity, meaning that the pads of his humbucker (a type of pickup) were turned toward the bridge of his guitar rather than toward the neck. This inversion produced the unprecedented, out-of-phase tone that is so sought after by guitarists. Several

guitar makers have suggested another possible cause for the change in tone—somehow the internal connections were reversed during the manufacturing stage.

Greeny Changes Hands

In 1970, young Northern Irish guitarist Gary Moore opened for Fleetwood Mac along with his band, Skid Row. Just as Green had idolized Clapton, Moore had long revered the Mac guitarist. "I saw Peter in Belfast for the first time and I had a huge impression, that I'd never heard such 'deep' guitar. At the age of 14 or 15, it's really something that blows you away: I'd heard a guitar before, but I'd never 'felt' it. This feeling invaded every space in the room, it was infectious, you just had to watch him play, read the joy on his face. His playing was so fluid…And when I got to know him, he helped me a lot."[13]

Indeed, Peter quickly took Gary under his wing. Shortly before leaving Fleetwood Mac in 1970, Green offered to lend Gary his guitar. Gary could not believe his ears, but he enthusiastically accepted and picked up the instrument from Peter's parents. Moore's only fear was that something might happen to his mentor's six-string. For this reason, he took no chances and took the guitar with him wherever he left his small, unlocked studio in London's Belsize Park. After a few days had passed, Peter contacted Gary and asked him what he thought of Greeny. The young Irishman was obviously ecstatic, and he was taken aback when Peter asked if he would be interested in buying Greeny from him. Green had no plans for making a long career in the music business, so knew he would not be needing the guitar. He opened up to Gary about his imminent departure from Fleetwood Mac.

Gary, who had a very limited budget, was afraid of making his mentor too low an offer. But Peter was not really interested in money. What mattered most to him was finding a good home for his instrument, where it would be

pampered and played in the purest blues tradition. And he sensed that Gary was one of the best. Peter invited Gary to sell his guitar—a Gibson SG—and to give Gary whatever he wanted in exchange. Moore bought it for £160. When he paid Peter the money, Peter gave him back around £50, explaining that he just wanted to break even. Touched, Gary thanked Peter warmly and told him that if he ever wanted his instrument back, he wouldn't keep it. But Peter was settled in his decision, and he told Gary that he would never touch Greeny again.

A Long Voyage

From this point on, Greeny became Gary Moore's instrument of choice, and he recorded some of his finest material with it, whether on Thin Lizzy's ninth album, *Black Rose: A Rock Legend* (1979), or on the unforgettable "Parisienne Walkways" track off his first album, *Back on the Streets*, which was released in 1978.

Moore made very few modifications to Green's guitar, contenting himself with changing the volume and tone knobs. The biggest transformation was necessitated by a car accident that shattered Greeny's neck.

Miraculously repaired, the guitar found itself at the heart of Gary Moore's 1995 album *Blues for Greeny*, in which the student paid tribute to the master by covering some of Peter Green's finest pieces, such as "If You Be My Baby," "Need Your Love So Bad," and "The Supernatural," among others.

Unfortunately, the love affair between Greeny and Gary Moore came to an end in 2006, when the Northern Irish guitarist was forced to sell the instrument for financial reasons. The capital gain was enormous, of course, and the sale of the guitar to vintage specialist Phil Winfield fetched between $750,000 and $1.2 million. Winfield soon put Greeny back on the market for around $2 million.

Greeny then passed from collector to collector until one fine morning in 2014. On that particular day, Metallica guitarist Kirk Hammett was in London and he received a message from a friend saying that he had a guitar he thought Hammett would want to see. Guitar dealer Richard Henry met Hammett in his hotel room with a case and a vintage Marshall amp. When Kirk's friend opened the case, the

Gary Moore playing "Greeny" during the Black Rose tour in May 1979. Opposite: Having passed through the hands of Gary Moore and Kirk Hammett, "Greeny" acquired the aura of a legendary guitar, on a par with Eric Clapton's "Blackie" or David Gilmour's "Black Strat."

Metallica guitarist immediately noticed the inverted pickups and realized what instrument he was dealing with. As soon as he played Greeny, he was blown away...but his enthusiasm was quickly tempered by the asking price, which was close to $2 million. Hammett consulted another legendary guitarist, Jimmy Page of Led Zeppelin, who urged him to buy Greeny without a moment's hesitation. Hammett was convinced, and the very next day he played Greeny onstage.

Back Home

A fan of Peter Green, Gary Moore, and Thin Lizzy, Kirk Hammett did not buy Greeny to leave it in a case or behind glass. He bought it so he could put it back to where it belonged: onstage. It was with this in mind that, at Mick Fleetwood's invitation, Hammett took part in a concert in honor of Peter Green, on February 25, 2020, at the London Palladium theater. During rehearsals for the show, Hammett picked up Greeny and covered "The Green Manalishi (with the Two Prong Crown)," which he played masterfully at the concert while being accompanied by ZZ Top guitarist Billy Gibbons. At the end of this first rehearsal session, Mick Fleetwood realized that it had been almost half a century since he had been on stage with Greeny. Kirk had brought her "home" and the circle was complete.

ALBUM

MR. WONDERFUL

Stop Messin' Round . I've Lost My Baby . Rollin' Man . Dust My Broom . Love That Burns .
Doctor Brown . Need Your Love Tonight . If You Be My Baby . Evenin' Boogie .
Lazy Poker Blues . Coming Home . Trying So Hard to Forget

RELEASE DATES
United Kingdom: August 23, 1968
Reference: Blue Horizon—7-63205
Best UK Chart Ranking: 10
Best US Chart Ranking: Did Not Release in the US

The press criticized the quality of the production and the redundancy of the melodies, but *Mr. Wonderful* ranked in the top 10 of UK album sales.

LACKING IN INSPIRATION

Without in any way detracting from all the obvious good qualities of *Fleetwood Mac*, that album's success was nonetheless a result of the sudden interest in British blues among that country's young people. At the beginning of 1968 things were looking good for Fleetwood Mac, although they were not yet as musically open-minded as the Rolling Stones, Pretty Things, or the Animals, mainly due to the doctrinaire stance adopted by Peter Green and Jeremy Spencer. As good apostles of the blues, the two musicians did not wish to deviate from their favorite genre by mixing it too much with other popular styles. However, the Latin-influenced single "Black Magic Woman," which was released in the UK in March 1968, seems to have triggered something in Spencer and Green, and perhaps it softened their rigorous vision of what the blues could be. At the beginning of 1968, the band began to incorporate rock'n'roll songs, such as Little Richard's "Long Tall Sally," into their live performances—something that would have been unimaginable just a few months earlier. Although the seed of novelty might have been planted, Fleetwood Mac's second album, *Mr. Wonderful*, still reflects a subservient fidelity to the blues that clearly hampers the band's ability to move forward.

Undermined Credibility

In April 1968, barely two months after the release of their first LP, Fleetwood Mac returned to CBS Studios in London to work on their second album. Peter Green was far from relaxed, and the pressure was beginning to weigh on his vulnerable shoulders. Green's fans considered him an equal to Eric Clapton, but Green did not feel he deserved such acclaim. He doubted not only himself but also his band, which didn't rehearse nearly enough for his tastes. The potential of Fleetwood Mac was obvious, but the members of the band too often lost themselves in on- and offstage behavior that wasn't always in the best of taste. In their early days, audiences raved about Fleetwood Mac's musical qualities, but as time progressed fans talked more about their onstage antics, which were often vulgar and often the fault of Jeremy Spencer, although the other band members let him get away with behaving poorly. Spencer used foul language, played with dildos, and occasionally filled condoms with beer or milk and then hung them on his guitar. By the end of March, the band was banned from playing at the Marquee in London, even though they had been playing there for several years.

Clifford Davis, who had recently become the group's manager and would remain in this role until 1974, was tearing his hair out trying to calm down other nervous venues. Davis had cut his teeth in the business with more disciplined acts, including the Beatles, whom Davis worked alongside as an assistant to Brian Epstein, their legendary mentor. At the time Clifford was known as Cliff Adams, his birth name, but he decided to change it in 1968–69 to avoid confusion with the vocal group the Cliff Adams Singers. At the beginning of 1968, Cliff joined Rik and John Gunnell's agency, which had been booking the band's tours since the band's inception. In his book *Fleetwood Mac: The First 30 Years* (1998), Bob Brunning writes that Peter and Cliff met at the agency shortly after the release of "Black Magic Woman" on a day when Green had come to the office to complain about the single's promotion. The two men hit it off, and soon Peter asked Cliff to take over the band's management. Once Davis accepted, one of his first tasks was to convince Green to include his name in the credits of his songs, a decision that would have repercussions in the future.

In the meantime, the band became a little more disciplined in the studio. Their recording sessions were short and grouped together over a few days in April 1968. In a way, this was fortunate, as the sessions became a source of occasional tension, particularly between the technical team and Green, who was extremely demanding.

Objective: Re-Creating the Sound of Chess Studios

From the outset, the musicians agreed on new recording methods that differed significantly from those used on their first album. They were uncompromising as they discussed their plans with Mike Vernon. They wanted their sound to be captured in the traditional way, with microphones positioned in front of their amps, but their quest for sonic

Phil Chess (far left), the emblematic founder of Chess Records, helped oversee the "Super Blues" sessions in January 1967, a record featuring (L to R) Bo Diddley, Little Walter, and Muddy Waters.

perfection was not an easy ask. At one point, sound engineer Mike Ross was instructed to achieve the darkest, muddiest sound possible. To do this, he was given a yardstick to help guide him while setting up the array of microphones that were erected around the studio. The idea was to make the listener feel as if they were in Chess Studios in the heart of the 1950s. In Peter Green's eyes, nothing could match the authenticity of the works recorded within the walls of that renowned Chicago label, which was founded by brothers Leonard and Phil Chess. Chess Studios produced the best works of Muddy Waters, Bo Diddley, Howlin' Wolf, Sonny Boy Williamson II, John Lee Hooker, and Memphis Slim. In short, a large part of Peter Green and Jeremy Spencer's personal pantheon of musical heroes all came from Chess Studios, and they dreamed of re-creating that legendary sound inside CBS Studios in London.

It was left to Mike Vernon and Mike Ross to fashion this sonic ideal, even though recording technology had evolved toward greater purity by the late 1960s. The first step was to position the microphones, which was Mike Ross's job. Mike Vernon left Ross in charge, recognizing that his own knowledge of the subject was limited. More importantly, Vernon was also not really interested. "I do know people who can tell the difference [by ear] and can say, 'Well that sounds to me like a Neumann…' which is extraordinary, really, but I'm not one of those people. I'm more of a feel merchant: if I don't have the right kind of feel from the band, the right kind of approach from everybody involved, then it's not much good to me. It won't make any difference what microphones I use, it won't sound any better!"[16]

So, Mike Ross found himself obliged to squirm around in the studio as he worked to position mics in every possible way, and to turn amps and speakers against the grain to "dirty up" the sound as much as possible. This was like asking a cleaner to sprinkle dust around a room instead of cleaning it up. The incongruity did not end there—to satisfy Fleetwood Mac's demands, Mike Vernon also had the idea of running the vocals through a Vox AC30 guitar amp, which degraded the signal and "dirtied" the sound. For the guitars, the plan was simpler: Some overdrive (distortion) was added to each amp. With these few ingredients, the band's sound objective was achieved; they recorded in mono since the equipment of the time was mostly designed for this type of listening, and the sound came out raw and distorted. Add to this a saxophone section that sometimes sounds inexplicably strange ("Need Your Love Tonight" can make the most fragile ears bleed) and a heterogeneous mix that detracts from the listening experience, and you have a record that sounds almost amateurish in its production quality. This approach proved unappealing to uninformed listeners, and while these aesthetic choices were based on artistic decisions, the resulting music was tasteless and unoriginal.

An Extended Lineup

On "Black Magic Woman," which had been recorded just a few weeks earlier, the band demonstrated its fabulous ability to marry genres, but on this new album Fleetwood Mac seems to show contempt for the listener, offering no fewer than four songs that all feature the same introductory riff ("Dust My Broom," "Doctor Brown," "Need Your

In 1968, Clifford Davis (pictured here in 1976), trained in management by Beatles' mentor Brian Epstein, took over the Mac's destiny.

Concert poster, Central London Polytechnic on April 27, 1968. This concert was recorded as a live album and released in 1986 by Thunderbolt.

Love Tonight," and "Coming Home"). These were all four Elmore James compositions suggested by Jeremy Spencer, whose limits in terms of inspiration had become quite glaring. These limits seemed to seal his fate within the band, since this would be his last major contribution to the group as guitarist and singer. However, Peter Green also bears some responsibility for this situation. Although he did not appreciate his guitarist's lack of commitment—particularly to his own songs—Green brooded over his grievances rather than engaging in conflict, and more often than not he found himself having to play both his part and Jeremy's.

For this new album, the team around the four central members of the group began to expand. A new recruit named Christine Perfect, the keyboardist from Chicken Shack, joined the roster and took over duties on the keyboard and piano. Perfect was not immediately promoted to full-member status within the group, but her guest appearances validated all the good things the members of Fleetwood Mac had already thought about her. With the possible exception of Jeremy Spencer, who did not take kindly to the arrival of a musician who was meant to play the piano, a privilege that was previously reserved for him. According to Spencer, he could have added piano overdubs himself.

In addition to Christine Perfect, the team also enjoyed the contributions of harmonica player Duster Bennett and, at Mike Ross's suggestion, alto saxophonists Steve Gregory and Dave Howard, and tenor saxophonists Johnny Almond and Roland Vaughan. This was a complete U-turn for Peter Green and John McVie, who had not appreciated the inclusion of horns into the Bluesbreakers during their time with that band. But, in Green's mind, this was all part and parcel of the Chicago blues sound, and therefore worth the sacrifice. These new contributions, which are mostly limited to the accompaniment on each track, remain far down in the mix and cannot mask the lack of originality in this album as a whole.

Between the obvious lack of inspiration and the questionable method of sound recording that managed to make Peter Green's guitar shriek (the last straw!), the final results of this new opus did not live up to the band's (or the critics') expectations. The very name of the album, *Mr. Wonderful*, could almost make one smile, given how out of step it is with the album's content.

Greater Than the Sum of Its Parts

The name of this second album is even more smile-provoking when combined with the Terence Ibbott photograph that was chosen for the cover, which captures Mick

At the Mac's request, John Peel wrote humorous comments about the band members as liner notes for *Mr. Wonderful*.

The compilation album *Fleetwood Mac: The Complete Blue Horizon Sessions 1967–1969* allows fans to fully immerse themselves in the recording of *Mr. Wonderful*. The compilation album includes false starts, outtakes, and studio discussions.

Fleetwood's bemused gaze. The cover had already been chosen before the album was finished, and we owe the album name to Bob Brunning. The group's founding bassist kept up excellent relations with his former bandmates; one day, while he and Peter Green were having lunch, they started joking about talk show hosts and the obsequious way that they buttered up their guests. They began imitating the hosts and their ridiculously flowery language: "[And here is] the truly wonderful…" and so on. The album title was thus born from their joking around, and it was chosen by default, after CBS categorically vetoed the original title that the group wanted: *A Good Length*. It's not known whether this title was meant to evoke a "good length" for the record, or for something else…

The album cover inaugurated a series of artworks all featuring Mick Fleetwood, and all capitalizing on his tall, lanky physique. He is shown shirtless, wearing a hat, with his eyes wide open like a deer caught in the headlights. People who purchased the record could unfold the album cover, revealing Fleetwood's lower body in the process. His anatomy is concealed by a loincloth made of branches, and he is shown holding a doll and a toy dog. Perhaps this is a nod to the dog that appeared on the cover of the band's first album? "Terence had the most imaginative mind, beyond belief,"[17] Mike Vernon later recalled. "The guy was just…weird. He was an extremely clever photographer and a great artist. Terence would come up with the

most daft ideas, some of which were just vulgar to the point of being irresponsible and unusable. But sometimes he came up with extraordinary pictures. The picture of Mick on the double-fold of *Mr. Wonderful* was extraordinary."[17]

The inside of the album gatefold jacket featured a jumble of photos of the band and an assortment of eccentric notes written by British DJ John Peel, who was assisted by his pet hamster, Biscuit. The hamster was credited for his contributions, and Peel's notes were presented as though they had been typed out on small scraps of torn paper.

Audiences and critics alike were reserved in their enthusiasm for the new album, which was released in August 1968. This muted reception did not prevent the record from posting very respectable sales numbers, including hitting the top 10 on the UK charts. The album didn't make the Billboard 200, though, because it was not distributed in the United States. Instead, a compilation album titled *English Rose* was released in December 1968 for the American market only. It featured six tracks from *Mr. Wonderful*, three nonalbum singles ("Jigsaw Puzzle Blues," "Black Magic Woman," and "Albatross"), two previously unreleased songs ("One Sunny Day," "Without You") that would eventually become part of *Then Play On*, and another previously unreleased song ("Something Inside of Me"). Mick Fleetwood's comic flair was once again put to good use on the cover of *English Rose*, where he appears dressed in drag.

The Chicken Shack keyboardist
(seated, with Stan Webb, Andy
Silvester, and Dave Bidwell) gradually
established herself as one of the
Mac's preferred collaborators.

STOP MESSIN' ROUND

Peter Green, C. G. Adams / 2:22

Musicians

Peter Green: vocals, guitar
John McVie: bass
Christine Perfect: piano
Mick Fleetwood: drums
Steve Gregory: alto saxophone
Johnny Almond: tenor saxophone

Recorded

CBS Studios, London, April 28, 1968

Technical Team

Producer: Mike Vernon
Sound Engineer: Mike Ross

Single:

Side A: Need Your Love So Bad / **Side B:** Stop Messin' Round
UK Release Date: July 5, 1968
Reference: Blue Horizon (45 rpm ref.: 57-3139)
Best UK Chart Ranking: 31

COVERS

The song inspired some fine cover versions. In 1990, Gary Moore revisited it on his album *Still Got the Blues*. Five years later, the guitarist from Savoy Brown, a band that also featured Kim Simmonds and, at one time, Bob Brunning, contributed an audacious jazz reinterpretation on the tribute album *Rattlesnake Guitar: The Music of Peter Green*, led by drums played with brushes. But the prize for originality goes to Aerosmith on *Honkin' on Bobo* (2004), the hard-rock combo's tribute to the blues. Unusually for the band, the lead vocals were left to Joe Perry, with Steven Tyler playing on harmonica.

Genesis and Lyrics

For the first time, Peter Green shares songwriting credits with another member of the team. In this case, that team member is the group's manager, Clifford Davis, who preserved his anonymity by crediting himself as C. G. Adams (Davis's birth name was Clifford George Adams). Supposedly, he is mentioned in the lyrics for his involvement—in reality, this was a trick by Davis. Davis led Green to believe that mentioning him as a co-writer of the song would enable Green to avoid certain taxes. Green, unfamiliar with legal matters, took this at face value and agreed. History is silent on whether this actually saved him any money. What is certain is that it was of little importance to the musician, who made it a matter of honor, once out of the band, to refuse his own royalties—sometimes violently so. C. G. Adams's contribution was therefore more than minor to lyrics that were just as minor. The phrases "Baby, please stop messin' 'round / You're messin' 'round all the time" form the backbone of this forgettable prose.

There is more reason to enthuse about the guitar playing that makes itself at home on this track, to the detriment of the vocals. Peter Green has constructed the number in such a way as to give his instrument as much space as possible. Only two of the twelve-bar verses feature lyrics, while the other four are left to Green's guitar, which multiplies solos on the pentatonic scale of *C* major.

As is often the case, Peter Green works from existing material. He takes his inspiration from "Stop Messin' Around," a melodically related song by Detroit bluesman Walter Mitchell in 1948, by setting up a question-and-answer system between his guitar and the saxophones, very similar to the back-and-forth between vocals and harmonica introduced by Mitchell in his song.

The first eight bars of Mitchell's blues spin can be found in a song that precedes it by three years: 1945's "Stop Breakin' Down." This Sonny Boy Williamson I track is itself an adaptation of a Robert Johnson song from 1938. In the latter, we find the same phrase construction, which testifies to the kinship between all the versions: "Stop breakin' down / Please stop breakin' down."

Production

For this track, Green includes Christine Perfect and two sax-ophonists. This kind of orchestration reflects his desire to re-create the Chicago blues sound. Jeremy Spencer, for his part, as on most of Peter Green's compositions, remains in the background. The session recordings, available on *The Complete Blue Horizon Sessions 1967–1969*, shed light on the sessions, and they include five takes for this song. Right from the start, Peter Green takes charge. He cuts through the chat-ter and gives his instructions, breaking down the structure of the song as he sees it. He begins to explain to the saxophon-ists the question-and-answer format he wants to establish between his guitar and their instruments. To Christine Perfect, who asks about his interventions, he says: "You play on every verse." Yet the musicians seem slightly lost. Although the guitarist has a clear vision of his song, he strug-gles to convey it to the other musicians. After a while, Mike Vernon steps in and begins the recording, convinced that the best thing to do is to get started and adapt incrementally. In the end, it took no less than five takes to complete the track.

On the first take, Christine Perfect, probably the one who best grasped Green's intention, sets up a boogie rhythm with her right hand, to which she then adds a few minor variations. On the second take, she adds triplets to great effect on the first verse. But as the end of this first verse approaches, Mick Fleetwood, who has managed to install an infectious swinging shuffle, is having trouble managing the drums' transition to the next verse. Peter

Green decides to add a series of guitar chords to ease the transition. But a certain cacophony ensues between the instruments, to the point where Mike Vernon suddenly decides to end the take. Peter is only moderately receptive to the producer's decision to cut the recording even though he feels that things are going well and the band is begin-ning to show some cohesion. Another attempt is made, but as if to show the producer how annoyed he is, this time Green seems less concerned. The dynamic is now gone. Not surprisingly, the other musicians, who follow the direc-tor's lead, also lack panache. The fifth take is the right one. All the musicians now know their parts, and Mick Fleetwood scrupulously reproduces the sequence dictated by Peter Green. Green once again demonstrates his drive and vigor on this track, with its sustained tempo (132 bpm). His guitar attacks are forthright and decisive. As for Christine Perfect, she sounds like Jerry Lee Lewis, bounc-ing her fingers frantically over the keyboard.

Unfortunately, the mix does her no credit. The keyboard and bass fall far behind vocals, guitar, and saxophones. As for the drums, they sound suboptimal, as we can hear only the cymbals and still less the other elements of the kit. Despite these obvious shortcomings, due in large part to Green's preferred mode of recording, Mike Vernon will admit that this is without doubt Fleetwood Mac's most suc-cessful attempt to achieve the famous live sound that Peter Green wanted to re-create in the studio.

Jeremy Spencer working on the vibration of the strings of his Kay Truetone Speed Demon under the pressure of his bottleneck.

I'VE LOST MY BABY

Jeremy Spencer / 4:18

Musicians: Jeremy Spencer: vocals, guitar, piano / John McVie: bass / Mick Fleetwood: drums / Dave Howard: alto saxophone / Roland Vaughan: tenor saxophone / **Recorded:** CBS Studios, London, April 1968 / **Technical Team:** Producer: Mike Vernon / Sound Engineer: Mike Ross

Genesis and Lyrics

A new love ends in tears, in the grand tradition of the blues. In this song Jeremy Spencer slips into the shoes of the man who is left behind, abandoned by the woman he loves. He does not know which way to turn. His day begins in total disbelief and continues in denial. "I'm waiting this morning / Waiting for my baby to come back home / You know she left me this morning / And I don't know where she gone." According to the unhappy, spurned man, she had assured him that she would never leave him, that she would stay by his side forever. So, what happened? Did he make a mistake and get abandoned? Not in the least; he blames his beloved, without holding her to account: "The time she mistreated me / And I don't know how many times she lied / Well, I love my baby / And I'll tell the world I do."

Production

Whatever one may think of his distinctive voice, Jeremy Spencer has absolutely mastered all the keys to Elmore James's style, to the point where you might think "I've Lost My Baby" is a cover of the Mississippi bluesman. The song opens with a mangled guitar riff, as though Spencer got his fingers twisted into a knot, but the authenticity of the genre sometimes requires some minor roughness around the edges. So, the take was retained, and Mick Fleetwood takes to the drums with a toms roll that may be a little clumsy but is still devilishly effective. A discreet piano follows after a few bars, while Jeremy Spencer's guitar becomes sharper. Inspired by Elmore James's playing on "The Sky Is Crying," Spencer's guitar distills a flurry of notes to break the relative calm. Indeed, while Spencer's guitar sometimes lacks precision, particularly in the first part of the song, this is undoubtedly due to the fact that Mick Fleetwood's drumming strays slightly from the initial tempo and drags the other musicians along. John McVie's bass, rather uninspired on this track, literally drowns out the almost inaudible saxophones. This is a pity, as their presence lends extra tension and melancholy to Spencer's tortured vocals and clever, if unspectacular, piano playing. No doubt the guitarist's vision was clear, but he struggled to unite his musicians, who might have been more cohesive under Peter Green's leadership.

Mick Fleetwood demonstrates that he is equally at ease on blues and rumba rhythms on "Rollin' Man."

ROLLIN' MAN
Peter Green, C. G. Adams / 2:54

Musicians: Peter Green: vocals, guitar / Christine Perfect: piano / John McVie: bass / Mick Fleetwood: drums / Steve Gregory: alto saxophone / John Almond: tenor saxophone / **Recorded:** CBS Studios, London, April 1968 / **Technical Team:** Producer: Mike Vernon / Sound Engineer: Mike Ross

Genesis and Lyrics

In the band's attempt to re-create the warmth and spontaneity of the legendary American studio recordings (Chess, Cobra Records, Sun Records…) that fed the imaginations of young white bluesmen, "Rollin' Man" comes close to achieving its goal, due to the track's overall cohesion and the musicians' infectious enthusiasm. At the same time, however, the band has abandoned what had been its identity since the very beginning: a blues without artifice, as authentic as possible and as close as possible to its original expression by the Delta bluesmen. This song turns toward another form of blues, represented by Otis Rush and the Chicago scene, with its fast tempo due to the space it reserves for piano and saxophones. It is quite a stretch to think of Peter Green's and John McVie's reticence concerning saxophones when John Mayall decided to have them in the Bluesbreakers.

In this track, Peter Green, who has no need to push his vocals, fully assumes his role as singer and narrator. He slips into the role of a seducer and rolls with the punches. His voice is at times enticing during the seduction phase ("Oh baby / Don't you want a man like me? / I could give you so much lovin' / More than one woman ever seen"), at other times impatient as he looks ahead to the lovemaking to come ("Oh baby / We're gonna make some love tonight / We'll be rollin' out the blankets / I'm gonna make you feel all right"). It is worth noting that the crooner is so sure that his cooing will succeed that he switches from the interrogative present tense in the first verse to the affirmative future tense in the second.

Production

The wanderings of the first track, which were due to the unpreparedness of the brass section, are no longer an issue on this second track. The structure of "Rollin' Man" is very clear to read, assisted by a rapidly emerging hierarchy of instruments. Christine Perfect's piano takes center stage, imposing its Ray Charles–inspired boogie rhythmic breath on the other instruments. Behind her, John McVie's smooth bass perfectly captures the essence of rhythm'n'blues. As for Mick Fleetwood, he plays one of his most seductive drum parts since he joined the band. Without overdoing it, he lays down a demanding rhythm, with ideal rolls between each part. Above all, he puts his best foot forward on the finale, driving the frenzied rumba section. With such a solid foundation, the song proves solid—without showing any crazy originality—and leaves plenty of room for the squealing guitar to express itself through its ascending motifs.

"Dust My Broom," one of the first songs in Elmore James's stage repertoire, was recorded in August 1951 during an audition for Trumpet Records.

TRUMPET
RECORDS

No. 146

DRC53
(Vocal)

DUST MY BROOM
(Elmo James)
ELMO JAMES

By 1968, a dozen groups and artists had already revisited Johnson's classic "Dust My Broom" on both sides of the Atlantic, including B. B. King, Ike and Tina Turner, and Canned Heat on the American side; and the Yardbirds, John Mayall, the Bluesbreakers (with Peter Green and John McVie), and the Spencer Davis Group on the British side.

DUST MY BROOM

Robert Johnson / 2:54

Musicians: Jeremy Spencer: vocals, guitar, piano / John McVie: bass / Mick Fleetwood: drums / Dave Howard: alto saxophone / Roland Vaughan: tenor saxophone / Elmore James: arrangements / **Recorded:** CBS Studios, London, April 1968 / **Technical Team:** Producer: Mike Vernon / Sound Engineer: Mike Ross

Genesis and Lyrics

"I believe I'll dust my broom" is an expression suggesting the notion of sweeping everything away and starting fresh, but Jeremy Spencer has done absolutely nothing of the sort on this Robert Johnson track from 1936. Instead, he gets as close as possible to the arrangement conceived in 1951 by Elmore James, of whom Spencer was a major fan. In so doing, he completes the circle started a few months earlier with the exploration of another Elmore tune, "I Believe My Time Ain't Long."

Like his idol, Jeremy takes the first verses of Robert Johnson's version but, as a master of recycling, he tempers the "sweep" intended by the narrator with a more conciliatory verse, identical to that of Arthur Crudup's 1949 version: "I believe, I believe my time ain't long / I ain't gonna leave my baby / And break up my happy home." In this way, he plays down the irreversibility and brutality of the "clean sweep," implying that he is not really ready to start afresh.

Production

There are few surprises in this very—perhaps overly—faithful reprising of the Elmore James version. Indeed, by

sticking to the latter's heels in this way, the comparison is obvious. However, while Jeremy Spencer struggles to reproduce the versatility of James's voice, and in particular his vibrato, which is as nonchalant as it is diabolically precise, he nonetheless possesses his own vocal style—more nasal, less powerful, and less energetic perhaps, but which enables him to deliver the song creditably. All the more so as his voice seems to have undergone a slight postproduction treatment, either by pushing the fader into the red or by assigning an effect to take it to the edge of distortion. On the guitar front, it is all very familiar from the musician, who gnaws every Elmore-esque riff to the bone, executing his parts "in the manner of" without quite attaining the stratospheric level of his idol.

The rhythm section delivers a masterful shuffle, but again, it's nothing like the one that accompanied Elmore James. Unfortunately, the saxophone players remain far behind in the mix, as is often the case on Jeremy Spencer's tracks, in contrast to the prominence given to them on Peter Green's. They wake up a little at the end of the song to comfortably accompany bass and drums toward the exit. The piano, though the repository of several fine sequences, also suffers from an overly muddled mix, surprisingly more disjointed than on the Elmore James version released seventeen years earlier.

1968

LOVE THAT BURNS

Peter Green, C. G. Adams / 5:04

Musicians: Peter Green: vocals, guitar / John McVie: bass / Mick Fleetwood: drums / Steve Gregory: alto saxophone / John Almond: tenor saxophone / **Recorded:** CBS Studios, London, April 1968 / **Technical Team:** Producer: Mike Vernon / Sound Engineer: Mike Ross

Genesis and Lyrics

There could have been no better apprenticeship for Peter Green than his time with John Mayall's Bluesbreakers. His skills were honed by his experience with the godfather of the British blues boom. Mayall defined the contours and laid the groundwork. So, when a bluesman of this lineage unrolls a slow, mournful blues like a funeral march, the immediate point of comparison is Mayall's "Double Trouble." Peter Green must have had this in mind when he was working on "Love That Burns." Burning, incandescent, luminous…One could roll out the lexical field of fire for this track as much as the red carpet, since it shines with a rare brilliance at the heart of a dull, featureless album. Even the lyrics, often neglected since the band's debut, are of some interest. Beyond the stereotypical use of vocabulary linked to the fire of love and the danger of seeing it extinguished, a battle for the possession of the other is at stake, through the use of pronouns. When the narrator asks questions, the second-person singular dominates: "Would you love me tomorrow / Like you say you love me now?" We switch to the first-person plural as soon as doubts arise about the survival of this love: "When the flames of our flesh have stopped burning / And the fire of our love has cooled down." Finally, as fears take over, the lover becomes more prescriptive, using the first-person singular: "Baby, give me your love in return." Similarly, the different phases of the lover's tormented mind are reflected in grammatical forms: the interrogative form to assess his partner's attachment, the imperative to keep a hold on this love, and the negative form when this control turns against him: "Please don't use me, don't use me as your fool."

Production

A swish of cymbals, and the guitar begins its phrasing and the whole band enters on the fundamental note…the magic happens right from the start. Under the influence of a well-rounded bass that would have merited a central place in the sound spectrum, the whole band enters a phase of contemplation. The saxophones lament in unison like the wails of professional mourners, women who until the mid-twentieth century were hired to follow a funeral procession. Opposite them, Peter Green's guitar multiplies fragmented phrasing and melancholy solos over a slow rhythm and breathy orchestration. As for his vocals, they illustrate the progress he has made. He fully embraces his character, punctuating the end of his phrases with a variety of effects. He alternates between sighs, light tremolos, and muffled sobs, adding to the track's drama.

Peter Green was sometimes unfaithful to Greeny, preferring this sunburst-finish Fender Stratocaster crafted from ash.

DOCTOR BROWN

Waymon Glasco / 3:48

Musicians
Jeremy Spencer: vocals, guitar
John McVie: bass
Mick Fleetwood: drums
Dave Howard: alto saxophone
Roland Vaughan: tenor saxophone

Recorded
CBS Studios, London, April 1968

Technical Team
Producer: Mike Vernon
Sound Engineer: Mike Ross

Singer and harmonica player Buster Brown (1911–1976) remains famous for having created "Fannie Mae" and "Doctor Brown."

Genesis and Lyrics

Often attributed to Waymon Glasco, "Doctor Brown" is actually the work of Buster Brown, an American blues singer who made a name for himself with his 1959 hit "Fannie Mae." No one really knows whether Waymon Glasco was his real name; a persistent rumor claims Glasco was his manager, who, after the death of his protégé, bought out his catalog, thus perpetuating the confusion. In any case, Buster Brown was assisted by another Brown, John Thomas, an American tenor saxophonist who had played in the bands of Elmore James and J. B. Lenoir, in the composition of "Doctor Brown." The Brown story was born in 1960 on the Fire Records label, and takes the form of a typical blues shuffle, with warm saxophones and a joyfully dissipated harmonica, interspersed with an energetic "Whoooo" in Buster Brown's virile voice.

The lyrics, taken up by Jeremy Spencer for the Mac version, extol the virtues of an unconventional doctor who believes he can cure his patients with his irresistible powers of seduction: "They call me that lovin' man," he boasts at the beginning of the song. He then goes on to "cure your ills" "without a prescription" and "no pills," citing womankind in general as evidence for this: "You just ask any woman / In my neighborhood / If Doctor Brown don't cure you / Nobody can do you no good."

Production

No, you are not dreaming...the intro riff to "Doctor Brown" is a note-by-note retread of the riff from "Dust My Broom," which appears two tracks earlier on the album. Jeremy Spencer's ploy is all the more astonishing given that the original version of "Doctor Brown" bears absolutely no resemblance to this. But Spencer adores Elmore James so much that he uses exactly the same riff on the following track, "Need Your Love Tonight," and a little further on, at the end of the record, on "Coming Home." It is only a short step from there to thinking that the guitarist's inspiration often ran on alternating currents, a step that the listener can easily take, annoyed to the point of feeling cheated. Gone, then, are the doo-wop references of the original version to the Silhouettes' "Get a Job,"

Jeremy Spencer, on the left, reworked "Doctor Brown" as "Dr. J" on his solo album *Precious Little* in 2006.

American blues singer and harmonica player Sonny Terry, or Brown's huge hit "Fannie Mae," whose venomous groove he tried to copy, as he had already done on "Don't Dog Your Woman." Certainly, Jeremy Spencer must have thought that a successful formula could be repeated indefinitely, and his version of "Dust My Broom" pleased him enough to forget an elementary concept: You do not put the same song, or at least the same arrangement, on the same album four times. Purists will argue that certain elements differ, since there is no piano on this track, for example. But the saxophone, which has little impact because it lacks any real artistic direction, is just as dispensable as before. And Jeremy Spencer's guitar serves up more or less the same dish on every verse, while the rhythm section carelessly wades through the mire, with the palpable impression of no longer knowing which song they are supposed to be playing. As for Spencer's voice, despite a slight processing that still places it on the edge of distortion, it can do nothing to touch the raw energy emanating from Buster Brown in the original version.

NEED YOUR LOVE TONIGHT

Jeremy Spencer / 3:29

Musicians
Jeremy Spencer: vocals, guitar, piano
John McVie: bass
Mick Fleetwood: drums
Dave Howard: alto saxophone
Roland Vaughan: tenor saxophone

Recorded
CBS Studios, London, April 1968

Technical Team
Producer: Mike Vernon
Sound Engineer: Mike Ross

John McVie lights up "Need Your Love Tonight" with his deep, precise playing.

Genesis and Lyrics

If one of Spencer's goals was to demonstrate that, with a good blues riff, all lyrics are interchangeable, and that the blues perpetually feeds on itself, then including two tracks with a common riff—"Dust My Broom" and "Doctor Brown"—should have been more than enough to make his point. But no, here Spencer recycles the same guitar riff for a third time. For the lyrics, Spencer, monomaniac to the point of caricature, also recycles from his favorite toolbox: Elmore James. He draws from several of his favorite bluesman's standards. He opens with the third verse of "Make a Little Love": "Oh baby, I'll buy you a diamond ring / If you let me darling / I'll give you almost anything." And since he is missing a line, he completes it with a poor rhyme and an out-of-context phrase: "Well it's early in the morning." Here he goes again with another song by his mentor, "Early in the Morning": "And my baby can't be found." To round off this medley, after exhausting himself with promises and laments, Spencer suddenly twists the narrative with this chilling phrase: "If she don't come back to me / I'll put her six feet in her grave." The experimental lyricist takes this line from a new Elmore James song: "I Believe." We shall not dwell on the incoherence of the sequence; if she runs away and does not come back, he is not likely to hurt her...

Production

From the same guitar riff, played with the same intentions, the same attack, and the same sound, the guitarist unfolds a new version. But in a game of spot the difference, the interest is limited. The saxophones are given a little more room to express themselves; the tempo speeds up; and John McVie's bass is pampered more by Mike Vernon: with a deeper sound. The proximity of the microphone that picks up this instrument allows you to hear the beat on the strings, the instrumental break that gives all the instruments free rein to express themselves, Mick Fleetwood's muscular playing concentrated on his snare drum and hi-hat, and the collective finale scratched with slide strokes. Does this justify a third version of "Dust My Broom"? Certainly not.

B. B. King (here in the late 1960s), revered by Peter Green as the absolute model for the fervor and inventiveness of his playing.

IF YOU BE MY BABY
Peter Green, C. G. Adams / 3:54

Musicians: Peter Green: vocals, guitar / John McVie: bass / Mick Fleetwood: drums / Christine Perfect: piano / Steve Gregory: alto saxophone / John Almond: tenor saxophone / **Recorded:** CBS Studios, London, April 1968 / **Technical Team:** Producer: Mike Vernon / Sound Engineer: Mike Ross

Genesis and Lyrics

Here, Peter Green is caught with smoke and mirrors. Where the greatest blues singers repeat the same phrases twice in a row to hammer home the idea of deep despair, for example, here Green goes over the top. The song's title, "If You Be My Baby," is repeated no less than fourteen times in almost four minutes. In addition to being utterly misogynistic ("Cook my meals in the daytime and love me all night long"), the lyrics are also distressingly banal, going no further than a promise of love and happiness in exchange for winning his coveted woman.

Production

Peter Green uses the old B. B. King blues of the early 1950s as a model, building up a throbbing, almost lazy rhythm section (John McVie and Mick Fleetwood do not seem overwhelmed by enthusiasm) that is bursting with saxophones. The latter fare better than poor Christine Perfect, who is visibly lacking in imagination on this track, where she is content to string together lazy triplets, unlike the other tracks on the album, where her playing was a real asset. Peter Green's guitar lines are fluid and relaxed, and despite everything he seems at ease in the context of the somewhat flawed arrangement.

With this "Evening Boogie," Fleetwood Mac nurtures the group's cohesion and places the pleasure of playing together at the forefront.

EVENIN' BOOGIE

Jeremy Spencer / 2:42

Musicians: Jeremy Spencer: guitar / John McVie: bass / Mick Fleetwood: drums / Dave Howard: alto saxophone / Roland Vaughan: tenor saxophone / **Recorded:** CBS Studios, London, April 1968 / **Technical Team:** Producer: Mike Vernon / Sound Engineer: Mike Ross

Genesis and Lyrics

After a medley of variations on the "Dust My Broom" theme, "Evenin' Boogie" is a welcome release. This is an adaptation of Elmore James's "Hawaiian Boogie"—did we expect any other source of inspiration from Jeremy Spencer? The song retains its instrumental dimension. It thus serves as a recreational interlude, more than a breath of fresh air, as it is so musically dense.

Production

"Evenin' Boogie" pulsates under the effect of John McVie's bass. He weaves a walking bass phrase over a major pentatonic scale, playing a note on each beat. A classic rock'n'roll pattern inspired by the blues, in which it is generally played more slowly. Spencer's playing becomes shriller than on James's original, mainly due to the recording requirements imposed by the musicians on their producer. This blurs the

listeners' ability to distinguish what is being played. As a result, the saxes have little room to frolic and vary their playing, as J. T. Brown might have done on the Elmore James original. But they make up for it on the break with a rather inspired solo. The Fleetwood Mac adaptation also suffers from the absence of Johnny Jones's piano part, which peppered the Elmore James version with high notes, Jeremy Spencer having objected to adding piano overdub. He must have felt that the track would suffocate under too many instruments with Mick Fleetwood already saturating the track with his sweeping strokes on the cymbals.

FOR MAC ADDICTS

Carried away by the frenzy of the track, one of the saxophonists makes a clumsy mistake and lets out a whistling noise at 0:53. But this is of no consequence amid the strident slide guitar of Jeremy Spencer, which covers it up.

LAZY POKER BLUES

Peter Green, Clifford Adams / 2:37

Musicians
Peter Green: vocals and guitar
John McVie: bass
Christine Perfect: piano
Mick Fleetwood: drums
Steve Gregory: alto saxophone
John Almond: tenor saxophone

Recorded
CBS Studios, London, April 1968

Technical Team
Producer: Mike Vernon
Sound Engineer: Mike Ross

Joe Bonamassa, a great admirer of Peter Green's Fleetwood Mac, defines their music as an "exotic kind of blues dressed as rock'n'roll."

Genesis and Lyrics

Peter Green takes on a role usually reserved for Jeremy Spencer: the lecherous braggart. An ode to idleness and lust, "Lazy Poker Blues" is unencumbered by concessions to propriety, barely concealing its subject matter behind salacious metaphors: "She puts some coal on the fire so I can keep my poker hot." The lyricist demonstrates slightly more deftness with this mischievous line: "Yeah, we stoke around all day long / And night time, we stoke around some more."

Production

Faithful to their aim of making a record as raw and as close to live conditions as possible, the band bypasses the usual musical conventions. "Lazy Poker Blues" starts off headlong, with no fade, no intro, and goes straight into Peter Green's voice. This eagerness infects the playing of his partners, who execute the track with their feet to the floor, galvanized by Mick Fleetwood's snare drum–infused trot. The musicians connect, commenting and encouraging one another. Christine Perfect seems to have found her place and is growing in confidence. She hammers her triplets into the high notes, infusing an anarchic energy into this jam that we do not want to end. Peter Green is enjoying the symbiosis he has sought throughout the sessions. This satisfaction spills over into his vocals, which he approaches in a lower register than usual, with a slightly contracted throat and a kind of voluptuousness in his voice. These warm, low vocals are in perfect harmony with the sound of the guitar, which has been given a thicker reverb at the musician's request. But the sound brightens up when, from the twelfth fret onward, the musician launches into a solo sprinkled with bends of diabolical precision.

American virtuoso Joe Bonamassa, who made his stage debut alongside B. B. King at the tender age of twelve, has boundless admiration for Peter Green. In 2022, he recorded a cover version of this track, rich in solos and playing effects, for inclusion on his album *Blues Deluxe Vol. 2.*

John McVie listening to the umpteenth variation on the same riff on "Coming Home."

COMING HOME
Elmore James / 2:41

Musicians: Jeremy Spencer: vocals, guitar, piano / John McVie: bass / Mick Fleetwood: drums / Dave Howard: alto saxophone / Roland Vaughan: tenor saxophone / **Recorded:** CBS Studios, London, April 1968 / **Technical Team:** Producer: Mike Vernon / Sound Engineer: Mike Ross

Genesis and Lyrics

The fourth and final insult to the listener's patience is "Coming Home," which also uses the riff from "Dust My Broom." But this time, the blame is shared; Elmore James himself reused it on "Coming Home," a song of repentance in love. This is a cover of another song by Spencer's muse, but in the context of an album where a quarter of the songs are based on this same slide plan, this is one too many. Whatever the extenuating circumstances—the desire to make this a signature sound for himself, or to spawn as many versions as possible to ensure that at least one makes it onto the album—the result is painful.

Production

Spencer himself seems to grow weary on this track. Only the piano survives in the midst of the slump. As for the rest, the slowed-down tempo, the saxophones that fade away in a fog of sound, and Spencer's nuance-free, full-throated vocals show a lack of commitment.

1968

TRYING SO HARD TO FORGET

Peter Green, Clifford Adams / 4:47

Musicians: Peter Green: vocals, guitar / Duster Bennett: harmonica /
Recorded: CBS Studios, London, April 1968 / **Technical Team:**
Producer: Mike Vernon / Sound Engineer: Mike Ross

Anthony "Duster" Bennett on harmonica on "Trying So Hard to Forget."
Peter Green played guitar on Bennett's solo album, *Smiling Like I'm Happy*,
in early 1968.

Genesis and Lyrics

A few weeks before the recording, in early 1968, Peter
Green had already recorded a demo of "Trying So Hard to
Forget" with Duster Bennett, at the latter's home in Surrey.
It would later appear on the 2002 collection of Peter Green–
era Fleetwood tracks, *Jumping at Shadows: The Blues Years*,
and before that on Bennett's 1995 album *Out in the Blue*, a
compilation of recordings by the singer and harmonica
player, who died in a car accident in 1976, aged just
twenty-nine.

The lyrics of "Trying So Hard to Forget" are not very
cheerful. The narrator sets out his bilious vision of life,
dwelling on the negative elements that punctuate it—to the
point that he considers disappearing, as he plainly sings:
"Maybe you'd be better off if you should die." The man is
clearly haunted by traumatic memories, possibly dating
back to childhood, as he explains that he was "a down-trod-
den kid." Despite his best efforts, he cannot escape them,
unable to "stop [his] mind wandering" ("And people I've
tried so hard to forget / But I can't stop my mind wandering"). While he envies the "good life" of some of his contemporaries, he is caught up by his demons, and it is death
that looms large. He now sees it more as a liberation than a
source of anguish, claiming that death would simplify his
life: "Yes, if I ever get to heaven / That sure would ease my
worried life / You know when I find that place in the sky /
People I'm gonna leave this old world behind."

Production

Although the demo recorded at the beginning of the year is
some thirty seconds longer than the version featured on *Mr.
Wonderful*, it seems shorter because it is undoubtedly more
spontaneous. Peter Green seems to have asked all the musicians to take some time off, so as to bring the album to a
close with a sad blues that sounds more like a conversation
between two seasoned musicians. Indeed, what could the
rhythm section, Christine Perfect, or the saxophones have
done on this track? Nothing, certainly, as Green's guitar is
loquacious and already very expressive, finely extending
the darkness and pessimism of the lyrics.

Yet he seems to be struggling to find a way to play as
fluidly and naturally as he did on the demo, where the
influence of Lightnin' Hopkins could be felt, particularly in
the rhythmic aspect, which was even more dragging and
tense than here. Green's approach on the demo was clearly
more relaxed, a bit like a simple jam, since the demo tapes
were not destined to ever be made public.

Here, Bennett has probably been instructed to "fill in
the gaps" on harmonica, that is, to play when he feels a
space is opening up and neither Green's voice nor his guitar are about to occupy it. Duster is skillful and perfect in
the role of the unobtrusive accompanist, trying to keep
things simple yet effective. For his part, Green delivers a
clever vocal interpretation, playing with silences, then suddenly accelerating his delivery. The result is a recording
that is less somber than the demo, and in any case ideal for
closing the album.

Albatross / Jigsaw Puzzle Blues
UK Release Date: November 22, 1968
Reference: Blue Horizon (45 rpm ref.: 57-3145)
Best UK Chart Ranking: 1
US Release Date: January 1, 1969
Reference: Epic (45 rpm ref.: 5-10436)
Best US Chart Ranking: Did Not Chart

Albatross / Need Your Love So Bad
UK Release Date: April 27, 1973
Reference: CBS (45 rpm ref.: CBS 8306)
Best UK Chart Ranking: 2

The Beatles (here in 1969) were captivated by the beauty of the instrumental "Albatross."

Side A

ALBATROSS

Peter Green / 3:07

Musicians: Peter Green: guitar / Danny Kirwan: guitar / John McVie: bass / Mick Fleetwood: drums / **Recorded:** CBS Studios, London, October 6, 1968 / **Technical Team:** Producer: Mike Vernon

FOR MAC-ADDICTS

Released on 1969's *Abbey Road*, the Beatles' "Sun King" bears an uncanny resemblance to "Albatross," suggesting that, for once, the Fab Four were more followers than forerunners. George Harrison acknowledged the borrowing in 1987: "At the time, 'Albatross' (by Fleetwood Mac) was out, with all the reverb on guitar. So we said, 'Let's be Fleetwood Mac doing "Albatross," just to get going.' It never really sounded like Fleetwood Mac, but that was the point of origin."[19]

Genesis

This song draws its majesty from many sources. It is a very free interpretation of Santo and Johnny's instrumental theme "Sleepwalk," which paved the way for surf rock when it became the last instrumental song of the decade to reach the top of the American charts, in September 1959. More surprising, "Albatross" also owes a great deal to Chuck Berry's 1957 track "Deep Feeling," which is far removed from the sharp riffs we know from the composer of "Johnny B. Goode." And with good reason, since Chuck had borrowed this tune from Andy Kirk and His Twelve Clouds of Joy and their song "Floyd's Guitar Blues," played by legendary jazz guitarist Floyd Smith.

If these streams of inspiration were not enough, Martin Celmins's book *Peter Green: Founder of Fleetwood Mac* reveals that Peter Green took the few notes that make up the song's central phrasing from an Eric Clapton solo but played them more slowly. He doesn't specify which solo he was referring to, but it could be "My Last Meal," a Jimmy Rogers song the Bluesbreakers covered onstage but never

recorded. Peter Green also cited it as an influence in Jon Kutner and Spencer Leigh's *1000 UK Number One Hits.*

A whole range of inspirations apparently flooded into Peter Green's mind and fed the imagination of this instrumental track, which sounds like a slowed-down calypso.

Peter Green, who is usually very conventional in the way he names his tracks, almost systematically repeating the intro phrase or a passage from the chorus, has to draw inspiration this time from the feeling that emanates from them. The aerial dimension, the amplitude of the notes, the impression of suspended time, and the plenitude it exudes lead him down the path of a bird. He thought of albatrosses, celebrated as "kings of the azure" with "giant wings" by Charles Baudelaire, but also glorified in a memorable poem by Samuel Taylor Coleridge, "The Rime of the Ancient Mariner" (1798), which Green read as a child: "At length did cross an albatross, / Thorough the fog it came; / As if it had been a Christian soul, / We hailed it in God's name."

Danny Kirwan, Peter Green, and John McVie in the studio.

Production

The "Albatross" had been nesting in Peter Green's mind for years, but it took the arrival of Danny Kirwan to enable it to blossom. The Fleetwood Mac front man could never have expected Jeremy Spencer to make such a contribution to one of his songs. The two musicians had tried in vain to work on it, but Spencer did not share Green's artistic vision at all. Spencer was trying to draw Green toward something more grounded. Stuck on the introductory part of the track, Green struggled to find a decent follow-up. The harmonies of the second part, proposed by Kirwan, opened up Green's horizons, enabling him to give free rein to his lyrical flights. With his Fender Stratocaster propped upon his knees and plugged into a Matamp Series 2000-amp head, he unrolled sumptuous slides, sustaining each note and the cleanness of his touch. The Les Paul is also called upon to give body to his guitar parts.

Mick Fleetwood had the fabulous idea of using timpani mallets (a kind of mallet with a wooden handle and a felt-covered head). With this covering, the sound is much softer, caressing. The vibrations created by Mick Fleetwood, which give the impression of an expanding space, imitate the rolling of the waves to complete the picture sketched by Peter Green. No need for sound effects—everything is about suggestion, appealing to the imagination. But the real trick is the linking of the toms, pared down as far as possible, to the deep, enveloping fundamental notes played by John McVie. This is where we understand the importance of Mick Fleetwood's playing, which makes up for his lack of technique by taking care of the feel of the song. Mike Vernon confirms that this was a collective effort in the liner notes to the compilation *The Blue Horizon Story, 1965–1970 Vol. 1*; he explains that the song was conceived by Peter and then adapted by John and Mick.

It was a shame to turn this instrumental track, magnificent as it was, into a single. But Hank Marvin and his Shadows had been there, and in 1960 their track "Apache" topped the British charts. Green and Vernon's gamble paid off, with "Albatross" taking pole position in the UK charts on its release. The Netherlands also succumbed, placing it at the top of its charts.

Albatross / Jigsaw Puzzle Blues

UK Release Date:
November 22, 1968
Reference: Blue Horizon
(45 rpm ref.: 57-3145)
Best UK Chart Ranking: 1
US Release Date:
January 1, 1969
Reference: Epic (45 rpm ref.:
5-10436)
Best US Chart Ranking:
Did Not Chart

Side B

The new Fleetwood Mac lineup favors guitar-rich instrumentations with the virtuosity of the three gunners (front row) Danny Kirwan, Peter Green, and Jeremy Spencer. Opposite: Peter Green in full swing.

JIGSAW PUZZLE BLUES

Danny Kirwan / 1:33

Musicians: Peter Green: guitar / Danny Kirwan: guitar / John McVie: bass / Mick Fleetwood: drums / **Recorded:** CBS Studios, London, October 6, 1968 / **Technical Team:** Producer: Mike Vernon

Genesis

While the two songs may not have much in common, Fleetwood Mac's "Jigsaw Puzzle Blues" was inspired by the 1933 piece of the same name by Eddie Lang and Joe Venuti. Danny Kirwan wanted to capture the essence of clarinetist Jimmy Dorsey's solo on his version. Very short, lasting just 1:33, this song could very well have found its way onto the Mac's next album, *Then Play On*, rather than as the B side of another instrumental track. But at this stage, other Danny Kirwan tracks recorded on the same day as "Jigsaw Puzzle Blues" seemed more suited to filling out the album, such as "Coming Your Way" or "Without You." As catchy as "Jigsaw Puzzle Blues" was, it seemed easier to offload such a short track on a B side rather than sacrifice potential A sides. Not to mention the fact that the real introduction of Danny Kirwan to the band's fans would be via *Then Play On*.

Production

Fleetwood Mac, at this particular period, was home to three fine guitarists (even though Jeremy Spencer was

very selective about his participation in certain sessions). Not every band has instrumentalists as versatile as Peter Green and Danny Kirwan, capable of "sacrificing" themselves to ensure the rhythm of a song on which the other is going to shine as a soloist. And the least we can say is that Green was not content simply to settle for business as usual, since his rhythm section proves to be very effective, even though he had little appetite for jazzy registers. Perfectly in place and solid, he provides the ideal foundation for Danny Kirwan, whose playing and touch prove as inspired as they are precise. The man who was nicknamed "Ragtime Cowboy Joe" by his new comrades (led by Peter Green) because of his slightly old-fashioned musical tastes, sees his playing here clearly inspired by the versatility of Django Reinhardt. But he doesn't hesitate to integrate typically bluesy elements, including numerous bends. Kirwan also shows off his exceptional, nuanced vibrato, which almost single-handedly validates Peter Green's choice to integrate him into Fleetwood Mac. As for the rhythm section, it does what it has to do with efficiency, even though Mick Fleetwood lacks the most elementary finesse behind his drums and John McVie does not have to take any ill-judged risks on bass.

Man of the World / Somebody's Gonna Get Their Head Kicked In Tonite (with Earl Vince and the Valiants)

UK Release Date: April 4, 1969
Reference: Immediate (45 rpm ref.: IM 080)
Best UK Chart Ranking: 2

Man of the World / Best Girl in the World (Danny Kirwan)

US Release Date: February 1976
Reference: DJM Records (45 rpm ref.: DJUS-1007)
Best US Chart Ranking: Did Not Chart

Peter Green contemplates his loneliness and vulnerability as a public figure in "Man of the World." Opposite: Handwritten lyrics by Peter Green.

Side A

MAN OF THE WORLD

Peter Green / 3:28

Musicians: Peter Green: vocals, guitar / Danny Kirwan: guitar / John McVie: bass / Mick Fleetwood: drums / **Recorded:** Tempo Sound Studios, New York City, January 8, 1969 / Kingsway Studio, London, February 18, 1969 / **Technical Team:** Producer: Mike Vernon / Sound Engineer: Martin Birch

Genesis and Lyrics

At the beginning of January 1969, Fleetwood Mac took a few days off to go to the studio in New York and work on a few new songs with which to wrap up *Then Play On*. They also had to finalize a new single in anticipation of the album's release. The first objective was not achieved, but the band did find its 45 rpm candidate: "Man of the World." Musically, it follows on from "Albatross." Its predecessor gave Peter Green a jolt. He realized that conventional blues was no longer fully satisfying him. He added new colors, in this case pop and atmospheric, to his palette. "Man of the World" is another step away from the blues of the early days, but also a step away from Spencer and toward Kirwan. The new guitarist had picked up on the desires that had been bubbling to the surface of Peter Green's playing, and that encouraged Kirwan in this new direction with his own artistic suggestions. But the most obvious change is in the songwriting of the leader and lyricist. Long gone are the bloated words of patriarchal clichés that plague falsely romantic laments. In "Man of the World," Peter Green cracks the shell and expresses his

deepest doubts. The first verse is symptomatic of this introspection, as it takes the form of a rhetorical question that leads to a dizzying and unexpected reflection: "Shall I tell you about my life? / They say I'm a man of the world / I've flown across every tide / And I've seen lots of pretty girls / I guess I've got everything I need / I wouldn't ask for more / And there's no one I'd rather be / But I just wish that I'd never been born." The "man of the world" is Peter Green himself, the public man, the adored artist. He is the object of desire and takes advantage of it. He has experienced everything (success, concerts, etc.). But is he happy? "I guess I've got everything" implies that he puts on a show when asked, but his achievements are not enough to make him happy. And so, the last sentence of the couplet is a resounding no-no: He wishes he had never existed. This extreme realization has an origin, and it is expressed at the end of the song: "And how I don't want to be sad anymore / And how I wish I was in love." The lack of love. This is the first time Peter Green has expressed it so sincerely, without posturing or grandstanding.

Production

From the very first take, the band performs a minor miracle, and the song assumes its almost definitive form. Only the guitar parts need fine-tuning. Green opens with a series of delicate chords. He is joined by McVie, who strides forward with his deep, voluptuous bass, and Kirwan, who fills the background with dreamy chords. At 0:20, three watery notes break the rapture and leave a kind of mystery hanging in the air. More twists of this kind follow: As the soft, melancholy vocals settle in, and small touches of blues are incorporated, Mick Fleetwood's drums make a discreet entrance on hi-hat and bass drum. Just when you think the track has found its cruising rhythm, the guitar switches to overdrive mode and takes off vertically at the same time as the vocals, which sound like a heart-rending wail. Both immediately fall back, and the song's heartbeat returns to normal. Peter Green's guitar fades out in a lovely arpeggio, and the band enjoys a few long seconds of silence. The guitarist takes off again on a succession of airy notes and activates his vibrato arm to place an almost Hawaiian vibrato into the spirit. At 1:30, he slides a note toward the bridge, and, as a delightful slide dialogue between Kirwan and Green unfolds, Fleetwood places a surprising roll. At this point, the band shifts into a more muscular rock vein. In contrast, Green's voice becomes warmer and warmer, and he turns into a true crooner. We realize that he has never sung better. The sweetness of the beginning is restored on the finale, which ends in the most beautiful of ways, on harmonics.

Rarely performed live by Peter Green, perhaps because of its intimate nature, this song remained in Fleetwood's repertoire until 2019, fifty years after its creation. The band, led by Neil Finn, covered it on August 11 in front of a stunned audience at the RAC Arena in Perth, Australia.

Man of the World / Somebody's Gonna Get Their Head Kicked In Tonite (with Earl Vince and the Valiants)

UK Release Date: April 4, 1969
Reference: Immediate (45 rpm ref.: IM 080)
Best UK Chart Ranking: 2

Jeremy Spencer's style of playing provides a perfect counterpoint to "Man of the World" in the reckless "Somebody's Gonna Get Their Head Kicked Tonite."

SOMEBODY'S GONNA GET THEIR HEAD KICKED IN TONITE

Jeremy Spencer / 2:38

Musicians: Jeremy Spencer: vocals, guitar, piano / John McVie: bass / Mick Fleetwood: drums / Peter Green, Danny Kirwan: backing vocals / **Recorded:** Tempo Sound Studios, New York City, January 8, 1969 / Kingsway Studio, London, February 6, 1969 / **Technical Team:** Producer: Martin Birch

Genesis and Lyrics

Unlike the 45 rpm "Albatross" / "Jigsaw Puzzle Blues," which combined two similar instrumental compositions, Fleetwood Mac opted this time to offer two diametrically opposed sides. The dreaminess of "Man of the World" is countered by the rockabilly fantasy of "Somebody's Gonna Get Their Head Kicked In Tonite." After the intense emotional charge of the A side, the musicians felt they needed to take the pressure off with a much lighter track. In Peter Green's case, it was even a defense mechanism: a good dose of humor to counterbalance the confession he had conceded. Jeremy Spencer is just the man for the job. The troublemaker takes on the task with pleasure. He creates an authentic rock'n'roll parody. Following in the footsteps of the Beatles and their fictional doubles, Sgt. Pepper's Lonely Hearts Club Band, he even goes so far as to rename the band for the occasion—Earl Vince and the Valiants. The Beatles' alter egos were a gentle choir. Fleetwood Mac's alter egos are the Teds, hard guys with greased, teddy-boy banana hairstyles, who whip out their switchblades at the slightest provocation. Like Elton John, who fantasized about being a troublemaker on 1973's "Saturday's Alright for Fighting," Jeremy Spencer gets people fired up for a fight. With Spencer, it starts on a Wednesday: "It's a Wednesday night / There sure is gonna be a fight / Somebody's gonna get their head kicked in tonite / Well the joint is jumpin' / Everybody's shouting for more." Cathartic for the lyricist, the text allows him to let loose and unleash his primal violence.

Production

They may jump into satire with both feet, but the musicians are perfectly credible in their role as rockers. In fact, they turn out to be excellent. The song is propelled by Mick Fleetwood's distinctive pattern, which perfectly captures the spirit (and perhaps misses its vocation). The guitars twang, the piano bounces, the bongos thunder…But the real surprise comes from Jeremy Spencer, who adopts a hitherto unknown timbre. With his deep, sensual voice, he plays the '50s crooners to perfection. In a way, he is used to it, since he already regularly performs "Blue Suede Shoes" and imitates Elvis Presley like no one else, right down to his mimicries and little pelvic wiggles. The only criticism that can be leveled at this song is the sometimes haphazard and muddled production, with the lead and backing vocals stepping on each other in the mix, all performed in the lower register. Backing vocals are supposed to stand apart from the main voice and provide a counterpoint, a harmony, which is not at all the case here. The backing vocalists, Peter Green and Danny Kirwan, miss the mark in trying to imitate Jeremy Spencer. The result might not have been the same had Vernon been involved in producing this track. He probably felt he had no time to waste on a minor track.

MYSTERY BOOGIE

Jeremy Spencer / 2:51

Musicians: Jeremy Spencer: guitar / Peter Green: bass (?) / Mick Fleetwood: drums / (?): brass / **Recorded:** CBS Studios, London, (?) / **Technical Team:** Producer: Mike Vernon / Sound Engineer: Mike Ross

The members of Fleetwood Mac are often at their best as soon as they release the pressure. Aware that they are not immortalizing the hit of the decade, and that this is a simple jam with no great scope, they let their art breathe. Jeremy Spencer, for example, takes the opportunity to remind us of his slide guitar skills, on a bluesy country track. The saxophones do not add much, but the guitar has a twangy, slightly vibrating sound, a color rarely heard on Fleetwood Mac. "Mystery Boogie" is an extension of "Evenin' Boogie," which appears on the record, but with less tension. The swing imparted by the rhythm section is more convincing on this piece, which receives so little consideration that it is truncated on the finale with a fade-out that deprives us of a longer solo by Jeremy Spencer. The boxed set *The Complete Blue Horizon Sessions 1967–1969* provides a fresh lease on life for this previously unreleased track.

I'M SO LONESOME AND BLUE

Jeremy Spencer / 3:55

Musicians: Jeremy Spencer: vocals, guitar / Peter Green: guitar, backing vocals / John McVie: bass, backing vocals / Mick Fleetwood: drums / **Recorded:** Aeolian Hall Studio 2, London, April 16, 1968 / **Technical Team:** (?)

Another doo-wop/rock'n'roll parody, which says as much about Jeremy Spencer's talent for imitating Elvis Presley, Gene Vincent, and Buddy Holly as it does about his passion for this particular genre. Indeed, rock was far more seminal for Spencer than the blues, with which he became enamored later in life.

THE WOMAN I LOVE

B. B. King, Joe Bihari / 4:43

Musicians: Peter Green: vocals, guitar / John McVie: bass / Mick Fleetwood: drums / **Recorded:** Carousel Ballroom, San Francisco, June 1968 / **Technical Team:** (?)

This track, sometimes listed as "My Baby's Skinny," remained unreleased for a long time, before it appeared on the 2019 collection *Before the Beginning (1968–1970 Live & Demo Sessions)*. And with good reason, since it was played only on the band's American tour in June 1968. Green spins a long, lazy one-minute shuffle before launching into his vocals. There is a great deal of improvisation in this track, which lacks coherence; the rhythm section and guitar seem to march in parallel, but not at the same speed.

INTERGALACTIC MAGICIANS WALKING THROUGH POOLS OF VELVET DARKNESS

Jeremy Spencer / 4:29

Musicians: Peter Green: vocals, guitar / Jeremy Spencer: vocals, guitar / John McVie: bass / Mick Fleetwood: drums / **Recorded:** 201 Piccadilly Studio 1, BBC, London, May 27, 1968 / **Technical Team:** (?)

The title itself speaks volumes about Jeremy Spencer's disregard for progressive rock bands and acid rock, which conceptualize rock too much for his taste (note that this song is sometimes referred to as "Delta Heads"). Cruel as this satire may be, we must admit that the name is evocative and would not be out of place in the discography of Arthur Brown, Pink Floyd, or other explorers of psychedelia. Spencer pinpoints the supposed lack of musicality of their experimentation, causing a hell of a din and distorting instruments and vocals with the resources available on the BBC console. Even more viciously, he openly mocks the Beatles' "I Am the Walrus" with the words: "I am here and you are there and we are going nowhere."

TALK TO ME BABY

Elmore James / 3:27

Musicians: Peter Green: vocals, guitar / Jeremy Spencer: vocals, guitar / John McVie: bass / Mick Fleetwood: drums / **Recorded:** Studio B Television Centre, BBC, London, July 19, 1968 / **Technical Team:** (?)

"Talk To Me Baby," part of Jeremy Spencer's study of Elmore James, is very special to the band. It was Fleetwood Mac's very first live performance, at the Windsor Festival on August 13, 1967. It also opens *Live at the Marquee* (1992), which was recorded two days later; a version recorded at the BBC appears on *The Vaudeville Years of Fleetwood Mac—1968 to 1970* (1998).

MIND OF MY OWN

Danny Kirwan / 3:00

Musicians: Danny Kirwan: vocals, guitar / Peter Green: guitar / Jeremy Spencer: guitar / John McVie: bass / Mick Fleetwood: drums / **Recorded:** 201 Piccadilly Studio 1, BBC, London, August 27, 1968 / **Technical Team:** (?)

Whether his first legitimate contribution to his new band, or a scrap from the repertoire of Boilerhouse, his previous band, "Mind of My Own" reveals Danny Kirwan's ability to melt into the Fleetwood Mac musical mold. With its raspy blues shuffle, chiming guitar, and asperity-laden voice, it sounds like a Jeremy Spencer composition. Even the postadolescent, slightly rebellious spirit of the lyrics could be that of Spencer. This first milestone was released in 2001 on the compilation *Show-Biz Blues 1968–1970 Volume 2* (2000).

A TALK WITH YOU

Danny Kirwan / 3:58

Musicians: Danny Kirwan: vocals, guitar / Peter Green: guitar / Jeremy Spencer: guitar / John McVie: bass / Mick Fleetwood: drums / **Recorded:** 201 Piccadilly Studio 1, BBC, London, August 27, 1968 / **Technical Team:** (?)

Like "Mind of My Own," "A Talk with You" illustrates the feeling of isolation of a Danny Kirwan stuck between two phases of his life, and still struggling to be taken seriously. Classic blues in its form, despite its surprisingly limping rhythm, this track suffers from the naïveté of its lyrics, in which its author tries to pass himself off as more experienced than he is. The first two lines are symptomatic, betraying his youth: "Hey woman, let me have a talk with you / Hey girl, let me have a talk with you."

SOMETHING INSIDE OF ME

Danny Kirwan / 3:54

Musicians: Danny Kirwan: vocals, guitar / Peter Green: guitar / John McVie: bass / Mick Fleetwood: drums / **Recorded:** Unknown location, October 6, 1968 / **Technical Team:** (?)

"Something Inside of Me" shares the same title as an Elmore James song that Jeremy Spencer once revisited with Fleetwood Mac, but this is a Danny Kirwan composition. A haunting blues track set in the minor register, with multiple breaks that provide breathing space for the voice, this song highlights the tenderness of Kirwan's slightly green but luminous vocals. Lacking power, they are almost overwhelmed by the drums. It could have been a welcome and much-need addition to *Mr. Wonderful*, but it comes too late.

ALBUM

THEN PLAY ON

Coming Your Way . Closing My Eyes . Fighting for Madge . When You Say .
Show-Biz Blues . Underway . One Sunny Day . Although the Sun Is Shining .
Rattlesnake Shake . Without You . Searching for Madge .
My Dream . Like Crying . Before the Beginning
Outtakes: Jeremy's Contribution to Doo-Wop . Every Day I Have the Blues .
Ýeath Bells . (Watch Out for Yourself) Mr. Jones . Man of Action

RELEASE DATES
United Kingdom: September 19, 1969
Reference: Reprise Records RSLP 9000
Best UK Chart Ranking: 6
United States: September 19, 1969
Reference: Reprise Records RS 6368
Best US Chart Ranking: 109

Brunel University Students' Union present

midnight rave again!

(or brunel's back at the Lyceum)

Midnight–7 a.m., Friday night, October 24th
at lyceum, strand, wc2

★ FLEETWOOD MAC ★
★ DEEP PURPLE ★
★ HOWLING WOLF ★
KEITH RELF'S RENAISSANCE ★ AARDVARK
ANDROMEDA ★ EXPLOSIVE SPECTRUM LIGHTS

Buffet   Licensed Bars till 3 a·m.
Tickets: £1 advance. Send s.a.e. and money to social sec., brunel university
students' union, acton, w.3 (tel. 01-992 5691)
N.B. Tickets on night (25/-) not guaranteed, and available to S.U. card holders only

After his first appearance on "Albatross," Danny Kirwan, the talented teenage guitarist (seated, right), has the opportunity to contribute his refined blues and folk playing to the band's third album.

THE GREAT TURNING POINT

The musicians of Fleetwood Mac were settled and enjoying a good lifestyle. Jeremy Spencer was happy in love since he had gotten married and become a father; and John McVie also took wedding vows, on August 3, 1968, when he married Christine Perfect. Meanwhile, Mick Fleetwood strengthened his relationship with Jenny Boyd, sister of the illustrious Pattie, who was married to George Harrison. Fleetwood and Jenny married in 1970 and he completed the pattern of "settling down" within the group. As for Peter Green, he was not yet completely consumed by feelings of guilt for becoming a rock star.

The Arrival of a New Guitarist: Danny Kirwan

Artistically, it was a different story. In the opinion of (almost) all the members of the band, it was out of the question to make another blues album and to continue paying tribute to Elmore James—much to the chagrin of Jeremy Spencer, of course. He reveals himself to be short of ideas, wrung out, uninspired—as if sterilized by his fascination for his idol. It must be said that he never really sought to build his own repertoire, and was content to deliver cover versions of his heroes. He and Peter Green were no longer speaking the same language, if they ever had to begin with. Thinking back to the lack of enthusiasm that Spencer had for contributing to Green's songs on previous albums and singles, this is indeed in doubt. It was in this context that Peter Green asked Danny Kirwan to join the group in August 1968, to bridge the growing distance between him and Spencer and to prevent the two guitarists from each leading a parallel

band with a rhythm section devoted to his own cause. There were high hopes that the five musicians would finally collaborate effectively, and this is shown in the quite fluid recordings made for the BBC at the end of August and September 1968, some of which would eventually land on the 1995 compilation *Live at the BBC*. Unfortunately, this is not the story that ended up going down in history.

Finding a New Language

On October 6, 1968, the band entered the studio for a big recording session that resulted in the birth of "Albatross" and "Jigsaw Puzzle Blues," the two single titles scheduled for release as they continued to record their next album. The band also laid down several songs for the new album during the same session, including "One Sunny Day," "Without You," and a first version of "Coming Your Way." Within two weeks, "Like Crying" was added to the list. However, it was difficult to know precisely what would become of these songs, because for the time being the artistic direction taken by Fleetwood Mac remained very unclear. Years later, Mick Fleetwood admitted that the band had no clear idea of what they wanted to do for their third album, except not to reproduce the indigence of *Mr. Wonderful*.

A new session was scheduled for the BBC on October 9, at the end of which it seemed obvious that the gap was widening between Jeremy Spencer and the Peter Green–Danny Kirwan duo. Spencer couldn't find his place and wanted to focus his energy on what he did best. At this point, it became clear that Jeremy would only appear in the credits of *Then*

1969

In love: Christine Perfect and John McVie.

Play On. Mike Vernon also offered to strike a deal with Spencer: He would distribute an EP along with the future album that would consist only of Spencer's tracks, which would all pay tribute to Spencer's heroes. The material for this EP, which was to be entitled *The Milton Schlitz Show,* was recorded on October 30. For the occasion, Spencer invented fictional bands to which his bandmates, with the exception of Danny Kirwan, contributed out of the goodness of their hearts, indulging in parodies of doo-wop (under the fictional name of "Ricky Dee and the Angels"), country blues (as "Texas Slim"), and acid rock (as "The Orange Electric Squares"). In the end, the EP was not released with the future album—it was finally included in the 1998 rarities compilation *The Vaudeville Years of Fleetwood Mac 1968 to 1970.* It was by not attaching this EP to the third opus of Fleetwood Mac that the group would make the world understand that it had much greater ambitions than being a mere cover band. This was a step forward that the group most ardently desired, and the October recordings confirmed that Spencer seemed completely out of the game. It was therefore up to Peter Green and Danny Kirwan to provide the bulk of the upcoming album. The problem was that Green had no new titles to pull out of the bag.

The Heavy Burden on Kirwan

Kirwan's gift for the guitar had already been revealed on "Jigsaw Puzzle Blues," the B side of "Albatross." Peter Green showed an ability to sniff out new talent when he enlisted him. However, as soon as he arrived, Kirwan immediately felt pressure to write half an album. Mick Fleetwood said, "Pete could have done all the writing himself, but instead he informed a shocked Danny that he was responsible for half the album. Danny couldn't believe it, but it was another example of Pete trying to shake the Green God image."[4]

Who could say where this would take the group? Kirwan was still a teenager, full of promise of course, but a teenager. He tackled the task with goodwill, perhaps being a little too cerebral in his approach, but he had to rely on someone more experienced to reach his potential. Peter Green was to Kirwan what Eric Clapton had been to Green, and Kirwan didn't want to disappoint his mentor. For his part, Peter was sparing with his advice; he preferred to let his protégé make his own decisions—even if he was wrong—and learn his own lessons.

The pressure was all the greater as the press, aware of the sessions for Spencer's EP, began to report that the band had planned to release their new album in January or February 1969. Journalists did not suspect in the least that, apart from the EP of parodies, the album was still very far from the finish line. The musicians themselves could not imagine how chaotic and fragmented the recording of *Then Play On* would be.

The band temporarily extricated themselves from their creative quagmire by participating in a new session for the BBC on November 1, 1968 (it would be broadcast on the 26th of the same month), then, on November 15, embarking alongside Chicken Shack on a tour of Scandinavia that saw them give seven concerts in Denmark and Sweden, which were recorded on a rare set of bootleg tapes.

The American Tour

At the very beginning of December, just after a whirlwind trip to France to participate in the show *Surprise Partie,* the group flew to the United States for their second tour of the country, where things really started to happen. Earlier the same year, their first tour of the US had seen the group visit California, Florida, and New York between June 7 and July 15. Mike Vernon, who had to stay in England, did not leave immediately with them, unlike Clifford Davis. Eighteen dates were scheduled between December 6 and 31, which obviously left very little time to compose. This was especially a problem for Peter Green, because if he told

John McVie, Jeremy Spencer, Peter Green, Danny Kirwan, and Mick Fleetwood, ready to travel the world preaching the blues.

journalists before leaving that half of the future album was already composed, it was not really his half, but that of the young Kirwan. With the dust tidily swept under the carpet, the group began their journey with a week in New York: playing two shows at the Fillmore East before four others at the Scene, where, according to legend, Jimi Hendrix spent some time with the musicians. Then they headed to Texas for several dates in Austin, Dallas, and Houston, then back to the East Coast with three dates at the Boston Tea Party. Rather than follow up with a date at Madison Square Garden in New York, where they would have shared a prestigious poster with Al Kooper, Moby Grape, and Paul Butterfield, Fleetwood Mac's tour then planned two dates in Detroit at the Grande Ballroom. On December 28, Peter Green and his accomplices were on stage at the Miami Pop Festival, where they performed a laborious 45-minute set. From the Florida sun they moved on to the harsh climate of Philadelphia, where they were to give two concerts.

The Chicago Dream

But for the members of Fleetwood Mac, who were not yet fully concerned with the recording of the future album *Then Play On*, there was no question of leaving the country without crossing paths with the blues musicians who influenced them. Fate played a part, since their tour program was very favorable to allowing such an experience to take place.

On January 1, 1969, Fleetwood Mac was in Chicago, at the Kinetic Playground, where they opened for one of their heroes, Muddy Waters. The next day, the band was in Chicago's Bronzeville neighborhood to open the show for B. B. King at the Regal Theater. Finally, on January 3, the band returned to Chicago with the intention of opening two new concerts for Muddy Waters. Between these two dates, the long-awaited opportunity presented itself: Mike Vernon heard that Chess Records was considering closing its legendary Chess Studios. Marshall Chess, son of label co-founder Leonard Chess, and Chess bassist and band-leader Willie Dixon had made an appeal for musicians. For many bluesmen, the season had not been very generous, and there were still bills to pay. Jumping at the opportunity, Vernon immediately blocked out the date of January 4.

Chess Studios, located at 320 East 21st Street on Chicago's Near South Side, was filled with illustrious ambassadors from the blues world: Otis Spann (Muddy Waters's musician) on piano and vocals, a young Buddy Guy on guitar, "Honeyboy" Edwards on guitar and vocals, Shakey Horton on harmonica, J. T. Brown (Howlin' Wolf, Rabbit's Foot Minstrels) on tenor saxophone and vocals, S. P. Leary (Muddy Waters, Howlin' Wolf) on drums, and Dixon on double bass. No one knew this yet, but the recordings made that day would be the last true blues music played by Fleetwood Mac, released in late 1969 on *Fleetwood Mac in Chicago*. In the United States, the record company did not

A relatively inexperienced sound engineer at this stage, Martin Birch (here in 1976) accompanies Fleetwood Mac in the conception of *Then Play On*.

want to release the band's blues albums and preferred instead to publish the compilation *English Rose*, which included "Albatross," a song that was supported by American FM stations. And in Europe, Fleetwood Mac was still determined to release a new album with a change in musical direction. For now, the enchanted Chicagoan session was a one-off and not at all intended to become the third official album from the group. However, time was running out.

In England, Fleetwood Mac triumphed with "Albatross" topping the charts. The band, still on tour in the United States, were among the last to understand the extent of their success, as it was sudden and unexpected. Even the Beatles would bow down to the talent of Peter Green, who gave them inspiration for "Sun King."

After two and a half months touring the United States, Fleetwood Mac returned home on February 14, 1969. The press had already announced for several weeks that the single called upon to succeed "Albatross" would be "Man of the World" and that it would be released on February 21 by Blue Horizon. But the timing would slightly deviate from this plan, since on February 18, three days before the supposed release date, the band was in the studio in London still completing the song, which had been started during a session in New York on January 8.

After making these last-minute additions, the band intended to rest a little, and there was no single ready to make an appearance on the expected date. Fleetwood Mac still went to give a few concerts in the Netherlands and West Germany, and in March they recorded new sessions for the BBC, before going on tour in Scandinavia.

Green's Confession and a Label Change

Peter Green was optimistic when he spoke to the press. As he explained to the *New Musical Express*, he felt that the band had returned more united than ever from the United States by enjoying hotel stays and talking together about existential themes such as life and death. Above all, he said that he had seen the light and now believed in God. The concept was vague, but it would soon become clearer—and if Green's optimism seemed sincere, the first signs of the depression that would affect him long term appeared in April 1969 in the group's new single, "Man of the World."

"Man of the World" was published not by Blue Horizon but by Andrew Oldham, former manager of the Stones, on his Immediate label. Blue Horizon's contract had indeed come to an end, and the record company did not trigger their option to extend at the end of 1968, simply because Vernon had not realized that it was expiring. This was an oversight that did not escape Clifford Davis, the band's manager, who told Blue Horizon that Fleetwood Mac was released from any commitment and that he would therefore apply for another label. This state of affairs suited Davis well, as he was on the lookout for a juicier contract—and if he couldn't find it, he could always come back to Blue Horizon and CBS (the distributor) to demand more money in exchange for a new contract. Vernon was convinced that as part of their collaboration, the musicians would stay with him. To prove his investment even beyond the end of the contract, he also extended his commitment to them until the recording of "Man of the World." But this changed nothing, and the song marked the beginning of the group's collaboration with Immediate. Offering a disturbing and

London's De Lane Lea Studios take their name from Jacques De Lane Lea, a French intelligence agent working for the British government who used the building in 1947 as a place to dub English films into French. During the 1960s, the building was adapted into recording studios to meet the needs of the growing music and advertising industries.

introspective confession, not really made of the stuff that usually connotes a hit single, against all odds "Man of the World" climbed to second place in the British charts and reinforced the feeling of misunderstanding and guilt in Peter Green.

A Recording Process That Kept Dragging On

Paradoxically, the success of "Albatross" and "Man of the World" proved Green right about his new, more adventurous artistic direction. Without a regular producer since the departure of Blue Horizon and the end of the collaboration with Vernon, Fleetwood Mac had to become self-producing, assisted by sound engineer Martin Birch. In fact, the responsibility obviously rested on the shoulders of leader Peter Green. The group used and abused the takes, and it seemed like a very long time since the days when they had wanted to record live. So after days of jamming, Peter was given the task of sorting through the group's best takes.

On April 18, the band took over De Lane Lea Studios in London and canned the definitive versions of "Coming Your Way," "Like Crying," and "Before the Beginning," along with a first version of "Although the Sun Is Shining." The foundations were now laid. Four more sessions were needed to complete *Then Play On*, the recording of which would stretch until the beginning of July, with the exception of one session on August 3 during which "Oh Well" was recorded. This completed the album in its "revised" American version released in November 1969, two months after the original album's release, and inaugurated Mac's contract with Reprise, a division of Warner.

A Mixed Report

Peter Green eventually wrote only five of the new tracks, including "Underway," which sounds like a reprise from "Albatross" resulting from several hours of improvisation in the studio. From this same session of June 8, 1969, were born the two instrumentals "Fighting for Madge" and "Searching for Madge," credited respectively to Mick Fleetwood and John McVie. "Show-Biz Blues" and "Rattlesnake Shake" bear the seal of Peter Green.

Danny Kirwan, for his part, rose to the occasion: You only have to hear the finesse of his playing, as well as his energy on "Coming Your Way," to be convinced. His talent still needed to be polished, because some of his titles, such as "When You Say," "One Sunny Day" and "Although the Sun Is Shining," do not compete with Peter Green's strength on "Rattlesnake Shake" or "Show-Biz Blues." But he could not use Green as a crutch, as he preferred to work separately.

The first half of 1969 would leave its mark. Peter Green's dominant mood was starting to become a worry within the band: While he had previously seemed frightened by his new status as a music star but almost ready to accept it as an inevitability, he now seemed disenchanted, not to say

A deluxe version of *Then Play On* called *Celebration Edition* will satisfy the appetite of Fleetwood completists. It includes the original track list flanked by four bonus tracks ("Oh Well Parts 1 and 2," "The Green Manalishi," and "World in Harmony.") The deluxe edition also includes a 16-page booklet with a foreword by Mick Fleetwood and new liner notes by Anthony Bozza, journalist and co-author of Mick Fleetwood's memoir, *Play On: Now, Then, and Fleetwood Mac.*

bitter, toward the fans who had brought him to this pinnacle. He did not know how to relieve himself of this heavy burden, especially since it was accompanied by a material comfort that he rejected and that led him to cling to spirituality, as evidenced by the dark "Show-Biz Blues" and even more directly in "Closing My Eyes" and "Oh Well."

It must be said that the concept of the rock star seeking divine favor was fashionable in the late 1960s, including with the Beatles and more particularly George Harrison, who closed the circle with "My Sweet Lord" in 1970. Eric Clapton, the absolute model for Peter Green, celebrated his newfound faith after getting lost in hallucinogenic drugs on the song "Presence of the Lord." The song appeared on the only album released by Clapton's ephemeral band Blind Faith, in the summer of 1969.

Peter Green was therefore not alone in his spiritual quest but in fact perfectly in tune with the times, especially since he would also begin to experiment with hallucinogenic drugs, which took him to the point of no return. But as early as the summer of 1969, two months before the release of *Then Play On*, an article in *Rolling Stone* reported Green and Spencer's desire to work on a joint album that would tell the story of Jesus: "We believe in God," Spencer said to journalists, "and this is a serious venture."[20]

Success Is Confirmed

The album was finally released on September 19, 1969. It was titled *Then Play On* as a nod to a line from the beginning of Shakespeare's *Twelfth Night* that poetizes the concept of music: "If music be the food of love, play on." The cover of the album showed a naked man riding a white horse, a detail of a painting from 1917 by the English artist Maxwell Armfield that adorned the dining room wall of a London home. Placed above the fireplace, the painting

The band (shown here in Los Angeles in 1969) worked on its cohesion during the recording of *Then Play On* with intense jam sessions led by Peter Green.

picked up the colors of the decorative elements of the room, such as the dominant yellow, inspired by the curtains. Since this same detail was published in *Suburban Life* magazine in February 1917 under the name "Domesticated Mural Painting," it is possible that this publication inspired the group.

Despite bright tracks and a greater focus on pop infused by Kirwan, *Then Play On* is often located by fans in the "soft belly" of Fleetwood Mac's discography. The opus suffers above all from an artistic offering that remains confused and lacks cohesion, with only the angst of Peter

Green as a common thread. But it is also the first Mac album to sell more than 100,000 copies in the United States, where the public definitely seemed more inclined to give a favorable reception to a British rock band than to a British band aping the American pioneers of the blues. Undoubtedly, this was a good sign for the future.

In Europe, the group finally enjoyed great success and seemed stabilized in the eyes of the public. However, it was about to cross over into a zone of unprecedented turbulence. Ever since the recording of "Oh Well" in midsummer, Peter Green had become more and more distant. The guilt of success gnawed at him, and he suddenly lost interest in Fleetwood Mac. He announced that he wanted to leave the group, but Clifford Davis pulled at his heartstrings and convinced him to stay for the salvation of his partners (as well as his own). Mick Fleetwood then had a close discussion with Green, during which the latter confided, "Ah, there's nothing in it to hold me. [...] I'm sick of playing the same fucking thing night after night. I want to jam, Mick. I gotta move on to something new."[4] The drummer understood: Peter Green was going to go, and it was only a matter of time.

Danny Kirwan tiptoes into the band he admires, unaware that he will soon become the ship's helmsman.

FOR MAC-ADDICTS

Upon his arrival in the group, Danny Kirwan was recognized by his bandmates for his original musical tastes and particularly for his fascination with retro music. They soon gave him a nickname: "Ragtime Cowboy Joe."

DANNY KIRWAN, LOVE AT FIRST SIGHT IN BATTERSEA

Danny Kirwan and Peter Green met in September 1967 when Boilerhouse opened for Fleetwood Mac at Nag's Head in Battersea. He met them again on November 8 at the King and Queen in Brighton and on December 29 at the Marquee. The connection between the two musicians was instantaneous and this was a great source of happiness for Kirwan, who saw Green as a role model. The young guitarist made sure to arrive early, long before the concert was scheduled to begin. He gave the roadies a hand to make himself look good and then jammed with Peter Green. Flattered, Green saw in Kirwan the fan he himself had been when he observed Clapton a few years earlier.

But unlike Green, Kirwan could not hope to shine and compete with his role model as part of his current band. Boilerhouse was struggling to rise above amateur status, due to Kirwan's playing partners being at a limited level. Still, Kirwan had a hard time bringing himself to separate from them. Dave Terrey, the drummer, was a high school buddy. The boys, who were only fifteen years old, were so passionate about music that they set out to repaint an unused room in the Brixton Boys Club so they could use it as a rehearsal room. They had even built a stage out of recycled materials.

A Tough Choice

Kirwan was immersed in jazz from an early age, thanks to his mother being a music lover and a singer herself. It was she who introduced him to the gypsy jazz of Django Reinhardt (whose influence shines through on "Jigsaw Puzzle Blues"), the chamber jazz of Eddie Lang, and the big bands of the 1930s. When his tastes began to assert themselves, he swore by Stratocaster magician Hank Marvin, the Shadows, and, of course, by Eric Clapton, the genius of the Bluesbreakers. Terrey and Kirwan found a third partner through an ad posted in the *Melody Maker*. Trevor Stevens, two years older, took over as bassist and completed the trio, an unusual format at the time, but one that Cream and the Jimi Hendrix Experience would soon popularize.

Kirwan was progressing fast, and his reputation as an exceptional musician soon preceded him and reached the ears of Mike Vernon, who invited himself to a rehearsal. "Danny was outstanding," Vernon said. "He had a guitar style that was totally unique. I seem to remember him playing this Watkins beginner's guitar and yet making these wild sounds that reminded me in a way of Lowell Fulson."[21] Vernon shared his discovery with Peter Green, who knew the producer's tastes; he had already set Jeremy Spencer on his way. It was again Vernon who proposed to schedule Boilerhouse to open for Fleetwood Mac. What Peter Green saw seduced him to the highest degree. Gradually, he became the unofficial manager of Boilerhouse, but the rest of the trio—Stevens and Terrey—pumped the brakes: They did not feel ready to leave amateur status behind in favor of moving to the big leagues.

Before joining Fleetwood Mac, Danny Kirwan played with Dave Terrey (drums) and Trevor Stevens (bass) in Boilerhouse (here on the stage at the Marquee, London, 1967).

Kirwan was pragmatic. He did not put all his eggs in one basket: He found a small job in insurance, working a schedule that was compatible with his artistic activities. If he ever realized that his dreams of being a professional guitarist were not coming true, he would always have a backup plan. But in the meantime, he was giving himself the means to succeed. The three young men of Boilerhouse eventually agreed that they would part ways. To seal the separation in a spirit of close friendship, they decided to make a recording to preserve the memory of their association. During the summer, they met at Dalmain Music Studio in Dulwich and immortalized five songs: "All Your Love (I Miss Loving)," a cover of Otis Rush; "Silly Mean Old World" by T-Bone Walker; "Tell Me Mama," a classic of the 1930s; and two compositions by Danny Kirwan, "Wet Weather Blues" and "Something Inside of Me."

Finding Your Place

With Kirwan's agreement, Green posted an ad in *Melody Maker* hoping to find new musicians for his young protégé for Boilerhouse. No fewer than three hundred budding musicians answered the call! Many auditions were conducted, but the contenders did not tick the right boxes. We do not know if it was Kirwan who rejected them, or Peter Green who set the bar very high for his protégé. Mick

Fleetwood's pragmatism then came into play: Why not integrate Danny into Fleetwood Mac, he proposed. Considering Spencer's lack of involvement when it came to working on Green's compositions, Danny Kirwan's help wouldn't be useless. Strangely, Peter Green, Kirwan's Pygmalion, was not convinced by this prospect. Not yet. Neither were McVie and Spencer. Fleetwood was unfazed by this and insisted on including Kirwan, until the others eventually gave in. The young guitarist was offered the position of third strummer in August 1968. By chance, the first concert with the new recruit was scheduled (August 14 or 18, depending on the source) at the Nag's Head Blue Horizon Club, where a few months earlier their paths had crossed for the first time.

Green quickly saw the benefits of adding Kirwan to the group. In addition to the fact that he was an excellent singer with a blues timbre that was sometimes melodramatic, he brought a jazz background and an identity different from that of Spencer and Green. Kirwan also had a great ability to listen, and the fact that Green was his elder gave Green built-in authority. Kirwan's integration into the band was therefore quite natural, and the three guitarists were not each trying to take all the credit when they performed on stage. "We are a group of five musicians, each with a definite approach to his own thing." Peter Green said in 1969.

The youth and inexperience of Danny Kirwan (left) were apparent when he joined the band in August 1968.

"Jeremy does his thing and we back him. The same with Danny Kirwan and myself. Having three lead guitarists gives us this variety."[22]

Whether by chance or on the whim of a musician under the influence of his idol, Danny Kirwan played in Fleetwood Mac on a Gibson Les Paul just like Peter Green's. Yet their instruments sound different. Kirwan managed to develop a sound of his own, as explained by Bernie Marsden, guitarist of Whitesnake, who was the same age as Kirwan and witnessed, as a spectator, the emergence of his counterpart. "That whole long-bend thing; I've always had the theory that Danny developed that just so he'd be different to Peter," picks up Marsden. "And that's a very wise move, because who in the heck could play like Peter Green in that period? In my mind, I think Danny developed that so you could distinguish them on record. Which of course, you always could after that. I mean, that one lick in 'Man of the World' [1969] which he plays in the middle—it's so obviously Danny."[22]

A real driving force on the album *Then Play On*, Danny Kirwan was often the most involved member of the group, arriving an hour before everyone else at each rehearsal or recording. Over time, he gained confidence and was more and more comfortable on stage. His confidence even pushed him to do things outside of Fleetwood Mac. He participated in the solo albums of Christine Perfect and Jeremy Spencer, which were released in 1970. When Peter Green left the band that same year, Kirwan found himself leading the group with Jeremy Spencer. After considering the possibility of separation, they continued and recorded *Kiln House* in 1970. But in the middle of a promotional tour, Jeremy Spencer abruptly left the band. The musicians, now supported by Christine McVie, then recruited guitarist Bob Welch, a rhythm'n'blues enthusiast. Together they recorded *Future Games* (1971) and *Bare Trees* (1972).

A Sad End

The pressure on his young shoulders led Kirwan to alcoholism, which made him taciturn and irritable. At a concert in August 1972, he was so out of control that the other musicians decided to part ways with him. Kirwan then went solo, recording a series of unsuccessful records: *Second Chapter* (1975), *Midnight in San Juan* (1976), *Danny Kirwan* (1977), *Hello There Big Boy!* (1979). This failure was at least partly due to his reluctance to play on stage. His mental health would continue to falter during the 1980s and 1990s as he divorced, fathered a son he did not see, and eventually became homeless. In 1993, Mick Fleetwood became so worried about his former friend that he contacted the Office of Missing Persons. Kirwan was eventually located at a homeless shelter, living only on social welfare and meager royalties. In 1998, although he was invited, Kirwan did not attend Fleetwood Mac's induction ceremony into the Rock and Roll Hall of Fame. Twenty years later, away from all the honors and accolades, Kirwan died in his sleep in London, on June 8, 2018, after contracting pneumonia.

Away from the control booths, Martin Birch developed a passion for martial arts. In November 1974, he posed for the *Kung Fu* TV series in Los Angeles.

MARTIN BIRCH, A HIGH-FIDELITY MAN

The British music producer was still just a young novice sound engineer, resident at De Lane Lea Studios in London, when, in February 1969, he assisted Fleetwood Mac for the first time during the recording sessions for the single "Man of the World." Although he was still in his apprenticeship, the Mac musicians immediately recognized in him an enthusiast with a discerning ear. They accepted him all the more readily for being of their generation (he was born on December 27, 1948, in Woking, Surrey). In the right place at the right time in the heart of a musical London teeming with talent, Birch went on to record *Beck-Ola* (the rock masterpiece by the guitar virtuoso Jeff Beck) in April of the same year, making the acquaintance of such greats as Rod Stewart, Nicky Hopkins, and Ronnie Wood. Also in 1969, the young "sound engineer" worked on the album *Concerto for Group and Orchestra* for Deep Purple, the future benchmark of hard rock. In 1972, he was part of the *Machine Head* epic, immortalizing the riff machines of "Smoke on the Water," "Lazy," "Highway Star," and "Space Truckin'." His commitment and technical skills earned him the position of co-producer on *Stormbringer* in 1974, an album on which he managed the mixing and sound engineering. Jon Lord, the band's keyboardist, would naturally call on him for his personal projects: *Gemini Suite* (1971) and *Sarabande* (1976). His collaboration with Deep Purple lasted until 1977, when he recorded the live album *Last Concert in Japan*.

Long-Term Collaborations
Birch's focus is on the human element, and he does not try to line up collaborations like so many lines on a résumé.

With Fleetwood Mac, too, the collaboration is built up over time. Present on *Kiln House* (1970) and *Bare Trees* (1972) as sound engineer, he was eventually promoted to co-producer on *Penguin* (1973) and *Mystery to Me* (1973). And if he had not got a little too close to Christine McVie—and thus threatened the balance of the band—he could have stayed on much longer with the Mac. Peter Green, who had worked with him on *Then Play On*, would also call on him for his solo album *The End of the Game* in 1970. At the same time, Birch continued to collaborate with some of the biggest names in hard rock and heavy metal. He earned the nickname "Headmaster" and soon became a specialist in the genre. He worked with Wishbone Ash (1970–1972), Rainbow (1975–1986), and Iron Maiden (1981–1992). For the latter, he produced the classic *The Number of the Beast* in 1982. Birch retired in 1992 after providing Bruce Dickinson's band with a final opus, *Fear of the Dark*.

When he passed away on August 9, 2020, at the age of seventy-one, the members of Iron Maiden paid him a heartfelt tribute that summed up the man and the professional. According to bassist Steve Harris, "He was just absolutely brilliant. He wasn't just a producer, he was a hands-on engineer too, so he knew how to get a great sound [and get] the best out of you. [...]"[57] "To me, Martin was a mentor who completely transformed my singing," added singer Bruce Dickinson. "He was a psychotherapist and in his own words a juggler who could mirror exactly what a band was. That was his special talent as a producer. He was not a puppeteer, he did not manipulate the sound of the band, he just reflected it in the best possible way. Apart from all of that he was a wonderful, warm & funny human being."[57]

Danny Kirwan / 3:47

COMING YOUR WAY

Musicians
Danny Kirwan: vocals, guitar
Peter Green: guitar
Jeremy Spencer: piano
John McVie: bass
Mick Fleetwood: drums, percussion

Recorded
De Lane Lea Studios, London, April 18, 1969

Technical Team
Producer: Fleetwood Mac
Sound Engineer: Martin Birch

Single
Side A: Rattlesnake Shake / **Side B:** Coming Your Way
US Release Date: October 1969 at Reprise (ref. 0860)
Best US Chart Ranking: Did Not Chart

Mick Fleetwood, responsible for a veritable rhythmic cavalcade on "Coming Your Way."

Genesis and Lyrics

When they went into the De Lane Lea Studios on October 6, 1969, the band had not set foot in the studio since April 1968. There was a lot of pressure on the young Danny Kirwan because Peter Green was going through a period of creative scarcity and arrived at this session with only one new title. (Luckily for Green, this new title, "Albatross," would become a future single that went to number one in the charts.) The young guitarist therefore had free rein to contribute new songs. He introduced "Coming Your Way," a touching title due to the message it carries.

For the lyrics, Kirwan repeats the same verses and simply changes the "I" from the first verse to "You" on two occasions: "I've got things to do" becomes "You've got things to do." But whether the busy party is "I" [Kirwan?] or "You" [the group?], in the last line of each verse it's always the narrator "I" who joins them to follow the same path: "I'm coming [or going] your way." These few verses say a lot about Danny's gratitude to his partners. Indeed, the lyrics can be seen as a way to thank the band members for having offered him the opportunity to join their group and for having considered him as one of their own from the beginning. Several ideas are at work: the awareness of arriving in a group that already has its own identity, the desire to integrate without upsetting the established order, and, finally, the awareness that he is the one who has to adapt, not the other way around.

Interestingly, that was probably not the original meaning, as the song was listed as "Going My Way." Danny Kirwan reportedly chose to replace the last three words of the fourth sentence for fear that they would be perceived as a form of arrogance and vanity, which did not correspond to his intentions. As short as it is, this text can be read in a completely different, less personal way, from the perspective of a narrator trying to find their place with their beloved, without rushing them.

Production

The setting up of the piece posed some difficulties for the musicians. Five takes were disposed of, and the sixth—the only one to have been preserved at the end of this session on October 6—was only used to keep track of the structure, because the natural interaction between Danny Kirwan and Peter Green demonstrated on "Albatross" was totally absent from this new effort. The song lacks momentum, and the two musicians were barely able to find their places on the coda. Only Mick Fleetwood's brilliant ride stands out, imprinting a masterful tribal rhythm on the toms and opening onto large imaginary spaces.

A new recording session was required to give the song its final form. In the meantime, the track was debuted on stage and saw its tempo significantly increased. But when it was time to put it on tape on April 18, 1969, the musicians chose to return to the markers of the first attempt with a slower pace. This time, everyone found their place without difficulty.

A sumptuous game of questions and answers began between the two Les Pauls, with Peter Green on the right channel and Danny Kirwan on the left and center. Mick Fleetwood again shows he can save the day with creativity, adding a game of bongos that gives a shamanic dimension to the whole. The rhythmic cavalcade thus created contrasts favorably with the tranquility of the guitars, slower and softer, full of reverb for a result with the taste of western rock. Once the vocal parts, repeated like a mantra, have subsided, the two guitars rush to a break where their complementarity becomes striking. Then Kirwan escapes for an inspired solo and Mick Fleetwood focuses on his drums, emphasizing the throbbing side by playing on a grand scale, hitting each element with force and regularly varying his blows. During the overdubs phase, Jeremy Spencer takes advantage of the fact that the percussion has bowed out to support the epic intensity of the finale by crushing piano chords with determination.

Police attempt to contain a crowd of Catholic students in Londonderry, August 1969.

CLOSING MY EYES

Peter Green / 4:50

Musicians: Peter Green: vocals, guitar, bass, organ, timpani / **Recorded:** De Lane Lea Studios, London, May 31, 1969 / **Technical Team:** Producer: Fleetwood Mac / Sound Engineer: Martin Birch

Genesis and Lyrics

Four days before the recording of "Closing My Eyes," Fleetwood Mac was in Northern Ireland where they were performing at the Camden Fringe Festival. This was a trip that was neither trivial nor without risk. A month earlier, in April 1969, acts of sabotage had shaken the country, prompting prime minister Terence O'Neill to step down. In August, clashes broke out in Derry that spread throughout the country, marking the beginning of a conflict that left nearly 3,500 people dead.

It was in this very tense atmosphere that Fleetwood Mac took to the stage on May 30, 1969. But the group was quickly forced to shorten its show because of the intrusion of skinheads who threw coins and bottles at them. Peter Green was greatly affected by this troubled context where nationalism and religion came together as a motive for civil war. The musician, who had begun to experience a deep spiritual awakening, chose to infuse his next song with spirituality. It clearly sounds like a prayer to God, and we can see the vocabulary of love mixed with amazement in the song's lyrics, but everything tends more toward praise. "And seeing you standing there" is the appearance of God,

theophany. "You've touched me with your love / And though you're in my heart / We're still a world apart." This evokes in a very clear way Earth and Heaven, the world of humans and that of the divine. "Someday I'll die, and maybe then I'll be with you": This time, the allusion is to the afterlife and the possibility of one's soul being welcomed by God.

Production

"Closing My Eyes," with its descending, delicately caressed acoustic guitar chords, spreads a sense of peace and introspection. The bass offers a nuanced support to the whole, while Green plinks the guitar, giving it an almost bell-like sound, playing at the top of the neck. His slips are sometimes approximate, but this contributes to the authenticity of the piece and the sensitivity of its interpretation. A slight crescendo settles with the arrival of a classical guitar sound that is stopped dead in its tracks by silence, as if Green were calling for a few seconds of prayer or introspection. On the last phrase, we note the presence of a ghostly organ, which slowly fades out. An accomplished multi-instrumentalist, which he had never fully revealed until then, Peter Green chose to provide the entire instrumentation himself, locked alone in the studio with Martin Birch. This is part of his introspection process. "Closing My Eyes" is his moment of communion with the divine.

The *Then Play On* sessions were the setting for long improvisations from which "Fighting for Madge," "Underway," and "Searching for Madge" were taken.

FIGHTING FOR MADGE
Mick Fleetwood / 2:45

UNDERWAY
Peter Green / 3:04

SEARCHING FOR MADGE
John McVie / 6:56

Musicians: Peter Green: guitar / Danny Kirwan: guitar / John McVie: bass / Mick Fleetwood: drums / **Recorded:** De Lane Lea Studios, London, June 8, 1969 / **Technical Team:** Producer: Fleetwood Mac / Sound Engineer: Martin Birch

Genesis

Although divided into three distinct pieces, separated by a few tracks, the three instrumental tracks "Fighting for Madge," "Underway," and "Searching for Madge" are inseparable because they come from the same jam. Eight days after locking himself in the studio with Martin Birch and without his partners to develop "Closing My Eyes," his heart-to-heart with God, Peter Green opted on June 8, 1969, for a radically different approach: He launched the idea of a jam session. Beyond a desire to ensure the group's cohesion, the approach was largely motivated by the pressure being exerted on the group. The album release was constantly being postponed, and eight months after the first recording session, the record was still far from being completed. This was mainly due to a lack of inspiration on the part of Peter Green, who, in desperation, thought that an improvisation session would perhaps overcome some blockages and generate something unexpected and good. He was inspired by observing the Grateful Dead's jam sessions during his stay in the United States. If they could do it, why not Fleetwood Mac?

The compilation *The Vaudeville Years* sheds light on the origin of these three songs, as well as on the relevance of appropriations that do not reflect reality. The session featured three segments: "The Madge Sessions—1" (annotated "Danny's Instrumental"), "The Madge Sessions—2" (annotated "Jam to Be Used"), and "Underway." The first two are credited to the entire group and the third to Peter Green. However, "The Madge Sessions—2" and "Underway" are the result of a collegial improvisation, unlike "The Madge Sessions—1," on which Danny Kirwan makes his guitars weep alone in cathedral-like silence. Logically, "The Madge Sessions—1" should be credited to Danny Kirwan and the

On "Searching for Madge," Mick Fleetwood unleashes a power that we had not heard from him before.

other two to the whole group. That said, during editing Peter Green pulled the substantive marrow from this set of more than thirty minutes. From the first session he extracted a song he titled "Searching for Madge," and arbitrarily attributed it to Mick Fleetwood. Also from this session he took another single, "Fighting for Madge," which he credited to John McVie. Finally, he kept the "Underway" introductory sequence (3:04 out of the total 16:13 length of the jam), which he attributed to himself. The Kirwan section ("The Madge Sessions—1") was forgotten. Unlike Kirwan, who saw his composition disappear without being tried in any other form, there was one who was delighted with the result of this improvisation session—John McVie. Against all odds, he showed a great interest in progressive music. He who could not stand jazz digressions within John Mayall's Bluesbreakers somehow appreciated songs that extended longer than was reasonable.

Production

On "Searching for Madge," the rhythm section of Fleetwood Mac appears transfigured. Driven by the bite of the guitars pushing out a frenzied rhythm, multiplying the rise of ranges and the effects of playing, Mick Fleetwood lets everyone have free rein—as if the horse on the album cover was suddenly galloping away. In this rock context, Mick Fleetwood seems to feel fully at ease. He hits his cymbals more often than usual, doubling their power. He even plays two rolls back-to-back at 1:43 after changing patterns, which says a lot about his confidence at that time. John McVie, also full of confidence, walks with diabolical precision on the whole of his guitar's neck at a speed not previously known from him. Only the production choices spoil the pleasure of such cohesion with untimely drops in volume. More explicit in the "Fighting for Madge" section, these choices shed light on "Searching for Madge" and its messy intentions. The false fade-out at the beginning and the eruption of strings in the middle of the finale clearly mark the desire to introduce a form of psychedelia into this jam, attesting to the initial inspiration of the Grateful Dead.

"When You Say" was released on 45 rpm in October 1969, with "No Road Is the Right Road" as Side B (Blue Horizon). We owe it to Christine Perfect McVie, who takes it up in a version enhanced with elegant strings.

WHEN YOU SAY
Danny Kirwan / 4:22

Musicians: Danny Kirwan: vocals, guitar / Peter Green: guitar / John McVie: bass / **Recorded:** De Lane Lea Studios, London, July 2, 1969 / **Technical Team:** Producer: Fleetwood Mac / Sound Engineer: Martin Birch

Genesis and Lyrics

Pressure was mounting on the group. The press relayed Peter Green's optimism that the album would be released in June. But the months passed, and still no opus was on the horizon. At the beginning of July, the group finally managed to carve out a short slot on its calendar and put it to good use. The priority was the completion of the record, but Peter Green, who was not much concerned about this, focused more on the publication of a new single. And he saw "When You Say" as a potential successor to "Man of the World." This was a very strange choice that was finally abandoned, but this is still a song that is nevertheless significant with its unexpected rhythmic signature and its folksy lullaby tune that make it feel unfinished. Musically, not everything on this track is mastered, and the famous "la-la-la-la-la," which seems to compensate for a lack of text, sounds a little false while giving the whole thing a kind of cynical detachment. Unwittingly, Kirwan established a distance from his words, as if he was trying to make them mere meanderings. However, by their blissful sincerity, they touch on a form of Lennonist universality of love: "When you say / That there'll always be / You and me." With the same disarming simplicity, he introduces reciprocity into the romantic relationship, repeating the same paragraph, but this time in the first person.

Production

De Lane Lea Studios were booked for three consecutive days. There was a time when it would have then been possible to get a whole record in the can, but at this point the process was more laborious. The track-by-track recording method forced the musicians, who had become their own producers, to be more meticulous. Every day was more or less devoted to one song, and the first to be completed was "When You Say"—although "completed" is a rather flattering term, because this song sounds more like a demo.

The rhythmic signature chosen, rather unexpectedly, has a lot to do with it. The two guitarists—Green on lead guitar and Kirwan on rhythm—seem to navigate a little by sight while John McVie, behind, ensures the foundations with authority. Mick Fleetwood is careful not to intervene so as not to highlight the small rhythmic wanderings that would be more visible with metronomic drums. All the feeling of the song and its beautifully naive dimension come through the singing, both innocent and dispassionate, which carefully follows the guitar and is cleverly dubbed.

Six takes were needed to complete this piece, which irritated Kirwan. Not satisfied with his performance, he continued to consult Peter Green for his opinion. The latter, anxious to push Kirwan to think for himself, preferred not to make any pronouncements and left Kirwan responsible for his own artistic choices while guiding him on the path he had chosen. If Kirwan liked it, it didn't matter what others had to say, Green advised. But this only fueled the frustration of the young musician, who felt completely lost.

Peter Green opts to take on "Show-Biz Blues" alone, excluding Danny Kirwan, pictured here, who could have brightened up the track with a few guitar flourishes.

SHOW-BIZ BLUES

Peter Green / 3:50

Musicians
Danny Kirwan: vocals, guitar
Uncredited: clappers, tambourine
Recorded
De Lane Lea Studios, London, July 3, 1969
Technical Team
Producer: Fleetwood Mac
Sound Engineer: Martin Birch

Guitarist and singer Sister Rosetta Tharpe was one of the first gospel artists to reach a rock'n'roll and blues audience.

1969

Genesis and Lyrics

Peter Green wasn't quite done with the blues. As though in the grip of a fever, he gets himself back into it with "Show-Biz Blues." The song has no feeling of intimacy except for the instrumentation, because the group is engaged, united around him, clapping their hands, waving the tambourine, or punctuating the performance with small shouts of encouragement. Peter Green long hesitated about the best way to showcase "Show-Biz Blues": Does it lend itself better to a solo or group performance? Or as a sermon, in the spirit of gospel? It is this last option that was eventually retained, but to get there it was necessary to go through long months of gestation.

Green had recorded his first draft on January 8, 1969, at Tempo Sound Studios in New York. The song was then called "Do You Give a Damn for Me." This first attempt, through a more vehement and syncopated interpretation, testified to a dark period for Peter Green. The introductory question, repeated in the title, sounded more like a reproach to the public. Then, as spirituality permeated Peter Green's life, the piece turned into a Rosetta Tharpe–style sermon. Thus "Do You Give a Damn for Me" became "Him and Me," put on tape on May 31 in the same De Lane Lea Studios that would host its third mutation—this being the definitive one, recorded on July 2 and 3 under the name "Show-Biz Blues." The title was key in shedding light on the lyrics, since we understand that they extend to the problem of notoriety, which was so suffocating for Peter Green—and which "Man of the World" had already addressed, though the malaise there was less prevalent than in this track. "Show-Biz Blues" is more about the memory of mad old times, first loves, being carefree. A familiar reference resurfaces at the turn of a verse: "I was a rambling pony / [...] I would roll from town to town" is word for word the beginning of the B side of Fleetwood Mac's very first single. This song is therefore told by a mature narrator who has since been successful, and who is taking a look at the last few years through the lens of experience. The song gets darker as it goes on, with Green addressing his discomfort with fans who see him as a superman. He abhors this deification and protests that he is a man like any other: "And you're sitting there so green / Believe me man, I'm just the same as you."

Production

The guitar's twang on "Him and Me" is less present in the high register on the final version and its singing freer, thanks to the inclusion of clappers and tambourines that guide it rhythmically. Green had been looking to include these ingredients in the album for some time. He did it for the first time on May 15, 1969, during the break of "Rattlesnake Shake." "Him and Me" was recorded for the first time on July 2, and the next day Peter Green played it many times to fix it in his mind and to get the most relaxed and natural take possible. But none of the takes were up to the one he had recorded the day before. Green tried to concentrate by talking to himself. The tapes from the recording sessions capture these words: "This has got to be good, this is the only bluesy thing on the whole fucking LP." When he finally tries to slow down the tempo slightly, he holds the right grip, and he is less aggressive and more authentic. This song offers a good balance between fervor, humor, and intensity.

Fleetwood Mac out on a sunny day in 1968.

ONE SUNNY DAY
Danny Kirwan / 3:12

Musicians: Danny Kirwan: vocals, guitar / Peter Green: guitar / John McVie: bass / Mick Fleetwood: drums / **Recorded:** De Lane Lea Studios, London, October 6, 1968 / **Technical Team:** Producer: Fleetwood Mac / Sound Engineer: Martin Birch

Genesis and Lyrics

Danny Kirwan, at this point too immature, followed the same beaten paths walked by his partners before him. This pitfall could probably have been avoided if the work had been more collective and the other musicians had responded to his call for assistance in his heavy task of writing half the album. Instead, the young artist jumped with both feet into the usual blues tropes: I have the blues, my wife left me, I did not treat her well enough. In three verses, Danny Kirwan ticks all the boxes on the writing grid of a classic blues tune: "Help me take my blues away / [...] See you walking away / [...] I shouldn't treat you this way." The rhymes do not shine with richness: "you/do," "know/go," "say/way," "away/day." Only the title, "One Sunny Day," stands out, leading on a false positive note; the brain retains the smiling dimension of "sunny" more than the "one" that restricts the expression to the single sunny day hoped for by the narrator. The first line, a desperate call, sweeps away any doubt about the situation: "Help me baby."

Production

Led Zeppelin had not yet hit the scene—their first album would follow three months later—but Fleetwood Mac was already smelling the zeitgeist. They brilliantly capture the natural evolution awaiting the blues, renewed thanks to a massive transfusion of rock into their veins. The effect of this mixture makes blues-rock become heavy, massive, threatening. Capturing this spirit, the band has never exuded such power as with "One Sunny Day." Green flirts with proto-metal under the impetus of a Mick Fleetwood, who has given considerable muscle to his playing on this album. He seems to have discovered that he has toms available in his kit and therefore uses them at the slightest opportunity. His primal playing, even martial, leads the gunners of the six-string on the path of war. Properly aligned, Kirwan and Green launch bursts of descending scales in a synchronized manner. Then, like a flare, one of the guitars goes into the treble with a piercing whistle, to draw a melodic line that the vocals take up scrupulously. This singing line then sounds like an incantation from the depths of the ages. With less success, the bridges are deployed on a more classic blues grid, from which only the bottleneck game extracts a little originality.

Thanks to Danny Kirwan's pop know-how, "Although the Sun Is Shining" is reminiscent of the Kinks (here on the 1960s pop music show *Thank Your Lucky Stars*).

ALTHOUGH THE SUN IS SHINING

Danny Kirwan / 2:25

Musicians: Danny Kirwan: vocals, guitar / Peter Green: guitar / John McVie: bass / **Recorded:** De Lane Lea Studios, London, May 15, 1969 / **Technical Team:** Producer: Fleetwood Mac / Sound Engineer: Martin Birch

Genesis and Lyrics

Under the impetus of Kirwan, the group made its first free foray into the field of pop with "Although the Sun Is Shining." In addition, Kirwan opted for an acoustic arrangement that is not the norm for the group. This song carries British pop in its DNA and some features recall the Kinks, given its singing, which exists on the borderline between melancholy and bliss. This kind of in-between-ness is well expressed in the lyrics. All the conditions are met for the narrator to serenely enjoy his love ("Although the sun is shining / High above," "When we're together / We will never part"). But like a hypochondriac about love, he tells himself that it cannot last and perceives bad omens where there are none ("I see a weeping willow / In the park / Like this there's sadness growing / In my heart"). He comes to fear a separation. This possibility gives rise to a strange inconsistency in the text. At best, it illustrates the confusion of the narrator; at worst, it is clumsiness on the part of the author: "We will never part / And if you leave me / It'll break, it'll break my heart."

Production

A first demo was made on April 18, but the final recording took place on May 15, the same day that "Rattlesnake Shake" was completed. The restraint that characterizes Kirwan's almost ghostly singing from "Although the Sun Is Shining" could pass for a lack of involvement, a guilty inexpressiveness. Yet it gives full depth to this acoustic confession. Its languor fits perfectly with the subject and the paranoia that gives birth to a gray cloud in an azure sky. This schizophrenic duet between Kirwan and himself is even tinged with sepia, pre-war tones, when the chorus begins with its sinusoidal vocalizations, or when it ends and the two voices descend together. For once, the guitars are not the center of attention; the chord sequences are simple (*Lam, Fa, Si7, E7* on the verse, then *Fa#7, Si7, Mi, Fa7*). Some small ornamentations simply brighten up the whole, such as the series of three descending chords à la Jim Croce, at 1:30.

ON YOUR HEADPHONES

At 0:47, the melody rises on the word "sadness" while the main voice travels a downward curve, thus creating very beautiful harmonic notes.

Mick Fleetwood is unperturbed by
Peter Green's "Rattlesnake Shake"
lyrics, which expose certain aspects
of the drummer's sexuality.

RATTLESNAKE SHAKE

Peter Green / 3:29

Musicians
Peter Green: vocals, guitar, six-string bass
Danny Kirwan: guitar
John McVie: bass
Mick Fleetwood: drums, tambourine (?)

Recorded
De Lane Lea Studios, London, May 15, 1969

Technical Team
Producer: Fleetwood Mac
Sound Engineer: Martin Birch

Single
Side A: Rattlesnake Shake / **Side B:** Coming Your Way
US Release Date: October 1969 at Reprise (ref. 0860)
Best US Chart Ranking: Did Not Chart

FOR MAC ADDICTS

Mick Fleetwood returned to this title that evoked his masturbatory habits on his solo album *The Visitor* in 1981, bringing in Peter Green on vocals and guitar. Bob Welch also played the song solo on "Live at the Roxy" that year. And it should be noted that the hard rock band Aerosmith included this song in their stage repertoire in 1973 and recorded a version of "Rattlesnake Shake" for the compilation *Pandora's Box* in 1991.

Genesis and Lyrics

On May 15, 1969, Fleetwood Mac returned to the studio. On this day, they worked on only two songs: "Although the Sun Is Shining," whose outline was produced a month earlier during a previous recording session, and a new composition by Peter Green, "Rattlesnake Shake." Subtlety does not stifle its author, who gratifies the listener with revelations about his playing partner, Mick Fleetwood—about the drummer's masturbatory habits, in fact. Peter Green's disinterest in his fame is so ingrained in him that revealing salacious details about his intimate life in his songs does not seem to frighten him in the least. Neither does he fear offending his friend, as the two men are complicit. "'Rattlesnake Shake' is an old Peter Green song about my ample habits as a young masturbatory male. I'd leap out of the van, they'd turn the lights on me, and I'd mimic the art of wanking."[14]

Was he offended to see his intimacy exposed in this way? Not in the least: "When the record came out, I took a lot of teasing about the lyric, but I didn't care. It had the frankness and ring of truth of everything that Peter Green did."

The text testifies to the fact that the hormones of the young musicians, just out of adolescence, were still at boiling point. It is the work of an artist who lives in isolation with his male bandmates almost twenty-four hours a day, including an agitator with a sharp tongue and provocative gestures, Jeremy Spencer. Without their producer and older-brother figure Mike Vernon to serve as a safeguard and to remind them of what was artistically acceptable and not, the band lets salacious private jokes spill over into their repertoire and even goes so far as to accept Clifford Davis's proposal to release "Rattlesnake Shake" as a single in the United States. Thus, in October 1969, this salacious piece without great musical finesse succeeded the very refined "Albatross" and "Man of the World." The song did not reach the top of the singles sales charts. However, it did earn a spot on Billboard's Mainstream Rock chart, peaking at number thirty.

A Phallic Symbol

Refinement is totally absent from this text, which begins with a "sexy" parade of the narrator: "Baby, if you got to rock / I got to be your rockin' horse." Note the references to rock'n'roll and blues during the two verses: "got to rock," "like to roll," "have the blues." After a series of insistent requests to a young woman whom the narrator covets, the verse ends pitifully for the character, who declares without an ounce of self-love that if he returns alone, he will pleasure himself: "But when I get home tonight / I guess I got to shake myself." The unsuccessful seducer assumes this failure by using the first person, but Peter Green indicates his friend Mick Fleetwood in the third verse by naming him directly and making him a "rattlesnake" charmer, a very graphic scene: "Now, I know this guy / His name is Mick / Now, he don't care when he ain't got no chick / He do the shake / The rattlesnake shake." It's hard not to think of the snake from Big Joe Williams's 1941 blues track "Crawlin' King Snake," covered by John Lee Hooker in 1949—especially in the rock interpretation, where it is given an obvious sexual subtext by Jim Morrison and the Doors in 1971.

Production

Such a subversive text requires setting to music in a similarly intense way. Peter Green thus set out to build a powerful and burning blues rock title. The song begins a cappella, before the entry of guitars with a crunching sound that creates a heavy atmosphere, even stifling, with a very slow rhythm. "Pete's chainsaw guitar lick, hard as nails and as immediate as a dog's bite, really defined our sound in those days," Mick Fleetwood said in 1999, forgetting that Fleetwood Mac had, on the contrary, at that time focused on a more aerial blues, even a refined pop rock.

Kirwan's guitar varies little, getting stuck on a chord, while Green's guitar draws serpentine sinuous phrases that serve the purpose perfectly. For a bit, it almost feels like hearing the beginnings of what would become stoner, the music of the California desert, in the 1990s: a penetrating heavy rock with throbbing guitars full of distortion. Two bass lines are present, one provided by Peter Green on a six-string and the other by John McVie, to reinforce this impression of sinuous and hypnotic lines that encircle the listener. An inventive break hosts claps that support the almost shamanic dimension of the song. In addition, there are rattlesnake noises, which would have been added in post-production from an audio tape—even if the sound is more reminiscent of a tambourine.

John Mayall in 1967.

WITHOUT YOU
Danny Kirwan / 4:35

Musicians: Danny Kirwan: vocals, guitar / Peter Green: guitar / John McVie: bass / Mick Fleetwood: drums / **Recorded:** De Lane Lea Studios, London, October 6, 1968 / **Technical Team:** Producer: Fleetwood Mac / Sound Engineer: Mike Vernon

Genesis and Lyrics
Before being inducted as a member of Fleetwood Mac, Danny Kirwan was an avid fan of the band and, even more, of Peter Green. He had studied Green's playing, devoured his record production, and knew his work with the Bluesbreakers quite well. The great resemblance between Kirwan's new composition, "Without You," and one of the songs from the time Green played with John Mayall, "Out of Reach," could not have escaped Green. The same melancholic effusion, the same very slow tempo, the same break in the voice—all were there. Danny Kirwan delivers his version with perhaps less passion than his role model, but with much more softness and delicacy and a shade more blues-pop than soul-blues. The young musician presented this title shortly after his arrival in the lineup, and the band played it during a visit to the BBC on August 27, 1968, at the Piccadilly studio, for broadcast on the show *Top Gear*. At that time, the working title was "Crazy for My Baby" (the first sentence of the lyrics), and it included a harmonica part played by Peter Green and piano played by Jeremy Spencer, which disappeared during the final recording of October 6 in favor of a second guitar, provided by Peter Green. The lyrics are without relief, with the author continually lamenting his loneliness by repeating "I'm so lonely babe" ad nauseam.

Production
With the silky touch of two talented guitarists like Danny Kirwan and Peter Green, there is no need for frills: Two instruments with a warm and crystalline sound are at work and give the song all its beauty. A slight vibrato on the rhythm guitar with a delicate reverb to make the sound of the solo guitar angelic is enough to draw out the quintessential Les Paul sound. It is through this treatment, light but essential, provided by Mike Vernon that we see the importance of his work—a finesse that the group will struggle to find once the producer is gone. John McVie's bass is smooth and slippery, evolving discreetly. Mick Fleetwood's interventions are almost nonexistent; the song could just as easily have been recorded without him. Drinking from the source of the blues, irrigated by soul, this title shines by its beauty more than its originality.

Danny Kirwan (right) at the helm on "My Dream," which defines his musical identity, somewhere between blues and airy pop.

MY DREAM

Danny Kirwan / 3:31

Musicians: Danny Kirwan: guitar / John McVie: bass / Mick Fleetwood: drums / **Recorded:** De Lane Lea Studios, London, July 2, 1969 / **Technical Team:** Producer: Fleetwood Mac / Sound Engineer: Martin Birch

Genesis

The musicians had no choice: The session at the beginning of July had to mark the end of the recording of the album *Then Play On*, whose release date has already been announced… and passed. On July 2, they worked on completing three songs: "When You Say," "Show-Biz Blues"—which would be completed the next day—and, at the end of the day, "My Dream." Time was running so short that this refined composition Danny Kirwan pulled out remained instrumental. And too bad if the record already has three compositions of this type (those of the "Madge Sessions"). Its melodic density exempts it from needing a singing line. At first, it was logically named "Danny's Instrumental." But it deserved better than this prosaic title, so the next day, the group came together to find a name: "My Dream." Kirwan emphasizes the dreamlike dimension of this piece with undulating lines on the guitar.

Production

The musical identity of the young Danny Kirwan asserts itself over the songs he delivers on this album. Admittedly, he may not have the unparalleled feeling and touch of Peter Green, but, as a fine melodist, he compensates with a pop sensibility and an inclination for surprising chord progressions. In order not to waste time, it was decided that Kirwan would play the different parts on this track himself, which he already had in mind, having worked on them alone before presenting them to his partners. The guitarist shows exceptional variety here, especially in his lead playing. He gives everything a go, whether vibrating with his left-hand notes or playing chords at the end of each phrase, and he continues with meticulously chipped arpeggios, places glissandos between chords, and elaborates upon elegant phrasing in a few notes. Kirwan doesn't make any blunders: Each note is of use and participates in the melodic construction of the piece. The song also owes a lot to Martin Birch, who went beyond his usual duties as a sound engineer. He recorded Danny Kirwan's guitar tracks one by one, and then, once the rhythm section was added, proceeded to do a thorough editing in which he combined guitar tracks, interweaving them to make a coherent whole. In this, he acted as a real producer, a task that normally fell to the musicians themselves since Mike Vernon was no longer in the studio with them.

Danny Kirwan and Peter Green provide vocals for "Like Crying."

LIKE CRYING

Danny Kirwan / 2:21

Musicians: Danny Kirwan: vocals, guitar / Peter Green: vocals, guitar / **Recorded:** De Lane Lea Studios, London, April 18, 1969 / **Technical Team:** Producer: Mike Vernon / Sound Engineer: Martin Birch

Genesis and Lyrics

Although the complementarity of their guitar playing is exemplary, Peter Green and Danny Kirwan rarely functioned as a pair of fusion songwriters such as Paul McCartney and John Lennon were in their early days. But "Like Crying" is an exception. Sung in two voices and played on two guitars, an unusual exercise for musicians, it exudes symbiosis, spontaneity, and complicity. And unlike the other compositions of the album, fomented by the two artists each in their corner and delivered in their raw form, this time the approach is more spontaneous. It was by hearing Peter Green humming in the studio, repeating the same line, "Woman's got the blues," that Danny Kirwan had the idea to make it a chorus and conceived the rest of the song from this very short tune, which reminded him of Bessie Smith. Nicknamed the "Empress of the Blues," this figure of female emancipation with an exceptional, powerful voice was a definitive role model for Janis Joplin. She died at only forty-three years old, as a result of injuries caused by a car accident. This song retained the name "Woman's Got the Blues" for some time, before it was permanently recorded on April 18, 1969, and

renamed. The text is not very developed, but it could possibly evoke Bessie Smith and her assumed bisexuality.

Production

A first version of this song, undated, was recorded in late 1968 by Mike Vernon. It eventually appeared on *The Complete Blue Horizon Sessions 1967–1969* and on *The Pious Bird of Good Omen*. It faithfully reproduced the warmth of the interpretation and the intimacy of the moment with the sounds of the strings and the wood, which were very audible. The second version, kept for the album *Then Play On*, was made on April 18, 1969, without the help of Mike Vernon, who had been sidelined as a collateral victim of Fleetwood Mac's departure from Blue Horizon. Peter Green and his group thought they could get by without the expertise of their technician. But their inexperience is unfortunately evident on this album. The new version of this song does not have the authenticity and sharpness that was first intended and is instead more muted. The placement of the microphones and the processing of the voices meant that on the first version, the two singers did not need to push their voices too far. In this second recording the sound is less natural, more forced. However, this does not detract from the beauty of the track, the exceptional playing of the guitars, and the obvious pleasure that the two musicians take from this. Moreover, from the first moments, in the introduction, we can hear them laughing.

1969

Peter Green (right) and the other musicians give life and depth to "Before the Beginning," an instrumental track conceived in New York.

BEFORE THE BEGINNING

Peter Green / 3:28

Musicians: Peter Green: vocals, guitar / Danny Kirwan: guitar / John McVie: bass / Mick Fleetwood: drums / **Recorded:** De Lane Lea Studios, London, April 18, 1969 / **Technical Team:** Producer: Mike Vernon / Sound Engineer: Martin Birch

Genesis and Lyrics

The change of air and the discovery of a new culture served as inspiration for Peter Green, who took advantage of the group's stay in New York, between December 1 and 11, 1968, to conceive the title "Before the Beginning." At the time, the song had not yet adopted its final name, and it was called "Blues in B Flat Minor" because at that stage it was only an instrumental. But it evolved strongly and when the band presented the song on stage at the Shrine Auditorium in Los Angeles on January 25, 1969 (this version is available on the live album *Shrine '69*), it had already undergone some major changes. It was introduced with a break overlaid with a solo full of fabulous soul, and had lyrics and a title, "Before the Beginning." It is amusing to note that the band chose a song so named to close its record. The first verse of the lyrics takes us on what seems to be yet another lament about the absence of the beloved. There is a fear of falling back into the ready-made formulas of ancestral blues, but Peter Green quickly changes course and refocuses the subject on himself.

Over the verses, he lifts the veil on his doubts, his anxieties, and what could appear with hindsight as the first clinical signs of madness: "And how many times must I be the fool?" The phrase can also mean "How many times must I be the one who gets fooled?" which would make sense in the context of a romantic relationship.

Production

This time, the absence of Mike Vernon is not too damaging. The demo of "Blues in B Flat Minor," which was recorded live, lacked brilliance, and Peter Green's guitar suffered cruelly from an absence in the bass. On the final version, the group did not hesitate to leave him the place of honor. The other side of the coin is that the dialogue with Kirwan's rhythm guitar no longer has the same flavor, being relegated to the back of the mix. We also lose in passing between the two recordings some inspired small flamenco ornamentations, placed here and there at the end of the sentence by Peter Green. But the song breathes better overall. The treatment of toms, which is more and more on this album the signature of Mick Fleetwood, is less deaf and less muted. Finally, Peter Green's voice is properly highlighted in the foreground, even if we can deplore an ugly echo that is too strong.

Rehearsing at the Royal
Albert Hall in London,
April 22, 1969.

JEREMY'S CONTRIBUTION TO DOO-WOP
Jeremy Spencer / 3:34

Musicians: Jeremy Spencer: vocals, guitar / John McVie: bass / Mick Fleetwood: drums / **Recorded:** De Lane Lea Studios, London, October 30, 1968 / **Technical Team:** Producer: Mike Vernon / Sound Engineer: Mike Ross

To spare the ego of Jeremy Spencer, who was not required to do much during the recording of *Then Play On*, the team offered him the chance to record a parody EP, consisting of covers played by fictional groups invented by Spencer for the occasion. The parody EP was supposed to be marketed with the LP. However, this strange project never materialized. Thanks to the compilation *The Vaudeville Years of Fleetwood Mac 1968 to 1970*, released in 1998, the public was able to discover what they had escaped. Spencer's talents as a comedian and impersonator are put to use in the prologue, which consists of the presentation of a fictional radio show that serves as a common thread throughout the EP. He plays an unbearable radio presenter with a nasal voice, Milton Schlitz (which he pronounces "Shitz"), and he introduces the first fictional band to appear on his show: Ricky Dee and the Angels performing "Jeremy's Contribution to Doo-Wop" (a nod to "Elmore's Contribution to Jazz" by Elmore James from 1957). It is nothing more than a parody of 1950s doo-wop modeled on Dion and the Belmonts' "I Wonder Why" (1958), with deliberately falsetto vocalizations.

EVERYDAY I HAVE THE BLUES
Memphis Slim / 4:23

Musicians: Jeremy Spencer: vocals, guitar, piano / John McVie: bass / Mick Fleetwood: drums / **Recorded:** De Lane Lea Studios, London, October 30, 1968 / **Technical Team:** Producer: Mike Vernon / Sound Engineer: Mike Ross

The joke continues with "Everyday I Have the Blues," introduced by the unmistakable Milton Schlitz, who plays carpet salesman by including commercials in his show. This time, the parody takes a more cynical turn: Instead of inventing another fictional group, Milton/Jeremy claims to be Alexis Korner, a very real artist whose response to this tribute is unknown. In a hoarse aristocratic voice, Spencer caricatures the father of the British blues boom without any hint of indulgence. The guitars sound fake, the setup is shaky. Nothing stands up in this dissonant jazzy song that Jeremy Spencer completes with a sadistic trumpet improvisation.

DEATH BELLS
Jeremy Spencer / 5:05

Musicians: Jeremy Spencer: vocals / Peter Green: guitar / **Recorded:** De Lane Lea Studios, London, October 30, 1968 / **Technical Team:** Producer: Mike Vernon / Sound Engineer: Mike Ross

"Death Bells" introduces some decency into the Milton Schlitz project with fake bluesman Texas Slim…who is from Texas, as the presenter aptly points out. In a deep voice that is deliberately unintelligible, Spencer plays the homegrown bluesman. He ends almost in tears, accompanied by Peter Green, who, even in a parody context, plays in the style of Lightnin' Hopkins as well as Hopkins himself.

(WATCH OUT FOR YOURSELF) MR. JONES
Jeremy Spencer / 3:35

Musicians: Jeremy Spencer: vocals, guitar / John McVie: bass / Mick Fleetwood: drums / **Recorded:** De Lane Lea Studios, London, October 30, 1968 / **Technical Team:** Producer: Mike Vernon / Sound Engineer: Mike Ross

Then come the Orange Electric Squitters, and hippies and other psychedelic rock worshippers become the target of the joke. This fake band is presented as enlightened, threatening to control the brain of their victim: Mr. Jones. Spencer's accusatory vocals overcome a crazy rock instrumentation on the finale—which, however, holds up perfectly and could create a more serious illusion in a completely different context.

MAN OF ACTION
Jeremy Spencer / 5:21

Musicians: Jeremy Spencer: vocals, piano / Mick Fleetwood: percussion / **Recorded:** De Lane Lea Studios, London, October 30, 1968 / **Technical Team:** Producer: Mike Vernon / Sound Engineer: Mike Ross

The last parody is saved for John Mayall, the man who nevertheless facilitated the emergence of Fleetwood Mac by bringing together Peter Green, John McVie, and Mick Fleetwood. Only the last participates in this ungrateful parody orchestrated by the clown of the group. The track, haunting and melancholic, would easily escape ridicule if Spencer did not sing it in the voice of a duck.

OUTTAKES

Green giving his all to a performance, even to outtakes.

MY BABY'S SWEET
Homesick James Williamson / 3:53

Musicians: Jeremy Spencer: vocals, guitar / Peter Green: guitar / John McVie: bass / Mick Fleetwood: drums / **Recorded:** BBC's Studio B Television Centre, London, July 19, 1968 / **Technical Team:** (?)

Often misidentified as "My Baby's Sweeter," this song appears on *The Vaudeville Years of Fleetwood Mac 1968 to 1970*. Performed regularly during concerts in 1968, this cover of Homesick James Williamson comes off as a little more muscular under the effect of Mick Fleetwood's insistent drumming, followed by McVie's elastic bass playing. Jeremy Spencer typically played piano on this song, but the BBC television crew wanted him to play guitar when this track was recorded in July 1968.

A benchmark for slide guitarists, Homesick James is one of the pillars of Chicago blues. He was a close collaborator of Sonny Boy Williamson II.

ONE SIDED LOVE
Danny Kirwan / 3:52

Musicians: Danny Kirwan: vocals, guitar / Peter Green: guitar / Jeremy Spencer: guitar / John McVie: bass / Mick Fleetwood: drums / **Recorded:** The Hague, February 28, 1969 / **Technical Team:** (?)

Haunting and languorous but lacking a little in body, "One Sided Love" nevertheless shines as a fully inhabited song with guitars that unite around bends that roar. This song was only played on stage during a concert in The Hague in 1969, and it only appears now on certain bootlegs.

(THAT'S WHAT) I WANT TO KNOW
Jeremy Spencer / 3:54

Musicians: Jeremy Spencer: vocals, guitar / John McVie: bass / Mick Fleetwood: drums / **Recorded:** September 1969 (?) / **Technical Team:** (?)

Very little is known about this delicious parody of Ricky Dee (aka Jeremy Spencer), which was most likely meant for inclusion on Jeremy Spencer's 1970 solo album. This song is included on *The Vaudeville Years of Fleetwood Mac 1968 to 1970* and it features Spencer in a register that seems totally foreign to him: that of a teen idol, which he interprets using a slender voice that sounds surprisingly credible.

FAST TALKING WOMAN BLUES
Peter Green / 4:02

Musicians: Peter Green: guitar / Danny Kirwan: guitar / John McVie: bass / Mick Fleetwood: drums / **Recorded:** De Lane Lea Studios, London, September 18, 1969 / **Technical Team:** Producer: Fleetwood Mac / Sound Engineer: Martin Birch

First appearing as "Drifting" in Fleetwood Mac's repertoire, "Fast Talking Woman Blues" was immortalized during a studio session that happened the day before *Then Play On* was released. After an intro reminiscent of Jimi Hendrix, the band plunges into a jam session as intense as it is slow. Green is given all the space required to let his talent speak, and he plays around the beats, rumbles his solos, slows down, and speeds up as needed. This piece appears on *The Vaudeville Years of Fleetwood Mac 1968 to 1970.*

TELL ME FROM THE START
Danny Kirwan / 2:02

Musicians: Danny Kirwan: vocals, guitar / Peter Green: guitar (?) / Mick Fleetwood: drums / **Recorded:** De Lane Lea Studios, London, September 18, 1969 / **Technical Team:** Producer: Fleetwood Mac / Sound Engineer: Martin Birch

"Ragtime Cowboy Joe" is officially back. The members of Fleetwood Mac gave Kirwan this gently mocking nickname owing to his somewhat outdated musical tastes, which included a love of ragtime. Accompanied by a tambourine, Kirwan could just as well have played this charming song all on his own, and its pairing of Kirwan's youthful voice with otherwise retro sounds is deliciously anachronistic. This track is included on *The Vaudeville Years of Fleetwood Mac 1968 to 1970.*

OCTOBER JAM #1
Danny Kirwan, Peter Green, John McVie / 5:01

Musicians: Peter Green: guitar / Danny Kirwan: guitar / John McVie: bass / Mick Fleetwood: drums / **Recorded:** De Lane Lea Studios, London, October 24, 1969 / **Technical Team:** Producer: Fleetwood Mac / Sound Engineer: Martin Birch

This song finds Fleetwood Mac in the middle of an improvisation session. The recording is delivered as is, without any edits, as part of *The Vaudeville Years of Fleetwood Mac 1968 to 1970.* This jam has some interesting dynamics and it certainly deserved to have been structured into a real song by the group. Peter Green twists his guitar's whammy bar to distort its sounds as much as possible, but as soon as he lets go and is joined by the rhythm section, John McVie's bass starts to build a tense rock sound. Mick's subtle cymbal playing sets up a fairly deft and constant note of tension. One might also be surprised by the quality of the sound on this track, as the spectrum seems more open than on the rest of *Then Play On.*

OCTOBER JAM #2
Danny Kirwan, Peter Green, John McVie,
Mick Fleetwood / 1:57

Musicians: Peter Green: guitar / Danny Kirwan: guitar / John McVie: bass / Mick Fleetwood: drums / **Recorded:** De Lane Lea Studios, London, October 24, 1969 / **Technical Team:** Producer: Fleetwood Mac / Sound Engineer: Martin Birch

Although this song's title implies otherwise, this track has nothing to do with "October Jam #1" except that it was recorded on the same day. A not uninteresting attempt at pop rock, this track sounds more like a coda than a song in its own right. It is built around a progression of ascending major chords, and like all the band's other untapped pieces from this era, this number appears on *The Vaudeville Years of Fleetwood Mac 1968 to 1970.*

LOVE IT SEEMS
Danny Kirwan / 2:39

Musicians: Danny Kirwan: vocals, guitar / Peter Green: guitar / John McVie: bass / Mick Fleetwood: drums / **Recorded:** De Lane Lea Studios, London, October 24, 1969 / **Technical Team:** Producer: Fleetwood Mac / Sound Engineer: Martin Birch

An unfinished track from Danny Kirwan, "Love It Seems" suffers for its similarity to "When You Say," another track that was included in *Then Play On.* This song remained unpublished until *The Vaudeville Years of Fleetwood Mac 1968 to 1970.* Here, two six-strings are at work; one is rhythmic and placed on the left of the spectrum, while the other takes the lead and is set on the right. Although seductive, this song suffers from a lack of charisma and body in Kirwan's voice, in addition to his unsuccessful use of "la-la-la-la" to fill in the gaps.

Oh Well (Part 1) / Oh Well (Part 2)

UK Release: September 26, 1969
Reference: Reprise Records (45 rpm ref.: RS.27000)
Best UK Chart Ranking: 2
US Release: November 19, 1969
Reference: Reprise Records (45 rpm ref.: 0883)
Best US Chart Ranking: 55

During an intense spiritual phase, Peter Green (here in a toga) fills his compositions, such as "Oh Well (Part I)," with religious imagery.

Side A

OH WELL (PART I)

Peter Green / 3:22

Musicians: Peter Green: vocals, guitar, dobro / Danny Kirwan: guitar / John McVie: bass / Mick Fleetwood: drums, cowbells, congas, claves / Jeremy Spencer: maracas / Sandra Elsdon-Vigon: recorder / **Recorded:** De Lane Lea Studios, London: August 3, 1969 / **Technical Team:** Producer: Fleetwood Mac / Sound Engineer: Martin Birch

Genesis and Lyrics

The musicians, finally relieved of the mental burden of the third album (whose sessions ended a month earlier), could now look forward to the release of a new single. The previous one, "Man of the World," dates back to April 1969. "Oh Well (Part 1)" was born of the exploitation of a Peter Green blues riff he did not really believe in. "Part 1" was intended to appear on Side B, but Clifford Davis—or the record company (?)—preferred this wild electric rock blues to its Hispanic-sounding counterpart ("Part 2"). The lyrics, conceived by Peter Green, correspond to his religious mood of the moment: They are about one mortal's judgment of another, and divine protection.

Production

"Oh Well (Part 1)" illustrates just how far Peter Green had come since his debut. He had mastered the art of the blues to such an extent that he could use it as a starting point for branching off into other musical landscapes.

The opening motif on the dobro, a particularly resonant instrument inextricably linked to the blues, sets an initial milestone to which the musicians return several times. But, in between each sequence, they move away from this into rock territory. It begins with a reprise of the motif on electric guitar, with the low E string sounding like a buzzing bell. The first burst of acceleration. Then the riff is modulated, before the band explodes the motif under the onslaught of saturated electric guitars, roaring and screeching, spurred on by percussion emerging from all sides. Rather than fade out the decibel deluge, Peter Green lets the last note of his outro ring out and continues with what was originally intended to be the start of "Oh Well (Part 2)."

ON YOUR HEADPHONES

At 0:42, Mick Fleetwood's two strokes of the cowbell serve a double purpose: They provide ornamentation, with a rustic feel that might recall ancestral blues such as skiffle. And amid the ambient chaos, they signal to the musicians the end of the sonic romp and the return of Peter Green's vocals.

The band moves into the realm of Western music with a cinematic "Oh Well (Part 2)."

OH WELL (PART 2)

Peter Green / 5:37

Musicians: Peter Green: classical guitar, electric guitar, cello, timbales, cymbals / Jeremy Spencer: piano / Sandra Elsdon-Vigon: recorder / **Recorded:** De Lane Lea Studios, London: August 3, 1969 / **Technical Team:** Producer: Fleetwood Mac / Sound Engineer: Martin Birch

Genesis

This composition was destined for a better fate, as it was originally intended to appear on Side A. This decision was undoubtedly motivated by the record company's (or manager's) reluctance to bet again on an instrumental after "Albatross." One does not always win twice on the same board! The idea for this composition came to Peter Green by chance, as he recounts in an interview with *Guitar Player* in 1994: "I got the idea after hearing a Hispanic guitar piece on the radio while riding in the back of a car. The song was written and played on a Ramirez guitar I'd just bought. I sold it shortly after recording the song."[24]

Production

"Oh Well (Part 2)" actually begins on the first side, as its length does not allow it to fit on a single side—thereby conferring an unexpected transition and additional originality upon "Part 1." The track ends with a bluesy classical guitar section, topped by a penetrating reverb on an electric guitar. A recorder is then played by Peter's girlfriend, Sandra Elsdon (later named Elsdon-Vigon). The young psychotherapist is the famous "Magic Mama" who inspired "Black Magic Woman." Her intervention gives this finale an Ennio Morricone–ish Western dimension. Indeed, at the end of the 1960s, the Italian Western was enjoying its golden age, with films such as *The Good, the Bad, and the Ugly* and *Once Upon a Time in the West*. They clearly inspired Peter Green and his team—especially the timpani playing, which lends dramatic intensity and a cinematic dimension to the whole.

ALBUM LIVE

BLUES JAM AT CHESS (VOL. 1 & 2)

Volume One: Watch Out . Ooh Baby . South Indiana (Take 1) . South Indiana (Take 2) . Last Night . Red Hot Jam . I'm Worried . I Held My Baby Last Night . Madison Blues . I Can't Hold Out . I Need Your Love . I Got the Blues . **Volume Two:** World's in a Tangle . Talk with You . Like It This Way . Someday Soon Baby . Hungry Country Girl . Black Jack Blues . Everyday I Have the Blues . Rockin' Boogie . Sugar Mama . Homework . **Bonus Tracks:** Bobby's Rock . Horton's Boogie Woogie . My Baby's Gone . Honey Boy Blues . Have a Good Time . That's Wrong . Rock Me Baby

RELEASE DATES

United Kingdom: December 5, 1969 (under the title *Blues Jam at Chess*)
Reference: Blue Horizon—7-66227
Best UK Chart Ranking: Did Not Chart
United States: 1969 (under the title *Blues Jam in Chicago*)
Reference: Blue Horizon—BH 4803
United States: 1971 (under the title *Fleetwood Mac in Chicago*)
Reference: Blue Horizon—BH 3801
United States: 1975 (under the title *Fleetwood Mac in Chicago*)
Reference: Sire Records—SASH-3715-2
Best US Chart Ranking: 118 (1975)

Chess Records' most famous
location was at 2120 South
Michigan Avenue in Chicago.

ONE LAST BLAST OF THE BLUES

In December 1969, Fleetwood Mac were in the midst of their American tour (November 21, 1969–February 13, 1970) when the Blue Horizon label decided to release a double live album recorded in Chicago's legendary Chess Studios eleven months earlier, during the band's previous visit to the United States (December 6, 1968–February 9, 1969). This is a brief perspective of that period.

Mike Vernon's Surprise

On December 28, 1968, the members of Fleetwood Mac left the seventy-degree warmth of Florida for Chicago, where the mercury dropped below zero in places, four days later. The thermal shock was brutal, even for Britons used to the harshness of their island climate. This was in addition to the moral fatigue that was beginning to set in among the band's ranks. The logistics of the tour were onerous and costly, and the label's promotional efforts in the United States seemed insufficient to Peter Green, who realized that Fleetwood Mac did not stand for much on the American side of the Atlantic as yet. But their producer Mike Vernon was counting on the musicians' renewed enthusiasm at the idea of meeting up in the Windy City, which Jeremy Spencer and Peter Green considered to be the epicenter of the blues. And he especially expected them to be excited at the prospect of taking to the stage at the Kinetic Playground to support their idol, Muddy Waters, for several concerts on December 31, 1968, and January 1, 3, and 4, 1969—all the more so as the producer had a small, late Christmas present for them.

Vernon had heard that the studios of Chess Records, the legendary home of Chicago blues, might be closing. It had been a tough year financially, and both locals and musicians needed to recharge. The producer jumped at the chance and booked the studios for January 4. He did not know what would come out of this hastily arranged recording, but he decided to invite local musicians to jam with the Mac members. He had in mind the principle of sessions organized by renowned American bluesmen who passed through London during the great period of the British blues boom and recruited young British musicians like Peter Green, John McVie, and Mick Fleetwood, who were then part of the Bluesbreakers or the Mac in its early days. Incidentally, Vernon thought this might put some fuel back into the tank, as the band was clearly running out of inspiration for its third album.

Unknown in Chicago

Willie Dixon, studio coordinator, resident double bass player, and composer of the famous "Hoochie Coochie Man" for Muddy Waters in 1954, was asked to recruit some Chicago bluesmen. But Mike Vernon's original ambition of building a genuine all-star band around his colts soon proved unattainable. Muddy Waters, Howlin' Wolf, Otis Rush, Junior Wells, and Magic Sam, at the top of the list sent to Dixon, all declined the offer. Most of the blues heavyweights were not available or willing to travel for a British band they had never heard of. They barely understood that Fleetwood Mac was not the name of a solo artist. Reality hit Vernon square in the face: While the band was already an institution in the UK, there was still a long way to go on the US side of the Atlantic. But this session could be just the first step toward the recognition they had been missing. Mick Fleetwood confirms: "None of them had ever seen or heard of us before and when they got a look at us, I could tell that they thought we were another loud, over-distorted, acid-rock blues band from England, the type who turned it up to mask their fairly basic skills. But we showed them otherwise; they saw that we were a tight little act who could put them through their pace[s]. Peter, of course, won the day with his taut soloing, his guitar tone and the deep soul in every bit of his playing."[2]

Different Experiences

Although not all the stars were there, the final cast was enough to make any blues fan salivate: legendary guitarist Buddy Guy; pianist Otis Spann, creative partner of Muddy Waters; harmonica player Shakey Horton, Chicago's first postwar soloist of the genre; saxophonist J. T. Brown, who worked with Elmore James; guitarist Honeyboy Edwards, a contemporary of Robert Johnson; Chess drummer S. P. Leary; and, of course, bassist Willie Dixon, who needs no introduction. The seven professionals were in the house.

Mike Vernon had drawn up a precise wish list but had not given much thought to how to get all the musicians to work together during this session, in particular his three guitarists (Peter Green, Danny Kirwan, and Jeremy Spencer)

1969

Debonair double bass player Willie Dixon, posing under a road sign honoring fellow bassist Muddy Waters, on Chicago's South Side.

with Buddy Guy or Honeyboy Edwards, when their turn came. An inevitable game of musical chairs ensued, the quality of which varied according to the profile of the outside contributor (guitarist, harmonica player, pianist, etc.). The multi-instrumental talents of Peter Green and Jeremy Spencer were an advantage for them, unlike John McVie, who was left out of half of the session. And for a specific reason: Willie Dixon, the master of the house, filled the rhythmic role as double bass player—a situation that did little to revive McVie's already subdued enthusiasm for this recording. He deplored the American musician's somewhat condescending attitude toward him, at least initially, as did Mick Fleetwood in his 1991 memoirs: "As soon as Pete's respect for their music became apparent, they stopped treating us like tourists."[4]

As the nice polite boys that they were, John McVie and Mick Fleetwood, the least concerned by the day's business, put on a good show, but nothing more. As for Danny Kirwan, he took a back seat. Less experienced than his partners in this kind of collegial exercise, the young musician failed to push his character to the fore. Jeremy Spencer was the one who enjoyed himself the most. "Jeremy about wet his pants over J. T. Brown, who had played with Jeremy's god, Elmore,"[4] Mick Fleetwood joked years later.

Strangely enough, Peter Green was on the sidelines, even though this day should have been a high point for him. He felt that something had changed in him. This session had come almost too late; he was no longer the same man, nor the same musician adoring his American elders. He aspired to something other than covering blues tunes that had become hackneyed through countless cover versions, for the sole pleasure of playing among connoisseurs. This unconditional fan of Robert Johnson and Elmore James had since discovered the Beatles and the Stones in his own country, and the horizons open to him were much wider than just the Mississippi bayou. Even the mythical Chess Studios, which reminded him of a school entrance hall, did not have as much appeal as he had imagined they would. The layout was spartan: The musicians were provided with folding chairs, acoustic screens were placed behind them, and cubicles were used to isolate the amps from each other. Most of the time, the musicians played in a circle, eye to eye. Only Mick Fleetwood stood a little way back, isolated in a booth behind the stalls.

All's Well That Ends Well...More or Less

As a warm-up for the long session that was to follow, Fleetwood Mac began with a tight lineup, without any guests, playing a track that Peter Green had been keeping hidden for some time, called "Watch Out." Then the tracks followed on at high speed, with no real preparation between them. The pleasure is palpable on certain passages, such as the shuffle of "Madison Blues," which, despite minor rhythmic inconsistencies on Mick Fleetwood's part, synthesizes the spirit of this session, notably through the inspired interventions of J. T. Brown on saxophone and Jeremy Spencer. The recording is riddled with imperfections, resonances, and approximations, but the subtle, precise touches of Willie Dixon on double bass and Buddy Guy on guitar counterbalance these shortcomings. Hosts and guests commune on tributes that get everyone on the same wavelength, like Howlin' Wolf's "Ooh Baby" or "Sugar Mama"; he had finally graced this singular session with his presence, in spirit. The atmosphere becomes much more relaxed and convivial, aided by the flowing scotch. Peter Green, who was not overly enthusiastic at the start, finally shines. Jeremy Spencer is jubilant. In the presence of J. T. Brown, he outdoes himself on "I Held My Baby Last Night," "I'm Worried," and "I Can't Hold Out." After a while, the guests ask the young Brits to play their signature songs. Shakey Horton, for example, gives his all, taking his

Peter Green at Chess Records' studios for some memorable Chicago blues sessions, January 4, 1969.

partners with him on "I Need Your Love" and "I Got the Blues." The same goes for Otis Spann on "Someday Soon Baby" and "Hungry Country Girl." At the end of the session, everyone went off to a South Side club, where Peter Green almost got himself mugged!

What Happens in Chicago, Stays in Chicago

In the press, Mick Fleetwood congratulated himself on this inspiring session, for which he credited Mike Vernon: "He understood the very nature of what Chicago meant to us— not a load of gangsters flying around, but the great Chicago Blues players."[28] But Vernon was to overshadow this fine initiative by deciding to release it as an album, despite the reluctance of the band, who regarded the session as an excellent souvenir, but not as something mature enough to be presented to the public.

On December 5, 1969, the Chess Studios session was released by Blue Horizon under the title *Blues Jam in Chicago, Volumes One and Two.* The album featured twenty-two tracks spread over two LPs and four sides. Only five songs featured previously unreleased material composed by Fleetwood Mac. For ease and owing to lack of time during the recording sessions, the musicians concentrated on blues standards, or on playing the guests' own tracks.

Ironically, this non-approved double album is Fleetwood Mac's last true blues record. Vernon's decision to override their wishes angered Peter Green. The day after the opus was released, on December 6, 1969, he opened up unreservedly to journalist Nick Logan in the *New Musical Express*: "The bulk of our fans won't like it, because a lot of the blues fans have dropped us, like they do, because we've been on television and had hits."[30] Two years later, the record was released in the United States, this time under the name *Blues Jam in Chicago.* The public proved Peter Green right, as the album failed to chart in the UK and barely made it to number 118 in the US— six years later, in 1975.

WATCH OUT

Peter Green / 4:10

Musicians: Peter Green: vocals, guitar / Danny Kirwan: guitar / John McVie: bass / Mick Fleetwood: drums / **Recorded:** Chess Ter Mar Studios, Chicago, January 4, 1969 / **Technical Team:** Producers: Marshall Chess, Mike Vernon / Sound Engineer: Stu Black / Assistant Sound Engineer: Willie Dixon, Neil Slaven

Fleetwood Mac record "Watch Out," a song that had languished in their repertoire since their early days. Indeed, an early bootleg from a concert at the Marquee on August 15, 1967, already referenced it. At the time, the band included Bob Brunning in its ranks, and guitar parts were shared between Peter Green and Jeremy Spencer. It had also been recorded in the studio, at CBS's New Bond Street offices, on November 22, 1967, this time as a trio with Green, McVie, and Fleetwood. The version recorded in the Chess studios appears slower, more laid-back, and better structured, due in part to Kirwan's discreet jazzy guitar. The rhythmic rigor of Kirwan and John McVie enables Peter Green to "knit" a long solo on the scale. Vocally, Green appears more menacing than on previous recordings, with a "Watch out" that grabs the listener.

RED HOT JAM

Peter Green / 4:36

Musicians: Peter Green: guitar / Buddy Guy: guitar / Honeyboy Edwards: guitar / Willie Dixon: double bass / Mick Fleetwood: drums / Shakey Horton: harmonica / **Recorded:** Chess Ter Mar Studios, Chicago, January 4, 1969 / **Technical Team:** Producers: Marshall Chess, Mike Vernon / Sound Engineer: Stu Black / Assistant Sound Engineer: Willie Dixon, Neil Slaven

With the 1969 *Blues Jam in Chicago* edition, the listener has access to the first aborted take of "Red Hot Jam." Mike Vernon explains to the guests that this is a Peter Green

instrumental, while one of the amps emits some nasty feedback. The setup is somewhat hesitant, with Shakey Horton feeling uncomfortable, hardly daring to get started. He even takes a back seat on the guitar solo. The second version is much more assured, and Shakey works wonders, responding brilliantly to Peter Green's prodigious solos. A pity, however, that the guitars are so lacking in body. The equalization lacks bass, and a little reverb would have given them more depth.

TALK WITH YOU

Danny Kirwan / 3:22

Musicians: Danny Kirwan: vocals, guitar / Peter Green: guitar / Otis Spann: piano / John McVie: bass / S. P. Leary: drums / **Recorded:** Chess Ter Mar Studios, Chicago, January 4, 1969 / **Technical Team:** Producers: Marshall Chess, Mike Vernon / Sound Engineer: Stu Black / Assistant Sound Engineer: Willie Dixon, Neil Slaven

This was one of the first Danny Kirwan songs played with Fleetwood Mac. It has never sounded better than in this context. The young artist is clearly gaining confidence, freed from his guitar constraints by Peter Green's control (very present in the mix) and Otis Spann's assurance. The latter slips into the tempo as if he had always known the song, anticipating Kirwan's transitions, while concentrating on his right-hand playing so as not to clutter up the space occupied by the guitarists.

1969

A session with Danny Kirwan, David "Honeyboy" Edwards, and Willie Dixon.

LIKE IT THIS WAY

Danny Kirwan / 3:45

Musicians: Danny Kirwan: vocals, guitar / Peter Green: guitar / Otis Spann: piano / John McVie: bass / Mick Fleetwood: drums / **Recorded:** Chess Ter Mar Studios, Chicago, January 4, 1969 / **Technical Team:** Producers: Marshall Chess, Mike Vernon / Sound engineer: Stu Black / Assistant Sound Engineer: Willie Dixon, Neil Slaven

Danny Kirwan gives a single instruction, which he repeats twice before giving the starting signal: "Fast." Green follows, but not everyone is on the same tempo. Kirwan then takes the time to tap the rhythm with his foot. The second attempt is the right one—or at least this is the one that sticks. The result is clearly not up to scratch. The track descends into a delirious cacophony, mainly due to the drums. The liner notes indicate that Leary stepped aside for Mick Fleetwood, whose playing is unrecognizable. Usually, he concentrates on two elements of his drums, three at most. Here, the drummer is all over the place, often to bad effect.

ROCKIN' BOOGIE

Jeremy Spencer / 3:45

Musicians: Jeremy Spencer: guitar / Peter Green: guitar / Honeyboy Edwards: guitar / Willie Dixon: double bass / Mick Fleetwood: drums / J. T. Brown: tenor saxophone / **Recorded:** Chess Ter Mar Studios, Chicago, January 4, 1969 / **Technical Team:** Producers: Marshall Chess, Mike Vernon / Sound Engineer: Stu Black / Assistant Sound Engineer: Willie Dixon, Neil Slaven

Recorded at the end of a grueling day, "Rockin' Boogie" displays an admirable freshness. Willie Dixon's taut playing and Mick Fleetwood's instinctive, energetic style provide the ideal rhythmic foundation for this joyous boogie. Jeremy Spencer, who officiates on slide, has found an ideal playing partner in J. T. Brown. A beautiful complicity is born between the two musicians. Brown recognizes Spencer as a fine blues connoisseur, and one senses that the two men are looking for each other to respond musically throughout the piece. A great moment of masterful improvisation.

Spearheading British blues,
Fleetwood Mac set out to
seduce American audiences.

THE BOSTON TEA PARTY CONCERTS: FLEETWOOD MAC AT THE HEIGHT OF THEIR POWERS

Following the release of *Then Play On*, the band left for the United States in mid-November 1969. The three-month tour (November 21, 1969—February 13, 1970) would see them play some thirty dates, some of them opening for Joe Cocker and the Grease Band or Jethro Tull. On promotional posters, the band is pompously billed as "the pride of England." As 1969 drew to a close, Fleetwood Mac's sales in the UK were buoyant: *Then Play On* was such a success that the British magazine *Melody Maker* announced on the front page of its December 27 issue that the group was "England's biggest seller," ahead of the Beatles. That was saying a lot. With this third US tour, Fleetwood Mac was determined to make a definitive impact across the Atlantic by winning over the American public.

A Tour Full of Twists and Turns

Still in the United States at the start of a new decade, the band played San Francisco's Fillmore West with the Byrds and bluesman John Hammond on January 2 and 4, 1970, followed by five nights at the famous Los Angeles club Whisky a Go Go from January 7 to 11. The day after their last show at the Fillmore West, on January 5, they rented Studio 2 at Western Recorders in Hollywood to record "The Green Manalishi (with the Two Prong Crown)" with sound engineer Martin Birch, who had flown in from England especially for the occasion. But nothing concrete emerged from this session, and the song had to be rerecorded in April.

In January, Jeremy's wife, Fiona Spencer, and John's wife, Christine McVie, joined them for the remainder of the tour, which was to last several more weeks and include stops in Seattle, Washington, Boston, and even Vancouver, Canada. Curiously, there was a persistent rumor about the imminent departure of Danny Kirwan, who was on his way to becoming the band's mainstay in place of Peter Green. The latter was gradually losing interest in Fleetwood Mac, so much so that their manager, Clifford Davis, was forced to issue a statement to the music press officially denying this departure.

On January 30, 1970, the band performed at the Warehouse in New Orleans for the inauguration of the venue, located at 1820 Tchoupitoulas Street, with the Flock and the Grateful Dead. Too wasted by acid at the end of the evening, the musicians decided not to follow the Dead back to their motel in the French Quarter after the show—fortunately for them, because the next morning at dawn, a police raid on the motel resulted in the arrest of nineteen people, including some members of Grateful Dead and Owsley Stanley, their sound engineer, also known as an underground chemist producing methamphetamine and purified LSD. For the members of Fleetwood Mac, arrest would have meant immediate expulsion from the country, and would have permanently compromised their American ambitions.

Peter Green's Obsessive Excesses

For several weeks already, acid consumption had become a regular occurrence within the band, particularly for Peter Green, who was slipping dangerously: "I was touring America and one night took the drug at a party," he would explain later. "Everyone else went to bed but I had this vision of a man watching TV. There were pictures of starving people in Biafra on the screen. I remember thinking, 'We can get TV cameras there, but we can't get them food.' And then the man in my dress got up, ready to go to bed, and just switched off the TV set. I realized I was at a crossroads. I had more money than I needed."[25]

For Peter Green, the American tour served as a kind of revelation. The man who dreamed only of freedom and seemed to have tasted it during his few weeks in the United States, was finding it increasingly difficult to face up to his responsibilities. He felt that the life of a rock star was not for him. His allusions to spirituality increased in intensity until they became obsessive. He spent all his spare time thinking about the new perspectives that acid consumption seemed to open up for him. Mick sometimes caught him crying in his hotel room, watching the news. One day, his bandmates learned that he had just donated £12,000 to charity, a considerable sum at that time. Jeremy Spencer was receptive to the guitarist's self-questioning, as was John McVie to a certain extent. But before long, Green explained in the press that he wished to see Fleetwood Mac become a charity band devoid of any financial interests. He

naively hoped that all the money generated by the band's musical activities would be used to improve the condition of those most in need.

Inevitably, John McVie became more skeptical. As for Mick Fleetwood, he was downright resistant to the idea. Beyond the tensions caused, the situation gave rise to some comical episodes. "There had been mumblings on the American tour; Peter started trying to persuade us to give all our money away," explained Mick Fleetwood in an interview—Mick sighs, the memory evidently still hanging heavy: "We had all these band meetings in hotels, and we'd sit there for hours, basically going over that whole Haight-Ashbury hangover. John and I would say, 'Well, you can do it, but we aren't giving our fucking money away.' Pete would say, 'You're wrong, you're wrong; it'll all come back on us, I'm telling you.' Once we were playing the Fillmore East and he came over to the drums and mumbled, 'We've got to do it.' I knew what he was talking about. He wanted us to play for no money, for nothing. Later on in the set, I called him over and said, while were still playing, 'I won't give my money away, Pete, but what we should do is continue doing what we're doing, but do with the money something constructive, like finance an orphanage.'"[26]

Three Legendary Concerts

When the band arrived in Boston from New Orleans, they were still recovering from the massive police raid on the Dead. In Boston, the three performances scheduled at the Boston Tea Party on February 5, 6, and 7 were intended to be recorded with a view to releasing a live album to the public later that year. The reason for this was simple: Clifford Davis intended to ride the wave of success that Fleetwood Mac was enjoying after several months on the road, but above all he hoped to compensate for the lack of artistic direction on the next studio album, which was proving very difficult to plan in the total absence of new songs. A live album could therefore serve to keep fans waiting and represent a kind of culmination for the Mac musicians, who saw it as an opportunity to respond to their friends in the Grateful Dead, themselves authors of the *Live/Dead* double album a few months earlier.

The band arrived in Boston somewhat refreshed—except for the little hot spot in New Orleans—following a number of days off. They could rest in the assurance that they would deliver three performances at the same venue, which they already knew well from having played there before. This had the added advantage of leaving room for combining the best takes from each evening to achieve an ideal result. The venue, a former synagogue, also boasted excellent acoustics and guaranteed the presence of an audience already familiar with, if not actually fans of, the Mac's music.

Over the course of the three evenings, the band remained true to themselves, giving free rein to long instrumental passages, pushing the boundaries of experimentation with disconcerting fluidity.

On the first night, the musicians hit the ground running with tracks such as "Black Magic Woman" and the Duster Bennett cover "Jumping at Shadows." Other tracks played on February 5 included "Like It This Way," "Only You," "Rattlesnake Shake," and the traditional "You Gotta Move," as well as "The Green Manalishi (with the Two Prong Crown)" in a quarter-hour-long version, plus the inevitable reverence to Elmore James, "I Can't Hold Out."

On the second night, the bluesman was again honored with covers of "Red Hot Mama" and "Stranger Blues." Little Richard was also honored with a cover version of his "Jenny, Jenny," while the band featured its own repertoire, including "World in Harmony," "Oh Well," and "Rattlesnake Shake." Above all, the audience was treated to a guest appearance by Joe Walsh and Eric Clapton, who accompanied the band on an almost fifteen-minute jam called "Encore Jam."

Another jam, this time without Clapton and Walsh, was on the menu for the first and third nights. Known as "On We Jam," it featured on February 7 in a set list made up of numerous covers, from Duster Bennett ("Jumping at Shadows") to B. B. King ("If You Let Me Love You"), Elmore James ("Madison Blues," "The Sun Is Shining," and "Can't Stop Lovin'"), Little Richard ("Tutti Frutti"), and Jerry Lee Lewis ("Great Balls of Fire"). The set lists for the three evenings are complex and therefore difficult to reconstruct faithfully, but they contained many surprises for the audience, and musical moments of rare intensity.

Two Memorable Jam Sessions

Although many of the tracks from these three Boston evenings testify to the caliber of Fleetwood Mac, the two jams known as "Encore Jam" and "On We Jam" are probably the most fascinating, as they retain their dark side. It is very difficult to say exactly who is doing what and when.

What is certain is that the band has no safety nets in these long improvisations, which is testimony to the perfect complementarity of the musicians. On the first night, for example, Danny Kirwan struggles to get his rhythmic feet under him a minute into "On We Jam." Immediately, Peter Green arrives in support and takes over the lead part, improvising freely over a midtempo rhythm well anticipated by the rhythm section. Kirwan then has plenty of room to get "back on track." In the same way, a little further on, he gradually steps back from the rhythm section and devotes himself more to the harmonic register, leaving time and space for Peter Green to experiment and conclude the piece on some lovely high notes. The guitarist is delighted with the audience's enthusiastic reception

The musicians, in tight formation, take full measure of their stage potential.

to this conclusion and cannot suppress a shout of satisfaction.

The second jam, "Encore Jam," is another of the most memorable moments of these concerts. Although it finally emerged in 1998 in an incomplete 13:25 version, mentioning the participation of Joe Walsh and Eric Clapton, it unfortunately lacks the audio quality to accurately discern the contributors among the (five!) guitarists purportedly on stage. Above all, some commentators, such as Richard Orlando in the third volume of his book *A Love That Burns*, seem to doubt that the performance recorded and available on disc is the one in which Clapton can be heard, implying that this jam took place over two evenings. Orlando also points out that Clapton is not listed in the credits of the piece published in 1998 in volume two of *Live in Boston: Remastered*, attributed to Green, Kirwan, Spencer, and Joe Walsh.

A Project Buried and Exhumed

As it turned out, with Peter Green's departure in May 1970, a new Fleetwood Mac lineup, and the release of a new studio album (*Kiln House*) a few months later, the live album project was finally buried. It would not be unearthed again until 1985, when the Shanghai Records label recovered the tapes and initially extracted seven tracks: "Oh Well," "Like It This Way," "World in Harmony," "Only You," "Black Magic Woman," "Jumping at Shadows," and—of course—an Elmore James track, "Can't Hold On."

Understatedly titled *Live in Boston*, the recording was augmented the following year by a double LP titled *Cerulean*, featuring fourteen more tracks recorded at the Boston Tea Party.

In 1998, the Snapper label released a three-CD boxed set entitled *Live in Boston: Remastered*, more definitive in that it included thirty of the tracks played by the band at the three concerts, nine of them previously unreleased. It was subsequently reissued twice, in 2003 as *Live at the Boston Tea Party* and in 2013 as *Boston*.

At no point, however, did a label decide to publish the three concerts in their entirety without modifying the set list, which would have provided the most realistic glimpse of the level reached on stage by Fleetwood Mac during this period. In hindsight, however, it is amusing to think that with this historical document many American fans, latecomers to the band's history, discovered that there was a Fleetwood Mac other than the one associated with the Stevie Nicks/Lindsey Buckingham duo. *Live in Boston: Remastered* is a far cry from the lush, polished pop aesthetics of the albums *Rumours* (1977) and *Tusk* (1979), which made them permanent *Billboard* residents.

The Green Manalishi (with the Two Prong Crown) / World in Harmony

UK Release Date: May 15, 1970, with Reprise Records (ref. RS.27007)

Best UK Chart Ranking: 10

US Release Date: June 3, 1970, with Reprise Records (ref. 0925)

Best US Chart Ranking: Did Not Chart

Side A

FOR MAC-ADDICTS

On the cover of the single, all the members of Fleetwood Mac appear, including Jeremy Spencer, who was not present when the song was recorded. Many years later, in the BBC TV documentary *Man of the World*, broadcast in 2009, Spencer explained that, although he did not take part in the recording, he was present at certain sessions, including the one where Peter Green recorded his spectacular moans.

THE GREEN MANALISHI (WITH THE TWO PRONG CROWN)

Peter Green / 4:34

Musicians: Peter Green: vocals, guitar, six-string bass / Danny Kirwan: guitar / John McVie: bass / Mick Fleetwood: drums, gong, maracas, claves / **Recorded:** De Lane Lea Studios, London, April 14, 1970 / **Technical Team:** Producer: Fleetwood Mac / Sound Engineer: Martin Birch

Genesis and Lyrics

Caught between the hammer of his rock star status and the anvil of his increasingly strong spiritual convictions, Peter Green knew as early as 1969 that his departure from Fleetwood Mac would be inevitable. He believed that taking mescaline soothed his demons—except when he came face to face with them.

One night, he was plagued by a terrifying nightmare in which he had a vision of a green dog visiting him. According to him, the dog was the color of banknotes. What could be more normal for a man who was constantly wondering about this aspect of life, and who, consumed by the obsession of divesting himself of all his material possessions and no longer deriving any financial benefit from music, was trying to convince his Fleetwood Mac partners to embrace his charity band project?

When he awoke from this nightmare in the middle of the night, he was paralyzed by fear, drenched in sweat, unable to move or breathe normally. He finally grabbed a guitar and a pen and paper and frenetically, almost automatically, wrote down the lyrics and chords of what was to become "The Green Manalishi (with the Two Prong Crown)." The lyrics, disturbing in the extreme, refer to darkness, Satan (even though no direct reference is made), the Bible, and Green's malaise, as well as the temptation to give up and sink into madness.

The band played the song live from the end of 1969, in full-length versions approaching or exceeding ten minutes.

Peter Green often introduced it to the audience in this way: "It's a song about the devil."

But how to approach such a monster in the studio? For the moment, Green refused to do so. This was about his demons and was therefore his song. It had no place being shared with the masses other than through the immediacy of the stage.

But when he made the decision to leave Fleetwood Mac (which materialized in May 1970), he finally changed his mind and decided to offer this last single to his partners as a farewell, and to the public as a musical testament. He would later say that he had not emerged unscathed from the experience of this powerful composition, and that it had taken him two years to recover.

Production

Less accessible than the group's previous singles, "The Green Manalishi (with the Two Prong Crown)" only reached number ten in the UK charts, a disappointing commercial performance given the band's momentum. And yet, at that very moment, it was certainly Fleetwood Mac's most ambitious and impressive work to date. Could it have been any different with Peter Green's swan song?

When the band entered the studio on April 14, 1970, they knew that "The Green Manalishi (with the Two Prong Crown)" was one of the most important singles in their history. Everyone was aware that Green's adventure with Fleetwood Mac would end with its release.

The guitars of Peter Green and Danny Kirwan that pierce a stifling atmosphere with their sharp riffs, Mick Fleetwood's menacing drumming as he lays into his toms with an ecstatic intensity, John McVie's heavy bass that gives the impression of a steady heartbeat—everything here concurs with the precise imagery of the madness

A shot of the band from the photo session for the cover of "The Green Manalishi" single.

against which the song's main protagonist struggles. His mental derangement is even more directly evoked by strange moans and chilling sound effects.

The production is perfectly mastered from start to finish: The storm rumbles constantly, from the first cymbals conscientiously crashed by Mick Fleetwood to the final intermingling of guitars.

Rarely, if ever, has Fleetwood Mac offered such a dense recording. The sound of the guitars is particularly elaborate, as evidenced by the thin layer of reverb applied to the song's opening chords, as if to subliminally lighten the narrator's distress.

Peter Green: Intransigent Director

When Peter Green starts singing, his voice is determined, literally bewitching. It becomes even more so when the reverb, previously applied to the instruments, envelops the voice in its turn, before disappearing and reappearing as the song progresses. This detail is far from left to chance, since the effect often occurs on specific words, as on "mad" at 1:14, clearly to accentuate the narrator's loss of orientation as he teeters on the brink of madness.

John McVie's bass plays a decisive role, as do Mick Fleetwood's toms, with all their tension, supporting the

unhinged guitars of Green and Kirwan. McVie and Fleetwood seem to be the only pillars left standing in the face of the darkness that assails their partners.

But the final result is complicated to achieve. John McVie, in particular, only partly appreciates the pressure put on him in certain parts, where Peter Green almost dictates what he should do. Green also plays six-string bass on the track, which accentuates its heaviness. But in doing so, he takes the place of John McVie, who could have played the six-string part himself.

Peter Green did not want to have any discussions; he had very clear ideas about the results he wanted to achieve. And since the decision to leave the band was already firmly in his mind, sparing his partners by being diplomatic was the least of his worries. He was just as intransigent, if not more so, with Martin Birch at the mixing stage. But everyone did their utmost to soothe Green's frustrations and enable him to realize his artistic ambitions.

In the end, no single could have provided a more mystical conclusion to Peter Green's career with Fleetwood Mac than "The Green Manalishi (with the Two Prong Crown)." But little did anyone suspect that, more than a nightmare, it was a prophetic vision of the dark and tragic destiny that lay ahead.

SINGLE

Side A: *The Green Manalishi (with the Two Prong Crown)*
Side B: *World in Harmony*
UK Release Date: May 15, 1970, with Reprise Records (ref. RS.27007)
Best UK Chart Ranking: 10
US Release Date: June 3, 1970, with Reprise Records (ref. 0925)
Best US Chart Ranking: Did Not Chart

Peter Green's last offering before his departure, "World in Harmony" resonates as a universal wish and a musical achievement.

Many bands have delivered their own renditions of this song. Among the most successful versions are those by the English heavy metal band Judas Priest in 1979 and by the American doom metal trio Melvins in 1999. Five years after Judas Priest, the American heavy metal band Corrosion of Conformity took up their predecessors' arrangement on their album *Eye for an Eye* (1984).

Side B

WORLD IN HARMONY
Danny Kirwan, Peter Green / 3:16

Musicians: Peter Green: guitar / Danny Kirwan: guitar / John McVie: bass / Mick Fleetwood: drums / **Recorded:** De Lane Lea Studios, London, April 16, 1970 / **Technical Team:** Producer: Fleetwood Mac / Sound Engineer: Martin Birch

Genesis

Two days after having wrapped up "The Green Manalishi (with the Two Prong Crown)," the musically and lyrically heaviest track ever recorded by the band, Fleetwood Mac were back in the studio to record its diametric opposite. The instrumental number "World in Harmony," as its name suggests, is resolutely positive and bright, as though a touch of hope needed to be added as a B side to such a dark A side. The band had already been playing this track (the only one co-written by Kirwan/Green) live since January. They had even worked on it a little during a fleeting studio interlude in the United States. But Peter Green had not made it a fundamental objective, feeling that it still lacked something to be completed and put down definitively on tape. With the decision to place the track on the B side of "The Green Manalishi," solutions had to be found quickly to the problems that had been carefully swept under the carpet until then.

Production

Initial attempts were inconclusive. The pressure had not really died down since the recording of "The Green Manalishi" two days earlier. The latter recording involved so much tension that the first takes of "World in Harmony" turned out to be rigid, whereas the piece requires a great deal of relaxation to express its full potential and convey its positive message through the sheer force of the music. This is what "World in Harmony" had always lacked: the perspective of some distance, a little sideways step. This was impossible with the hectic pace of the tour—even more so now that everyone knew Peter Green's journey with Fleetwood Mac had to come to an end. It was out of the question to record countless live takes and keep the best one. Every available resource had to be used, as on "The Green Manalishi," which meant building the song track by track. Each of the two guitarists played his part and was assigned a channel in the stereo field: Danny Kirwan can be heard on the right-hand side of the spectrum, while Green is on the left, which makes it easier not only to appreciate their individual approaches, but also to understand the complexity of the song's structure. A few additional guitar tracks, drowned in reverb, discreetly complete the light, airy texture of "World in Harmony," which is also supported with an insidious bass by John McVie and an effective beat by Mick Fleetwood. A complete success, which would long nourish the nostalgic regrets of fans for this Fleetwood Mac lineup.

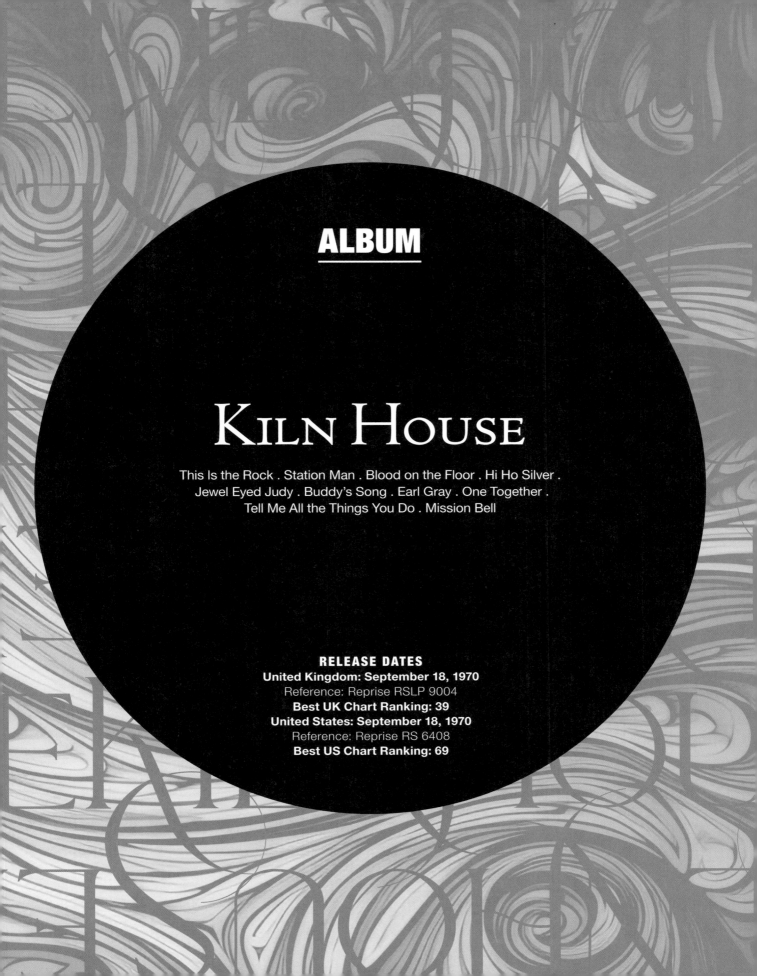

ALBUM

KILN HOUSE

This Is the Rock . Station Man . Blood on the Floor . Hi Ho Silver .
Jewel Eyed Judy . Buddy's Song . Earl Gray . One Together .
Tell Me All the Things You Do . Mission Bell

RELEASE DATES
United Kingdom: September 18, 1970
Reference: Reprise RSLP 9004
Best UK Chart Ranking: 39
United States: September 18, 1970
Reference: Reprise RS 6408
Best US Chart Ranking: 69

Peter Green, changed by a March 1970 visit to a German commune, announced his departure from the band two months later.

LIFE WITHOUT PETER GREEN

1970

Having only just returned from their American tour, the members of Fleetwood Mac were about to embark on another series of concerts, this time in Europe, in March and April 1970. It was around this time, in March, that Jeremy Spencer, his wife, Fiona, and John and Christine McVie decided to rent a six-bedroom house together in Hampshire. A little later, Mick Fleetwood, Danny Kirwan, their respective girlfriends, and a large part of the Fleetwood Mac touring team took up residence in this large building, a former hop-drying house nicknamed Kiln House. Until then, Danny had lived in Brixton, Jeremy in Paddington, Mick in Kensington, and it was always difficult to get together to rehearse. Moving to London would have been suicidal: The city abounds in temptations. Curiously, while the prospect of a bucolic retreat might have suited Peter Green's ideals, the guitarist chose to go it alone and take no part in this shared adventure, staying with his parents until they left for Paris, where they were to kick off their new European tour with a concert at the Olympia on March 7, 1970.

On the first dates of the tour, the musicians gave the impression of drifting apart, speaking little together, while Peter Green became increasingly isolated. Ever since he had realized that the other band members would not go through with his charitable idea, he had changed radically: He grew his hair and beard, wore togas, sported a gigantic wooden crucifix, and now only talked about God in the

interviews he gave. In articles, his comments were at best garbled and at worst taken out of context, making him seem like a crank. Peter Green made no secret of the fact that he was frustrated by the limited room for maneuver his role within Fleetwood Mac allowed him, and began to consider a solo career. He knew that a successful band, under pressure from fans, restricted his creative scope and took fewer risks. Like many before him, he wondered to what extent he could remain true to his ideals once the long-awaited success arrived.

A Strange Incident in Munich

On March 18, 1970, the band was in West Germany for a series of six concerts. Peter Green, although frustrated at not being able to convince his partners to fully embrace his ideals, seemed to be rediscovering his enjoyment of playing, not only on his own songs but also on those of Kirwan and Spencer. In reality, he was quite moody and had good and bad days: While his mood seemed bright in Hanover on March 18, Berlin the next day revealed a darker, more introverted Peter Green. Over the next few days, Fleetwood Mac played in Hamburg, Düsseldorf, and then Munich, with a view to a final concert in Nuremberg on March 24. In Bavaria, the concert was scheduled for Sunday, March 22, at Circus Krone. The show was marred by a number of incidents, including clashes between police and spectators.

Fleetwood Mac at the airport in Berlin, March 1970. Tired, serious faces betray the weariness and unease generated by Kirwan and Green's visit to a German commune, also known as the "Munich incident."

1970

After the concert, Peter Green and Danny Kirwan were spirited away by two beautiful women from a hippie community known as the Haifisch Kommune (or High-Fish Commune, a play on the German word for shark, *Haifisch*, and the English word "high"—that is, "stoned fish"). These enigmatic characters led them to a manor house secluded in the middle of the forest, where a hallucinatory psychedelic party was taking place. The two musicians stayed there for two days, ingesting gargantuan doses of LSD. Escorted by the band's road manager, Dennis Keane, Mick Fleetwood finally went to the mansion to extricate them. He found Peter in the middle of a trip, but lucid enough to tell him to get lost. Green explained to Fleetwood that he was not going to follow him, that he was going to stay and live in the community, that there was everything he needed here. Diplomatically but firmly, Mick finally persuaded him to return to the hotel, explaining that Peter could return to the community once all his obligations had been discharged. "And then the drugs…He was one person who didn't need any of that shit. He was so sensitive anyway [...] The Fleetwood Mac story is one of survival. What you would say about Peter was, he was not

able to survive. I'm just saying that he was not equipped. He was not equipped for that journey. For whatever reason, I may never quite know. But it certainly was about a gentleman who was incredibly sensitive, and had been hurt as a young boy. Y'know, being Jewish in the East End of London, he'd had a rough time, way more even than the stories he would tell me. I don't think he ever properly got over that."[27] Nor would Danny return unscathed from the Munich trip. "Peter Green and Danny Kirwan both went together to that house in Munich [...] both of them took acid, as I understand. Both of them, as of that day, became seriously mentally ill."[31]

They did not know it when they left, but the Munich episode was going to change the destiny of the band and, above all, the lives of Peter and Danny, for whom it can be said that there was a "before" and an "after" Munich.

Peter Green's Departure

This event precipitated the departure of Peter Green, who left Fleetwood Mac at the end of May. It was not a spur-of-the-moment step as he had been wanting to do it since the previous US tour, and everyone knew it. He wanted to

Peter Green (in white toga, center) and Jeremy Spencer (right) were to experience mystical epiphanies that affected their participation in the band.

explore new musical horizons, in particular new instruments such as bass and percussion, and to get rid of all his material possessions. While some see the "Munich incident" as the cause of his departure, others see it as one of the first consequences of the mental problems that had been plaguing him for several months. Once his decision to leave the band had been made and announced, Green nonetheless assumed his responsibilities by completing their tour and fulfilling his contractual obligations, including the delivery of a final single, "The Green Manalishi (with the Two Prong Crown)." He offered Fleetwood Mac this last track, written after a nightmare. The track, full of strange moans and chilling sound effects, reinforced Peter Green's mystical, enigmatic side in the public eye. But it once again demonstrated his immense talent, following in the footsteps of "Albatross," "Man of the World," and "Oh Well."

Years later, Mick Fleetwood still wondered how his partner, who had once shared the same goals, could have rejected them to such an extent when he was so close to getting everything he had ever wanted. "Well I don't think we ever did [realize that he was ill]. [...] We got the sense when it was too damn late," he explained, adding: "And I

don't think we would have been, in retrospect, equipped to do anything about knowing how to help him anyhow. He intimated that he was done. We were on a tour in America and he said: 'We've got to give all our money away.' Of course, we didn't know that his illness was starting then. And he disowned himself. Disowned what he'd done. Said that he'd stolen everything he'd ever created. Of course, it's nonsense. But then suddenly it was like: 'Oh shit, he's fucking leaving.'"[27]

A Rudderless Ship

Back in London at the end of the tour, Peter was about to take the plunge: Some of the German hippies who had latched on to him followed him to the English capital and moved in with him. Together they continued tripping on acid. Green, who saw his departure from the band as a renaissance, was quick to announce the forthcoming release of a solo album (*The End of the Game* would hit record stores in the early winter of 1970). He also had ambitions to jam with many other artists, but this was a pipe dream. He was now a broken man, and the abyss lurking in front of him grew deeper every day.

As for the rest of the band, they were mired in uncertainty: Without Green, they were like a rudderless ship, a crew without a compass. Fleetwood Mac may still have been afloat, but it urgently needed to find a captain and set a course. Perhaps this was the opportunity for Danny Kirwan or Jeremy Spencer to assert himself as leader in place of Peter Green, who had been the leader in soul and artistry?

The press soon began to wonder about the band's future. Some journalists argued that its members were traumatized and would never recover; an imminent split was frequently mentioned. Other, more optimistic observers predicted that Christine McVie would join the band, alongside her husband. But manager Clifford Davis was quick to dispel all rumors, insisting that Fleetwood Mac would continue as a quartet. In fact, he claimed, this was the configuration under which the band had signed its contracts for the American dates in August. In any case, Fleetwood Mac needed to get back on their feet quickly, as the new album had to be completed before they left for America, where they were due to tour throughout August.

A Summer Fraught with Danger

At Kiln House, Fleetwood Mac's "headquarters," morale was low, but living together enabled the band to close ranks quickly. Although he was not the creative leader, Mick Fleetwood took charge, supported by John McVie, who was determined to get things back on track.

Mick Fleetwood and Jenny Boyd's wedding took place on June 20, 1970, without their best man, Peter Green, who was absent at the time of the ceremony. He finally arrived late and made a point of telling the newlyweds that he did not believe in marriage. Despite this happy event, there was no question of a honeymoon, as the album composition sessions could not wait.

The four official members met in the kitchen, converted for the occasion into a rehearsal room. A lot of hashish went up in smoke to help overcome the tensions linked to the uncertainty.

Peter Green's departure left an immeasurable void and the band needed a new leader. Mick Fleetwood had that soul, but as a drummer, he was not the combo's creative engine. Danny Kirwan should have been the one to take on this responsibility, but he seemed to shrink from the challenge. Jeremy Spencer did not feel like a leader either, and his compositional skills were limited, at least in terms of what he had shown so far. "Jeremy had not really made huge inroads to writing," said Mick Fleetwood. "So we went into Jeremy's rock'n'roll world."[27] Jeremy agreed: "I didn't feel I could do it. All I could play was rock 'n' roll. Peter was a developed musician. I couldn't do the stuff that people now expected us to play."[29]

But he had no choice: He had been chosen to become the band's creative leader, and he would have to write about his life and experiences, not just cover the old blues of his idols. Danny Kirwan, meanwhile, was given the onerous task of succeeding Peter Green as the band's lead guitarist.

The pressure mounted at Kiln House, which became a veritable pressure cooker. One night, a clash erupted and everyone decided to quit the band: Neither Danny nor Jeremy wanted to take on the mantle of leader, which was too big for them. Even the placid John decided he wanted to stop playing bass and become a roadie instead. That night, Mick, who refused to throw in the towel, spent over four hours bringing his bandmates to their senses, one by one. He was persuasive, convincing them that something positive could come out of the ordeal, that a new creative phase could be opened up for them. His words had the desired effect, and once the psychodrama had passed, the composing stage could resume in peace.

A Collective Opus

Reinvigorated, the band returned to De Lane Lea Studios in London, where they were reunited with sound engineer Martin Birch. The album, logically named *Kiln House*, was recorded between the end of June and mid-July 1970.

The musicians had before them a dozen or so tracks straddling blues rock, rock'n'roll, and tentatively baroque pop. Jeremy Spencer and Danny Kirwan shared the songwriting, with support from John McVie and Mick Fleetwood on "Station Man" and "Jewel Eyed Judy." Peter Green's departure had at least one beneficial effect: the emergence of collective contributions. However, with Jeremy Spencer's

1970

The new Fleetwood Mac: Mick Fleetwood, John McVie, Danny Kirwan, Christine Perfect, Jeremy Spencer.

return to the forefront of the music scene, covers such as "Hi Ho Silver" (Big Joe Turner) and Donnie Brooks's "Mission Bell" also returned.

To a certain extent, *Kiln House* (and, by extension, Fleetwood Mac) owes its survival to Jeremy Spencer's solo album, recorded in 1969 and released in early 1970. Forced to confront the exercise of composition, which he had previously scrupulously shunned, Spencer was obliged to call on other musicians, notably members of Fleetwood Mac, including Danny Kirwan, to support him. Kirwan was fully committed to his work, and the two learned to work together and even enjoyed it.

Yet their musical worlds had never been so different. Spencer might have broadened his scope with rock'n'roll-inflected tracks like "This Is the Rock," "Blood on the Floor," and "Buddy's Song," as well as with the country folk "One Together" and the rhythm'n'blues "Hi Ho Silver," but there was still a huge gap between his work and Kirwan's creative pop, even when tinged with these same influences. Even a neophyte can tell by ear whether a composition on this album is by Kirwan or Spencer. The album, produced at a time of crisis, is marked by the team's reflexive retreat back to the basics—rock'n'roll,

blues rock, country—especially Spencer. Without the pressure of Peter Green's gaze, Kirwan experiments a little more, but timidly.

The production on this album is clearly superior to its predecessors. The band, learning on the job in the same way as their young sound engineer, Martin Birch, made enormous progress in microphone placement, recording management, balance between instruments, and their place in the mix (with one guitar less—Peter Green's—the problem is simpler). The album was completed a fortnight before they set off on tour in the United States at the beginning of August.

Christine McVie's Growing Role

The creative duo formed by Kirwan and Spencer on this album soon became an unofficial trio with the arrival of Christine McVie.

The keyboardist, who had announced her retirement from the music industry, finally sang and played on a number of tracks on *Kiln House*, as well as put her drawing talents to good use by creating the cover illustration. The cover reflects the bucolic atmosphere of Kiln House. It shows two children accompanied by a dog in a rural setting

With Peter Green's departure, the three-guitar lineup became a thing of the past. The band would have to get to grips with that loss during the recording of *Kiln House*.

1970

populated by animals and incongruous little characters of varying degrees of visibility: birds, a slug, a snail, a teddy bear, even a trio of elves in the tree on the right of the drawing. Starting out with a realistic illustration, Christine McVie soon drifted into incorporating a few whimsical elements, perhaps under the influence of the joint she was smoking at the time, as she admitted in a 2004 interview with Robin Eggar for *S*, the *Sunday Express* magazine supplement.

Musically, Christine McVie's contribution to this album was essential: Her piano playing was perfectly suited to the new tracks, and she filled the harmonic space left vacant by Green. Despite this decisive contribution, she is not credited as a member of Fleetwood Mac on the album.

At the end of July, just as the band was about to leave for the United States, Mick Fleetwood took advantage of a dinner party at Kiln House, where everyone was gathered, to ask Christine if she would officially join the band. He felt that the band's live sound had lacked density since Peter's departure, and that Christine was the ideal person to remedy this problem. Moreover, in addition to her obvious talent, she already knew all the songs. The young woman did not hesitate to take to the stage for the first time as an official member of Fleetwood Mac on August 8, 1970, at the Warehouse in New Orleans.

Farewell to Kiln House

But before leaving for three months, the group had to vacate the house. A chapter in their story drew to a close;

the lease was terminated. Like a fleeting spell, the magic of Kiln House quickly faded. Jeremy and his wife, Fiona, spent long hours reading the Bible, and Mick's pregnant wife, Jenny, was already thinking of taking a break from their relationship. She found it hard to find her place among the group of artists, with whom she was spending time but who did not really know her.

It would not be long before Kiln House was no longer the sun-drenched, flower-filled garden that saw Fleetwood Mac reinventing themselves at the start of summer. But Mick felt that the experience had been beneficial both artistically and practically, if not personally. So, fearing that the band would split up again and not be able to find each other, he suggested creating a collective fund and buying a house with the *Kiln House* advance.

Mick was tasked with finding the new house. He fell in love with a secluded hilltop Victorian mansion called Benifold. Also in Hampshire, not far from Kiln House but not quite as rustic, it was a vast nineteenth-century building with twenty rooms, formerly owned by an ecumenical society that welcomed believers of all faiths for spiritual retreats. It overlooked seven hectares (seventeen acres) of land, including a forest and a dilapidated tennis court surrounded by pretty trees. A billiard room and a music room, so that the group could rehearse at any time of the day or night, completed this little paradise. However, this did not suit Mick's wife, Jenny, who dreamed of making a home with him, not joining a community. Without thinking for a second about following him on tour, or even

waiting three months for him in this gigantic mansion, she decided to pack her bags and spend some time with her mother in Devon.

So the departure for the United States was not exactly an easy one. But for a first tour without Peter Green, things went well, and Christine quickly adapted. Jeremy, for his part, was allowed to play some old blues in the second half of the concert and even to imitate Elvis Presley, after presenting the new tracks from *Kiln House*, scheduled for release in early autumn. Having just returned from America, the band embarked on a series of European tours.

Kiln House hit record stores in mid-September 1970. Although well received by critics and fans, it was not a commercial success (39 on the UK charts, 69 in the United States). Admittedly, none of the ten songs on the album had the makings of a hit, but Fleetwood Mac had nonetheless salvaged things and given themselves the means to survive—with an unexpected heroine, Christine McVie, who quickly became the central pivot of Fleetwood Mac's new lineup. The band that had been ready to throw in the towel only a few months previously had just unknowingly embarked on a new, long voyage, with an uncertain destination but with renewed motivation.

A return to rock fundamentals for Jeremy Spencer, who had made blues his main vector of artistic expression.

A balance gradually emerges between Kirwan's and Spencer's compositional contributions.

THIS IS THE ROCK

Jeremy Spencer / 2:45

Musicians
Jeremy Spencer: vocals, guitar
Danny Kirwan: guitar, backing vocals
Christine McVie: backing vocals
John McVie: bass
Mick Fleetwood: drums, percussions

Recorded
De Lane Lea Studios, London: June–July 1970

Technical Team
Producer: Fleetwood Mac
Sound Engineer: Martin Birch

Genesis and Lyrics

With Peter Green gone, it was time to move on, whatever the cost, even with scaled-back artistic ambitions. As a result, Fleetwood Mac deviated from its musically ambitious trajectory, abandoning Peter Green's cosmic blues pop and returning to the basics, such as rock. Rock was an essential component of Jeremy Spencer's musical identity. He had mastered it to perfection. So he returned to the original source, rock'n'roll, and put his gift for imitation to good use by slipping, for the duration of "This Is the Rock," into the leather of a slick 1950s singer—Gene Vincent, for example—as he did for the aborted EP *The Milton Schlitz Show*, but without the satire. The title says it all: "This Is the Rock." Spencer launches into a definition of the concept, for want of more profound lyrics. But the approach worked, since fifties rock itself often remained on the surface, self-congratulatory in its lyrics, extolling the virtues of its energy, dance, and so on. In his lyrics, Jeremy Spencer describes rock as both a musical genre and a mode of expression: "The rock / Makes you jump and shout […] It makes you lose / All your troubles and cares / You'll lose your blues." With a certain malice on the part of a musician who devoted his early years to the blues, he plays on the word's meaning, implying that by playing rock, he "loses his blues"—both the melancholy and the musical style.

Production

There is a discrepancy between the text and the music. No raging or yelling, just good old-fashioned rock'n'roll, lightly sprinkled with bluegrass on one of the guitars, the one that launches the song in the first few seconds. It is played through a small, low-powered amp with a high resonance, giving the impression of using a dobro. The second guitar, which has to rely on the bridge pickup for its more piercing, drier sound, plays a relaxed little motif. This fits in perfectly with the easygoing mood of John McVie's walking bass and Mick Fleetwood's relaxed shuffle rhythm on the brushes. The song's rock'n'roll identity is essentially due to the vocals: on the one hand, backing vocals inherited from doo-wop, sung together without any real chord work; and on the other, Jeremy Spencer's unrecognizable vocals. His nasal side has completely disappeared; he croons wonderfully in the low registers on the line "That knocks you right out," and does some nice dropouts when he goes into the high registers with a full, expressive voice. This track, on which the musicians appear relaxed, has no great ambition other than to diffuse enjoyment. Placed as an opener, it sounds like a declaration of intent for the album: The band is fully aware that it is embarking on a record of resilience, but it cannot be expected to sink into the doldrums. The group retains its dignity, even though it cannot compete with what it was just a few weeks previously.

STATION MAN

Danny Kirwan, John McVie, Mick Fleetwood / 5:49

Musicians
Danny Kirwan: vocals, guitar
Jeremy Spencer: vocals, guitar
Christine McVie: keyboards, backing vocals
John McVie: bass
Mick Fleetwood: drums, congas

Recorded
De Lane Lea Studios, London: June–July 1970

Technical Team
Producer: Fleetwood Mac
Sound Engineer: Martin Birch

Single
Side A: Jewel Eyed Judy / Side B: Station Man
US Release Date: January 6, 1971, with Reprise Records (ref. R 0984)
Best US Chart Ranking: Did Not Chart

The "Jewel Eyed Judy" single's Side B, "Station Man," became a staple of the band's set list and was played live 121 times.

Genesis and Lyrics

After going back in time to the 1950s, Fleetwood Mac was back with the flow, playing rhythm'n'blues firmly rooted in the present times. This is Christine McVie's first album in the spotlight. She is "only" a musician on this track, which is contributed by Danny Kirwan and completed with the help of John McVie and Mick Fleetwood. Yet it is she who breathes life and groove into it, with the syncopated playing for which Chicken Shack is famous. The track's very particular rhythm and management of silences make it seem to progress in fits and starts. In this way, it reproduces the jolts of a train as it starts off. The effect is deliberate, since it is mentioned in the lyrics. It is the train, rather than the stationmaster who gives the song its name, that is the focus of attention.

As in "Although the Sun Is Shining," we can legitimately wonder whether Danny Kirwan is guilty of clumsiness or deliberately blurring the lines in service to his song's meaning. In the first verse, the narrator asks the stationmaster for the departure time. Then, "Midnight train / Now is leaving / Engine screaming." But further on, the narrator sees it coming ("I see it's coming..."). Is he confusing the issue (or in this case the rails), suggesting that there may be several trains? Is he implying that arrival at the desired destination—that of love, since he refers to it as the "train of lovin'"—depends on the choice he makes? Similarly, he does not clearly establish his narrator's state of mind, except that he is impatient. Does calling the vehicle the love train mean that he has already found love and does not know where it will take him ("Where I'm going I don't know"), or does it mean that he is reunited with a former love ("From ages past")? Or does it mean that he has been waiting a long time ("I've been waiting") for the love that never came? In any case, he takes up a chestnut of blues and later of beat literature: the eternal theme of the train, which marks a change of life, a flight toward a better future. In this context, the time of departure is significant: midnight, the boundary between two days, between past and future.

Christine McVie's syncopated, groovy playing radiates from tracks like "Station Man."

Production

In journalist and filmmaker Revel Guest's 1971 documentary *Black, White and Blues* (published by VAP Transatlantic Films), featuring Fleetwood Mac, Savoy Brown, Chicken Shack, and Muddy Waters, we see a short clip of a Mac rehearsal at Kiln House. The band is playing "Station Man." The musicians appear highly focused and visibly tired, their features drawn. But the setup is already very close to the final version. John McVie is seated for the sake of comfort and precision playing, concentrating on what appears to be a Gibson Non-Reverse Thunderbird bass. His playing is much more fluid than Spencer's edgy and taut style (but he has to deal with slide and picking). He faces Danny Kirwan, whose dark eyes and three-day beard are a far cry from the hairless face he sported on the previous album—he looks ten years older. Christine McVie, behind her imposing Wurlitzer 200A, sits opposite Mick Fleetwood, waving his

arms around his snare drum and hi-hat. The same cohesion emerges from this session as from the recording made shortly afterward at De Lane Lea Studios. The sound is much more honed and polished. The band, as much as Martin Birch, has made immense progress in this area, spending time rigging amps and drums to reproduce the warmth and proximity of the instruments—even though their production choices may still be questionable, such as the idea of a very long fade-in that would only make sense if the instrumental intro were prolonged. What is more surprising is the flexibility of Spencer's slide playing, which has gained in clarity, economy, and precision. He also proves to be an excellent vocal partner, harmonizing perfectly with Danny Kirwan. What Fleetwood Mac loses in originality (Mick Fleetwood's congas are just a little extra), it gains in quality of execution.

John McVie plays with authority and subtlety on bass, as on "Blood on the Floor."

BLOOD ON THE FLOOR

Jeremy Spencer / 2:44

Musicians: Jeremy Spencer: vocals, guitar / Danny Kirwan: guitar, backing vocals / Christine McVie: keyboards, backing vocals / John McVie: bass / Mick Fleetwood: drums / **Recorded:** De Lane Lea Studios, London: June–July 1970 / **Technical Team:** Producer: Fleetwood Mac / Sound Engineer: Martin Birch

Genesis and Lyrics

With "Blood on the Floor," Jeremy Spencer walks a fine line between sincerity and parody. This was the problem with an artist who had so far demonstrated his versatility in many styles, but who had only ever shown deference to the blues. And then some: Even on the abandoned EP *The Milton Schlitz Show*, intended to accompany the album *Then Play On*, Spencer pinpointed the blues of Alexis Korner and John Mayall. Similarly, he had always been an admirer of rock and country, but whenever he played it, it was for satirical purposes. So how do we know that "Blood on the Floor" is based on honorable intentions? On the strength of its inclusion on the track list alone? Spencer has never commented on this.

It is difficult to base an opinion on the lyrics. Whether in jest or not, Jeremy Spencer, a poor lyricist, takes refuge in the stereotypes he has identified in the style he tackles. For him, the shortcut is obvious: He views country music through the prism of outlaw country alone, a bloody universe where criminals repent and spill their grief over their guitars in the corner of a grove just long enough to give their nag a rest while the sun sets over an arid plain. In this vein, the first line is a farewell: "Well goodbye world." But his sense of storytelling collapses in the second line, as he feels compelled to comment on the veracity of what he has yet to announce: "It's sad but true." He then tells us that he has an appointment with his executioner because he killed his girlfriend, whom he caught in bed with another man. Repentance is not on the agenda: "They say I've done wrong / I don't say I'm sorry." The crooner's accents and the velvety quality of his voice point to Ricky Nelson as the model for this track, but the word "jailhouse" and the high notes are also reminiscent of Elvis Presley and his "Jailhouse Rock."

Production

Mick Fleetwood, who is not much called upon in this number, is content to mark time with a half-hearted beat. John McVie, on the other hand, holds the song single-handedly. He uses his partner's snare drum as a guide, and between each beat, he rises and falls incessantly. This is what makes the melody so rich, since the vocals themselves follow these inflections. Danny Kirwan's acoustic guitar provides a conventional but effective accompaniment, backed up by a second guitar, played on slide by Jeremy Spencer. Christine McVie has all the space she needs to express herself, preferring to play right-handed in the high range, as the bass range is already pretty well filled.

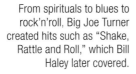

From spirituals to blues to rock'n'roll, Big Joe Turner created hits such as "Shake, Rattle and Roll," which Bill Haley later covered.

HI HO SILVER

Big Joe Turner / 3:05

Musicians: Jeremy Spencer: vocals, guitar, piano / Danny Kirwan: guitar, backing vocals / John McVie: bass, backing vocals / Mick Fleetwood: drums / **Recorded:** De Lane Lea Studios, London: June–July 1970 / **Technical Team:** Producer: Fleetwood Mac / Sound Engineer: Martin Birch

Genesis and Lyrics

During the preparatory work sessions at the Kiln House residence, the rock'n'roll direction of the album began to take shape. Jeremy Spencer suggested paying tribute to one of the musical genre's pioneers, Big Joe Turner, a rhythm'n'blues singer who helped build a bridge between blues and rock'n'roll in the early twentieth century. Having lost his father at just four years of age, Big Joe Turner earned money for his family by singing in the streets during his younger years, before leaving school to perform in Kansas City clubs. To attract passersby on the street, and then customers in these establishments, one had to impose oneself and sing loud enough to hold their attention. This is how the church singer learned the virtues of boogie and blues when they show their power of projection. Singing hard, playing fast—this is what counts in the interpretation of "Honey Hush," his biggest hit along with "Shake, Rattle & Roll." He recorded this song in 1953, and it topped the American Billboard rhythm'n'blues charts.

The song, part of Jeremy Spencer's record library, became "Hi Ho Silver" under his auspices. The expression appears in the lyrics of the chorus and is repeated over and over on the finale. The text includes elements of slang, but the message remains crystal clear: The man is in charge at home and the woman must obey him, says the narrator. In case of rebellion: "I'm holding a baseball bat." The text, from another era, seems inconceivably violent today.

Production

The original relied heavily on a punctuation motif provided on the trombone, played by Pluma Davis, the band leader who accompanied Big Joe Turner during the recording session. The instrument seemed to respond to Big Joe Turner's vocals, creating a dialogue. But the most loquacious of all was James Tolliver's boogie piano, knitting incessant lines at full speed in the background. In Fleetwood Mac's version, the piano is still present, but it does not perform the same function, serving above all as ornamentation. The accompaniment is provided mainly by Danny Kirwan's biting guitar rock. Played on the basis of a classic twelve-bar blues, it draws its originality from its saturated tones, which attract attention right from the intro, and from its frank, incisive attack. The trombone's interventions are echoed by Jeremy Spencer's slide guitar and his powerful, aggressive vocals that recall John Lennon's voice in certain aspects—notably his unrestrained screams, as on the finale, which features a note held for almost six seconds at the end of the coda.

JEWEL EYED JUDY

Danny Kirwan, Mick Fleetwood, John McVie / 3:17

Musicians
Danny Kirwan: vocals, guitar
Jeremy Spencer: vocals, guitar
Christine McVie: keyboards, backing vocals
John McVie: bass, backing vocals
Mick Fleetwood: drums

Recorded
De Lane Lea Studios, London: June–July 1970

Technical Team
Producer: Fleetwood Mac
Sound Engineer: Martin Birch

Single
Side A: Jewel Eyed Judy / **Side B:** Station Man
US Release Date: January 6, 1971, with Reprise Records (ref. R 0984)
Best US Chart Ranking: Did Not Chart

FOR MAC-ADDICTS

Almost three years later, penned by Bob Welch, Fleetwood Mac quotes itself on the opening track of *Mystery to Me*, "Emerald Eyes." "Find emerald eyes in the night / Gleamin' shiny and bright / As if covered with silver" strongly recalls "and jewels that gleam / Would your eyes still sparkle then / If we were, once again?"

Genesis and Lyrics

The creative divide was widening between Jeremy Spencer and Danny Kirwan. While the former was familiarizing himself with the compositional process, the latter was a step ahead, more creative and adventurous than his partner. "Jewel Eyed Judy," for example, is full of pop, folk, and rock influences. This track even appears to be a precursor of the modern form that rock would later adopt: the famous sequence of calm verse, violent chorus (and so on) that we would find in the pattern of alternative rock or grunge in the 1980s and 1990s, for example.

The lyrics on this track are a little more detailed than usual. Its lyricist even tries to move away from conventional writing with impressionistic sketches. He skips certain verbs and joins two ideas together to create a contextual link between them, as in the first line: "Moonshine time, thoughts of you." Danny Kirwan also delves into the lexical field of brilliance to spin the metaphor ("shine," "gleam," "sparkle," "glistens"), and lists the sources of light emission or reflection ("moonshine," "jewels," "eyes," "stars," "moonlight"). The overall effect is still academic but reflects a notable poetic effort by the young author to give depth to this evocation of a man, under the moon, directing his thoughts to the woman he loves.

Attributed to John McVie, Mick Fleetwood, and Danny Kirwan, according to Mick Fleetwood's autobiography, *Play On,*[2] the song was written jointly by his wife Jenny Boyd (then four months pregnant) and Christine McVie. The song was written about one Judy Wong, nicknamed "Jewel Eyed Judy," who was the wife of Jethro Tull guitarist Glenn Cornick. Jenny later wrote in her autobiography, published in 2020, that "Although I never mentioned it, I was disappointed that I wasn't credited as a co-writer [on "Jewel Eyed Judy"]. Their manager put me under the name Mick."[44] Judy Wong, who worked for a long time as a manager and secretary for Fleetwood Mac, remained very present in the group even after her departure. She was so enmeshed that she became known to some as "the mother of the group." In particular, she compiled the programs from their numerous tours and introduced them to Bob Welch in 1971.

In 1987, Fleetwood Mac dedicated their album *Tango in the Night* to the magnetic Judy Wong, who inspired "Jewel Eyed Judy." Here, the band's stage manager and secretary was photographed by Baron Wolman in 1968 for *Rolling Stone* magazine.

Production

Whereas "Station Man" opens with a very long fade-in, "Jewel Eyed Judy" kicks off without a warning shot, on what might sound like the end of a phrase. The second guitar, Spencer's in particular, seems to have begun its arpeggio just before the tape starts. It seems very disciplined, executing this arpeggio by alternating well-defined notes with others in glissando. John McVie scrupulously follows this progression on the bass, playing groups of two notes that follow the melody. Danny Kirwan's guitar is given free rein. The musician shows intelligence and finesse in his interventions, not playing over every bar. Above all, each of his appearances brings a different color to the beginning of the song. On a bend, he instills a country tinge; on a slide or a track cleverly dubbed by Martin Birch, he sounds like George Harrison.

Kirwan's own vocals are dubbed identically, to give them more body and power. And if the voice sounds slightly tired, with a few borderline vibratos as you sense that he is at the end of his tether, this little imperfection creates additional depth, a welcome emotion. Guitar licks played back and forth launch the chorus, which literally takes off with the intervention of guitars saturated to the max, almost verging on a hard rock that would not be disowned by the likes of the Who or Led Zeppelin. At 1:14, the chorus also features what appears to be a short, compressed Wurlitzer climb that comes to a screeching halt.

For its catchiness, the song was chosen as a single in the United States to promote the tour of the country that began the following month, but it failed to penetrate the charts despite its undoubted qualities.

BUDDY'S SONG
Ella Holley / 2:08

Musicians
Jeremy Spencer: guitar, vocals
Danny Kirwan: guitar, backing vocals
Christine McVie: backing vocals
John McVie: bass
Mick Fleetwood: drums

Recorded
De Lane Lea Studios, London: June–July 1970

Technical Team
Producer: Fleetwood Mac
Sound Engineer: Martin Birch

Buddy Holly, rock'n'roll pioneer and the inspiration for "Buddy's Song," tragically died in a plane crash at the age of 22 on February 3, 1959.

Genesis and Lyrics

No doubt running short of Elmore James songs, whose repertoire he had already plundered, Jeremy Spencer prefers to honor the pioneers of rock on *Kiln House*, and in particular one of the most famous: Buddy Holly. Tragically, Holly died at the age of twenty-two in a plane crash, along with fellow stars of the era the Big Bopper and Ritchie "La Bamba" Valens, on February 3, 1959, a date immediately dubbed "the day the music died." Buddy Holly, rock'n'roll's great hope, instantly became one of its first martyrs. Jeremy Spencer, of course, had not forgotten this traumatic episode. "Buddy's Song" was credited to Ella Holley, Buddy Holly's mother (Buddy's real name was Charles Hardin Holley) by Jeremy Spencer so that she could benefit from the royalties. In reality, the song is essentially a reworking of Holly's "Peggy Sue Got Married," with new lyrics listing a number of Holly's song titles, including "Rave On," "That'll Be the Day," "Maybe Baby," and, of course, his biggest hit, "Peggy Sue."

Production

Musically, this tribute to the youthful ambassador of rock'n'roll is faithfully based on the original "Peggy Sue Got Married" arrangement. However, the tempo is slightly slower on Fleetwood Mac's version, and above all, the drums are much less refined, as Mick Fleetwood's playing is less varied than that of Jerry Allison, the drummer of the Crickets (Buddy Holly's band), a true master behind the drums. The guitar parts are also more muddled than on the song by the singer with the big glasses, whose precise, catchy chops embody real originality. Here, Danny Kirwan and Jeremy Spencer encroach on each other's territory, at least until the first solo at 1:21. The saturated guitar part, on the other hand, is an interesting initiative, but ultimately little exploited beyond a few placed chords. As for the backing vocals, they provide "Buddy's Song" with the rock'n'roll backing for this reverential, if not completely original, tribute. Even if they are not always brilliantly accurate, they remain completely "in the spirit."

1970

EARL GRAY

Danny Kirwan / 4:05

Musicians
Danny Kirwan: guitar
Jeremy Spencer: guitar
Christine McVie: piano
John McVie: bass
Mick Fleetwood: drums

Recorded
De Lane Lea Studios, London: June–July 1970

Technical Team
Producer: Fleetwood Mac
Sound Engineer: Martin Birch

Christine McVie gradually finds her place first at the heart of the band's instrumentation, eventually taking over the composition too.

Shorter by half (2:18), the first demo for "Earl Gray" was recorded on April 20, 1970, at London's De Lane Lea Studios, under the name "Farewell." Danny Kirwan sings a few la-la-la's to signal the moment when a vocal should be inserted; this suggests that the track was not originally intended as an instrumental. The demo was released in 1998 on the compilation *The Vaudeville Years of Fleetwood Mac 1968 to 1970*.

Genesis

Following in the footsteps of Fleetwood Mac's previous instrumental releases, including "Albatross," "Underway," and "Oh Well, Part 2," all by Peter Green, Danny Kirwan decided to confront the master in his absence by producing an instrumental piece of his own. For him, having joined the band at a very young age to accompany his mentor, it was a question of "killing the father" by trying his hand at an exercise at which the latter excelled and that brought Fleetwood Mac commercial success and critical acclaim. As "Earl Gray" is an instrumental, its name is the only information on its mood; however, it has never been explained. The most obvious interpretation would be that it was named after the Earl Grey variety of tea, which probably had its devotees at Kiln House, but this theory is impossible to confirm. However, the title does include a play on words, since "Gray" is spelled with an *a* (not the standard British *e*), suggesting a form of melancholy and languor that pervades the song.

Production

The guitar is at the heart of this soothing instrumental track. Its repetitive motif progresses throughout the four-minute track, while the arrangement gradually fleshes out. John McVie's bass is perfectly minimalist, merely supporting the fundamentals on the chord changes, and Mick Fleetwood's drums deliberately take a back seat while remaining very audible thanks to the matte sound of the snare drum he obtains by slightly holding back on his strokes during the recording. Christine McVie's delicate yet discreet piano acts like the cement of a fortress; it enriches the overall sound and brings melodic variety when the track could have lost interest after two minutes. Despite its gently bluesy, even country tone—due to the twangy guitar bridge—"Earl Gray" fails to match the epic quality of Peter Green's instrumentals. But Danny Kirwan proves his inventiveness with this contemplative track, perfect for watching nature unfold before our eyes on a road trip, for example. It is also an expression of his artistic maturity, since there was no better way to avoid being perpetually compared to the master than to take his cue from him.

ONE TOGETHER

Jeremy Spencer / 3:23

Musicians
Jeremy Spencer: vocals, guitar
Danny Kirwan: guitar, backing vocals
Christine McVie: backing vocals
John McVie: bass
Mick Fleetwood: drums
Recorded
De Lane Lea Studios, London: June–July 1970
Technical Team
Producer: Fleetwood Mac
Sound Engineer: Martin Birch

Jeremy Spencer shows more subtlety than in the past, showcasing his talent on hybrid tracks of country, folk, and gospel, such as "One Together."

Genesis and Lyrics

Jeremy Spencer had no choice. If he was to replace Peter Green and potentially take on the mantle of Fleetwood Mac's creative leader, he had to put away his Elmore James pastiches and start writing real songs, drawing on his personal life and experiences, which the other band members gently but firmly invited him to do. More inclined to draw on his rock references from the 1950s and early 1960s, he came up with several tracks on *Kiln House*, the most introspective of which is certainly "One Together," a ballad blending folk, country, and gospel. Already tormented by spiritual aspirations that were hardly in keeping with the rock-star lifestyle, Spencer sometimes lived in seclusion at Kiln House, spending long hours reading the Bible with his wife, Fiona. Undeniably, "One Together" sounds like the beginnings of a manifesto for Spencer: While it seems clear that he is addressing a loved one, this person may not be a woman, as a first reading might suggest, but God. Both interpretations are possible: "How can my heart be filled with doubts of you / When you can fill me with a love that's true?" or "I want to see you more and more each day / I really need you, you're my only way." If he was still wondering what he could do ("What can I do?"), he would find the solution in February 1971.

Production

Almost unrecognizable, Jeremy Spencer's voice is surely the most striking element of this recording. Gentle and measured, at the opposite end of the spectrum from the loud, sometimes vulgar energetic man he could be on stage, it is above all wrapped in a benevolent arrangement. Accompanied by acoustic guitar and bass leaning on the fundamentals, this self-doubting Jeremy Spencer is comforted by Mick Fleetwood's warm, minimalist toms playing. From 1:57 onward, the slide guitar takes center stage with a real solo, whereas up until then it had served only to color the instrumental passages. The backing vocals, very much in evidence, are reminiscent of a gospel choir, reinforcing the song's probable religious significance.

Strangely enough, whereas one might have thought that "Tell Me All the Things You Do" would become a standard in Fleetwood Mac's stage repertoire, the song only remained there for as long as Kirwan was in the band. It reappeared in 2018 on the "An Evening with Fleetwood Mac" tour, with Neil Finn and Christine McVie sharing the lead vocals.

TELL ME ALL THE THINGS YOU DO

Danny Kirwan / 4:10

Musicians: Jeremy Spencer: vocals, guitar, keyboards / Danny Kirwan: vocals, guitar / John McVie: bass / Mick Fleetwood: drums / **Recorded:** De Lane Lea Studios, London: June–July 1970 / **Technical Team:** Producer: Fleetwood Mac / Sound Engineer: Martin Birch

FOR MAC-ADDICTS

Less than a year after the release of *Kiln House*, the British rock band the Hollies went into the studio to record the album *Distant Light*, released on October 8, 1971. Putting aside their usual vocal harmonies, they recorded "Long Cool Woman in a Black Dress," which clearly builds on "Tell Me All the Things You Do."

Genesis and Lyrics

Jeremy Spencer and Danny Kirwan were often criticized for their lack of charisma compared to the magnetism emanating from their former leader Peter Green. Expectations were especially high for Kirwan, who joined Fleetwood Mac when he was just eighteen and was destined to become the band's main songwriter after Green's departure. He takes his new role to heart on *Kiln House* and makes a notable contribution on many tracks, including "Jewel Eyed Judy" and "Station Man." But there are just two for which he is the only one to be credited: "Earl Gray" and especially "Tell Me All the Things You Do," strangely sent to the end of the album when it could probably have become a Fleetwood Mac classic. But then again, while Kirwan is a fine singer and guitarist, he is not exactly a first-rate lyricist. "Tell Me All the Things You Do" therefore suffers from the extreme weakness of its lyrics, which can be summed up on a Post-it note: "Tell me / Tell me all the things you do / I'll tell you / Tell you all the things I do." Basically: If you promise to tell me all the things you do, I promise to tell you all the things I do. Not enough to be compelling, obviously, as well as employing a recurring device in Kirwan's lyrics: the repetition of the same phrase, only changing the personal pronouns from one verse to the next.

Production

Immediately rooted in rock, "Tell Me All the Things You Do" quickly flirts with proto-hard rock, even swamp rock (a mix of rock, boogie, and country), recalling the bubbling of bands like Cream or Credence Clearwater Revival. The skillful interweaving of incendiary electric guitars, not short on inventive riffs, innovative breaks, and inspired solos, using distortion and wah-wah alike, is not unlike the overexcited atmosphere that pervades the song. In the opening bars, Kirwan's vocals display a lovely vibrato and a softness that contrasts intelligently with the sharpness of the guitars. The chemistry between the two guitarists, Kirwan and Spencer, has never been more palpable, while the rhythm section, led by the feeling of John McVie and the power of Mick Fleetwood, demonstrates impeccable discipline. On the finale, with the amps smoking and nearing breaking point, Jeremy Spencer's heartfelt interventions on the Wurlitzer add even more density to what is certainly the most melodic track on *Kiln House*. Indeed, it is impossible to finish listening to the album without humming it. Spencer recorded this keyboard part in an attempt to reproduce the style of Ray Charles. He was not entirely satisfied with the result, but the recording was kept that way.

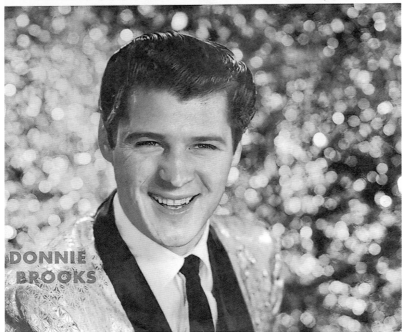

"Memphis" came from the same popular Donnie Brooks album as the huge hit "Mission Bell," which inspired Jeremy Spencer to cover it less than a decade later on *Kiln House*.

1970

MISSION BELL

William Michael, Jesse Hodges / 2:33

Musicians
Jeremy Spencer: vocals, guitar
Danny Kirwan: guitar, backing vocals
Christine McVie: keyboards, backing vocals
John McVie: bass
Mick Fleetwood: percussions

Recorded
De Lane Lea Studios, London: June–July 1970

Technical Team
Producer: Fleetwood Mac
Sound Engineer: Martin Birch

Genesis and Lyrics

"Mission Bell" was originally recorded by American pop singer Donnie Brooks in 1960. Written and composed by William Michael and Jesse Hodges, the song was an unexpected success, reaching number seven on the Billboard charts. Prior to this, Brooks's stage performances had been generally acclaimed, but he lacked a hit to establish himself with the public. That was "Mission Bell." Brooks relies on his velvety voice, enchanting female backing vocals, and a sparkling arrangement, with plenty of strings and, of course, a chime simulating a mission bell, the common thread running through the song. This type of bell is a legacy of the first Catholic missionaries who landed in California between the seventeenth and nineteenth centuries. Traveling from Spain, they built structures called "missions" all along the Pacific coast, which served as both military forts and churches, and were equipped with tall bell towers. These can still be seen along the famous El Camino Real driving route between Sonoma (north of San Francisco) and San Diego (near the Mexican border).

The lyrics are not particularly original. The song is about a love story, completely idealized by one of the two protagonists. He implores the other to abandon herself to him in return, guaranteeing that he will be worthy of this trust and that his love will never end: "Say you love me / Say those three words and / I will give my love to you / My love is higher than a mission bell."

For hundreds of years, mission bells have hung high, in a tower or a wall as is pictured here. They were the inspiration for the song "Mission Bell."

The famous mission bell referred to in the song inspired more than just Donnie Brooks (and Fleetwood Mac in turn) in the history of music, as the Eagles also mention it in their 1977 hit "Hotel California." The narrator sings: "I heard the mission bell / And I was thinking to myself / This could be heaven or this could be hell."

Production

This time, Fleetwood Mac, or rather Jeremy Spencer, does not exhume an obscure, little-known blues track as he follows in the footsteps of the many artists who have already delivered a reworking of this title, released barely a decade before. Among them, Ronnie Hilton (1960), Gary Miller (1960), Jimmy Velvet (1964), P. J. Proby (1965), Wes Dakus and the Rebels (1966), and Gene Pitney (1967) all had varying fortunes, but never quite managed to rise to the level of Donnie Brooks. Nor does Spencer intend to show any great originality, since his version clearly follows in the footsteps of the original. John McVie's round bass is the main attraction of this honest retelling, marked by a slightly psychedelic approach. Indeed, the backing vocals in particular are much less frontal in the mix than on Brooks's version. Wrapped in a deep reverb, they give an impression of floating, reinforced by the few guitar notes, slightly slid on the finale, embellished by small touches of piano in the background. As in Brooks's version, the chimes simulating the mission bell are omnipresent. Spencer's voice is nowhere near as hushed and precise as Donnie Brooks, but his performance remains convincing. As for Mick Fleetwood, whose sobriety benefits the entire arrangement, he makes do with delicate, perfectly matched percussion. Ideal for closing the album, "Mission Bell" is not so much original as suggestive of a gateway to a more pop universe, which Fleetwood Mac would gradually incorporate in the years to come.

Dragonfly / The Purple Dancer

UK Release Date: March 12, 1971, with Reprise Records (ref. RS 27010)

Best UK Chart Ranking: 52

The single was released in Germany and the Netherlands. Both editions feature specific sleeves. The Dutch version, in sober black and white, features a photograph of the five members of Fleetwood Mac. The German version, more in the spirit of psychedelia, is illustrated by a drawing of a dragon with red-ribbed wings spitting flames. Is this a deliberate pun or a literal interpretation of *dragonfly*?

Side A

Welsh poet and writer William Henry Davies documented his life on the American road from 1893 to 1899 in *The Autobiography of a Super-Tramp* and wrote a collection of popular poetry titled *Georgian Poetry*. One of his poems inspired the song "Dragonfly."

Opposite: A group photo taken in Los Angeles, in August 1970, used to illustrate several single covers, including "Dragonfly."

DRAGONFLY

Danny Kirwan, William Henry Davies / 2:45

Musicians: Danny Kirwan: vocals, guitar / John McVie: bass / Mick Fleetwood: drums / **Recorded:** De Lane Lea Studios, London: late 1970 / **Technical Team:** Producer: Fleetwood Mac / Sound Engineer: Martin Birch

Genesis and Lyrics

After the challenge of recording a full album without Peter Green, it was time for a new single. Danny Kirwan took on the task. Experiencing recurring difficulties with lyric writing, he decided that the best way around the problem was to draw on literature, and chose a poem by Welsh writer William Henry Davies, author of *The Autobiography of a Super-Tramp*. In truth, it was the man as much as the work that fascinated the young musician, who drank in the texts of this wandering poet, a beatnik before his time. He appreciated the richness, urgency, and audacity of Davies's poems, which reveal the darker sides of his personality. Such an ambivalent writer, mixing light and darkness in his verses, intrigued the complex character that is Kirwan, torn between the call of work and that of debauchery.

Danny chose "The Dragonfly," a poem close to his heart that, against all odds, does not tend toward the dark side. On the contrary, it is a pastoral, bucolic ode to roses about to bloom and a majestic dragonfly that has come to rest on an apple leaf in a lovely garden before setting off again. While not the most profound of poems, its syntax, the conciseness of its words, and the sharpness of its images make it an ideal text for a musical setting. Kirwan was also seduced by the calming ambience radiating from his lyrics. They ideally match the melody he had in mind, which veers toward the flowery psychedelic pop of San Francisco. However, the musician took the liberty of changing the order of some verses and leaving others out, to best adapt this poetic text to the prosody of his song. He even skipped an entire paragraph for which he had no use, ultimately retaining just two strophes.

Production

The recording date is not precisely documented, but it was shortly after the start of the UK tour, which kicked off in Leeds on November 6, 1970. Danny Kirwan teamed up with John McVie and Mick Fleetwood for this track, which turned resolutely toward the rock'n'roll, blues, and country of *Kiln House*. This new track is steeped in American psychedelic culture yet bears the stamp of Kirwan's elegantly melancholic pop sensibility. The two guitar tracks he performs carry this duality. One is rhythmic and acoustic, but with a brilliant arpeggio sound, while the other is louder in the mix. The latter, with its delightful reverb, is delicately vibratoed with whammy bar strokes over the chords, followed by a stunningly beautiful ascending phrasing. The whole is a sumptuous harmonic interlacing tracery. The bass plays a supporting role, remaining in the background, while Mick Fleetwood adds a few taps on the toms to a melody that hardly needs any artifice. For the vocals, Danny Kirwan superimposes two tracks, a technique already tried and tested on *Kiln House*. Perhaps this is the

mistake that makes the song remote, preventing it from becoming a hit. Admittedly, the atonal, wispy vocals are in tune with the psychedelic, intimate dimension of the track, but they lack presence and never take off, remaining in the background on the same level as the instruments. This takes away from the track's personality.

The single failed miserably, reaching number fifty-two in the UK charts. It was a vertiginous fall, since Fleetwood Mac had not missed landing a single in the UK top 10 for three years: "Albatross" (number one in 1968), "Man of the World" (number two in 1969), "Oh Well" (number two in 1969), and "The Green Manalishi (with the Two Prong Crown)" (number ten in 1970). The musicians interpreted this fiasco as a public response to Peter Green's absence. Green, however, had a very positive opinion of the song: "I like Danny Kirwan's thing—'Dragonfly'—which was done when I first left. I think that's the best thing they did. But I was just glad to get out of that group,"[32] he concludes, without regret.

Dragonfly / The Purple Dancer
UK Release Date: March 12, 1971, with Reprise Records (ref. RS 27010)
Best UK Chart Ranking: 52

THE PURPLE DANCER

Danny Kirwan, John McVie, Mick Fleetwood / 5:42

Musicians: Danny Kirwan: vocals, guitar / Jeremy Spencer: vocals, guitar / Christine McVie: piano, backing vocals / John McVie: bass / Mick Fleetwood: drums / **Recorded:** De Lane Lea Studios, London, end 1970 / **Technical Team:** Producer: Fleetwood Mac / Sound Engineer: Martin Birch

Genesis and Lyrics

Relegated to the B side despite its obvious effectiveness, "The Purple Dancer" unites the entire band. In this respect, the song is a historical landmark that the members of Fleetwood Mac were not yet aware of: As the first single to induct Christine McVie as an official member, it was also the last recorded by Jeremy Spencer, who abruptly resigned before its release.

After citing difficulties in writing lyrics that hold up on "Dragonfly," Danny Kirwan wrote a convincing lyric for "The Purple Dancer." He proclaims his love for a dancer. As he shares a dance with her, a flurry of questions assails him: "Will I leave her, will I wonder? / Will I fall down to the ground? / Is it love that is the answer?" At least the answer to the question "Will I ask myself questions?" is obvious: Yes, since almost the entire text is a sequence of questions. Only the esteemed dancer can help: "She can surely know the answer."

FOR MAC ADDICTS

For years, "The Purple Dancer" was the only track in the band's catalog not to be released on CD. Indeed, it was not until 2020 that it was included in the 8-CD box set *Fleetwood Mac: 1969 to 1974*.

Production

"The Purple Dancer" adopts a different, more ethereal approach to psychedelia than "Dragonfly." The B side asserts itself for what it is: rock with its feet firmly planted on the ground. Benefiting from Jeremy Spencer's racy playing, which does not lose itself in the hallucinogenic swirls of psychedelic pop, and with a touch of boogie from Christine McVie, the track could have claimed A-side status in the same way as "Dragonfly."

The band's energy is lively, boosted by a fast tempo. Kirwan starts off with a guitar-vocal lead. Mick Fleetwood opts for a classic but effective buildup, hitting the snare drum to a crescendo before landing on the cymbals. A second guitar replays note by note the melodic line of the vocals just performed, before launching into a short but spirited solo. Christine McVie introduces a new theme and a new, more boogie rhythm. Accustomed to sometimes rushed backing vocals, this time the band spends some time fine-tuning them, and it shows. Lead vocals, counter-vocals, and backing vocals are perfectly in tune. Accuracy, which is not always the order of the day, is—for the moment—not the band's great specialty, but the track offers a greater variety of vocals. At over five minutes, this guitar-heavy track stands out as one of Fleetwood Mac's most accomplished in a long time.

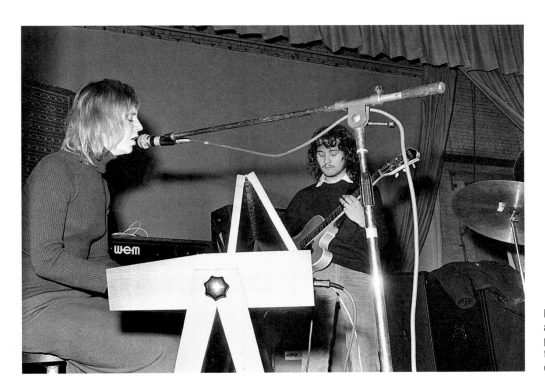

Prior to Christine Perfect's arrival, Jeremy Spencer played the keyboards. After that, he was free to focus on his six-string.

LONELY WITHOUT YOU
Christine McVie / 5:13

Musicians: Christine McVie: vocals, keyboards / Jeremy Spencer: guitar / Danny Kirwan: guitar / John McVie: bass / Mick Fleetwood: drums / **Recorded:** (?) / **Technical Team:** Mastering: Denis Blackham

The crew assembled on *Kiln House*—notably the co-involvement of Christine McVie and Jeremy Spencer—was short-lived. Spencer disappeared both literally and figuratively from the scene in February 1971.

A rare example of close collaboration between the two musicians, "Lonely Without You" was never recorded in the studio. All that remains is a live record of this piece, whose origin and date have not been established. The song was included on the compilations *Madison Blues* (Shakedown Records) which in 2003 featured studio sessions by the Christine Perfect Band and Fleetwood Mac, as well as the latter's live performances, and *Crazy About the Blues* (Secret Records Limited), which in 2010 featured tracks recorded live by Fleetwood Mac and the Christine Perfect Band.

This ballad, written and sung by Christine McVie, blossoms in a relaxing blues atmosphere imposed by cottony keyboards. This is the first Fleetwood Mac song to feature her deep, powerful lead vocals, imbued with an obvious blues culture. Jeremy Spencer lays down his slide guitar lines in complete tranquility. We sense his diligence and care, a far cry from the Spencer of the early days, who consistently gave the impression of someone trying to start a fire by rubbing his bottleneck against the strings.

DOWN AT THE CROWN
Danny Kirwan / 3:04

Musicians: Christine McVie: vocals, keyboards / Danny Kirwan: vocals, guitar / Jeremy Spencer: vocals, guitar / John McVie: bass / Mick Fleetwood: drums / **Recorded:** (?) / **Technical Team:** Mastering: Denis Blackham

Recorded in 1970, with no indication of its origins, "Down at the Crown" also features on the twin compilations *Madison Blues* from 2003 (Shakedown Records) and *Crazy About the Blues* from 2010 (Secret Records Limited). This Danny Kirwan–crafted track is specially designed for the stage. A country blues treat with a steady tempo, it does not show any great originality, but it does testify to the cohesion between the musicians and the mimicry of Kirwan's bouncy guitar playing and Christine McVie's keyboards. Their complicity is even evident in their vocals, coordinated on the first part. They instinctively follow the guitar's clean strokes as they are played back and forth. Kirwan's right-hand playing is the metronome of a song whose value lies in its rhythm. At 0:45, Kirwan unexpectedly introduces a syncopated reggae rhythm.

LIVE AT THE BBC

Disc 1
Rattlesnake Shake
Sandy Mary
I Believe My Time Ain't Long
Although the Sun Is Shining
Only You
You Never Know What You're Missing
Oh Well
Can't Believe You Wanna Leave
Jenny Lee
Heavenly
When Will I Be Loved
When I See My Baby
Buddy's Song
Honey Hush
Preachin'
Jumping at Shadows
Preachin' Blues
Need Your Love So Bad

Disc 2
Long Grey Mare
Sweet Home Chicago
Baby Please Set a Date
Blues With a Feeling
Stop Messing Around
Tallahassee Lassie
Hang On to a Dream
Linda
Mean Mistreatin' Mama
World Keeps Turning
I Can't Hold Out
Early Morning Come
Albatross
Looking for Somebody
A Fool No More
Got to Move
Like Crying Like Dying
Man of the World

Release Dates
United Kingdom: 1995
Reference: Castle Communications—EDF CD 297
Best UK Chart Ranking: 48
United States: 1995
Reference: Castle Communications—CASTLE114-2
Best US Chart Ranking: Did Not Chart

Radio Stars

During its first years of existence, Fleetwood Mac was a favored guest of the BBC, recording numerous sessions for British radio, thanks in particular to John Peel, the legendary disc jockey and host of BBC Radio 1's *Top Gear*. Won over by the band's first single, Peel programmed them on the strength of these two tracks alone, and continued to do so regularly from 1967 to 1971, becoming their best promoter. *Top Gear*, launched in 1967—which he co-hosted in the early months before taking sole control—was the first radio program to give Fleetwood Mac national airplay. Other BBC programs followed, including *Night Ride* (BBC Radio 2), *Star Club*, and *Symonds on Sunday*. These recording sessions, carried out in various BBC studios between November 1967 and January 1971, gave the band the opportunity to experiment in a relaxed atmosphere, while saving on expensive studio days. In 1995, BBC Worldwide released a compilation box set of these sessions, simply entitled *Live at the BBC*.

Of exceptional sound quality, more flattering than many of the live performances recorded by the band, the recordings taken as a whole cover four years of Fleetwood Mac's life, roughly up to the departure of Peter Green and Jeremy Spencer in 1971. They are a formidable testimony to the stylistic and technical evolution of the Mac, to the transformation of a promising young band into a mature and adventurous group that managed to shed its dogmatic and inflexible vision of the blues to gradually branch out and diversify its influences between rock'n'roll, folk, and blues rock, as attested by the BBC recording of July 7, 1970, which preceded the release of the band's fourth studio album, *Kiln House*.

Four Years of Sessions in the Can

On November 7, 1967, four days after the release of its first single, "I Believe My Time Ain't Long / Rambling Pony," Fleetwood Mac was invited to the BBC studios in Maida Vale, London, to record six of its songs for broadcast on *Top Gear* on November 12: "Long Grey Mare," "Baby Please Set a Date" (an Elmore James cover), "Looking for Somebody," "I Believe My Time Ain't Long," "Got to Move" (a Homesick James Williamson reworking), and "A Fool No More."

On January 16, 1968, the band returned to Aeolian Hall Studio No. 2, this time to lay down a few tracks for the *Top Gear* broadcast on January 21. In the meantime, they had completed the recording sessions for their debut album, scheduled for release on February 24. Of the six tracks recorded that day in the BBC studios, only two were

British DJ John Peel helped launch Fleetwood Mac, regularly inviting the band to perform at the BBC studios.

included in the *Live at the BBC* box set: "I Can't Hold Out" and "World Keeps Turning" (also known as "The World Keep on Turning"). Yet Fleetwood Mac were far more prolific that day, performing three covers—B. B. King's "Sweet Little Angel," Elvis Presley's "Don't Be Cruel," Elmore James's "The Sun Is Shining"—and an unreleased one with a name that would challenge any radio host: "Bee-I-Bicky-Bop Blue Jean Honey Babe Meets High School Hound Dog Hot Rod Man." On January 16, 1968, Eddie Boyd was also invited to the session. Peter Green, Mick Fleetwood, and John McVie joined the pianist and singer to play three of his songs, "Where You Belong," "Blue Coat Man," and "The Stroller." With the keyboardist's post occupied, Jeremy Spencer logically took a back seat. Fleetwood Mac received a fee of £30 from the BBC for the full performance that day.

The band returned to BBC Radio 1 on April 9, 1968, this time for the *Saturday Club* program, but none of the three songs ("Worried Dream," "Please Find My Baby," and "Peggy Sue Got Married") played that day and broadcast on April 13 made the cut for *Live at the BBC*.

The musicians returned to the Aeolian Hall studios on April 16, 1968, to record for a broadcast the following day, this time Radio 1's *Night Ride*. Despite the interest of this session, which focused on covers (B. B. King's "How Blue Can You Get?," Homesick James Williamson's "My Baby's Sweeter," and Louis Jordan and B. B. King's "Buzz Me Baby"), it did not make it onto the compilation either, but it

was included in its entirety on the *Show-Biz Blues 1968–1970 Volume 2* compilation in 2000.

Of the following session, recorded on May 27, 1968 (broadcast June 2) for *Top Gear*, only "Mean Mistreatin' Mama"—a composition credited to Leroy Carr and Elmore James—made an appearance on the live album. The session also included a version of "That Ain't It (I Need Your Love)" from the repertoire of Jimmy Rogers and Big Walter Horton, Tommy Roe's "Sheila," Robert Johnson's "Dead Shrimp Blues," and the psychedelic parody of entertainer-in-chief Jeremy Spencer's "Intergalactic Magicians Walking Through Pools of Velvet Darkness."

Two days after a concert in Hyde Park on August 24, 1968, Fleetwood Mac were welcomed back by the *Top Gear* team on August 26 and 27 at Piccadilly Studio 1. Since their previous appearance on the BBC, the band had been beefed up, with Danny Kirwan present, and guest Christine McVie on backing vocals and possibly keyboard (sources differ on the latter). No fewer than sixteen songs were recorded on tape for airplay on September 1. "Need Your Love So Bad," "Preachin' Blues," and "Stop Messin' Around" were extracted from this marathon session to garnish the copious *Live at the BBC* menu.

On October 9, 1968, Danny Kirwan's "Like Crying Like Dying" (named as such on the record, but of course this is "Like Crying," which is present on the *Then Play On* opus), Tom Hardin's folk cover "Hang On to a Dream," and

The Playhouse Theatre, opened in 1882 in London's West End, served as the BBC's recording studio between 1951 and 1976.

FOR MAC ADDICTS

The *Top Gear* radio program served as an unexpected platform for Fleetwood Mac. In return, the band honored John Peel, the BBC show's iconic host, by quoting him in the liner notes to *Mr. Wonderful*. The band is referred to as "almost a resident group on *Top Gear*."

Fleetwood Mac's unmissable instrumental "Albatross" were recorded at the Playhouse Theatre for the Radio One Club show. "Unmissable"—but not for everyone. John Peel did not appreciate it at all and was more inclined to play Side B of this single, "Jigsaw Puzzle Blues," in his playlist. Off-air, he even mocked "Albatross," ironically renaming it "Albert Ross."

On November 1, "Sweet Home Chicago" was played in the presence of Alexis Korner, radio host for the occasion at Studio 1 of Aeolian Hall for a program called *Rhythm'n'Blues*.

On March 10, 1969, Fleetwood Mac again recorded a series of songs for *Top Gear*, six of which were retained for the 1995 compilation: Jeremy Spencer's "You Never Know What You're Missing," Danny Kirwan's "Early Morning Come," and four covers: Lloyd Price's "Can't Believe You Wanna Leave," Conway Twitty's "Heavenly," "Tallahassee Lassie," popularized by Freddy Cannon and Rabon Tarrant, and Jack McVea's "Blues with a Feeling."

On March 17, Peter Green, Christine and John McVie, and Mick Fleetwood played again, this time for *Symonds on Sunday*, with Alexis Korner on guitar and Duster Bennett on harmonica. On June 10, they recorded "Man of the World" and "Jumping at Shadows" by the same Duster Bennett, and "Linda," a new song by Jeremy Spencer. In the midst of promoting *Then Play On*, Fleetwood Mac paid another visit to Radio 1 to perform two tracks, also included on *Live at the BBC*, "Although the Sun Is Shining" and "Oh Well," released shortly before as a single on September 26, 1969.

The 1970 sessions would make up the bulk of Disc 1 of the double album. It was based first and foremost on the concert recorded by the BBC at London's Paris Cinema on April 9, 1970 (broadcast on the nineteenth and again on the twenty-second), with "Rattlesnake Shake" opening the compilation. That evening, the master of ceremonies, Dave Symonds, was put to the test by his guests, who spared him nothing: He announced "Under Way" as the first track, but the band had changed its set list without warning him and began "Rattlesnake Shake" before moving on to the planned track. Shortly afterward, Symonds attempted to interview Danny Kirwan, but had his fingers burned in the process, as the poor man who was feeling very ill at ease only answered yes or no, which quickly made the exchange sterile and awkward.

Another radio appearance followed, at London's Playhouse Theatre on April 27 (broadcast on May 23), with "Sandy Mary" by Peter Green and "Only You" by Danny Kirwan.

But the main source of songs for *Live at the BBC* was the July 7 session (broadcast on August 22, 1970), which followed Peter Green's departure and preceded the summer recording of *Kiln House*, which testifies to the rock'n'roll turn taken in preparation for this final album. Spencer and his band invoked Buddy Holly on "Buddy's Song," the Everly Brothers on "When Will I Be Loved," and Big Joe Turner on "Honey Hush." Kirwan also slipped in a new song, "When I See My Baby," and Spencer aired his "Jenny Lee." But the session also says a lot, through the Mac's choices, about the band's disorientation at the time. The band opted for covers and included only two original tracks that each barely meet the two-minute mark. After this rock'n'roll passage, the last word goes to the blues with the latest recording (from January 23, 1971): "Preachin'," a tribute to the great Son House. These are the songs by Fleetwood Mac that remain unreleased outside this *Live at the BBC*.

YOU NEVER KNOW
WHAT YOU'RE MISSING
Jeremy Spencer / 2:53

Musicians: Jeremy Spencer: vocals, piano / Peter Green: guitar, backing vocals / Danny Kirwan: guitar, backing vocals / John McVie: bass / Mick Fleetwood: drums / **Recorded:** Playhouse Theatre, London, March 10, 1969 / **Technical Team:** (?)

On the day this radio session was scheduled, another band-related event monopolized the attention of the music microcosm: Their manager, Clifford Davis, officially announced that Fleetwood Mac would not be extending their contract with Blue Horizon. This was probably why he kept his flock so busy—to keep them away from the studios and minimize their contact with Mike Vernon, who might have convinced them to stay. Davis was aiming for competition between record companies in the hope of securing a more lucrative contract. Fleetwood Mac was busy. On March 10, the band spared no effort, recording no fewer than six songs for the *Top Gear* TV show, including "You Never Know What You're Missing."

The band was often relaxed about the credits, so it is not surprising to see this song attributed to Jeremy Spencer, when all he had done was rearrange a Ricky Nelson track first recorded ten years earlier, in June 1959. Whether or not deliberately, John Spencer conceals the use of the future tense by renaming the track, which was originally called "You'll Never Know What You're Missing." There is something very spontaneous about this version, which opens with hesitant claps and charming doo-wop backing vocals. There is also something moving about Spencer's interpretation. He slows down the tempo considerably compared to the original, which favors a deeper, more sensual vocal. In this way, the performer comes closer to Ricky Nelson's source of inspiration, Elvis Presley's "Treat Me Nice," than to Ricky Nelson's own version.

EARLY MORNING COME
Danny Kirwan / 2:29

Musicians: Danny Kirwan: vocals, guitar / **Recorded:** Playhouse Theatre, London, March 10, 1969 / **Technical Team:** (?)

This Danny Kirwan composition, never immortalized in the studio and very rarely played, also comes from the March 10 session. This recording is thus a precious testimony to this little strumming blues gem. The simplicity of its structure, as well as the variations in intensity of the vocals, give this composition its charm. Despite the fragility of the interpretation, the text displays a self-assurance not often seen in Kirwan, who usually prefers the role of the spurned lover. This time, he is the object of desire, creating an imbalance in the love relationship: "Everything you do / I know you wanna please."

LINDA
John Spencer / 2:03

Musicians: Jeremy Spencer: vocals, guitar / Peter Green: guitar, backing vocals / Danny Kirwan: guitar, backing vocals / John McVie: bass / Mick Fleetwood: drums / **Recorded:** Piccadilly 201 Studio 1, London, June 10, 1969 / **Technical Team:** (?)

On discovering "Linda" on *Chris Grant's Tasty Pop Sundae* on June 10, 1969, listeners might have thought it was a (rather strange) new Fleetwood Mac composition. Pounded under a martial rhythm, it emerges timidly as a high sugar content bubblegum pop ballad, topped by a thin, almost cartoonish voice. In reality, "Linda" is just the umpteenth fantasy from Jeremy Spencer, who could not get enough out of his *Milton Schlitz* EP to express his desire for satire. This time, he added Tommy Roe to his roster of parodies. Spencer must have heard of Roe's hit "Dizzy," which reached number one in the UK Singles Chart on its release in March 1969. This certainly gave him the idea of tackling another of his hits, "Sheila," created at the start of his career and taken to the top of the charts by American audiences. The same galloping drums and the same melodic line are to be found. The imitation is so credible and the melody so catchy that the humorous dimension almost disappears.

Jeremy Spencer was well aware of this and included the song in the track list of his solo album (released on January 23, 1970), before releasing it as a single on October 17, 1969, with "Teenage Darling" on Side B.

WHEN I SEE MY BABY

Danny Kirwan / 2:12

Musicians: Danny Kirwan: vocals, guitar / Jeremy Spencer: guitar / John McVie: bass / Mick Fleetwood: drums / Christine McVie: backing vocals / **Recorded:** London (?), July 7, 1970 / **Technical Team:** (?)

Given the recording date, July 7, 1970, one wonders whether "When I See My Baby" was intended for *Kiln House* or whether it was destined to feed the frustrations of a Kirwan who had been very productive since joining Fleetwood Mac but had to leave a number of compositions by the wayside. Still, this song would not have been out of place in this track list, given Jeremy Spencer's and Danny Kirwan's fine dual guitars. Despite a few inaccuracies and hesitant notes, the latter's solo shows great inventiveness. Christine McVie's interventions on the doo-wop backing vocals are regrettable, however, as they underline the fact that she is at her best on lead vocals.

SANDY MARY

Peter Green / 5:01

Musicians: Peter Green: vocals, guitar / Jeremy Spencer: guitar, piano / Danny Kirwan: guitar / Mick Fleetwood: drums / Nick Pickett: fiddle / **Recorded:** Playhouse Theatre, London, April 27, 1970 / **Technical Team:** (?)

A solid track with powerful attacks, "Sandy Mary" sees Fleetwood Mac shed all its usual nuances of playing to give way to the energy of rock. With all its muscles on display, the song compares favorably with the firepower of the Kinks. Unfortunately, Peter Green's confidence at the microphone is not contagious, and the track gradually disintegrates, losing some of its superb sound due to a poorly handled fatal bridge. The sound does not really help, either. The wah-wah pedal, too infrequently used by Green, is not exploited as it should be, and Spencer's piano disappears beneath the sonic magma, crushed by low frequencies, as does Nick Pickett's fiddle, credited but nonexistent. The band first played "Sandy Mary" live on their US tour, during one of their performances at the Whisky a Go Go, the Los Angeles club, in January 1970. Three months later, Peter Green gave his composition an unflattering radio baptism on this April 27, 1970, recording for *Top Gear*.

ONLY YOU

Danny Kirwan / 2:51

Musicians: Danny Kirwan: vocals, guitar / Peter Green: percussion, guitar (?) / Jeremy Spencer: guitar (?) / John McVie: bass / Mick Fleetwood: drums / Nick Pickett: fiddle / **Recorded:** Playhouse Theatre, London, April 27, 1970 / **Technical Team:** (?)

"Only You," debuted onstage in Stockholm on November 4, 1969, was a regular feature in Fleetwood Mac's sets over the following months, until April 27, 1970, the day they recorded a new performance for *Top Gear*, for broadcast on May 23. This was the band's last moment with Peter Green, and on this track they offer an admirable moment of cohesion that makes one miss this lineup all the more.

The first few seconds of the track are a little unsettling: The drums seem too fast and full for Danny Kirwan's guitar phrasing. But when he reaches the bridge, he introduces abrupt tonal changes, bringing out the song's danceable Latin rhythm, underlined by the percussion. A remarkable guitar duet then takes shape on the finale, testifying to the great complicity between the musicians. Fiddler Nick Pickett (ex–John Dummer Band) is credited on fiddle, although he is not audible.

JENNY LEE

Jeremy Spencer / 2:20

Musicians: Jeremy Spencer: vocals, guitar / Danny Kirwan: guitar, backing vocals / John McVie: bass / Mick Fleetwood: drums / **Recorded:** (?) / **Technical Team:** (?)

Included in the set that the post–Peter Green Fleetwood Mac recorded on August 22, 1970, "Jenny Lee" stands out from the rest of the tracks for its acoustic, pop lightness. And with good reason: It is not a Mac track but a Jeremy Spencer one. It comes from the guitarist's first solo album, released in January 1970, but he performs it with his band, who were with him when the record was made.

This retro-tinged pop bluette evokes the sweetness of 1950s teenage songs, such as those by the Everly Brothers or the more confident Jan and Arnie, who themselves released a track called "Jennie Lee" in 1958. The tempo might have been faster and the lyrics might have been different, but their carefree atmosphere and chastity, in stark contrast to Jeremy Spencer's personality, lead us to believe that he had heard of it and was inspired by it. Given his taste for subversion, it is no coincidence that his song is named after a 1950s pin-up known for her burlesque shows.

With the departures of Peter Green and Jeremy Spencer, *The Original Fleetwood Mac* is a sampling of the band's highly productive period from 1967 to 1968.

THE ORIGINAL FLEETWOOD MAC

Drifting
Leaving Town Blues
Watch Out
A Fool No More
Mean Old Fireman
Can't Afford to Do It
Fleetwood Mac
Worried Dream
Love That Woman
Allow Me One More Show
First Train Home
Rambling Pony No. 2

Bonus Tracks
Mighty Cold
Jumping at Shadows
Somebody's Gonna Get (Their Head Kicked In Tonite)
Man of Action
Something Inside of Me
One Sunny Day
Without You
Coming Your Way

Release Dates
United Kingdom: May 1971
Reference: CBS—63875
United Kingdom: 1990
Reference: Castle Communication/Essential! Records—ESSLP 026
United Kingdom: 2000
Reference: Snapper Music / Original Masters—156072; Artisan Recordings—SMA CD 832
United Kingdom: 2004
Reference: Columbia—5164482
Best UK Chart Ranking: Did Not Chart
United States: 1977
Reference: Sire—SR 6045
Best US Chart Ranking: Did Not Chart

The Jewel Box

In May 1971, a year after Peter Green's retirement, CBS—who retained the distribution rights to the band's early recordings—filled a gap in the band's discography by releasing a compilation of twelve previously unreleased tracks: *The Original Fleetwood Mac*. Initially released in the UK, it gives visibility to previously unexploited tracks. This is hardly surprising, given that the band's first incarnation—the 1967–1968 lineup featuring Peter Green, Jeremy Spencer, John McVie, and Mick Fleetwood—recorded many tracks outside their official studio albums (Bob Brunning is featured on "Rambling Pony No. 2"). The "fault" lies in their overflowing activity, their almost unlimited access to Decca Studios and then CBS Studios

thanks to producer Mike Vernon, and the prolixity of the two guitarists, Green and Spencer, who were constantly vying to come up with a new composition or a cover of an American blues tune.

In this body of work, studio recordings and live recordings coexist, with original compositions such as "Drifting," "Leaving Town Blues," "Watch Out," "A Fool No More," "Fleetwood Mac," "Allow Me One More Show," "First Train Home," "Rambling Pony No. 2," and blues covers such as "Mean Old Fireman," "Can't Afford to Do It," "Worried Dream," and "Love That Woman."

Two "enriched" editions later completed this publication. One, in 2000, featured four additional tracks:

"Mighty Cold," "Jumping at Shadows" (in a live version), "Somebody's Gonna Get (Their Head Kicked In Tonite)," and "Man of Action." The other, in 2004, essentially featured alternative versions and extended the time spectrum to the Kirwan period, disregarding the coherence of the product: "Watch Out," three takes of "Something Inside of Me," "One Sunny Day," "Without You," and "Coming Your Way."

This compilation symbolically closes the British chapter of the Mac: the band's genesis, and the passage of the Peter Green comet and its rather lunar satellite, Jeremy Spencer.

DRIFTING

Peter Green / 3:30

Musicians: Peter Green: vocals, guitar / John McVie: bass / Mick Fleetwood: drums / **Recorded:** CBS Studios, London, 1967 / **Technical Team:** Producer: Mike Vernon / Sound Engineer: Mike Ross / Assistant Sound Engineer: Richard Vernon

Peter Green never got to the end of this song, recorded during Fleetwood Mac's first year of existence, at one of the many late-night work sessions at CBS Studios. It seems finished, but its linearity and the absence of a second verse indicate its incompleteness. The guitarist's idea was to play it as a group, spinning this standard twelve-bar blues structure over a 12/8 rhythm and waiting for the inspiration of the moment to do the rest. But, despite the excellent acoustic conditions set up by Mike Vernon—the resonance of the drums and the richness of the bass sound are exemplary— this title in *G* minor stays low, in every sense. Peter Green's guitar lead performs some fine feats, but it relies on a first track, also recorded by him, that lacks originality. Hopelessly limp at this tempo, the rhythm guitar confines itself to the execution of a pentatonic scale, locking in any inventiveness or velocity for the solo.

A spiritual heir to Peter Green's blues, Rory Gallagher pays tribute to him with a fabulous cover of "Leaving Town Blues." A daring and unexpected choice, this rare track is acoustic, which is not the Irish electric blues virtuoso's preferred terrain. Its reworking, like that of "Showbiz Blues," was later included on the *Peter Green Songbook* album, a tribute compilation featuring Larry McCray, Ian Anderson, and Kim Simmond. It was released in 1995, the year of Gallagher's death.

which evoke the passage from childhood to adulthood through the image of the train journey. This classic blues narrative tears the narrator away from his mother and his land. Fully immersed in Delta culture, Peter Green imagines himself in the shoes of one of those Mississippi bluesmen who left for Chicago to make a living as a musician: "Now, when I go to Chicago / Blues don't you follow me." (This sequence is cleverly constructed: Either there is a clear break between the two lines [meaning that he is addressing the blues when he says "don't you follow me"], or the lyricist spans between the two lines [meaning that the narrator is joining the "Chicago blues"]. In which case, "don't you follow me" would be addressed to his mother, as the narrator does throughout the rest of the song.)

LEAVING TOWN BLUES

Peter Green / 2:51

Musicians: Peter Green: vocals, guitar / John McVie: bass / Mick Fleetwood: drums / **Recorded:** CBS Studios, London, December 11, 1967 / **Technical Team:** Producer: Mike Vernon / Sound Engineer: Mike Ross / Assistant Sound Engineer: Richard Vernon

Four false starts threw the band's concentration, and they managed to finish the song only on the fifth take. Obviously, the drums were a problem. In fact, the song was finished on December 11, 1967, without the band having reached a satisfactory solution. Combining hi-hat and cross stick, Mick Fleetwood's drum shuffle takes up too much space and seems out of step with the song's rootsy, bluesy Delta ambience, which does not require such rhythmic support. It is surprising that Green did not try to include a harmonica part, a reflex he often indulged in during the first year of the Mac's existence. The rural blues atmosphere of the first half of the twentieth century is palpable in the lyrics,

A FOOL NO MORE

Peter Green / 4:33

Musicians: Peter Green: vocals, guitar / Jeremy Spencer: guitar / John McVie: bass / Mick Fleetwood: drums / **Recorded:** CBS Studios, London, November 22, 1967 / **Technical Team:** Producer: Mike Vernon / Sound Engineer: Mike Ross / Assistant Sound Engineer: Richard Vernon

"A Fool No More" is certainly the most accomplished and convincing track in this series of previously unreleased material. During the recording sessions for the first album, it appeared to be Peter Green's first step on the road to an airy blues that would lead him to "I Love Another Woman" and "Albatross." If we go a step further, the intense, deep, reverb-laden sound, the precise, melodious play on the bends, and the incredible sustain prefigure David Gilmour's most introspective Pink Floyd tracks. The bitterness of the lyrics, following the adultery of the narrator's girlfriend, contrasts with the melancholy of the melody.

Blues guitarist Lizzie Douglas, better known by stage name Memphis Minnie.

MEAN OLD FIREMAN
Jeremy Spencer / 3:44

Musicians: Jeremy Spencer: vocals, guitar / **Recorded:** CBS Studios, London, November 22, 1967 / **Technical Team:** Producer: Mike Vernon / Sound Engineer: Mike Ross / Assistant Sound Engineer: Richard Vernon

"Mean Old Fireman" appears on *The Original Fleetwood Mac* but also found a place twenty-eight years later, on *The Complete Blue Horizon Sessions 1967–1969*, another retrospective compilation, released in 1999. Surprisingly, the booklet of this boxed set credits the song to Arthur Crudup. Yet nothing in the bluesman's discography seems to link "Mean Old Fireman" to any of his compositions except perhaps "Mean Ole Frisco," for the similarity of its title but nothing else. The kinship with Son House's work is much more relevant, if we compare it to a track like "Depot Blues," for example.

On this recording Jeremy Spencer does not have to strain his voice, and he can remain in a natural low register. This enhances the authenticity of his performance. In this respect, he proves that he is never more convincing than when he is not overacting. His bottleneck playing on an acoustic guitar with f-shaped sound holes, sounding almost like a dobro, also relies on economy. The positioning of the microphones, which capture every detail of the playing, allows for nuances and prevents an overly aggressive style. Like "Leaving Town Blues," the text exploits the theme of the train that leaves the station and changes the life of the person who takes it, but this time it is approached from the angle of love. This could have given rise to two different interpretations. Jeremy Spencer chooses despair over anger, expressing resentment toward the "Mean Old Fireman" who plays stationmaster and whistles the train's departure, ensuring the rupture between the narrator who remains on the platform and his wife who leaves.

CAN'T AFFORD TO DO IT
Homesick James Williamson / 2:00

Musicians: Jeremy Spencer: vocals, guitar / Peter Green: guitar, backing vocals / John McVie: bass, backing vocals / Mick Fleetwood: drums, backing vocals / **Recorded:** CBS Studios, London, 1967 / **Technical Team:** Producer: Mike Vernon / Sound Engineer: Mike Ross / Assistant Sound Engineer: Richard Vernon

While the slide guitar playing of Homesick James Williamson (Elmore James's preferred partner) was already at the heart of the original instrumentation on "Can't Afford to Do It," it was primarily piano driven. In Jeremy Spencer's version, the guitars have taken over, eliminating the piano part in favor of a change of tempo. The higher tempo takes the song into boogie-rock territory, where Mick Fleetwood is at home. He sets up a rousing shuffle punctuated by a few well-judged variations. This acceleration gives the track a vital, lifesaving boost. Mike Vernon's production makes it easy to distinguish each instrument without any of them taking precedence. Once again, Jeremy Spencer does not need to raise his voice, which tends to become brittle and nasal when pushed to its limits. He is probably the one who condemns the song to the status of a novelty. He misses the beginning of the solo and fails to land on his feet. Mike Vernon seals the fate of the recording by making it die in a miserable fade-out that limits the damage. The track would not be reworked in the studio (no doubt because of its melodic proximity to "Shake Your Moneymaker"); it was discarded and would remain unreleased.

COMPILATION

FLEETWOOD MAC

Peter Green / 3:52

Musicians: Peter Green: guitar / John McVie: bass / Mick Fleetwood: drums / **Recorded:** Decca Studios, London, 1967 / **Technical Team:** Producer: Mike Vernon / Sound Engineer: Mike Ross / Assistant Sound Engineer: Richard Vernon

This instrumental may not be the most intense or original track on the Fleetwood Mac compilation, but its story is inseparable from that of the band to which it gave its name and set a course. Peter Green said, "The name just came to me: I thought Fleetwood sounded like an express train and groups were starting to call themselves after musicians. Then, we were in the studio recording an instrumental that sounded like a train."[21]

Recorded during a session at Decca Studios in 1967, before the band was even a project, this song unites Peter Green, John McVie, and Mick Fleetwood around a groove, in a feverish interpretation of the blues. Backed by McVie's rumbling, groovy bass, Mick Fleetwood stabilizes the rhythm as much as he decorates it, adding subtle variations here and there. Peter Green, for his part, already demonstrates fabulous dexterity and instinctive, transcendent playing.

WORRIED DREAM

B. B. King / 5:20

Musicians: Peter Green: vocals, guitar / Christine Perfect: piano / John McVie: bass / Mick Fleetwood: drums / **Recorded:** CBS Studios, London, April 11, 1968 / **Technical Team:** Producer: Mike Vernon / Sound Engineer: Mike Ross / Assistant Sound Engineer: Richard Vernon

It did not take Peter Green long to get hold of "Worried Dream." The B. B. King track on the album *Blues on Top of Blues*, released in January 1968, was still warm when Green, who had bought the record as soon as it came out, began trying to reproduce it. At the April 11 session to finalize "Need Your Love So Bad," Green arranged to include "Worried Dream" in the day's schedule. The band seems to have had much less trouble recording this reinterpretation than the single.

As evidenced by the complete rendition of the two takes that appear on the compilation *The Original Fleetwood Mac*, Mike Vernon began by asking the band to play twelve bars to settle in and test the sound of each instrument. The

musicians comply, then launch into the song, but the producer cuts them off mid-stream. Green seems irritable. He rants, presumably because of noises outside the studio, then turns to Mick and says, "Mick, I don't like the brushes."[33] Without flinching, the drummer puts them away and takes up his sticks again. He had something to argue about, since playing with brushes is more suited to this smoothly evolving track, but Mick knows that with Peter there are times when he has to silently comply. Then, in an authoritative voice, Peter Green demands that the studio door should be closed. The next take is the right one. Christine Perfect (just a guest at this stage of Fleetwood Mac's existence) shows admirable inventiveness. She relieves Peter Green of his guitar duties by occupying the melodic space with her keyboard, which allows him to concentrate more on his vocals. Not only that; she also shows herself to be very attuned to the lyrics. In the second verse, when Peter Green sings, "Last night, I dreamed about my baby," she takes the initiative and adds a few high notes to emphasize the dreaminess. As for Green, he makes his guitar weep like no one else on this edgy blues number.

LOVE THAT WOMAN

Otis Rush / 2:25

Musicians: Jeremy Spencer: vocals, guitar, piano / John McVie: bass / Mick Fleetwood: drums / **Recorded:** CBS Studios, London, April 1968 / **Technical Team:** Producer: Mike Vernon / Sound Engineer: Mike Ross / Assistant Sound Engineer: Richard Vernon

Credited to Otis Rush, "Love That Woman" was actually composed by his pianist, Lafayette Leake, and recorded in June 1957. Under the guidance of Willie Dixon, a luxurious orchestration was put in place to support the song: guitar, piano, brass, harmonica, and more. While the guitar and piano are retained, Spencer strives to return the song to its blues essence, stripping it of some of its arrangements and removing the typical Chicago-style color that made it so special.

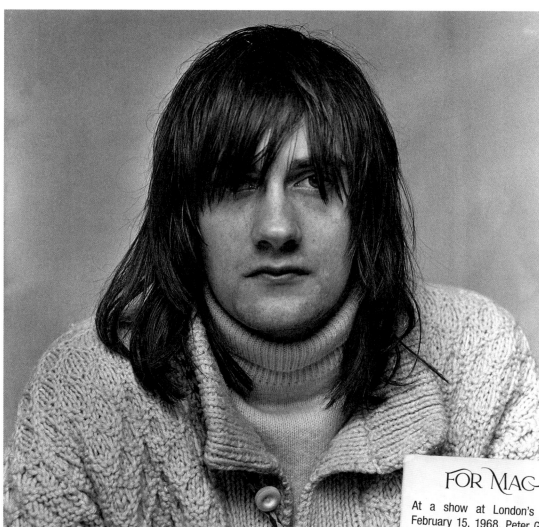

Mick Fleetwood receives a heartfelt tribute to his groove from Peter Green, baptizing "Fleetwood Mac," one of their first instrumental compositions.

ALLOW ME ONE MORE SHOW

Jeremy Spencer / 2:57

Musicians: Jeremy Spencer: vocals, guitar / **Recorded:** CBS Studios, London, 1968 / **Technical Team:** Producer: Mike Vernon / Sound Engineer: Mike Ross / Assistant Sound Engineer: Richard Vernon

Jeremy Spencer takes on this song alone in guitar-vocal format, and it is an even more convincing success than "Mean Old Fireman." The way he lets his voice linger on the descending phases at the end of a phrase lends an unexpected melancholy to the song, giving depth to the

FOR MAC ADDICTS

At a show at London's Middle Earth Club on February 15, 1968, Peter Green announced that he was going to try his hand at B. B. King's "Mean Old World." In passing, he praised the cover by "Tony Bennett," when he meant Duster Bennett. He wrongly attributed it to B. B. King, who in fact borrowed it from T-Bone Walker. Green was very absent-minded that evening. The musician, who was working on his cover of "Worried Dream," made a revealing slip of the tongue during his rendition of "Mean Old World," singing "worried mind" instead of just "mind."

narrator's plea for help in mourning his wife's departure. "I've got the blues so bad, Mama / Poor ol' heart is sore," he sings in a suitably American accent. Because, of course, Spencer has once again sought his inspiration on the other side of the Atlantic. "Allow Me One More Show," for example, is a reworking of Blind Willie McTell's "Mama, 'Tain't Long fo' Day," in which he has kept the tune but changed the lyrics. But Spencer does deserve some credit for his interpretative inventiveness with his complex acoustic guitar playing, between the bottleneck that rubs the *E* string and the other strings played in picking.

Duster Bennett, composer of "Jumping at Shadows," concentrates on his Gibson Les Paul Gold Top at the Royal Albert Hall, April 22, 1969.

FIRST TRAIN HOME
Peter Green / 4:04

Musicians: Peter Green: vocals, guitar, harmonica / John McVie: bass / Mick Fleetwood: drums / **Recorded:** Decca Studios, London, 1967 / **Technical Team:** Producer: Mike Vernon

"First Train Home," like the "Fleetwood Mac" instrumental, harks back to the band's prehistory, when Peter Green, John McVie, and Mick Fleetwood were still working with John Mayall. It might well have been at the end of an April 1967 recording session for the Bluesbreakers that Vernon immortalized the track as part of a demo for Decca Records. But the version that ended up on *The Original Fleetwood Mac* compilation could just as easily have been rerecorded later. Indeed, Mike Vernon mentions in the liner notes of *The Complete Blue Horizon Sessions 1967–1969* the possibility of a recording of the song (and the "Fleetwood Mac" instrumental) in August 1967. In any case, "First Train Home" says a lot about Peter Green's vision for his band-in-the-making. His model, at the time, was a trio like Buddy Guy's, and this track sounds like an attempt to emulate the sound of the bluesman's band. But the British combo's youth and immaturity prevent it from reaching the model's intensity, despite Peter Green's fine guitar performance. The latter is less at ease on the microphone, with a few false notes of the kind that are, fortunately, not heard from him again.

RAMBLING PONY #2
Peter Green / 2:57

Musicians: Peter Green: vocals, guitar, harmonica / John McVie: bass / Mick Fleetwood: drums / **Recorded:** Decca Studios or CBS Studios, London, August 1967 (?) / **Technical Team:** Producer: Mike Vernon

Once again, the date of this session is uncertain, as is its location. It could date back to August 1967. It is a variant of the song "Rambling Pony," chosen as Side B for the very first single in Fleetwood Mac's career, "I Believe My Time Ain't Long." The main difference lies in the tempo, which is much faster than the version chosen for the 45 rpm. Obviously, it loses all the charm of its original intention, which was to evoke slave songs, since the incantations are less profound. The initial adrenaline quickly fades in the face of the riff's linearity. Green's own vocals get lost in a muddled mix, tiring the eardrums with every passing second.

MIGHTY COLD

Doc Pomus, Mort Shuman / 2:21

Musicians: Jeremy Spencer: vocals, guitar, piano / John McVie: bass / Mick Fleetwood: drums / **Recorded:** (?) / **Technical Team:** Producer: Fleetwood Mac

Spencer seems to be once again donning the parodic teen rocker character, Ricky Dean, that he created during the *Milton Schlitz* sessions, this time taking on "Mighty Cold (To a Warm, Warm Heart)," a track released by teen idol Fabian (Forte) in May 1959 as Side B to his hit "Tiger." The track was written by two compositional giants: Doc Pomus and Mort Shuman, a well-known creative duo from the Brill Building, the nerve center of the New York music industry in the 1950s–1960s, which spawned a number of hits for the Drifters, Elvis Presley, and Dion DiMucci.

Fleetwood Mac's livelier, rock'n'roll version, propelled by an unstoppable piano, attests to Jeremy Spencer's immoderate love of fifties rock and his total mastery of its codes.

JUMPING AT SHADOWS (LIVE)

Duster Bennett / 4:02

Musicians: Peter Green: vocals, guitar / Danny Kirwan: guitar / John McVie: bass / Mick Fleetwood: drums / **Recorded:** Boston Tea Party, Boston, February 5, 6, or 7, 1970 (?) / **Technical Team:** Producer: Clifford Adams

"Jumping at Shadows" is one of Fleetwood Mac's finest borrowings. Peter Green makes Duster Bennett's delicate ballad his own. A member of the Blue Horizon stable, this singer, guitarist, and harmonica player developed a close relationship with the members of the Mac over the years. They had helped him put together his first album, *Smiling Like I'm Happy*, in 1968. Originally a session musician, Bennett also benefited from the support of John Mayall, who offered him the chance to open for the Bluesbreakers.

The Brill Building refers both to a subgenre of pop and to its place of creation, a New York building occupied by a team of professional songwriters who flooded the pop music of the late 1950s and early 1960s with their creations, which were sung by the stars of the moment. Neil Sedaka, Neil Diamond, Doc Pomus, and Burt Bacharach were the great architects of this ephemeral genre, giving a luxurious, orchestral dimension to teenage love songs.

Peter Green, who usually covers only old songs, puts all his soul and talent into reinterpreting this contemporary track, as if he had composed it himself. He turns it into a vehicle for his buried emotions, projecting his own mental confusion and deepest anxieties into the lyrics. To make the song his own, Green even modified the lyrics in small (but significant) ways when he performed it live onstage. This can be heard in the recording made during one of the three Boston Tea Party concerts (February 5–7, 1970) chosen for the compilation, in which he changes "Lord have mercy" to "Somebody help me," as if he did not yet know whether to place his faith in God or man, or when he utters this terrifyingly premonitory line in retrospect: "I think I'm going insane."

"Jumping at Shadows" features one of Peter Green's finest guitar performances, including a marvelous crescendo that, although executed on a conventional blues pattern, encapsulates the purity, scope, and feeling of his playing. First performed onstage in Copenhagen on March 25, 1969, it was to become a staple of the band's set list over the following year, culminating in the Boston Tea Party performances. This passage gives a discographic existence to this track, which was never recorded in the studio.

ALBUM

FUTURE GAMES

Woman of 1000 Years . Morning Rain . What a Shame . Future Games
Sands of Time . Sometimes . Lay It All Down . Show Me a Smile .
Outtake: Stone

RELEASE DATES
United Kingdom: September 3, 1971
Reference: Reprise Records—K44153
Best UK Chart Ranking: Did Not Chart
United States: September 3, 1971
Reference: Reprise Records—RS 6465
Best US Chart Ranking: 91

The band welcomes a newcomer in
Bob Welch (center), a guitarist with
a jazz background, a musical trait
the band never exploited.

DOUBLE OR QUITS

By 1971, the British blues boom was running out of steam. It had lost one of its main ambassadors in Peter Green, and some of the early pioneers like John Mayall were beginning to give in to the siren song of jazz. Even Eric Clapton was roundly criticized in 1970 when he released his long-awaited first solo album, *Eric Clapton*, which purists regarded as a betrayal of his blues roots. The release of the magnificent *Layla and Other Assorted Love Songs* with his band Derek and the Dominos a year later did little to help his cause; he was soon perceived as being associated with bands such as Savoy Brown and Ten Years After, accused of abandoning the blues in favor of catchy guitar riffs played at high volume, which would soon become the basis of heavy metal.

Fleetwood Mac was not there yet. But neither was it part of the group of songwriters in vogue at the time, with artists like James Taylor, Carole King, or Joni Mitchell, or even the new glam rock stars with the androgynous style that was beginning to emerge on both sides of the Atlantic, like David Bowie, Rod Stewart, or Alice Cooper, or a band like T. Rex. To say that Fleetwood Mac had hit rock bottom would be an exaggeration. The band, passing through a kind of no-man's-land at that time, was working to change its image by getting rid of the labels and pigeonholing that clung to it.

Heading for America

The months following the release of *Kiln House* found the band settled into a fairly comfortable routine. Now based in a vast mansion in Benifold, Hampshire, the musicians enjoyed its luxurious facilities when not on tour.

After struggling to overcome the departure of Peter Green, the band's true creative soul, Fleetwood Mac got back on track with *Kiln House*, while initiating a restrained turn in the direction of pop. The Jeremy Spencer–Danny Kirwan duo were at the helm, and Christine McVie's regenerating arrival in the band was made official. The album might have saved the day, but the band now had to work on forging a new image. And this quest for identity would involve America. For the British public, Fleetwood Mac had probably already given everything. So the only way to get the ball rolling again was to cross the Atlantic, where much remained to be done. So, in January 1971, the band set off for a three-month tour of the United States, where Clifford Davis had set up a string of engagements. Mick Fleetwood had just enough time to visit his wife—who had given birth to a baby girl—before taking off for California.

On the surface, everything was going well: *Kiln House* did better in the United States than in England, and the first date at San Francisco's Fillmore West looked promising. Another pleasant surprise: Carlos Santana was making a big splash on American FM with his reworking of "Black Magic Woman," sparking new interest in Fleetwood Mac. However, as soon as they arrived in California, Mick realized that something was not right with Jeremy Spencer: "He and Danny had taken some mescaline upon arrival, and Jeremy didn't seem to come off it for a long time" the drummer would later explain. "Since I roomed with him on the road, I just knew he wasn't doing all that well. He was always a dreamer to begin with; lately he had been immersed in the Bible and all kinds of books on philosophy and changing your life. I could see something might happen."[4] But what was most worrying was that he was putting less and less heart into his work. Before he played at the Fillmore West on February 14, 1971, everyone kept reassuring him for fear that he might not make it onto the stage. That night, against all odds, Spencer probably played his best concert with the Mac. And also his last.

The Sudden Disappearance of Jeremy Spencer

With Fleetwood Mac due to leave San Francisco the following morning for a series of dates at the Whisky a Go Go in Los Angeles, Jeremy confided to Mick, in the privacy of their bedroom, that he would not be traveling with them. The earthquake that struck the San Fernando Valley (not far from Los Angeles) a few days earlier, killing some sixty people, had shaken him to the core. He could not explain it very clearly to Mick, but he was distraught. On the verge of tears, he admitted he had a premonition that something terrible might happen there. Mick tried to reassure him, but he was convinced that Los Angeles was an evil place. Jeremy finally agreed to board the plane, but not without some trepidation. Once settled into his suite at the Hollywood Hawaiian, Jeremy seemed to have calmed down. He then turned to Mick and told him he wanted to go for a walk on Hollywood Boulevard, to find a bookshop he had visited in the past. Mick offered to go with him, but Jeremy preferred to go alone. He never returned.

After a few hours, it became clear that something had happened, and Jeremy had disappeared. Everyone was looking for him, and they were worried. At 6 p.m., the decision was made to cancel the evening concert. A member of the staff remained glued to the phone, just in case...The band scoured the surrounding area, questioning shopkeepers and passersby, but no one had seen Jeremy. Clifford Davis decided to call the police to report his disappearance. He thought either Jeremy had a bad encounter and had been kidnapped or—and this was still the most likely—he had broken down and joined one of the many sects or hippie communities that tried to attract new followers on Hollywood Boulevard every day. Their recruitment technique was aggressive: They claimed that the end of the world was near, and that it was necessary to turn to God in the hope of being saved. Their pitch might well have convinced a self-doubting Spencer, who was ripe for this kind of approach. As the days passed, the Whisky gigs were canceled one after the other, while Clifford Davis maintained contact with the police.

The band was shocked by this sudden departure, which felt like a betrayal. Was Jeremy Spencer really that unhappy? The worst thing was not knowing. His photo was soon broadcast on TV, and the FBI and Interpol were alerted. By the end of the fourth day, a caller suggested to investigators

that Spencer might be with the Children of God sect in Los Angeles, where he was already living under another name.

Clifford Davis, accompanied by road manager Phil McDonnell, went there that evening. After an hour of parleying with cult members who claimed Jeremy was not there, he finally appeared—and was now calling himself Jonathan. His long hair was gone; his head was shaved, and he was dressed in old clothes. For part of the night, Clifford and Phil listened to him explain that he did not want to work anymore, that the earthquake heralded the end of the world, and that he wanted his soul purified before that happened. Fleetwood Mac had become the least of his worries. When Clifford and Phil told him that if he did not resume touring, the band would not survive, he did not bat an eyelid. As for his wife and children, he was not worried about them, either. He was convinced that Jesus would protect them.

The Temporary Return of Peter Green

Back at the hotel, Clifford reported to the rest of the band on the latest tragic news, which could have spelled the end of Fleetwood Mac. There were still six weeks of touring left. It was impossible to abandon the tour without risking bankruptcy. And one could simply not extricate Spencer by force. The operation would be too dangerous. Besides, it was not as if he went to the Children of God under duress. That was his choice. A little later, he flew to a sect property in Texas, where he was joined by Fiona and their son, while their second child remained in Benifold with Fiona's mother. "Jonathan's" job from now on was to recruit new souls to the ranks of the Children of God.

At this time, only one person seemed in a position to come to the group's rescue: Peter Green. An ocean separated them, as he was in England. According to the latest reports, he was in a bad way: His solo album *The End of the Game* was a flop, and he had reportedly sold all his instruments and had become a gravedigger. But Fleetwood Mac were up against it, and Clifford Davis resolved to pick up the phone. He explained the situation to a very detached Peter Green, who was about to take a job as a farmhand. The prospect of returning to the stage did not excite him, but out of friendship he agreed to join the group in the United States. Two days later, he was up and running, but the band, clueless, had to improvise its set every night, with

a heavy emphasis on jamming. Peter did not talk much but was clearly having fun with his friends.

At the end of an eventful eight-week tour, Fleetwood Mac might have been in the doldrums. But when all was said and done, their finances were excellent. There had been very few cancellations, and the arrival of Peter Green clearly helped the band to stay on track and gain in popularity in the United States. Quite simply, it was their best tour ever.

But morale was quickly dampened: Once Peter Green left, no one knew what the future would hold. But there was no question of giving up. The band's entourage advised them to change their name and start afresh. But while half of Fleetwood Mac's original members might have left, the other half were still there and felt they had a right to decide the band's future. Back in Benifold, all options were considered, including begging Jeremy Spencer to come to his senses. Christine McVie was very reluctant to accept this idea, even though, like Danny Kirwan, she could not imagine Fleetwood Mac without a third songwriter. One thing was certain: Clifford Davis had scheduled a UK tour starting June 4. The band had a month in which to come up with the rare gem they needed.

Bob Welch: A Breath of Fresh Air

Jeremy Spencer's sudden departure would trigger the arrival of Bob Welch, a young Californian hippie with a rather well-to-do mother who was an actress and a father who was a film producer. The band's first American, this kid, accustomed to hanging out at Paramount Studios and Hollywood parties, was to become the symbol of the "new" Fleetwood Mac, ready to conquer America in the new decade.

In the spring of 1971, Bob Welch, who had played guitar for the unsuccessful bands Seven Souls and Head West, flew to England. His friend Judy Wong had arranged an audition with Fleetwood Mac, who were still looking for a new guitarist. He was not the first to apply. Welch spent several days in Benifold without actually being auditioned. "Bob never actually played a note," recalls Christine McVie. "All we did was sit around and talk until dawn, and we just thought he was an incredible person. I remember saying to Mick that I didn't even care what his playing was like, he was such a good person. If we'd

hated his guitar work, it would have been a real drag."[34] In fact, the band's main need was reassurance. Still traumatized by the successive departures of Peter Green and Jeremy Spencer, they wanted to be sure that Bob Welch was stable and willing to make his mark on the team. Welch, who hadn't played a single note in a few days, was selected for the job, continuing the Fleetwood Mac tradition of recruiting without an audition.

Welch took advantage of an initial advance from Clifford Davis to buy a new guitar, a Gibson ES-345, which he would use mainly on the record. He then moved to Benifold. The guitarist was surprised by his first steps with Fleetwood Mac. He had expected an approach that was familiar to him in the United States: It was up to the band to provide fresh material, and then he would play what was written for his parts. Instead, he soon realized that he needed to get more involved in the composition, as Danny Kirwan and Jeremy Spencer had been asked to do when recording *Kiln House*. He was given a great deal of freedom. The only order of the day was to get away from the blues. Welch seized the opportunity; he could see that the band's morale was low, and that a new artistic direction needed to be established. Reinventing themselves did not seem to be beyond Fleetwood Mac, but they needed to regain their confidence, and he might well be that long-awaited breath of fresh air.

Martin Rushent controlled the console for *Future Games*. Trained as a sound engineer, he went on to produce for other bands, including the Stranglers and Telephone.

FOR MAC-ADDICTS

There are two different shades for the jacket, depending on the year of publication. The first pressing in 1971 featured a predominantly orange-yellow color. The following year, the record was reissued with a water-green jacket, much to the delight of collectors.

In the Studio, Looking to the Future

From June and July 1971 onward, Welch was put through his paces on the band's UK dates. The hardest part for him was singing songs he had written in front of a large audience, something he had never really done before. But he managed it well, and the songs he came up with appealed to everyone. The band took advantage of this good run to record *Future Games* at Advision Studios in London.

No producer was on hand to direct operations. Only Martin Rushent, the sound engineer, was available to assist. Only twenty-three years old, he had little experience. After arriving at Advision Studios as a projectionist, he began working in the audio department as a tape operator alongside Tony Visconti. He was then drafted in as engineer on a major project, *Jesus Christ Superstar*, in 1970, followed by T. Rex's legendary *Electric Warrior* in 1971.

In the studio, decisions were taken collegially, even though the unpredictable Danny Kirwan sometimes disappeared without warning, only to reappear a few days later with a new song. Bob Welch found it hardest to bond with him, but for the time being, they managed to cooperate.

Musically, their contributions were different. Welch, for his part, steered Fleetwood Mac definitively toward Californian pop rock with "Lay It All Down," but above all with "Future Games," an epic title track lasting more than eight minutes. It is impossible not to hear the influence of Crosby, Stills, Nash & Young in it, as well as the evocation of the wide-open spaces of the American West. Welch was also clearly responsible for introducing the chiseled vocal harmonies. It was he who came up with the idea of interweaving and equalizing female and male vocals, a process that was to become the band's

trademark. Without this starting point, without Bob Welch, it would probably have been impossible to imagine the grafting of Lindsey Buckingham and Stevie Nicks to the band a few years later.

Assuming a more central role, Danny Kirwan created a kind of progressive soft rock, a little like Wishbone Ash, but with a penchant for long, sometimes slightly hazy instrumental passages, as evidenced by the uneven "Woman of 1000 Years," "Sands of Time," and "Sometimes."

As for Christine McVie, with "Morning Rain" and the pop ballad "Show Me a Smile," she made a most promising official entry into the band. "What a Shame" was co-written by the whole band, and its title sounded like a collective message to Jeremy Spencer, expressing the disappointment caused by his departure.

New Beginning

With its eight tracks, *Future Games* is both a transitional album and a new beginning. Its cover features Kells and Tiffany—the children of Mick Fleetwood's sister Sally. They are playing happily in the River Nadder, not far from Salisbury. The metaphor is obvious: The children crystallize the hopes that the band is pinning on its new opus, the aptly named *Future Games*, after choosing to give their own future a new artistic direction. On the back cover, each of the musicians has his or her own photo, with the exception of John McVie, who prefers to be represented by a penguin, an animal that fascinated him to such an extent that he later had one tattooed on his arm. In any case, it was from this moment on that the creature became a permanent part of Fleetwood Mac's imagery.

Photographed with his bandmates in the woods near Kiln House, Bob Welch (far left) shared composition work with Danny Kirwan and, to a lesser extent, Christine McVie.

In England, the release of *Future Games* went relatively unnoticed, but on the other side of the Atlantic, Fleetwood Mac managed to invent a future for themselves by entering the Billboard 200 at number ninety-one. Nevertheless, the critics were sometimes harsh, such as *Rolling Stone* journalist Lloyd Grossman, who described the record as "thoroughly unsatisfactory"[35] on its release. He went even further: "It is thin and anemic-sounding and I get the impression that no one involved really put very much into it. If Fleetwood Mac have tried to make the transition from an energetic rocking British blues band to a softer more 'contemporary' rock group, they have failed. If they have simply lost interest, I hope they regain it in time to salvage what was once a very promising band."[35]

One thing was certain: Never before had Fleetwood Mac sounded so far removed from the original band, and that was exactly what they wanted. A new US tour in support of the album was on the horizon, and Fleetwood Mac intended to use it to relaunch themselves once and for all.

However, not all the problems went away with the arrival of Bob Welch. Firstly, Clifford Davis was not convinced Welch was the right choice, and the two men did not like each other. John McVie's conduct (and in particular his relationship with alcohol) was also of great concern to Christine, who was becoming less and less tolerant of his excesses. It was not unusual for tension to mount between them. The others were well aware of this—a new start, especially for Christine, would doom the group. As the captain of a band that was as anarchic as they came, Mick Fleetwood managed to calm the young woman down. The McVies had to get along at all costs, since Fleetwood Mac's survival depended on it. The next few months would clearly be crucial.

Despite staying in the charts for twelve weeks after its release in the United States, the commercial success of *Future Games* was slow in coming. It was not until October 4, 2000, that it was certified a gold disc by the Recording Industry Association of America, rewarding half a million copies sold in the country.

CHRISTINE McVIE, THE PERFECT ARTIST

Born on July 12, 1943, in Bouth, Lancashire, Christine Anne Perfect spent her early years in the rather gloomy industrial city of Birmingham. Her father, Cyril Perfect, was a university lecturer as well as a musician, playing violin in the Birmingham Symphony Orchestra. Cyril's own father was once organist at Westminster Abbey. This was doubtless a portent of the golden destiny awaiting Christine at the keyboard. Her mother, Beatrice, could have foreseen this, as she claimed to be a medium and a healer. Sometimes she went ghost hunting with other members of the local psychic research association, much to the dismay of little Christine, who dreamed of having a "normal" mother.

A Complete Talent

The little girl's daily environment was lulled by music. She learned to play the piano at the age of four, then took classical lessons for several years. She was introduced to Fats Domino by her older brother, and she took up the guitar and started singing whenever she could.

By the age of sixteen, she was regularly heading for London with friends to try her luck in the capital's talent agencies. She sang a few Everly Brothers tunes to make a good impression, but for the time being it was not enough. So, like many good musicians of her generation, she headed off to art school in Birmingham, where she met Spencer Davis, an impressive specialist in German literature but above all an excellent musician. She fell for him to some extent, she jokingly admitted, to the point of secretly starting a diet. She and Davis led the university jazz band for a while until Davis was thrilled to discover the talent of fifteen-year-old Steve Winwood, who played blues piano in the Chapel Pub at lunchtime. Along with Winwood, Davis formed the Spencer Davis Group, which soon took off.

Christine dreamed of doing the same with her own band. In 1964, at the age of twenty-one, she joined another local band, Sounds of Blue, in which she played keyboards with Andy Sylvester on bass, Stan Webb on guitar, and Chris Wood on saxophone. The adventure lasted only a year, but it left a lasting impression, as the group developed a repertoire that nobody else in the Midlands was playing, largely inspired by Mose Allison, Ray Charles, and Amos Milburn.

The Chicken Shack Adventure

Well educated and well presented, she had no trouble finding a job in London, on Regent Street, at Dickins & Jones, a well-known clothing store. But the atmosphere was not good, and the job of window dresser not very fulfilling. In fact, she was bored out of her mind. Her friend Andy Sylvester, the bassist with Sounds of Blue, called her in 1966 to ask her to join Chicken Shack, the band he was about to form with guitarist Stan Webb. It was the signal she had been waiting for to change her life. Admittedly, she was not yet a blues piano specialist, but on Andy Sylvester's recommendation, she assimilated the entire Freddie King discography, and King was accompanied by the excellent pianist Sonny Thompson, whose style she meticulously studied. Initially a mimic, she gradually developed her own technique and quickly became one of the pillars of Chicken Shack's success. Few women were involved in the blues scene in 1967, and the beautiful Christine soon made her mark. At the time, blues bands were often judged on the virtuosity of their guitarists, and Chicken Shack was no exception with Stan Webb. His unkempt, gangly figure was no real threat to guitarists of the caliber of Peter Green or Eric Clapton, but he had enough drive to attract attention, and Christine Perfect's extraordinary voice, at once sweet and plaintive, but also stunningly in tune, did the rest.

Meeting John McVie

Christine Perfect first met John McVie at a Fleetwood Mac concert in early 1968. He did not really catch her eye that night, as she was more interested in Peter Green. "But John asked me if I wanted a drink and we sat down and had a few laughs before they went on stage,"[36] Christine recalls. "Then after the concert he came over and said, 'Shall I take you out to dinner some time?' I went, 'Whoa, I thought you were engaged or something.' He said, 'Nah, it's all over.' I thought he was devastatingly attractive but it never occurred to me to look at him."[36]

They went out for a short time, before John went off on Fleetwood Mac's first US tour. "By this time I was really crazy about him," Christine recalls. "But I didn't really know what was happening with him."[36] The romance was put on hold when Christine left for Germany with Chicken Shack. There, a brief affair with a German disc jockey made her realize her feelings for John. She decided to write him a long letter about it. On her return to England, the two lovebirds reunited. John proposed to Christine, and the ceremony took place ten days later, in August 1968, so that Christine's dying mother could attend.

She became tired of the touring life, which was clearly getting in the way of her dream of a more or less normal family life. So Christine McVie decided to leave Chicken

The much-missed Christine McVie, as discreet as she was essential, passed away on November 30, 2022.

Shack and become a housewife. However, Mike Vernon convinced her to take part in sessions for a solo album in the autumn of 1969. While Chicken Shack enjoyed huge success in Europe (and even its only real hit) with Christine's vocals on "I'd Rather Go Blind," she let herself be tempted by one last turn on the dance floor, put together a band after a few auditions—which she christened the Christine Perfect Band—then set off on tour again. But this tour did not rekindle the flame. Worse still, it went badly, and it was not uncommon for Christine to leave the stage in tears. With her self-confidence badly shaken, the young woman decided to take a further step back from the music world… just as her album *Christine Perfect* was released by Blue

Horizon. The lack of success of this first opus confirmed her decision. However, her retirement was not to last long. In the summer of 1970, just two months later, she joined her husband in Fleetwood Mac to make up for Peter Green's departure. First unofficially on the recorded album *Kiln House* (she had already appeared on the previous album, *Then Play On*, without being credited), then as a full member on the ensuing US tour.

She immediately proved to be an indispensable musical asset to the band, writing or co-writing some of their biggest hits, including "Don't Stop," "Little Lies," "Everywhere," "You Make Loving Fun," "Over My Head," and "Say You Love Me."

She knew how to adapt and was able to move from blues to pop with ease when the band embarked on their new direction with the release of their five American albums between 1971 and 1974. With the help of Bob Welch, she introduced Fleetwood Mac to vocal harmonies, which reached their peak of mastery with Lindsey Buckingham and Stevie Nicks, and rivaled those of the Beatles or Crosby, Stills & Nash. Christine also gave the impression of never forcing a composition: She never struggled, she wrote quickly, earning the admiration of the rest of the band. "Songbird," for example, took just thirty minutes to compose.

But Christine was not only a great musician with an extraordinary ability to adapt: She was also an invaluable stabilizing element over the following decades, marked by departures, feuds, ego wars, and divorces (including her own, in the middle of a tour in 1976, largely due to John McVie's alcoholism). Her ability to accept situations and analyze them coolly, and her stoicism, were as important as Mick Fleetwood's energy in keeping the band on course. Although not an angel, she managed to avoid falling into the yawning abyss that lurked for those in her company who abused drugs and alcohol.

A Life-Saving Departure

Between *Mirage* (1982) and *Tango in the Night* (1987)—the only two albums released by Fleetwood Mac during this decade—she found time to release a second solo opus, *Christine McVie*, whose two hits "Love Will Show Us How" and "Got a Hold on Me," landed at number thirty and number ten, respectively, on the US Billboard charts, and proved to the world her talent as a songwriter, even outside Fleetwood Mac.

But in the midst of the chaos, after *Tango in the Night* and the sudden departure of Lindsey Buckingham, she and the rest of the band struggled to regroup for the 1990 album *Behind the Mask*. The album, like its successor in 1995, *Time*, did not meet her expectations. Between these two albums, Christine, exhausted, took a break from the band.

But in between the two albums, she was honored when her song "Don't Stop" was chosen by Democratic candidate Bill Clinton for his presidential campaign, and on January 20, 1993, as he was inaugurated as the forty-second president of the United States, a specially reformed Fleetwood Mac took to the stage at the White House to perform it. This adventure paved the way for *Time* as well as for the album *The Dance* and its tour, in 1997. With Fleetwood Mac back at the top of the charts, and the band inducted into the Rock and Roll Hall

of Fame in 1998, Christine again felt the need to take a step back. She was exhausted from touring: Going onstage was no longer as exhilarating, the lights blinded her, she felt disoriented, and she needed to find some peace and quiet. Few were worried at the time, telling themselves that, as usual, she would be back after one or two years. But her break lasted fifteen years. And she never really missed music.

"I was tired of living out of a suitcase,"[37] she confided. "My father was sick. I'd reached a point when I felt I needed to get back to my roots." There was also her fear of flying, which limited her travel and touring options. "It was a clear-cut decision to move back to England. I relinquished my green card and moved lock, stock, and barrel back to England. They tried to persuade me not to leave, but my mind was made up."[37] "She was just in need of a radical life change,"[38] Lindsey Buckingham explained in an interview with *Rolling Stone* in 2013. "She pretty much burned all her bridges in Los Angeles. She sold her house, ended her relationship, quit the band and moved back to England."[38]

Christine settled in Canterbury, where she was content with a daily routine punctuated by long walks with her dogs, hours indulging her passion for painting, restoring her seventeenth-century redbrick home, and watching TV. The woman who admitted during the wild Fleetwood Mac years that she never hesitated to raise a glass (or several) of champagne in the late evenings, was now content with a cup of tea and a small chocolate before bedtime, usually around 9 p.m. She interrupted her semiretirement in 2004, when she released her third solo album, *In the Meantime*, in the company of her nephew Dan Perfect, whom she wanted to please. It was also a therapeutic choice, as Christine tried to overcome the failure of her second marriage to Portuguese musician Eddy Quintela.

Christine had not cut ties with her Fleetwood Mac friends, however. Whenever the band performed in London, she watched them from backstage before meeting up with them again after the show. But at no point did she feel that she had made the wrong decision—quite the contrary.

The Last Dance

It all led up to that evening in 2013, when she joined Fleetwood Mac onstage at London's O2 to perform "Don't Stop." She felt overwhelmed. After several days, she decided to pick up the phone and call Mick. What would he, and of course the rest of the band, think if she decided to return to Fleetwood Mac? After a few internal discussions on the

Christine McVie at the Paramount Theatre in Denver, Colorado, July 27, 2017.

terms of her reintegration, everyone was obviously enthusiastic, including Stevie Nicks, who had been living without her best friend all this time: "It was very hard for me," said Nicks. "It became very much the boys' club, a lot of testosterone."[39] The musician's return was the occasion for a gigantic world tour, "On with the Show," with seventy-eight sold-out dates. By this time, a new Fleetwood Mac album was even being considered. Christine and Lindsey contributed material, and in the studio, John and Mick seemed to be on board. However, Stevie did not take part, and Christine and Lindsey decided to turn it into an album of duets, entitled *Lindsey Buckingham Christine McVie*. It was released in 2017, and John and Mick were listed in the credits.

The following year, the internal quarrels between Lindsey and Stevie came to a head, leading to the guitarist's acrimonious departure, and he was replaced by Mike Campbell and Neil Finn. Despite this, Christine did not leave Fleetwood Mac for all that, and would never leave again, acquitting herself with a major tour in 2018–2019. By this time, she was already suffering from severe back pain caused by scoliosis. She now sometimes played sitting down, much to her chagrin. And although Mick pushed to reunite the classic lineup in 2021 and, why not, record a new album, the miracle was never to happen.

Almost resigned, Christine modestly confided to journalists that, as she approached her eightieth birthday, all she could hope for was to have a few more years ahead of her. In the midsummer of 2021, she began to detach herself from her glorious past and sold most of her rights to

Hipgnosis, including those to the hits "Say You Love Me," "Little Lies," "Don't Stop," "You Make Loving Fun," "Think About Me," and "Save Me." Shortly before the summer of 2022, when asked about Fleetwood Mac's future plans, she replied with a touch of disillusionment, first mentioning the replacements for Lindsey Buckingham, Mike Campbell, and Neil Finn: "Those guys were great," said McVie. "We have a great time with them, but we've kind of broke up now, so I hardly ever see them." Fleetwood Mac fans were even more disappointed when they read the rest of Christine's confidences: "I don't communicate with Stevie [Nicks] very much either," she says. "When we were on the last tour, we did a lot. We always sat next to each other on the plane and we got on really well. But since the band broke up, I've not been speaking to her at all."[40]

Everyone understood that Fleetwood Mac no longer really existed, even though Christine left a small window open, without really believing it: "We might get back together, but I just couldn't say for sure. [...] I don't feel physically up for it," she said. "I'm in quite bad health. I've got a chronic back problem which debilitates me. [...] The mind is willing, but the flesh is weak."[40] But here again, there would be no miracle. A few weeks later, on the morning of November 30, 2022, Christine McVie died at the age of seventy-nine.

Mick Fleetwood wrote a poignant tribute to the woman who had spent so many years with the band, concluding with the words: "The best musician anyone could have in their band and the best friend anyone could have in their life."

BOB WELCH, THE CALIFORNIAN POP-ROCK SOUND

Bob Welch, whose real name was Robert Lawrence Welch Jr., was born on August 31, 1945, in Los Angeles, California, into a family with deep roots in local show business. His father, Robert Lawrence Welch Sr., was a Hollywood producer and screenwriter for Paramount Pictures, spending his days with such well-known actors as Bob Hope and Bing Crosby. His mother, Templeton Fox, started out as a singer before becoming an actress, working mainly for Metro-Goldwyn-Mayer productions.

Heading Toward a Future as a Studio Musician

Although little Bob spent most of his time on the set waiting for his parents, he soon developed a taste for the arts himself, first learning the clarinet, and then, like most teenagers of the time, the guitar. He showed as much interest in jazz as in rhythm'n'blues and, a little later, rock. Admitted to the prestigious Georgetown University (a Catholic institution of higher learning run by the Jesuits), he instead headed for France and Paris, where he studied at the Sorbonne. Or so he would have his parents believe—in reality, he spent most of his time in cafés or smoking hashish with older students. Having been summarily repatriated to the United States, he made a few unconvincing appearances at the University of California (UCLA) to study French. The young man soon decided to devote himself to his true passion: music. Starting in 1964, he found a position as guitarist in the group the Seven Souls, which, despite a few good songs such as "I'm No Stranger" and "I Still Love You," made its mark mainly as a backing band for soul stars such as Aretha Franklin and James Brown, who sometimes traveled without their own musicians.

The group disbanded in 1969 and, after a lackluster ending, Bob took drummer Henry Moore and organist Robert Hunt on board to try his luck in Europe with a new R&B trio, Head West. The trio did not last long either; it released a single eponymous album on Vogue in France in 1970, before dissolving into anonymity.

GIBSON LOVER

Bob Welch loved Gibson guitars, even though he sometimes opted for Fender. Faithful to the Les Paul, he often played an SG Custom during his years with Fleetwood Mac and, occasionally, an EDS-1275 twin.

Four Years with Fleetwood Mac

In 1971, just as Bob was about to return to the United States to take up a guitarist's job at Stax Records in Memphis, his friend Judy Wong (the "Jewel Eyed Judy" of the song), Fleetwood Mac's office manager for many years and a friend of the rock stars of the day, informed him that the band was looking for a guitarist following the unexpected departure of Jeremy Spencer. She organized the meeting, even though Fleetwood Mac had already held a few unsuccessful auditions. Bob flew to Benifold. After several days, the guitarist was accepted and became the band's first American member.

Bob Welch's arrival marked the beginning of a new era for Fleetwood Mac, enabling them to evolve from their blues-rock roots toward a Californian pop-rock sound. He was also the man who convinced the Mac to move to Los Angeles and make their mark there for good. His guitar playing was precise and versatile. Sometimes swift, sometimes delicate, he adapted to a wide range of styles depending on the circumstances. This jazzman, also a fan of blues and folk, was particularly fond of two-guitar playing, creating superb combinations, notably with Danny Kirwan, even though Welch did not really like him.

Welch remained with the band from 1971 to 1974, contributing to five albums. He also wrote some hits, including "Sentimental Lady" and "Ebony Eyes." Four years during which he was under a great deal of pressure, from studio sessions to long tours. Four years during which he experienced a great deal of friction with Danny Kirwan (who threw in the towel in 1972). Four years during which he began to drink heavily and damaged his marriage. At the

Bob Welch left a lasting imprint on Fleetwood Mac's repertoire, penning such iconic songs as "Future Games," "Sentimental Lady," "Hypnotized," and "Emerald Eyes."

end of 1974, exhausted, Bob Welch decided to resign from Fleetwood Mac.

A Tragic End

Even so, he was not finished with music. In 1975, he formed the short-lived trio Paris with former Jethro Tull bassist Glenn Cornick and former Nazz drummer Thom Mooney. Two albums were released but were not commercially successful. He then embarked on a solo career, with a debut album entitled *French Kiss* in 1977, which included a cover of his hits "Sentimental Lady" and "Ebony Eyes." Welch released a number of albums in the 1980s. His manager was none other than Mick Fleetwood, confirming that relations with his former Mac comrades remained friendly.

They became more acrimonious in 1994, however, when Bob sued the band and Warner Bros. Records for breach of contract, claiming nonpayment of royalties owed to him. Although the lawsuit was settled out of court in 1996, not everything seems to have been resolved: When the band was inducted into the Rock and Roll Hall of Fame in 1998, Bob Welch was not one of the musicians nominated. According to Welch, he had been "forgotten" because of his recent differences with the band, even though he had been instrumental in saving it in the early 1970s.

He eventually reconnected with his ex-colleagues, notably Mick Fleetwood, in the early 2000s. But weakened by spinal surgery in the early spring of 2012 and undermined by doctors' diagnoses of short-term disability, he chose to end his life on June 7 of that year, shooting himself in the chest in his Memphis home. The sixty-six-year-old guitarist left a multipage suicide note and a love letter to his wife, Wendy, who outlived him by only four years.

WOMAN OF 1000 YEARS

Danny Kirwan / 5:28

Musicians
Danny Kirwan: vocals, guitar
Bob Welch: vocals, guitar
Christine McVie: keyboards, backing vocals
John McVie: bass
Mick Fleetwood: percussions

Recorded
Advision Studios, London, June–August 1971

Technical Team
Producer: Fleetwood Mac
Sound Engineer: Martin Rushent

A poem by Rupert Brooke, known for his pacifist works, directly influenced Danny Kirwan's writing of "Woman of 1000 Years."

Genesis and Lyrics

Kirwan had already demonstrated his interest in poetry on "Dragonfly," a song released as a single in 1971, for which he had overtly borrowed the words of Welsh poet William Henry Davies. On "Bare Trees," in 1972, he appropriated a text by Rupert Brooke for "Dust," this time covertly. In between the two, the guitarist tried his hand at poetic art on his own, with relative success. "Woman of 1000 Years" is one of those vaguely lyrical attempts that show a gap between intentions and results. The song was recorded at a time when the band, wishing to make a major stylistic change, was riding the progressive rock wave that was flourishing at the time in the wake of such seminal works as King Crimson's *In the Court of the Crimson King* (1969), Genesis's *Trespass* (1970), and Jethro Tull's *Aqualung* (1971).

Formats were stretched, soundscapes were expanded, and lyrics became tinged with mysticism. Love relationships are no longer treated in the same way as in the blues. The blues love story—Manichean (dualistic)—was too often limited (at least for the models chosen by the Mac) to treating the theme of the breakup through the lens of judgment: who was at fault, who was the more deserving. Progressive rock, on the other hand, opened onto a poetry of medieval, mystical origin, where the female figure is depicted as a diaphanous, fragile, inaccessible beauty. The love story is as timeless as a tale passed down orally through the ages. The tragic and the cursed invite themselves in, as if to magnify the legend of its protagonists.

Kirwan's lyrics and his mysterious, allegorical title "The Woman of 1000 Years" is right in line with this trend. The enigmatic dimension is quickly dispelled, however. First of all, we understand that the half-aquatic, half-aerial being as described by Kirwan, somewhere between a mermaid and a sylph, has left a man who has spent his life mourning her. "Your silvered ways / As you go down to the sea" validates the vision of a marine creature with shiny scales. Whereas "Flying down from a high / She is gone and then appears" is more suggestive of a winged figure. But the truth may lie elsewhere, and it could be the moon: its silvery reflections ("your silvered ways"), its movements in the sky ("as you go down to the sea"), its role as a guide for the "fisherman."

On "Woman of 1000 Years," Mick Fleetwood abandons his drum kit to demonstrate his facility on percussion (1973).

Production

With this composition, Kirwan can finally express the musical desires that drive him. The shadow of Peter Green has receded, and the American folk color brought by Bob Welch's playing is more in keeping with his universe than that of Jeremy Spencer. The summery recording is also a perfect match for the sunny mood of the track. While the band is still predominantly British, the transition to Californian rock is underway with this track, which displays a rarely achieved refinement. It opens with the tender caress of strumming acoustic guitar. With great skill, Martin Rushent gradually builds up its presence in the mix, gracing it with ever-greater resonance. The melodious instrumental background and finely honed vocal harmonies are unmistakably reminiscent of Crosby, Stills & Nash. Mick Fleetwood aptly introduces bongos and woodblocks to give the whole an Asian, psychedelic feel. A more apt choice than drums played with the brushes. This would have weighed the whole thing down and broken the airy fragility of the track. The melodic, dreamlike odyssey progresses with variations in key dictated by the guitar. Each time, Kirwan chooses the chord that will create the thrill and surprise, without ever disrupting the harmony. The track thus meanders between melancholy and grace, a sensation largely due to the fact that the track tilts neither into minor nor into major, but stands on the fine line between the two, as the introduction is based on *Sus2* (suspended) chords.

MORNING RAIN

Christine McVie / 5:39

Musicians
Christine McVie: vocals, keyboards
Danny Kirwan: guitar, backing vocals
Bob Welch: guitar, backing vocals
John McVie: bass
Mick Fleetwood: drums

Recorded
Advision Studios, London, June–August 1971

Technical Team
Producer: Fleetwood Mac
Sound Engineer: Martin Rushent

FOR MAC-ADDICTS

The song was unveiled at the start of the year, on January 5, 1971, during one of the BBC sessions. It was then called "Start Again," a title even more transparent in terms of its theme.

Christine McVie's personality and influence shine in her composition "Morning Rain."

Genesis and Lyrics

Christine McVie, who does not feature prominently on the album's first track, distinguishes herself with "Morning Rain," a curmudgeonly pop number that shakes things up as much by its music as by its message, and contrasts sharply with the ethereal enchantment of "Woman of 1000 Years." In this song, Christine seems to address the band bluntly. She sweeps aside past procrastination and calls for the band's renewal: "We've got to start again […] / There's no use complaining / It's the only way / There's no use feeling dissatisfied / Cause how can you know until you've tried?" In case her injunction to ignore the past and look to the future is not clear enough, she dots the *i*'s and crosses the *t*'s by singing: "The future's new and the past is dead." She also hints at the meaning of the album's name, *Future Games*. Although recently made an official member of the Mac, the musician was far from a novice, having regularly contributed to the band's songs as a guest since the second album. She thus enjoys a privileged status as intermediary between the "old" founding members and the newcomer, enabling her to call for a clean sweep of a past to which she is not overly attached while enjoying the legitimacy to drive change.

Production

To create a break with the ethereal ambience of the first track, the decision was taken to make a very abrupt start by opening with a percussive-style keyboard part by Christine McVie. The newcomer, who does not hesitate to take the reins on this track, installs a very rich melodic line that Kirwan chooses to reproduce identically. A slight gap is maintained between the two tracks, so that they do not interfere with each other and give body to the melody. The guitar, serving only as a support, is then pushed to the back of the mix. A far more logical choice than that of passing Bob Welch's guitar through a wah-wah. Emerging little by little, the effect brings real rhythmic added value and diversifies Fleetwood Mac's instrumental panorama. Until then, only Peter Green had used it, and then only rarely and only on recordings. Unfortunately, after this guitar had burst through the left channel and into the right, the band chose

Christine McVie seeks to shock her bandmates awake, rejecting their general despondency following Danny Kirwan's departure.

to reduce it to a mere whisper in the mix. Instead, a fuzz guitar is used for solid, biting, powerful solos.

Christine McVie's vocal performance starts off on the cautious side during the verses, only to bounce back on the bridge. In the midst of the boiling sound, her voice emerges, strong and passionate. She plunges with ease into the lower register, preserving both roughness and harmony. Her partners' voices become more present in the finale, when everyone sings "do, do, do, do" at the top of their voices. More than an onomatopoeia, given the content, these lyrics are above all an incitement to action.

John Perfect also contributed to his sister Christine's solo album, *In the Meantime*, released in 2004. The album assumes the character of a family reunion, with John's son, Daniel, also contributing backing vocals.

FOR MAC-ADDICTS

Render unto Caesar what is Caesar's: Peter Green finally got to exploit the riff he had left uncultivated, and which Fleetwood Mac hastened to cultivate in his absence. He created "Just for You," a 1979 track included on his *In the Skies* album.

WHAT A SHAME

Bob Welch, Mick Fleetwood, Danny Kirwan, John McVie, Christine McVie / 2:20

Musicians: Danny Kirwan: guitar / Bob Welch: guitar / Christine McVie: keyboards / John McVie: bass / Mick Fleetwood: drums / John Perfect: saxophone / **Recorded:** Advision Studios, London, June–August 1971 / **Technical Team:** Producer: Fleetwood Mac / Sound Engineer: Martin Rushent

Genesis

They say that the sequence of tracks on an album shapes a story. After Christine McVie's motivational speech calling for a collective effort in "Morning Rain," all the members join forces to create "What a Shame," a two-minute, twenty second instrumental. So much for the legend. The reality is more prosaic: This collective work, improvised during a jam session, was recorded at the end of the session to make up for the lack of tracks that had been pointed out by the record company. Seven tracks, however long they may be, are not enough to constitute an album worthy of the name, and the band was ordered to complete the set list. The result is a spontaneous creation taken from an eight-minute jam session that has been known since it was unveiled as a bonus track on the album's 2020 reissue. As a collective work, all the members of the band are credited on "What a Shame," as well as saxophonist John Perfect, called upon specifically for this track by his little sister, Christine McVie.

To launch this improvisation, a riff, a pattern, a phrasing was needed. Annihilating all the fine intentions sketched out by Christine McVie's speech in the previous song about the need to move forward and bury the past, Kirwan finds nothing better than to engage in musical spiritualism and invoke the ghost of Peter Green. Indeed, the guitarist remembers an old, unused riff by his bandmate and leads the whole band down this path.

Production

John Perfect, no doubt anxious not to overplay his guest role on this track and distort Fleetwood Mac's identity, is initially content to reproduce the theme developed by one of the guitars. But during the mixing stage, the saxophone's contribution is emphasized to the detriment of the guitars, giving the impression that the saxophonist is calling the shots. All the more so when, in the middle of the track, the theme has shifted enough for him to indulge in a jazzy solo.

On the other hand, the funky guitar, undoubtedly played by Welch, which provides the groove and soul of the track, is inexplicably buried in the mix. A highly unfortunate decision, since the instrument formed a highly effective partnership with Christine McVie's Fender Rhodes–like keyboards. The only merit of this mix is that it enhances the rhythm section, which works wonders in the lower end of the spectrum. The bass, in particular, delivers its groove with authority in the lower registers. The mix turns out to be dubious, but not as dubious as the editing, which cuts just two minutes and twenty seconds from an improvisation that lasted more than eight minutes. This damaging salami-slicing leaves out the most interesting and meaty parts, notably the introduction and finale, which contained intense, technical guitar passages. It is clear that the song has been rushed and sacrificed on the altar of the record company's demands, to the detriment of artistic interest. The song would have required longer maturation and should not have become an instrumental. A lead vocal had in fact been envisaged on the eight-minute first version. In the middle of the mash, the phrase that gave the song its name emerged: "What a shame." A fitting interjection.

Bob Welch would revisit his composition eight years later, on his solo album *The Other One* (1979), as well as on *His Fleetwood Mac Years and Beyond* (2003).

FUTURE GAMES

Bob Welch / 8:14

Musicians: Bob Welch: vocals, guitar / Danny Kirwan: vocals, guitar / Christine McVie: keyboards, backing vocals / John McVie: bass / Mick Fleetwood: drums / **Recorded:** Advision Studios, London, June–August 1971 / **Technical Team:** Producer: Fleetwood Mac / Sound Engineer: Martin Rushent

Genesis and Lyrics

"Future Games," the title track of this fifth album, is the bravura moment of Bob Welch's first contribution to Fleetwood Mac. From the outset, the singer and musician sets out to make his mark with this epic track, which spans more than eight minutes—a record length in Fleetwood Mac's studio discography. The musician takes the band down the path of cosmic progressive pop, a path the band had never taken before "Woman of 1000 Years," from the same session. Bob Welch thus asserts his personality and maturity; his lyrics do not lapse into the blissful, sentimental platitudes that the cottony melody he has fashioned for the occasion might induce.

In fact, it is from his words, which take up the notion of the future, that the album's name is born: "I know I'm not the only one / [...] playing future games." He echoes Christine McVie's lyrics in "Morning Rain," and he seems to display the same apparent optimism, believing that the band's destiny lies in the hands of the musicians: "You invent the future that you want to face." An ambiguous and unsettling sentence, as it hints at a form of uncertainty. Yes, we are masters of our own destiny, but it may not be as bright as we had hoped. He also injects a form of universalism into his text, following the trends of the time, inspired by lyricists such as John Lennon: "I know I'm not the only one" thus responds to Lennon's "But I'm not the only one" from "Imagine," recorded a few weeks earlier.

Production

Danny Kirwan and Bob Welch display an admirable cohesion on this track, even though their conceptions of music later proved irreconcilable and their characters incompatible. They take the lead in turns, showing off their extraordinary touch and inventiveness. The two musicians combine their guitar playing to perfection, maintaining groove and imagination. Particularly Welch, who, after the intro (on which he plays all the strings in alternating directions), sprinkles the melody with typically jazz-oriented, totally unexpected chord sequences. Bob Welch was "one of those jazz guitarists that could just play any chord in the

Bob Welch composes a first piece worthy of his immense guitar talent with the psychedelic, ethereal title song of *Future Games*.

world,"[41] said Stevie Nicks, who performed with him onstage. The track opens with a majestic chorus that sounds like it was crafted by the Beach Boys. It exits on the chiming chords of the introduction. Kirwan's blues sensibility then comes to the fore with a velvety-smooth phrasing that echoes the main theme. This gradually builds to a crescendo that reaches its climax in the coda, featuring a solo by John McVie. Apart from this intervention, the bass remains relatively discreet, an exception on an album on which it benefits from an advantageous mix. Christine, for her part, is content to provide accompaniment, installing aerial, futuristic layers with sounds reminiscent of Ray Manzarek (the Doors). Welch's vocals are doubled, and Martin Rushent adds a slight echo. This method adds a little flesh to the vocals, which were sounding a little thin. Bob Welch's vocals have the same qualities and shortcomings as Danny Kirwan's: very pure, beautiful vocals, which work perfectly in rich choral arrangements, but which lack scope and power on their own. But both Welch and Rushent were well aware that an exceptional track like this could not suffer from such a weakness.

All the sensitivity and complexity of Danny Kirwan's character are expressed on "Sands of Time."

SANDS OF TIME

Danny Kirwan / 7:24

Musicians: Danny Kirwan: vocals, guitar / Bob Welch: guitar, backing vocals / Christine McVie: keyboards, backing vocals / John McVie: bass / Mick Fleetwood: drums, percussions / **Recorded:** Advision Studios, London, June–August 1971 / **Technical Team:** Producer: Fleetwood Mac / Sound Engineer: Martin Rushent

Genesis and Lyrics

Challenged by Welch's display of talent on *Future Games*, Kirwan's songwriting reaches new heights of subtlety on "Sands of Time." His song makes a fine play on the contrasts between light and darkness, as much in the musical mood as in the lyrics. This is reflected in the way he composes: He often switches between major and minor keys within the same song, abruptly changing the mood from happy to sad with a simple change of chord. The same pendulum effect can be found in the text. Just as a magical night is taking shape due to the presence at the narrator's side of the woman he loves, the prospect of her departure obscures this moment of happiness: "And before you go show me / All the words of love." The second verse continues in the same fatalistic vein with "And the falling sands of time / blow my wind…" The "falling sands" is that of time inexorably running out, bringing the narrator closer to the end of his romance. "Wondering what the host will send" adds uncertainty and mysticism to the situation. "The host" could mean a deity or fate. Faced with elements beyond his control, the narrator chooses to enjoy the present moment with his loved one. They decide to go to the sea, which is clever as the word "sand" implies a double meaning, referring to both the hourglass and the beach.

Production

Skilled in mood and key variations within the same composition—he alternates between *G* major and its complement, *E* minor—the musician brings together two distinct sections: one with two complementary melodious riffs with a folk sensibility, and another introduced by a violining effect that erases the attack and plays on the progression of the volume. Time is cleverly doubled on this darker, more hypnotic section. Mick Fleetwood, for his part, envelops the wide variety of guitar licks and the multitude of arpeggios with meticulous cymbal playing.

Danny Kirwan was so influenced by George Harrison (here with the Beatles on the roof of Apple Corps Studios, January 30, 1969) that some of his solos, such as the one in "Sometimes," bear the hallmarks of Harrison's guitar work.

SOMETIMES
Danny Kirwan / 5:27

Musicians: Danny Kirwan: vocals, guitar / Bob Welch: guitar / Christine McVie: keyboards / John McVie: bass / Mick Fleetwood: drums / **Recorded:** Advision Studios, London, June–August 1971 / **Technical Team:** Producer: Fleetwood Mac / Sound Engineer: Martin Rushent

Danny Kirwan's admiration for the Beatles extends beyond his own compositions, with a surprising reggae version of "Let It Be" on his 1976 solo album *Midnight in San Juan*. But he is not the only Mac member to have revisited the repertoire of George Harrison's band. Among other tributes, Bob Welch covered "I Saw Her Standing There" on *Three Hearts* (1979), Billy Burnette appropriated "I've Just Seen a Face" on *Soldier of Love* (1986), and Lindsey Buckingham played "Here Comes the Sun" on an ABC New Year's Eve TV show in 2001.

Genesis and Lyrics

"Sometimes" sounds like Danny Kirwan's most blatant attempt to write a radio hit, structured as such with catchy verses, a solid bridge, a unifying chorus, an air-splitting solo, and heady backing vocals. All the ingredients are there, including a touching confession that goes straight to the hearts of the listeners: the story of a man who has lost his love and looks back on the moments he spent with his partner. This time, the lyricist manages to avoid lapsing into pathos, using simple language and images to express the emptiness that grows inside him.

Yet Kirwan abhorred the very principle of radio-friendliness. For him, a song had to exist in its own right before it could be marketed. As he confided to *Melody Maker* in 1969: "Don't listen to radio! I'm interested in songs, and I don't hear that many good ones about. I like good melodies and arrangements—heavy music. I thought that the Beatles last album was a good one, so that's what I'm listening to."[42]

Production

The omnipresence of the keyboards and the swaying rhythm would suggest that this is a new Christine McVie composition, but the elegant arabesques of the country guitar—and, above all, the bridge with its surprising descending chord sequence, strongly reminiscent of John Lennon's "Isolation" (1970)—reveal that it is in fact the work of Danny Kirwan. The former Beatle's imprint is evident even in the vocals: The guitarist does not hesitate to test the limits of his voice's restricted range, as at 1:48 when he shades off in search of high notes that are a little out of reach. But he had learned from listening to Lennon records that imperfections sometimes give a song its fragility and charm. The guitar solo that follows, at 2:00, has the air of a George Harrison flourish, highly melodic and expressive. The lack of vocal accuracy is even more jarring on the upbeat chorus, which could have been the climax of the track's progression but is in fact a weak moment. A great pity, considering the admirable guitar part with a refreshing vibrato that follows.

LAY IT ALL DOWN
Bob Welch / 4:31

Musicians: Bob Welch: vocals, guitar / Danny Kirwan: guitar, backing vocals / Christine McVie: keyboards / John McVie: bass / Mick Fleetwood: drums / **Recorded:** Advision Studios, London, June–August 1971 / **Technical Team:** Producer: Fleetwood Mac / Sound Engineer: Martin Rushent

Genesis and Lyrics

Bob Welch expresses his musical identity through this second contribution, which is minor in comparison with the title track but is useful for its invigorating singularity. Rhythm'n'blues to the core, it stands out in the midst of a mostly quiet, introspective opus, and it has the merit of injecting an energy that this record lacks. Before it surprises with its indelicate petulance amid the ballads of Danny Kirwan and Christine McVie, it does so through the lyrics themselves, which constitute a veritable religious sermon. An unusual (even clumsy) choice for a newcomer, to say the least, when you consider the recent history of Fleetwood Mac, which had recently lost two of its major members, Peter Green and Jeremy Spencer. Both chose a spiritual path that took them away from the band for good. And yet, the band gave Bob Welch carte blanche to follow through on his idea.

The musician draws his inspiration from gospel music to re-create its positive, galvanizing energy. But he does not content himself with the form, writing a veritable homily from the Bible. He slips into the shoes of a Baptist or Pentecostal minister addressing his flock: "Let me retell / A story of old / About a man named Moses / Who lived long ago." All the clichés of the genre are present: the call to

brotherhood ("Let all your sons and your daughters"), the use of the imperative, repeated over and over again ("Lay down your burden"), and the liturgical vocabulary ("prophesied," "golden calf," and "paradise here on earth").

Production

Bob Welch does not push the caricature too far, but his intention is there. And if the song assumes more of a form of a funky rhythm'n'blues, this is because it is the closest thing to the markers of energetic gospel in the guitarist's musical culture. This bouncy jam builds on Bob Welch's fat, punchy, opening riff. It leads the way for the bass, penetrating and groovy, which finally gives John McVie the chance to make the strings vibrate and let loose with percussive attacks and supple playing. Christine McVie would have expected nothing less to deploy her vital, syncopated playing. But it is Mick Fleetwood who is enjoying himself the most. While he is never more inventive than when constrained by a quiet song that forces him to play brushes or bring out a variety of percussion instruments, he also revels in the more energetic tracks, which make greater demands on his bass drum kicks and snare drum slamming. Not to be outdone, Danny Kirwan crosses swords with Bob Welch on a number of solos; the two men divide up their contributions with ease and find ways to coexist intelligently on the tracks. While the cohesion was never real in the studio, on record, and particularly on this track, the two partners give the illusion of being as one, with similar sounds and instinctive, energetic playing.

FOR MAC ADDICTS

The *1969 to 1974* box set brings together the six albums produced during this period, with bonus tracks. It includes an alternative mix of "Lay It All Down," which is clearer and more balanced. The guitars are more polished, the vocals better processed, but the preeminence of the keyboards is lost. The box set also includes the single version of "Sands of Time," other mixes of "Sometimes" and "Show Me a Smile," the "Stone" outtake, and the long, unedited version of "What a Shame."

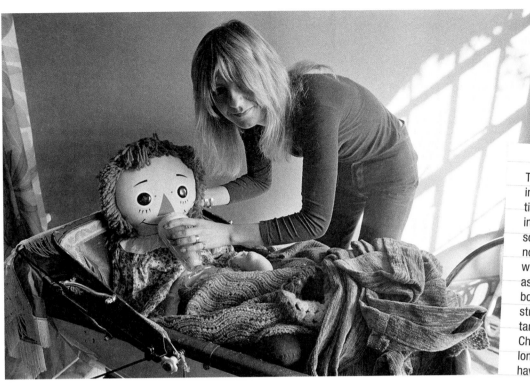

The use of the crash cymbal in this song raised questions within the group, leading to another version of the song being produced but not used. This version, which was released in 2020 as part of the 1969-1974 boxed set, appears more stripped back, with the guitars more to the fore and Christine McVie's voice no longer doubled as it may have been in the original.

SHOW ME A SMILE

Christine McVie / 3:21

Musicians: Christine McVie: vocals, keyboards / Danny Kirwan: guitar / Bob Welch: guitar / John McVie: bass / Mick Fleetwood: drums /
Recorded: Advision Studios, London, June–August 1971 /
Technical Team: Producer: Fleetwood Mac / Sound Engineer: Martin Rushent

Genesis and Lyrics

On March 21, 1978, three weeks after signing the papers for her divorce from John McVie—they had been separated for two years—Christine confided in journalist Garth Pearce: "I have reached the stage when my lifestyle and frame of mind is no longer cut out for babies. Where would they fit in?"[43]

She continued: "I have two godchildren, a half brother, and a half sister who is 11. It's great to have them around the house when they visit from England. [...] I can always wave them goodbye at the end of the visit and it makes me realise that I could not take kids on now. With my career, there's no place for them."[43]

This did not stop the musician from showering them with her benevolent, protective gaze, which shines through in "Show Me a Smile" just as it did in her drawing, chosen to illustrate the cover of *Kiln House*. Childhood is the seat of innocence and happiness, according to her tender lyrics: "Shine me a light from your eyes dear / Don't let me see a single tear / [...] Show me a smile / Soon you'll be a man / My little one / So have fun while you can." It thus synthesizes the red threads of the album highlighted by the cliché on the cover: childhood, the need to seize the moment and the future. But like Kirwan in "Sands of Time," she tempers her enthusiasm, implying that the future is uncertain, that adulthood can be cruel, and that it is better to enjoy it while you can: "So have fun while you can / Or there'll be none."

Production

"Show Me a Smile" closes the album just as "Woman of 1000 Years" had opened it, in an atmosphere of consummate gentleness, amid subtle, dreamy, penetrating guitars to which Danny Kirwan points the way. Despite the guitarist's imprint on this song, Christine McVie balances out the number of credits, taking two on the album, as many as Bob Welch. She puts her instrument totally at the service of the song, deliberately choosing a soft, chiming tone for her keyboards that blends with Kirwan's and Welch's clean guitars. A judicious choice that gives the impression of a myriad of notes emanating from a single instrument. The sharpest sound in the midst of this melodic harmony is that of Mick Fleetwood's crash cymbal. Although not very discreet, its diffusive power is essential: With each stroke, the sound seems to disperse in slow motion, accentuating the effect of weightless melody.

Bob Welch had to shelve his acoustic "Stone," as it was incomplete to include on *Future Games*.

STONE
Bob Welch / 2:34

Musicians: Bob Welch: vocals, guitar / Danny Kirwan: guitar /
Recorded: Advision Studios, London, June–August 1971 /
Technical Team: Producer: Fleetwood Mac / Sound Engineer:
Martin Rushent

Forced to record an additional song, "What a Shame," at the insistence of the record company, the Fleetwood Mac musicians had no other song in reserve except "Stone," which was deemed too embryonic and irrelevant to feature on the final disc. Recorded with just two guitars, this track takes the form of a charming acoustic ballad performed by Bob Welch. The raw recording preserves the track's authenticity and lends it an appealingly intimate dimension. One of the two men—certainly Bob Welch—can be heard initiating the count and then setting off into a simple chord progression, while Kirwan provides a discreet accompaniment in keeping with the fireside spirit of this little folk gem. Welch's voice is not always quite right, but it is nuanced and carries with it the tenderness and melancholy of the occasion. If this song had been more polished and set off with careful counter-vocals, it could have made the final selection without blushing. Instead, this unreleased track would have to await the release of the *1969 to 1974* box set in 2020 to emerge from the obscurity to which it had been consigned.

"Open the Door," a Danny Kirwan composition, was immortalized only on stage.

OPEN THE DOOR

Danny Kirwan / 3:04

Musicians: Danny Kirwan: vocals, guitar / Jeremy Spencer: guitar, backing vocals / Christine McVie: keyboards / John McVie: bass / Mick Fleetwood: drums / **Recorded:** January 1971 (?) / **Technical Team:** (?)

Immortalized live and included on the live compilations *Preaching the Blues* and *Madison Blues*, "Open the Door" did not find favor with a studio recording despite its obvious qualities. This lament, written by Danny Kirwan and calling for a love that rejects him, assumes the form of a languorous blues rock dotted with mournful guitar solos, with which Jeremy Spencer mixes his inspired slide strokes. The two men demonstrate a fine unity, especially vocally; Spencer provides support on every second phrase, adding to the track's dramatic dimension.

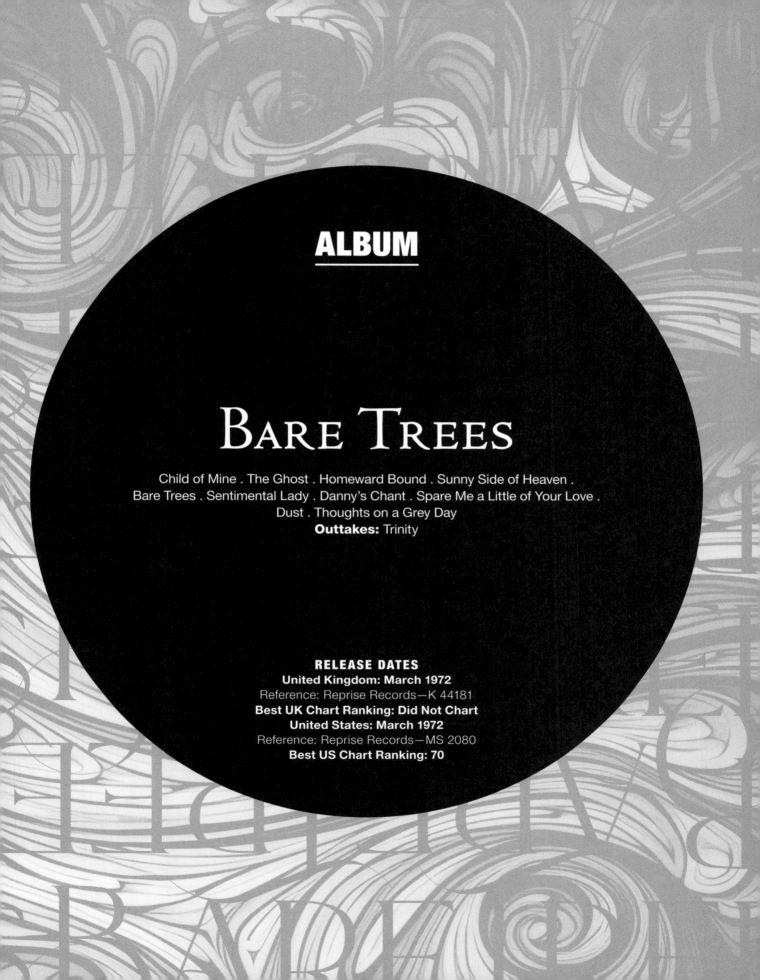

ALBUM

BARE TREES

Child of Mine . The Ghost . Homeward Bound . Sunny Side of Heaven .
Bare Trees . Sentimental Lady . Danny's Chant . Spare Me a Little of Your Love .
Dust . Thoughts on a Grey Day
Outtakes: Trinity

RELEASE DATES
United Kingdom: March 1972
Reference: Reprise Records—K 44181
Best UK Chart Ranking: Did Not Chart
United States: March 1972
Reference: Reprise Records—MS 2080
Best US Chart Ranking: 70

On the cover of *Bare Trees*, the band chooses a forest of leafless trees to create ambience before the first note is played.

Sinking inexorably into depression and excess, the affable Danny Kirwan exited the band of his own accord.

KIRWAN'S FAREWELL

As soon as it was released, *Future Games* confirmed that the fate of Fleetwood Mac was now in the hands of the United States, especially since the arrival of Bob Welch. Indeed, while the record was firmly anchored in the Billboard 200 chart, in ninety-first position, an American tour began on October 13, 1971. The group shared the bill with Deep Purple, Van Morrison, Savoy Brown, and Long John Baldry. Extended by two weeks, it ended on November 26, 1971. The lights appeared to be green when Fleetwood Mac recorded their follow-up album, *Bare Trees*, at the end of 1971.

A Quick Recording

Recording was done at a brisk pace. The album was completed during one of the band's rare weeks off, during the month of January 1972, at De Lane Lea Studios in London, with Martin Birch at the helm once again. But even though the recording went without any noticeable hitches, the situation within the group had deteriorated a lot over the course of the American tour. John McVie was drinking a lot, as was Danny Kirwan. John's drinking threatened his relationships with Christine and with the group. As for Kirwan, he gradually alienated himself and seemed to take an almost perverse pleasure in being in conflict with everyone, including having fun systematically hiding cigarette packs.

Though Kirwan composed the bulk of the new album, it became more and more obvious that he was at the end of his journey with the Mac. Tensions were growing with the other members, especially Bob Welch; he had especially established good relations with the McVies and Mick Fleetwood, but he remained the last real "supporter" of

Danny in the group. The last one who would speak to him again, too.

Year after year, the Mac went on tour in the United States for several months, starting on February 25. A most stressful unexpected event occurred that complicated the release of *Bare Trees* (scheduled for March on both sides of the Atlantic) and caused a big scare to the group. The album's master tapes, sent to the United States, were demagnetized and partially erased by the new X-ray machines at the New York airport. Long and agonizing days of studio remixes in this city were required to recover the tapes and get the album into the bins as planned.

Thirty-Five Disconcerting Minutes

As soon as it was released, *Bare Trees* struggled to confirm the artistic choices made by the band in its previous album, even as the band attempted to seduce the American audience with a soft-rock sound. This Fleetwood Mac now had little in common with the original band, apart from the name and the rhythm section, still composed of Mick Fleetwood and John McVie.

If *Bare Trees* does not immediately arouse enthusiasm, it is nevertheless endearing. Shorter than its predecessor at just over thirty-five minutes, it offers a more rock-like sound, thanks in part to the experiments of Danny Kirwan, whose melancholy is palpable, and a quite cleverly constructed track list. The egos of the composers were in fact spared, as each of the three (Kirwan, Welch, McVie) had the opportunity to place one of their titles in the opening trio.

The stylistic contrast between guitarists Danny Kirwan and Bob Welch appeared more blatantly here than on *Future Games*. But though the two men had very little

Christine McVie, John McVie, Mick Fleetwood, and Bob Welch will soon have to cope with the absence of Danny Kirwan (here in Los Angeles, 1973).

chemistry between them, their playing and their position-ing in Fleetwood Mac were perfectly complementary: Welch generally leaned toward rhythm and blues with a slight jazz influence, where Kirwan provided a more melodic and progressive approach, greatly helped by an exceptional mastery of vibrato, a taste for experimentation, and a thorough knowledge of the blues. The result was melodious and gave the impression of total harmony between the two men, which was very far from the reality. Welch and Kirwan might never have become friends, but the secret of *Bare Trees*—like that of *Future Games*—is the musical symbiosis between the melancholic artist from Brixton and the hippie from Hollywood. Their guitars intertwine strangely, turn around, and chase each other ele-gantly, and even their voices weave silky patterns together.

A Chilly Reception

In England, the reception of *Bare Trees* was rather cautious: The critics accused Fleetwood Mac of playing too much by ear and focusing on the sensations of the moment, whether they were named T. Rex, Slade, Humble Pie, Don MacLean, Gilbert O'Sullivan, or Elton John. Some even go hard, as Mick Fleetwood recalls: "*Bare Trees* did well in America, unlike in Europe, where one critic defined it as 'another nail in the coffin of Britain's greatest blues band.'"[4] When it was released, only Welch's hit "Sentimental Lady" seemed to do well, as well as Christine McVie's songs, which were considered to be promising. The potential that emerged clearly showed that the musician had become an excellent composer and a convincing singer, sometimes compared by critics of the time to Sandy Denny or Dusty Springfield. For some observers, there was no doubt that she could, if she wanted to, pick up the thread of her solo career. As for the concluding track of the record, it baffled fans and critics to say the least, there was nothing musical about it.

In the United States, Bob Welch's contribution made itself felt and the group was quietly making its mark. However, it is there, during the *Bare Trees* tour, that the next psychodrama would be played. If Welch's arrival kept Fleetwood Mac from sinking during the storms of 1970–1971, it was now the personality of Danny Kirwan—the more sensitive and withdrawn of the two guitarists, who had become the unofficial central figure of Fleetwood Mac since the departure of Jeremy Spencer—that would threaten the stability of the group.

Deeply marked by the absence of his biological father, Danny Kirwan expresses himself in "Child of Mine."

CHILD OF MINE

Danny Kirwan / 5:28

Musicians: Danny Kirwan: guitar, vocals / Bob Welch: guitar, backing vocals / Christine McVie: keyboards, backing vocals / John McVie: bass / Mick Fleetwood: drums, percussion / **Recorded:** De Lane Lea Studios, London, January 1972 / **Technical Team:** Producer: Fleetwood Mac / Sound Engineer: Martin Birch

Genesis and Lyrics

Danny Kirwan is one of the essential links in *Bare Trees*. His compositions were much more rock oriented than anything he had recorded before. He also seems much more comfortable and adventurous than on *Future Games*. In "Child of Mine" (which bore the heavy responsibility of opening the album), he tackles head-on, even if in a somewhat disjointed way, an event that greatly marked his childhood: the absence of a biological father who was never part of his life. Kirwan is the name of his stepfather. To address this personal theme, he chose rock'n'roll exuberance, which contrasts with the intimacy of the subject: "Little child of mine / You'll be lovin' like your little Mother did / Heard it somewhere before / I won't leave you no not like

my Father did." An artistic choice that is justified by reading certain lyrics; we understand that even if the wound had never really healed, the guitarist has chosen to move forward and not to present as a victim: "I miss you again / I let the sunlight through my eyes / I won't cry."

Realization

With his roaring bass and cunning line, John McVie gave the impression of starting the engine of a racing car. "Child of Mine" is indeed a concentrate of rock with accents of the blues, which is reminiscent of the bluster of the first Rolling Stones tracks, or even some songs by Cream (Eric Clapton's power trio), such as "Rollin' and Tumblin'." Very assured, Danny Kirwan's voice harmonizes perfectly with an explosive duo of skillfully intertwined guitars. Danny Kirwan and Bob Welch answer each other mischievously, each nestling on one side of the stereo spectrum to ensure more efficiency and clarity (so listen to all their inventive little frills on headphones!). In this shattering opening track, the guitars appear fierce, the solos sharp, and the breaks totally mastered. Mick Fleetwood immediately delivers a high-flying performance, as evidenced by his playing in the choruses. He is muscular and tribal on the rolls of toms and also conquering and ingenious when he puts his bass drum foot down; he imposes an ever more breathless tempo. As for Christine McVie's performance behind her keyboards, it is very representative of her great instinct as a musician. She is able to slip with discretion (but with formidable efficiency) into the gaps left by the other instruments, with a velvety sound that always blends best with them. Very coherent musically, "Child of Mine" is certainly one of Danny Kirwan's most underrated tracks. There was no better way to open *Bare Trees*.

Bob Welch sketches out a highly visual, cinematic track with "The Ghost."

THE GHOST

Bob Welch / 4:02

Musicians: Bob Welch: vocals, guitar / Danny Kirwan: guitar, backing vocals / Christine McVie: keyboards, backing vocals / John McVie: bass / Mick Fleetwood: drums, percussion / **Recorded:** De Lane Lea Studios, London, January 1972 / **Technical Team:** Producer: Fleetwood Mac / Sound Engineer: Martin Birch

Genesis and Lyrics

As a child, Bob Welch was immersed in the world of cinema thanks to his parents. His father, a film producer and screenwriter (at Paramount Pictures), and his mother, an actress, introduced him to Hollywood film sets. There, the privileged young man spent long hours in contact with stars and the technicians responsible for running the dream factory. It is therefore no coincidence that the lyrics of "The Ghost" are very visual. The Californian depicts the wide-open spaces of the American West. A certain nostalgia emerges as the harshness of the cold, gray British winter takes hold outside at the time of recording. Some metaphors thus appeared comforting for Welch, who formed in his mind, thanks to sleep, blue hills and a desert, contrasting with the austere countryside, bare trees, and rain of Benifold: "Blue hills are lookin' good to me / I go there, when I'm fast asleep / Ghost town, and the desert wind / Strange sounds, at the worlds end."

Realization

Beginning with a convoluted riff played simultaneously on acoustic guitar and bass, "The Ghost" immediately plunges the listener into a mysterious atmosphere. This is reinforced by the appearance of electric guitar chords powerfully layered by Danny Kirwan and a haunting flute part, actually played by Christine McVie on her Mellotron. The instrument offers more depth to the dreams described by Bob Welch in the lyrics. The guitarist gives an intense vocal performance, in osmosis with the flute dancing all around. Danny Kirwan offers a discreet score on guitar, leaving more space for Christine McVie's keyboard, a true pillar of the song. The rhythm section is not to be outdone, with an inventive proposal on the chorus, itself very melodic: John McVie's slippery bass is venomous while Mick goes over the top in the verses with his omnipresent toms without abusing the cymbals on the choruses. Far from mistreating them, he caresses them delicately, as if to follow the contours of the narrator's dream. On the finale, Bob Welch's voice gradually fades, like a night that ends with regret at letting a dream escape whose sweetness has rocked one to sleep.

Christine McVie expresses
her aversion for the stage
for the first time in
"Homeward Bound."

This is the first time Christine McVie expresses her weariness of touring, including the long-haul flights and the boredom that comes with them. She will also refer to it in 1997 in "Temporary One," just a few months before retiring from Fleetwood Mac to enjoy a more peaceful life.

HOMEWARD BOUND

Christine McVie / 3:24

Musicians: Christine McVie: vocals, piano, keyboards / Danny Kirwan: guitar / Bob Welch: guitar / John McVie: bass / Mick Fleetwood: drums, percussion / **Recorded:** De Lane Lea Studios, London, January 1972 / **Technical Team:** Producer: Fleetwood Mac / Sound Engineer: Martin Birch

Genesis and Lyrics

Danny Kirwan and Bob Welch both began *Bare Trees* with relatively personal lyrics: the first on the absence of a father, the second on homesickness. So it was then the turn of Fleetwood Mac's third regular composer to load the barrel and reveal herself in "Homeward Bound," a song evoking the boredom inherent in touring. Unfortunately, it suffered from the lack of depth of its subject. The narrator longs for her good old rocking chair and complains of wasting precious time: "I wanna sit at home in my rockin' chair / I don't want to travel the world / As far as I'm concerned I've had my share / But time's more precious than gold / I don't wanna see another aeroplane seat / Or another hotel room." Poor Christine still did not know that she would

spend the next twenty-six years on the road before her voluntary withdrawal in 1998. In "Homeward Bound," she was already asking for a quieter life and a return ticket, instead of "another drink and another cigarette."

Realization

If Christine makes listeners smile with her idle and homey lyrics, she demonstrates her constant progress as a composer with the melody of "Homeward Bound," which owes its effectiveness to a virtuoso crossover of cavernous organ and boogie piano. This one will force the bass of her husband, John, to be relatively withdrawn on the track. Mick Fleetwood is immediately required, since he breathes out from the first bars a gripping tension with his bell. A clever process that allows him to expand the solo parts of his colleagues on guitar or keyboard a little further. His frequent descents of the fierce toms serve as revivals of his solid playing, enriched with martyred cymbals on the choruses.

The guitar solos are also part of the highlights of this song with a successful balancing act: At 2:22, Danny Kirwan delivers with perfect feeling a relatively conventional score, but it expands from 2:42 with a second guitar. The two harmonized six-strings respond to each other in the stereo spectrum, requiring careful synchronization, while John McVie's bass, very discreet until then, comes to knit a strong line in the background. Something that was not noticed before, the acoustic guitar seems to appear in the last bars to extinguish the rock'n'roll fire, which had been lit and maintained a few minutes earlier. If the arrangement is spectacular, what can we say, finally, of Christine's voice, which is self-sufficient and requires no choir? Her weariness expressed in the lyrics transpires every time she opens her mouth. One of the best songs on *Bare Trees*, for sure.

"Sunny Side of Heaven" features John McVie's deep, hypnotic four-string playing.

SUNNY SIDE OF HEAVEN

Danny Kirwan / 3:11

Musicians: Danny Kirwan: guitar / Bob Welch: guitar / Christine McVie: keyboards / John McVie: bass / Mick Fleetwood: drums / **Recorded:** De Lane Lea Studios, London, January 1972 / **Technical Team:** Producer: Fleetwood Mac / Sound Engineer: Martin Birch / **Single:** Side A: Sentimental Lady / Side B: Sunny Side of Heaven / **US Release Date:** May 1972 / **Reference:** Reprise Records (ref. REP 1093) / Best US Chart Ranking: Did Not Chart

Genesis

"Sunny Side of Heaven" intervened to calm the debates after a trio of nervous titles at the opening of *Bare Trees*. This instrumental—a heavenly folk-rock melody written by Danny Kirwan—was new proof of the guitarist's success with this type of exercise. He had already shown his taste for instrumental arrangement on several occasions, notably with "Earl Gray" on *Kiln House* (1970) or "My Dream" on *Then Play On* (1969).

Realization

Shaped by Danny Kirwan to offer the best of his qualities as a guitarist, "Sunny Side of Heaven" featured an electric guitar with a sunny tremolo, played in the style of Hank Marvin, guitarist and soul of the Shadows. Sensitivity and humanity emerge from a captivating sound. The main motif is intended to be warm, but the high notes that gradually invite themselves are more piercing and powerful, while remaining plaintive. Kirwan's touch is quite remarkable in both registers, and he places himself at the heart of a piece on which his colleagues consciously play the utilities. John McVie plunges his hypnotic bass into soft and reassuring depths, Mick Fleetwood wedges a pleasant rhythm in the background, and Christine McVie expresses herself discreetly via her organ with its velvety sound. Not really a staple of Fleetwood Mac's stage repertoire, "Sunny Side of Heaven" was, however, rehabilitated in the mid-1970s by Lindsey Buckingham, who would then enjoy playing it during a few concerts.

The fog-shrouded British winter countryside inspires the writing of "Bare Trees."

BARE TREES

Danny Kirwan / 5:05

Musicians: Danny Kirwan: vocals, guitar / Bob Welch: guitar, backing vocals / Christine McVie: keyboards, backing vocals / John McVie: bass / Mick Fleetwood: drums / **Recorded:** De Lane Lea Studios, London, January 1972 / **Technical Team:** Producer: Fleetwood Mac / Sound Engineer: Martin Birch

Genesis and Lyrics

This new contribution by Danny Kirwan would be the album's title track. "Bare Trees" features a man up at dawn who goes for a walk "in the cold of a winter's day," contemplating on his way "bare trees" bathed in "a grey light." Enveloped by this gloomy ambiance, he imagined his sweetheart who has stayed warm, nestled in a cozy bed. "Bare Trees," with its creeping melancholy, is directly inspired by John McVie's photograph that adorns the album cover, as well as the poem responsible for closing it, "Thoughts on a Grey Day"—a composition by a certain Aileen Scarrott, the band's neighbor in Headley, Hampshire. More specifically, the song "Bare Trees" relays a particular line from Mrs. Scarrott's poem, saying: "With trees so bare, so bare." Perhaps Danny Kirwan chose, like her, to use this to support a reflection on age, the passing of time, and by extension death. It would therefore not be a simple walk in the cold and foggy English countryside in winter, but the inevitable departure of one of the two halves of a couple while the other had no choice but to accept this cycle of life and continue along its path.

Production

It is surprising to think that Danny Kirwan was only twenty-two years old when he composed this very mature title. His guitar makes sparks and is never stingy, with a small effective ornamentation at the end of the verse or chorus, while Bob Welch supports it effectively. The idea of playing the same venomous riff as the bass to increase the tension is also clever: It gives John McVie the opportunity to place a heavy, rough line that fits perfectly with the excited tambourine and pressing bass drum played by Mick Fleetwood. He delivers a clear strike on his snare drum with a flat sound that serves as a foundation for the group throughout the song. Christine McVie's Wurlitzer fleshes out the moments of tension and places a few flights with the most beautiful effect. As for the choirs, they only support Danny Kirwan's voice, which is very clear, on very short sequences. If the theme of the song is rather dark, Fleetwood Mac manages to make it a country-rock number full of vitality, full of warm, funky riffs that bring hope and a certain form of completeness to the narrator.

Overlaid with Christine McVie's inspired keyboard playing, "Sentimental Lady" has a catchy soft-rock sound.

SENTIMENTAL LADY

Bob Welch / 4:36

Musicians: Bob Welch: vocals, guitar, backing vocals / Danny Kirwan: guitar / Christine McVie: keyboards, piano, backing vocals / John McVie: bass / Mick Fleetwood: drums / **Recorded:** De Lane Lea Studios, London, January 1972 / **Technical Team:** Producer: Fleetwood Mac / Sound Engineer: Martin Birch / **Single:** Side A: Sentimental Lady / Side B: Sunny Side of Heaven / **US Release Date:** May 1972 / **Reference:** Reprise Records (ref. REP 1093) / Best US Chart Ranking: Did Not Chart

Genesis and Lyrics

No doubt about it, "Sentimental Lady" was the title that most openly demonstrated the change of style made on this album by Fleetwood Mac, a band then going with its desire to gain a more consistent commercial success. This soft-rock ballad by Bob Welch, mixing the carefree and the nostalgic in love, stood out with its romantic lyrics, which refer to Nancy (Bob's first wife). The narrator insists on his total dependence on the "sentimental lady": "All I need is you," he sings, adding that all the things he had always wanted run through his head when he is in her presence. This "sentimental lady" reconciles him with love: "Sentimental gentle wind / Blowing through my life again."

Production

Bob Welch, who had already demonstrated with "Future Games," on the previous album, that he was perfectly comfortable playing in the register of ballads with celestial choruses, was convinced that he could do even better. Starting with an acoustic guitar with precise arpeggios supported by a few piano notes, "Sentimental Lady" was immediately enriched with a minimalist rhythm section, but one in which John McVie's deep bass is particularly illustrated. On the pre-chorus, the bass increases as Danny Kirwan places some backing vocals, leading the band into a splendid chorus. There, Bob Welch's soft voice combines beautifully with Christine McVie's in stunning vocal harmonies. From 2:23, a celestial guitar solo with slight jazzy accents, filled with tremolo, brings more delicacy to an already very silky arrangement. Christine McVie's cottony-sounding organ, always on a strong footing, reinforced the angelic feeling of a scarily effective melody. The sober playing of Mick Fleetwood, who delicately whips his cymbals on the choruses, is also no stranger to this general impression of sweetness and romanticism.

It is therefore difficult to understand how the Fleetwood Mac label failed to make this single an authentic hit in the United States, because "Sentimental Lady" obviously ticked all the boxes of commercial success. It seems that Warner preferred to promote Arlo Guthrie's new single, released at the same time, by muting this one from Fleetwood Mac. Disappointed, Bob Welch rerecorded a new version for his solo album *French Kiss* in 1977. With Mick Fleetwood, Christine McVie, and Lindsey Buckingham to assist him, he would be rewarded with eighth place in the US Billboard 200 chart.

A master of shuffle boogie, Mick Fleetwood diversified his playing, creating a score with tribal accents in "Danny's Chant."

DANNY'S CHANT

Danny Kirwan / 3:16

Musicians: Danny Kirwan: vocals, guitar / Bob Welch: guitar, backing vocals / Christine McVie: keyboards, backing vocals / John McVie: bass / Mick Fleetwood: drums / **Recorded:** De Lane Lea Studios, London, January 1972 / **Technical Team:** Producer: Fleetwood Mac / Sound Engineer: Martin Birch

Genesis

Asserting himself as the focal point of Fleetwood Mac on *Bare Trees*, and eager to bring greater testimony of his sound experiments, Danny Kirwan gave birth to a second instrumental title with "Danny's Chant," a midtempo blues rock with massive rhythm.

Production

It starts with a deluge of electricity contained by the guitarist's wah-wah pedal. John McVie's roaring bass, supported by Mick Fleetwood's tribal toms, then comes on the scene, while scat vocals and distant backing vocals add up to create one of Fleetwood Mac's most harrowing intros. This section then sets up its heavy atmosphere by developing a dark theme, illuminated by some vivid guitar flashes. John McVie and Mick Fleetwood meanwhile remain on their tribal motif of departure, while Christine McVie's keyboard stays in support, very far back in a mix that particularly accentuates the guitars. The interlacing formed by the raging six-strings of Bob Welch and Danny Kirwan is another proof of their perfect, mutual musical complement. In hindsight, it is quite surprising that their names were not more often associated with other guitar heroes of the time. Especially the inventive Danny Kirwan, whose remarkable work on *Bare Trees* would certainly have guaranteed him posterity on the following albums, had he not exploded in midflight at only twenty-two years old.

Rock'n'roll icon, singer, and songwriter Jackie DeShannon.

SPARE ME A LITTLE OF YOUR LOVE

Christine McVie / 3:48

Musicians: Christine McVie: vocals, piano / Danny Kirwan: guitar, backing vocals / Bob Welch: guitar, backing vocals / John McVie: bass / Mick Fleetwood: drums / **Recorded:** De Lane Lea Studios, London, January 1972 / **Technical Team:** Producer: Fleetwood Mac / Sound Engineer: Martin Birch

Genesis and Lyrics

As Mick Fleetwood says about Christine McVie: "The great thing about her songs is that she always finds such novel ways to say, 'I love you.'"[4] Here, she asks the loved one to keep some feelings about her, because loving her has made her a more fulfilled, more accomplished person. It's hard not to see Christine's desperate attempt to get the attention of John, who was descending more and more into alcoholism at the expense of his relationship. At the time of recording, the problem had been entrenched for several months already. Every time they approached it, the McVies ended up arguing and, inevitably, fur flew. Still in love, Christine tried to save him and keep him by her side, and she wrote these comforting words, as if to rekindle in her mind the many reasons she had fallen for John: "And it's not the same as before / It gets stronger everyday / [...] Now I know how the sun must feel / Every time it shines / And now I know this is real / And I want you to be mine."

Production

Undoubtedly, "Spare Me a Little of Your Love" had, like "Sentimental Lady," the potential to become a single, and even a hit. A midtempo ballad mixing folk, country, soul, and gospel, it starts with Christine McVie's delicate organ, supported by a benevolent rhythm section and some promising guitar hooks. The warm and sensual voice of the young woman demonstrates all her virtuosity, starting on the verses with a low register to gradually rise in the treble and reveal an irresistibly soft melody that reaches its climax on the chorus, when the chords of Danny Kirwan and Bob Welch, perfectly chiseled, come to support her. At 1:44, Danny Kirwan splits a very nice guitar solo, bathed in a light wah-wah, demonstrating once again all his technical mastery. The finale, quite inexplicably, accelerates without it really bringing anything to the song.

The record label, Reprise Records, considered releasing "Spare Me a Little of Your Love" on 45 rpm in the UK, with "Sunny Side of Heaven" as Side B. This was then canceled at the last minute, without any official reason being given, although a pressing number had already been assigned to it. Reprise's motivation was probably cooled by the very disappointing sales figures of the latest single, "Sentimental Lady." This did not prevent "Spare Me a Little of Your Love" from becoming a Fleetwood Mac live classic in the following years. Proof of its intrinsic value, the song even ended up being covered by several artists, including Johnny Rivers on his album *New Lover and Old Friends* in 1975.

DUST

Danny Kirwan / 2:41

Musicians
Danny Kirwan: vocals, guitar
Bob Welch: guitar, backing vocals
Christine McVie: piano, backing vocals
John McVie: bass
Mick Fleetwood: drums

Recorded
De Lane Lea Studios, London, January 1972

Technical Team
Producer: Fleetwood Mac
Sound Engineer: Martin Birch

> The British poet Rupert Brooke suffered a dark fate. At only twenty-seven years old, in 1915 he became infected by a mosquito bite that turned septic. He died on April 23, 1915, aboard the hospital ship *Duguay-Trouin*, anchored off the island of Skyros, Greece, while fighting with the British navy in the Battle of the Dardanelles. He is buried there in a field of olive trees.

Rupert Brooke, described by fellow poet and playwright W. B. Yeats as "the handsomest young man in England."

Genesis and Lyrics

Consumed by his self-destructive tendencies, the mind of young Kirwan (who was then only twenty-two years old) was engaged in a dangerous dance of seduction with death. This theme and its symbols are at the heart of "Dust," the same as in "Bare Trees." This time, Kirwan borrowed the words of Rupert Brooke, whose poetry he had already highlighted in "Dragonfly."

In a striking coincidence, the British poet, also precocious in his need to evoke death, was the same age as his admirer when, between December 1909 and March 1910, he conceived the poem "Dust." Danny Kirwan drew from this the substance of the two verses of this song. The original poem was about two lovers so ecstatic in their devotion to each other that not even death could separate them. By the time it reached its conclusion, the poem completely transcended its melancholic opening, transforming death, a dark event, into a joyful and luminous celebration. Danny Kirwan, however, limited his borrowing to the opening of the poem—precisely very dark and melancholic, but also very graphic. He speaks of "the white flame in us" that is gone, the loss of "the world's delight," bodies which "stiffen in darkness, left alone," and the two lovers who "crumble in our separate nights." No salvation, hope, or light at the end of the tunnel, therefore, in the version retained by Kirwan, who whispered gloomily and repeatedly: "When we are dust…" He captured the essence of the beginning of Brooke's poem and concocted a completely adapted musical setting.

Production

Delicate acoustic guitar arpeggios played on the pick open the piece. They are quickly joined by a discreet rhythm, also played on acoustic guitar, but rubbed with the fingers, then sent during mixing into the right channel of the stereo spectrum. A plaintive electric guitar then makes its entrance playing a few notes, supported by John McVie's minimalist bass. A relatively rare process for Fleetwood Mac but nevertheless very effective: Mick Fleetwood's sober and benevolent drums start at the same time as Danny Kirwan's singing. In a very American soft-folk-rock atmosphere (proof that the formula is not only the prerogative of the American of the group, Bob Welch), Danny Kirwan weaves a melancholic atmosphere with very skillful (if not technically impressive) guitar

Danny Kirwan was only 22 at the time of *Bare Trees*, but his face bears the marks of adulthood torments.

lines. His voice, perfectly supported on the chorus by Bob Welch and Christine McVie, reveals a sweetness rarely heard before. The melody he manages to shape is absolutely exquisite and does full justice to Rupert Brooke's text, even if it is only partially used. It is, however, bizarre (not to say a little ungrateful) that Danny Kirwan, unlike what he did for W. H. Davies on "Dragonfly," did not credit Brooke for the song. "Dust" would be the last song performed by Danny Kirwan on a Fleetwood Mac album.

Mick, tape recorder in hand, immortalizes his neighbor's reading of her poem in "Thoughts on a Grey Day."

FOR MAC-ADDICTS

Some have claimed—wrongly—that the recording of Mrs. Scarrott's poem "Thoughts on a Grey Day" was made by Mick Fleetwood himself trying to replicate the voice of an old lady. Actually, we can hear Mick and Aileen Scarrott talking together at the end of the recording.

THOUGHTS ON A GREY DAY

Mrs. Aileen Scarrott / 1:42

Musicians: Aileen Scarrott: reading / **Recorded:** Mrs. Scarrott's home, Headley, Hampshire, January 1972 / **Technical Team:** Producer: Fleetwood Mac / Sound Engineer: Martin Birch

Genesis and Lyrics

Undoubtedly accustomed to gray and gloomy weather, nobody equals the English in finding beauty and romance in all circumstances. At the end of "Dust," which was as melancholic as possible, there could not be a more beautiful (and atypical) conclusion to *Bare Trees* than the poem that had inspired Danny Kirwan to write the song "Bare Trees," and also give the band their winter concept of the album. This poem is the work of Aileen Scarrott, the group's charming neighbor in Hampshire.

The sixty-eight-year-old Eastbourne resident was a poet in her spare time. Mick, literally bewitched by her texts, one day went to her house with a tape recorder and asked her to read one into the microphone. She then chose to recite a few stanzas on love and the austere beauty of winter.

"It was exquisite, and so very, very English," Mick explained. "She asked that her poem be entitled 'Thoughts on a Grey Day,' and it mirrored the midwinter ambience of our feelings when we made this record as aptly as John McVie's eloquent cover photograph of bare trees standing guard in the fog."[4] She gave a perfect account of the unique atmosphere during which daylight hours diminish while a current of arctic air blows over Benifold, where the windows are adorned with frost. "God bless our perfect, perfect grey day," she exclaims, before redoubling her enthusiasm when evoking "With trees so bare, so bare / But oh so beautiful, so beautiful."

Production

Perhaps Aileen Scarrott was a little too eager to make the reading of her poem a touch monotonous. But the effect sought by the drummer is there, the same as that wanted by Simon and Garfunkel on their album *Bookends* in 1968, with the interlude "Voices of Old People": to carry the voices of the elders, and through this their wisdom. With all the displacement that this implies in the heart of the tribulations of a rock band. Married three times when she acquiesced amicably to Fleetwood Mac's request, Aileen Scarrott answers at the end of her poem to her husband, Harry (also married for the third time) and whose voice can be heard behind her. Like Fleetwood Mac, she has lived many lives. She now thanks God for "perfect love and peace." The Mac will not taste this right away. The group still had violent storms to face ahead.

The holy compositional trinity of Christine McVie, Bob Welch, and Danny Kirwan in its final moments on *Bare Trees*.

TRINITY

Danny Kirwan / 4:07

Musicians: Danny Kirwan: vocals, guitar / Bob Welch: guitar / Christine McVie: keyboards, piano / John McVie: bass / Mick Fleetwood: drums / **Recorded:** De Lane Lea Studios, London, January 1972 / **Technical Team:** Producer: Fleetwood Mac / Sound Engineer: Martin Birch

Recorded for *Bare Trees*, "Trinity" was in the end not selected by the band to appear on the album, and it was not until the 1992 release of the box set *25 Years—The Chain* that it was discovered by the public. Written by Danny Kirwan, it is proof of the musical maturity reached by the guitarist. His very short lyrics (barely two verses) which were also very obscure, depict a boy who "came down from Trinity," forced to leave his home "walking miles" to find a way. The song was not really convincing. "Trinity" essentially takes the form of a big jam session with Mick Fleetwood focused on his percussion for a good minute really taking off on drums, at the moment when John McVie, solid, makes himself heard on bass. Danny Kirwan and Bob Welch exchange guitar pleasantries, competing in ingenuity, with riffs and solos, while Christine McVie puts chords behind her keyboards without any real imagination. If "Trinity" is a new demonstration of the Kirwan-Welch musical "compatibility," it seemed too unfinished to claim a place on *Bare Trees*.

ALBUM

PENGUIN

Remember Me . Bright Fire . Dissatisfied . (I'm a) Road Runner .
The Derelict . Revelation . Did You Ever Love Me . Night Watch .
Caught in the Rain

RELEASE DATES
United Kingdom: March 1, 1973
Reference: Reprise Records—K 44235
Best UK Chart Ranking: Did Not Chart
United States: March 1, 1973
Reference: Reprise Records—MS 2138
Best US Chart Ranking: 49

The penguins at London Zoo, inspiration to John McVie.

The new album introduces two new faces to the team: guitarist Bob Weston (with cap) and singer Dave Walker (far right, behind the dog).

FOR MAC-ADDICTS

Penguin officially enthrones John McVie's animal totem as the band's mascot. The Fleetwood Mac bassist fell in love with the penguin when he and Christine McVie lived near the London Zoo at the beginning of their marriage. The musician, a member of the Zoological Society, would spend hours observing them and studying their behavior.

THE LEAP INTO THE UNKNOWN

Danny Kirwan was a shadow of the introverted, diligent young guitarist he once was. His behavior, made erratic by alcohol abuse, had become incompatible with band life. Irascible to an extreme, he could not stand being in the presence of the other members of Fleetwood Mac and vice versa. Only Mick Fleetwood was still willing to draw on his diplomatic resources to maintain dialogue and make certain journeys with him during the US tour, which was paused on May 28, 1972, and resumed on August 14. However, during the month of August, Kirwan managed to break down the last barrier keeping him from the exit.

An Inevitable Separation

Before a concert at an American university, Danny started an argument with Bob Welch over some nonsense about an allegedly out-of-tune guitar. Kirwan lost his temper and deliberately banged his head against the wall. Blood flowed. He grabbed his beloved Gibson Les Paul and smashed it in a rare fit of violence. Perfectionist that he was, he set about scrupulously smashing everything in his dressing room. Stunned, the other members refrained from intervening. They let him get on with it. When he had finished, panting, he turned to them and announced, determinedly, that he would not be going onstage that night. Yet the crowd was already roaring, and the band was expected any second. They had no choice but to perform without him.

Bob Welch, his hands full, tried to maintain a semblance of structure to the songs by improvising as best he could a mix between his guitar parts and Kirwan's. By the end of the show, Kirwan's voice had gone. He waited quietly in his dressing room for his colleagues. The musicians, having just done their entire set on the fly, might have been expecting a session of contrition. If so, they were in for a surprise. Kirwan, whose defiant look did not bode well, told them in the most natural way possible that he had observed the concert from the sound console and noticed many mistakes: tempos not respected, opportunities to improvise missed, etc. This was one affront too many. Mick Fleetwood, who had protected Kirwan for too long, managed to restrain himself from jumping down Kirwan's throat.

In the absence of manager Clifford Davis, who had stayed behind in England, leadership fell to Mick. That evening, he sought advice from Jon Lord, keyboardist with Deep Purple, with whom Fleetwood Mac shared the bill. Lord confirmed what Fleetwood already knew: Kirwan's dismissal was inevitable. "No-one [had] ever been fired from Fleetwood Mac before," recalled Mick Fleetwood. "Danny was the first, but he wouldn't be the last. I went to his room, knocked on the door, sat on the bed and flumbed my way through it. I told him that we all knew he wasn't happy with us and that we weren't happy either, and the best thing would be for him to leave the band. Danny didn't say a word, he just sat there silently. When I asked him if he understood, he nodded, and that was it, Danny was out. I then went upstairs to John and Christine's room and was crying before I even got to the door."[4]

Kirwan's Downfall

After Kirwan's departure, his alcoholism worsened and, combined with depression, led to his decline. He did try his hand at a few musical experiments, as in 1974, when he formed a band with one of his replacements, Dave Walker. Called Hungry Fighter, the band was seen as a club for bitter former Fleetwood Mac members. In any case, it would last for only one concert. It did not take Walker long to realize the extent of Kirwan's problem, and that Fleetwood Mac had parted company with him for a reason.

Kirwan knew that he alone was responsible for his ousting from Fleetwood Mac. His resentment toward his former bandmates quickly faded after his eviction. In 1974, he even played again with Mick Fleetwood during the recording sessions for Tramp's second album, *Put a Record On*, the band led by another ex–Fleetwood Mac member, Bob Brunning. The atmosphere was very friendly, and Kirwan proved to be involved and cooperative. He went on to build a solo career with the ironically named *Second Chapter* (1975), followed by *Midnight in San Juan* (1976, released under the title *Danny Kirwan* in the United States). His melodic sense remained intact, even though the songs were simpler and less spiritual than in the past. His galloping alcoholism and the minor exposure of his albums gradually sapped his motivation. Yet he had the full support of Clifford Davis, who remained his manager, and his label, DJM Records (renowned for having accompanied the rise of Elton John). But they could do nothing to prevent the artistic wreck of *Hello There Big Boy!* (1979), for which Kirwan no longer had the strength or inclination to play. The guitarist subsequently sank into total destitution, ending up homeless.

Two New Recruits for the Price of One

Fleetwood Mac had lost a first-rate composer and the guarantor of the Fleetwood Mac sound after the departures of Green and Spencer. For the band, it was a leap into the unknown.

The remaining musicians were distraught by this latest defection. They knew that while the decision to keep Kirwan would have inevitably led them into the wall, his departure might just as easily have condemned them to an artistic death. The band did not consider for a second continuing as a four-piece when Bob Welch, as singer and guitarist, would have had the ability to take over the leadership. But fear held them back. So, to replace Danny, they made a choice that showed their nervousness by recruiting not one but two musicians.

The first, Dave Walker, singer and harmonica player, came from Savoy Brown, a band well-known to Fleetwood Mac. The two groups started out at the same time, during the expansion of the British blues boom. They often shared the same stages, and Savoy Brown welcomed bassist Bob Brunning to its ranks in 1967. This time, it was up to Kim and Harry Simmonds's to supply one of its members to the fraternal formation. A year and a half after joining Savoy Brown, Dave Walker, already feeling out of favor with the Simmonds brothers, seized the opportunity to join Fleetwood Mac in September 1972. "Things had *always* been a bit shaky with the personnel in Savoy Brown," commented the defector. "I heard from somebody who was *very* much in the know in New York that I was going to be replaced. I wasn't making a lot of money with Savoy Brown, and I had had an argument with Harry Simmons [*sic*] about that! The next thing I knew, I got a call from John McVie in New York saying that Danny Kirwan was leaving the band and Fleetwood Mac needed a different kind of front man. Was I interested in joining Fleetwood Mac? I was!"[5] Walker was a charismatic singer. The artist with the hippie look was a stage beast who took all the limelight. Qualities that Kirwan lacked.

The second, Bob Weston, was offered the guitarist's post. He had been working as a touring musician and studio session musician for Long John Baldry. The members of Fleetwood Mac were able to see Bob Weston in action during joint concerts with Baldry in 1971: "We trotted off to America. It was wonderful!" recalls Bob Weston, the guitarist with the large sideburns. "But the money was terrible. £60 per week. We often opened for Fleetwood Mac, however. Mick Fleetwood was being particularly friendly at the time. I thought, 'Nice people, very charming.'"[5]

Mick Fleetwood's phone call in September 1972 came at just the right time. Bob Weston was stony broke. At first he thought it was a joke and hung up. But he did not let the opportunity slip away on the second call. "Of course I said yes. It was an ideal musical situation for me. I was well tweaked up, already playing every night of the week, and with my blues influences, it was a natural progression for me to join Fleetwood Mac."[5]

A Difficult Adjustment

In October 1972, the band took advantage of a break in their touring schedule to meet and work with their new members at their Benifold estate. The aim was not only for Dave Walker and Bob Weston to familiarize

A blues guitarist permeated by pop, Bob Weston had the skill to make his mark with Fleetwood Mac, but his stay turned sour.

Dave Walker was recruited to take over vocal leadership, but his contribution was reduced to two songs.

themselves with the usual stage repertoire, but also for them to participate from the outset in the songwriting effort for the next album, whose recording was scheduled for January 1973.

While the new recruits should have been the ones having to find their bearings, strangely enough, it was the older members of the band who felt uncomfortable. They were not getting anywhere, and they were not playing well, which logically led to tensions. Bob Welch was the most productive of the old-timers, while Christine McVie still seemed to be struggling to come to terms with her role as songwriter. But things gradually improved, even though there was no real symbiosis.

On October 28, 1972, shortly after the first songwriting sessions, Christine McVie gave an optimistic interview to *Melody Maker*. After dismissing the question about Danny Kirwan by claiming that he just wanted to do solo material and sweeping all the problems under the carpet, she described the results of the writing sessions as follows: "The new material we are coming up with seems a lot harder, probably because Danny was always writing the softer, more melodic material."[45] Diplomatically, Christine

McVie implied that Fleetwood Mac would not be placing themselves at the service of Dave Walker. The musicians did try to adapt to Walker's voice during the first rehearsals, but this had forced the composers (mainly Christine McVie and Bob Welch) to adapt their songs to Walker's deep, powerful voice by changing the key. But McVie and Welch felt this distorted the songs. So there was no other solution than to drastically reduce the role of the man who was to be the new stage leader.

A "Homemade" Recording

The band had on the other hand provided themselves with the means of a natural and friendly integration by choosing to record at home, in Benifold, Mick Fleetwood's vast manor house lost in the Hampshire countryside. The musicians came up with an original solution. They decided to rent the Rolling Stones' mobile studio. It was a technological innovation for its time. The idea of a fully equipped studio installed inside a truck, enabling any location to be transformed into a professional studio, was born in 1968. At the time, the Stones were looking for a flexible solution that would allow

It was on the stage that Dave Walker showed the full extent of his charisma. In the studio, he rarely had a chance to express himself.

them to record or compose whenever they wished at Mick Jagger's country estate in Stargroves (UK) without being constrained by schedules. It also meant avoiding astronomical professional studio bills. Their pianist, Ian Stewart, had suggested the idea and consulted the best producers of the day for their opinions. The Stones then entrusted the design to Helios Electronics. The British band soon saw the benefits of renting out the machine to other bands. Some of the greatest albums in history were recorded on this machine: Led Zeppelin's *III* (1970) and *IV* (1971), The Rolling Stones' *Sticky Fingers* (1971) and *Exile on Main Street* (1972), the Who's *Who's Next* (1971), and Deep Purple's *Machine Head* (1972).

The two large rooms on the first floor of Benifold were partly emptied to become a real recording studio. Fleetwood Mac's musicians stacked up their amps and instruments, while retaining the existing furniture. The acoustics of the rooms were ideal, and the reverberation was well metered, much to the astonishment of Martin Birch, who was expecting to have a hard time calibrating all his microphones. It was a relief that he was now the official producer, after having worked as engineer on *Then Play On*, *Kiln House*, and *Bare Trees*. Martin Birch then ran all the cables through the front door to the machine parked out front, which served as a control booth.

Finally, Christine McVie imposed her voice on three fresh tracks with a radio immediacy that lay the groundwork for what would become Fleetwood Mac pop in the 1970s, without yet reaching the quality level: "Remember Me," "Dissatisfied," and "Did You Ever Love Me." This last song, which provides the album's dose of originality with the intervention of steel drums, is shared with co-composer Bob Welch. Welch also performed his own compositions, which showed greater confidence in his abilities: the jazzy "Bright Fire," the Latin groove "Revelation," and the Crosby, Stills & Nash–inspired folk gem "Night Watch."

Bye-Bye Blues

The newcomers seemed underutilized: Bob Weston composed only the instrumental "Caught in the Rain," and Dave Walker sang only on the Junior Walker and the All Stars cover, "(I'm a) Road Runner," and on his own country-rock composition, "The Derelict." On the former, in particular, he did not spare himself, as if to prove that he was not there by chance, but the musicians at his side lacked conviction. After declaring their desire to bring in a strong leader to put an end to the band's lack of vocal personality, Fleetwood Mac gave the impression of going against the grain and extinguishing the ambitions of the singer they believed to be trying to turn the band into Savoy Brown II. Dave Walker did not feel integrated: "The bulk of the writing was being done by Christine and Bob Welch. [...] They were better at it. But I found it frustrating not really feeling like a part of the creative process."[46] Walker consoled himself by drinking more than he should have, in the company of his new drinking partner, John McVie. Bob Weston was more welcomed, and he showed himself more willing and more energetic in the studio. He showed the band the versatility of his playing (notably with slide guitar on "Remember Me") and demonstrated his banjo skills on "The Derelict." But his songwriting involvement was minimal. He spent as much time in the studio as he did making friends with Jenny Boyd, Mick Fleetwood's girlfriend, who had finally found someone to talk to. She felt terribly alone, whether on tour or in Benifold, living on her baby's schedule, totally out of step with her musician husband. This growing closeness led to an affair, which cut short Weston's involvement with Fleetwood Mac.

The result was a profound discrepancy between the band's intentions when recruiting its two new members and the final result. During the composition and recording process, the members realized that recruiting two blues

For the first time, Fleetwood Mac became a sextet: Christine McVie, Dave Walker, Bob Welch, Mick Fleetwood, Bob Weston, John McVie.

The photo immortalizing the ephemeral lineup, located inside the gatefold album jacket, was taken at Ludshott Common and Waggoners Wells, a vast nature reserve of about 704 acres in eastern Hampshire.

musicians was not going to help their integration, simply because Fleetwood Mac was no longer a blues band. It had become difficult to define, at least on this album, as it explored so many musical avenues that it seemed disjointed.

An Interminable Transition

The nine tracks, totaling around thirty-five minutes, are packaged under the title *Penguin*, a tribute to John McVie's favorite animal. The creature adorning the cover was painted by artist Chris Moore, a twenty-six-year-old illustrator who graduated in graphic design from Maidstone College of Art, then from the Royal College of Art. The future illustrator of renowned science-fiction books had set up his company only a few months before he was contacted by Fleetwood Mac. This was to be one of his first commissions in the music industry, but not his last—he would go on to design the covers of Rod Stewart's *The Vintage Years 1969–70* and three Status Quo albums (*Just Supposin'...*, *12 Gold Bars*, and *Never Too Late*).

Since Peter Green's departure, press and public alike had seen each Mac album as a work of transition, but the band

struggled to come up with a new artistic vision. They seemed to be more affected by events than overwhelmed by them. Heralded as being set to last, this lineup had an expiration date—the new singer, Dave Walker, was already considered to be a problem. In the meantime, Fleetwood Mac wasted another cartridge with *Penguin*, a shot which fell far short of its predecessors. Fortunately for the group's future, sales remained decent, at least in the United States (forty-ninth on the chart), as it no longer existed commercially in the UK. The touring schedules showed that the band was on the road almost all the time in the United States, confirming the mutation of the British band into a US band.

The critics were rather lenient, accepting the band's lack of musical coherence. Robert Christgau, a journalist with *Newsday* at the time, even enthused: "I love it. I also like all of Christine McVie's husky laments. But could rilly do without Bob Welch's ever-mellower musings."[55] In the *New Musical Express*, journalist Tony Stewart commented two months after its release, in May 1973: "Obviously Mac have found a musical direction both pleasing to the ear and musically satisfying. My only misgiving is that perhaps they will obscure their own talents and become another prettily-sounding band."[56]

PORTRAIT

Despite his onstage charisma, Dave Walker had a patchy career marked by many short-lived appearances with bands, including Fleetwood Mac, Raven, and Black Sabbath.

DAVE WALKER, THE ETERNAL STAND-IN

The mandate given to Dave Walker by the members of Fleetwood Mac in September 1972 was not the least of tasks: to provide the lead vocals and, above all, to take over the leadership—at least on stage—of the band. In other words, to become, for years to come if possible, the face and soul of Fleetwood Mac. This is a tall order when talented predecessors were unsuccessful, including Peter Green, one of the most gifted guitarists of his generation, Jeremy Spencer, the slide ace, and Danny Kirwan, the six-string lace-maker. Three guitarists with distinct sensibilities, each able to imprint their own artistic personality on the band while ensuring continuity. Walker, who was not a guitarist, was expected to do the same. Unfortunately, this was not to be.

Right Place, Wrong Time

Dave Walker's failure was not due to a lack of personality, for the man radiated insane energy as soon as he picked up the microphone, and boasted a powerful, expressive voice that set him apart from other singers. Unfortunately for him, the rest of Mac was not up to Walker's standards. Christine McVie and Bob Welch had to go through this casting error to realize that they had within them the breath of inspiration Fleetwood Mac needed, and that the personality they wanted to give the band was their own.

In the end, Walker, who stayed with the band for about a year—between the summers of 1972 and 1973—including numerous tour dates, the recording of *Penguin*, and the beginning of the recording of *Mystery to Me*, would leave behind him only a meager discographic trace: a cover, "(I'm a) Road Runner," and a composition of no great scope, "The Derelict," whose DNA was too far removed from Fleetwood Mac. "I was pretty burned out and was having problems of my own at the time which restricted my effectiveness in all areas of my life, both professional and personal,"[46] Dave admitted in an interview in 2000. It was neither the first nor the last bad experience for this artist, who never managed to make a lasting contribution to the bands he did not found. On the other hand, he had built up an impressive résumé. Who can boast of having sung in Humble Pie, Fleetwood Mac, and Black Sabbath?

From Guitar to Vocals

Nothing predestined this artist, born on January 25, 1945, in Walsall, Staffordshire, for a career in rock'n'roll. In fact, rock'n'roll was totally outlawed in the home of his grandmother, who raised him. He was only allowed to sing in the Methodist church. As a teenager, Dave Walker was given more autonomy and was able to play in a skiffle band with his twin brother, Mick. The two young aspiring musicians followed each other in the rhythm'n'blues band the Redcaps—in which Dave first played rhythm guitar, then vocals, and Mick played bass—between 1960 and 1965. The Redcaps were lucky enough to open for the Beatles four times and released three singles: a cover of the Isley Brothers' "Shout"; a Chuck Berry cover, "I'm Talking About You"; and an original composition, "Funny Things." None of them managed to chart. This failure led Dave Walker to change his tune. Until 1969, he played in Beckett, the resident band of a Birmingham nightclub whose career was limited to a stage existence.

In 1970, Jeff Lynne abandoned his first project, the Idle Race, before joining the Move and launching his famous band, Electric Light Orchestra. The Idle Race continued without its founder and recruited Dave Walker on vocals. He took part in the *Time Is* album (wrongly credited as Richie Walker) before resigning in 1971. He was not inactive for long, however, as Savoy Brown's guitarist Kim Simmonds, who had just seen all his partners throw in the towel to form Foghat, decided to carry on. To this end, Simmonds recruited a new team, made up of three members of Chicken Shack, and entrusted the microphone to Walker. In the space of just over a year, between 1971 and 1972, the new band put together three albums: *Street Corner Talking*, *Hellbound Train* (number thirty-four in the United States in 1972), and *Lion's Share*. This is where Fleetwood Mac came in. It was not to be, however, as Walker failed to convince his partners and was fired during the recording of *Mystery to Me*. Against all odds, in 1974, he joined forces with Danny Kirwan (another ex-Mac man) to launch Hungry Fighter. A small gig and then off: A road accident following the gig resulted in the destruction of the band's equipment. In any case, the band was already questioning the reliability of its guitarist, a confirmed alcoholic.

250

Dave Walker then had a brief stint with Raven, after moving to San Francisco. With two band members, guitarist Greg Douglass and bassist Skip Olsen, he joined the glam-rock band Mistress in 1976. At the same time, he took part in Danny Kirwan's solo album, *Midnight in San Juan*, writing the song "Look Around You." The following year, he received an offer he could not refuse. Tony Iommi, guitarist of the legendary heavy metal band Black Sabbath, whom he had met in Birmingham, offered him the singer's position vacated by Ozzy Osbourne. As soon as he was hired, Walker worked on the new songs composed by the remaining members of the band, with a view to a new opus. But once all the lyrics were down on paper, he learned that

Ozzy was planning to make a comeback. In 1978, Osbourne resumed his position with no one to object, and, refusing to accept any material conceived in his absence, brushed aside the lyrics written by Dave Walker.

In 1979, Walker formed the Dave Walker Band, but soon gave up and retired from music for a while. He made a brief comeback with Savoy Brown from 1986 to 1991, then again from 1999 to 2003 with a semi-amateur psychedelic garage band, Donovan's Brain. Four years later, he reactivated his idea of the Dave Walker Band, which helped him shape the tracks on his solo album *Walking Underwater* (2007) for the stage. Since then, he has been touring with his band, made up of musicians from his hometown in Montana.

The guitarist with the sideburns composed "Caught in the Rain" and took part in the conception of "Forever."

BOB WESTON, THE MAN OF THE SHADOWS

Like Mick Fleetwood, Bob Weston grew up with family members who dedicated their lives to their country. The Fleetwoods had been in the Royal Air Force, and the Westons were in the Royal Navy. Born Robert Joseph Weston on November 1, 1947, in Plymouth, Devon, Bob started out playing the violin before switching to the guitar at the age of twelve after a revelation when he discovered the blues. In the mid-1960s, he headed for London, convinced that he could make a living from his passion. He reached Paris, where he joined the beat group the Kinetic. With them, he opened for Jimi Hendrix and Chuck Berry when they visited France. Benefiting from the arrival of the beat wave in France, the group was signed by the local label Disques Vogue. The label released the album *Live Your Life* and the EPs *Live Your Life* and *Suddenly Tomorrow* in France in 1967. Despite their potential, the band split up the following year, and Bob returned to London in April 1968. He found himself a band more in tune with his musical desires: Black Cat Bones, which played a heavy rock style. He took the position of lead guitarist, previously held by Paul Kossoff. But the collaboration did not last, and Bob left the group at the end of 1968. He then opted for a less exposed but more financially secure position: He became a session musician, working in the studio as well as on stage. This led to a string of gigs with Ashman Reynolds, Chimera, Graham Bond, and Long John Baldry.

The Fleetwood Mac Experience

Weston's ongoing collaboration with Baldry led to regular meetings with Fleetwood Mac, with whom the blond rhythm'n'blues giant shared the bill. Weston caught the eye of the group formed by Fleetwood, McVie, and Welch. So, when Danny Kirwan was ousted, his replacement was ready-made. The pairing of the two Bobs was a promising one. Weston's versatility enabled him to move off the blues track with ease, his playing was skillful and instinctive, and he was capable of playing other instruments, as he demonstrated by playing harmonica and banjo on "The Derelict," a composition by the other September 1972 recruit, Dave Walker. However, the artistic freedom promised by the Fleetwood Mac musicians was not forthcoming. Christine McVie and Bob Welch retained control of the songwriting and Bob Weston found himself with only one instrumental, "Caught in the Rain," at the end of the recording of *Penguin*. He gritted his teeth, telling himself that if he gave a satisfactory performance, he would be given more responsibility on *Mystery to Me*. Despite some memorable contributions (such as his slide intro on "Why") and a joint composition

("Forever"), his inspiration was blocked by the other musicians. However, his past as a session musician had given him a sense of self-denial and he persisted with the band, carving out a niche for himself with some very convincing live performances. Unfortunately, it was a non-musical matter that was to disrupt the harmony that was beginning to settle in the Mac. Since his arrival in the Fleetwood Mac family, Bob Weston had always been very close to Jenny Boyd. Suffering from being sidelined, she found in him a sympathetic ear. Their platonic friendship soon turned to physical passion. Mick, who got on very well with Weston, finally found out in 1973. He thought he could overcome the ordeal and continue to work with Weston, but the taste of betrayal was too bitter. He opened up to the group, who agreed that a split was inevitable.

Return to Anonymity

Bob Weston returned to London at the end of 1973. There was talk of a possible collaboration with George Harrison, the ex-Beatle who was now going solo, but it did not materialize. Instead, he began to play for Murray Head, both on tour and in the studio, contributing to the hit album *Say It Ain't So* in 1975. That same year, he joined the cast of Steve Marriott's All Stars, but was soon dropped when Marriott decided to take on the lead guitar himself. Weston returned to his shadowy role of session musician. In 1979, the creative bug took hold of him again and he set about recording his first solo album, *Nightlight*, at Basing Street Studios and Roundhouse Studios. The opus was supported by the single "Silver Arrow," but it failed to gain recognition. He persisted in 1980 with a second album, *Studio Picks*. Against all expectations, Mick Fleetwood graced the song "Ford 44" with his presence, demonstrating that the hatchet had been buried between the two comrades. Once again, however, the charts evaded the singer and guitarist. He tried one last time to break through, with a more pop single, "Desire," in 1985, but it was not a success. Bob Weston gave up and again returned to the life of a session musician. He did, however, diversify, working in film and television throughout the 1980s and 1990s. In 1999, he nevertheless offered a third installment to his solo discography with *There's Heaven*. His career ended in anonymity as he only occasionally played with an amateur band, Mad Dog Bites.

The musician died in the early hours of 2012 in complete solitude, following a gastrointestinal hemorrhage due to cirrhosis. His body was discovered by the police on January 3, 2012. He was sixty-four years old.

REMEMBER ME
Christine McVie / 2:41

Musicians
Christine McVie: vocals, keyboards
Bob Welch: guitar, backing vocals
Bob Weston: guitar
John McVie: bass
Mick Fleetwood: drums, percussion

Recorded
Rolling Stones Mobile Studio, Benifold, Hampshire, January 1973

Technical Team
Producers: Fleetwood Mac and Martin Birch
Sound Engineer: Martin Birch

Single
Side A: Remember Me / Side B: Dissatisfied
US Release Date: May 1973 with Reprise Records (ref. REP 1159)
Best US Chart Ranking: Did Not Chart

Christine McVie opened up in "Remember Me," a song that was directed toward her husband.

Genesis and Lyrics

Danny Kirwan was no longer there to provide his share of songs for Fleetwood Mac, and Christine McVie, who until then had only contributed a few tracks, albeit promising ones, had to give more of herself and assume her role as composer and leader. "Remember Me" finds her making an urgent, almost desperate plea to her partner, in a voice that is both passionate and sensual. Her relationship with John McVie—which had become increasingly complicated with the bassist's chronic alcoholism—is obviously at the heart of this track, even if his name is never mentioned. "I want you and I need you" is how she sums up the situation. She accepts the doubts and even the pain, because she feels she loves him more than he loves her: "I'm just hoping that maybe / You're feeling the same way too." Feeling that she has been patient for a long time, she makes a thinly veiled threat and sets limits to her love: "It may not be love / Or an everlasting feelin'." She calls him to order, urging him to do something about a situation that is no longer tenable.

Production

"Remember Me" clearly anticipates Fleetwood Mac's *Rumours* period. If the song is often cited as one of Christine McVie's best compositions, it is of course down to its catchy melody, but also to the question-and-answer game with magnificent backing vocals on the chorus. These are judiciously isolated in the left-hand part of the stereo spectrum, accentuating the light, airy feel of the track, a real pop delicacy calibrated for radio. Newcomer Bob Weston's slide guitar is perfectly in tune with his assured lines, while the solid rhythm section is supported by Christine's versatile playing at the piano. Fleetwood Mac's sound is compact and intense on this album opener, illustrating the band's successful transition to pop, which would stabilize definitively a few years later. The guitars are biting, and the two Bobs (Welch and Weston) make sure they do not step on each other's toes. Aesthetes of the six-string, they weigh up each note so that it benefits the song, as on the subtle passage with harmonics at 1:20, before Weston goes on the attack with his incendiary slide guitar. Like "Morning Rain" or "Just Crazy Love," "Remember Me" is one of those Christine McVie songs

Bob Welch and Bob Weston complemented each other's vocals in "Remember Me."

Christine McVie performed "Remember Me" at Bob Welch's Live from the Roxy concert in 1981.

that offered Fleetwood Mac a future, and whose reminiscences will be heard on later tracks such as "Over My Head" or "Say You Love Me." However, the single failed to chart in the United States.

John McVie delivered complex, melodic bass lines in "Bright Fire."

BRIGHT FIRE

Bob Welch / 4:32

Musicians: Bob Welch: vocals, guitar / Bob Weston: guitar / Christine McVie: keyboards, backing vocals / John McVie: bass / Mick Fleetwood: drums, percussion / **Recorded:** Rolling Stones Mobile Studio, Benifold, Hampshire, January 1973 / **Technical Team:** Producers: Fleetwood Mac and Martin Birch / Sound Engineer: Martin Birch

Genesis and Lyrics

"'Bright Fire' was very loosely referring to the Vietnam war, and in general to the terrible suffering that man inflicts upon himself,"[47] Bob Welch explained to Fleetwood Mac fans in 1999, thereby justifying the song's precise references to "the dust," "the future burn," and "green magnesium fire." In writing this FM pop ballad, the guitarist's main aim was to highlight the fact that, in life, violence solves nothing, unlike love. Right from the first verse, he calls on everyone to form their own opinion before entering into a conflict-filled relationship, and not to follow the movement like a sheep. He urges the listener to "stop thinking about yesterday," because time, in his view, is simply "a region to be passed," and the only thing that seems to matter in this world to him is to "look where the roses grow." It is all about turning negative experience into positive action.

Production

A clear, reverb-laden guitar, coupled with Christine McVie's ethereal keyboard, gives the introduction to "Bright Fire" a slightly psychedelic feel. However, it is John McVie's bass that takes center stage on this FM-calibrated track. Slippery, acrobatic in places, it relies effectively on Mick Fleetwood's drums, somewhat in the background, and on a few subtle guitar lines by Bob Weston. Almost banal on the verses, the melody becomes catchier on the chorus, where Bob skillfully lets the words hang in the air. Christine McVie's distant backing vocals, seeming to extend the lament of her organ, bring Bob Welch's gentle voice to the fore in a final, downright haunting sequence on which the two sing: "Look where the roses grow / Look where the roses lie." But Bob Welch's songwriting, with this new, very "American" track, once again points the way to a possible future for the band.

"Dissatisfied" was Side B to "Remember Me," but "Dissatisfied" followed the same theme and, thus, remained in the shadow of the single.

Mick Fleetwood made his swing speak and adopted a jazz approach in "Dissatisfied."

DISSATISFIED

Christine McVie / 3:43

Musicians: Christine McVie: vocals, keyboards / Bob Welch: guitar, backing vocals / Bob Weston: guitar / John McVie: bass / Mick Fleetwood: drums, percussion / **Recorded:** Rolling Stones Mobile Studio, Benifold, Hampshire, January 1973 / **Technical Team:** Producers: Fleetwood Mac and Martin Birch / Sound Engineer: Martin Birch / **Single:** Side A: Remember Me / Side B: Dissatisfied / **US Release Date:** May 1973 with Reprise Records (ref. REP 1159) / Best US Chart Ranking: Did Not Chart

Genesis and Lyrics

Christine McVie, as she did in the opening of "Remember Me," recalls her chaotic relationship with John McVie. But rather than wallowing in self-pity, she tries to pique her husband's interest and provoke a reaction. By explaining that she is "dissatisfied" with their marriage, she hopes to make him feel guilty enough to admit his problem and try to return to being the man she loved from the start. Wondering why he is "still so sad," she tries to restore his faith in himself, confessing that he is "the only reason for all my joy." Nor is she afraid to openly question her dependence on John. Helplessly, she explains that she would do "anything / Just to see you smile again" and "take away a little pain." Using a lovely metaphor, she says she hopes to be able to "make the sun shine through" and restore their shared happiness

Production

Despite a distressing theme—that of a failing love affair—Christine McVie takes the opposite tack, opting for a bouncy, upbeat melody. The guitars of Bob Welch and Bob Weston perform a perfect duet, knitting ingenious lines to a swaying rhythm section without ever encroaching on each other's territory. The disciplined Mick Fleetwood beats time with a light swing, giving the impression of breaking his wrist on his cymbals to muffle them with finesse like jazz drummers, while John McVie remains a pillar of this warm groove with a round, groovy bass. At 1:48, a typical country-rock guitar solo, brilliantly played with the finger, lights up the track, while the highly addictive chorus runs right through to the finale, with the millimeter accuracy of the backing vocals picking it up, accompanied by a mischievous little electric guitar gimmick. Finally, Christine McVie's voice manages to keep its balance on this emotional roller coaster, forcing her to sing lightly on a very personal theme.

"(I'm a) Road Runner" has been covered by bands other than Fleetwood Mac: The Jerry Garcia Band delivered their own rendition, along with James Taylor, Steve Gaines (guitarist with Lynyrd Skynyrd), and Peter Frampton, with Frampton including it on his 1977 album *I'm in You*.

FOR MAC-ADDICTS

In the original version of "(I'm a) Road Runner," Junior Walker ran into a key problem. The saxophone allowed only two, which did not match the key of his vocals. So it was necessary to speed up the saxophone. Walker's harmonica, which replays this musical sequence, posed no such problem.

(I'M A) ROAD RUNNER

Brian Holland, Lamont Dozier, Eddie Holland Jr. /
4:52

Musicians: Dave Walker: vocals, harmonica / Bob Welch: guitar, backing vocals / Bob Weston: guitar / Christine McVie: keyboards, backing vocals / John McVie: bass / Mick Fleetwood: drums, percussion / **Recorded:** Rolling Stones Mobile Studio, Benifold, Hampshire, January 1973 / **Technical Team:** Producers: Fleetwood Mac and Martin Birch / Sound Engineer: Martin Birch

Genesis and Lyrics

A trio of American soul songwriters and producers, Brian Holland, Lamont Dozier, and Eddie Holland were key to the success of the Motown label in the 1960s. They penned a number of hits by artists from the Detroit stable, including the Supremes, Marvin Gaye, the Four Tops, the Temptations, and the Miracles. The trio was also responsible for "(I'm a) Road Runner," originally recorded in 1965 by Junior Walker & the All Stars, which reached number twenty on the Billboard charts. The lyrics refer to the great freedom enjoyed by roadrunners, the species of bird popularized by the Wile E. Coyote and Road Runner cartoons, in which Wile E. Coyote sets various traps in the path of his antagonist, the Road Runner. In the song, the narrator explains that he too is a roadrunner, with no need for money or ties, and that all he needs is a toothbrush and "let me live a life free and easy." He warns that he "don't want no woman to tie me down / [...] You can love me at your own risk."

Production

For their first album with Fleetwood Mac, Bob Weston and Dave Walker struggled to contribute songs to the group effort. Weston only managed to deliver one instrumental, "Caught in the Rain," on the closing track of *Penguin*, but his involvement was less problematic than that of Dave Walker, designated as singer and supposed leader. The latter did not fit in, and only sang on two tracks: a composition called "The Derelict" and this cover, "(I'm a) Road Runner." But this track had no real purpose other than to give him a little credit. Dave Walker himself admitted as much, answering a fan who asked if this was, as he had often read, one of Fleetwood Mac's worst recordings: "I thought 'Road Runner' was a decent choice of song for me to sing but again, it was done very quickly and the vocals did leave a lot to be desired. I have never heard it referred to as the worst Fleetwood Mac recording ever and in my own defense I could probably come up with a couple of those silly sickly sweet songs written by other members of the band that might qualify for that dubious distinction. After I was fired from the band I bumped into Ritchie Blackmore in London and he told me he really liked it."[46] Dave Walker also plays the harmonica on this cover, replacing the saxophone originally played by Junior Walker. As for Christine McVie, she acquits herself very creditably on piano, while the others are content to carry on with business as usual. Not at ease, Dave Walker was not to last long with the Mac: "With regard to the whole Fleetwood Mac experience, most of the memories are sad as I realized very early on that I just did not fit in but was afraid to admit it to them or to myself."[46]

THE DERELICT

Dave Walker / 2:43

Musicians: Dave Walker: vocals / Bob Welch: guitar / Bob Weston: guitar, banjo, harmonica / Christine McVie: piano / Mick Fleetwood: drums, percussion / **Recorded:** Rolling Stones Mobile Studio, Benifold, Hampshire, January 1973 / **Technical Team:** Producers: Fleetwood Mac and Martin Birch / Sound Engineer: Martin Birch / **Single:** Side A: Did You Ever Love Me / Side B: The Derelict / **UK Release Date:** July 6, 1973, with Reprise Records (ref. K 14280) / Best UK Chart Ranking: Did Not Chart

Dave Walker's only compositional contribution, "The Derelict," illustrated the difficulty of his integration into the band.

Genesis and Lyrics

"The song 'The Derelict' was written from a life experience and did have personal connotations for me at the time,"[46] explains Dave Walker. Very short and light, it tells the story of a person who has lived "in a derelict," moving from squat to squat before settling down with a partner who gives him everything he needs: love. Although relatively short, the lyrics of "The Derelict" are so sincere that everyone can identify with them. Walker depicts the sad daily life of a protagonist who "ate off the floor" and spent his days "wrapped in a blanket," until an encounter that literally saves him and gives him hope for a better life: "So I moved in with you, and you loved me." It is hard not to see this as a metaphor for his short-lived career with Fleetwood Mac: that of a man who simply wanted to be loved.

Production

"The Derelict" is probably one of the most neglected songs in Fleetwood Mac's repertoire. The bass of John McVie, who did not participate in the recorded version of the song, is not heard. Christine McVie's piano is very discreet: "With regard to 'The Derelict,' the song on the album was never finished, as there was no bass track and there was no real production,"[46] lamented Dave Walker in an interview in 2000. He is right, and it is a pity, because it was certainly the best track on *Penguin*. The rhythmic acoustic guitar is diligent and Mick Fleetwood's drums are invaluable with their warm matte sound, while Bob Weston comes into his own with a facetious banjo and a simple but incredibly comforting harmonica part. Dave Walker also shows off his touching voice on a very catchy melody. The delightful country-rock flavor emanating from "The Derelict" can only highlight the regret of those who feel that Dave could have given much more if he had remained with Fleetwood Mac.

Bob Welch was present on all fronts, on guitar and bass, on this deeply intriguing track.

REVELATION
Bob Welch / 4:55

Musicians: Bob Welch: vocals, guitar, bass / Bob Weston: guitar / Christine McVie: keyboards, backing vocals / Mick Fleetwood: drums, percussion / **Recorded:** Rolling Stones Mobile Studio, Benifold, Hampshire, January 1973 / **Technical Team:** Producers: Fleetwood Mac and Martin Birch / Sound Engineer: Martin Birch

Genesis and Lyrics

Bob Welch is the man behind this track, with its ominous lyrics and apocalyptic theme. He explained in 1999 (emphasis his): "I was at the time, and still AM, interested in things like 'why are we here, does it have a purpose, or is it, are WE, just an accident.' How, and why (if there is a why) did the universe come about? If there is no 'God,' then it's ok to just go around and do whatever we want, right? Just live for ourselves, right? Are there other beings in the universe who are as intelligent as we are? Is this reality we see every day the ONLY reality, or is there something or somewhere that we can't see, feel, taste or touch with our five physical senses? To me, all this stuff IS what the '60s were all about… people were trying to EXPAND their horizons, their ways of thinking."[47] The lyrics of "Revelation" also reflect this mysticism and dizziness in the face of existential and metaphysical questions, with the help of a few lines that say little about their real meaning, such as: "The future gives a warning of the fire that burns below / He puts his hands together, cause his faith is strong." In this respect, the song's title is somewhat misleading, since if there is a revelation, it remains very vague. Because, despite the presence of a laughing demiurge at the helm in the opening verses, seeming to control everything and to whom the human being can calmly surrender, the fire is smoldering. We do not know who is responsible, man or God, and who is in a position to put it out.

Production

In this technically skillful blend of rock and jazz, the first thing that stands out is the rounded, loquacious, and mysterious bass—a bass the likes of which John McVie has never recorded before. And with good reason: Here, the master of groove is not the usual initiator of the low frequencies, since he is absent from the recording, but Bob Welch. Dave Walker confirms that John may well have been at the bar with him when the song was wrapped up: "It may well be that Bob Welch did play the bass track on *Revelation*, but I cannot be sure as I was in the bar. Whether John was with me or not, has long since been erased from my memory bank."[46] While Mick Fleetwood displays his stamina on the toms, it is Bob Welch who officiates on this impressive bass part, but obviously this did not make him want to change his role in Fleetwood Mac for good: "I LOVE to invent bass parts, and love playing the bass, but McVie is the true workmanlike and steady bass player among us. I just dabble!"[47] he admitted in 1999. Guitars also play a key role in this track, which captures the essence of the adventurous spirit of the late 1960s with inventive gimmicks and solos and finely chiseled arpeggios. While Bob Welch's voice is mysteriously bewitching—if not very charismatic—the backing vocals on the chorus have an unsettling edge to them when they deviate from the main melody, which is already not very catchy.

John McVie was confronted with Christine's questioning and bitterness in her new compositions.

DID YOU EVER LOVE ME

Christine McVie, Bob Welch / 3:39

Musicians: Bob Weston: vocals, guitar / Bob Welch: guitar, backing vocals / Christine McVie: keyboards, vocals / John McVie: bass / Mick Fleetwood: drums, percussion / Ralph Richardson: steel drums / Russell Valdez: steel drums / Fred Totesant: steel drums / **Recorded:** Rolling Stones Mobile Studio, Benifold, Hampshire, January 1973 / **Technical Team:** Producers: Fleetwood Mac and Martin Birch / Sound Engineer: Martin Birch / **Single:** Side A: Did You Ever Love Me / Side B: The Derelict / **UK Release Date:** July 6, 1973, with Reprise Records (ref. K 14280) / Best UK Chart Ranking: Did Not Chart / **Single:** Side A: Did You Ever Love Me (Mono) / Side B: Did You Ever Love Me (Stereo) / **US Release Date:** September 1973 with Reprise Records (ref. REP 1172) / Best US Chart Ranking: Did Not Chart

Genesis and Lyrics

Co-written by Christine McVie and Bob Welch, "Did You Ever Love Me" sees Christine return to her complex relationship with her husband, John McVie, as she had already done in "Remember Me" and "Dissatisfied." Of the three tracks, "Did You Ever Love Me" is probably the one that brings out the most bitterness and regret in the young woman. In it, she underlines everything that now separates them and that once united them. She even questions the sincerity of this love: "Do you ever wonder or worry about me? / Did I ever love you? Did you ever love me?" The lyrics also reveal the narrator's powerlessness to preserve this love, as she explains: "So all I wanted slips through my hands." She also dreads a separation she considers to be inevitable, while recalling moments of happiness: "You made me happy but time has gone by."

Production

While *Penguin* is, by all accounts, a rather disjointed album, and the assimilation of Dave Walker and Bob Weston was less than optimal, "Did You Ever Love Me" is one of the few satisfying highlights. This chic pop-rock ballad is imaginatively arranged with luminous steel drums. It was Mick Fleetwood's idea to incorporate them, and to call on session musicians to perform them. However, despite its beautiful melody, the song, chosen as a single, failed to chart in either the United States or the UK. The public may have been taken aback by Christine McVie's bold choice of melody: a rather smiling one, in contrast to the song's theme of despair in love.

Christine arrived in the studio with a few piano chords, quickly joined by the two Bobs, with whom she began jamming. Nothing was really planned, but eventually Welch helped complete the lyrics over the next few days, while Bob Weston was asked to sing a few sequences with Christine. Why him and not Welch? "[W]e just wanted to give Bob a little vocal showcase,"[49] explains Welch diplomatically.

NIGHT WATCH

Bob Welch / 6:09

Musicians: Bob Welch: vocals, guitar / Bob Weston: guitar / Peter Green: guitar / Christine McVie: keyboards, backing vocals / Steve Nye: keyboards / John McVie: bass / Mick Fleetwood: drums, percussion / **Recorded:** Rolling Stones Mobile Studio, Benifold, Hampshire, and AIR studios (overdubs), London, January 1973 / **Technical Team:** Producers: Fleetwood Mac and Martin Birch / Sound Engineer: Martin Birch

Genesis and Lyrics

Some of the tracks on Bob Welch's Fleetwood Mac albums take on paranormal themes, as in "Night Watch," about unidentified flying objects referred to as "magic shadows." "['Night Watch'] was about the 'big' UFO landing, where they come down, everybody sees them, and everything changes (hopefully) for the better,"[47] Bob explains concerning the song. It has to be said that in the early 1970s, the subject aroused a growing fascination, nurtured and encouraged by the popularity of books like Erich von Däniken's *Chariots of the Gods?* (1968). The song's narrator, as a witness to these paranormal phenomena, sees in them a personal note of hope, as he suffers from loneliness and sings of his despair: "Well I have wondered why I live." He bases all his expectations (or otherwise) on the arrival of these "magic shadows" that hypnotize him completely, and with which he hopes to soon become one: "I'll step aboard with you one day."

Production

The atmospheric ambiance of "Night Watch," which stretches painfully over six minutes, seemed completely anachronistic when the album was released. Four years earlier, the timing would certainly have been perfect for Bob Welch and Fleetwood Mac, but by 1973, the psychedelic wave had already passed and been largely digested. With its bewitching keyboards, distant guitars drowned in reverb, hypnotic percussion, plunging bass, and ethereal backing vocals, "Night Watch" arrives after the battle, at the risk of making Fleetwood Mac seem like brontosaurs

of rock. While technically well produced and convincingly inhabited by Bob Welch, the track once again highlights the band's lack of artistic coherence on this decidedly disjointed album. The only real attraction is the surprise (and anecdotal) presence of the returning Peter Green on the fade-out: "Pete was at the studio all day as I remember, just sitting in the corner, not saying anything. I don't know whose idea it was, but he went down into the echo-chamber in the basement, and played along with 'Night Watch' from there," Bob Welch explains, before adding, "We couldn't see him or anything, and he just did what he wanted. It was very late at night, and we'd all had quite a bit to drink. Pete didn't make any comments after he recorded."[49] Dave Walker was also present, and his version more or less corroborates that of his colleague: "We were in Air London Studios, doing over-dubs for the *Penguin* album and Peter Green showed up with his guitar which was surprising because at the time he was refusing to play with anyone and was going through a difficult period in his life. There was one part in the tune that needed something special and with no disrespect to Bob Welch or Weston, it was not happening musically. Who persuaded him or how he was persuaded to play I do not clearly remember, but I think he nailed the track on the second take. Truly magical."[46]

Peter Green was in Benifold for a day to say hello to his old partners and took the opportunity to lay down a guitar (uncredited) on "Night Watch." According to Dave Walker, "[He] showed up with his guitar which was surprising because at the time he was refusing to play with anyone and was going through a difficult period in his life... but I think he nailed the track on the second take. Truely magical."[46]

Bob Weston's creative space was restricted, as Bob Welch and Christine McVie took over the composition of *Penguin*.

CAUGHT IN THE RAIN

Bob Weston / 2:35

Musicians: Bob Weston: guitar, backing vocals / Christine McVie: piano, backing vocals (?) / **Recorded:** Rolling Stones Mobile Studio, Benifold, Hampshire, January 1973 / **Technical Team:** Producers: Fleetwood Mac and Martin Birch / Sound Engineer: Martin Birch

Production

This instrumental by Bob Weston has the tricky task of closing *Penguin*, an album that was so very unbalanced. This is the only piece in Fleetwood Mac's repertoire for which the guitarist is given full credit, since the other track where his name is mentioned as composer is "Forever," on the *Mystery to Me* album, alongside Bob Welch and John McVie. With all due respect to Bob Weston, "Caught in the Rain" turns out to be pretty unremarkable, boiling down to a few chords and harmonics played on acoustic guitar, basic piano—which we cannot be certain was played by Christine McVie—and ethereal backing vocals. The ambiance is not unpleasant, but compared to previous Fleetwood Mac instrumentals, whether by Peter Green or Danny Kirwan, "Caught in the Rain" is sorely lacking in subtlety. Ironically, as Bob Welch explains, "I think while Bob was doing 'Caught in the Rain,' I was in the pantry, 'chalking my dickie.' Sorry, that's from an old joke, I couldn't resist!;-)"[47]

ALBUM

MYSTERY TO ME

Emerald Eyes . Believe Me . Just Crazy Love . Hypnotized . Forever . Keep on Going .
The City . Miles Away . Somebody . The Way I Feel . For Your Love . Why .
Outtake: Good Things (Come to Those Who Wait)

RELEASE DATES
United Kingdom: October 15, 1973
Reference: Reprise Records—K 44248
Best UK Chart Ranking: Did Not Chart
United States: October 15, 1973
Reference: Reprise Records—MS 2158
Best US Chart Ranking: 67

For his 2003 album *His Fleetwood Mac Years & Beyond*, Bob Welch reinterpreted three of his contributions: "Emerald Eyes," "Hypnotized," and "Miles Away." In the next installment in 2006, released only in digital format, he added new versions of "The City" and "Somebody."

A DECEPTIVE CALM

Fleetwood Mac did not wait for the release of *Penguin*, on March 1, 1973, to set off crisscrossing America. The band followed the schedule drawn up by Clifford Davis, with the backing of the musicians, to continue its expansion in the United States, a welcoming land, unlike England, which no longer paid them much attention. The Mac began the tour to promote *Penguin* on February 23, 1973, in Upper Darby, Pennsylvania, and completed it on May 31 in Davis, California. On stage, the band confirmed its newfound format, with Dave Walker in fine form, never better than when he was performing live.

Marriage and Music: Bad Bedfellows

While the concerts went well, the atmosphere backstage was a different matter, as Clifford Davis recalls: "It was a very successful tour! Walker was known from his Savoy Brown days and Bob Weston was also up front on stage a lot of the time. Then suddenly there seemed to be a lot of resentment. Because Dave was hogging the spotlight and picking up a lot of girls, stealing the show, you know!"[5] Whereas in the past they had turned a blind eye to Jeremy Spencer's worst stage outrages, now Fleetwood Mac were decrying Dave Walker for overdoing it. His penchant for the bottle was also criticized—a bit rich when John McVie cultivated the same vice. "Yes, I probably was the outcast," Walker explained in an interview in 2000. "Adversarial is

probably too strong a word to use as overall there was a friendly atmosphere most of the time, of course, I never heard what was said when I wasn't there, and they were a little timid about looking a person in the eye and speaking their mind."[46]

As the concerts progressed, the band adjusted their set list to play songs that did not require Dave Walker's intervention, thus reducing his presence on stage to a minimum. Walker was not fooled by this and understood what was going on. This added to his malaise, which expressed itself in ever more alcohol and ever more tension, particularly with his wife, who was accompanying him on the American tour.

He was not the only one for whom love and a musical career had trouble coexisting. Her husband's excesses and the inherent difficulty of working together continued to inspire the worried lyrics of Christine McVie's compositions, which are featured on this next album, such as "Believe Me," fueled by questions about their relationship; "Just Crazy Love," which evokes passion (incipient or dying); and "The Way I Feel," which speaks of the need to express one's feelings. Jenny, for her part, felt totally sidelined by Mick, whether she was on tour or not. As for Bob Welch's wife, who remained in California, she constantly reproached him for Fleetwood Mac's incessant touring. And when he was not on the road, he was recording in Benifold.

A Very Tense Start to Recording

In June, just six months after the last recording of *Penguin*, the band returned to the fold to put the finishing touches on a new opus. Given the lack of critical acclaim for *Penguin*, the musicians decided not to wait before conceiving its successor. The convenience provided by the Rolling Stones' mobile studio was so much appreciated during the January sessions that Fleetwood Mac opted for the same system. The truck was available, as was Martin Birch, now virtually the seventh member of the Mac, who was reappointed producer. The band was delighted to rediscover the sound conditions they had enjoyed so much on *Penguin*. "The sound in there was amazing, just massive, like a concert hall, resounding off the trees and all through the grounds,"[4] recalls Mick Fleetwood. Bob Weston adds enthusiastically: "Being at Benifold [...] was ideal, a great rehearsal situation, plenty of space, lots of lovely food, and a great little pub down the road."[48]

Soon, however, the focus shifted from new compositions to internal tensions. With work on the album only just getting under way, and despite the unfavorable timing, Mick, John, and Christine made the decision to end their collaboration with Dave Walker. As a result, the singer was not credited. "There were two tracks that I originally recorded vocals on, one was Christine's song and I think one was Bob Welch's, but after so long, the titles escape me. I would doubt that my tracks were kept although if my memory serves me well, my performances were good."[46]

Fleetwood Mac's triumvirate commissioned Clifford Davis to do the dirty work and break the bad news to the singer. This lack of courage galled the manager, who agreed, but only on condition that all three musicians were present—after all, it was their decision—and they had to accept it. This did not spare them the insults of Walker, who reproached them for their cowardice. After this episode, the singer, whose self-confidence had been seriously damaged, spent six months unable to sing and sank into depression.

Progress at Benifold

The band tried to put this episode behind them and immerse themselves in the work of recording the new album. Bob Welch was the most involved, and with good reason: He had taken the lead from Christine McVie as a songwriter, penning seven compositions (and co-writing an eighth). He puts his stamp on this album, which takes an increasingly obvious American soft-rock turn. For the first time, he really succeeded in imposing his sonic identity, whereas previously he had seemed restrained. As lead guitarist, his playing shone as never before. His jazz approach finely colored his subtly honed pop songs, and his musical complicity with Bob Weston illuminated tracks such as "Hypnotized," on which the guitar ornamentation sounded like sung parts.

This opus is also Fleetwood Mac's most eclectic work, with multiple influences such as the funk of "The City" and the reggae of "Why." Bob Welch worked closely with Martin Birch to give this record a highly polished, radio-calibrated production. The mobile studio had a state-of-the-art Helios console that would not be out of place in a traditional studio. Only the Tannoy speakers seemed a little light in terms of sound reproduction capacity for listening comfort, but apart from that, Birch had everything on hand that would be required to produce a top-quality record. The co-producer confirmed that he was the right man for the job. By now, he knew everyone's playing style, their taste in sound, and the equipment they used. As a result, he got the best out of the musicians and their instruments, and signed off with a highly polished, radio-friendly production.

Martin Birch's post—the control booth—soon became a refuge for Christine McVie, who spent most of her time there to escape spats with John. Inevitably, the sound engineer and the pianist started to bond, and Christine's incessant quarrels with her husband were forgotten in Birch's arms. Threats rained down. Regularly, each in turn, the spouses demanded the other's departure from the band. Bob Welch, the neutral element, showed his annoyance during these tense moments, threatening to leave and

Bob Weston paid a heavy price for his affair with Mick Fleetwood's wife: He was ousted from the band after *Mystery to Me*.

embark on a solo career. His productivity on this album led the other members to take his declarations seriously. The tension subsided, only to flare up again shortly afterward.

As for Mick, he was constantly on the move, supervising the recording sessions and then going off to listen to Birch's rough cuts in the truck. Totally absorbed in these tasks, the drummer neglected his wife, Jenny. In fact, they were not really a couple anymore. Jenny spent a lot of time with Bob Weston, and a kind of platonic love had developed between them. The guitarist, as a result, was a little less involved than the others in the sessions, assuming his role as a performer, but he played his guitar parts so brilliantly that no one thought to reproach him for his distancing.

A "Toasty Warm" Atmosphere

Miraculously, the album took a turn for the better, displaying stylistic coherence and solid, catchy compositions with sweet melodies. In the final analysis, a deceptive harmony emerged from the album while the band was taking on water from all sides for personal reasons. "Christine was flirting (to say the least) with the engineer/producer Martin Birch," Bob Welch would explain years later, "which made for a toasty warm atmosphere and strong sensuous undercurrent during the recording of the whole album."[47]

The album's songs and titles bear the stamp of this amorous muddle. *Mystery to Me* is taken from a line in the opening song, "Emerald Eyes": "She's still a mystery to me." In his 1991 autobiography, Mick Fleetwood explains: "The title of the album came from Jenny. She's told me since that the mystery was how she'd begun to feel for Bob Weston. The two of them would go on long walks or hang out together in the house. I didn't see it at all, to me it looked as if Jenny had found a friend in the band. I was happy, actually. I figured that if she felt more comfortable, she'd come on tour more, allowing us to be together."[4]

Beware the Gorilla

The strikingly original cover, designed by Modula, the agency already responsible for the cover of the previous album (*Penguin*), is as dubious as it is surprising, adding to

Another whiff of adultery, this time between Martin Birch and Christine McVie, contaminated the recording sessions.

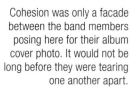

FOR MAC-ADDICTS

A mistake was made on the cover of the first pressing of *Mystery to Me*: The track listing indicated "Good Things (Come to Those Who Wait)" as the penultimate song on Side 2, when in fact it had been replaced at the last minute by "For Your Love." The error was rectified on subsequent pressings.

the mystery suggested by the title. It shows an imaginary ape with the body of a gorilla and the head of a mandrill on a dreamy beach, licking his lips with the white topping of a cake in which he has just dipped his paw. He has also taken a bite out of a book lying on the sand. A tear rolls down his cheek. The image continues on the back cover. When unfolded, the full image appears: Opposite the "gorilla" stands an old man in a white toga, obviously a sage, with books placed before him. Behind his back is the penguin, adopted as Fleetwood Mac's mascot from the previous opus. It seems that the "gorilla" has abandoned the book (symbolizing knowledge) and prefers to feast on the cake (pleasure). A comment by Bob Welch posted in 1999 in response to a fan question validates this interpretation: "The meaning I think was sort of supposed to be: 'no matter how much knowledge you get, everything is still a mystery, and you're still a monkey.'"[47]

Fierce Criticism

Sales figures were modest. The album peaked at number sixty-seven in the US, selling around 250,000 copies. In the UK, the situation was even more desperate, as the album failed to chart. Critical reception was lukewarm at best, if not downright cruel. On January 3, 1974, *Rolling Stone* journalist Gordon Fletcher wrote a vitriolic review: "Though they're all probably excellent musicians with talent coming out of their ears, the fact still remains that ever since Fleetwood Mac lost its three guitarists extraordinaire, they've become increasingly less interesting. Things that are better felt than expressed have brought Fleetwood Mac to a point where the band just doesn't seem to matter much anymore. Though performed with great proficiency and occasionally enlightening subtlety, the first side of *Mystery to Me* turned out to be so abysmally dismal that I gave serious consideration to just stopping it right there and chucking the damn thing out the window at a passing bird. All the songs were the same faceless blend of tired, low-key English rock. [...] Side two turned out to be considerably better though hardly comparable to the fire associated with the name Fleetwood Mac during the residencies of Messrs. Green, Spencer and Kirwan."[50] A cold shower for the musicians, who were aware that they had undergone a decisive transformation and had high hopes for this record, which had seemed destined for glory.

Jenny Boyd was the subject of numerous men's desires, including Bob Weston and Bob Welch.

EMERALD EYES

Bob Welch / 3:37

Musicians: Bob Welch: vocals, guitar / Bob Weston: guitar / Christine McVie: keyboards, backing vocals / John McVie: bass / Mick Fleetwood: drums / **Recorded:** Rolling Stones Mobile Studio, Benifold, Hampshire, June 1973 / **Technical Team:** Producers: Fleetwood Mac and Martin Birch / Sound Engineer: Martin Birch / Assistant Sound Engineers: Desmond Majekodunmi, Paul Hardiman

Genesis and Lyrics

To open *Mystery to Me*, Bob Welch composed a folk-rock ballad in honor of an emerald-eyed woman who brings him comfort and serenity by her very presence. Apart from Mick Fleetwood, who was blind to the romance going on behind his back, no one was fooled as to the identity of the young mystery woman: This is Jenny Boyd. The narrator constantly praises her qualities of discretion and honesty, as well as the way she "makes your day to day life easy." He praises her role within Benifold, too often ignored by the other members of the group. The narrator

also feels enhanced by the light emanating from this almost celestial being in his eyes: "Find emerald eyes in the night/Gleamin' shiny and bright." "A lot of times in my songs, I used 'she' to symbolize 'longing,' spiritual or otherwise…'Emerald Eyes' is like the science fiction 'super-female' with light beams coming out of her eyes, who has all-knowledge, all-sensuality, all-beauty wrapped up in 'her' one super-person."[47] It is this song that gives the album its title, with the line "She's still a mystery to me." Whether intentionally or not, the song's vocabulary of the gaze and the light recalls "Jewel Eyed Judy," co-written by Jenny and Christine McVie in 1970 for *Kiln House* (although they were not credited at the time).

Production

It is impossible not to think of Crosby, Stills, Nash & Young, America, or Neil Young's fabulous *Harvest* album (released in 1972) when listening to "Emerald Eyes." This very American-sounding track clearly confirms the imprint that Bob Welch wishes to leave on Fleetwood Mac, and paves the way, already begun, that leads the English band toward the great spaces of the West. Over a slow, confident rhythm, layers of guitar build up, and Bob Weston's solo playing proves as luminous as the emerald eyes referred to in the song. While John McVie's bass relies essentially on fundamental notes to give depth and impact to Mick Fleetwood's powerful drums, Christine McVie's cottony keyboards add density to the overall sound at the end of the chorus, often after Weston's guitar interventions (from 2:46 onward, for example), when Bob Welch's warm voice resurfaces. Welch's warm vocals are admirably supported by Christine's backing vocals, which add sweetness to the soothing melody.

BELIEVE ME

Christine McVie / 4:12

Musicians: Christine McVie: vocals, keyboards, backing vocals / Bob Welch: guitar, backing vocals / Bob Weston: slide guitar, backing vocals / John McVie: bass / Mick Fleetwood: drums / **Recorded:** Rolling Stones Mobile Studio, Benifold, Hampshire, June 1973 / **Technical Team:** Producers: Fleetwood Mac and Martin Birch / Sound Engineer: Martin Birch / Assistant Sound Engineers: Desmond Majekodunmi, Paul Hardiman

Genesis and Lyrics

Throughout her songs, Christine McVie talks about her turbulent relationship with her husband John. She expresses her doubts, her questions, her incomprehension, and sometimes her anger. "Believe Me" marks a new chapter of self-assurance for her, symptomatic of the evolution of their relationship. In this song, the narrator reaffirms her love for her partner, "Even though you've stopped the sun from shining." She refuses to feel any more guilt, believing, "Well I've tried my best, but it may not be enough." Both lovers have been through difficult times, but she has no intention of giving up. Her only hope is that life will become simpler and that their love can finally be lived normally.

Production

After a gentle piano introduction, "Believe Me" speeds off into a rock'n'roll mood, buoyed by Christine's nonchalant vocals on the verses. She is joined by some fine backing vocals on the more remonstrative chorus. Mick Fleetwood and John McVie are particularly prominent on this feverishly paced track: the former with drums that can be heavy in places, and the latter with an elastic bass line that fits perfectly with Christine McVie's driving piano. The two Bobs' guitars are also in the spotlight, complementing each other brilliantly. At 1:47, Bob Weston's country slide guitar delivers a long solo until 2:10, before a final verse is introduced by charming, harmonized backing vocals. A real break occurs in the song from 2:43 until the finale for a long instrumental sequence: Mick Fleetwood's drums become more intense, with a snare drum gaining in power and depth, and toms playing that is both rich and very courteous as it offers more space to Christine McVie's enchanting piano and the screaming guitars in the distance.

JUST CRAZY LOVE

Christine McVie / 3:22

Musicians: Christine McVie: vocals, keyboards, backing vocals / Bob Welch: guitar, backing vocals / Bob Weston: guitar, backing vocals / John McVie: bass / Mick Fleetwood: drums / **Recorded:** Rolling Stones Mobile Studio, Benifold, Hampshire, June 1973 / **Technical Team:** Producers: Fleetwood Mac and Martin Birch / Sound Engineer: Martin Birch / Assistant Sound Engineers: Desmond Majekodunmi, Paul Hardiman

Genesis and Lyrics

In "Just Crazy Love," Christine McVie unleashes her pen as a passionate lover of a man to whom she promises the exclusivity of her irrational love: "You know you'll always be the only one / And if you'll let me say / You'll never be a lonely one." She consciously devalues herself, perhaps feeling unable to compete with other women: "And I'll do anything if you'll let me be your baby / Even when everybody tells me / I'm just being a fool / Something inside says I've got to have you." In this dizzying game of love, there is probably a subtle reference to her clandestine affair with producer Martin Birch, as she acknowledges that "I can't play by the rules." She implores the object of her desire to give her a chance to make it up to him, but the lyrics do not say whether she succeeds in being heard.

Production

"Just Crazy Love" is a forerunner of the pop direction that would catapult Fleetwood Mac to the top of the charts in the years that followed. Christine McVie demonstrates her skills as a songwriter. She seems perfectly poised for the imminent takeoff to stardom. Without a doubt, with "Just Crazy Love" and its unstoppable chorus, Christine stands out as the future lethal weapon of the Mac. Beyond her airy, playful vocal delivery, her piano playing appears invigorating and refreshing. Like a precious stone patiently polished, the luminous melody of "Just Crazy Love" is reminiscent in its effectiveness of other little pebbles "Tom Thumb" McVie left on her path, such as "Spare Me a Little of Your Love" on *Bare Trees* (1972) or "Remember Me" on *Penguin* (1973). A veritable master class in concise pop, "Just Crazy Love" seems to be ahead of its time, with guitars that are sometimes untidy but have a communicative energy, a frenzied rhythm section, and, above all, backing vocals that are perfectly calibrated on the chorus.

HYPNOTIZED

Bob Welch / 4:48

Musicians
Bob Welch: vocals, guitar
Bob Weston: guitar, backing vocals
Christine McVie: keyboards, backing vocals
John McVie: bass
Mick Fleetwood: drums

Recorded
Rolling Stones Mobile Studio, Benifold, Hampshire, June 1973

Technical Team
Producers: Fleetwood Mac and Martin Birch
Sound Engineer: Martin Birch
Assistant Sound Engineers: Desmond Majekodunmi, Paul Hardiman

Single
Side A: For Your Love / **Side B:** Hypnotized
UK Release Date: 1973 with Reprise Records (ref. REP 1188)
Best UK Chart Ranking: Did Not Chart
US Release Date: 1973 with Reprise Records (ref. K 14315)
Best US Chart Ranking: Did Not Chart

The Pointer Sisters covered "Hypnotized" in 1978 on their fifth studio album, entitled *Energy*. During a 1999 Q&A session on FleetwoodMac.net, Bob Welch admitted his surprise at the choice. "I was flattered, of course, since they were a wonderful group, but I sometimes wonder if they could've made any sense of the lyrics, which were pretty [...] obscure."

Genesis and Lyrics

While Christine McVie is often considered an essential link in Fleetwood Mac's metamorphosis into a veritable pop hits factory, Bob Welch also had a lot to do with it. "Hypnotized" is without doubt the best song he ever gave Fleetwood Mac, and perhaps one of the best of his entire career. As Welch himself admitted in 1999, "My favorite song that I wrote from the old days is 'Hypnotized.'"[47]

Guided by the Californian guitarist's fascination with UFOs, the song "was primarily inspired by Castaneda's books, the Hickson Pascagoula Miss UFO sighting, some stories told to me by friends, and some personal experiences."[47] Welch's passion for supernatural phenomena led him to study the work of Carlos Castaneda, the American doctor of anthropology and author of a dozen books on South American Indian shamanic teachings, from which he benefited. Although his works—bestsellers in the 1960s—were widely debated and even contested, he enjoyed a certain cult following among artists such as singers Jim Morrison and John Lennon and beat writer William S. Burroughs. In his text, Bob Welch evokes hypnosis and dreams: "Because there's no explaining what your imagination / Can make you see and feel / Seems like a dream / They got me hypnotized." The lyricist also refers to the case known as the Pascagoula Abduction, the alleged abduction of two men by aliens in Mississippi in 1973, shortly before the recording of "Mystery to Me." Charles Hickson and Calvin Parker, two shipyard workers from Pascagoula, claimed to have been abducted and studied by humanoid creatures aboard a UFO, before being released after some twenty minutes so that they could recount their experience to their fellow workers. The high-profile affair undoubtedly troubled Bob Welch, even though he somewhat romanticizes their encounter of the third kind: "Two friends having coffee together / When something flies by their window / [...] Now it's not a meaningless question / To ask if they've been and gone."

The oblique lyrics referring to a strange, glass-smooth pond in the heart of a North Carolina forest contribute to the mystique of "Hypnotized." Bob Welch would later explain where he got the idea: "A guy that I used to work with from Winston-Salem told me the story of he and some friends riding dirt bikes 20 miles or so out in the woods when they came upon a strange 'crater' in the ground with smooth sides like melted glass. It was a 'pond' in the sense that there was some rainwater in it, I guess. There were no

Disco and R&B luminaries the Pointer Sisters delivered a stunning cover version of Fleetwood Mac's "Hypnotized" in 1978.

access roads or caterpillar tracks, so it wasn't a construction site. I think the location must have been near Winston-Salem. They all immediately got the feeling they should get out of there. Maybe it was a meteor impact? I just liked the imagery for the song."[61]

Finally, Benifold's mysterious ambiance probably also influenced the somewhat catch-all lyrics: "There was an odd, ethereal mood around those grounds all the time, and a feeling that anything could happen," said Bob. "I was reading about, as the lyric says, 'a place down in Mexico where man can fly over mountains and hills,' and one night I had a vivid dream that a UFO piloted by a Navajo shaman landed on our overgrown grass tennis court one moonlit night."[4]

Production

"Hypnotized" proved to be one of the band's most musically adventurous pieces of the pre-Buckingham years, taking them down the path of hybrid jazz. Initially, it was a blues track in 6/8 time, intended to be sung by Dave Walker. But once Walker was out of the family picture, Bob Welch reworked and adapted it so that he could sing it himself. "Chris helped a lot with the new tempo and the mood," Bob explained. "I remember listening to the playback with her. She looked at me and said, 'It gives me the willies, Bob.' I felt the same way, even after a hundred playbacks."[47] In addition to Bob Welch's penetrating, haunting vocals—which greatly accentuate the hypnotic dimension of the song—"Hypnotized" is distinguished by Christine McVie's luminous harmonies, as well as by the jazzy guitar solo, which was played by either Bob Welch or Bob Weston; we do not really know which. Indeed, Weston's work was downplayed by Welch, who was a master of the art of irony, and whose following statement is therefore open to question: "My guitar style, is best exemplified by the stuff in 'Hypnotized,' which was all me, with some moral support from Weston who at the time I think was clinging, with a mixture of admiration and disgust, to my leg…"[47] But the song's real tour de force

is the Dantesque drums part by Mick Fleetwood, inspired by a drum machine loop: On the recording, explains Bob Welch, "'Hypnotized' is NOT a drum 'loop,' but is actually Mick playing straight through […] I don't know how he did it! This was in the days long before anybody thought of using drum loops, and Mick was one of the few drummers who could have pulled off being a 'human drum loop.' The cymbals etc. are all what Mick played on the spot, not recorded later etc."[47] According to Mick, though, it was not all that complicated: "I started playing a groove during the session, then the rest of the band joined in when it was time to rehearse. It's so damn simple. Ba-ba-ba-bom, ba-ba-ba-bom, ba-ba-ba-bom, ba-ba-ba-bom. No drum fills, nothing. It's so simple, but drummers used to ask me how to do it. It's nothing but a snare drum and the rest of the beats are on a bass drum, fairly briskly played, yet they never cop it."[8] Despite the track's effectiveness, Warner did not think "Hypnotized" had the qualities of a single, and decided it would make a perfect Side B. So, the band was asked to record a cover of "For Your Love" to appear on Side A.

Eager to explore, the band attempted a foray into pre-disco with "Keep on Going."

Bob Welch ventured into new, reggae-infused territory with "Forever."

FOREVER

Bob Weston, John McVie, Bob Welch / 4:04

Musicians: Bob Welch: vocals, guitar / Bob Weston: guitar, backing vocals / Christine McVie: keyboards, backing vocals / John McVie: bass / **Recorded:** Rolling Stones Mobile Studio, Benifold, Hampshire, June 1973 / **Technical Team:** Producers: Fleetwood Mac and Martin Birch / Sound Engineer: Martin Birch / Assistant Sound Engineers: Desmond Majekodunmi, Paul Hardiman

Genesis and Lyrics

Light and swaying, rooted in reggae with its sunny melody, "Forever" is unlike anything Fleetwood Mac had released up to that point. At no point does it sound like it was recorded in the English countryside between rain showers. "Forever" takes us to the heart of the Caribbean. Unenthusiastic about going to work, the narrator lets his procrastinating side get the better of him and admits to being "slow, too lazy for anything." Charmed by the luminosity of the day, entranced by the quiet ballet of "boats that keep sailing past me, but not too fast," he is content to observe them. Unwilling to let himself be carried away by the mad rhythm of a working day, he continues, taking the listener into his confidence with a knowing "You know": "I wish this day could keep on going and last forever / [...] Please don't fool with my happiness." Too tired to write these few lines, Fleetwood Mac decided that this blessed man's profession of faith was already long enough and stopped after eight lines.

Production

"We tried not to do 'throwaway' tunes on records, but we did (and still do, speaking for myself) like to have a variety of moods and feels on songs so things wouldn't all sound the same," explained Bob Welch concerning "Forever," adding that "'Forever' is one of those little 'mood' pieces that wasn't written at all beforehand, and was the result of a 'jam' between me and John. John McVie was one of the most inventive bass players I ever worked with. He really made his bass lines COUNT, they're almost like little songs within the song."[47] Indeed, it is John's bass line that guides the melody of this reggae, not necessarily destined for posterity, but which spreads good vibes for over four minutes. According to John's recollection, he was in Benifold's large ground-floor room, playing a line on a drum machine loop, when Christine joined him: "I think it was Chris who heard the riff I was playing," recalled John McVie. "She liked it and took it from there. I think Bob Weston had a part in that as well."[51] McVie confirms that Mick Fleetwood was not asked to record "Forever," the band having preferred to start from the drum machine loop: "If memory serves," said Bob Weston in 2003, recalling the importance of the other Bob's involvement, "it was one of the more up-market models [...] I remember that John and I developed the basic riffs to the song, and couldn't quite get it to arrive at its final point; so we called in the Wizard Welch who did the business. He was great like that; he could always pull something out of the fire, which otherwise might have turned to ashes."[48]

KEEP ON GOING

Bob Welch / 4:04

Musicians: Christine McVie: vocals, keyboards, backing vocals / Bob Weston: guitar / Bob Welch: guitar, bass / Mick Fleetwood: drums, percussions / Richard Hewson: strings arrangements / **Recorded:** Rolling Stones Mobile Studio, Benifold, Hampshire: June 1973 / **Technical Team:** Producers: Fleetwood Mac and Martin Birch / Sound Engineer: Martin Birch / Assistant Sound Engineers: Desmond Majekodunmi, Paul Hardiman

Genesis and Lyrics

Composed by Bob Welch, "Keep on Going" breaks with Fleetwood Mac's tradition of having the person who writes the song sing it. Feeling that the key was not suited to his own range, Bob asked Christine to try her hand at it. The singer's performance was unanimously acclaimed. And so she was the one to give life to the lyrics of this ode to resilience: "'Keep On Going' is about 'truckin' through the madness and NOT selling out for a $,"[47] explained Bob Welch. Welch admits he has no regrets about leaving "his" song to Christine: "Christine sung 'Keep On Going' because she liked it, and sounded better on it than me....I've always written some things that I personally couldn't sing particularly well."[47] In the text, the narrator believes that he must "keep on the way I'm going" and not allow himself to be influenced by his environment, which pushes him to ask questions he does not want to answer. He is convinced that abandoning his ideals is anything but a guarantee of peace and wisdom: "For every crime, there's retribution / And every valley has a mountainside [...] That kind of deal won't turn out right."

Production

Christine McVie's somewhat nonchalant vocals take center stage in an arrangement that blends funk and soul. It also features a bouncy bass with an irresistible groove, which, for once, is by Bob Welch, not John McVie. Another novel element in Fleetwood Mac's musical environment is the massive but not intrusive presence of dramatically contoured strings, offering the band an early foray into pre-disco, a musical color that the dance floor–style drums played by Mick Fleetwood only reinforce. "The strings," explained Bob Welch, "are a real orchestra, I think arranged by Paul Buckmaster, who did a lot of the early Elton John albums."[47] Yet the credits make no mention of Paul Buckmaster as arranger, but of Richard Hewson instead. To Bob Welch's credit, the two men were among the sharpest triggers in the realm at the time and sometimes worked on the same records, such as Claire Hamill's *One House Left Standing* in 1972, shortly before *Mystery to Me*. So it is not out of the question that both were asked to write, but only one of them was credited: "I probably 'hummed' some lines to either Buckmaster or his 'copyist' just to give him an idea of the kind of thing we wanted on the song,"[47] concludes Welch, without really removing any doubt. One should also mention Bob Weston's beautiful acoustic guitar solo from 2:15 onward.

THE CITY

Bob Welch / 3:35

Musicians
Bob Welch: vocals, guitar
Bob Weston: guitar
Christine McVie: piano
John McVie: bass
Mick Fleetwood: drums

Recorded
Rolling Stones Mobile Studio, Benifold, Hampshire, June 1973

Technical Team
Producers: Fleetwood Mac and Martin Birch
Sound Engineer: Martin Birch
Assistant Sound Engineers: Desmond Majekodunmi, Paul Hardiman

From Bob Welch's point of view, New York City and its skyscrapers were dehumanizing and alienating. They offered no redeeming features in "The City."

Genesis and Lyrics

Everything pits these urban giants against each other, as they turn their backs on each other at the western and eastern ends of the United States, one looking toward the Pacific, the other toward the Atlantic: Los Angeles versus New York City. Bob Welch, a native of the City of Angels, has chosen his side, preferring the gentle kiss of the Californian sun to the proud buildings that claw at the eastern sky. As the son of a producer and screenwriter, he favors the dreamers and artists of Hollywood, the golden beaches and freeways of this sprawling city, rather than the inhabitants of the city that never sleeps. To the Californian's ears, New York's urban symphony takes the form of an angry, "claustrophobic" blues that leaves no time to breathe. Listening to its violently hammered riff, one cannot help but think of "Going Down," Freddie King's incendiary track conceived in 1971 with the help of producer Leon Russell as an overt attempt to seduce the rock audience.

The text of "The City" leaves no doubt as to the songwriter's low opinion of the Big Apple. Each of the three stanzas begins in much the same way, with slight variations: "Gonna stay out of New York," "Well, there's something wrong with New York," "I won't go back to New York." Welch draws up a list: the madness, the lack of air, the absence of sunshine, the so-called sophistication. "New York was having one of its worst periods in history when I wrote 'The City,'"[47] he recalls. "The city was nearly bankrupt, they were having 'garbage strikes,' and homeless guys were coming out at every stoplight to try to clean your windshield for a dollar. All the English people in our touring crew, including the roadies, used to be really paranoid about being 'mugged' or something whenever we went there."[47]

In the liner notes to his album *His Fleetwood Mac Years and Beyond Vol. 2* (2006), which featured a cover of this song, Welch explained that his girlfriend had been assaulted. He is careful to point out, however, that he has since radically changed his mind about the town. He no doubt remembers the outraged reaction he provoked among the band's New York fans with this song.

Fleetwood Mac, back to being a quintet during the time of *Mystery to Me*.

Production

In New York, noise was everywhere. "The City" could only blossom a thousand miles away from soft rock. Welch built this track with the intention of making it a sonic firebrand. He quickly conceived it as a raging blues riff driven by Hendrix-like fire. The proximity to the sound of "Voodoo Child" owes much to the use of wah-wah on Welch's lead guitar. The musician sets the song alight with his guitar as much as he seems to detach himself from it through the vocals, with a voice that is sometimes atonic, sometimes melancholy. The wah-wah applied to his instrument twists his groove and gives it a whiff of funk and brimstone. The effect is so powerful that it almost sounds like a talk box, a device with a tube placed in the mouth to modulate the guitar signal and simulate the human voice. Bob Weston takes charge

of the rhythm section, which remains bluesy in tone, with elegant, well-placed slides. Christine McVie diligently follows the same melodic progression as the guitar, solidifying it and ensuring that it does not confuse the listener.

For the rhythm section, a track like this is a treat. John McVie's finger-style bass is deep. It does not stray far from the fundamentals, except for a few well-felt descents, but its interest comes mainly from the agile, precise rhythmic playing of the right hand.

Mick Fleetwood has the right logic for this groovy onslaught. He favors solidity, setting up an almost rigid pattern on the snare drum, but in so doing he gives off an impression of mechanical, crushing force, which fits in well with the theme of the stifling, claustrophobic city.

MILES AWAY

Bob Welch / 3:47

Musicians: Bob Welch: vocals, guitar / Bob Weston: guitar, backing vocals / Christine McVie: piano, backing vocals / John McVie: bass / Mick Fleetwood: drums / **Recorded:** Rolling Stones Mobile Studio, Benifold, Hampshire, June 1973 / **Technical Team:** Producers: Fleetwood Mac and Martin Birch / Sound Engineer: Martin Birch / Assistant Sound Engineers: Desmond Majekodunmi, Paul Hardiman

Genesis and Lyrics

The position of "Miles Away"—which comes just after "The City," the opening song on the album's Side B—makes sense lyrically. After depicting New York in the most pejorative of ways, Bob Welch here revisits the theme of the repulsive city, but this time to evoke the need to get away from it, as he explained in 1999: "['Miles Away' is about] escaping to a safe place, away from the craziness of modern life."[47] Although it is not mentioned by name, the Big Apple is described in the form of Andy Warhol, one of its most eminent artistic figures of the 1970s: "Now there's too much Warhol hanging off the wall." It is not so much the emblematic artist of pop art that Welch nails in his text, but rather the consumerism—denounced in the painter's work—that is eating away at the art world. In New York, avant-gardism soon became fashion and the norm. And so did nonconformism, which, in the guitarist's eyes, lapsed into caricature with "all those Hare Krishnas turned out to be a joke." By 1973, the Summer of Love was long gone, its spirit diluted into a cool lifestyle that had nothing to do with the counterculture of the previous decade. At the risk of sounding like a reactionary, Bob Welch takes his cue from the hippie types and their "cloud of smoke." A position he reaffirmed in 1999: "'Miles Away' was essentially a stream of consciousness thing about the whole 'peace and love' thing of the 60's"[47] that he says disappeared by the following decade.

Production

On the subject of taking to the road and swallowing up the miles to reach a calmer, more authentic destination, the style that best lent itself to this evocation was southern rock. The first twenty seconds take us down this road, with Bob Weston delivering multiple sharp Pete Townshend–style attacks. Mick Fleetwood ensures the sequence's originality with some killer rolls. But then, abruptly, the bass breaks the established rhythm and opens into a jazzy digression. John McVie, weaving a captivating soundtrack, becomes the heart and engine of the song. His spirited phrasing evokes John Entwistle's heyday with the Who. While he does not achieve his legendary dexterity, the impetus given by this bouncy line is reminiscent of his approach. Contrary to rumor, and given the fact that the bass was, against all odds, Bob Welch's favorite instrument, he did not write the bass score. He merely suggested a few adjustments to the line conceived by John McVie. Welch's talent is expressed in these surprising guitar lines, alternating between jazzy phrasing with unexpected turns (at 0:33), swift soloing (at 1:37), suspended notes with astonishing sustain (at 2:07 and especially 3:03), and admirably controlled feedback (at 2:34). His vocals are just as surprising, close to spoken words, on the verses. The atonality of these passages contrasts with the galvanizing moments on the choruses, where he is joined by energetic, precise backing vocals from Christine McVie and Bob Weston. After the blues funk of "The City," this rock and jazz fusion gives the album an invigorating variety.

FOR MAC-ADDICTS

Mick Fleetwood regards himself as an inquisitive percussionist. The broad spectrum of the percussion family is as much a challenge to him as a source of amusement. This frivolity and his taste for showmanship prompted him in the 1990s to ask producer Jimmy Hotz to design a special jacket for him. With the help of Atari, Mick was able to activate different MIDI (musical instrument digital interface) sounds by pressing certain parts of the garment.

SOMEBODY

Bob Welch / 5:00

Musicians: Bob Welch: vocals, guitar, backing vocals / Bob Weston: guitar, backing vocals / Christine McVie: keyboards, backing vocals / John McVie: bass, backing vocals / Mick Fleetwood: drums /
Recorded: Rolling Stones Mobile Studio, Benifold, Hampshire, June 1973 / **Technical Team:** Producers: Fleetwood Mac and Martin Birch / Sound Engineer: Martin BirchvAssistant Sound Engineers: Desmond Majekodunmi, Paul Hardiman

Genesis and Lyrics

The second side of *Mystery to Me* assumes a more groovy, jazzy tone than the first, which alternated between introspective soft rock and stylistic explorations of funk and reggae. Bob Welch follows up with a third track that puts the groove front and center, after "The City" and "Miles Away." But the theme of "Somebody" breaks with the previous two tracks and prevents the whole from being seen as a triptych. The only narrative trait the three songs have in common is the narrator's lucidity and mistrust in the face of bad vibes, given off by a place in "The City" and "Miles Away," and by a person in "Somebody." The neutrality of this word, "somebody," preserves the anonymity of the individual described in the text. We can imagine that it is someone close to him or her, and that Welch does not want anyone, rightly or wrongly, to recognize him- or herself. This anonymity allows the lyricist to pour out his reproaches without reserve: "I saw desires that burned in you / The need for power to be a king," who expresses himself to the detriment of the love demanded by those around him, first and foremost the narrator. This quest for power and fame leads the character to play with his own life. There is talk of madness ("I found out / That you was the crazy kind"), decadence, and domination. This last aspect seems to dictate the character's relationship with others. He expects those closest to him to be at his service, which the narrator categorically refuses. He expresses this in the medieval metaphor of allegiance: "I'm not gonna kiss your ring."

Production

Simple and effective, the riff is based on a *G-F-D#-D* sequence. The deep, enveloping bass interjects, playing only the fundamentals and trying to respect the silences. On these foundations, Bob Welch adds a few half-blues, half-jazz guitar ornaments. The track then opens with a more boogie-like sequence, during which the bass becomes more loquacious and takes control of the song. The ear picks up on Mick Fleetwood's signature percussion, which sounds like it could be a rattle. Mick Fleetwood, no specialist in the genre, loves to have fun with percussion, as he confesses: "I'm told that what I do as a percussion player is all sort of back-to-front, where the fills are usually not in the obvious places, and it's because I don't really know what I'm doing. I just do it spontaneously."[51] Another intriguing element is the treatment of Bob Welch's voice. A slight chorus effect can be heard. This coloration perfectly serves the groovy ambiance of the track, which is adorned with backing vocals that are not always melodious, but the rising phrase they utter ideally serves the track's dynamics.

The precarious balance of the McVie couple was at the center of many of Christine's compositions.

THE WAY I FEEL
Christine McVie / 2:43

Musicians: Christine McVie: vocals, keyboards / Bob Welch: guitar / Bob Weston: guitar / **Recorded:** Rolling Stones Mobile Studio, Benifold, Hampshire, June 1973 / **Technical Team:** Producers: Fleetwood Mac and Martin Birch / Sound Engineer: Martin Birch / Assistant Sound Engineers: Desmond Majekodunmi, Paul Hardiman

Genesis and Lyrics
"The Way I Feel" is the complete opposite of the rejectionist movements expressed in Welch's three compositions at the start of Side B ("The City," "Miles Away," and "Somebody"). Christine McVie's songs give voice to her sensibility and refocuse the debate around the theme that consumes her mind musically and in her private life: love. And more precisely, her sentimental confusion. With John McVie mute and struggling to express his feelings, the keyboardist brings out her torments through the channel her husband is likely to hear best: music. Christine McVie opens with the universality of the feelings she is going through: "Once in everyone's life / You know a feeling has to grow." The lyricist then tightens the focus, using "you" on the pre-chorus to include the listener, allowing them to identify with the song, and finally to include them in the confidence. This comes in the second verse. The musician addresses her love partner directly, reminding

him of the strength of her love. The pre-chorus immediately drowns out this sentimental impulse, as she tells herself that it is too late and that she is deluding herself. As if trying to apologize for talking too much, she concludes the chorus with "I can't conceal the way that I feel"—the unwritten reproach suggesting that John McVie was adept at such concealment.

Production
The break with the previous tracks is also a stylistic one. Christine McVie sets Fleetwood Mac back on the soft-rock path in the most dazzling way, with a ballad of accomplished sweetness. Bob Welch and Bob Weston instantly grasp what the composition needs. Devoid of bass—Christine's left-hand playing fills the bill perfectly—and drums—which would make the song heavier—the aim is to bring finesse and lightness to the piano score. Since it is already very melodic, there is no need to depart from this. Two acoustic guitars, playing the same tune, are added, but they take up the melodic line of the keyboard. The preciousness of their sounds and the delicate touch of both Bobs are enough to give the piece the extra finesse it needed.

"For Your Love," a cover of the Yardbirds hit song, appeared on *Mystery to Me* and was chosen as a single.

The Yardbirds obtained "For Your Love" from a Denmark Street (London) publisher who held the rights to this composition written by Graham Gouldman, future member of the Hollies and 10cc. Gouldman joined the Yardbirds as guitarist in 1984, almost 20 years after the song's release.

FOR YOUR LOVE

Graham Gouldman / 3:44

Musicians: Bob Welch: vocals, guitar / Bob Weston: guitar, backing vocals / Christine McVie: keyboards, backing vocals / John McVie: bass, backing vocals / Mick Fleetwood: drums / **Recorded:** Rolling Stones Mobile Studio, Benifold, Hampshire, June 1973 / **Technical Team:** Producers: Fleetwood Mac and Martin Birch / Sound Engineer: Martin Birch / Assistant Sound Engineers: Desmond Majekodunmi, Paul Hardiman / **Single:** Side A: For Your Love / Side B: Hypnotized / **UK Release Date:** 1973 with Reprise Records (ref. REP 1188) / Best UK Chart Ranking: Did Not Chart / **US Release Date:** 1973 with Reprise Records (ref. K 14315) / Best US Chart Ranking: Did Not Chart

Genesis and Lyrics

At the end of the recording process, the band felt they had produced an album of exceptional variety and polished production. It seemed to the musicians that they had achieved the quintessence of their art under difficult conditions, having had to part company with one of their members, Dave Walker. So it was with a light heart that the troupe headed to Warner's Los Angeles offices to let the management team hear the fruits of their labor. They, too, were fully satisfied, but did point out one shortcoming. In their opinion, none of the tracks on the track listing was worthy of a single release, not even "Hypnotized," which they saw as the centerpiece of *Mystery to Me*. So the band had to return to Benifold to record a new song right away, but they did not have another composition that was mature enough to be finalized quickly. Bob Weston suggested recording a cover version. He had in mind a Yardbirds song that might suit them: "For Your Love." The proposal was enthusiastically received by Bob Welch, who considered it

one of the best songs by a band that had included some of the best six-string blasters of all time (Eric Clapton, Jeff Beck, Jimmy Page). The Yardbirds were on hiatus at the time, so there was no risk of overshadowing them, and "For Your Love" had already proved its commercial potential, reaching third place in the British charts on its release in 1965. By including this new track, Fleetwood Mac offloaded a previously recorded track from the track list, which seemed a little weaker than the others: "Good Things (Come to Those Who Wait)."

Production

The original version, with its distinctive guitar riffs and fast tempo, embodies the characteristic energy of the British Invasion. Carried by Keith Relf's voice, the song captivates with its blend of rock and pop. But the production was poorly honed, as the studio equipment was rudimentary. The giant leap made in eight years in this respect is obvious on Fleetwood Mac's version. The band's approach to this new version differs from that of their contemporaries: The instrumentation is less energetic and more subtle. Witness the guitar harmonics in the introduction, and the congas added by Mick Fleetwood to support his drums. The drummer also has the idea of bringing in the break with the sudden change of rhythm with massive timpani strokes, which Martin Birch takes pleasure in highlighting by pushing their volume. Christine McVie reproduces the harpsichord tones (originally provided by Brian Auger), making them sound like harp notes. The major difference, however, is the quality of the vocal harmonies and the inventiveness of the guitar solo in the middle of the piece.

Ironically, Warner's flair proved to be lacking, as radio stations shunned "For Your Love," preferring its Side B, "Hypnotized," which received more airplay.

Christine McVie closes the album with "Why," on a bitter, fatalistic note about her relationship with John.

FOR MAC-ADDICTS

Richard Anthony Hewson already had a solid pedigree when Fleetwood Mac asked him to write "Why." The British arranger specialized in jazz-funk on a personal level (he had a respectable success with RAH Band) and he'd worked with James Taylor on "Carolina in My Mind" (1968), the Beatles on "I Me Mine" and "The Long and Winding Road" in 1970 (under the supervision of Phil Spector), and the Bee Gees on *Melody* (1971).

WHY

Christine McVie / 4:56

Musicians: Christine McVie: vocals, piano, backing vocals / Bob Welch: guitar, backing vocals / Bob Weston: guitar, backing vocals / John McVie: bass, backing vocals / Mick Fleetwood: drums / Richard Hewson: strings arrangements / Orchestra: uncredited / **Recorded:** Rolling Stones Mobile Studio, Benifold, Hampshire, June 1973 / **Technical Team:** Producers: Fleetwood Mac and Martin Birch / Sound Engineer: Martin Birch / Assistant Sound Engineers: Desmond Majekodunmi, Paul Hardiman

Genesis and Lyrics

The album closes on a bittersweet note. Wrapped in delightful instrumentation, this ballad marks the end of the emotional roller coaster drawn by Christine McVie's lyrics throughout the record. The five compositions she has penned for this opus—"Believe Me," "Just Crazy Love," "Keep on Going," "The Way I Feel," and "Why"—depict a woman deeply in love, but also worried, even fatalistic, about the outcome of her love. She needs reassurance about her partner's feelings but runs into a wall.

The conclusion is terrible: "It's all over," "I just can't carry on." She preserves a glimmer of optimism: "The hurt I feel will simply melt away," but it is more about her ability to get back on her feet than the survival of her relationship.

Production

"Why" is introduced by a country-style sequence featuring slide guitar and open chords played by Bob Weston. The guitarist was fully involved in the composition of this track, working out all the guitar parts, including those to be played by Bob Welch. But Weston would not be credited: "I asked one or two of the band to give me an hour or so while I finished the guitar parts, as Christine was getting a trifle concerned about the way her song was going. Upon their return, everyone had a smile on the dial. Sadly, I missed out on the arrangement credits as they brought in a string arranger who had my parts played, practically note for note, on strings, and he took the credit."[48] In spite of this injustice, posterity will remember Weston's fantastic work on this track, with its abundance of guitar parts, which provide an infinitely delicate setting for Christine McVie's full, warm voice, taking the song into softer rock territory after the country opening.

GOOD THINGS
(COME TO THOSE WHO WAIT)

Bob Welch / 4:35

Musicians: Bob Welch: guitar, vocals / Bob Weston: guitar / Christine McVie: backing vocals / John McVie: bass / Mick Fleetwood: drums /
Recorded: Rolling Stones Mobile Studio, Benifold, Hampshire, June 1973 / Mixing: Advision Studios, London / **Technical Team:**
Producers: Fleetwood Mac and Martin Birch / Sound Engineer: Martin Birch / Assistant Sound Engineers: Desmond Majekodunmi, Paul Hardiman

Genesis and Lyrics

"Good things come to those who wait" is a proverb that encourages patience, better advice than haste when you really want something badly. The words reflect the profound introspection of the narrator, who does not know how to act in the face of the voices he hears in his head advising him to act quickly to achieve "this dream that [I] keep having." He describes a schizophrenia-like malaise when he sings: "Hold out a candle and look in my eyes / You'll see a prisoner learnin' to lie / How do I know? / It's like a whisper on the wind / And a voice that gets louder before it disappears again." He manages to temporize, however, letting the voices evaporate, but he senses that they will return and torture him again: "Good things come to those who wait / But don't wait too long."

Production

Recorded during the *Mystery to Me* sessions, this Bob Welch composition, heavily influenced by Steely Dan, was eventually dropped from the album's track listing, to be replaced at the last minute by a cover of the Yardbirds' "For Your Love," suggested by Bob Weston. Warner was looking for a single, and the one suggested, "Hypnotized," did not fully satisfy the label, which preferred to "play it safe" by placing "For Your Love" on Side A and "Hypnotized" on Side B.

This is a pity, because "Good Things (Come to Those Who Wait)" certainly had the necessary qualities to feature on the album. Bob Welch's haunting vocals, seemingly from beyond the grave, shine through in the midst of a dense arrangement where Mick Fleetwood's tribal, hypnotic drums, mostly played on toms, add substance to the roaring guitars of the two Bobs and John McVie's heavy bass. Christine McVie's distant backing vocals complete this cryptic, mysterious track.

"Good Things (Come to Those Who Wait)" disappeared from Fleetwood Mac's repertoire and was only played live once, on September 23, 1973, at the PNE Garden Auditorium in Vancouver, Canada. After that, we had to wait until 1979, when Bob Welch recorded a totally different version of the song, "Don't Wait Too Long," for his solo album *Three Hearts*. Fleetwood Mac's version would reemerge remastered in 2020 (eight years after Bob Welch's death) on the reissue of *Mystery to Me*. Fans who had bought the first pressings of the album in 1973, on which the song was mentioned and the lyrics published, could finally know what it was all about; the puzzle was finally complete. On the following album, *Heroes Are Hard to Find* (1974), the song "Bad Loser" obviously recycled some of the ingredients of "Good Things (Come to Those Who Wait)."

THE "FAKE MAC" AFFAIR

October 23, 1973. After a concert in Nebraska, Mick Fleetwood announced to the other members of the band, in the absence of the main person concerned, that he no longer wished to play with Bob Weston, who was having an affair with his wife, Jenny Boyd. The band decided to fire Weston. Bob Welch was immediately dispatched to call the manager, Clifford Davis, to inform him of the tour's postponement: "Clifford? Can you hear me? Listen, we've got a big problem. We've had to fire Bob Weston, and Mick's not doing too well. We're suspending the tour for a while until we can get together again."[4] Tired of the incessant internal quarrels and previous job losses, Clifford Davis turned on his heels and threatened the band directly: "So, Bob, it's all over, is that it? Listen to me: I just want to remind you that if you screw up this tour like you did the others, you'll never get another chance. Not with me, anyway. [...] You'd better listen to me now. If you stop touring, it'll destroy my reputation with the promoters and tour managers I have to rely on to survive in this fucking business, and I swear I'm not going to let myself be sunk by the whims of a bunch of irresponsible musicians. [...] If you pull out of this tour, there will be no next album, because your careers will be over. Let me make that perfectly clear."[4]

Davis's "New" Fleetwood Mac

The band, stunned, decided to ignore their manager. Little did they suspect the enormity of how things would turn out. After all, Davis had no intention of allowing himself to be dispossessed of what he considered to be "his" band. Over the following weeks, the manager put together a new lineup comprising Elmer Gantry (singer), Kirby Gregory (guitar), Paul Martinez (bass), David Wilkinson (piano), and Craig Collinge (drums), which he sold to tour managers as Fleetwood Mac... "I want to get the idea out of people's heads that Fleetwood Mac is Mick Fleetwood's band," Davis explained, before concluding: "This band is my band. It's always been my band."[53] Davis spread the idea that Mick, as the band's leader, had simply decided to fire everyone except himself. According to the manager, the drummer would have been part of this new adventure had he not

backed out in mid-January 1974, when personal problems forced him to give way to Craig Collinge at the last minute.

Mick denied that he had ever planned to join Davis's project. At the end of February 1974, after the "false" Fleetwood Mac had been touring the United States for more than a month, sowing confusion wherever it went (many spectators, and even promoters, were furious and demanded their money back), Bob Welch, Mick Fleetwood, and John and Christine McVie decided to organize a fight-back after consulting lawyers. Welch—who has since left the band but returned to England for the occasion—told *Rolling Stone*: "It's a scam. The manager formed a band very quickly using the Fleetwood Mac name before we had time to do anything about it."[53] Welch was adamant that Davis took advantage of Mick's divorce following the "Jenny affair," and the period of uncertainty created by the cancellation of the rest of the tour, to take control unilaterally. "We all received letters from Davis indicating his intention to put a new band back on the road. He gave us an ultimatum."[53] This was an ultimatum that none of the historic members of the band could accept, since they intended to go back on the road when *they* decided to do so, after a necessary period of reflection and restructuring following Weston's departure.

A Legal Imbroglio

At Warner Bros., there was obvious panic. Executive director Don Schmitzerle was tearing his hair out over who had exclusive rights to the band's name. For his part, Clifford Davis asserted with aplomb that people have always misinterpreted the name Fleetwood Mac as being a contraction of the names Mick Fleetwood and John McVie, whereas in his eyes, it was first and foremost the name of the song written by Peter Green when he played with John Mayall. Not held back for a moment by any sense of bad faith, he pointed out that Mick Fleetwood was the only remaining member of the original band, since John McVie was not the original bassist (that was Bob Brunning).

Bob Welch, for his part, fulminated: "If [Davis] has the rights to the band's name, he can, theoretically, put anyone

FOR MAC-ADDICTS

In January 1979, guitarist Kirby Gregory of the "fake Fleetwood Mac," took part in the recording of Danny Kirwan's third album, *Hello There Big Boy!* In this context he rubbed shoulders with Bob Weston, under the management of Clifford Davis, who became producer for the occasion.

in it. He can recruit four barking dogs on a leash and call it Fleetwood Mac. Basically, if you want to sum up the situation, the manager has flipped. We're going to take legal action."[53] To fight this legal battle, which promised to be long and intense, the troops would have to be remobilized. Mick was still in the doldrums and would soon be off to Zambia to recharge his batteries. As for Christine, she was (already!) expressing her tour fatigue and talking of retiring, or even opening a small business.

In the end, the British band took legal action, while the "new" Fleetwood Mac continued its American tour, facing an increasingly hostile public and suspicious tour operators anxious to limit financial losses (the tour was sold for thirty-nine dates in thirty-eight cities by American Talent International). Mick Fleetwood and his bandmates quickly obtained an injunction to prevent Clifford Davis and his band from touring under the Fleetwood Mac name. Lawyers and courts could now deliberate on who was the real Fleetwood Mac. This first victory reassured Mick Fleetwood: "When things like this happen," he explained, "many bands don't have the stamina to cope. It's very easy to say to yourself, 'Good God, it's just not worth it.' I'm sure Clifford never thought for a moment that we'd get through it. Right now we are managing ourselves."[54] Following the release of the *Heroes Are Hard to Find* album on September 13, 1974, the band embarked on a new tour (September 19, 1974, to June 8, 1975), which almost resembled a vacation, as it enabled the musicians to avoid the legal dispute. This now pitted only Fleetwood Mac against its former manager, Clifford Davis, with the "fake" Fleetwood Mac having thrown in the towel. Elmer Gantry and Kirby Gregory became members of the Davis-funded band Stretch in 1974. Stretch even scored a minor hit (number sixteen in the charts) with the single "Why Did You Do It?," whose lyrics castigated Mick Fleetwood for not joining the band on tour. According to Stretch, Fleetwood had committed to joining the band but then backed out, denying any knowledge of the project. "In the end, as I understand it," Mick asserted in 1991, "the 'fake Mac' only played two weeks of a ten-week tour. To this day, I don't know the names of the musicians involved, and I don't want to. Years later, the band's singer contacted us to apologize. He swore that [they] had been told I'd join them on the road after a few gigs, so they went ahead."[4]

An "Amicable" Agreement

Meanwhile, the dispute between Fleetwood Mac and Clifford Davis dragged on in the English courts, crystallizing around three claims: the ultimate right to use the name, publishing rights, and Fleetwood Mac's desire to rehabilitate the honor of its name, which had been considerably tarnished by the affair. This last point was backed up by the fact that some tour managers acknowledged that the public who came to see Davis's band felt cheated and that this had damaged the credibility of the Fleetwood Mac name. In 1978, Mick Fleetwood, the McVies, and Bob Welch also claimed royalties from Clifford Davis's company, Leosong, which had been owed to them since 1973.

Finally, on a chilly spring morning, the dispute was resolved in an office where Mick Fleetwood, John McVie, Clifford Davis, and their respective lawyers met. The atmosphere was heavy. "There was so much hatred in the room that you could have cut it with a switchblade," Mick explained, adding that: "Despite the cold, the office felt like a sauna after five minutes."[4] Despite the many disputes, everyone was aware that enough money had been spent on this legal skirmish that made little sense.

With heavy hearts, Fleetwood Mac agreed to an out-of-court settlement: "I was beginning to sound like a lawyer myself," said Mick. "Even though we had no desire to give this man anything, we finally said: 'Look, this is hurting us unnecessarily, let's just give him his fucking money and be done with it.'"[4] Parliament had passed a new copyright bill, which went Davis's way. So, for many years to come, Davis would continue to receive royalties on Fleetwood Mac's old hits, such as "Albatross" and many others. But in return, at the end of this sordid tale—probably one of the saddest episodes in the history of the music industry—Fleetwood Mac kept its name and won its freedom for good.

ALBUM

HEROES ARE HARD TO FIND

Heroes Are Hard to Find . Coming Home . Angel . Bermuda Triangle .
Come a Little Bit Closer . She's Changing Me . Bad Loser . Silver Heels .
Prove Your Love . Born Enchanter . Safe Harbour

RELEASE DATES
United Kingdom: September 13, 1974
Reference: Reprise Records—K 54026
Best UK Chart Ranking: Did Not Chart
United States: September 13, 1974
Reference: Reprise Records—MS 2196
Best US Chart Ranking: 34

Bob Welch advertises his affiliation with Warner Bros., Fleetwood Mac's record company.

THE SURVIVAL INSTINCT

With another traumatic departure—that of Bob Weston in October 1973—Fleetwood Mac spared no expense and put their survival instincts to the test for the umpteenth time. Clifford Davis, tired of managing a band that had gone through seven incarnations since 1967, began a new chapter in Fleetwood Mac's fabulous adventures by sending out on the road a "fake" group of unknown musicians, using a name of which he believed he was the sole owner. In so doing, he declared war on his former protégés Mick Fleetwood, John and Christine McVie, and Bob Welch, who had been carefully excluded from the "new" Fleetwood Mac project. The latter had had their hands full since they had decided to fire Bob Weston and put their tour on hold. Although they told Davis of their intention to resume touring at a later date, their heads were understandably elsewhere, and they were ignoring the warnings of their soon-to-be ex-manager, who was taking advantage of this slight headwind to methodically implement his plan.

The Mac members scattered all over the world. Mick went as far as Africa to rest his mind and forget his wife Jenny's infidelity with Bob Weston. Welch left to recharge his batteries in his hometown of Los Angeles. As for the McVies, they were taking advantage of this truncated tour to put several thousand miles between them for the first time in a long time. At this stage, there was no talk of divorce as yet, but of a well-deserved vacation on their own. John flew to Hawaii, while Christine returned to England. Jenny, for her part, was convinced that her relationship with Mick could still be saved. She ended up sending him a telegram in Africa, begging him to come back. Mick was happy to give his marriage another chance.

Having spent most of their time on the road in the early seventies, the band decided to settle in California.

America or Die

But on his return, Mick Fleetwood was faced with chaos. With this "fake" Fleetwood Mac on the road, and Clifford Davis more uptight than ever and determined to protect "his" property, Fleetwood and his band soon realized that everything they had spent years building was about to be shattered. A powerful man, Davis even influenced the decisions of Warner Bros. Records; he was, until proven otherwise, Fleetwood Mac's manager, and it was he who had negotiated with the label and controlled the band's recording contract. The "official" musicians would therefore need a very good lawyer and a mountain of money to thwart his plans. The problem was, they had neither. And time was running out, because Warner, fearing that the outcome of a trial would be favorable to Davis, froze not only all projects but also all funds linked to Fleetwood Mac, so as to be able to release them quickly to the party determined by the judge.

For the band, the situation was even critical, as they were stunned to learn that they had renounced the publishing rights to their songs when they signed their contracts in the late 1960s. For several months, they languished in Benifold, unable to publish anything under the Fleetwood Mac name or even tour to promote *Mystery to Me*, which had been well received in the United States. Everything was blocked by the legal situation and the resulting inertia. Clifford Davis, for his part, knew that disputes take a long time to be settled in England, and he intended to stifle his former protégés via the slowness of the judicial system, not

suspecting for a moment that they would show unfailing determination to thwart his plan.

But to do so, the group had to leave Benifold and England. It was Bob Welch who started the ball rolling: He had never really liked communal life or Fleetwood Mac's house in the English countryside; he was a Californian and wanted to go home. From Los Angeles, where he had taken up residence again, Welch was constantly on the phone to motivate his friends back in England. He was convinced that the West Coast sunshine and a booming Californian music scene would do his band a world of good. And he eventually found the decisive argument: Fleetwood Mac needed to get closer to Warner Bros. Records to rebuild trust with their label. For Bob Welch, it was America or the demise of the band.

Mick, who felt guilty personally and professionally, was becoming the catalyst for many changes. Everything he and his friends had worked so hard for was being called into question because he had let his guard down on his marriage, and on the band. Invigorated by long phone conversations with Bob Welch, he finally surrendered to Welch's arguments about the need to relocate Fleetwood Mac to California: "I got off the phone and looked around. England in winter seemed desultory, bare, and gray. I felt depressed," Mick Fleetwood wrote in his autobiography in 1991. "Finally I said, look, let's get out of England and go to America. The record company's there, and we have to tell them that we're still here, let's make an album. Neither Christine nor John

1974

Mick in the recording studio in 1974.

was keen to do it. I said, let's do it and treat it as a trial period. All we know about America is hotel rooms and gigs and wanting to go home after five months. I said, let's all get apartments and see what it's like. I said, all we ever do is work over there all the time anyhow. We've gotta get out of England and make a record or we're finished. Let's just go over, have a sniff, and see how it is."[4]

While John was quickly won over to the cause, Christine, not exactly a fan of California, resisted. It has to be said that she had invested a lot of her time in Benifold, where she was happy, and she would have preferred not to be away from her family. "But I begged her to try it for six months," Mick continued. "I swore that we would come back to England if she didn't like it. And, of course, she saw that it was a good thing to do. We were demoralized from sitting at home for months and needed shaking up. We hadn't made any music or gone anywhere. We needed this."[4] Cautious, the band kept Benifold for several years before selling it.

(Re)Born in the USA

The band set foot on American soil in April 1974. Mick and Jenny found refuge in Laurel Canyon, a neighborhood of Los Angeles popular with folk and rock musicians such as Neil Young, Canned Heat, Joni Mitchell, and James Taylor. They tried to patch up their marriage in the comfort of a picturesque cottage. As for John and Christine, they also opted for the Hollywood Hills. Far from the bucolic solitude of Benifold, bustling Californian life was the exact opposite of what they had known until then, but everyone seemed to be getting used to it. A first step had been taken, and now it was time to raise their heads professionally: to face up to emergencies and set a new dynamic in motion.

With just over $70,000 in their pockets, the group would have to win its legal battle and, for the umpteenth time, reinvent itself. They were almost starting from scratch, with no equipment and no manager. Their credibility had been damaged not only with tour managers but also with some of the public by the "fake" Fleetwood Mac, and they had no

Nick DeCaro was recruited for his arrangement expertise on *Heroes Are Hard to Find*.

record label until an agreement had been renegotiated with a very wary Warner Bros.

Mystery to Me could have bolstered the coffers if numerous concerts had followed, but that was impossible. While the band had obtained an injunction prohibiting the fake Fleetwood Mac from touring, Clifford Davis's lawyers had obtained another prohibiting the "real" Fleetwood Mac from playing until the end of the legal proceedings. Of course, nothing prevented the musicians from writing and recording, but they could not release an album, tour, or earn money as Fleetwood Mac.

While some in their entourage advised them to change their name and start afresh, Mick Fleetwood and his band refused to capitulate. But Clifford Davis, convinced that he "owned" Fleetwood Mac and that the name had value in itself, no matter who played the music, had no intention of giving in.

A New Album Against All Odds

Having had their fingers burned, Mick, John, Christine, and Bob decided to stop using a manager and to manage their careers themselves via a new company called Seedy Management. As a result, they could now sit down at a table to negotiate a new contract with Warner, provided they hire a lawyer to officially represent them. This would be Michael Shapiro, an acquaintance of Bob Welch's from his days with Seven Souls. The lawyer helped the band

reach an agreement with the record company, but the firm remained cautious, demanding compensation in the event of Clifford winning the case and the band being held legally liable. With their backs against the wall, the musicians accepted these conditions.

At the end of June 1974, Fleetwood Mac moved into the Angel City Sound studio in Los Angeles to rehearse new material for a new opus, *Heroes Are Hard to Find*. Aside from *Fleetwood Mac in Chicago* in 1969, this was the first of the band's albums not recorded in England. It was co-produced by Fleetwood Mac and Bob Hughes, Angel City Sound's in-house producer. The latter had previously worked for Vanilla Fudge (*Near the Beginning* in 1969), the Flying Burrito Brothers (*The Flying Burrito Bros* in 1971), Billy Joel (*Cold Spring Harbor* in 1971), and Spencer Davis (*Mousetrap* in 1972).

Bob Welch wrote most of the album, but not without difficulty: "We struggled with material," he recalled, "because nobody at that point could really articulate a clear direction. We wanted to do modern, no-cliché music, and had many long philosophical discussions about what we should do."[4] It was Christine McVie who came up with the title track, an upbeat rhythm'n'blues number with horns doped with Californian sunshine. The song set the creative process in motion but did not necessarily set the tone for the final album, which was torn between Christine's concern for immediacy and Bob Welch's clear desire to explore

1974

Fleetwood Mac worked with Tom Wilson, who produced the greatest albums by Bob Dylan, Simon and Garfunkel, and The Mothers of Invention.

psychedelia and progressive rock. The band gave itself the means to achieve its ambitions. As on *Mystery to Me*, it repeatedly required the services of an orchestra, led in this case by Nick DeCaro—a talented arranger and A&M Records regular who worked wonders on Gordon Lightfoot's *Sit Down Young Stranger* (1970).

During the time of the recording sessions in July 1974, Fleetwood Mac seemed to be rebuilding itself, coming together in the face of hardship, ignoring the courts where its future was at stake. To retain control of the Fleetwood Mac brand, Clifford Davis had not given up on the idea of destroying the band. He was determined to prevent the release of the new album, and, by extension, the promotional tour that was to follow. He took the case to court, which rejected his injunction. This was an initial victory for Fleetwood Mac, which reassured Warner, and the release of *Heroes Are Hard to Find* was officially scheduled for September 1974. The horizon seemed to be clearing.

"The Real Fleetwood Mac Stands Up"

Without being euphoric, the critics were pleasantly surprised, agreeing on the greatest successes of this new opus: the rhythmic "Heroes Are Hard to Find"; the exquisite "Prove Your Love"; the magnificent "Come a Little Bit Closer," reminiscent of the Beach Boys; the hypnotic "Bermuda Triangle"; and the vindictive "Bad Loser," aimed exclusively at the band's number one enemy: Clifford Davis.

The mysterious, eye-catching cover features Mick Fleetwood and his daughter Amy, photographed by Herbie Worthington III. Mick wears a pair of lace panties that belonged to one of his friends, named Sandra. Inflating his chest to the max, he reveals his ribs and holds his three-year-old daughter at arm's length as she steps on his shoes. Taken in a mirror, the final image gives the impression of three sides, with three Micks back-to-back. For Bob Welch, "The 'Heroes Are Hard…' cover, which came directly from Christine's song of the same name […] was Mick, with his ribs sticking out, being a 'hero' to his daughter who was looking up at him with adoration. So it was like, even supergeeks like the one Mick portrays on the cover, is a hero to SOMEBODY." The back of the disc, meanwhile, shows a photo of the band in a state of hilarity, not without reason according to Bob Welch: "I think we were all laughing because Nixon had just resigned!"[47]

The Mac musicians set off on tour to defend *Heroes…*, feeling serene on the musical front, if not totally serene on the legal front—the lawsuit with Davis would last a few more years. Some forty dates awaited them between now and December 1974, with a dual objective: to reassure fans and sell them the new album, but, above all, to put the band back at the center of the music industry and reestablish the trust that had been lost with agents and tour managers. To achieve this, any and all concerts would do, even if it meant drastically reducing the band's fee as part of this reconquest operation.

The end of the year was exhausting for the musicians, who sailed from one Holiday Inn to the next, fearing that Davis would come up with yet another twist.

In November, however, the gamble seemed to be about to pay off when *Rolling Stone* magazine put Fleetwood Mac on its front cover with the headline "The Real Fleetwood Mac Stands Up." In the eyes of everyone, the band was rehabilitated.

The Defection of Bob Welch

However, this difficult period left more scars than it might seem, especially on Bob Welch himself, who spared no effort to keep the band's head above water. He was exhausted after having written the bulk of the last two albums, especially as he had also invested a great deal of time in bringing Fleetwood Mac back to the United States and fighting against the persecution of Clifford Davis. Furthermore, his marriage was on the rocks, and the fact that he was constantly on the road did not do much to reconcile the couple. The icing on the cake was the fact that, although the album was well received by the critics, it failed to live up to the Mac's expectations of commercial success. Mick Fleetwood even went so far as to say ironically that it had barely sold enough copies "to pay Warner Brothers' electric light bill."[8] That was a slight exaggeration, since it did better in the US than any of their previous albums, reaching number thirty-four on the Billboard charts. At the time, it was a tremendous boost to the band's morale. And if Warner was wondering whether Fleetwood Mac still had an audience, the message sent by this result was very positive.

The Mac musicians were nevertheless concerned about Bob Welch. Welch had reached an impasse and his departure seemed inevitable. In December 1974, just as Fleetwood Mac's four-year search for a new musical identity seemed to be coming to an end, Welch announced his intention to leave the group. "I had come to the point where I didn't feel I had anything else to offer the band," he explained a few years later. "I had just burned it out. Faced with the prospect of making another Fleetwood record, I wouldn't have known what to do. I had a certain type of thing that was liked, but it wasn't any great success. The whole band was just chugging along on one cylinder, and my attitude was that after four years of ups and downs, something had to give."[25] The departure was all the more regrettable in that Bob Welch left behind some splendid songs that not only heralded his future solo successes, but also set a new standard for something bigger within Fleetwood Mac.

Mick Fleetwood had grasped this, and he did not want to waste any more time. Like Peter Green, Bob Welch would not change his mind—there was no point holding him back. During a rest day on tour in Van Nuys, Mick had visited Sound City Studios, with the idea of recording the next Fleetwood Mac album. As fate would have it, a spellbinding duo came his way: While his ears were drawn to Lindsey Buckingham's guitar, his eyes were caught by the beauty of the young singer, Stevie Nicks.

So, when Bob Welch made his departure official, Mick Fleetwood called recording engineer Keith Olsen to ask for the guitarist's contact. Olsen told him that recruiting Buckingham would be an excellent idea—and that he would certainly not be coming alone, but with his girlfriend, Stevie Nicks. An emotional turmoil for Mick, because replacing a guitarist with a guitarist and a singer was not part of the plan. And yet, he was about to open a radiant new chapter in the history of Fleetwood Mac.

1974

An ARP String Ensemble keyboard model.

On "Heroes Are Hard to Find," Christine McVie makes her first use of the ARP String Ensemble keyboard, which emulates a range of instruments (violin, cello, double bass, etc.), and for good reason: It is a novelty. This polyphonic gem from Eminent BV was first marketed in 1974 and was quickly adopted by many keyboardists, including Richard Wright ("Shine on You Crazy Diamond") in 1975 and Elton John ("Someone Saved My Life Tonight") the same year.

HEROES ARE HARD TO FIND

Christine McVie / 3:35

Musicians: Christine McVie: vocals, keyboards, backing vocals / Bob Welch: guitar / John McVie: bass / Mick Fleetwood: drums / Nick DeCaro: direction and arrangements / Orchestra: uncredited / **Recorded:** Angel City Sound, Los Angeles, July 1974 / **Technical Team:** Producers: Fleetwood Mac and Bob Hughes / Sound Engineer: Bob Hughes / Assistant Sound Engineer: Doug Graves / **Single:** Side A: Heroes Are Hard to Find / Side B: Born Enchanter / **UK Release Date:** February 28, 1975, with Reprise Records (ref. K 14388) / Best UK Chart Ranking: Did Not Chart / **US Release Date:** November 20, 1974, with Reprise Records (ref. RPS 1317) / Best US Chart Ranking: Did Not Chart

Genesis and Lyrics

As the album's title track, "Heroes Are Hard to Find" conveys the general meaning of this ninth opus. Who are the heroes evoked in this title that sounds like a definitive statement? They are plural. In fact, Fleetwood Mac multiplies the avenues of interpretation. There is the everyday hero, the loving parent who serves as a role model for his child, as illustrated by the cover featuring Mick Fleetwood and his daughter. There are the band members themselves, always at the helm despite the many blows of fate, who, in a fit of self-congratulation, refer to themselves as "hard-to-find" heroes compared to the pale illegitimate copies who replaced them on tour. And then there are the heroines, sung by Christine McVie in this fundamentally feminist track, written by a woman for the women she apostrophizes from the very first word, "Girls." She then gives voice to all those who have been abused by the manipulations of their partners and crushed by a patriarchal model that has run its course. The strength of her text lies in its universality, even if it means setting aside all nuance: "They're all the

same." The backing vocals, provided by the singer and keyboardist, give depth to her message, as the women seem to express themselves through them. These voices are much more than harmonic support, as they comment, in the style of gospel or soul, on the lead vocal's lyrics and add their own point of view: "don't believe him," "such a shame," or "he's just lying."

While such an attack is not unprecedented—Aretha Franklin cried out for "Respect" in 1967 when she twisted Otis Redding's version, and Carly Simon settled her score with "You're So Vain" in 1972—it is an important milestone in the long march toward gender equality.

Production

In a way, this track validates the choice made to continue with four musicians, with, for the first time, a single guitarist. Rather than impoverishing the formula melodically, the absence of a second guitar leaves room for the band's creativity. On this track, that creativity is expressed by a brass section led by Nick DeCaro, a renowned Los Angeles–based producer and arranger who cut his teeth at A&M Records. This addition lends vigor to the track and highlights the natural groove of Christine McVie's keyboard playing. At the end of the track, she completes her composition with a layer of synthetic strings. "Heroes Are Hard to Find" has all the hallmarks of a potential hit: a lively, swaying rhythm; a galvanizing energy; a capacity to appeal to the widest possible audience thanks to its positioning at the confluence of styles between rhythm'n'blues, funk, and pop; a strong message delivered by a voice that is just as strong; and a chorus that is instantly memorable. Logically chosen as a single, the song failed to chart in either the US or the UK.

Bob Welch sacrificed himself to progressive rock with "Coming Home."

FOR MAC-ADDICTS

Interestingly, two Fleetwood Mac songs share the name "Coming Home." One of the tracks on *Mr. Wonderful*, borrowed from Elmore James and sung by Jeremy Spencer, already had this title. The parallel between the 1968 blues track and this psychedelic experimentation says a lot about the band's musical evolution over the span of six years.

COMING HOME

Bob Welch / 3:52

Musicians: Bob Welch: vocals, guitar / Christine McVie: keyboards / John McVie: bass / Mick Fleetwood: drums / **Recorded:** Angel City Sound, Los Angeles, July 1974 / **Technical Team:** Producers: Fleetwood Mac and Bob Hughes / Sound Engineer: Bob Hughes / Assistant Sound Engineer: Doug Graves

Genesis and Lyrics

The only guitarist in place since Bob Weston's ousting, Bob Welch, who was now an old hand in the band, enjoyed a great deal of compositional freedom. No longer simply a musician at Fleetwood Mac's service, his musical universe was now one with that of the band. On "Coming Home," the jazz aficionado leads his three partners in this direction. But he takes them off on a different path, developing a long, psychedelic, experimental introduction during which he distorts the sound of his guitar while mumbling a sort of incomprehensible utterance. Only a few snippets emerge, which seem to be: "I want you all to know, I cannot find any impossibilities to destroy you." It is very reminiscent of Pink Floyd's "One of These Days" (1971) and its terrifying words: "One of these days I'm going to cut you into little pieces." In 1999, Bob Welch humorously tried to muddy the waters: "On 'Coming Home,' what sounds like prophesying in an unknown language, is probably me talking to the dry cleaner or something. [...] Or...I may have been saying something heavy and profound, which now escapes me, or telling the engineer to turn my headphones up...."[47] In any case, none of this seems to correspond to the content of the message. It is worth noting that the band was used to recording everything: song ideas, of course, but sometimes also banal or funny conversations, in restaurants or elsewhere—for memory's sake, or to integrate snippets into their music and create sound effects, as is the case on "Coming Home." As for the rest of the song's lyrics, they are a hodgepodge of supposedly poetic surrealist imagery, once again referring to "heroes": "All the heroes in the bright burning truth."

Production

Since 1973, the year preceding the recording, marked by the massive commercial success of progressive rock—with the triumph of Moody Blues (*Seventh Sojourn*) and Pink Floyd (*The Dark Side of the Moon*) both topping the Billboard charts—the fashion was for experimentation. And Fleetwood Mac dove in headfirst. Mick Fleetwood picks up mallets and places some ominous rolls, while Bob Welch ratchets up the tension with hammer-on guitar. The guitar is drowned in reverb and assigned a flanger effect. Bob Hughes, for his part, swirls the instrument around the spectrum, passing it rapidly from left to right to create a sense of vertigo for the listener. Christine McVie, far from her usual register, improvises random notes. Then, kick-started by a new roll from Mick, bass and keyboard develop an oppressive theme. Bob Welch's guitar steps in with a jazz sequence that totally changes the mood and tonality of the piece. The progression (*Dom9, F#7, F#7/Eb, Lab7, C#7sus4, E#7, F7, Bbm7, Lab7, C#7*) with seventh chords (major and minor thirds, perfect fifths, and major and minor sevenths) adds richness to the melody and breathes life into the claustrophobic track.

ANGEL
Bob Welch / 3:55

Musicians
Bob Welch: vocals, guitar
Christine McVie: keyboards
John McVie: bass
Mick Fleetwood: drums

Recorded
Angel City Sound, Los Angeles, July 1974

Technical Team
Producers: Fleetwood Mac and Bob Hughes
Sound Engineer: Bob Hughes
Assistant Sound Engineer: Doug Graves

Genesis and Lyrics

The psychedelic experimentation of "Coming Home" was immediately answered by the seemingly straightforward rock of "Angel." This feverish song emerges at the end of a long fade-in, like a sequence taken from the middle of an intense jam session. Inspired by its hypnotic dimension—and by the name of the recording studio, Angel City Sound—Bob Welch scribbled off the song's text in one go. Once again, he veers into the esoteric, but with more skill than usual. The ghostly apparitions are in no way frightening; quite the contrary. He attributes feminine traits to them, giving his story a romantic twist. Sometimes his boorishness becomes delicate as he describes the evanescence of the "angel of my dreams." The nature of their relationship is platonic, secretive, and dotted with missed appointments: "I still look up / When you walk in the room / I've the same wide eyes / Now they tell the story / I try not to reach out / When you turn round / You say hello / And we both pretend."

Production

Alongside "Coming Home," "Angel" seems surprisingly straightforward. This is far from the case. Its construction is a model of its kind. Mick Fleetwood lays a solid foundation, setting up a varied pattern punctuated by cymbal strikes at the end of each bar. A throbbing groove is set up by a playful bass, alternating between fundamental and melodic scales, almost guitar-like. As for Bob Welch's bass, it seems to multiply between the track that forms the rhythmic foundation (with its muffled sound in the background of the mix) and the one that accommodates his twirling phrasing. These ornaments never last more than two or three seconds, but they vary constantly, lending richness and delicacy to the track. In the midst of this sonic fireworks display, Christine McVie manages to bring the keyboard to life by taking advantage of the rare harmonic spaces and completes the sound space with apt timing.

Mick Fleetwood provided the rock foundation for "Angel" with assurance and authority.

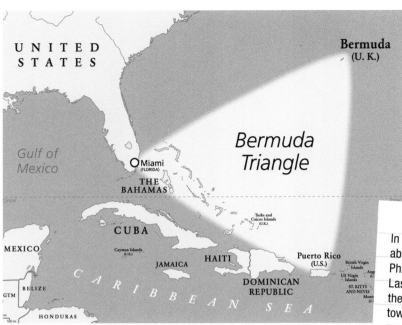

The Bermuda Triangle, the source of so many mysteries and vague theories, inspired Welch's song with the same name.

In 1976, Mort Shuman released a song in France about the Bermuda Triangle, with lyrics by Philippe Adler, as Side B to his single "Save the Last Dance for Me." In this song, which evokes the disappearance of a plane, we hear the control tower desperately calling the pilot by his code name: "Allô, Papa Tango Charley?"

BERMUDA TRIANGLE
Bob Welch / 4:08

Musicians: Bob Welch: vocals, guitar, vibraphone / Christine McVie: keyboards, backing vocals / John McVie: bass / Mick Fleetwood: drums, percussions / **Recorded:** Angel City Sound, Los Angeles, July 1974 / **Technical Team:** Producers: Fleetwood Mac and Bob Hughes / Sound Engineer: Bob Hughes / Assistant Sound Engineer: Doug Graves

Genesis and Lyrics
Bob Welch has never made any secret of the fact that esotericism, the paranormal, and the supernatural fed his imagination as much as his work, preferring the enigmas of his time to sentimental platitudes. In 1974, the Bermuda Triangle became a hot topic of conversation and media attention, following the publication of several articles and books devoted to the subject. These articles were so successful that they marked the beginning of a series of investigations and counter-investigations into the subject and led to a renewed focus on this area located inside a triangle formed by the Bermuda archipelago, Miami in Florida, and San Juan in Puerto Rico.

With this song, Bob Welch takes his turn to express his views on this enigma, taking the listener as witness: "I guess you've heard about the Bermuda Triangle / There's something going on / Nobody seems to know just what it is." In what sounds more like a long commentary declaimed in a soft, velvety voice than a song lyric, Welch cites food for thought such as "a hole down in the ocean" and "a fog that won't let go."

Production
"Bermuda Triangle" was born by accident. The musicians were looking for a drum rhythm for another song (they have since forgotten which one it was) when Mick Fleetwood played what would form the basis of "Bermuda Triangle." It did not suit what they were looking for, but the hypnotic, robotic rhythm was worth exploring. Bob Welch called in the sound engineer and asked him to artificially increase the speed of Mick's drum loop by 20–25 percent. On this basis, the guitarist began to build a new jazz-fusion track with a Hispanic guitar. The musician perfected its exoticism by adding an introduction over which congas and Asian-accented guitar respond, then, later in the song, discreet touches of vibraphone.

1974

FOR MAC ADDICTS

"Sneaky Pete" was an obvious choice when it came to finding a guitarist capable of playing slide on this track. Pete Kleinow, a member of country-rock outfit the Flying Burrito Brothers, masters the pedal steel guitar like no other. The whole of Laurel Canyon called on him, including Linda Ronstadt, Joni Mitchell, Jackson Browne, and Frank Zappa. His greatest feat before joining Fleetwood Mac was his work on John Lennon's *Mind Games* album.

COME A LITTLE BIT CLOSER

Christine McVie / 4:45

Musicians: Christine McVie: vocals, keyboards, backing vocals / Bob Welch: guitar, backing vocals / Sneaky Pete Kleinow: guitar / John McVie: bass / Mick Fleetwood: drums / Nick DeCaro: direction and arrangements / Orchestra: uncredited / **Recorded:** Angel City Sound, Los Angeles, July 1974 / **Technical Team:** Producers: Fleetwood Mac and Bob Hughes / Sound Engineer: Bob Hughes / Assistant Sound Engineer: Doug Graves

Genesis and Lyrics

Despite the popularity of its namesake "Come a Little Bit Closer" (a number by Jay and the Americans that reached number three on the US charts in 1964), Christine McVie's composition has nothing in common with that hit, except the thematic one of a lascivious dance. Christine McVie's—performed to what she calls "a simple melody," with a clever "infinite regress"—is tinged with deep melancholy. For this shared moment of intimacy, when bodies come together, resonates like an emotional memory. It is evoked by the lyricist to rekindle, if still possible, the fire of passion in her partner (John McVie, as everyone knows).

Production

From the outset, "Come a Little Bit Closer" seemed to have great potential as a single. So much so, in retrospect, that it seems incomprehensible that Warner did not choose to bank on this track, even against the backdrop of Fleetwood Mac's legal imbroglios. At the opposite end of the spectrum from Bob Welch's sonic experiments, which would make any artistic director looking for a bankable artist falter, this track is immediately legible, built with exemplary efficiency right from the start. For if we isolate the piano part conceived by the composer, Christine McVie, the song can be performed on its own as a piano-vocal. The introduction contains the melody in its most complete form, with the four basic chords F, C, $a\#$, Dm, and all the ornamental notes. It is played in a slow, contemplative rhythm. The motif ends with a short climb, and its arrival at the top is greeted by a cymbal blast from Mick Fleetwood, the starting signal for the entry of the other instruments and the beginning of the orchestral part added at overdub moments. We can imagine the enthusiasm of the musicians when we first hear Sneaky Pete Kleinow's airy slide guitar part—reminiscent of Bob Weston's light guitar playing, but also of George Harrison's with its long ascending curves and stairstep descents—and even more so with the epic momentum breathed into the piece by the string orchestra conducted by Nick DeCaro. This momentum is further enhanced by the rhythm. The sweeping attacks and ringing chords recall the construction of some of the Who's iconic songs of the same period (Fleetwood Mac admirers the Smashing Pumpkins also drew inspiration from this). The verse simplifies the melody set out in the introduction, with just the two placed chords of F and $a\#$. Christine McVie then reintroduces the missing chords on the exhilarating chorus, carried by a voice so natural that the note-holding seems easy to master, as much as the prosody—which is by no means obvious, the singer speeding up the flow, for example, when she pronounces the verse that gives the song its name. As for the crystalline backing vocals, most of which she provides herself, they add the right touch of romanticism.

Laurel Canyon, California, influenced the musical mood of "She's Changing Me."

SHE'S CHANGING ME
Bob Welch / 2:58

Musicians: Bob Welch: vocals, guitar, backing vocals / Christine McVie: keyboards, backing vocals / Sneaky Pete Kleinow: guitar / John McVie: bass, backing vocals / Mick Fleetwood: drums / Nick DeCaro: direction and arrangements / Orchestra: uncredited / **Recorded:** Angel City Sound, Los Angeles, July 1974 / **Technical Team:** Producers: Fleetwood Mac and Bob Hughes / Sound Engineer: Bob Hughes / Assistant Sound Engineer: Doug Graves

Genesis and Lyrics
Behind its melodically obvious character, "She's Changing Me" is shrouded in a halo of mystery. Who is behind the "she" that so influences the narrator's destiny? Is it a woman, as the pronoun suggests, or the personification of drugs, or death? Elements of explanation are few and far between. We know that, in the text, "she" is associated with danger, as the singer urges the listener to beware. The narrator declares that we only understand the meaning of her gaze when she comes to us, and that behind her eyes lies the road we must follow. This creature, reminiscent of the Gorgons, carries an ambivalence: She can "take away the sadness in your heart," as much as "she can destroy." The key element could be the woman's nickname: "They call her the sweet omega." Omega is the twenty-fourth and last letter of the Greek alphabet. As opposed to alpha, it represents the end and could therefore,

in Bob Welch's mind, symbolize death. But don't count on him to dispel the mystery. In 1999, Welch said the words "sweet omega" referred to Jesuit priest and philosopher Teilhard de Chardin's concept of Omega Point, or the pinnacle of spirituality or the point of convergence of the consciousness of humanity. The concept, he said, was similar to American writer and philosopher Terence McKenna's "singularity at the end of history," the Christian rapture, the Buddhist enlightenment, or the Monroe Institute's "reassembling of the cluster"[47] of consciousness.

Production
The gentle Californian lifestyle and the bubbling counterculture that animated Laurel Canyon were the new living environment for Fleetwood Mac's musicians. This atmosphere is distilled in this song by local native Bob Welch. "She's Changing Me" is a fresh, uplifting little folk-rock gem, worthy of the Byrds, with backing vocals à la Crosby, Stills & Nash or the Beach Boys. Mick Fleetwood and Christine McVie agree to synchronize the rhythm of their entrance playing. Bob Welch then takes the lead with strumming over an acoustic guitar, very classical except for the change of key induced by the arrival of the brass band, which is surprisingly discreet.

In vindictive mode, Christine expressed all the resentment accumulated against Clifford Davis, Fleetwood Mac's former manager and the "bad loser" in the song.

BAD LOSER

Christine McVie / 3:25

Musicians: Christine McVie: vocals, keyboards, backing vocals / Bob Welch: guitar, backing vocals / John McVie: bass, backing vocals / Mick Fleetwood: drums, percussions / **Recorded:** Angel City Sound, Los Angeles, July 1974 / **Technical Team:** Producers: Fleetwood Mac and Bob Hughes / Sound Engineer: Bob Hughes / Assistant Sound Engineer: Doug Graves

Genesis and Lyrics

They got the feather; he got the tar. One way or another, the bile had to come out. The overflow was too great after the series of assaults orchestrated by Clifford Davis against his ex-protégés. It was better for everyone—the band and Davis alike—if they were done creatively. If the former Fleetwood Mac manager wanted to take away the musicians' freedom of movement by preventing them not only from performing but also from marketing their creations under their own name, the members did still have their writing. Surprisingly, it is the discreet Christine McVie, usually the band's balancing element, who kicks off the hostilities. She begins her text by recalling the repeated failures of the "bad loser" in question in his vile attempts to control them. In the second stanza, she castigates his relentlessness and promises him the same failure in his next attempts. In the next verse, she explains that his conscience will never leave him in peace and ends with the sentence that breaks all ties with the past: "You're no friend of mine."

Production

It would have been easy to set off the sonic wildfire with a roar of guitars to express the anger of the entire team. But Fleetwood Mac had almost established the counterintuitive as an immutable law. This diatribe therefore adopts an unexpected musical form: a song shrouded in mystery, with its descending endings, penetrating female backing vocals, Christine McVie's deep, confident voice, and its western color. But what really catches the attention is the clear retreat of her keyboard in favor of the guitars—a choice that does not correspond to the usual characteristics of her compositions and sounds more like the work of Bob Welch—and the omnipresence of Mick Fleetwood's work, which combines drums and tambourine to impart a lively, continuous rhythm. "I think 'Bad Loser' sounds like me, because Mick played one of his 'jungle' drum trademark things on it and he didn't often do that on one of Christine's songs,"[47] Bob Welch wrote in 1999.

Etta James, winner of seventeen Blues Music awards, influenced Bob Welch's chorus.

SILVER HEELS

Bob Welch / 3:25

Musicians: Bob Welch: vocals, guitar / Christine McVie: keyboards, backing vocals / John McVie: bass / Mick Fleetwood: drums / **Recorded:** Angel City Sound, Los Angeles, July 1974 / **Technical Team:** Producers: Fleetwood Mac and Bob Hughes / Sound Engineer: Bob Hughes / Assistant Sound Engineer: Doug Graves

Genesis and Lyrics

Peter Green, Jeremy Spencer, and Danny Kirwan—Fleetwood Mac's three least talkative songwriters—could have written "Silver Heels" as a threesome, but they would not have written nearly as much as the loquacious Bob Welch. Unlike his three predecessors, who looked back admiringly on the blues' glorious past, Bob Welch prefers to soak up the zeitgeist. In 1974, funk was booming and diversifying (jazz funk, P-funk, disco funk...), and dress codes were changing. Hippie fashion had had its day, and the flannel-sandals-patchouli combo had been replaced by "boots" with "silver heels," "diamond rings," and "fox fur," as Welch describes them in this text. These elements make up the wardrobe of a young woman on whom he has a crush, and whom he compares to a hurricane for the devastating effect she has on his mind. For the first time in a Fleetwood Mac song, elements of contemporary culture are

included: Welch cites Paul McCartney and Etta James as unattainable role models in terms of the former's vocal quality and the latter's funky attitude (a prominent figure in R&B, soul, and jazz, she released an album called *Etta James Sings Funk* in 1970).

Production

The reference to Paul McCartney is not confined to the lyrics but extends to the music, which leans toward Wings with its mix of rock and pop and its incendiary groove. The track kicks off without preamble with the combined attack of Bob Welch's incisive guitar chord and Mick Fleetwood's clattering cymbal—a striking entrance ideal for accompanying the appearance of the young woman compared to a hurricane. The verses and choruses are clearly distinguished by their melodic progression: The first appear descending, the second ascending, ensuring a varied progression for this original track, which has an insidious, never frontal groove. It also features interesting little variations in construction, such as the break at 0:55, which leaves the guitar alone on stage, with claps as its sole rhythmic accompaniment.

The estrangement between Christine and John continued to fuel the keyboardist and singer's lyrics.

PROVE YOUR LOVE
Christine McVie / 3:57

Musicians: Christine McVie: vocals, keyboards / Bob Welch: guitar / John McVie: bass / Mick Fleetwood: drums / Nick DeCaro: direction and arrangements / Orchestra: uncredited / **Recorded:** Angel City Sound, Los Angeles, July 1974 / **Technical Team:** Producers: Fleetwood Mac and Bob Hughes / Sound Engineer: Bob Hughes / Assistant Sound Engineer: Doug Graves

Genesis and Lyrics
Little by little, Christine McVie's texts were evolving in both content and form. They are still about the imbalance in a love relationship—and her feeling of giving far more than she receives—but she was now adopting a much more purposeful attitude. She was no longer the young woman lamenting her fate in the hope that her complaints would resonate with John McVie. The vocabulary used is significant. The personal pronouns "I" and "me" are at the center of the discourse, associated with the language of possession and satisfaction. "I want," "the place for me," "to please me." By contrast, the second-person singular is linked to obligations: "You've got to prove." Suddenly, the roles are reversed.

Production
"Prove Your Love" is an instant classic at first hearing. The nonchalant beat struck by Mick Fleetwood (alone for the first few seconds) is not at all engaging, and Bob Hughes's choice not to cut this part may come as a surprise, but it does offset the entry of the bass and keyboard, which enter together on a cymbal stroke from the drummer. The vocals also kick in without delay, in the form of enchanting vocalizations. These are the central element of the song, as it is this melodic motif that the mind retains. Christine's vocals are admirable in their own right; suave and light, they detach themselves effortlessly from the air, played on the keyboard to create an autonomous melody. The confident voice drives the relays between parts, as at 1:09 when the musician sings over the drums before resuming her full, groovy performance on the Fender Rhodes electric piano. The second part of the song is enhanced by elegant string arrangements, discreet except for the sequence where the violins build to a crescendo and lead to a classy finale, accompanying the keyboard's melodic ascent toward the treble range.

The Fender Rhodes affects the sound in "Born Enchanter" to great advantage under the touch of Christine McVie's fingers.

BORN ENCHANTER

Bob Welch / 2:54

Musicians: Bob Welch: vocals, guitar / Christine McVie: keyboards, piano / John McVie: bass / Mick Fleetwood: drums / **Recorded:** Angel City Sound, Los Angeles, July 1974 / **Technical Team:** Producers: Fleetwood Mac and Bob Hughes / Sound Engineer: Bob Hughes / Assistant Sound Engineer: Doug Graves / **Single:** Side A: Heroes Are Hard to Find / Side B: Born Enchanter / **UK Release Date:** February 28, 1975, with Reprise Records (ref. K 14388) / Best UK Chart Ranking: Did Not Chart / **US Release Date:** November 20, 1974, with Reprise Records (ref. RPS 1317) / Best US Chart Ranking: Did Not Chart

Genesis and Lyrics

Bob Welch's humor and creative freedom are at work here. Completely freewheeling, the guitarist does not shy away from provocation or experimentation, as though already aware that he is engaged in a gallant "last stand." Here he is, parading around with his characteristic second degree, a seducer of the ladies, spreading his charm like an evangelist spreading the good word. In fact, he includes religious elements in his speech, addressing the "Lord" in the second verse. The narrator asks him to let him go to "my city of dreams." We can guess that this city (perhaps Los Angeles?) embodies vice and temptation and is in danger of driving him away from his faith.

Production

"Bob's writing was strong as well, on songs like 'Born Enchanter,' which was a bluesier variation of the jazzy, esoteric-pop style he'd achieved so well on 'Hypnotized.'"[2] This analysis is by Mick Fleetwood and emphasizes the versatility of Bob Welch's playing. This doesn't take into account the soulful mood that runs through the track, instilled by several elements. First, the vocals: A world separates Welch's early Mac efforts—the track "Future Games," for example, where his frail, listless voice was lost in the mix—and this "Born Enchanter," where he fully embodies his born seducer persona. In the latter song, he takes vocal risks and discovers a wider range than he thought possible. He sings much higher than usual, and masters his breath, projection, and intonation sufficiently to remain expressive and instill a typically soulful sensuality. On this terrain straddling blues, jazz, and soul, Christine McVie is in her element, twirling her right hand like a piano bar performer. Her idea was to combine a jazz-sounding acoustic piano track with a more soulful electric piano (a Fender Rhodes) track.

At the instigation of Bob Welch (seated), Fleetwood Mac returned to long improvisations, a habit previously encouraged by Peter Green.

SAFE HARBOUR

Bob Welch / 2:32

Musicians: Bob Welch: vocals, guitar / Christine McVie: keyboards / John McVie: bass / Mick Fleetwood: drums / **Recorded:** Angel City Sound, Los Angeles, July 1974 / **Technical Team:** Producers: Fleetwood Mac and Bob Hughes / Sound Engineer: Bob Hughes / Assistant Sound Engineer: Doug Graves

Genesis and Lyrics

As Bob Welch attempts to recall things in 1999, "I have an idea which consists of some partial lyrics, and chord changes for something which will wind up being 'Safe Harbor.' I don't have any idea what anything else will be like, when I just start playing with Mick, John, Chris, Bob Weston—whoever,"[47] mistakenly including Weston in the picture, whereas in June 1974, when "Safe Harbour" was composed, he had left it. The guitarist proposes a "creative jam" to his partners, based on two chords that he loops over and over, whose lightness and elegance he loves: "They just start playing whatever comes into their minds, while STILL keeping to the rough 'outline' that I've sketched musically. There are usually very FEW words spoken when you are 'working up' songs. Most of the communication is done musically, or with looks, gestures, head nods…stuff like that. Maybe somebody will shout, 'G minor, not G major!' but that's about it. In a way, it's sort of like making love, it's all (mostly) NON-verbal, you communicate with your body language, and your instrument."[47]

Production

The hypnotic, repetitive dimension of this quasi-instrumental piece comes from the conditions in which it was created: a long improvisation in which everyone tries to find their place. Obviously, John, Christine, and Mick do not take any risks: John plays the fundamental notes, without any further embellishments, but the title, a slow, dreamlike progressive blues, does not call for anything more. Christine's rhythmic playing is totally restrained here. She opts for simple, vaporous strings. As for Mick, he immediately understands the mood of the track and responds to his partner's needs with a very discreet use of cymbals, the most logical in the circumstances. "One of the things about working with talented people, like the members of Fleetwood Mac, is that you don't really have to 'explain' things like 'atmosphere' etc. to them. They are all good enough musicians, and have trained their musical sensitivities to a point where they just sort of know, intuitively, what is needed for a certain mood."[47]

ALBUM

FLEETWOOD MAC

Monday Morning . Warm Ways . Blue Letter . Rhiannon . Over My Head . Crystal .
Say You Love Me . Landslide . World Turning . Sugar Daddy . I'm So Afraid

RELEASE DATES
United Kingdom: July 11, 1975
Reference: Reprise Records—K54043
Best UK Chart Ranking: 23
United States: July 11, 1975
Reference: Reprise Records—MS 2225
Best US Chart Ranking: 1

The second self-titled *Fleetwood Mac* continued the band's tradition of never appearing as a whole band on album covers.

In this 1975 group photo, John McVie, in a nod to the album cover, places his hands around Mick Fleetwood's head as if consulting a crystal ball.

FOR MAC-ADDICTS

Fleetwood Mac was nicknamed the White Album because of its cover color, and to differentiate it from the previous eponymous LP, released in 1968.

INTO ORBIT

On December 31, 1974, Mick Fleetwood picked up the phone to call Lindsey Buckingham. He had little left to lose. His band was once again on the brink of collapse following the departure of Bob Welch, marking the abrupt end of Fleetwood Mac's ninth lineup. Producer Keith Olsen—whom Mick had met a few weeks earlier at Sound City Studios when he was looking for a place to record the next album—had extolled the guitarist's virtues. Olsen played Mick "Frozen Love," a track from Lindsey's album with Stevie Nicks, which Olsen produced. Mick was immediately impressed. So, when the horizon darkened again for Fleetwood Mac, the drummer considered Lindsey Buckingham for the position vacated by Bob Welch.

The Perfect Couple

After some hesitation, the stubborn Lindsey—who still harbored hopes of breaking through as a duo with Stevie Nicks—agreed to join the band with his partner. The latter, tired of their unsuccessful musical project and financial woes, welcomed the opportunity to join the band. If it did not work out, they could always go back to working as a duo, Stevie thought. For his part, Mick, who initially intended to hire only Lindsey, wanted to make sure that Christine McVie would not take offense at the arrival of a second singer, even though Christine was not particularly looking for the spotlight. To make sure the two women hit it off, he arranged a meeting at a Mexican restaurant in Los Angeles. A pleasant surprise: The two singers immediately

struck up a rapport. After a few margaritas, Mick turned to Lindsey and Stevie and officially asked them if they wanted to join Fleetwood Mac. After a brief glance at each other, the couple smiled and answered in the affirmative. The band's tenth incarnation was born. "I've always felt a sense of depth and destiny about Fleetwood Mac. We always did everything on instinct," Mick explains in his autobiography. "Nobody ever auditioned for Fleetwood Mac, and that's one of the reasons nothing ordinary ever happened to this band. Somewhere up there, I've always felt, was a little magic star, looking out for us. People were *meant* to be in this group."[4]

A few days after their first meeting, Christine McVie returned to England to visit her family, while John and Mick took the opportunity to invite Lindsey to rehearse in a garage on Pico Boulevard in Santa Monica. The session was idyllic. The three musicians hit it off instantly. But the moment of truth came on Christine's return, when the Mac got together for their first rehearsal. From the outset, the osmosis was obvious. The vibes were right, the energy was there, and the two newcomers fit right in: Lindsey's versatile guitar playing impressed, and Stevie's charisma, a blend of endearing beatnik poet and cowgirl, lent a mystical dimension to this new version of the band. Everyone sensed that Lindsey Buckingham and Stevie Nicks were about to permanently alter Fleetwood Mac's DNA, injecting pop precision and naked emotion into a lineup that was in dire need of a creative spark.

Going with Sound City

A few weeks later, at the beginning of February 1975, Fleetwood Mac moved into Sound City Studios to record their new album.

Located in a former Vox factory building in the disreputable Los Angeles suburb of Van Nuys, the studios had opened in 1969 under the impetus of Joe Gottfried and Tom Skeeter, entrepreneurs with ambitions of creating a record label and management agency. The two men soon turned their attention to recording and began to make their mark in the business. The original venue boasted excellent acoustics, but more important, Skeeter and Gottfried invested in state-of-the-art equipment, acquiring a Neve Model 8028 28-input Class A console, a space-station-style control desk (with ninety-six automated faders!) that recorded music on analog tapes. There are only four or five of these models in the entire world. But only the model at Sound City Studios had been customized by manufacturer Rupert Neve himself. It quickly won over all the producers who had the opportunity to work on it, and it became an important factor in the famous Sound City sound. Renowned for the quality of its acoustics, equipment, and production, as well as for its family-friendly atmosphere, Sound City Studios welcomed an impressive number of bands and artists until its closure in 2011, making it a cult venue for American music production.

The first to inaugurate the Neve 8028 were Stevie Nicks and Lindsey Buckingham with the song "Crying in the Night" (on their album *Buckingham Nicks*), recorded in 1973 with the help of Keith Olsen. But it was Fleetwood Mac, who chose Sound City to record their tenth studio opus, that gave the Van Nuys studio its first claim to fame. Mick Fleetwood fell under the spell of the place on his first visit. "It's a church. By the luck of whatever, I had the ability to open that door."[77]

Keith Olsen: The Hitmaker

Mick Fleetwood was in charge of production, assisted by Keith Olsen, who also worked as sound engineer, seconded by David DeVore. Olsen has been praised by all the musicians who have worked with him for his efficiency and his ear for detail. Trained as a double bass player and a fan of jazz, classical music, and rock, Olsen's ability to spot the songs that are going to be big hits right from the demo stage earned him the nickname of "hitmaker." Rick Springfield credits him with his greatest success: "He didn't produce all those hits for all those musicians for no reason. He had a golden ear and helped so many people reach their potential. I remember playing him my demos and he picked 'Jessie's Girl' out of a batch of 15 songs and said, 'This is a hit.' I doubted him and thought there were better songs in my demo reel. Proof right there of his gift."[81]

When he took over the *Fleetwood Mac* sessions, Olsen was thirty years old and still had only limited experience. Fascinated by the work of Brian Wilson—whom he had had the good fortune to meet at the very start of his career—he was a fan of meticulous productions that re-created the studio listening experience as closely as possible. Over the following three decades, Olsen built up a reputation as a producer, and his résumé soon included collaborations with the Grateful Dead, Santana, Pat Benatar, Sammy Hagar, Ozzy Osbourne, Scorpions, and Emerson, Lake & Palmer. His discography includes more than thirty-nine gold albums and twenty-four platinum albums.

SOUND CITY, THE HOME OF ALTERNATIVE ROCK

Sound City. The name of the studios that gave birth to so many legendary albums has become as mythical as those of Abbey Road, Electric Lady, Sun, Capitol, Chess Records, and Muscle Shoals.

A Studio with a Legendary Sound

Opened in 1969, Sound City Studios, with its two recording spaces (Studios A and B), quickly gained a reputation for quality recording, to the point of becoming a key venue for many of the music industry's biggest names in the late 1970s. This old-fashioned venue, with its carpeted walls, Jack Daniel's bottles, and cigarette butts, might not have looked like much, but it had three essential qualities: unique acoustics, cutting-edge equipment, and, above all, an exceptional staff, both technical and human. As a result, Sound City not only survived four decades of change but also produced albums that set new standards in rock music under the leadership of producers such as David Briggs, Keith Olsen, Butch Vig, and Rick Rubin. Following sessions in the 1970s by Neil Young for *After the Gold Rush* (1970), Elton John for *Caribou* (1974), Fleetwood Mac for *Fleetwood Mac* (1975), the Grateful Dead for *Terrapin Station* (1977), and Tom Petty and the Heartbreakers for *Damn the Torpedoes* (1979), Sound City Studios give birth to revolutionary behemoths over the following three decades: Guns N' Roses' *Appetite for Destruction* (1986), Nirvana's *Nevermind* (1991), and Rage Against the Machine's eponymous *Rage Against the Machine* (1992).

The acoustics of the venue are particularly exceptional for drumming, as all the greatest drummers, from Jeff Porcaro to Dave Grohl and Lars Ulrich, have discovered. Lars Ulrich, a drummer with Metallica, listened to samples of bass drum recordings made in different studios, then made a "blind" choice of the one he recorded at Sound City Studios for *Death Magnetic* (2008).

An Analog Museum

In 2011, the studio closed its doors to the public and much of its equipment was sold, including the famous Neve Electronics 8028 console, bought by Dave Grohl, former drummer with Nirvana and current leader of Foo Fighters. A devotee of vintage analog gear, Grohl installed the massive analog console in his own California studio, the 606, in Northridge, California. Two years later, Grohl shot a documentary (his first as a director) on the history of Sound City Studios, where he'd played a key role as drummer for Nirvana.

Also in 2011, Fairfax Recording leased Studio A for the exclusive use of its in-house artists. Leaving the studio in its original state, Fairfax renovated the control room, equipping it with analog equipment even older than the famous Neve 8028 console, including an ARP 2600 semimodular analog synthesizer, a Wurlitzer 140B electric piano, and equalizer modules designed for Columbia CBS Studios in New York.

In 2017, the studio's doors reopened to all artists with a partnership between Sandy Skeeter, daughter of founder Tom Skeeter, and Olivier Chastan. While digital technologies were integrated into the control booths, it still houses an impressive collection of vintage analog equipment, including two of the eleven Helios Type 69 consoles still in operation (one for each of the studio control rooms). Studio B also boasts a Helios Type 69 audio mixer, which equipped Island Studios in 1969 and was used by Led Zeppelin and Black Sabbath, among others. This time, the premises underwent a significant facelift, getting immaculate white walls and checkerboard-patterned flooring. Until then, the venue had been kept exactly as it was. Ever since it opened in 1969, no one had dared touch the old carpet that lined the walls or the outdated linoleum that covered the floor, for fear of altering the venue's legendary acoustics.

The bright smiles of the five musicians, confident in the future of this new incarnation of the band.

Everyone Contributes

The Buckingham Nicks duo did not come to Olsen empty-handed. The two "cursed" artists (who had already been working for some time on new compositions for their next album) showed up at the recording sessions, Lindsey's four-track Ampex under their arm, to play Mick, John, and Christine the first versions of "Rhiannon" (probably the best of all), "I'm So Afraid" (a track for which Lindsey had been working on guitar harmonies for several years), "Monday Morning," as well as two tracks salvaged from the duo's *Buckingham Nicks* album sessions: "Crystal" and "Landslide." The band's reaction to these tracks was mixed. In the eyes of John McVie, they represented a major stylistic shift, and he was hesitant (although the last few albums had been moving in this musical direction). Keith Olsen, a close friend of Buckingham and Nicks, tried to convince him with a cynical argument: "We're doing pop rock now. It's a much faster way to the bank."[70] Mick Fleetwood, in his usual good-natured way, was enthusiastic. "[They] were showstoppers, even as rough sketches recorded on Lindsey's four-track,"[70] recalled the drummer in 2004. Christine McVie, equally inspired, contributed two of her most memorable tracks, written on an old Hohner portable electric piano in their new Malibu apartment overlooking the Pacific Ocean: "Say You Love Me" and "Over My Head," as well as a lullaby for lovers, "Warm Ways," and a blues number called "Sugar Daddy."

In addition to Christine McVie's proven talent, Fleetwood Mac now boasted two gifted new songwriters.

The newcomers brought not only their own songs but also their respective talents. "Lindsey was the most creative guitar player we'd had since the days of the Green God,"[4] admitted Mick Fleetwood in his autobiography. Indeed, with his guitar, he could handle any rock style with authority and credibility, as well as the most seemingly undemanding acoustic situations. As for Stevie, recalls Mick, who was already anticipating success at the time, "as I watched Stevie dance around the rehearsal room I had a feeling that audiences were going to devour her."[4]

The White Album (as the band's fans would call it) would reveal the full extent of Nicks's and Buckingham's talent for meticulous arrangements and effective use of vocal harmonies. These were Fleetwood Mac's new lethal weapons, which would make them one of the behemoths of American music.

This also made it possible to exploit Christine McVie's songs to the full. Since her early days in the band, the musician had always been able to write melodies with great potential, but now the musical setting could rely on some high-quality artistry.

Ephemeral Consensus

Unlike the band's recent recordings—and despite the massive presence of cocaine and alcohol to fuel the long hours of work—the *Fleetwood Mac* sessions proceeded with ease. There were a few bumps in the road, often caused by Lindsey Buckingham, but nothing to dampen the mood, as everyone was still on their toes. Lindsey did make an effort to contain himself, but sometimes he just could not help it: Since he could play just about any instrument, it seemed only natural for him to stand in front of the drums to suggest a rhythm to Mick (who rarely took offense), or to grab a bass to show John McVie (who was much less complacent about the musician he found a little too directive for his taste). One day, when Lindsey presumed to suggest a rhythmic chord, John had no hesitation in putting him in his place. As Mick Fleetwood recounted in his book *Play On*: "'Hang on a sec,' he said, interrupting Lindsey who'd picked up a bass guitar and started playing a rhythm line. 'You realize who you're talking to, right?' 'Well, yeah,' Lindsey said, smiling, a bit unsure. 'I'm McVie,' John said. 'The band

1975

The set list for the first Fleetwood Mac Tour dates included two songs by the Buckingham-Nicks duo, "Crystal" and "Frozen Love." They usually played the latter during the encore, before "Hypnotized," which closed the set.

Mick Fleetwood, Stevie Nicks, and Lindsey Buckingham at the Inglewood Forum show in 1975, to be released in 2023 as *Rumours Live.*

you're in is Fleetwood Mac. I'm the Mac. And I play the bass."[2] Once this clarification has been made, the bassist retreated into his usual silence and things went back to normal. This was a new situation for Lindsey, who had been used to calling the shots. As the days went by, the energy rose and the enthusiasm grew. So much so that once the eleven tracks were on tape, the members of Fleetwood Mac were amused by the anxious calls from Warner Bros.

The record company, scalded by multiple dramas, changes of musicians, canceled concerts, and falling sales, was not yet aware of the symbiosis that had been created over the previous few weeks. Mick went out of his way to reassure them: He sincerely believed that the album was going to be the most important recording chapter in the Mac's career. He personally visited the office of Mo Ostin (then boss of Warner Bros.), accompanied by the band's lawyer, Mickey Shapiro, to demand support, if not the freedom, to find another, more suitable label. He tried to persuade the record company that the album would revolutionize the way Fleetwood Mac was perceived. And, incidentally, boost financial revenues.

Onstage, Before the Album's Release

Fleetwood Mac was undoubtedly on the road to a successful facelift. In anticipation of the album's release, the band decided to put its new lineup to the test onstage in the spring of 1975, without even waiting for the release or having publicly announced the arrival of two new members. They embarked on a mini-tour of Texas (May 15 to June 8), then of the American Midwest and Northeast, against the advice of Warner, who feared that old demons would resurface, and the musicians would be torn apart again on the road. The first concert took place in El Paso, Texas, on May 15, 1975. That night was a trial by fire, as the Mac played its new songs (which nobody knew) and introduced

its two new recruits for the first time. The audience soon realized that this new lineup, led by the sensuality of Stevie Nicks and the virtuosity of Lindsey Buckingham, was about to become something huge.

Contrary to the record company's fears, the dynamics of the live shows followed in the same manner as those of the studio sessions: The machine was launched, and everything seemed to fall into place naturally. Reassured, the band returned to Sound City Studios to mix the album before showing it to Warner, but not without a final scare. The album master was briefly mislaid, causing a moment of justifiable panic, before being found in extremis at the top of a pile of cassettes about to be erased. Warner's top brass were on their guard. One cannot really blame them, given the band's habit of changing lineups with each new record or tour. So it was with some difficulty that the label, accustomed to releasing 250,000 copies (or at most 300,000) of Mac albums, agreed to a 350,000-copy release in the record stores.

Illustrated with a black-and-white photo by Herbert W. Worthington, the cover chosen for the new opus was as stunning as it was eye-catching. As usual. It shows Mick Fleetwood, accompanied this time by his bandmate John McVie, posing in a scene that is both zany and enigmatic. In front of an art deco–style door frame, Mick Fleetwood, dressed to the nines, cane in hand, sips a flute of champagne, while John McVie, on his knees, stares at a crystal ball suspended in the air—as if he had thrown it to start juggling.

Fatal Tour for the Couples

Fleetwood Mac hit the record stores in July 1975 and was initially a modest success. Convinced of its potential, the band decided to step up their concert schedule and embark on a new tour in order to win over the public and reassure

The new Fleetwood Mac reached artistic fulfillment with the arrival of the Buckingham Nicks duo, combining pop pragmatism and hippie mysticism.

Warner. The Fleetwood Mac Tour took them across the United States and Canada for five long months (July 25 to December 20, 1975). As was often the case with Fleetwood Mac, tours exacerbated existing rifts, and this one, despite its enormous success, was no exception. In the end, it got the better of the McVie couple. But could it have been any other way? After all, Christine and John had been working, playing, and living together since the early days of the band. And it was already a miracle that they had not yet split up after all those years of stress, turmoil, and Christine's warnings (in song) that had gone unheeded. By the autumn of 1975, the point of no return had been reached. John and Christine could no longer even stay in the same room. But they had too much respect for the Fleetwood Mac institution to sabotage the current tour and decided to remain professional to the end. Their friends watched helplessly as their marriage slowly and inevitably foundered. Although the legal divorce would take some time, the McVie marriage was well and truly over.

The McVie relationship was not the only one to come to an end on this tour. Mick, too focused on Fleetwood Mac and with insufficient time for his family, saw 1976 take its toll on his relationship with Jenny, who, after a fit of hysteria at a barbecue, left the marital home with their two children. Mick, powerless, just had to resign himself to seeing them leave his life.

Finally, Lindsey and Stevie's relationship, which had already been stormy for several months, also took a serious turn for the worse. After her little slump, Stevie was back on the right foot and had totally blossomed, concert after concert, to the point where Lindsey, previously used to talking for two, could only become a spectator of this metamorphosis.

The couple's dynamic inevitably changed now that they were part of a larger group and no longer a duo. As Stevie took her place and began to claim more space, on the stage and off, Lindsey still craved her attention. Beneath his tough exterior was a person who had grown accustomed to having a supportive Stevie by his side. Sometimes, he even reproached her for being too sexy on stage, with her tantalizing dances, thus adding to the anxiety that she was going to leave him.

The Metamorphoses of Stevie

The big winner of this tour—apart from the band itself, which enjoyed an incredible success—was Stevie Nicks. The young woman emerged from this period armed with a maximum of hard-won self-confidence. She was able to come out of her shell through contact with other musicians, whereas until then she had relied solely on Lindsey the perfectionist. She overcame many hardships on this tour. She suffered from vocal cord problems and had to face vitriolic criticism from certain journalists. Not least Bud Scoppa, in a September 25, 1975, article in the influential *Rolling Stone* magazine. After praising Christine McVie's role, the journalist wrote: "Nicks, on the other hand, has yet to integrate herself into the group style. Compared to McVie's, her singing seems callow and mannered, especially on 'Landslide,' where she sounds lost and out of place—although to be fair, this is more a problem of context than of absolute quality. Her 'Rhiannon,' colored by Buckingham's Kirwan-style guitar, works a little better and 'Crystal,' on which

The quintet took the top position on the Billboard charts for the first time. Although it lasted only a week, it was the first step in their bid to conquer the American market.

Buckingham joins her on lead vocal, suggests that she may yet find a comfortable slot in this band."[58] Stevie, convinced that Mac had chosen her only as part of a package deal because they really wanted Lindsey Buckingham, began to doubt herself. Above all, the routine of the tour quickly took its toll: Sleeping on the amps in the back of the truck, always cold, and relying on only a few decent meals, she lost weight.

And to make matters worse, cocaine had become an integral part of the tour's daily routine. When the tour passed through Stevie's Phoenix stronghold, her family saw her onstage and became alarmed. At times, she thought she should give it all up, but each time, Mick pulled her back, explaining that she was now a pillar of the band. Sometimes, she would sit alone backstage and fill the pages of her notebook with future song lyrics. It was at this time that she wrote the first snippets of "Sisters of the Moon," the future hit on *Tusk* (1979).

But in November 1975, she was definitively invigorated by the unexpected entry of "Over My Head" in the Billboard Hot 100 chart (number twenty), and gradually managed to transform her blues into something creative and beautiful. This song, on which Stevie's voice plays an important role, becomes Fleetwood Mac's very first American hit single. She realized that if the public had no reservations about her singing style, she was not going to let the poisoned pens of the critics drag her down.

Definitively a New Band

There is no doubt that Fleetwood Mac, run by men from the start, had reached a turning point in its history with the *Fleetwood Mac* album and its promotional tour. From then on, women had their say: "I think we just had a product that everybody wanted at the time," Christine McVie modestly explains. "It was a very versatile album, and on stage the band projected a kind of exciting image—a new sort of image which hadn't been seen before. It was unique to have *two* women in a band who were not just back-up singers, or singers *period*. Stevie sings, sure, but she also does other musical/movement things which are aesthetic. The five characters on stage became five *characters* as opposed to just five members of a band."[5] While a few lowbrow musicians on the road were quick to mock John and Mick at the bar when they saw that they were touring with two women, Fleetwood Mac had finally found a strong image to accompany their music.

All these efforts were rewarded, as *Fleetwood Mac* quickly exceeded the 250,000 sales expected by the record company. In September 1976, fifteen months after its release and at the cost of a grueling tour, the album topped the charts, having also produced three hit singles: "Over My Head" (number twenty in the US), "Rhiannon" (forty-six in the UK and eleven in the US), and "Say You Love Me" (forty in the UK and eleven in the US).

From then on, the band spoke on a weekly basis with Warner, who provided invaluable support in the battle they were still waging against their former manager, Clifford Davis. This restored trust also meant that they could look to

1975

the future with peace of mind, with a new status for this new band…Warner now believed in the commercial potential of this new version of Fleetwood Mac, and contract renegotiations were easy between the two parties: The band obtained a substantial increase in royalties and a substantial cash advance on the next album. As for Stevie and Lindsey, they saw their status evolve from mere "employees" to true partners with the other musicians.

Time, finally, was to give full posterity to *Fleetwood Mac*. Far from being just a transitional album, it has now sold more than 7 million copies and is considered one of the cornerstones of the Mac discography, as well as one of their best records.

However, not everything was rosy after this tour. While Fleetwood Mac had finally reached the upper echelons of the charts, the musicians' lives had been permanently disrupted by an incessant ballet of discord and pain that would probably have killed off the band in the past. These disastrous consequences would soon play a major role in the development of the next album. In the year they were about to record the album that would change their lives, all the Fleetwood Mac musicians had either divorced or separated. But it was obviously too late to stop; from where they now stood, they could finally see the summit.

LINDSEY BUCKINGHAM, THE GAME OF SOLITAIRE

Lindsey Adams Buckingham was born on October 3, 1949, in sunny Palo Alto, a midsized American town in Santa Clara County, California. Pushed into swimming by his father, the owner of a prosperous coffee factory, little Lindsey, whose only interest seemed to be music, looked like a black sheep next to his two older brothers, who were nicknamed the "Swimming Buckinghams." At the age of five, he spent most of his time drawing guitars, while his two brothers were swimming laps in the community pool in Atherton, the comfortable, conservative Californian suburb on San Francisco Bay where the family now lived.

Self-Taught Guitarist

When Elvis Presley came into his life, Lindsey's obsession with the guitar took precedence over everything else. His parents gave him a Harmony worth no more than $35. From then on, with astonishing self-discipline, the young boy spent hours deciphering his brother Jeff's 45s by ear. There he found a haven of rock'n'roll and learned from the best—Elvis, Buddy Holly, the Everly Brothers, Chuck Berry, Eddie Cochran—experimenting with a wide range of musical styles and instruments. So while his brother Greg methodically trained for the Olympic Games—where he won a silver medal in Mexico in 1968—Lindsey devoted most of his free time to perfecting his technique and velocity, particularly in fingerpicking.

This style of playing was to become his trademark. Unlike other rock guitarists, he rarely used the pick, except in the studio when he wanted to achieve a particular strumming sound. His "Travis picking," inspired by Merle Travis, gives his playing a cohesive, melodic richness. But he also covers the rhythmic aspect, through the use of the thumb, often marking the rhythm on the first or second string, as on a banjo, an instrument he has mastered since childhood.

With his high school diploma in hand, and after a quick stint at San José State University, Lindsey, who had never learned to read sheet music or taken guitar lessons, felt ready to take the plunge. But far from putting on a bathing cap and splashing around, he grew his hair and joined a rock band, the Fritz Rabyne Memorial Band (often abbreviated to Fritz). He became the bassist for the young band, formed with a few friends from high school, as the guitarist's position was already occupied. In any case, his guitar playing, inspired as much by folk as bluegrass or classical, used fingerings that were too unusual in the rock sphere of the time, which tended toward a psychedelic sound requiring the use of numerous effects.

For Lindsey, Fritz lacked a feminine element, that is, a female vocalist. Many local rock bands of the time relied on female figures such as Grace Slick or Janis Joplin. Lindsey remembers the evening in 1966 when, at a student party, a young woman with long blond hair—Stevie Nicks—joined him at the piano to sing the chorus of "California Dreamin'" by the Mamas and Papas in perfect harmony. He decided to call her and offer her the job of singer. This unexpected interest took her by surprise, but she was excited at the prospect of entering the world of rock'n'roll, and she was ready to shelve her initial goal of becoming a teacher.

Over the next three years, the band became a regular on the Bay Area circuit, opening for such West Coast talents as Jefferson Airplane, Quicksilver Messenger Service, Moby Grape, the Charlatans and, of course, Big Brother and the Holding Company, with a magnetic Janis Joplin, who would forever change Stevie's perception of music. Lindsey and Stevie grew closer, but their relationship remained platonic for some time. In 1971, Fritz's fusion of folk and more-or-less psychedelic rock was no match for the new pop behemoths: The previous year's big hits were the Beatles' "Let It Be," Mungo Jerry's "In the Summertime," and Simon and Garfunkel's "Bridge over Troubled Water." With no hits of this caliber in sight, the band broke up. Lindsey and Stevie, who had begun a romantic relationship, began writing together with a view to becoming a real duo.

Birth of a Duo

To pursue their dream, the lovebirds decided to move to Los Angeles in search of a recording contract. But Lindsey contracted a severe case of mononucleosis, which forced him to stay in bed for several months and thwarted their plans. The musician took advantage of this misfortune to write new songs. He bought an electric guitar so he could work on his lead playing, as well as a professional Ampex four-track tape recorder, which his father allowed him to install in one of the offices at his coffee-roasting factory. Lindsey never counted the hours and developed a real obsession for audio engineering work, dwelling on all the details that would later make him a meticulous and demanding producer.

He and Stevie recorded the first demos of their Buckingham Nicks duo, until Lindsey deemed them perfect. Once Lindsey was back on his feet, the couple finally headed for Los Angeles, where they befriended producer Keith Olsen and his assistant Richard Dashut, a close collaborator of Fleetwood Mac.

The early days were hard. Stevie was forced to take a job as a waitress, while Lindsey, with Keith Olsen's help, prepared the recording of their first album, *Buckingham Nicks*, released in September 1973 on Polydor. The situation created an imbalance and tension between Stevie, who was close to the realities of everyday life, and Lindsey, who was more actively nurturing his dream. In the absence of the expected commercial success, Polydor broke its contract

A self-taught guitarist, Lindsey Buckingham became known for his folk fingerpicking.

with the devastated duo. While Stevie, weary of odd jobs, began to think about going back to school, Lindsey continued to polish new demos, hoping that the tracks that were starting to get radio airplay would finally enable the album to take off. It was around this time that Mick Fleetwood called Lindsey. They had bumped into each other at Sound City Studios some time earlier, and Mick had enjoyed the *Buckingham Nicks* samples he heard.

Fleetwood Mac, the Ideal Implant

Convinced that Lindsey would be an ideal replacement for Bob Welch (who had left a few months earlier), Mick Fleetwood offered him the guitarist's job. Lindsey accepted on condition that his girlfriend, Stevie Nicks, could come along, too. Mick accepted his request and proposed a meeting in a Mexican restaurant with the rest of the band. Before going to the meeting, Buckingham, seized by doubt, called his session musician friend Waddy Wachtel to ask him what he thought. Wachtel, who understood before Lindsey did that destiny was calling him to something big, convinced him to accept the Mac's proposal: "Lindsey [...] you're on the wrong phone call! Call Mick Fleetwood back and tell him yes! This is it, man. This is your shot right here. This is it. This doesn't happen again!"[59]

During this interview, the bohemian couple made a strong impression on the band. Sure, Stevie looked gorgeous, but so did Lindsey, with his curly hair and piercing eyes. The first rehearsals came quickly. "It was going to work and we all knew it," Mick Fleetwood later explained. "Lindsey had never been backed by a rhythm section as interwoven and nuanced as John and me, and his playing positively took off. I knew immediately that we'd never need another guitarist; Lindsey could do it all—leads, rhythm, moving effortlessly between the two, and all while singing, no less. I'm not sure anyone realizes just how gifted he is."[2]

Lindsey had no trouble fitting in with Fleetwood Mac, which he already knew about from Peter Green, and whose favorite album was *Then Play On*. His and Stevie's arrival undoubtedly marked the beginning of a new era for the band. But this new era, prolific and captivating as it was, put an end to Stevie and Lindsey's already stormy relationship. In 1977, around the time of the *Rumours* album, they parted ways.

A Parallel Solo Career

After the relative success of *Tusk* in 1979, and before returning with a new Fleetwood Mac album, *Mirage*, in 1982, Lindsey launched his solo career with the opus *Law and Order*, which recorded collaborations with Mick Fleetwood and Christine McVie, and offered sounds closer to lo-fi or new wave. In 1984, as his relationship drew to a close with Carol Ann Harris (a former model and sound engineer he had met in 1977, just before the release of *Rumours*), Lindsey released his second solo album, *Go Insane*, whose title track enjoyed great success in the American charts, reaching number twenty-three. Lindsey's intense passion for Carol Ann Harris came to an end after seven long years of embracing the rock'n'roll lifestyle, which unfortunately included cocaine. "Probably, if I had known what I was getting into, I would have thought twice about it," Harris explained in 1984. "But I fell in love with him [Lindsey]. I had no choice. It's not a life I would have chosen for myself."[60]

Now single and a millionaire before the age of thirty-five, Lindsey lived alone in a house worth more than two

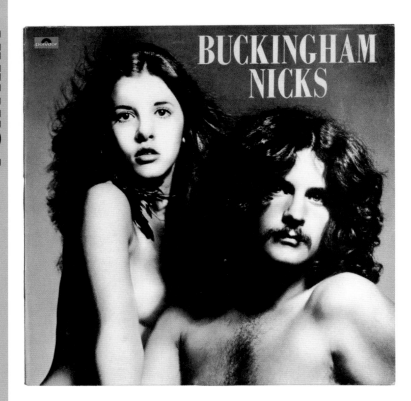

Although it failed to win over a wide audience, the Buckingham Nicks duo's only album, released in 1973, marked the start of an ongoing collaboration with Richard Dashut.

million dollars, tucked away at the end of a cul-de-sac in Bel Air, high above Los Angeles. He had everything anyone could dream of: a sumptuously decorated house with swimming pool, beautiful cars, and, most important for him, a magnificent 24-track recording studio right across the street from his bedroom. The warm Southern California sun streamed in through the huge bay windows but failed to brighten the gray daily life of a lonely man who nevertheless indulged in a slightly arrogant attitude, a way for him to avoid ever fully revealing himself.

A true Stakhanovist in the studio, this solitary soul spent his afternoons locked away with his instruments and electronic equipment, experimenting with new ideas. Music was the only thing he still took very seriously, driven by his obsessive desire to invent new things. "I'm trying to break down preconceptions about what pop music is," the man who played all the instruments and provided all the vocals on *Go Insane* confessed to *Rolling Stone* magazine in 1984, before concluding anxiously: "I'm struggling to be original."[60]

A Difficult Cord to Cut

Despite his desire to become a solo artist in his own right, Lindsey was unable to cut the cord with the Mac once and for all. It was partly for this reason that, in 1987, he agreed to give the band several songs that were to feature on his third solo album to their fourteenth album, *Tango in the Night*. Co-producer of the album with Richard Dashut, Lindsey did his utmost with his usual thoroughness, but refused, despite the album's commercial success (number seven in the US and number one in the UK), to take part in the promotional tour. "He didn't want to go out on the road, and we knew that, and he kept putting us off," explained Mick Fleetwood in 1990. "We said, You—out of anyone

with the amount of work you put into this album—you're not going out on the road? That's crazy! You want to piss this down the drain? Don't you want people to hear this?" Under pressure, Lindsey accepted the idea of taking part in the tour on condition that two or three new guitarists and percussionists were added. Everyone agreed to the new formula, and Lindsey gave the go-ahead. "But he changed his mind after we booked the tour," lamented Mick, before adding, "He'd realized he'd been forced into a situation and had cracked. He said that touring would have destroyed him and been hell for everyone else."[61]

Trapped by his difficult relationship with the other band members—notably Stevie Nicks—and struggling to express his true emotions, Lindsey provoked a real fistfight on August 7, 1987, when he announced his departure from the Mac to the other band members. A violent altercation broke out with Stevie Nicks. Mick Fleetwood later recounted in his autobiography that the musician had slapped his ex-girlfriend that evening. Lindsey always denied having laid a hand on Stevie. In any case, that same evening, Lindsey was replaced by two new guitarists, Rick Vito and Billy Burnette.

A Roller-Coaster Relationship

The war of egos between Lindsey and Stevie never really ended, and the musician, often described as irascible and moody, alternated ups and downs with the young woman and the band, juggling his solo career with Fleetwood Mac until 2018.

From 1987 to 1992, Lindsey devoted himself to recording his third solo album, entitled *Out of the Cradle* (1992). It included the song "Wrong," a public protest against his ex-partner Mick Fleetwood's misinterpretation of the night in 1987 when he chose to leave the band.

From the very first studio sessions, Lindsey Buckingham exposed his perfectionist streak and a desire for experimentation.

That same year, he joined his former bandmates on stage at the request of newly elected US president Bill Clinton, who asked the Mac to perform his campaign song, Christine McVie's "Don't Stop." However, disagreements still ran deep, and there was still no talk of a re-formation. Stevie Nicks, who never missed an opportunity to air her grievances with Lindsey through the media, declared in 1994: "We did not break up friends, and we have never been friends since. He is not really able to have any kind of relationship with me. I just bug him to death. Everything I do is abrasive to him. He's scary when he gets mad."[63]

In 1997, the hatchet seemed to have been buried with The Dance tour, which marked Lindsey's return to Fleetwood Mac and resulted in a live album of the same name. In 1998, Lindsey and his bandmates were inducted into the Rock and Roll Hall of Fame. The clouds seemed to have parted for good, especially as the guitarist's life took on a calmer tone with the birth of his first son in 1998, his marriage in 2000 to his son's mother, Kristen Messner (twenty-one years his junior), and the birth of two more children in 2000 and 2004.

The 2000s saw Lindsey add to his personal discography with 2006's *Under the Skin*, 2008's *Gift of Screws*, 2011's *Seeds We Sow* and 2017's *Lindsey Buckingham Christine McVie*, a duet with Christine. Fleetwood Mac added only one more studio album, 2003's *Say You Will*.

One Smile Too Many

On January 26, 2018, the band was celebrated at the MusiCares Person of the Year gala in New York, playing a short set that included notably "The Chain," "Little Lies," "Tusk," "Gold Dust Woman," and "Go Your Own Way." On the surface, all seemed well. But this was the last time Lindsey Buckingham would play as a member of Fleetwood Mac. Indeed, during one of Stevie's speeches, Lindsey briefly raised his eyes to the sky and flashed a smile that Stevie interpreted as ironic. Backstage, the tension was palpable. When Lindsey reminded the others that he wanted to take a few months off to tour solo before considering going on the road with them, none of the band members seemed willing to accede to his request—especially not Stevie Nicks, who was still very upset after what fans came to call the "smirking incident." So, on April 9, Lindsey was fired and replaced by Neil Finn (ex–Split Enz, ex–Crowded House) and Mike Campbell, Tom Petty's longtime partner in the Heartbreakers. Once again, Fleetwood Mac's most successful lineup failed to stick together: Lindsey walked out and returned to his solo career, but not before suing the band for unfair dismissal, which was eventually settled "out of court" (in a manner of speaking, of course).

The End of the Illusions

A year later, Lindsey's vocal cords were damaged during surgery. The possibility of a reunion was out of the question. Little by little, the musician returned to the studio and, although his stage activity was reduced, in 2021 he released a new solo opus, *Lindsey Buckingham*. On this occasion, he looked back with some bitterness on his last moments with Fleetwood Mac: "Recording with the band was like a movie production, you had to have a schedule, a script, and negotiate everything, a constant push and pull. Working by myself, it's more like making a painting. [...] There's less drama."[64] As he explained to *Rolling Stone*'s Stephen Rodrick in 2021: "I think she wanted to shape the band in her own image, a more mellow thing, and if you look at the last tour, I think that's true." He also said, "I think others in the band just felt that they were not empowered enough, individually, for whatever their own reasons, to stand up for what was right."[64]

STEVIE NICKS, THE ENCHANTRESS

"I could not pronounce the word 'Stephanie' when I was little. My pronunciation of it came out as 'TeeDee,' which was [eventually] turned into Stevie. My mother still calls me TeeDee."[66] It was "Stevie" that one of the most emblematic figures in American pop-rock music chose for her stage name. For the record, her name is Stephanie Lynn Nicks, born on May 26, 1948, in Phoenix, Arizona. Under the watchful eye of her grandfather, country singer Aaron Jess Nicks, she first sang at the age of four. He introduced her to dozens of 45s, which they listened to religiously together. He was tempted to take her on tour with him but gave up in the face of her parents' categorical refusal.

A Traveling Spirit

Stevie's childhood was punctuated by constant moves due to the professional obligations of her father, a vice president at the bus company Greyhound. Arizona, New Mexico, Texas, Utah, California…These numerous stops forged Stevie's highly sociable character. In each city, she was "the new girl" and had to make friends quickly, even though she knew she would lose them six months later. At home, her room was a sanctuary filled with music and images of ballerinas and fairy tales. Her parents, initially wary of her passion for music, realized her talent and gave her their full support. A month before her sixteenth birthday, they gave her a small Goya classical guitar and paid for her first lessons. A few weeks later, she had already composed her first song, "I've Loved and I've Lost, and I'm Sad But Not Blue."

During high school, in Arcadia, California, Stevie joined a folk group called the Changing Times, heavily influenced, as the name suggests, by Bob Dylan, as well as the Mamas and the Papas. In 1966, Stevie moved again and attended high school in Atherton, California. It was there that she met Lindsey Buckingham. In the summer of 1967, the guitarist invited her to join the psychedelic Fritz Rabyne Memorial Band—usually shortened to Fritz—as a singer. In one fell swoop, the folk singer found herself with both feet in rock. With such moorings—a band and a budding love affair—Stevie left her family in 1968 to move to Chicago and stayed in California, where she planned to continue her studies at the University of San José to become an English teacher. She eventually abandoned this goal in favor of music. Fritz's trajectory was ascendant: The band regularly opened for renowned artists such as Santana, Jefferson Airplane, Creedence Clearwater Revival, Jimi Hendrix, and, above all, Janis Joplin. Stevie was captivated by Joplin's talent and the way she could enthrall crowds with her energy and frenetic voice alone. All she could think about was following in her role model's footsteps. Unfortunately, the band was unable to secure a record deal and broke up in 1971. The tensions were too great anyway: Stevie's charm and voice were attracting all the attention, and the other musicians felt she was overshadowing their musical talents.

An Empty Stomach and a Head Full of Dreams

Stevie stays in touch with Lindsey, who doesn't share the band's mistrust of her. A romance begins between the two young artists. Partners in the city, they became partners onstage, performing as a duo. In 1973, they landed a contract with Polydor Records, which released their joint album, *Buckingham Nicks*. They recorded it largely on their own: "I sat in a room with Lindsey for nine months, in his father's coffee plant, a little tiny room […] while we did half of the songs on that record on a four track. Like we'd go when the workers went home. We'd go at seven o'clock and we'd stay until six thirty all night long."[67] Their symbiosis was total, and this could be heard above all vocally. Their voices blend naturally and harmoniously. However, despite Lindsey Buckingham's provocative choice of having them pose bare-chested on the album cover—a traumatic experience for Stevie—the record failed to sell and the label ended their contract. The couple had no money left, and Stevie had to work as a waitress to pay the bills. They often experienced the ache of hunger. The singer gave herself another six months for things to turn around. If they didn't, she'd return to her parents and resume her studies.

The couple moved in with Keith Olsen, the producer of their first album, who had become a close friend. He would be with them again for the *Fleetwood Mac* sessions in 1975. But even the sessions' boost did not solve everything. Stevie began to use cocaine, and her relationship with Lindsey deteriorated. Their passionate love turned into a continuous roller-coaster ride. This inspired Lindsey to write the song "Landslide," which became part of the White Album along with "Rhiannon," which had been conceived by Stevie around the same time. Fleetwood Mac entered the lives of the two star-crossed lovers at just the right moment—before they finally threw in the towel and Stevie gave up music.

Fleetwood Mac: A Lifeline

The combination of forces—Nicks and Buckingham on one side, Christine McVie and Mick Fleetwood on the other—was ideal. As luck would have it, Stevie was very familiar with Fleetwood Mac's recent repertoire and adored the band. The admiration was soon mutual, according to Mick Fleetwood: "I recognized Stevie right away as a writer and she reminded me of my dad, because she was writing in her journals all the time. Stevie wanted to bring mysticism into the band, which I supported completely because I do believe that there are many aspects to our existence greater than we are."[2]

The two newcomers, ideal replacements for guitarist Bob Welch, were to accompany the band on the path already taken in the previous albums, leading to an accessible and effective pop that was to offer Fleetwood Mac an unexpected renaissance and massive worldwide success. *Fleetwood Mac*, number one in the US. *Rumours*, number

While visiting the Wallingford Vehicle Rally (UK) in September 1975 for a radio show, Stevie Nicks posed for Fin Costello by leaning against driver Larry Clouatre's Chevelle, nicknamed Matter of Time.

one everywhere, selling 40 million copies! *Tusk*, number one in the UK. *Mirage*, number one in the US. America courted the young woman. Aware of the importance of her image, the singer conceptualized her clothing style during this period, calling on designer Margi Kent to create bohemian-style outfits for her. She embodied a character halfway between angel and witch. With Nicks and Buckingham at its heart, nothing seemed to stand in Fleetwood Mac's way. Not even their romantic relationships. The couple eventually broke up during the recording of *Rumours*, for which Stevie wrote "Dreams," "I Don't Want to Know," and "Gold Dust Woman," poetic tracks with silky melodies nourished by Californian pop as well as the folk of her early days. In 1977, Stevie Nicks fell into the arms of Mick Fleetwood, who was married to Jenny Boyd. But the singer quickly put an end to this affair to avoid jeopardizing the band's survival.

Multiple Collaborations

In 1978, Stevie took her first step toward a solo career: Although uncredited, she provided lead vocals alongside Kenny Loggins on "Whenever I Call You 'Friend'" (number five in the US). Throughout her career, Nicks participated in outside recordings. The highest-ranking of these collaborations is not the one in which she is most featured: For example, she is only mentioned in the backing vocals on "Separate Lives," by Phil Collins and Marilyn Martin, which reached number one in 1985. That same year, she appeared alongside Tom Petty and the Heartbreakers on a live version of "Needles and Pins" (number thirty-seven). A decade later, in 1996, she teamed up with Mick Fleetwood and Lindsey Buckingham for "Twisted," which featured on the soundtrack to the film *Twister*. In 2002, she hailed Sheryl Crow as one of her equals, singing "C'mon, C'mon," "Diamond Road," and "You're Not the One" with her. In the decade that followed, Stevie enjoyed surprising original associations with artists from other generations and musical universes: "Dreams" with the house duo Deep Dish (2006), "You Can't Fix This" with the rock band Foo Fighters (2013), "Golden" with the country pop group Lady Antebellum (2013), "Beautiful People Beautiful Problems" with pop singer Lana Del Rey (2017), and "Midnight Sky" with Miley Cyrus (2020). She then lent her voice to Maroon 5's pop song "Remedy" and assisted Gorillaz on "Oil" in 2023. That same year, she brought out an unreleased song from her repertoire, "What Has Rock and Roll Ever Done for You," which she finalized with Dolly Parton.

Overflowing Inspiration

Stevie composed relentlessly, building up a substantial stock of songs. In 1979, during the *Tusk* sessions, she conceived essential new songs—including "Sara" and "Sisters of the Moon," both released as singles and charting at number seven and number eighty-six, respectively, in the US. This burst of inspiration continued even during the album's world tour. So much so, in fact, that she found herself at the helm of a substantial number of songs that she knew perfectly well would never make it into the Mac repertoire because she shared the songwriting duties with Christine McVie and Lindsey Buckingham.

All this previously unreleased material was grouped together in Stevie Nicks's first solo album, *Bella Donna*, which she released on Modern Records, a label founded for the occasion with the help of Paul Fishkin, her new partner. The label would host five of her solo albums recorded between 1981 and 1994. *Bella Donna* featured ten tracks, including two duets—"Stop Draggin' My Heart Around" with Tom Petty and the Heartbreakers, and "Leather and Lace" with Don Henley, singer and drummer of the Eagles, with whom she had a furtive affair in the late 1970s—and "Think About It," a song written by Stevie in 1975 in support of Christine (whom she now considered a sister), just as she was about to leave John McVie. *Bella Donna* hit the record stores on July 27, 1981, to the disapproving gaze of the other Fleetwood Mac members, who saw it as a threat to the group's equilibrium. Stevie did her best to reassure them, promising that she would implement both projects without the band suffering. "My relationship with Fleetwood Mac will never change," she declared in 1983. "I will always be the baby sister, the one that is left out a little bit. My solo work allows me not to feel bad about it and enjoy them [Mac] for what they are, instead of worrying about not being included enough."[68]

The Glory and the Heartbreak

Bella Donna was a resounding success. The album reached number one on the Billboard 200 chart, and Stevie became the figurehead of Fleetwood Mac. But this solo interlude left the young woman bereft. This was due as much to the intense pace of her work as to her excesses of all kinds. To make matters worse, on the day her album was announced as number one, Stevie learned that her best friend, Robin Anderson (who was pregnant), was suffering from leukemia. Robin gave birth to a baby boy—for whom Stevie was godmother—before passing away in 1982. That same year, Stevie cut short

the White Winged Dove Tour and met the other members of Fleetwood Mac in France, at the Château d'Hérouville, to record *Mirage*, which was released on June 18. In 1983, Stevie Nicks recorded her second solo album, *The Wild Heart*, dedicated to Robin. She called on Jimmy Iovine once again, even though he no longer worked with him. The album featured a host of musicians, including Benmont Tench on keyboards; David Foster on piano; Prince on synthesizers; Steve Lukather, Don Felder, and Tom Petty on guitar; and Mick Fleetwood on drums. Containing the singles "Stand Back" and "Nightbird," and the duet with Sandy Stewart, "If Anyone Falls," *The Wild Heart* was released on June 10, 1983. It reached number five on the Billboard 200 chart, confirming Stevie Nicks's growing status on the American scene.

As prolific as ever, the young woman took advantage of the Wild Heart Tour (in 1983) to write and record demos for her next album. She was able to concentrate fully on her solo career because the band was on an extended hiatus, with everyone going about their own business. More up-tempo, with synthetic arrangements, Stevie's new opus, finally christened *Rock a Little*, was released on November 18, 1985. Its success was less phenomenal than that of its predecessors; it peaked at number twelve on the US chart, and one of its singles, "Talk to Me," reached number four.

Years of Comings and Goings

During the tour that followed in 1986, Stevie Nicks opened her eyes to her drug addiction and realized that it could cost her life. She entered rehab at the Betty Ford Center in California. Due to the tour and this unforeseen stay, the singer was unable to participate fully in the conception of Fleetwood Mac's *Tango in the Night* album. She did, however, send a few demos by post. The album was released in April 1987. It was a huge success, but internally, things were not going well. Buckingham quit after yet another argument with Nicks. He was replaced by Rick Vito and Billy Burnette for the Shake the Cage Tour (1987). As for Stevie, she was once again forced to rest due to overwork and addiction to Klonopin (clonazepam), an anxiolytic and sedative usually used for anxiety and bipolar disorders. She got back on track in 1988 to prepare her fourth solo album, *The Other Side of the Mirror*, recorded with her partner at the time, Rupert Hine, and released in May 1989.

The following year, she continued to come and go, taking part in Fleetwood Mac's *Behind the Mask* album and promotional tour. At the end of the tour, she walked out on the Mac following an argument with Mick over a song, "Silver Springs," which she intended to include on her compilation *Timespace: The Best of Stevie Nicks* (released on September 3, 1991), celebrating her ten-year solo career.

Nicks reunited with her partners in 1992 for the inaugural gala of President Bill Clinton. Between 1992 and 1993, she put the finishing touches to *Street Angel*, a new solo opus, which she released on May 23, 1994. Two years later, while working on her next solo project, she called on Mick Fleetwood and John McVie. It was the little spark she needed to give the band the desire to reunite. This happened in 1997 with the Dance tour, immortalized by a live album.

Stevie Nicks seized upon Bohemian imagery and its mystical symbolism to create her stage persona.

TAMBOURINE GIRL

Stevie Nicks has made the tambourine her signature onstage accessory. But more often than not, in concert with the Mac, the cymbalettes were fixed with gaffer, to prevent the sound from interfering with the music. This led to an embarrassing moment at Bill Clinton's inauguration concert. Nicks handed the tambourine to the president as a gift. He understood that she wanted him to play it, and he shook it without making a sound.

"My Own Little 'Rumours'"

Just before the release of a boxed set called *Enchanted*, Stevie Nicks put the finishing touches to *Trouble in Shangri-La*. The album benefited from the contribution of Sheryl Crow, who produced several songs and provided guitars and backing vocals. Debuting at number five on May 1, 2001, the album marks Nicks's commercial renaissance. The track "Planets of the Universe" even earned her a Grammy nomination for Best Rock Vocal Performance in 2001. That same year, she rejoined her Fleetwood Mac partners.

Nicks spent most of the 2000s performing solo or with the Mac. It was not until 2011 that she graced audiences with a new studio album, *In Your Dreams*, released ten years after its predecessor. She conceived it with the support of Dave Stewart, half of the Eurythmics duo, who composed most of the tracks from poems by the singer.

Stevie chose to promote it via the single "Secret Love," an initial demo which she had recorded at the time of *Rumours*, in 1977. "My own little 'Rumours'"[69] was how she liked to describe this album. It was enthusiastically received by the public, who propelled it to number six on the Billboard 200 chart.

She reunited with Fleetwood Mac in 2014—and especially with her good friend Christine McVie, back with the band—for the On with the Show Tour.

In 2018, Stevie Nicks was inducted into the Rock and Roll Hall of Fame, becoming the first woman artist to be honored twice, as a member of Fleetwood Mac, and for her solo career. In 2020, she released the album *Live in Concert: The 24 Karat Gold Tour*. In 2023, the whole of her impressive solo career was compiled in a boxed set (sixteen vinyl records or ten CDs), entitled *Complete Studio Albums and Rarities*.

MONDAY MORNING
Lindsey Buckingham / 2:48

Musicians
Lindsey Buckingham: vocals, guitar
Christine McVie: keyboards
John McVie: bass
Mick Fleetwood: drums
Stevie Nicks: backing vocals

Recorded
Sound City Studios, Van Nuys, California: February 1975

Technical Team
Producers: Fleetwood Mac, Keith Olsen
Sound Engineers: Keith Olsen, David DeVore

Single
Side A: Say You Love Me / **Side B:** Monday Morning
UK Release Date: October 8, 1976
Reference: Reprise Records (45 rpm ref.: K 14447/RPS 1356)
Best UK Chart Ranking: 40
US Release Date: June 9, 1976
Reference: Reprise Records (45 rpm ref.: RPS 1356)
Best US Chart Ranking: 11

The demo version heard by Christine, John, and Mick in the early days of the *Fleetwood Mac* work sessions was unveiled on the release of the album's deluxe edition in 2018.

1975

Genesis and Lyrics
Like a symbol, "Monday Morning" is the opening track on Fleetwood Mac's album, which awakens to the dawn of a new day. The theme of the song, however, is neither a birth nor a renewal. The song, written and sung by Lindsey Buckingham, has a more personal, romantic dimension. It evokes the musician's troubled relationship with Stevie Nicks. On Mondays, Stevie Nicks presents a pleasant face, but on Fridays, at the end of a week spent with the young woman, the narrator is thinking of taking a trip. He reserves the beautiful role for himself, showing himself to be the stable element in the couple, while his partner declares her love for him one day and vanishes into thin air the next. Buckingham longs for a little peace and serenity. He is self-congratulatory, pointing out that no one but him could endure such a situation: "But I don't mind." He does, however, brandish this threat: "You know I can't go on believing for long."

Production
Stevie and Lindsey master the song perfectly, having had the opportunity to try it out on stage during the few concerts they gave as Buckingham Nicks, accompanied by Tom Moncrieff on bass, Bob Aguirre (a former member of Fritz) on drums, and drummer Gary Hodges on percussion—the three musicians who were to accompany them in the studio to record their second album. The downside was that Lindsey, who had a very precise idea of his song—which he had time to fine-tune—tended to tell the other band members how to play. While Stevie was aware of Lindsey's perfectionist nature and control-freak tendencies, the others were sometimes annoyed by it. Buckingham shifted his vision somewhat after assessing the qualities of his partners. For example, the guitar, which featured prominently on the demo version, fades into the background here, leaving more room for the other instruments. "I wasn't even sure what my role was gonna be at that point," explained Buckingham in 2018. "Obviously it was kind of a lesson in adaptation for me, and maybe giving up on certain things and concentrating on other things which were maybe strengths for the good of the band. So part of the exercise of joining Fleetwood Mac was adapting down to not only fit

a sound, but I had to get off the guitar I was using and get on to a Les Paul. Their sound was very fat, and the nature of the playing with Christine (McVie) and John (McVie), there was a lot of space taken, so you had to sort of take what was left and fit into it."[71] The bass, in particular, a "forgotten" element in the first version, takes on more fullness and roundness under John McVie's fingers. Mick Fleetwood scrupulously reproduces the very present roll imagined by Lindsey, which gives the song its liveliness.

Christine McVie on keyboards during a recording session in 1975.

"Warm Ways" was only released as a single in the UK because the record company felt that "Over My Head" was better suited to the American market.

WARM WAYS

Christine McVie / 3:50

Musicians: Christine McVie: vocals, keyboards / Lindsey Buckingham: guitar / John McVie: bass / Mick Fleetwood: drums / **Recorded:** Sound City Studios, Van Nuys, California: February 1975 / **Technical Team:** Producers: Fleetwood Mac, Keith Olsen / Sound Engineers: Keith Olsen, David DeVore / **Single:** Side A: Warm Ways / Side B: Blue Letter / **UK Release Date:** November 7, 1975 / **Reference:** Reprise Records (45 rpm ref.: K 14403/REP 3675) / Best UK Chart Ranking: Did Not Chart

Genesis and Lyrics

A radical change in the ongoing narrative of Christine McVie, who usually draws on the source of her torments of love to irrigate her lyrics. This time, the imbalance of feelings that torments her is swept away by a feeling of infinite bliss. In a few words, she depicts the pleasure that runs through her body and mind after a night of lovemaking in the arms of her lover. All she needs are a few adjectives: "easy," "gentle," "warm." The use of this last word is particularly clever, as it maintains a certain ambivalence. Christine is not one to use overly direct images to express sexual desire. Instead, she maintains a sense of propriety. So "warm" can be taken to mean either "warm" or "hot." In the sense of "warm," the lyricist preserves a semblance of chastity. But if the listener understands "warm" in the sense of "burning," the evocation becomes more torrid. It is up to the listener to make up their own mind, even though the phrase "You made me a woman tonight," says it all about the intensity of the night.

Production

Translating the ecstasy described in the song's lyrics into music is a task within Lindsey Buckingham's grasp, especially when it comes to creating a gentle setting, as the lyrics of "Warm Ways" require. Mick Fleetwood builds on the slow, languid rhythm imposed on his matt timbre drums as he creates a voluptuous, satiny instrumentation. To achieve this, he combines an acoustic guitar played with delicate strumming and a clean-sounding electric guitar, but with a special nuance provided by a chorus effect. This enveloping effect lends an almost oceanic color to the track, especially when enhanced by a beautiful reverb, as is the case here. The prominence of the clean guitar takes precedence over the melody unfurled by Christine McVie on her Fender Rhodes, but the young woman illustrates herself in other ways, with her contralto vocals of exemplary mastery.

FOR MAC-ADDICTS

Although it was rehearsed in the run-up to the *Fleetwood Mac* promotional tour—including backing vocals by Stevie Nicks—"Warm Ways" did not make it onto the set list. Despite its status as a single, it was never played live.

BLUE LETTER

Richard Curtis, Michael Curtis / 2:31

Musicians: Lindsey Buckingham: vocals, guitar / Christine McVie: keyboards / John McVie: bass / Mick Fleetwood: drums / Stevie Nicks: backing vocals / **Recorded:** Sound City Studios, Van Nuys, California: February 1975 / **Technical Team:** Producers: Fleetwood Mac, Keith Olsen / Sound Engineers: Keith Olsen, David DeVore / **Single:** Side A: Warm Ways / Side B: Blue Letter / **UK Release Date:** November 7, 1975 / **Reference:** Reprise Records (45 rpm ref.: K 14403/REP 3675) / Best UK Chart Ranking: Did Not Chart

Genesis and Lyrics

As the sessions drew to a close, Mick Fleetwood added a last-minute song to the track list. He was seduced by the music filtering in from a nearby studio—racy country rock, heir to Buffalo Springfield or the Eagles—composed by the Curtis Brothers, Michael and Richard, whom Stevie and Lindsey knew well having played with them on several occasions. The four musicians even recorded two demos together: "Seven League Boots" (which Crosby, Stills & Nash reappropriated in 1982 under the title "Southern Cross") and "Blue Letter." The latter particularly appealed to Mick, who decided to include it on their new album. This spontaneity, these initiatives guided by the simple desire to play together— the musicians had not experienced such intensity since the early years of the Mac, and this was a good thing for the McVie-Fleetwood team.

The pleasure felt is inversely proportional to that of the song's narrator, who has just received a letter from his partner announcing the end of their relationship. She does so abruptly, mentioning her age and suggesting that she is now looking for younger arms to hold her. The narrator, however, thinks he perceives between the lines of this missive the desire of his companion to spend one last night with him. An invitation he accepts with reticence: "Baby when your day goes down / I won't be waitin' around for you." Many fans saw in this song an evocation of the chaotic relationship between Lindsey Buckingham and Stevie Nicks, as well as a draft of the future "Go Your Own Way," forgetting on the way that the lyrics had been written by Michael and Richard Curtis.

Production

Fleetwood Mac plunges headlong into the Californian rock that, until now, they had been content to skim over. The band's new architect, Lindsey Buckingham, is at the helm with his confident, energetic vocals and abrasive guitar sound, whose sharp edges have been rounded off and polished so as not to irritate the ear. While this track is obviously rooted in country—as evidenced by the guitarist's chord playing and John McVie's bass line—its interpretation is more along the lines of Californian country rock, with its softened, catchy, moderate tempo and its radiant, even solar dimension. The lyrics might have suggested a downbeat interpretation, but this is not the case. We can imagine Lindsey and Stevie smiling as they recorded their respective vocal parts. Here, for the first time—in track list order—the young woman makes a notable appearance, hinting at the harmonic possibilities of her association with Buckingham. A last-minute guest on the album, this track was honored with a place on Side B of the single "Warm Ways," but the combo went completely unnoticed in the British charts when it was released in November 1975.

John McVie, Lindsey Buckingham, Christine McVie, Stevie Nicks, and Mick Fleetwood in October 1975.

RHIANNON

Stevie Nicks / 4:12

Feeling she had spoiled the story of Rhiannon by missing out on the Mabinogion, Stevie made her the heroine of "Angel," one of the tracks on *Tusk*.

Musicians
Stevie Nicks: vocals
Lindsey Buckingham: guitar, backing vocals
Christine McVie: keyboards, backing vocals
John McVie: bass
Mick Fleetwood: drums

Recorded
Sound City Studios, Van Nuys, California: February 1975

Technical Team
Producers: Fleetwood Mac, Keith Olsen
Sound Engineers: Keith Olsen, David DeVore

Single
Side A: Rhiannon / Side B: Sugar Daddy
UK Release Date: April 30, 1976
Reference: Reprise Records (45 rpm ref.: K 14430)
Best UK Chart Ranking: 46
US Release Date: February 4, 1976
Reference: Reprise Records (45 rpm ref.: RPS 1345)
Best US Chart Ranking: 11

Rhiannon originated from a collection of medieval prose poems collectively called *The Mabinogion*.

Genesis and Lyrics

In 1974, on the advice of a friend who knew of her taste for the supernatural (her version varied, sometimes referring to an impulse purchase in an airport store), Stevie Nicks immersed herself in reading the novel *Triad: A Novel of the Supernatural*, by Mary Bartlet Leader. Published two years earlier (1972), it tells the story of a woman, Branwen, stricken by the loss of her child, who encounters strange phenomena and ends up possessed by a witch named Rhiannon. Stevie Nicks emerged from this reading fascinated by the mysticism emanating from this name of Welsh origin. She dreamily told herself that if she ever had a daughter, she would like to name her Rhiannon. In the meantime, she gave the name to a song she was beginning to compose on the piano for the second album she was planning to record with Lindsey Buckingham. She had no idea of the mythological dimension of Rhiannon, a character from Welsh folklore. "It wasn't until 1978 that I found out about the Mabinogion [Welsh medieval prose tales drawing on Celtic mythology], and that Branwen and Rhiannon are in there, too, and that Rhiannon wasn't a witch at all; she was a mythological queen," Stevie explained in 2013. "But my story was definitely written about a celestial being. I didn't know who Rhiannon was, exactly, but I knew that she was not of this world."[72] Rhiannon is indeed an indefinable figure, an unattainable sylph, who appears on starless nights and escapes our vision. In so doing, Stevie lays the groundwork for the character she is building for herself.

Production

Like its inspiration and namesake, "Rhiannon" was a difficult song to capture. It took many hours and countless takes to finalize the song—more so than for any other of the band's tracks up to that point. But the musicians were well aware that it was worth the effort, and that they were undoubtedly dealing with a classic in their repertoire. In any case, the recording of the album was flowing so smoothly that a little challenge did not frighten them. To give themselves a boost and to help them forget about lunch breaks, they reached for some coke and booze…

"['Rhiannon'] was one of those songs that took over a day to get the basic track, and we're on analogue tape…"

Five years after writing "Rhiannon," Stevie received from a fan four novels by Evangeline Walton based on *The Mabinogion*. Stevie acquired the rights and, in 2020, began work on a TV series that never came to fruition.

recalled producer Keith Olsen. "The first pass was kind of magical but had too many mistakes. The second pass was pretty good, but didn't have the magic and from there it went downhill. But I kept those two."[73] Work continued late into the night, but to no avail. The new takes were not satisfactory. Everyone fell asleep, and the musicians agreed that it would be better to start again, a little fresher, the following afternoon. The band parted company, but Keith remained firmly planted in his seat. He wanted to try one last thing. "I started editing the two-inch tape," said the producer. "And I created loops with certain sections to transfer it to another machine. So if you listen to the end of 'Rhiannon,' you'll perceive a mini sonic rift on the crash cymbal that's heard every time the loop ends. It took like 14 or 15 cuts to put this song together. It was very complicated."[73]

The next day, the musicians discovered the producer's nocturnal work. He had pieced together the best parts of the previous night's recordings and achieved the long-awaited result. Lindsey Buckingham's mutated chords sound as intriguing and enveloping as ever. Stevie's slightly broken voice rises and falls with a form of despair in the intonation that immediately provokes a shiver, while Christine McVie's chiming notes herald the surprising key change of the second part. Euphoric when she heard the final result, Stevie Nicks did not want the song to be released as a single. She was attached to the song and feared it would fail in the charts. It did not, however, and reached an impressive eleventh place on the Billboard Hot 100 chart, accelerating the album's success.

FOR MAC-ADDICTS

Widely known simply as "Rhiannon" and named as such on the album, the single was released in the US under the name "Rhiannon (Will You Ever Win)."

Christine McVie's "Over My Head" topped the US charts.

ON YOUR HEADPHONES
At 0:18, Lindsey Buckingham adds subtle harmonics, unfortunately masked in the mix. A live performance of the track enables us to better appreciate this delectable ornamentation, as well as his snappy picking.

OVER MY HEAD

Christine McVie / 3:34

Musicians: Christine McVie: vocals, keyboards / Lindsey Buckingham: guitars, backing vocals / John McVie: bass / Mick Fleetwood: drums, percussions / Stevie Nicks: backing vocals / **Recorded:** Sound City Studios, Van Nuys, California: February 1975 / **Technical Team:** Producers: Fleetwood Mac, Keith Olsen / Sound Engineers: Keith Olsen, David DeVore / **Single:** Side A: Over My Head / Side B: I'm So Afraid / **UK Release Date:** February 27, 1976 / **Reference:** Reprise Records (45 rpm ref.: K 14413) / Best UK Chart Ranking: Did Not Chart / **US Release Date:** September 24, 1975 / **Reference:** Reprise Records (45 rpm ref.: RPS 1339) / Best US Chart Ranking: 20

Genesis and Lyrics

In early December 1974, Fleetwood Mac wrapped up the promotional tour for their album *Heroes Are Hard to Find* in Long Beach, California, virtually at home. Christine and John McVie returned to their Malibu apartment to take a breather and regain their strength. But the keyboardist never strayed from her instruments for long. So she took with her a Hohner electric piano of modest dimensions and, above all, portable. In her spare time, she tapped away on the keyboard and found the first chords of "Over My Head." Once the skeleton of her score was established, the lyricist poured out her heart in what seemed to be a new confidence addressed to John McVie. As usual, the object of her love is portrayed as blowing hot and cold on their romantic relationship. She burns with desire for him but comes up against his coldness and moody behavior. Yet the face of the lover is not the one we think it is, if we are to believe Christine McVie, who revealed in a documentary broadcast in 2022 by the BBC that she was actually thinking of the new boy, Lindsey Buckingham, and his beguiling good looks.

Production

The melody imposed by the keyboard maintains two main chords for part of the song, but on certain sequences Christine places a descending sequence that gives the melody all its originality. The celestial backing vocals themselves follow this downward trajectory. Lindsey distills clusters of slightly modified, delicately played notes. But the one who really stands out is Mick Fleetwood, who brings out the full artillery and showcases his percussion talents, bringing variety to a song that could have been a little too linear. He adds bongos, cowbell, and shaker. The song was chosen as the first single from the *Fleetwood Mac* album, but it was given a minor facelift before being released as a 45. The long fade-in is cut to suit radio broadcast requirements, and the guitar level is raised on the choruses. The finale is also shortened, stopping at the third bar.

CRYSTAL

Stevie Nicks / 5:12

Musicians: Lindsey Buckingham: vocals, guitar / Christine McVie: keyboards / John McVie: bass / Mick Fleetwood: drums / Stevie Nicks: backing vocals / **Recorded:** Sound City Studios, Van Nuys, California: February 1975 / **Technical Team:** Producers: Fleetwood Mac, Keith Olsen / Sound Engineers: Keith Olsen, David DeVore

Genesis and Lyrics

During the first collective work sessions, each of the "camps" presented their compositional ideas for the new album. In addition to Stevie and Lindsey's demos of "Landslide," "Rhiannon," and "Monday Morning," they also discussed "Crystal." The context of this latter song was different from the other three. It was not an unreleased piece, having already been immortalized on Buckingham and Nicks's album. But in Stevie's eyes, this charming ballad deserved better treatment, the kind of production Fleetwood Mac could offer. The idea of revisiting it was unanimously supported by the band. Stevie Nicks, who took lead vocals on only two other tracks, could have taken the microphone on this composition, which she had written. Instead, she gave Lindsey the honor of performing it again because she felt that the guitarist's suave, expressive voice was perfectly suited to this track. Stevie made a notable sacrifice here, as the lyrics were so close to her heart. Indeed, she wrote it with her father and grandfather in mind. She evokes their benevolence and praises their presence by her side, against all odds. In contrast to romantic love, she believes that paternal love is not subject to the ravages of time: "How the faces of love have changed / Turning the pages / And I have changed / Oh but you, you remain ageless."

Lindsey Buckingham provided the vocals on "Crystal" that were intended for Stevie Nicks. Producer Keith Olsen considered Lindsey's timbre more suitable for the song.

Production

The strong guitar attacks, whose high notes were too prominent in the *Buckingham Nicks* version, are considerably toned down in the *Fleetwood Mac* version. The musicians agreed that the song needed nuance to reveal its full potential. As a result, Lindsey refines his vocals and delivers a much more intimate performance. He sings closer to the microphone, which picks up his every breath. Keith Olsen was careful to preserve these elements, giving authenticity and closeness to the final result. John McVie's round, melodic bass also adds warmth. Christine McVie chooses to play a Mellotron, whose tones blend ideally with Buckingham's guitar. But it is when Stevie Nicks's voice comes into play that the song enters another dimension, and the vocal harmonies that she builds with Lindsey Buckingham reach a level of perfection that the band had never before experienced.

Once again, bassist John McVie (here in the studio in 1975) is at the heart of a desperate song written by his wife.

SAY YOU LOVE ME

Christine McVie / 4:11

Canada also welcomed the single with open arms, placing it at number twenty-nine on the RPM Top Singles chart in 1976, even though New Brunswick folk singer Shirley Eikhard had beaten them to it with a new version of the song, reaching a respectable number thirty-four.

Musicians
Christine McVie: vocals, keyboards
Lindsey Buckingham: guitar, banjo, backing vocals
John McVie: bass
Mick Fleetwood: drums
Stevie Nicks: backing vocals

Recorded
Sound City Studios, Van Nuys, California: February 1975

Technical Team
Producers: Fleetwood Mac, Keith Olsen
Sound Engineers: Keith Olsen, David DeVore

Single
Side A: Say You Love Me / Side B: Monday Morning
UK Release Date: October 8, 1976
Reference: Reprise Records (45 rpm ref.: K 14447/RPS 1356)
Best UK Chart Ranking: 40
US Release Date: June 9, 1976
Reference: Reprise Records (45 rpm ref.: RPS 1356)
Best US Chart Ranking: 11

1975

Her tumultuous union with John McVie inspired Christine to write numerous songs designed to reawaken their mutual feelings.

Genesis and Lyrics

Christine McVie reached the heights of romantic songwriting in many ways. But there was one aspect that she never tackled: the religious dimension of this feeling. In "Say You Love Me," she does so in a highly original way, addressing her love partner as a deity with authority over her human condition. From the very first verse, she combines the sacred and the profane: "Have mercy, baby." She throws herself at his feet, imploring his help and mercy. The entire lexical field of supplication is used, as well as the weakness that defines her, in contrast to the one she implores. The love relationship is thus totally unbalanced by this mixture of devotion and penitence.

Production

In January 1975, the first work session with Fleetwood Mac's most popular lineup began with "Say You Love Me." "That was my first rehearsal with Stevie and Lindsey," recalled Christine McVie. "They were in the band, but I'd never played with them before. I started playing 'Say You Love Me,' and when I reached the chorus they started singing with me and fell right into it. I heard this incredible sound—our three voices—and said to myself, 'Is this me singing?' I couldn't believe how great this three-voice harmony was. My skin turned to gooseflesh and I wondered how long this feeling was going to last."[4]

"Say You Love Me" would thus outline what would become Fleetwood Mac's new secret weapon, making them one of the behemoths of American music: vocal harmonies. This is particularly apparent on the catchy bridge, where the perfectly mastered vocals hit the nail on the head. But Christine's melodious, rhythmic playing remains the main attraction of this track, which moves between soft rock and country. Lindsey Buckingham's simple, flowing playing—which shifts between acoustic guitar, banjo, and twelve-string guitar—also contributes to the song's catchiness. The musician particularly stands out on the finale, which ends in a fade-out as he continuously spins his delicious, chiming arpeggios. Released as a single, this track achieves the same performance as its predecessor, "Rhiannon": number eleven on the US Billboard Hot 100 chart—the highest position reached by the Mac in the country.

Because of its intimate dimension, "Landslide" regularly gave rise to moments of intense closeness onstage between Stevie Nicks and Lindsey Buckingham, as in 1997, during The Dance tour.

LANDSLIDE
Stevie Nicks / 3:05

Musicians
Lindsey Buckingham: guitar
Stevie Nicks: vocals
Recorded
Sound City Studios, Van Nuys, California: February 1975
Technical Team
Producers: Fleetwood Mac, Keith Olsen
Sound Engineers: Keith Olsen, David Devore

A classic in Fleetwood Mac's repertoire, the studio version of "Landslide" was not released as a single.

Genesis and Lyrics

Stevie Nicks was just twenty-seven when she wrote "Landslide" in 1974. Yet when you listen to the lyrics, she seems to have already lived several lives. This powerful introspection came at a pivotal moment in her career. Shortly before this, the Buckingham-Nicks duo had released their first and only album, whose failure prompted Polydor to release them from their contract. Stevie was exhausted by the odd jobs she had to do to support the couple, and questioned the wisdom of pursuing a career that was really not taking off. Perhaps she should go back to school after all? But her father convinced her to give it another six months, in view of all the energy she'd already invested. He told her that should the tide still not turn, her parents would still be there to help her.

Reassured, at the end of 1974, Stevie accompanied Lindsey to Aspen, Colorado, where he rehearsed with Don Everly for two weeks before going on tour with him for three months. During this time, Stevie decided to stay in Aspen with a friend in a house they had borrowed. The living room provided an incredible view of the Aspen valley, and, impressed by the amount of snow surrounding her, the young woman realized that she could easily be swept away without being able to do anything about it, should an avalanche occur. Overwhelmed by this idea, she began to think about the notion of unconditional love and the sacrifices one can make for a loved one or for one's children. Within minutes, she had written "Landslide," a powerful metaphor for the fragility of life and the power of feelings: "What is love? / Can the child within my heart rise above? / Can I sail through the changin' ocean tides?" Three months later, the phone rang at Stevie and Lindsey's house. Mick Fleetwood made them a proposal that would, at least for a while, dispel any doubts about the existential questions the young woman had been asking herself.

Production

Early critics were not kind to Stevie Nicks's voice when *Fleetwood Mac* was released, but it was her distinctive timbre, at once confident and melancholy, that made "Landslide" so special, a song that would become a mainstay of the Fleetwood Mac repertoire. Over the years, it

even became one of the band's most frequently performed songs, giving rise to often unique stage moments between the two ex-lovers, Stevie Nicks and Lindsey Buckingham, as they quarreled or unexpectedly reunited. Composed at a time when the couple were at rock bottom, before being offered the chance of a lifetime by Fleetwood Mac, "Landslide" is without doubt the song that most characterizes their resilience.

Intended to appear on Stevie and Lindsey's second album—which never saw the light of day—"Landslide" was naturally recorded by the couple under the admiring gaze of the other band members, who had no real place in this intimate track. Beyond Stevie Nicks's serious interpretation, Lindsey Buckingham's crystalline arpeggios appear like a bubble of comfort, a woolen sweater placed gently on the shoulders of her companion, chilled by the sight of all that snow.

Surprising as it may seem given the song's popularity today, "Landslide" was never released as a single when *Fleetwood Mac* was first released in 1975. Instead, Fleetwood Mac released a live version of "Landslide" from the album *The Dance* in 1997 as a single, and this time the song climbed to number fifty-one on the Billboard Hot 100 chart, becoming the band's twenty-fourth chart entry.

"World Turning" gave its name to the World Turning Band, a Fleetwood Mac tribute band formed in early 2013. It has become a resident of Nashville's 3rd & Lindsley venue, where it performs about every two months to crowds of Fleetwood Mac fans, and more often than not to sold-out audiences. It covers all the big hits written by the Mac, as well as the best solo hits by its members.

WORLD TURNING

Christine McVie, Lindsey Buckingham / 4:25

Musicians: Lindsey Buckingham: vocals, guitar, dobro, backing vocals / Christine McVie: vocals, keyboards, backing vocals, maracas / John McVie: bass / Mick Fleetwood: drums, tama / Stevie Nicks: backing vocals / **Recorded:** Sound City Studios, Van Nuys, California: February 1975 / **Technical Team:** Producers: Fleetwood Mac, Keith Olsen / Sound Engineers: Keith Olsen, David DeVore

Genesis and Lyrics

The first real collaboration between keyboardist Christine McVie and guitarist Lindsey Buckingham, "World Turning" was actually an adaptation of Peter Green's "The World Keep on Turning," which appeared on Fleetwood Mac's first album in 1968. McVie and Buckingham, who share the lead vocals, have completely transformed it to the point where they are now the only credited songwriters. In Peter Green's blues version, he sang of his worries, but also of his yearning for a woman. "World Turning," much more pragmatic, is rooted in reality: "Everybody's got me down," "World turning / I gotta get my feet back on the ground." The main protagonist feels lost and needs someone to help him get back on his feet and find his bearings. Although his morale is fragile, he is determined to carry on, and hopes to find "somebody to help me through the night."

Production

Propelled by Buckingham's searing bluesy fingerpicking on his dobro, "World Turning" was created in the studio in less than an hour, as a result of the budding chemistry between Christine McVie and Lindsey Buckingham. Stevie Nicks was annoyed, even a little jealous, at having been left out of the composition of this track, as producer Keith Olsen explained: "Stevie was a bit upset over the writing team…but she got over it."[74] Lindsey kicked things off, bringing that haunting metallic country-blues gimmick to the dobro. But above all it was the interplay of his voice with Christine McVie's that was striking: The guitarist showed that he could sing the blues without having to blush at the former Chicken Shack singer, a specialist in the genre. Buckingham's efforts brought Fleetwood Mac the guitar and vocal presence the band had lacked since the departure of Danny Kirwan, with no offense to Bob Welch. As for Mick Fleetwood, he seemed truly inspired as, two-thirds of the way through, he took the song into another dimension by increasing the tempo. One of the band's most frequently played live tracks, "World Turning" also enabled the drummer to incorporate his frenetic "solo moment," armed with his tama (nicknamed the "talking drum"), a West African instrument introduced to him by a Nigerian musician in London in 1969. Incontestably, "World Turning" creates a clear dividing line between the "old" Fleetwood Mac and the new guard.

1975

SUGAR DADDY

Christine McVie / 4:09

Musicians: Christine McVie: vocals, keyboards / Lindsey Buckingham: guitar / John McVie: bass / Mick Fleetwood: drums / Waddy Wachtel: guitar / **Recorded:** Sound City Studios, Van Nuys, California: February 1975 / **Technical Team:** Producers: Fleetwood Mac, Keith Olsen / Sound Engineers: Keith Olsen, David DeVore / **Single:** Side A: Rhiannon / Side B: Sugar Daddy / **UK Release Date:** April 30, 1976 / **Reference:** Reprise Records (45 rpm ref.: K 14430) / Best UK Chart Ranking: 46 / **US Release Date:** February 4, 1976 / **Reference:** Reprise Records (45 rpm ref.: RPS 1345) / Best US Chart Ranking: 11

Genesis and Lyrics

The term "sugar daddy" generally refers to a man who provides for a younger person ("sugar baby"), in a romantic or an intimate relationship. He provides her with financial support, gifts, or other benefits in exchange for companionship, attention, or whatever has been arranged with her. This is exactly what Christine McVie—the very opposite of the character she describes—describes in the song "Sugar Daddy." In the first and second verses, the narrator expresses the need for a sugar daddy who could provide her with "a little money," food ("And when I get a little hungry / He could give me all I could eat"), and booze. However, she warns him that her affections lie with another man. She points out that he gives her the love she needs, so she does not need her sugar daddy for that: "But when it comes to love / He'd better leave me alone." In the third verse, the narrator imagines herself being driven around in a luxury car by her sugar daddy.

The song depicts a woman's desire for financial security while emphasizing that fulfillment in love remains essential to her life. While it is impossible to rule out the idea of a metaphor on the part of the band, who were seeking Warner's support at the time and more financial guarantees from the label, Christine McVie admits she did not look that far: "I don't recall it being about anybody," she declared, adding that: "Most of my songs are based on truth, and real people, but a lot of them are just fantasies, really."[75]

Production

"Sugar Daddy" is often described as one of the weakest—or at least most inoffensive—songs on *Fleetwood Mac*. Yet its warm arrangement is a real success, and its melody, not to mention Christine's enthusiastic interpretation, proves ever more catchy with each successive listen. The Fleetwood–John McVie tandem's upbeat, swaying rhythm section blends effortlessly with the young woman's cottony keyboards, while Lindsey Buckingham's guitar solo, while admittedly unexpected, is remarkably well-written. Even the backing vocals, which come in only on the finale, at the end of which you can hear Christine laughing, spread an infectious good vibe. In the notes accompanying the following album, *Rumours*, Stevie Nicks confided that "Sugar Daddy" was one of her favorite Christine songs. Much lighter than Christine's usual Fleetwood Mac productions, the song failed to become a staple for the band, who never played it live. Its main feature is that it is one of the few songs in this lineup to feature a guest—in this case Waddy Wachtel, who played rhythm guitar, and was credited as "Waddy" on the album jacket.

Lindsey was attached to "I'm So Afraid," which he had written and had been perfecting since the early 1970s. It was a highlight of his 1992–1993 Out of the Cradle tour.

Drummer Mick Fleetwood's heavy, martial drumming contributes greatly to the somber, plaintive atmosphere of "I'm So Afraid," which flirts with hard rock.

I'M SO AFRAID
Lindsey Buckingham / 4:15

Musicians: Lindsey Buckingham: vocals, guitar / Christine McVie: keyboards / John McVie: bass / Mick Fleetwood: drums / Stevie Nicks: backing vocals / **Recorded:** Sound City Studios, Van Nuys, California: February 1975 / **Technical Team:** Producers: Fleetwood Mac, Keith Olsen / Sound Engineers: Keith Olsen, David DeVore / **Single:** Side A: Over My Head / Side B: I'm So Afraid / **UK Release Date:** February 27, 1976 / **Reference:** Reprise Records (45 rpm ref.: K 14413) / Best UK Chart Ranking: Did Not Chart / **US Release Date:** September 24, 1975 / **Reference:** Reprise Records (45 rpm ref.: RPS 1339) / Best US Chart Ranking: 20

Genesis and Lyrics

Given Lindsey Buckingham's propensity for sidelining Fleetwood Mac at various times during their collaboration, his compulsive perfectionism and his desire to be omnipotent, the lyrics of "I'm So Afraid"—especially at the start of his adventure with the band—seem almost prophetic. The guitarist describes a man who has been plagued by loneliness and anguish for years but has no intention of changing his ways: "I've been alone / All the years / So many ways to count the tears / I never change / I never will." There seems to be no possible happy ending in the bleak existence of this man with a doomed soul. His paranoia causes him to slide into an abyss of sadness, an inexorable fall that leads to a fatal outcome: "Agony's torn at my heart too long / So afraid / Slip and I fall and I die."

Production

First and foremost, the lead rhythm section dominates the rich arrangement of the song, one of the heaviest in Fleetwood Mac's discography. Mick Fleetwood plays mostly toms at the beginning, imposing a dark, unbreathable climate, reinforced by John McVie's deep bass. Christine McVie, a little in the background with her shadowy keyboards, adds even more depth to this track, repatriated by Lindsey from the Buckingham-Nicks era. Over the years, he worked on harmonizing his guitar parts to the point where, thanks to this meticulous interweaving, they now resemble a veritable orchestra in their own right. Lindsey Buckingham has always claimed that he could never see himself improvising a new solo like Jimi Hendrix every night. So he had already thought through the details of how he would perform "I'm So Afraid" on stage. He knew it would be a wonderful showcase for his undulating, virtuoso playing. As for his voice, it proves as sensitive as it is vulnerable when it rises into the high register. For all these reasons, this song, one of Fleetwood Mac's most frequently performed onstage, would never be performed without Lindsey Buckingham. Relegated to the final track of *Fleetwood Mac*, it stands out for its emotional intensity, and is reminiscent of one of Fleetwood Mac's other brutal and anguished songs, Peter Green's "The Green Manalishi."

On April 25, 1976, Fleetwood Mac played to a crowd of 57,000 at the Oakland–Alameda County Coliseum, as part of the *Day on the Green* festival.

ALBUM

RUMOURS

Second Hand News . Dreams . Never Going Back Again . Don't Stop . Go Your Own Way .
Songbird . The Chain . You Make Loving Fun . I Don't Want to Know . Oh Daddy .
Gold Dust Woman
Outtake: Silver Springs

RELEASE DATES
United Kingdom: February 4, 1977
Reference: Warner Bros. Records—K56344
Best UK Chart Ranking: 1
United States: February 4, 1977
Reference: Warner Bros. Records—BSK3010
Best US Chart Ranking: 1

Advertisement in the May 14, 1977 issue of *Billboard* promoting *Rumours*. This was the lineup's second album, and the band in this format would soon be known as the "Rumours Five."

FLEETWOOD MAC'S MASTERPIECE

It is impossible to pinpoint the precise moment when the interpersonal problems of the Mac members began to profoundly affect the atmosphere within the band, but despite appearances and unexpected commercial success, 1976 was a stormy year.

A Whirlwind of Emotions

Mick Fleetwood had resigned himself, heartbroken, to Jenny's departure. Nothing could distract him from the mission he had set himself—to keep the Fleetwood Mac ship afloat—especially after conceding so much to avoid it going under. Even though the arrival of Stevie Nicks and Lindsey Buckingham had given the band a new lease on life, Mick was aware of the need to strike while the iron was hot, and he set about producing a new album without delay. His aim was to provide materially for his family, although he couldn't be present for them. Moreover, he did not know it yet, but the gestation of *Rumours*, the title of the Mac's eleventh studio album, was going to be long, complex, and very demanding, both emotionally and artistically. "Much of what has been said about *Rumours* has assumed a mythical dimension. Some things are true, others exaggerated," Mick explained in an interview with *Le Monde* in January 2013. He added: "Yes, we were all in an intense emotional turmoil, undermined by marital problems, with relationships within the band. Yes, alcohol and cocaine overwhelmed us. Yes, we sometimes did not leave the studio for several days, and ended the sessions exhausted, bordering on madness. [...] This recording could have ended in tragedy. To this day, I don't know how we survived it."[81] In his 2014 autobiography, Mick clarified: "We'd all be dead already if we weren't made of stronger stuff. What nearly did us in was the way we handled our emotions as our personal relationships came apart. But we refused to let our feelings derail our commitment to the music, no matter how complicated or intertwined they became. It was hard to do, but no matter what, we played on through the hurt."[2]

All this pain and emotional chaos would be expressed in song after song, resulting in a legendary album that has sold more than 40 million copies worldwide, making it one of the ten best-selling albums of all time.

A Chronicle of Broken Relationships

By the time the band began writing *Rumours*, the lives of all its members were falling apart. After more than seven years together, John and Christine McVie drifted apart irretrievably, Stevie Nicks and Lindsey Buckingham's relationship exploded, while Mick Fleetwood and Jenny Boyd began divorce proceedings. Yet breaking up was clearly not an option. All the musicians were aware of Fleetwood Mac's moment of glory, and none of them wanted to let the opportunity pass. Loyalty to the band transcended personal traumas. "After ten years of struggling, it would have been silly to throw it all away," explained Christine. "We proved to each other that we had a pretty strong character as a band, that we could cope with the problems and surmount them, which we did."[5]

Lindsey Buckingham, Stevie Nicks, and Christine McVie drew inspiration for their new songs from their recent love affairs. For the most part, they deal with lost loves, failing couples, betrayals, bitter regrets and anger. "That wasn't conscious either," said Lindsey Buckingham. "I mean you just write about what's happening. All the songs, really, seem to relate to each other. They're all about each other."[5] Sensitivities and ego conflicts were exacerbated by the uninterrupted microscopic scrutiny during their first few weeks in the studio; the couples tore each other apart live on radio and television, making *Rumours* the diary of the end of love affairs within Fleetwood Mac.

A Recording Under Extreme Tension

In the early hours of January 1976, as "Rhiannon" began to climb the charts and *Fleetwood Mac* passed the symbolic million-copy mark, Mick Fleetwood wanted more than ever

1977

The facade of Record Plant Studios in Sausalito, California, where *Rumours* was recorded.

to keep the band together on the road to success, and he decided to repeat the *Kiln House* experience. He set out to find a place where the musicians could live together and still be creative. Attracted by the growing reputation of the Record Plant studio in Sausalito, the drummer decided to bring everyone to the San Francisco Bay Area. The Plant, conceived as a soundproof cocoon where artists could easily withdraw from the outside world to immerse themselves body and soul in music, had opened its doors three years earlier. With its exceptional facilities, it quickly became one of California's most sought-after recording studio venues. Two limousines were at the musicians' disposal at any time of the day or night, as well as a speedboat, a conference room, a jacuzzi, and a games room.

The band then headed for San Francisco, where they rented a house perched on a hill not far from the studios. Mick, in a spirit of optimism, booked the Plant for just two months. A tall order, given that the previous album took three months to complete and that relations between the Mac members were much more strained than they had been at that time.

A New Duo at the Controls

The band, keen to retain control over the production of its album, did not renew its confidence in Keith Olsen. They even decided to dispense with the services of Kelly Kotera, the Plant's sound engineer, after a disastrous day's work with him during the mixing of the radio version of "Rhiannon" on January 18, 1976. Kotera proved incapable of mastering the new API mixing console equipped with 550A equalizers, a computerized and automated jewel of technology that he was to use for the recording of the album. Fleetwood Mac dismissed him and called in Richard Dashut, who had already worked with Stevie Nicks and Lindsey Buckingham. Dashut accepted on condition that he be assisted by sound engineer Ken Caillat. So, in the middle

of one of the wettest winters in Northern California history, Caillat joined the band in Sausalito with his faithful companion, Scooter, in the passenger seat. Scooter was a beagle who would soon become one of the Mac's mascots, appearing on the cover of 1979's *Tusk*. Caillat had never heard of the band until a fortnight earlier, when he was asked to remix an hour-long set recorded by Fleetwood Mac for the *King Biscuit Flower Hour* radio show. Years later, he still marveled at having been asked to work on such a seminal album: "I know how crazy that sounds in retrospect, especially considering that I was already something of a music industry insider. But Fleetwood Mac had yet to have a hit song in America. By the end of my journey making *Rumours*, though, I knew that my life would never be the same."[78]

As planned, John, Lindsey, and Mick took up residence in the rented house not far from the studio, as did producers Richard Dashut and Ken Caillat, who shared a room. But after a few days, Stevie and Christine decided to keep their distance and rented adjoining apartments overlooking the harbor. "There were girls everywhere [in the house] and everybody was completely drunk the whole time," recalled Stevie Nicks. "Me and Chris decided we couldn't be there. The next day we moved out and got two matching apartments next to each other." But some nights, after leaving the studio, alcohol-soaked John McVie would come looking for Christine, weary of trying to find solace among the groupies. "He'd be walking up and down the corridor, very upset, screaming her name, and she'd be hiding in my room,"[36] she added. "I had to avoid John McVie like the plague for a few months," Christine confirms, "unless we were playing, when it was all right."[79]

High-Tension Sessions

The sessions began on Wednesday, January 28, 1976. First to arrive, Richard Dashut and Ken Caillat took the time to

get to know the reception staff and the team of assistants before discovering the exceptional equipment at their disposal. The first few days were devoted to finding the best configuration for instruments and microphones. The two sound engineers decided to place the instruments in a semicircle facing the control room so that the musicians could see each other and the technical crew behind the control room glass. So they set up Mick's giant drum kit on the right-hand side of the room (as seen from the booth), then John's gear in the right-hand corner, as close to Mick as possible, on his right. Then Lindsey's guitar area was defined opposite the booth. Finally, on the left side of the recording room, Christine's keyboard station with her clavinet, Fender Rhodes, and Hammond organ. A microphone was placed in front of each of the three instruments so that she could sing while sitting and playing. Stevie, for her part, would stand in the middle of the studio, waving a tambourine above her head to the beat of the music, even if it was not recorded. Only Mick's tambourine parts were recorded for the album. To the left and right of the arched control room were two secluded cabins with large windows providing views of both the studio and the control room. The one on the left was for recording acoustic instruments, such as Lindsey's grand piano and guitars, as well as quieter elements such as vocals and tambourines. The one on the right was for loud guitars, bass amps, and organ speakers.

But after five days, Ken Caillat was still not fully satisfied with the setup and realized he was spending far too much time on each element separately. Pressure began to mount on his inexperienced shoulders, as he sensed the impatience of the musicians, who were champing at the bit to get the show underway. Ken decided that the best way to achieve a coherent overall sound was to have the musicians play and adjust the settings according to how the instruments complemented each other. After these meticulous preparations, the Mac members could begin recording.

Their working method was by now well established: The three songwriters usually approached the rest of the band with a gimmick and snippets of lyrics (or even a simple idea for the subject of a song), and it was up to everyone to come up with suggestions. Christine and Mick were often the quickest to make suggestions. The latter sometimes waited until the last phase of the recording to try out percussion to "color" an arrangement. Sometimes John did not finalize his bass parts until he was fully aware of the song's subject. In fact, it was not uncommon for him to ask to redo his parts once the vocals had been laid down, believing that his placement would be all the better that way in relation to the melody. The fact that recorded songs were about the people who record them did not make things any easier, and sometimes the lyrics did not come into play until very late in the creative process, so as to avoid adding fuel to the fire. Lindsey fine-tuned his lyrics

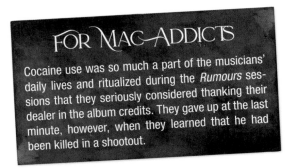

FOR MAC-ADDICTS

Cocaine use was so much a part of the musicians' daily lives and ritualized during the *Rumours* sessions that they seriously considered thanking their dealer in the album credits. They gave up at the last minute, however, when they learned that he had been killed in a shootout.

and arrangements on his own right up to the last minute, and everyone has to adapt to this, even if it meant radically revising what they had already recorded. Stevie and Christine, on the other hand, were more direct in their writing and interpretation, and if they made adjustments, they were less drastic. Nonetheless, the songwriters were slow to release their lyrics, which exasperated Mick and John, who only cared about playing.

The early stages were laborious, as communication between certain band members proved volcanic from the outset: John, who was soon to appear on the arm of Sandra Elsdon (Peter Green's ex-girlfriend), hardly spoke to Christine at all. The first few days' attempts at being civil to each other were followed by terse, tense conversations, which Christine usually cut short with this injunction: "John, you're being ridiculous. You've had too much to drink. Now leave me alone and just concentrate on your bass part."[78] As for Stevie and Lindsey, they scrupulously avoided agreeing on anything. Lindsey took their breakup very hard. His only way of dealing with the situation was to go on one date after another to forget Stevie. For her part, Stevie began a relationship with Don Henley (of the Eagles), barely a month after leaving Lindsey, which did little to ease the atmosphere between the two ex-lovers.

Simple sessions designed to find the right arrangements were stretched out over many hours, each time interspersed with slamming doors, flying objects, and interminable arguments. So what should have taken five hours instead took twenty, and day after day, it took a long time for the heated tempers to cool down to the right temperature and get back to work productively.

Even though the only thing that still united the members of Fleetwood Mac was the music and the desire to make *Yesterday's Gone*—its working title—a great album, the goal was going to prove increasingly difficult to achieve, given the way things were going.

The increase in drug use—with everyone helping themselves to a small black velvet bag placed on Ken Caillat's mixing desk—was taking its toll on the musicians' powers of concentration, as were the incessant parties organized by the inevitable parasites who had moved in around them since the Mac's rise to fame.

Backtracking

After nine weeks of recording, the band decided to take a break to recover from their mental fatigue and returned to Los Angeles. The first two months were particularly trying for everyone. "The communication was very bad," Lindsey recalled. "It's not that anyone was fighting, it's just that no one was quite together enough to get a really healthy start."[5] A sentiment widely shared by co-producer Richard Dashut: "It took two months for everyone to adjust to one another. Aside from equipment problems, there were psychological problems in that the band were going through a tremendous upheaval."[5]

After several weeks' rest, the musicians took stock before resuming the recording sessions. Due to scheduling constraints, they had to find new premises. They started scouring studios for a place to rework their raw material. They finally found it on a run-down stretch of Hollywood Boulevard: sound engineer Wally Heider's Studio 3, where Ken Caillat had worked before joining them in Sausalito. They stayed there from mid-May to mid-June. During one session, when Lindsey nonchalantly blurted out to Mick, "Well, things don't seem to be going exactly the way I would like them to go," the drummer replied curtly, "Well, maybe you don't want to be in a group."[60]

Tensions with Lindsey were not confined to Stevie or Mick. Lindsey's relationship with John, courteously strained up to that point, became downright stormy the day the bassist, exasperated by the guitarist, threw a glass in his face, which Lindsey barely had time to dodge. The musicians were unable to accept responsibility for the poor impressions they experienced when listening to the first tapes, so the listening system was blamed. "More or less all that we kept from the Sausalito sessions in the end were my drum tracks," confessed Mick Fleetwood. "We took the tapes and stripped every song down to those, then set about overdubbing all of the instruments and vocals. We basically remade the record from scratch, forcing every member to relive all the heartache inherent in those songs that we'd lived and breathed for nine weeks, nearly twenty-four hours a day."[2] Richard Dashut confirmed this: "It wasn't necessary or even expedient for them all to be in the studio at once, ever. Only two tracks on *Rumours* were recorded

1977

and played at the same time. In other words, virtually every track on that album is either an overdub, or lifted from a separate take of that particular song. What you hear on the record is the best pieces assembled, a true aural collage."[5] He also said, "Lindsey and I did most of the production. That's not to take anything away from Ken or the others in the band—they were all involved. But Lindsey and myself really produced that record and he should've gotten the individual credit for it, instead of the whole band."[108]

But despite great efforts and real progress, the record had made little headway by the time summer arrived. By June, tracks such as "Don't Stop," "I Don't Want to Know," and "The Chain" had not yet been completed, while others, such as "Oh Daddy," had not even been written. For some tracks, notably "The Chain" (originally called "Keep Me There"), the band kept coming back to it, without ever being able to really bring it to fruition as the weeks went by.

The '76 Summer Tour

Another break in the album's work sessions came at the beginning of the summer, with Fleetwood Mac due to hit the road on June 18, 1976, for a summer tour (which had begun with two isolated dates on May 1 and 3). *Fleetwood Mac* continued to climb the charts, and public demand for the album grew ever stronger. It was also an opportunity for the musicians to vent all the frustrations they had built up over the past six months onstage, and to rub shoulders with the rest of the music industry's elite, sharing the bill with the likes of Jeff Beck, Jefferson Starship, Ted Nugent, and the Eagles (who had been on a roll since the release of

"One of These Nights" at the beginning of June). Unexpectedly, no major incidents disrupted the tour. Cocaine was served onstage between songs, and alcohol flowed freely every night backstage. Artificial paradises, combined with the clamor of a delighted audience, seemed to act like a soothing balm on the band. But the interlude was short-lived. No sooner had the tour ended than Warner blew the whistle, reminding the musicians that it was time to return to the studio to finish the album, of which none of the label's executives had yet heard a single note.

The concert series concluded in Tampa, Florida, on July 4. The Mac members had six days before they left for a concert in Philadelphia on July 12, so they took the opportunity to book a few days at Criteria Studios in Miami. They then returned to Wally Heider's studios for further sessions from August 4 to 22 (and again in October). Countless recordings, overdubs, and adjustments took place during these summer sessions.

Warner's Concerns

When the *Fleetwood Mac* album reached number one on the Billboard 200 on September 4, 1976, Warner's pressure on the band, and especially on Mick Fleetwood as manager, did not abate. Quite the contrary, in fact. Not knowing anything about the progress of the sessions or the artistic directions that emerged from them was a source of great concern to the studio, especially as the bill was starting to mount. "If it had been a little shaky, we might not have spent a lot of money recording it," Mick Fleetwood would later explain. "But we felt it was warranted because we

Cartoon of Mick Fleetwood by Ron Coddington, 1977.

In addition to being a hit machine, Fleetwood Mac also established itself as a formidable live act (here in July 1977).

WOODEN BALLS

It is impossible not to notice the crotch ornament worn by Mick Fleetwood on the cover of *Rumours*. Much commented on and criticized, the wooden balls hanging from his belt were originally the handles of a chain flush toilet. The drummer had stolen them from a club toilet during one of his first concerts. Having become a real good-luck charm for him, they found a buyer for more than $120,000 at an auction in December 2022.

were working on making what was good better and better. And the record company was really very good. They called a couple of times about hearing things, and I said, 'You're not hearing *anything* till we've finished.' They said, 'Do you realize how much money you're spending?'"[5]

And again, Warner did not know the whole story. Also in September, Richard Dashut and Ken Caillat realized that the tapes they had been working on twelve hours a day for nine months were gradually losing quality through intensive listening, and were in danger of wearing out, which would be dramatic at this stage. No band had ever taken so long to record an album. The playback heads were probably heavily clogged and damaging the tapes. The team panicked. Fortunately, another master (the tape from which copies can be made) existed. But this master did not contain the most recent and interesting overdubs made by the band. So they had to act fast before disaster struck.

The team went to ABC-Dunhill in Los Angeles, which had two 24-track consoles. The idea was to transfer only the overdubs on the oldest master, playing them on one machine and recording them on another. But this operation was a first. The most complicated part was to achieve perfect synchronization at a time when, of course, time codes had yet to appear on machines. Song by song, track by track, it took a long night of anguish to save the album (and the band). Richard Dashut recalls: "We wore out our original 24-track master. We figured we had 3,000 hours on it and we were losing high end, transients and much of the clarity. The drums were valid and maybe a couple of guitar parts. We ended up transferring all the overdubs on the master to a safety master. We had no sync pulse to lock the two machines together, so we had to manually sync the two machines—ten tracks by ear using headphones in twelve-hour sessions. People thought we were craze [*sic*] but it turned out really good."[108]

A European Interlude

Aware of the need to improve Fleetwood Mac's commercial approach to reassure Warner, Mick decided to spend ten days in England with the band before returning to the studio. The main aim of this lightning trip was to promote *Fleetwood Mac* across the Atlantic and exploit its potential to the full in lands that had been neglected for some time. Once there, the musicians were surprised to see Peter Green arrive at their hotel. The former Mac leader was staying with them for a few nights. He appeared scruffy and had put on a lot of weight. He glared at his former bandmates and talked to them aggressively, which upset them, especially John. Another ghost from the past resurfaced: Danny Kirwan. Here again, the post–Fleetwood Mac bill was a steep one: Danny quickly abandoned his short-lived solo career and became a homeless alcoholic. He disappeared as quickly as he reappeared.

After this brief European interlude and flashback to the past, it was time to get back to work on *Rumours*. New recording sessions took place at Davlen Sound Studios in Hollywood in September 1976. After several months of hard work, everyone was confident with the technical team, and in particular with Ken Caillat, who did his best to smooth things over with everyone. He was never short of ideas: "I made every instrument sound its most unique and fitting for [each] song," he explained. "I loved creating the sound and that's actually how they ended up promoting me to producer because the sounds I was making were changing the trajectory of the songs themselves; I was having an effect on the production of the songs by the engineering that I was doing."[80]

The Final Touch

The final phase enabled many songs to be given a final touch: Lindsey recorded the final solo on "I Don't Want to Know," as well as the acoustic guitar part on "Second Hand News." Christine added an organ to "Silver Springs"—which did not make it onto the album, much to the dismay of Stevie Nicks, who wrote the song and regretted its use on Side B of the first single, "Go Your Own Way." For the time being, Stevie finished "coloring" the vocal harmonies on "Dreams."

A visit to the Record Plant (in Los Angeles) in November 1976 enabled final adjustments to be made, shortly before the mixing stage, which took place at the Producer's Workshop (on Hollywood Boulevard), then at Sound City Studios (where the band had recorded their previous album, in November and December). Fleetwood Mac reunited with Keith Olsen, who was entrusted with the role of mixing engineer. Even at this stage, last-minute additions were made to certain songs, including "The Chain," "Don't Stop," "Gold Dust Woman," and "Dreams." In the end, the usual process of creating a record (recording, overdubs, editing, mixing, mastering) was not respected at all. The various stages were totally blurred and mixed up, to the point where it became very difficult for even the band and crew to document the chronology of the different interventions on each track.

Consultations continued after mixing to determine the most coherent order in which the songs should appear in the track list. Although decisive, this phase was not the most complicated, but it still became a phenomenal headache. Should there be a ballad after "Go Your Own Way" or not? Is "Don't Stop" in the right place? Does the album really flow? Everything had to be perfect. Every second of the record.

Before the finishing line, the album's title was changed from *Yesterday's Gone* to *Rumours*, based on an idea by John McVie. This was his way of poking fun at the gossip that had fueled the music industry for many months about Fleetwood Mac. Some of this gossip was completely far-fetched: Stevie Nicks was said to have left the Mac to indulge her true passion, black magic; everyone was sleeping with everyone else; the band was breaking up; over-consumption of drugs was crippling the band's productivity; Christine and Lindsey were leaving to form their own band...Tired of being questioned about the validity of this or that rumor, John came up with the perfect response with a fitting album title: *Rumours*. While it cannot be identified with any particular song, it perfectly captures the mood of the album.

The cover was also designed in November by Herbie Worthington, who had already worked on the previous album. The proofs arrived at the beginning of December, creating a new controversy within Mac. The best photo of the collection was obvious to everyone, but there was a problem: It did not include all the band's members. It was in fact an artistic extension of the previous album cover, at Mick's request, who wanted it to resemble a work of art. But it shows only the drummer and Stevie Nicks. She is wearing a black dress with trumpet sleeves, which she stages in an elegant dance movement, while Mick, holding her hand, stands in front of her, one foot on a small stool, two wooden spheres dangling from his belt. Lindsey expressed his disappointment at not being featured on his band's album cover. No matter how much Herbie explained that it was not a question of promoting one member over another, the guitarist was offended and held a long-standing grudge against the photographer. Ironically, the photo on the back of the album this time shows all the Mac members hugging and kissing, as if they no longer really knew who they were supposed to be with.

Timed to the Nearest Second

As 1976 drew to a close, work on the album came to a close. The mix was still being fine-tuned, song by song. Each one was listened to for six to eight hours, and everyone was given the chance to make final (but tiny) suggestions, whether on equalization, panning, or effects. The mix was not finished until everyone was happy. Between Tuesday, January 4, and Friday, January 7, 1977, pushing perfectionism to the limit, the band completed its almost yearlong adventure by choosing the number of seconds of silence to leave between each song...If the pause was too short, the transition would seem too abrupt and disrupt the flow. If it was too long, the listener's experience might be impaired. Each of the musicians left with a private copy of the album to listen to at home, and Stevie Nicks organized a big end-of-album party to let close friends hear it. The record would not be mastered for a few days, but already the guests were showing their enthusiasm by whistling and applauding.

Warner was thrilled with the result. The songs were powerful, the songwriting accomplished, and the arrangements meticulously crafted. Lindsey Buckingham's guitar playing, in particular, crystalized the band's demanding and audacious style: "On *Fleetwood Mac* he was more laid-back," explains Christine, "not so sure of himself, still very good. But on this album, his playing has come up much more forcefully. There's more power and dominance in the guitar and the aggressiveness of the guitar changes the characteristics of the songs."[5] Undoubtedly, Buckingham went far beyond his role as a musician, taking an active part in the production and arrangements, so much so that he would later declare "I can't figure out why I didn't ask for production credit."[60] A view shared by Dashut.

The Tidal Wave

The album was preceded by the release of the first single, "Go Your Own Way," which was an immediate radio hit. In the wake of this good start, record shops went into overdrive, preordering *Rumours* en masse in readiness for the official release on February 4, 1977. With eight hundred thousand albums, it was the biggest order ever

1977

John McVie, Christine McVie, Mick Fleetwood, Stevie Nicks, and Lindsey Buckingham at the Rock Music Awards ceremony in September 1976.

received by Warner for an album. Even before its release, *Rumours* seemed well on the way to dethroning its predecessor, the label's bestseller until then. And that was just the beginning…In the months that followed, *Rumours* established Fleetwood Mac at the top of the charts on both sides of the Atlantic. The album remained number one in the US for almost three years without interruption. In just a few days, 1 million albums were sold. By the end of the year, 7 million were sold in the US alone, and 2 million in the rest of the world. By 1980, worldwide sales had reached 13 million copies.

"In retrospect," Ken Caillat said later, "it's a miracle that we were able to finish *Rumours*. But later, I came to understand that *Rumours* probably succeeded because it was brilliant group therapy in which we all—wittingly or unwittingly—participated. It's possible that if it hadn't been for all of the sexual and relationship turmoil in the band, you wouldn't know this record any better than some of the previous Fleetwood Mac records."[78] Indeed, with *Rumours*, the band definitively changed gear: In people's minds, they were no longer that hard-working blues-rock outfit, but became a factory of pop-rock hits perfectly calibrated for radio.

During the promotional *Rumours* Tour (February 24, 1977, to August 24, 1978), Fleetwood Mac's outrageousness took hold, and they opted for out-of-control pomp. The musicians definitely abandoned old station wagons for private jets and black limousines, obviously filled with industrial-size quantities of cocaine. Mick Fleetwood and, above all, Stevie Nicks would be the two main cocaine users over the next few years. A turning point in Fleetwood Mac's career, *Rumours* took a whole year of hard work, constant tension, and numerous studios to complete, and cost just over a million dollars.

But on May 21, 1977, when the album ousted the Eagles' *Hotel California* from the top spot on the Billboard charts, none of this mattered. For the general public, *Rumours* had become an optimistic post-hippie fantasy, the hope that these civilized adults could be kind in sorrow and even empathetic, building a new community out of the ashes of the old. Yet Fleetwood Mac's art of psychological torture would soon resurface, and contrary to appearances, *Rumours*, a finely polished diamond with a thousand facets and shining in any light, would have nothing of a happy ending where everyone ended up becoming friends after the ordeals. On the contrary, this diary of a series of acrimonious breakups, all occurring just as the band was about to really take off, foreshadowed a future of struggles, betrayals, and new wars of egos.

KEN CAILLAT, SOUND COLORIST

Ken Caillat came very close to turning down the offer that would open the door to the production of *Rumours*, which would become the ninth best-selling rock album of all time. At the time, Ken was a sound engineer at Wally Heider Studios in Hollywood. The twenty-nine-year-old San José native (born Kenneth Douglas Caillat on August 12, 1946) had been working there for five years and was beginning to enjoy a certain reputation in the business. He was known for being a workaholic, a trait inherited from his father, a NASA engineer. His father instilled in him from an early age that nothing is impossible for the Caillats, once they set their minds to it.

The Choice of Music

"When I was in college, I'd considered becoming a psychiatrist," he explains in his 2012 book devoted to the making of *Rumours*, "so I called a couple of prominent shrinks in the San Jose area and asked whether I could talk to them about their career choice. One of them said to me, 'You hear other people's problems all day long, and you have to be careful to let it go at night, or else it will stay with you and build up inside you. And that can destroy you.' That was all I needed to hear. I immediately looked for a career that would lift people up, something positive. So I chose a career in music."[78] With this decision made, Ken Caillat headed for Los Angeles, scouring recording studios and labels for a job. He imagined that if he got a foothold in the business, he would be able to use the facilities for his personal projects and record his demos, as he played guitar and composed his own songs.

In 1971, he walked through the door of Wally Heider Studios, renowned for the quality of its live recordings. He was welcomed by the owner, Wally Heider himself, a truculent, paternalistic character who was immediately attracted by the young man's profile and hired him. Over the next few years, Ken worked as a sound engineer with the 5th Dimension ("Living Together, Growing Together," 1973), George Carlin (*Occupation: Foole*, 1973), and Joni Mitchell

(*Miles of Aisles*, 1974). "With Crosby and Nash, I learned what the brilliance of production and artistry can do," Ken Caillat explained in 2013. "With Joni, I learned that if I was given the perfect set of colors, I could paint a masterpiece."[78] For Paul McCartney and Wings, he had the opportunity to record a string section on the album *Venus and Mars* (1975).

When Destiny Calls

On January 15, 1976, Ken Caillat received a phone call from the manager of Wally Heider Studios, informing him that Fleetwood Mac had booked the premises for the mixing of a one-hour live performance by the band on DIR Radio Network's *King Biscuit Flower Hour* broadcast. Caillat, who knew nothing about the band, was reluctant to take on the project, but two of his fellow sound engineers, more familiar with the Mac's reputation, told him it would be madness to turn down such an opportunity. The sound engineer agreed and bought their then-latest album: *Fleetwood Mac*. He was won over by the sophisticated pop he discovered— just as he was by Richard Dashut, the second sound engineer on the *Buckingham Nicks* album, who had been asked by Fleetwood Mac to assist Caillat with the *King Biscuit* mixing session.

Dashut arrived with the tapes under his arm, and the two men set to work. A solid bond of cooperation developed between them during the session. When the musicians joined them, the work was already well underway, and he was immediately praised by the whole band. Stevie Nicks danced on "Rhiannon"—the best indicator that the result was pleasing. She has already forgotten Caillat's inaugural blunder—during their introductions, he called her "Lindsey," misled by the androgynous first names of the two new band members. At the end of the recording session, Mick Fleetwood walked up to Caillat and told him that he would have loved to call on him for their next record, but that they had already hired Record Plant Studios sound engineer Kelly Kotera. Ken, who was less

Ken Caillat, catapulted at a very young age in the role of engineer and co-producer of *Rumours*, one of the ten best-selling albums of all time, recounted this formative experience in a book published in 2012.

experienced, understood perfectly, but appreciated Mick's consideration.

The day after mixing was completed, Ken received a phone call from his new friend, Richard Dashut. Dashut has just been promoted to producer on *Rumours* following Kelly Kotera's dismissal after a very messy first day of recording. Dashut asked Caillat to join the team as sound engineer. The young man's blood ran cold. He was not given to jumping in headlong, but he felt he could not let this offer pass him by. With Wally Heider Studios off his back, he jumped behind the wheel of his car, put his dog Scooter on the passenger seat, and headed toward his destiny.

A Winning Duo

The Dashut-Caillat duo worked perfectly. Fully committed, both men stayed with the musicians in the rented house in the hills adjacent to the studios throughout the sessions. Caillat managed to make the most of the equipment at his disposal, mastering the API mixing console with 550A equalizers to give color to the takes, which were a little dull for his taste due to too much sound insulation in the recording room. He was promoted to co-producer during the recording process. When tape problems arose, Caillat and Dashut opted to handle the overdubbing and mixing themselves. Their work was rewarded in 1978 with the most coveted Grammy Award: Best Album of the Year. The quality of the production, the clarity of the melodies, the care given to each instrument, the magnificence of the vocal harmonies…Their work became a benchmark for many professionals at the time.

The collaboration with Fleetwood Mac naturally continued on *Tusk* (1979), the album that divided fans for its experimental dimension. But no one would question Caillat's exemplary production. He lavished the album with a full, refined sound, delicate treble management, deep bass, and clean drum strokes…Meanwhile, via the Mac, he assisted Bob Welch with the conception of *French Kiss*, his

1977 solo album. In 1980, he proved his skills for the band on the live circuit with *Fleetwood Mac Live*, and two years later was back in the studio with them for *Mirage*.

Ken Caillat's name became synonymous with success, and the biggest stars sought his services. He was involved in the sound effects for "Dancing on the Ceiling," the title track of Lionel Richie's 1986 album. Then he hit the big time when he was recruited as sound engineer on Michael Jackson's multi-million-selling *Bad* album, released in 1987.

In the late 1990s, Ken Caillat launched his own company, 5.1 Entertainment Group, which specialized in surround-sound management. The company worked on numerous star projects, from Alice Cooper to Billy Idol to Sting. In 2012, Caillat published a book, *Making "Rumours": The Inside Story of the Classic Fleetwood Mac Album*, a memoir of his experience during the recording of the legendary album. The following year, he diversified his activities and launched the Sleeping Giant Records label (which he sold in 2018). In 2016, as custodian of the memory of the Record Plant studios in Sausalito, he invested financially in the restoration of the premises.

RICHARD DASHUT, "THE RIGHT MAN FOR THE JOB"

"Looks like you'll be in charge of our next record," Mick Fleetwood told Richard Dashut after he pulled him aside in the Record Plant parking lot at the end of January 1976. The ground was now shifting beneath the feet of the twenty-five-year-old technician whose experience was, at this stage, virtually nonexistent—apart from a role as assistant sound engineer on Lambert and Nuttycombe's *As You Will* (1973) and as second sound engineer to Keith Olsen on Buckingham Nicks's first opus a few months earlier. "Three years ago, I was cleaning toilets," Richard Dashut retorted in a panic. "I can't do this by myself!" But a determined Mick Fleetwood would not take no for an answer, having already told him, "You're the right man for the job."[78]

From the Studio Floor to the Top of the World

This unexpected appointment was like a poisoned chalice for Dashut, who had to replace Kelly Kotera at a moment's notice. Kotera, the Record Plant's in-house producer, was initially recruited to record *Rumours*. But Kotera, as experienced as he was, had lost his nerve and his job—in just twenty-four hours—thanks to the new API mixing console he was unable to tame. As usual in such circumstances, Mick took matters into his own hands in the face of urgency and made the most unlikely of choices—just as he did when he recruited Stevie Nicks and Lindsey Buckingham without auditioning them—entrusting the album to a man more experienced in handling mops than mixing consoles.

Indeed, Richard Dashut (born September 19, 1951) had indeed started out a few years earlier as a cleaner at Sound City Studios in Los Angeles, where he met producer Keith Olsen and the Buckingham Nicks duo, who gave him his first steps as a sound engineer. But it has to be said that Mick hits the nail on the head every time, and it is hard to tell whether he has sheer good luck or an incredible flair.

With Mick Fleetwood leaving him little choice, Richard Dashut agreed to be catapulted into the producer's chair, on one condition: He would have Ken Caillat with him, the sound engineer he had met while mixing a live session for a national broadcast. The two men had become such good friends behind the console at Wally Heider Studios that Richard could think of no better recruit to help him with this titanic task. In addition to his friendship, he knew that Ken's strong point was his knowledge of microphones. Ken was unsurpassed when it came to finding the best placement or selecting the best equipment to achieve the desired sound.

The two men complemented each other perfectly. Dashut's work was empirical and intuitive, relying largely on his sensitivity, while Ken's was based on a more

Richard Dashut (far left) was a simple maintenance technician at Sound City studio, but he went on to co-produce an album that would sell nearly 40 million copies.

technical knowledge. The result was a sound of exemplary cleanliness and clarity.

Accepting responsibilities that would have frightened a more seasoned producer, Richard Dashut rose to the challenge beyond imagination, winning (with Ken Caillat) the Grammy Award for Best Album of the Year for *Rumours* in 1977.

A Member of the Family

"Dick Dash" (Mr. Clean), as Dashut was known at the time, became a full member of the extended Fleetwood Mac team, with whom he spent almost his entire career, becoming the band's regular producer and sound engineer until 1995. The year *Rumours* was released, he took part as sound engineer in the recording of "Sentimental

Lady," included on Bob Welch's *French Kiss* album. Before tackling the monumental *Tusk*, he assisted Walter Egan on *Not Shy* in 1978, under the orders of Lindsey Buckingham, who produced the album. The following year, he accompanied Mick, Lindsey, and John on the recording of "Rock Sugar," a track from *Uprooted*, Rob Grill's solo album. He also produced Bob Welch's new opus, *Three Hearts*. He had his first major live experience with *Fleetwood Mac Live* in 1980, and in the following years produced the various members of the Mac in their solo adventures: Lindsey on *Law and Order* (1981), "Holiday Road" (1983), "Time Bomb Town" (1985), and *Out of the Cradle* (1992); Mick Fleetwood on *The Visitor* (1981) and *I'm Not Me* (1983); and Christine McVie on "Can't Help Falling in Love" (1986).

Dashut took part in the *Mirage* adventure alongside his friend Ken Caillat in 1982. Then he moved to the other side of the studio glass, co-writing *Book of Love, Empire State,* and *Oh Diane* with Lindsey Buckingham. The singer-songwriter's trust in Lindsey continued on 1987's *Tango in the Night*, as the two men formed a new production duo in Ken Caillat's absence. He even extended his influence a little further, by coming up with the concept for the album cover. The band entrusted him with the reins one last time, on *Time* (1995). Having left the Fleetwood Mac fold, he gradually withdrew from music, appearing only in the credits of experimental duo Rambient's "So Many Worlds" in 2001. His choice confirms the loyalty of a man who knew he owed his career to Fleetwood Mac and wished to devote his life to it.

SECOND HAND NEWS
Lindsey Buckingham / 2:43

Musicians
Lindsey Buckingham: vocals, guitars, percussion, toms
Christine McVie: keyboards, backing vocals
John McVie: bass
Mick Fleetwood: drums, percussion, marching drum
Stevie Nicks: vocals

Recorded
Record Plant Studios, Sausalito: January 27–April 10, 1976
Wally Heider Studios, Hollywood: May 14–mid-June 1976, August 4–22, 1976, October 1976
Criteria Studios, Miami: July 5–11, 1976
Davlen Sound Studios, Hollywood: September 1976
Record Plant, Los Angeles: November 1976

Technical Team
Producers: Fleetwood Mac, Ken Caillat, Richard Dashut
Sound Engineers: Ken Caillat, Richard Dashut
Assistant Sound Engineer: Chris Morris

When Lindsey Buckingham drew inspiration from the Bee Gees for the rhythmic aspect of "Second Hand News," he probably didn't imagine that *Rumours* would overtake *Saturday Night Fever* among the best-selling albums in history.

FOR MAC-ADDICTS
The upbeat, energetic tone of "Second Hand News" earned it a special place in Fleetwood Mac's stage set. With more than six hundred appearances in their shows over the years, it is naturally one of their most-played songs.

Genesis and Lyrics
Was it Lindsey Buckingham's intention to play it cool, or was it to save Stevie Nicks from the acid rain that was about to descend on her when she read the "Second Hand News" lyrics? Whatever the case, the songwriter, aware of the potential crisis that would ensue from his violent attack on his musical and romantic partner, initially chose to present the piece to the rest of the band as an instrumental. At this stage, it was called "Strummer." But it was clear that Buckingham already had a vocal line and lyrical framework in mind. This is evidenced by one of the very first takes, included in 2013 on CD 4 of the deluxe version of the *Rumours* album. The musician performs it on an acoustic guitar at a high tempo. He is accompanied only by Christine McVie, who recorded several tracks of keyboards to accompany the melody. The singer mumbles familiar endings to phrases like "nothin' on you."

When he finally gave the lyrics their final shape and delivered the song to Steve Nicks, who was to accompany him vocally on the verse, she found it hard to take. She remained silent, but her livid complexion spoke volumes about the violence of the affront. This was a cruel situation for the young woman, who had to take it upon herself to sing this violent message addressed to her.

The first words formalized the separation, even though no one had any doubts about it. (During the stay, Lindsey took solace in the arms of Christina Conte, a young woman he met in a bar, and Nicks is said to have started dating Eagles drummer and singer Don Henley.)

Settling Scores
Lindsey points the finger of blame at Stevie: "Someone has taken my place." He then blows hot and cold, immediately following up with an indecent proposal: to have a good time together in the tall grass, and too bad if there are no more feelings…The real clarification comes in the third verse: "I ain't gonna miss you when you go / Been down so long / I've been tossed around enough." The lyricist finishes off his victim by asking her to leave him alone to go about his business—by which he means music. He targets a reproach often made by Stevie Nicks, who resented Lindsey for putting his music ("my stuff") ahead of everything else.

A kind of coolness coupled with condescension emanates from this song, tasting like Buckingham's perverse victory over Nicks. "We were all trying to break up and when you break up with someone you don't want to see him," explains Stevie Nicks, who in a way legitimizes her former lover's gall. "You especially don't want to eat breakfast with him the next morning, see him all day and all night, and all day the day after…"[87]

Production

In 1976, the world was still under the spell of the disco wave that had broken the previous year with the soundtrack to *Saturday Night Fever*, largely provided by the Bee Gees. More than the eponymous hit, Lindsey Buckingham could not get over the groove of "Jive Talkin'" (by the Gibb brothers), and in particular the mutated guitar rhythm that gave the melody an edgy, jubilant quality. Listening to the track, he realized that this was the key element missing from the future "Second Hand News" to make it more seductive. "I think we had a working title of 'Strummer,'" said Lindsey Buckingham. "I think because it did start off as a kind of a strummy, acoustic feel. But I think the intent for that song was to be kind of a dance beat."[96] Lindsey therefore set about injecting this form of disco groove into his composition. The result is convincing, but he wanted to push the

percussive aspect even further. The trouble was that Mick Fleetwood was not at ease on this track and did not manage to translate musically what Lindsey Buckingham had in mind. "Mick's first inclination of the drum feel was to go more folky," recalled the guitarist and composer. "He had kind of a press role [*sic*], a loose pattern, an Irish approach, which was a more literal approach of what the song really was and what it was giving off in its initial stages. It had quite a few interesting textures on it. A lot of people remarked on the snare sound [in the final version], which was kind of ringy and thin. It wasn't exactly what was considered state of the art and it was kind of retro…and that was cool."[96]

But that was not enough. Lindsey then had a bright idea: He spotted a chair made of Naugahyde (an artificial leather) in the studio and played the rhythm on it. The dull sound was just what he had in mind. His annexation of the rhythmic terrain did not stop there. Unhappy with the bass line recorded by John McVie, the guitarist took advantage of a day when his partner was away to play it his own way. He opted for a very simple, direct, unadorned phrasing. John could very well have played it, but Lindsey Buckingham is never better served than by himself. He delivered the song just as he had imagined it, a lively, danceable, catchy opener.

DREAMS
Stevie Nicks / 4:14

Musicians
Stevie Nicks: vocals, backing vocals
Lindsey Buckingham: guitars, backing vocals
Christine McVie: keyboards, vibraphone, backing vocals
John McVie: bass
Mick Fleetwood: drums, percussion

Recorded
Record Plant, Sausalito: January 27–April 10, 1976
Wally Heider Studios, Hollywood: May 14–mid-June, 1976, August 4–22, 1976, October 1976
Criteria Studios, Miami: July 5–11, 1976
Davlen Sound Studios, Hollywood: September 1976
Record Plant, Los Angeles: November 1976

Technical Team
Producers: Fleetwood Mac, Ken Caillat, Richard Dashut
Sound Engineers: Ken Caillat, Richard Dashut
Assistant Sound Engineer: Chris Morris

Single
Side A: Dreams / **Side B:** Songbird
UK Release Date: March 1977
Reference: Warner Bros. Records (45 rpm ref.: K 16969)
Best UK Chart Ranking: 24
US Release Date: March 1977
Reference: Warner Bros. Records (45 rpm ref.: WBS 8371)
Best US Chart Ranking: 1

Stevie Nicks and Lindsey Buckingham onstage in May 1977. "Dreams" is the band's only number one single and its second-most-played live track, behind "Rhiannon."

Genesis and Lyrics

One afternoon, toward the end of the first recording sessions in Sausalito, Stevie Nicks decided to isolate herself to work on a melody that had been in her head for a while. She disappeared into a small room at the Record Plant nicknamed "the Pit," where she used to hide when she had nothing to record. In fact, it was a former 140-square-foot office that had been transformed into a studio at the request of Sly Stone, the funk star and Sausalito regular. The sound engineer's console and controls were located directly in the building's foundations, almost ten feet below ground level, surrounded on all sides by small spaces for the musicians. The floor—but also the walls, the ceiling, and the small staircase—were covered with a soft-looking, predominantly red, fur-like covering. "It was a black-and-red room, with a sunken pit in the middle where there was a piano, and a big black-velvet bed with Victorian drapes,"[83] Stevie recalled.

The singer settled in with her Fender Rhodes and a cassette player. She quickly found a rudimentary drum pattern and pressed the Record button. In the space of ten minutes, Stevie composed "Dreams." Aware that there was something special about the song, the young woman joined the rest of the team in the main studio, eager to have the fruits of her labor heard: "I knew when I wrote it that it was really special. I was really not self-conscious or insecure about showing it to the rest of the band."[84]

Her partners were not initially enthusiastic. "I think Stevie had the capability just to play the chords that make her happy, that make her sing,"[85] Christine McVie explained in an interview with *Rolling Stone* in 2012. She added: "She comes in with her passion and her melody and puts her basic chords on it, and Lindsay has this phenomenal understanding of what she means…and I don't. She comes to me with a song and I go, 'I don't know what the fuck you mean.' You know? I don't get that at all. But Lindsey does. Like 'Dreams,' for example, sounded like the most simplistic thing in the world. She played it to me when we were doing the *Rumours* album, and I said to her, 'This is boring, this is really boring.' And she said, 'No, I only made three segments out of two chords…' and it was the only Number One hit single we ever had! There's two chords!"[85]

Once Stevie had composed the songs, "it would be Lindsey that comes in and translates her songs into chords. Then he comes to me, and he and I would work together. 'Cause he and I have a fantastic musical connection. Chemistry, as well. It's a different kind of chemistry from Stevie and Lindsey."[85]

One of the components of the song is its ambiguity: Are the reproaches expressed by Stevie Nicks in the lyrics, amid a sea of anger and sorrow, addressed to herself or to someone else? The latter seems the more likely scenario. Indeed, if *Rumours* is the diary of the ends of love affairs within Fleetwood Mac, then "Dreams" is unquestionably one of its most beautiful chapters. From the very first words of the song, Stevie Nicks seems to be responding directly to one of the first songs worked on in Sausalito, Lindsey Buckingham's "Go Your Own Way": "Now here you go again / You say you want your freedom / Well, who am I to keep you down?" Similarly, Stevie's repeated warnings about going mad from loneliness are obviously addressed to Lindsey: "But listen carefully to the sound / Of your loneliness / Like a heartbeat…drives you mad / In the stillness of remembering what you had." Stevie would

later say that she wished their breakup had been less acrimonious: "I told him that, in my heart, 'Dreams' was open and hopeful, but in 'Go Your Own Way,' his heart was closed. That's how I felt. That line, 'When the rain washes you clean,' to me that was like being able to start again, and that's what I wanted [for] Lindsey. I wanted him to be happy."[83]

Production

Along with Stevie Nicks, Lindsey Buckingham is the other man behind the success of "Dreams," a track on which he gives one of his finest guitar performances for Fleetwood Mac. He creates a splendid, meticulous accompaniment using a volume pedal, giving his playing a kind of nonchalance. His guitar part is the perfect complement to Nicks's narrative. Initially, Lindsey was not entirely satisfied with his performance. His first takes were done with a very clean sound, and he felt that there was not enough difference between the verses and the choruses, for which he was looking for a catchier sound. He spent several hours with Ken Caillat at the controls before achieving a satisfactory result. The entire track is based on just three

FOR MAC-ADDICTS

The word *dreams* appears only three times in the lyrics: "It's only me / Who wants to wrap around your dreams and… / Have you any dreams you'd like to sell? / Dreams of loneliness…"

An unexpected viral video released in 2020 sparked a resurgence of interest in "Dreams," returning it to the charts (number twelve in the US). An illustrious unknown by the name of Nathan Apodaca filmed himself skateboarding in the middle of traffic while sipping a bottle of fruit juice and singing the Fleetwood Mac track. As a nod of recognition, Stevie, Mick, and Lindsey each reproduced the video in their own way.

1977

chords. It features a warm acoustic guitar and John McVie's deep, steady bass throughout. On drums, Mick Fleetwood delivers a solid groove enriched by a few congas, while Christine elegantly dresses up the arrangement with discreet but essential keyboards whose sounds she mixes: the emblematic Hammond organ and the famous Fender Rhodes.

But while the song's structure gives the impression of flowing seamlessly, it was in fact the subject of some serious reworking by Lindsey Buckingham. Christine McVie recalls: "The Lindsey genius came into play and he fashioned three sections out of identical chords, making each section sound completely different. He created the impression that there's a thread running through the whole thing."[83]

Stevie's vocal performance is also one of the key cogs in the song's success. One of her first takes was preserved (along with the drums), despite the countless overdubs she subsequently made for *Rumours*. Ken Caillat recalls: "She did this one vocal take and she was just so inspired that there was a part of that take that she could never repeat later. We tried maybe 25 times to go back and re-record it but there was one part that she could just never do better

than she had already done the first time. I don't know what that says, but it shows you there's something about people—they get so inspired and are so moved, it's beautiful. As a producer, you need to realize that you're in that position of creating something from a performance."[80] Stevie, on the other hand, kept redoing her backing vocals on the song, from month to month, from studio to studio, and she didn't put the finishing touches to it until October 1976.

Despite its instant effectiveness, "Dreams" initially struggled to convince critics such as *Rolling Stone*'s John Swenson, whose pen proved as incisive as it was short-sighted: "But Nicks has nothing on *Rumours* to compare with 'Rhiannon,' her smash from the last album. 'Dreams' is a nice but fairly lightweight tune, and her nasal singing is the only weak vocal on the record."[86]

Incredible as it may seem considering the success of *Rumours*, "Dreams" is the only Fleetwood Mac single to have reached number one in the charts. Indeed, the song reached number one in the United States and Canada, and was in the top 40 in other countries, including England (number twenty-four), Australia (number four), New Zealand (number six), Ireland (number twenty-three), and the Netherlands (number eight).

NEVER GOING BACK AGAIN

Lindsey Buckingham / 2:02

Musicians
Lindsey Buckingham: vocals, guitar
Recorded
Sound City Studios, Van Nuys, California: November 1976

Technical Team
Producers: Fleetwood Mac, Ken Caillat, Richard Dashut
Sound Engineers: Ken Caillat, Richard Dashut
Assistant Sound Engineer: Chris Morris

Single
Side A: You Make Loving Fun / Side B: Never Going Back Again
UK Release Date: September 30, 1977
Reference: Warner Bros. Records (45 rpm ref.: K 17013)
Best UK Chart Ranking: 45

Single
Side A: Don't Stop / Side B: Never Going Back Again
US Release Date: July 6, 1977
Reference: Warner Bros. Records (45 rpm ref.: WBS 8413)
Best US Chart Ranking: 3

Bassist Brian Yale and his bandmates in Matchbox Twenty delivered a stunning reworking of "Never Going Back Again" in 1998.

Genesis and Lyrics

"Never Going Back Again" is a graceful, light-hearted interlude that gives the album a breath of fresh air...more so than for Lindsey Buckingham and Ken Caillat, who exhausted themselves trying to achieve the brightest possible sound on this frugal piece of instrumentation that, in theory, should not have required much time. Written on the road during the summer of 1976—after the band had left the Sausalito studios for a few tour dates (May 1 to August 30)—"Never Going Back Again" features Lindsey Buckingham alone in a tête-à-tête with his acoustic guitar and his thoughts, directed toward a young woman he had briefly known: "It was written about a girl that I had met in New England and spent a very short amount of time with."[96] At least, this is what he says, although it is possible that it could also have been Stevie. In these lapidary lyrics, Lindsey recalls the ephemerality of their feelings and sealing the end of their relationship with a laconic "I'm never going back again."

To protect Stevie Nicks from his trenchant words, Lindsey initially deliberately concealed the lyrics of "Never Going Back Again," making the song seem to be an instrumental. This was how it came to be known as "Brushes," after the initial contribution of Mick Fleetwood and his brushes. The discovery of the content when the vocals were recorded was all the more painful for the musician.

Production

One of the last songs composed for *Rumours*, "Never Going Back Again" was originally intended to be more substantial. "It did go through its own evolution of trying other things," Lindsey testified. "I think the initial attempt was going to be a more orchestral approach, a more layered approach."[96] One of the initial versions, included on the deluxe version of *Rumours*—released in 2013 for the thirty-fifth anniversary of the album's initial release—attests to the intention to have more substantial instrumentation. Mick Fleetwood was to play his snare drum, but with brushes to preserve the delicacy of the track. This working version also featured a long introduction that Buckingham had sprinkled with refined harmonics, a passage that was eventually deleted, as the guitarist was not convinced by the addition. Preferring a more raw approach, Lindsey started the song directly with an enchanting Travis picking on acoustic

1977

Lindsey Buckingham, backstage with John McVie, warming up a few minutes before going on stage, July 1977.

guitar. This fingerpicking technique (Lindsey rarely uses a plectrum) owes its name to Merle Travis, the first musician to popularize this style based on alternating bass notes and syncopated rhythm. But this picking posed serious difficulties. After a few takes, Ken Caillat realized that Lindsey's guitar was losing its brilliance. As much a perfectionist as the musician himself, the sound engineer demanded that the strings should be changed three times an hour, throughout the recording day. "I'm sure the roadies wanted to kill me. Restringing the guitar three times every hour was a bitch. But Lindsey had lots of parts on the song, and each one sounded magnificent."[88] When Ken and Lindsey finally got the takes they wanted (two guitar takes, one on the left of the mix, the other on the right), the latter started on the vocal parts. But he was horrified to discover that his guitar part was not in the right key, and he was forced to rerecord it entirely.

"In the end his vocal didn't quite match the guitar tracks," confirmed Chris Morris, the assistant sound engineer, "so we had to slow them down a little."[109] And change the key of the instrument if his voice could not be changed. The guitar is therefore tuned in drop D (an open chord in which the key of the first string is lowered to D instead of E), with a capo placed on the fourth fret.

Matchbox Twenty contributed to the tribute album *Legacy: A Tribute to Fleetwood Mac's "Rumours"* (1998) with a new version of "Never Going Back Again." The track is oppressed by an ominous bass for a result that flirts with postgrunge.

DON'T STOP

Christine McVie / 3:11

Musicians
Lindsey Buckingham: vocals, guitars
Christine McVie: vocals, piano, keyboards
Mick Fleetwood: drums
John McVie: bass
Stevie Nicks: tambourine, backing vocals

Recorded
Record Plant Studios, Sausalito: January 27–April 10, 1976
Wally Heider Studios, Hollywood: May 14–mid-June 1976;
  August 4–22; 1976, October 1976
Criteria Studios, Miami: July 5–11, 1976
Davlen Sound Studios, Hollywood: September 1976
Record Plant Studios, Los Angeles: November 1976

Technical Team
Producers: Fleetwood Mac, Ken Caillat, Richard Dashut
Sound Engineers: Ken Caillat, Richard Dashut
Assistant Sound Engineer: Chris Morris

Single
Side A: Don't Stop / Side B: Gold Dust Woman
UK Release: April 1, 1977, with Warner Bros. Records (ref. K 16930)
Best UK Chart Ranking: 32

Single
Side A: Don't Stop / Side B: Never Going Back Again
US Release: July 6, 1977, with Warner Bros. Records (ref. WBS 8413)
Best US Chart Ranking: 3

Christine McVie and Lindsey Buckingham sing the chorus of "Don't Stop" in unison, giving it a unifying dimension.

Genesis and Lyrics

If we are to believe his statements, John McVie was unaware that "Don't Stop" had been written by Christine for him. "I never put that together," he said. "I've been playing it for years, and it wasn't until someone told me, 'Chris wrote that about you.' Oh, really?"[88] Yet it was hard for him to ignore it. In his autobiography, Mick Fleetwood gives John a contradictory account: "I'd be sitting there in the studio while they were mixing 'Don't Stop,' and I'd listen to the words which were mostly about me, and I'd get a lump in my throat. I'd turn around and the writer's sitting right there."[4] The lyrics of "Don't Stop" are explicit, and have all the makings of sunny, optimistic advice from Christine to John at the end of their marriage. They also reflect her own happiness, as she is currently dating the band's lighting director, Curry Grant: "All I want is to see you smile / If it takes just a little while / I know you don't believe that it's true / I never meant any harm to you."

"Don't Stop" can also be interpreted as a call to the band to keep its unity and look to the future after going through so many difficult moments. This is supported by Christine herself when she declares: "It just seemed to be a pleasant revelation to have that 'yesterday's gone.' It might have, I guess, been directed more toward John, but I'm just definitely not a pessimist."[88]

Production

The expressive piano, biting guitars, and solid drums are the main markers of this intense rock sound, built on a blues shuffle, which immediately gets the toes tapping while disseminating an optimistic feeling. Basically, on a shuffle, the hi-hat has the feel of a triplet, and the bass drum and snare drum are activated on beats 1 and 3. This makes the hi-hat sound faster, while the rest of the drums play at mid-tempo. This is known as a half-time shuffle.

The song was originally called "Yesterday's Gone," but after a few weeks of hearing Christine and Lindsey sing the chorus together, everyone started calling it "Don't Stop." And while the original plan was for Christine to sing alone, Lindsey's insistence prompted them to share the lead.

Fleetwood Mac onstage at the Oakland Coliseum in 1977.

The vocals are therefore split between Christine McVie and Lindsey Buckingham, who each take a verse and share a wickedly catchy chorus. Buckingham delivers a lovely, understated solo in the middle of the song.

The arrangement is full of little tricks, like the sudden stop near the end of the song (at 2:16), the repeated guitar notes, and the honky-tonk piano, which makes its presence felt without ever overdoing it. From 2:42 onward, light backing vocals add an airy touch to the finale, which concludes with a final piece of advice, repeated until it wears thin: "Ooh, don't you look back." Without doubt, "Don't Stop" liberated Christine McVie's songwriting, as Ken Caillat recognized: "On 'Don't Stop,' I could really see that everyone in the band was starting to collaborate and work together [...] everyone had an unswerving faith in Lindsey's visionary ideas and production sense. Lindsey, in turn, knew that he could push the other members of the band to give their best; not just Stevie, but also Christine. After six years of being in a blues band, Christine felt liberated by

the band's shift to a more pop sound. That better suited her songwriting style."[78]

The third single from the album, the song reached number three on the Billboard singles chart, and became one of Fleetwood Mac's most enduring hits. It enjoyed a resurgence in popularity when it was used by US presidential candidate Bill Clinton for his first campaign.

FOR MAC-ADDICTS

After winning the election, President Clinton managed to persuade the band, at that time separated, to re-form and perform the song on stage at his inaugural gala in 1993.

GO YOUR OWN WAY

Lindsey Buckingham / 3:38

Musicians
Lindsey Buckingham: vocals, guitar, backing vocals
Christine McVie: keyboards, backing vocals
John McVie: bass
Mick Fleetwood: drums, percussion
Stevie Nicks: backing vocals

Recorded
Record Plant Studios, Sausalito: February 4–April 10, 1976
Wally Heider Studios, Hollywood: May 14–mid-June 1976;
   August 4–22, 1976; October 1976
Criteria Studios, Miami: July 5–11, 1976
Davlen Sound Studios, Hollywood: September 1976
Record Plant Studios, Los Angeles: November 1976

Technical Team
Producers: Fleetwood Mac, Ken Caillat, Richard Dashut
Sound Engineers: Ken Caillat, Richard Dashut
Assistant Sound Engineer: Chris Morris

Single
Side A: Go Your Own Way / Side B: Silver Springs
US Release: December 20, 1976, with Warner Bros. Records
   (ref. WBS 8304)
Best US Chart Ranking: 10

Single
Side A: The Chain / Side B: Go Your Own Way
UK Release: February 4, 1977, with Warner Bros. Records
   (ref. SAM 361)
Best UK Chart Ranking: Did Not Chart

Single
Side A: Go Your Own Way / Side B: Silver Springs
UK Release: February 11, 1977, with Warner Bros. Records
   (ref. K16872)
Best UK Chart Ranking: 38

Genesis and Lyrics

During the tour preceding the recording of *Rumours* (October 27–November 11, 1975), the band rented a house in Florida to compose new songs before hitting the road again. But the musicians were not in good spirits. The atmosphere was deleterious. Each of them was turning over a new leaf in their love lives. Christine, who was having an affair with lighting director Curry Grant, was no longer keeping a low profile, which irritated the rest of the band and sent John into a tailspin. The situation cost Grant his job, even though he was one of the best professionals on the circuit. As a result, Christine had a grudge against John, who left their Malibu home as soon as the tour was over.

It was during this decisive stage in Florida that Lindsey Buckingham wrote "Go Your Own Way" for Stevie Nicks. One night, he grabbed a guitar and spontaneously sang the first words of the song to the stunned crowd: "Loving you / Isn't the right thing to do." The melody appealed to them enormously.

Three months later, on February 4, 1976, at the stroke of midday, the members of Fleetwood Mac entered the Record Plant, one after the other. Lindsey Buckingham and Richard Dashut had already discussed the cassette demo of "Go Your Own Way" that morning. Dashut could not hide his enthusiasm. He shared this with everyone by playing the tape over the studio speakers for the others to enjoy. Despite the poor sound quality and incomplete lyrics, everyone agreed on the potential of this composition. John McVie was the first to take the plunge. He asked Lindsey to pick up an acoustic guitar while he grabbed his Fender Bassman. Immediately, Buckingham's fingers came to life and sketched out a country-tinged score. It was too overloaded to be kept. But the melody was inspiring.

Behind the facade of smiles, heavy resentments began plaguing the band members, particularly Lindsey and Stevie, which fed into the writing of "Go Your Own Way."

"Play Like an Animal"

The other members settled in, Christine behind her Hammond organ, Mick behind his Ludwig kit. Lindsey finally opted for an electric, a 1959 Fender Stratocaster. He showed the others the structure of the song, then gave Mick a few personalized pointers as an aside. The drums were to be the keystone of the song's dynamics. The guitarist expected his partner to play a tribal rhythm, ideally on the toms, in the manner of the Rolling Stones' "Street Fighting Man." Ken Caillat remembers: "The right drum approach was crucial. One day, Lindsey came in and said he heard 'Street Fighting Man' by the Stones, and he thought that kind of feel would work well. I remember watching him guide Mick as to what he wanted—he'd be so animated, like a little kid, playing these air tom fills with his curly hair flying. Mick wasn't so sure he could do what Lindsey wanted, but he did a great job, and the song took off."[91] Before Mick recorded his part, Lindsey slipped him a hint: "Play like an animal." He wanted the listener to feel the anger that drives the text through his playing, which, even though it was not finished, would convey the deep resentment Lindsey harbored toward Stevie Nicks. In the end, Mick was unable to reproduce Charlie Watts's

pattern on "Street Fighting Man," but his own fit the spirit of the song very well and was retained.

In the lyrics, Lindsey poses as a victim, denouncing his love partner's lack of consideration: "If I could, maybe I'd give you my world / How can I / When you won't take it from me?" before following up with the killer line: "You can go your own way." But the final blow comes with the line: "Packing up / Shacking up is all you want to do." Stevie was mortified. She demanded, to no avail, that he retract the line: "I very, very much resented him telling the world that 'packing up, shacking up' with different men was all I wanted to do. He knew it wasn't true. It was just an angry thing that he said. Every time those words would come out onstage, I wanted to go over and kill him. He knew it, so he really pushed my buttons through that. It was like, 'I'll make you suffer for leaving me.' And I did."[89]

Production

The euphoria of the beginning gave way to weariness as the recording dragged on for four long months, necessitating visits to several studios, constant backtracking and rerecording during overdubs. By mid-November, everyone was back at square one, where it all began almost a year

Stevie Nicks develops a captivating stage presence, combining grace and mystery.

The drum pattern of "Go Your Own Way" was dictated to Mick by Lindsey, but the drummer had the opportunity to personalize the score by adding a few variations, notably on the toms.

earlier, at Wally Heider Studios, mixing the first mono and stereo versions of the future single "Go Your Own Way" and its Side B, "Silver Springs."

Electric and acoustic guitars finally coexist on the first part, developing the melody together right from the introduction. In a slightly nasal but powerful voice, Lindsey intones his lament, accompanied by the famous martial drum pattern that prepares the sonic explosion to come on the chorus. Mick Fleetwood provides his playing at the start of this segment, then Lindsey and Stevie's voices take off. In perfect harmony—at least musically—they let their anger explode on the end of phrases that the two performers drag out, accentuating the hymnal dimension of the chorus. On the dizzying finale, a guitar solo tears up the sound space. Although played by Lindsey Buckingham, it owes much to Ken Caillat. In the home stretch before the release of "Go Your Own Way" as a single, the sound engineer and producer is hard at work on his track, determined to resolve the final difficulties posed by this segment. Patiently and meticulously, he put together an original solo from scratch, based on numerous takes made by Buckingham. Thanks to Ken's magic, there is no trace of all this. To complete the piece's conclusion, Mick Fleetwood adds maracas and cymbals to give rhythmic depth to this sonic firework.

Entering at number seventy-one on the US Billboard charts on January 8, 1977, "Go Your Own Way" climbed steadily to its best-ever performance at number ten on March 12. In all, the single spent eleven weeks on the US charts. The following year, it earned Fleetwood Mac a Grammy nomination for Best Vocal Arrangement for Two or Three Voices. But the title eluded them and instead went to the Eagles' "New Kid in Town."

FOR MAC ADDICTS

In 1977, during the promotional tour for *Rumours*, Fleetwood Mac shared the bill with Boz Scaggs. Scaggs's drummer, Jeff Porcaro (later in Toto), was intrigued by Mick's unconventional playing on "Go Your Own Way." He asked him what he was playing on each bar. Mick explained that having suffered from dyslexia must have influenced his playing. Porcaro thought it was a joke, but Fleetwood was convinced that it was the secret of his unorthodox playing.

1977

SONGBIRD

Christine McVie / 3:20

Musicians
Christine McVie: vocals, keyboards
Lindsey Buckingham: guitar

Recorded
Zellerbach Auditorium, Berkeley: March 3–4, 1976

Technical Team
Producers: Fleetwood Mac, Ken Caillat, Richard Dashut
Sound Engineers: Ken Caillat, Richard Dashut
Assistant Sound Engineer: Chris Morris

Single
Side A: Dreams / Side B: Songbird
UK Release: March 1977, with Warner Bros. Records (ref. K 16969)
Best UK Chart Ranking: 24

Single
Side A: Dreams / Side B: Songbird
US Release: March 1977, with Warner Bros. Records (ref. WBS 8371)
Best US Chart Ranking: 1

Only Lindsey was authorized by Caillat, who wanted an intimate atmosphere, to play on "Songbird" alongside Christine.

Genesis and Lyrics

"I wrote [*Rumours* standout] 'Songbird' in half an hour," said Christine McVie in 2017. "I've never been able to figure out how I did that. I woke up in the middle of the night and the song was there in my brain, chords lyrics melody, everything. I played it in my bedroom and didn't have anything to tape it on. So I had to stay awake all night so I wouldn't forget it and I came in the next morning to the studio and had [producer] Ken Caillat put it on a 2-track. That was how the song ended up being. I don't know where that came from. I wished it would happen more often, but it hasn't. [laughs]"[90] The producer was immediately won over by the song and the intimacy of this first draft. He suggested that the musician should record it alone to emphasize the melodic power of the title and the subject matter—a pure, direct, authentic declaration of love. The contrast is striking with the song that precedes it on the track list, "Go Your Own Way." While the two tracks have a verse in common, their meanings are fundamentally different. "Go Your Own Way" is distorted by the desire for revenge, while the other marks the narrator's desire to ensure the happiness of the person she loves: "Baby, I'd give you my world"; "To you, I'll give the world." In the first case, Lindsey uses the conditional tense; and in the second, Christine chooses the future tense. "To place it right after 'Go Your Own Way' was just so great," enthused Lindsey in 2005. "I actually remember when the album was done…and one of the local radio stations had played the whole album […] And Richard Dashut and I were in our car when we still lived on Putney, and listened to this. I can remember when 'Go Your Own Way' came in and we were so aggressive at the end and it was a great thing. That song came off, and then 'Songbird' came on. And the masculinity and aggressiveness that was the end of 'Go Your Own Way' transformed into that intimate female, introspective side of 'Songbird' which followed. I honestly remember that the DJ that addressed the listeners before playing Side Two, you could tell she'd been crying!"[96]

Production

Ken Caillat imagined a special treatment for "Songbird": He wanted to give the impression that the track had been

recorded on stage. He was confident, and not afraid of breaking the coherence of the sound with the other tracks. Caillat had recorded this type of performance before, notably with Joni Mitchell, in the Berkeley Community Theater, a theater located on the campus of the renowned Berkeley High School. The sound engineer tried to book this venue, but it was not available. Instead, he obtained the Zellerbach Auditorium on the campus of the University of California, Berkeley, for March 3, 1976. Ken wanted to put Christine in the best possible conditions. He planned a delicate touch: He had ordered a bouquet of flowers and asked for it to be placed on her Steinway grand piano. He also asked the lighting designer to shine a spotlight vertically onto the bouquet, so that the pianist's attention would be drawn to the flowers. "Christine sat on the stage and played a nine-foot Steinway, and she sounded magnificent. I used 15 tracks for the piano—two close mics and the rest were distant mics. For something like 'Songbird,' I wanted the room to really speak."[91] Lindsey Buckingham eventually accompanied the musician on acoustic guitar, but his contribution remained very discreet. The idea was above all to give the pianist a rhythmic cue so she would not lose the tempo. While Ken did give Christine exceptional treatment, he was no less demanding. Live conditions call for a one-shot session. The session would last until the next morning in order to achieve the desired result.

THE CHAIN

Lindsey Buckingham, Mick Fleetwood, Christine McVie, John McVie, Stevie Nicks / 4:28

Musicians
Lindsey Buckingham: vocals, guitar, dobro
Stevie Nicks: vocals, backing vocals
Christine McVie: keyboards, backing vocals
John McVie: bass
Mick Fleetwood: drums

Recorded
Record Plant Studios, Sausalito: January 27–April 10, 1976
Record Plant Studios, Los Angeles: November 1976

Technical Team
Producers: Fleetwood Mac, Ken Caillat, Richard Dashut
Sound Engineers: Ken Caillat, Richard Dashut
Assistant Sound Engineer: Chris Morris

Single
Side A: The Chain / Side B: Go Your Own Way
UK Release: February 4, 1977, with Warner Bros. Records
(ref. SAM 361)
Best UK Chart Ranking: Did Not Chart

Single
Side A: Paper Doll / Side B: The Chain
US Release: December 1992, with Warner Bros. Records
(ref. 7-18661)
Best US Chart Ranking: Did Not Chart

Single
Side A: Love Shines / Side B: The Chain (Previously unreleased
alternative mix)
UK Release: January 25, 1993, with Warner Bros. Records
(ref. W 0145)
Best UK Chart Ranking: Did Not Chart

Single:
The Chain
US Release: 2009, with Warner Bros. Records (digital release)
Best US Chart Ranking: 81

Genesis and Lyrics

On Monday, February 2, after five long days of preparation, Ken Caillat finally kicked off the *Rumours* sessions. A Christine McVie composition opens the recording: "Keep Me There" (also called "Butter Cookie" for a while). But this first song was also one of the last on the album to be finalized, as the band returned to it again and again over the following months, never really completing it until November 1976. Such were the musicians' transformations and contributions to the initial track that it was renamed "The Chain," in reference to the amalgam of the various fragments that make it up. It is the only song in Fleetwood Mac's repertoire to be attributed to all five members of the band in the late 1970s.

The involvement of the other musicians began with the setting up of the structure, deemed too linear. "We decided it needed a bridge, so we cut a bridge and edited it into the rest of the song."[99] Lindsey Buckingham explained in *Rolling Stone* in 1977. The band agreed on a ten-note bass passage played by John McVie and a slow crescendo of drums played by Mick Fleetwood. Ken Caillat found the keys to the right balance in five minutes. He pushed the bass—a new fretless Alembic that John had just acquired—to the same level as the bass drum, positioned the electric guitar completely to the left and increased its treble to give it an acerbic bite, and finally, positioned the organ on the right of the spectrum, taking care to maintain its brilliance. He placed the voice, logically, in the center, and added a subtle reverb. Dashut and Caillat realized that there was no point getting lost with trying to achieve the perfect sound for each instrument, and that the priority was the balance of the whole. The musicians expressed their pleasure with this setup: Lindsey nodded rhythmically on his Stratocaster, Christine winked in the direction of Dashut and Caillat, Mick gave a satisfied thumbs-up when John stood in front of Mick's kit to enjoy the instrument's vibrations.

With this first song, the band had found its unity and could begin recording, without realizing that it would still be a long way to the conclusion. It was hard to imagine at this stage that "Keep Me There," a piece of angst-ridden, keyboard-driven pop, would be reworked a hundred times

1977

until it lost all connection with the original idea and became "The Chain." Only the mythical bass line and the guitar finale survived this mutation.

Production

"Keep Me There" has a classic format: verse, chorus, verse, chorus, instrumental break, chorus. But the band soon realized that the key moment comes in the finale, an explosive moment that should release the tension built up throughout the track. The musicians rehearsed the song twice before launching into the first take. "I remember John's great bass solo, 'Doe daaaa doe da da doe doe doe doe da dooooooooe.' And it's like the monsters are coming! And we all loved that,"[78] said Stevie. On the break, after John's

memorable line, Lindsey improvised a short, heartrending solo that was right on target. As soon as the take was over, everyone took off their headphones and joined the producer duo in the mixing booth. Everyone was smiling and congratulating each other. They had the feeling that they had an anthology piece on their hands. However, in a hurry to get on with other compositions, the musicians left the incomplete track aside. "We didn't get a vocal and left it for a long time in a bunch of pieces," Lindsey recalls. It almost went off the album. Then we listened back and decided we liked the bridge, but didn't like the rest of the song. So I wrote verses for that bridge, which was originally not in the song, and edited those in. We saved the ending. The ending was the only thing left from the original track."[99]

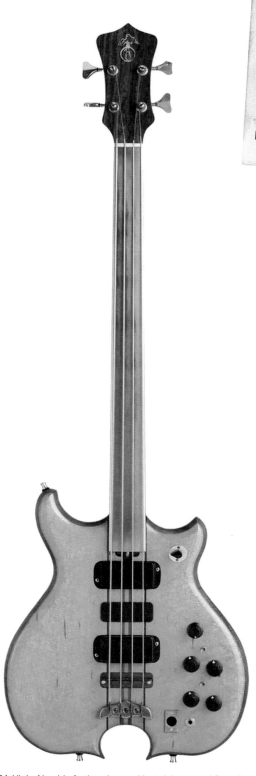

1977

John McVie's Alembic fretless bass with stainless steel fingerboard.

Starting It All Again from Scratch

On November 1, 1976, the band met at Record Plant Studios in Los Angeles. Lindsey arrived all smiles: He had an idea to save the abandoned title. But it involved drastic cuts. Indeed, only the finale was perfect in his eyes, and he suggested that the others should rewrite the entire verses and chorus, which suffered from an obvious lack of originality, but with as few instruments as possible. Dashut and Caillat prepared the recording session by adding enough blank tape before the chorus (as well as a segment of paper in between so that this new recording did not inadvertently erase the chorus) to contain the new opening and verse directly inspired by the introduction to "Lola (My Love)," a song from the *Buckingham Nicks* album. Only Mick and Lindsey played at the start. Lindsey used a dobro, while Mick reduced the beat to bass drum hits, following the click (a rhythmic sound indicator) created for him by Ken Caillat. After the take, Caillat cut the tape to paste the new verse onto the chorus. The spirit of the song was totally transformed. Then Stevie, Lindsey, and Christine sat down around a piano and started writing lyrics to go with the new verse. Stevie drew on the draft of another composition and incorporated snippets of it to form the new text for "The Chain"—a powerful, evocative text, which in a few verses sketches out all the ambiguity of the love and friendship relationships linking the members of Fleetwood Mac: The chain is an indestructible bond, made of a metal that withstands even the acidity of their arguments. But it is also the shackle that symbolizes their imprisonment. For better or worse, for love or hate, the members of Fleetwood Mac would remain united by this chain.

As the first song to be captured on tape for *Rumours*, it was also the last. With its rare dynamic for a pop song of this caliber, evolving from a calm, sober intro to an edgy finale with heartrending guitar and passionate backing vocals, "The Chain" made a lasting impression and established itself as one of the most important links in Fleetwood Mac's discography.

Until 1974 an advocate of the Fender Jazz Bass and Precision Bass, John McVie accompanied the band's turn toward pop with a growing interest in Alembic basses, particularly the Series I, as seen here in 1980.

John's memorable solo, which leads into the final sequence, was used in the UK as the main theme for Formula 1 race broadcasts in the 1990s.

The dissensions that arose
within the group leading up to
the recording of *Rumours* were
partly responsible for the lyrics
of this legendary album.

Christine McVie / 3:31

YOU MAKE LOVING FUN

Musicians
Christine McVie: vocals, keyboards, clavinet
Lindsey Buckingham: guitars, toms, backing vocals
John McVie: bass
Mick Fleetwood: drums, percussion, wah-wah pedal
Stevie Nicks: tambourine, backing vocals

Recorded
Record Plant Studios, Sausalito: February 8–April 10, 1976
Wally Heider Studios, Hollywood: May 14–mid-June 1976;
   August 4–22, 1976; October 1976
Criteria Studios, Miami: July 5–11, 1976
Davlen Sound Studios, Hollywood: September 1976
Record Plant Studios, Los Angeles: November 1976

Technical Team
Producers: Fleetwood Mac, Ken Caillat, Richard Dashut
Sound Engineers: Ken Caillat, Richard Dashut
Assistant Sound Engineer: Chris Morris

Single
Side A: You Make Loving Fun / **Side B:** Never Going Back Again
UK Release: September 30, 1977, with Warner Bros. Records
   (ref. K 17013)
Best UK Chart Ranking: 45

Single
Side A: You Make Loving Fun / **Side B:** Gold Dust Woman
US Release: 1977 with Warner Bros. Records (ref. WBS 8483)
Best US Chart Ranking: 9

1977

Genesis and Lyrics

Since she had begun recording *Rumours*, Christine had been playing the same riff over and over on her keyboard—a catchy, funky tune to which she had already assigned a name, "You Make Loving Fun," even before completing it. On February 8, 1976, while Stevie Nicks, Christine McVie, and Ken Caillat were waiting for the others, the latter suggested they start working on the song to keep themselves busy. Stevie, in a joyful mood, proclaimed that she would play the tambourine on it. Christine took her place behind her Fender Rhodes and played the melody with gusto, pounding the keys mercilessly. Ken Caillat was impressed by the velocity of her playing but found the sound of the Rhodes too mellow. He wanted something rougher. To obtain this result, he had the idea of running the keyboard through an amp to "dirty up" the sound a little, and through a pre-amp to beef it up. Christine was astonished by the result and remarked to Ken that it almost sounded like a clavinet. This struck a chord in the technician's mind, and he planned to add this harpsichord-like instrument, which sounds ideal in a funk context, to the overdubs. The other musicians arrived in the meantime. John, drunk since the early hours, was able to play but not lucid enough to understand that the text was talking about Christine's lover, Curry Grant, the band's lighting engineer. And he swallowed whole the young woman's (white) lie that the song was about her dog, which she made up in order to spare him.

Production

The first take, done without Lindsey Buckingham—who was absent that day—proved convincing, even without the guitar. The team then decided to overdub a clavinet track and connect a wah-wah pedal to the instrument, which would then be sent directly to the console. A great idea, but how could Christine manage the rhythm of the clavinet and the pedal at the same time? The tempo keeper, Mick Fleetwood, was then put in charge of the pedal, sitting next to the keyboardist so that she only had to worry about her

playing. The method was unconventional, but the musician devoted herself totally to her score, without having to constantly raise and lower the pedal. "It's got a real nice R&B feel to it," Lindsey commented. "It actually took a turn for the ethereal and sweet that you wouldn't expect from where it was going in the beginning. I remember being up at Wally Heider's and just trying to make that 'never did believe' section go somewhere else and then make it snap back into place."[96] The groove generated by the recording triggered a desire among the musicians to add a host of elements: Stevie got her tambourine track, Mick added castanets and wind chimes, and Lindsey added toms, in addition to his rhythm guitar part, played on a muscular Gibson Les Paul through a Leslie cabinet. As for John, who was tipsy on the first take, he had to re-record his parts later, as they were too rough on the first attempt.

I DON'T WANT TO KNOW

Stevie Nicks / 3:11

Musicians
Stevie Nicks: vocals, claps
Lindsey Buckingham: vocals, guitars
Christine McVie: keyboards
John McVie: bass
Mick Fleetwood: drums, percussion

Recorded
Wally Heider Studios, Hollywood: September–early October 1976

Technical Team
Producers: Fleetwood Mac, Ken Caillat, Richard Dashut
Sound Engineers: Ken Caillat, Richard Dashut
Assistant Sound Engineer: Chris Morris

FOR MAC ADDICTS

All the songs on *Rumours* were performed live by Fleetwood Mac, with the exception of "I Don't Want to Know," which was only performed by Lindsey Buckingham and Stevie Nicks as a duo before they joined the band.

Genesis and Lyrics

For Stevie Nicks, "I Don't Want to Know" had the foul taste of betrayal. Musically, she liked it a lot, but that was not the point. She was not fundamentally against the idea of resurrecting her composition, which dates back to the preparation of the Buckingham-Nicks duo's second album in 1974, then envisaged for a time for the *Fleetwood Mac* album the following year. But the conditions of this return to favor deeply wounded the composer. The decision to include this track in the track list to replace "Silver Springs"—another song written in her own hand, considered too long and perhaps also a little too slow—was made in the home stretch of the sessions, in September, without her being consulted. Everyone on the team knew about it except her. Worse still, the recording of "I Don't Want to Know" was done without her knowledge, with Lindsey Buckingham on vocals; Mick Fleetwood presented Stevie Nicks with a fait accompli. "But I don't want that song on this record," she insisted to Mick, who replied, 'Well, then don't sing it,'" as she recalled. "And then I started to scream bloody murder and probably said every horribly mean thing that you could possibly say to another human being, and walked back in the studio completely flipped out. I said, 'Well, I'm not gonna sing "I Don't Want to Know." I am one-fifth of this band.' And they said, 'Well, if you don't like it, you can either (a) take a hike or (b) you better go out there and sing "I Don't Want to Know" or you're only gonna have two songs on the record.'"[92] So it was with "a gun to my head,"[92] as she puts it, that Stevie found herself in front of the microphone, having to marry her voice to Lindsey Buckingham's and simulate a complicit vocal on this up-tempo song with its joyful melody and catchy claps. Ken Caillat gives a slightly less harsh version of events: "So we gave her the option that we could cut one of the slow songs down so we could have room for the other ones or we could take one of the other songs off and she said, 'Let's do it.' She wanted to keep all of the other songs more than 'Silver Springs.'"[93]

"I Don't Want to Know" gave rise to a heated argument between Stevie Nicks and Mick Fleetwood, with Stevie resenting the fact that this song had been recorded without her.

Production

The recording of the instruments, before Stevie finally took over the vocals, was done quickly, in just five hours (only part of the lead guitar was added at the beginning of October), due to the simple three-chord structure of the song. Furthermore, it had been almost two years since it was composed and performed live. This shows how well Lindsey Buckingham mastered it. It did not take him long to re-create it in the studio. All the more so as his twelve-string guitar occupied most of the sound space and made up the bulk of the track. There was no need for the other instruments—bass, drums, and keyboard—to go overboard. They are content with simple scores. Mick only added a tambourine—usually reserved for Stevie—for fun. Lindsey completed the recording with his voice and backing vocals; all that remained was to convince Stevie to add her voice. As its last-minute addition to the track list suggested, despite its strengths, "I Don't Want to Know" lacks the stature of the other tracks, as Mick Fleetwood pointed out: "That song often gets forgotten about in terms of it being part of *Rumours*. I think it's really unique. You get those voices [Stevie and Lindsey] together. And that was their style."[96]

The first version of "I Don't Want to Know," recorded by the band members without Stevie Nicks, was unveiled to the public in the super deluxe edition of *Rumours* released in 2012 to mark the album's 35th anniversary.

OH DADDY

Christine McVie / 3:54

Musicians
Christine McVie: vocals, piano, keyboards
Lindsey Buckingham: guitars, backing vocals
John McVie: bass
Mick Fleetwood: drums, percussion
Stevie Nicks: backing vocals, castanets, gong, Hammond B3, Moog, vocals

Recorded
Record Plant Studios, Sausalito: February 5–April 10, 1976
Wally Heider Studios, Hollywood: May 14–mid-June 1976;
August 4–22, 1976; October 1976
Criteria Studios, Miami: July 5–11, 1976
Davlen Sound Studios, Hollywood: September 1976
Record Plant Studios, Los Angeles: November 1976

Technical Team
Producers: Fleetwood Mac, Ken Caillat, Richard Dashut
Sound Engineers: Ken Caillat, Richard Dashut
Assistant Sound Engineer: Chris Morris

At the end of one of the takes, Christine, trying to attract the attention of the engineers in their control booth, played a few disordered notes. The rest of the band found this chance improvisation interesting and kept it.

FOR MAC-ADDICTS

During the sessions, the song was nicknamed "Addy" by the team due to a technical incident: Caillat's mishandling had damaged the tape in one of the takes, and on listening, the first D of "Oh Daddy" could no longer be heard.

Genesis and Lyrics

"Oh Daddy," a lonely, eerie ballad, is "probably my favorite Christine song of all time,"[70] Stevie Nicks confided in the liner notes to the 2013 reissue of *Rumours*, "and probably one of the only dark songs she wrote."[94] Both Lindsey Buckingham's ex-girlfriend Carol Ann Harris and Stevie Nicks biographer Zoë Howe have claimed that the song was about Christine McVie's then-relationship with the band's head lighting designer, Curry Grant. But Christine claims she wrote it with Mick Fleetwood in mind—not only because he was the only one to experience the joys and difficulties of fatherhood in the band, but also because he became a real father figure to the other members of the Mac, whom he had saved from the many storms of the last few years.

This was all the more true when the *Rumours* sessions got underway, at a time when the McVie and Buckingham/Nicks couples were falling apart. Once again, Mick had to be strong for everyone, even though his relationship with his own wife, Jenny, was falling apart. Christine had thus sought to comfort her friend with "Oh Daddy," whose lyrics speak of mistakes made and regretted, with the narrator admitting her wrongs ("If there's been a fool around / It's got to be me"). Christine's idea was also to reassure him about his choices and reinforce him as the band's tutelary figure: "Why are you right when I'm so wrong / I'm so weak but you're so strong / Everything you do is just alright / And I can't walk away from you."

Production

On February 5, 1976, the day after a snowy night, Christine arrived at Sausalito Studios. After shedding her winter clothes, she rushed to the piano to introduce the other musicians to her new composition, "Oh Daddy," which she had created during the first few days in the studio. First she played it alone, then everyone worked on their part until they thought they had it. Then the piece was played four or five times. After each attempt, the musicians discussed tempo and switched instruments to test the different sounds. Lindsey alone had about fifteen electric guitars and a dozen acoustic instruments. In the end, he opted for a

Mick Fleetwood (here onstage with a tama) has an extensive taste for percussion. On "Oh Daddy," he includes castanets and a gong.

safe bet, the Fender Stratocaster, to which the producers added a reverb and several delays.

The tempo was also the subject of lengthy research. From the very first tests, the problem occupied all the musicians' attention: "When we played it too fast, it felt rushed and congested; when we played it too slow, the song became lethargic," [78] explained producer Ken Caillat. One day, Caillat suggested that Christine should come and listen to two versions of the song in order to choose the right tempo, but she lost her temper with the two technicians: "We don't want to have to come in and listen every time we try out something different," Christine said firmly. "We want you guys to start paying attention to tempos and keys and tuning and other important things and help us out here." [82] The message got through, and soon the tempo was set, leaving plenty of room for the musicians to express themselves. Ken Caillat and Richard Dashut, who had sensed the wind in their sails, began taking notes at every take, to be able to answer Christine's questions and make suggestions. They pointed out to Lindsey and the pianist that they were on the same key and that it was difficult to distinguish their parts. Then they suggested that Christine pass the sound from her keyboard through a Leslie cabinet, but with a very slow rotation. The song, which had been largely cleared on February 5, 1976, underwent changes as the studios changed. In its final version, it opens very softly with a synthetic flute sound and two acoustic guitars, before the first piano chord of absolute gravity. John McVie's bass line floats pleasantly throughout. "That just came out," commented the musician modestly. "I couldn't think of anything else to do. I still think it's too busy behind her voice. It works I guess." [96] There are some nice guitar touches, both electric and acoustic (the subtle harmonics at 1:43 or 1:58, for example). As for the dull sound of the snare drum, this was the result of careful research by Mick Fleetwood, who wanted to bring warmth to his playing. On the second verse, the snare drum is slightly out of tune, but the team liked the resulting singular sound and left it like that. Mick also sought to bring originality to percussion. He added castanets (which remain marginal) and a gong to his panoply.

The atmosphere is certainly not as bare as that of "Songbird," but the sobriety reinforces the sincerity and effectiveness of the message. Christine's voice proves to be both moving and technically sound, with its light but well-placed vibrato, and extremely gentle, notably on the subtle passages at 1:37 and 2:38: "And I can't walk away from you / Baby, if I tried," or the suspended moment on the final "Yes, it's got to be me" at 3:18. Everything was done to enable the musician to achieve the ideal vocal take: "We recorded that song in an empty university auditorium in Berkeley," explained Mick Fleetwood," because we wanted the song to sound like Chris was singing it at the end of the night, after a show to an empty house. It needed that solitude sonically." [2]

GOLD DUST WOMAN

Stevie Nicks / 4:51

Musicians
Stevie Nicks: vocals
Lindsey Buckingham: guitars, dobro, backing vocals
Christine McVie: keyboards, backing vocals
John McVie: bass
Mick Fleetwood: drums, percussion, electric harpsichord
  (processed), sound effects

Recorded
Record Plant Studios, Sausalito: March 1976
Wally Heider Studios, Hollywood: May 14–mid-June 1976;
  August 4–22, 1976; October 1976
Criteria Studios, Miami: July 5–11, 1976
Davlen Sound Studios, Hollywood: September 1976
Record Plant Studios, Los Angeles: November 1976

Technical Team
Producers: Fleetwood Mac, Ken Caillat, Richard Dashut
Sound Engineers: Ken Caillat, Richard Dashut
Assistant Sound Engineer: Chris Morris

Single
Side A: Don't Stop / **Side B:** Gold Dust Woman
UK Release: 1977 with Warner Bros. Records (ref. K 16930)
Best UK Chart Ranking: 32

Single:
Side A: You Make Loving Fun / **Side B:** Gold Dust Woman
US Release: 1977 with Warner Bros. Records (ref. WBS 8483)
Best US Chart Ranking: 9

"Gold Dust Woman" is said to be derived from the street name Gold Dust Lane in Wickenburg, Arizona (Maricopa County), where Stevie lived as a child.

Genesis and Lyrics

In a 2022 interview, Stevie Nicks looked back on the genesis of the songs on *Rumours*. "All of those problems, and all of those drugs, and all of the fun, and all of the craziness all made for writing all those songs," she confessed, before adding: "If we'd been a big healthy great group of guys and gals, none of those great songs would've been written, you know?"[88]

So it was with the lyrics of "Gold Dust Woman," in which Stevie evokes—among other things—drug use (and its dangers), and more precisely *her* use. "Well, the gold dust refers to cocaine, but it's not completely about that, because there wasn't that much cocaine around then," she said. "Everybody was doing a little bit—you know, we never bought it or anything, it was just around—and I think I had a real serious flask of what this stuff could be, of what it could do to you. The whole thing about how we all love the ritual of it, the little bottle, the little diamond-studded spoons, the fabulous velvet bags. For me, it fit right into the incense and candles and that stuff. And I really imagined that it could overtake everything, never thinking a million years that it would overtake me."[95]

"'Gold Dust Woman' is about cocaine, of course, but it is also about the daily grind of the rock'n'roll scene, the difficulty of overcoming a breakup and the difficulty of taming sudden success. "After all these years—since I haven't done any cocaine since 1986 I can talk about it now you know. [...] I don't think I had ever been so tired in my whole life as I was when we were like—doing that [*Rumours*]. [...] It was so much work and it was so everyday intense you know. Being in Fleetwood Mac was like being in the army. It was like you have to be there. You have to be there and you have to be there as on time as you can be there. And even if there's nothing you have to do, you have to be there."[110] Some of the song's passages also take a jab at Lindsey Buckingham, such as the famous line: "Rulers make bad lovers / You better put your kingdom up for sale." "So 'Gold Dust Woman' was really my kind of symbolic look at somebody going through a bad relationship, and doing a lot of drugs, and trying to just make it—trying to live—you know trying to get through it to the next thing." Finally, the song addresses the issue of success and the

In its initial form, Stevie Nicks's "Gold Dust Woman" was a folk tune, stretching out over eight minutes. The other musicians turned it into a rock song with experimental elements. To achieve the sound, producer Mick Fleetwood donned a protective suit before striking panes of glass with a hammer.

"power" it confers metaphorically. "I was definitely swept away by how big Fleetwood Mac was and how famous I suddenly was," Stevie testified. "Me, who couldn't buy anything before, could now go in any store, and buy anything I wanted. And I wondered what that would do to me on down the line. I might be [a] ruler, but maybe I'd be a lousy lover." "Black widow / Pale shadow, she's a dragon / Gold dust woman." The singer explained: "That just means an anger. The black widow, the dragon thing, is all about being scary and angry."[95]

Production

"Gold Dust Woman" was the perfect dramatic finale to *Rumours*, the album of all the excesses. The more the band worked on the song, the more obvious it became that it was gaining in intensity. "We'd been in Sausalito for a month, and were beginning to get urgent phone calls from Warner Bros., who were wondering how we were doing,"[4] recalls Mick Fleetwood. Against this backdrop of intense pressure, "For me it was Stevie, physically the most fragile of us all, who exemplified the drive to create and prevail." The drummer continues: "I recall that she did her first vocal track of "Gold Dust Woman" in a fully lit studio. The song needed both a mysterious power and a lot of emotionality."[4] As the takes progressed, Stevie withdrew into herself, as if searching for the magic within. Richard Dashut came up with the idea of dimming the lights to help her along the way. A chair was

brought in for her to sit on. It was three o'clock in the morning; the session was a long one and the musician had to save her strength. Weeks of sleep deprivation and overwork had weakened her body, but she was determined to persevere despite a cold and a slight sore throat, which she fended off as best she could with lozenges, inhalers, tissues, and mineral water. "She wrapped herself in a big cardigan sweater to ward off the predawn chill," Mick continued. "An hour later she was almost invisible in the shadows, elfin under big headphones, hunched over in her chair."[4] Gradually, Stevie gained total control of her song. And by the eighth take, "Gold Dust Woman" was in the can. Exhausted but exhilarated, Stevie had just sung the lyrics from start to finish to perfection.

The track opens with a fade-out of strange, sitar-like sounds accompanying the acoustic guitars. It is another subtle arrangement, patient in the way it builds, taking place with Mick's haunting drums and John's venomous bass, but perhaps lacking the atmosphere of "Rhiannon."

Stevie Nicks makes the most of her fast, fairy-tale vibrato and is joined by Christine McVie and Lindsey Buckingham on backing vocals in perfect harmony, right up to that banshee cry where every note seems unreachable by the average person. After experimenting with several instruments, Lindsey Buckingham finally chose the dobro to flesh out his guitar parts, which undoubtedly added to the song's mystique.

FOR MAC ADDICTS

The idea of calling the song "Silver Springs" was born in Stevie's mind during a road trip with Lindsey. As they drove through Maryland, she noticed a sign that read "Silver Spring" (without the "s"). "And I loved the name...Silver Springs [*sic*] sounded like a pretty fabulous place to me. And uh, 'You could be my Silver Springs...'"[96]

SILVER SPRINGS

Stevie Nicks / 4:33

Musicians
Stevie Nicks: vocals
Lindsey Buckingham: guitars, backing vocals
Christine McVie: keyboards, backing vocals
John McVie: bass
Mick Fleetwood: drums

Recorded
Record Plant Studios, Sausalito: January 27–April 10, 1976
Wally Heider Studios, Hollywood: May 14–mid-June 1976;
 August 4–22, 1976; October 1976
Criteria Studios, Miami: July 5–11, 1976
Davlen Sound Studios, Hollywood: September 1976
Record Plant Studios, Los Angeles: November 1976

Technical Team
Producers: Fleetwood Mac, Ken Caillat, Richard Dashut
Sound Engineers: Ken Caillat, Richard Dashut
Assistant Sound Engineer: Chris Morris

Single
Side A: Go Your Own Way / Side B: Silver Springs
US Release: December 20, 1976, with Warner Bros. Records
 (ref. WBS 8304)
Best US Chart Ranking: 10

Single
Side A: Go Your Own Way / Side B: Silver Springs
UK Release: February 11, 1977, with Warner Bros. Records
 (ref. K 16872)
Best UK Chart Ranking: 38

Single
Side A: Silver Springs (Edit) / Side B: Go Your Own Way
UK Release: 1997 with Reprise Records (ref. 7-17300)
Best UK Chart Ranking: Did Not Chart

Genesis and Lyrics

Until late in the album's production process, it was agreed that Stevie Nicks would be credited with three tracks on *Rumours*: "Dreams," "Gold Dust Woman," and "Silver Springs." But the latter was to bear the brunt of what the musician experienced as an underhand maneuver on the part of her partners to stifle her artistic talents and further restrict her influence within the band. "It was at the Record Plant," Stevie Nicks recalled for the BBC in 1991. "Mick said, 'Stevie, I need you to come outside to the parking lot cause I need to talk to you for a minute.' And I knew it was really serious 'cause Mick never asks you to go out to the parking lot for anything. So we walked to the huge Record Plant parking lot and he said, 'I'm taking "Silver Springs" off the record.'"[92] In the booklet for the 2013 reissue of *Rumours*, she clarifies Mick's words: "'I'm taking Silver Springs off the album because it's too long.' Needless to say, I didn't take it well. I asked: 'What song are you going to put on the album instead?' They said, 'We recorded "I Don't Want to Know," and I think Lindsey thought it would suit me because I'd written that song, but it didn't suit me at all."[92]

"I wrote 'Silver Springs' with Lindsey in mind,"[96] Stevie explained on the Classic Albums DVD in 2005. The song's protagonist evokes her partner, whom she has to let go, and expresses her pain and regret at the situation, lamenting that he did not let her love him. She reflects on her inability to save the relationship and make him stay.

Squaring the Circle

At the end of the recording sessions, Ken Caillat was faced with a mathematical problem: fitting all the songs onto two twenty-minute sides. "We were in our ninth month of recording by this time, and we were starting to look ahead to what songs we'd have for the album," recalls the sound engineer. "And we realized we had

some long songs, like 'Go Your Own Way,' and some slow songs and medium slow songs. We were concerned that we might have too slow an album."[78] Against this backdrop, "Silver Springs" was singled out for its too-low tempo, but also for its excessive length (4:33). "Stevie is so prolific, all of her songs were initially about 14 minutes long," Caillat says in the documentary *Stevie Nicks: Through the Looking Glass*. "She would just go on and on and on […] So it was my job to sit with her and cut them down to three or four minutes. And there were tears."[98] For the other band members, a song like "I Don't Want to Know" seemed a better fit, as it was more dynamic and shorter. Stevie Nicks was beside herself. She sensed Lindsey's shadow behind this decision. She told herself that he probably did not appreciate being the subject of this song, as she had not appreciated being the subject of "Go Your Own Way" or "Second Hand News." He perfectly understood that "did you say that she loved you?" referred to his love affairs, and that "I'll begin not to love you" made their breakup official. The news of the "Silver Springs" withdrawal was hard for the young woman to take, for many reasons: everything had been decided behind her back, including the recording of "I Don't Want To Know"; she had put a lot of herself into this track, her favorite on the album; and she planned to give the publishing rights to her mother, Barbara.

Production

A refined violining effect played on guitar opens "Silver Springs," to which a heavy, well-rounded bass responds. Christine McVie intervenes with a few dreamy notes, accompanied by the harmonics of Lindsey Buckingham, who particularly enjoyed such ornamentation. As for Mick Fleetwood, his cymbal strikes are sparingly distilled, more to accessorize the melody than to mark the rhythm. In this magical soundscape befitting the personality of its composer, Stevie Nicks, her voice emerges, pure and airy, before evolving into a hoarse, raging tone on the final section. Her versatility makes this performance arguably the best on the album.

The song was relegated to Side B of Buckingham's December 1976 single "Go Your Own Way," but was on Side A in 1997 when it appeared as a single on the live album *The Dance*. This version of the song was nominated for a Grammy Award for Best Pop Vocal Performance by a Duo or Group in 1998.

"Silver Springs" also made an impact as the only outtake from the ninth-best-selling album of all time. It has continued to resonate with generations of female singers: It was covered in 2016 by Courtney Love—at the Fleetwood Mac Fest at the Fonda Theatre in Los Angeles—then cited by Lorde as the main influence for her second album, the 2017 *Melodrama*.

ALBUM

Tusk

Over & Over . The Ledge . Think About Me . Save Me a Place . Sara .
What Makes You Think You're the One . Storms . That's All for Everyone . Not That Funny .
Sisters of the Moon . Angel . That's Enough for Me .
Brown Eyes . Never Make Me Cry . I Know I'm Not Wrong . Honey Hi . Beautiful Child . Walk a
Thin Line . Tusk . Never Forget

RELEASE DATES
United Kingdom: October 12, 1979
Reference: Warner Bros. Records K 66088
Best UK Chart Ranking: 1
United States: October 17, 1979
Reference: Warner Bros. Records 2HS 3350
Best US Chart Ranking: 4

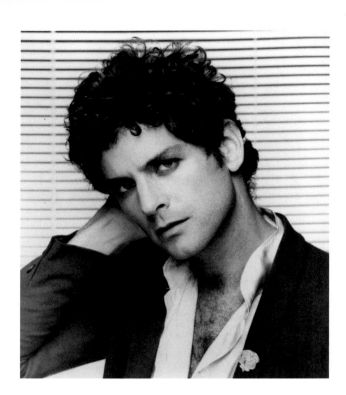

Shorter hair and bigger ideas for Lindsey Buckingham as he tackled *Tusk*.

Big winners at the American Music Awards in January 1978, Fleetwood Mac walked away with trophies for Best Pop/Rock Group and Best Pop/Rock Album for *Rumours*.

FOR MAC-ADDICTS

Tusk was reissued by Warner Bros. in Europe on vinyl in 1981 and on CD in 1987, and in the US on CD the same year. In 2015, a deluxe version was released, featuring the original album; a disc of singles, outtakes, and demo versions; and a disc of alternative mixes.

A TASTE FOR RISK

All the hours sacrificed on *Rumours* in the service of Lindsey Buckingham and Ken Caillat's perfectionism were rewarded a hundredfold by the ecstatic reception by the public. Fleetwood Mac had become the world's most lucrative pop band, and everything its musicians touched turned to gold or platinum. Christine McVie, Mick Fleetwood, and Lindsey Buckingham lent a hand to Bob Welch on *French Kiss*; the album reached number twelve on the US charts. John and Mick contributed to "Werewolves of London," the single from Warren Zevon's album *Excitable Boy*, which climbed to number eight on the Billboard charts. Lindsey Buckingham and Richard Dashut took on the production of Walter Egan's single "Magnet and Steel": It climbed into the top 10. Mick Fleetwood also tried to have Peter Green benefit from his state of grace by offering him a large check to finance his solo album *In the Skies* (1979), but the guitarist, whose playing had lost its luster, declined the offer in the name of his integrity.

The Eye of the Storm

But behind the scenes, the euphoria of success had already given way to disenchantment. The frantic pace of the second leg of the North American Rumours tour (May 1–October 4, 1977) was tearing Mick Fleetwood and Jenny Boyd apart. Relations between the musicians were also chaotic, even tempestuous. Fatigue affected both minds and bodies: Stevie's voice faded as the gigs wore on. The clouds gathered until the thunderclap of August 1977. Mick received a call from his mother informing him that his father, suffering from cancer, would not survive long. Very close to his parents—who accompanied him at many concerts and showered the whole band with affection—Mick was devastated. He tried to take refuge in work and alcohol, but this only increased his anguish. He found comfort in Stevie Nicks. She was a gentle haven in the midst of the storm. Little by little, their close friendship evolved into physical passion. Their feelings grew and their adventure began to take a serious turn. For all that, the two musicians were determined to keep it a secret. Stevie had a boyfriend (artistic director Paul Fishkin), and Mick was still married to Jenny. The marriage was no longer based on much of anything, but a deep affection still bound the drummer and his wife together, especially as she was there for her in-laws to help them cope with his father's illness. How, against this backdrop, could Mick and Stevie bring their developing love out into the open? Hindered by this disastrous timing, the two lovers decided after a few months to put an end to their relationship, without damaging their friendship or jeopardizing their coexistence within Fleetwood Mac. The end of this affair enabled another romance to take shape: Mick Fleetwood fell in love with Stevie's best friend Sara Recor, whom he had also been seeing during his secret fling with the musician. This time, he was able to bring this new love out into the open. This umpteenth sentimental imbroglio is documented—in part—in the song "Sara."

Lindsey Takes Control

When the musicians began work on *Tusk* in May 1978, they faced unprecedented pressure. This time, there was no question of saving the band's skin after the umpteenth defection of one of the members. The team remained unchanged. Instead, the concern of Fleetwood Mac's members was of a different order: how to stay at the top, both creatively and commercially. The answer seemed obvious, but Lindsey Buckingham would have none of it. There was no question of taking the easy way out and serving up to the public a "*Rumours II*." For him, that would be the fast track to artistic sclerosis in the medium term. He felt that he had every right to be the driving force behind the revival. He considered himself to be the most creative member of the band and was heavily involved in the discussions leading up to the creation of the successor to *Rumours*. Alongside Mick Fleetwood, he lobbied for the next album to be a double—even before the composition phase had begun. A triple would even be ideal, so that each of the three composers (Buckingham, Nicks, and McVie) would have their own personal project. But the record company would never agree.

Lindsey was very much attuned to new musical trends and had recently become obsessed with the emergence of the punk and new-wave movements. The Clash, the Sex Pistols, Talking Heads, and Blondie took center stage, giving rock behemoths like the Rolling Stones and Led Zeppelin a run for their money. Lindsey feared that Fleetwood Mac would pay the price for this younger spirit, and he intended to bring his band's next creations into line with the times. He could even see himself as the exclusive composer, especially as he was teeming with experimental ideas for the recording. Mick Fleetwood, far from squelching Lindsey's ambition, was ready to give him this artistic freedom. He sensed an aspect of the enthusiasm and taste for experimentation Peter Green had shown when he embarked on the *Then Play On* album. John and Christine were a little more circumspect but did not refuse outright. A half-hearted agreement was all Buckingham needed. In any case, denying Lindsey this freedom would have exposed the band to another split: "Basically," Dashut told *Rolling Stone*, "if Lindsey hadn't been allowed to do what he did on *Tusk*, I think that you wouldn't have had a band. Or that they would have got another guitar player."[60]

A Tailor-Made Studio

Lindsey began working alone on the new album, in his home studio. In this artistic immersion, the handsome Adonis discovered an extreme concentration and euphoria of experimentation. But although he could carry out this groundbreaking work in solitude, the band would need a professional studio for the recording. Mick Fleetwood pondered the question. Considering how long it had taken to make *Rumours*, and the band's desire to make a double album this time, he was worried that the rental bill would go through the roof. Would it not make more sense to have a custom-built studio built and owned by the band? The musicians were enthusiastic about the idea, but could not envisage it without the financial backing of Warner Bros. However, the record company categorically refused. Mick came up with the solution after talking to one of his friends, Geordie Hormel, the wealthy heir to a food industry giant who owned Village Recorders (aka the Village), an ultra-modern recording studio housed in a vast building at 1616 Butler Avenue, in West Los Angeles. Mick imagined pooling some of their advance on the album and teaming up with Geordie to build an annex equipped to their tastes, which they could then rent out to other bands. But the other members of the Mac did not see it that way. Geordie took charge of the cost of the new studio, which would amount to $1.4 million! In return, the musicians would have to pay substantial rental bills for the duration of the recording. When they agreed, they had no idea that the sessions would last thirteen long months...and that the final rental cost would far exceed the initial investment had Fleetwood Mac gone into partnership with Geordie.

In May 1978, the band moved into the brand-new "Studio D." "In the studio we had two ivory tusks as tall as Mick on either side of the console," Stevie recalled in 2003. "The board became 'Tusk.' If something went wrong it was, 'Tusk is down.' Those 13 months working in that room were our journey up the sacred mountain to the sacred African percussion, uh, place, where all the gods of music lived."[100]

1979

Built by the Masonic Order in 1922, the building at 1616 Butler Avenue in Los Angeles became the property of Maharishi Mahesh Yogi, who transformed it into a transcendental meditation center. In 1968, it was sold to composer Geordie Hormel, who turned it into a recording studio.

Inspired by these two "defenses," Stevie improvised as an interior decorator and set about personalizing the control room, hanging rich, wide drapes over the console, hanging paintings and Polaroids on the wall, and installing lights of every color everywhere. "It became very vibey, mystical, incensy and perfumed,"[100] she enthused. The musicians were like roosters. The new millionaires lived in a bubble of luxury: "The studio contract rider for refreshments was like a telephone directory," commented Christine McVie. "Exotic food delivered to the studio, crates of champagne. And it had to be the best, with no thought of what it cost. Stupid. Really stupid. Somebody once said that with the money we spent on champagne on one night, they could have made an entire album. And it's probably true."[36]

Champagne was not the only fuel for the band and the keyboardist. Cocaine was consumed in industrial quantities. Some of it went up the nostrils of Christine's new boyfriend, who was very present at the recording sessions: Dennis Wilson, the charismatic drummer—and surfer—of the Beach Boys. Or rather, the formerly charismatic surfer, because the man Christine had taken in was nothing like the sportsman adored by groupies. His square-jawed face

was overgrown with hair, and his gentle features faded behind a hippie look that testified to his nonconformism. Ill-regarded by his cousin and musical partner Mike Love, he suffered from not being able to express his musical talent within the Beach Boys. Until the album *Pacific Ocean Blue* (1977), no one suspected that Dennis, self-appointed guardian of the Wilson siblings, might have been concealing an inner Atlas. When the "other Wilson," Brian, went down under the effects of acid, it was Dennis who held up what could still be held up—a habit developed during childhood to protect his brothers from their father's tyranny and violence. In the studio with the Mac, Dennis strolled around like a drunkard, reeking of alcohol, his pitcher of orange vodka in hand. His presence, a burden for the other members, would nevertheless offer Lindsey Buckingham a unique privilege: access to the tapes of the *Smile* album, according to music historian Domenic Priore, who mentions it in his book *Smile: The Story of Brian Wilson's Lost Masterpiece* (2005). The record has become legendary—it was begun in 1966 but was abandoned and remained unreleased until 2011. This listening experience is said to have strongly influenced the composition of "That's All for Everyone" and "Walk a Thin Line."

Beach Boys mastermind Brian Wilson, whose creative ideas and unbridled perfectionism inspired Lindsey Buckingham, is pictured here during the recording of "Pet Sounds."

Musical Experiments of Every Kind

Lindsey Buckingham joined the other members of the Mac in Studio D at Village Recorders, with crazy tracks like "The Ledge" and "Not That Funny" under his arm. As the sessions progressed, he—like Brian Wilson—moved into a world where nothing mattered but the music, and he began to lose sight of the overall impression, drowning in production details. "He was a maniac," Ken Caillat attests. "The first day, I set up the studio as usual. Then he said to turn every knob 180 degrees from where it was now and see what happens." His idea was to distort the sound of the instruments as much as possible to create a constant sensation of strangeness in the listener, even if this meant creating irritating sounds. "He'd tape microphones to the studio floor and then get into a sort of push-up position to sing. Early on he came in and he'd freaked out in the shower and cut off all his hair with nail scissors. He was stressed. And into sound destruction."[102] Obsessed by the quest for a unique sound, he demanded that a bathroom be installed on the premises that would replicate the one in his home, to achieve the same acoustics as at home.

The main pillar of the Fleetwood Mac edifice he decided to tackle was the drums. He did everything he could to get as far away from the instrument's usual sounds as possible, by various means: altering the recording, as on "What Makes You Think You're the One" (the drums are picked up with the microphone of a Sony boombox, to give it a lo-fi color), or replacing the snare drum with a box of Kleenex on the title track, "Tusk." A heresy for Ken Caillat, who had gone to such lengths on the previous opus to achieve the most perfect sound possible for each instrument. But Lindsey knew what he was doing: He involved Caillat fully in the work of deconstructing the production, flattering his ego by evoking the greatest pioneers of the profession, Phil Spector and Brian Wilson. They spent hours together in the Beverly Hills house Lindsey shared with Carol Ann Harris (his new partner). Together, they deconstructed records by the Ronettes and "Pet Sounds" by the Beach Boys, attempting to unlock the secrets of these sonic geniuses' productions. Engaging Ken Caillat in such an exploration gave Lindsey Buckingham the feeling of making his mark on musical history. And if that meant unlearning one's craft, then so be it. In the intimacy of the home studio, the two men were free to indulge in all manner of experimentation: slowing down the rhythm of the tapes, speeding them up, placing a microphone on the bathroom floor. Lindsey's imagination knew no bounds.

Thirteen Difficult Months

In the studio, with the rest of the band, the atmosphere was not so conducive to cohesion. The sentimental stories at the heart of *Rumours* had sharpened the enmities between the members. Under these conditions, it was a balancing act involving negotiation and psychology, which Dashut and Caillat had a hard time mastering. How many times did John McVie have to calm Lindsey Buckingham down so he could master his bass parts? This gave the bassist good reason to slip away whenever he could and escape for a few hours on his yacht. Gestures of kindness between Nicks and Buckingham were also very rare. The only peaceful moments between the two former lovers were those of denial. Faced with the impossibility of communicating with

Under Lindsey Buckingham's leadership, the band threw itself wholeheartedly into the conception of *Tusk*, an album that was the antithesis of its predecessor.

Lindsey, Stevie chose to distance herself from him. But distancing herself from the musician, Fleetwood Mac's creative epicenter on this album, also meant distancing herself from the band itself. The recollections of Ken Caillat and Stevie Nicks could not be more at odds on this point. The producer claimed that the young woman only came in once a week to record her song and left just as quickly. Stevie, on the other hand, claims that she was "there in the studio every day—or almost every day—but I probably only worked for two months. The other 11 months I did nothing, and you start to lose it after a while if you're inactive. You see, Lindsey, Chris, John, and Mick all play, and I don't. So most of the time I'd be looking at them through the window in the control room. After four or five hours, they'd forget I was even there, they'd be so wrapped up in little details. It was very frustrating,"[103] said Stevie in 1981. Yet the singer had plenty of ideas to spare. Stevie's fertile mind bubbled over, and she churned out song after song without her partners paying the slightest attention. Her creative impulses were systematically extinguished. So she stored up the material for her first solo album, *Bella Donna*, in 1981. This was a project fomented in the wake of *Tusk*, for which she recruited Irving Azoff (the Eagles' manager) on the sly and, with Paul Fishkin and Danny Goldberg, founded the Modern Records label to accommodate her personal project.

In July 1978, the band had been locked in Studio D for three months. For their sanity, the musicians needed a break. Mick suggested playing a handful of dates, to allow the band members to recover their cohesion on stage and regain some automatisms after several weeks of forgetting their fundamentals in the name of their experimental approach. But this "break" was not to prove a restful one. On July 25, Mick's father passed away. The drummer had just enough time to jump on a plane to join him in his last moments. The album is dedicated to him. Five days later, during a visit to Philadelphia, Buckingham collapsed in the bathroom of his hotel room, victim of an epileptic seizure. He was paying for his long sleepless nights. The doctor advised him to take it easy and, if possible, to play seated on stage, a recommendation that the guitarist greeted with derision. Fortunately, the prescribed treatment quickly put an end to the problem. The tour ended on August 30, 1978. The band then headed back to the studio for months of experimentation, nerve-racking for each of the musicians, who were also under pressure from the record company. Mick was in charge of trumpeting to Warner Bros. boss Mo Ostin that all was well, that they were to be trusted, and that the millions of dollars invested were worth it.

In June 1979, the recording finally came to an end. The Mac finished recording the horn section for the title track and shot the video at Dodger Stadium with the Trojan Marching Band from the University of Southern California. For the occasion, Nicks brought out her high-school majorette baton, and Fleetwood struck his bass drum at the head of the procession. A final touch was added to "I Know I'm Not Wrong," the last song to be finalized. And so, after thirteen long months of countless takes and endless trial and error, the twenty-track album was finally complete.

Fleetwood Mac's thirteenth studio album was logically christened *Tusk*. While the word *tusk* has the sense of "elephant's tusk," in slang it also refers to the male sexual

An album of excess, *Tusk* was considered a commercial failure, despite selling 4 million copies worldwide.

In a return of karma for Stevie Nicks, whom the name "Scooter" seemed to pursue, a German band called Scooter sampled the track "Stand Back" from her solo album *The Wild Heart* (1983) in their dubious techno track "No Way to Hide" (2012).

organ. In 2015, Stevie Nicks confessed her aversion to this choice: "I didn't understand the title, there was nothing beautiful or elegant about the word 'tusk.' It really brought to mind those people stealing ivory. Even then, in 1979 you just thought, the rhinos are being poached and that tusks are being stolen and the elephants are being slaughtered and ivory is being sold on the black market. I don't recall it being (Mick's slang term for the male member), that went right over my prudish little head. I wasn't told that until quite a while after the record was done, and when I did find out I liked the title even less!"[104] The title was also inspired by the artwork of one of the photographers who worked on the album booklet: Peter Beard, an American specializing in Africa and wildlife photography.

While the choice of title was questionable in the eyes of Stevie Nicks, so was that of the visual selected for the cover. No musicians were present this time. Only Ken Caillat's dog Scooter, biting his trousers, appears against a beige background. Stevie did not like the fact that Caillat's dog was featured on the cover to the detriment of the band, and she cursed the animal, going so far as to express her satisfaction at its death a few years later.

Audacity or Sabotage?

On October 17, 1979, this amorphous object finally appeared, made up of fragments of strange music and experimental sounds, mixed with more-classical compositions that seemed to emanate from different groups. On the one hand, the urgent rhythm of Lindsey Buckingham's "The Ledge," in a completely deranged percussive stomp style, the restrained rage of "What Makes You Think You're the One"; and on the other, the ballads set with backing vocals by Christine McVie on "Over & Over" and "Brown Eyes," as well as the soothing, dreamlike touch of Stevie Nicks on "Storms," "Sisters of the Moon," and the sumptuous "Sara." And so the record unfolded, between the unexpectedly whimsical and the familiar, between the rough and the smooth. Despite his stranglehold on the album, with claimed authorship of nine tracks compared with six for Christine McVie and five for Stevie Nicks, Lindsey Buckingham spared no effort in embellishing the compositions of the two young women with vocal harmonies and brilliant arrangements. In this respect, the album does not reflect the internal conflicts that marred the whole recording process: Everyone was able to put aside their grudges to serve the collective, for the good of the music.

Tusk was released shortly before Pink Floyd's *The Wall* and the Clash's *London Calling*. It had a hard time finding its place, surrounded by these two recording monsters. The band's risk-taking disconcerted fans and buyers of *Rumours* alike.

With four million copies sold, the double album was not a total commercial failure—thanks in part to a higher sales price—but compared to its predecessor, it bordered on an industrial disaster. Could such musical experimentation, so adventurous as to verge on artistic suicide, have hoped for a better outcome?

One of the few shots of Christine McVie playing a guitar.

OVER AND OVER

Christine McVie / 4:35

Musicians: Christine McVie: vocals, keyboards / Lindsey Buckingham: guitars, backing vocals / John McVie: bass / Mick Fleetwood: drums, percussion / Stevie Nicks: backing vocals / **Recorded:** Village Recorders, Los Angeles: May 1978–June 1979 / **Technical Team:** Producers: Fleetwood Mac, Ken Caillat, Richard Dashut / Sound Engineers: Ken Caillat, Richard Dashut / Assistant Sound Engineers: Rich Feldman, Hernán Rojas

Genesis and Lyrics

Christine McVie's personal history, as she moved from an affair with lighting director Curry Grant to one with Beach Boys drummer Dennis Wilson, surfaced in the lyrics of "Over & Over." Burning with desire for the man she covets, the young woman struggles to contain her impatience: "Don't waste our time, tell me now." Filled with uncertainties (manifested in numerous questions throughout the text), she dares not believe in the possibility of being the chosen one: "Could it be me? / Could it really, really be?" Even before she gets an answer from the man she loves, the worried lyricist contemplates the worst: "Don't turn me away / And don't let me down, yeah / What can I do / To keep you around? (Ooh)."

Production

A sublime, languorous ballad to start the album, "Over and Over" benefits from a simple yet effective production by Lindsey Buckingham. "By the time we got to this we knew we had [an album] that was not by the book," explained the guitarist. "When it came to the sequencing we felt this song had a certain familiarity to it, something that people were going to be able to latch onto on one level and yet set them up for some of the other, more untraditional things. Where this got untraditional was leaving it in a fairly raw state, not too glossy in the production."[105] In the stereo spectrum, everything is therefore perfectly audible and well distributed: Lindsey's inspired electric guitar touches, the brilliance of his acoustic guitar, John's deep bass, Christine's delicate keyboards, but also Mick's soothing drums, which set a slow but driving rhythm thanks to the matte, reassuring sound of his snare drum. Christine's voice sounds inconsolable, well supported by plaintive backing vocals. All good reasons to open the album with this track.

Despite (or because of?) its exuberant, jubilant, nervous, and slightly disjointed feel, "The Ledge" became a filler track, with little to make it a commercially viable single.

Entirely conceived by Lindsey Buckingham, "The Ledge" required external support from only the backing vocals of Stevie Nicks and Christine McVie.

THE LEDGE

Lindsey Buckingham / 2:02

Musicians: Lindsey Buckingham: vocals, guitars, bass, drums / Christine McVie: backing vocals / Stevie Nicks: backing vocals / **Recorded:** Village Recorders, Los Angeles: May 1978–June 1979 / **Technical Team:** Producers: Fleetwood Mac, Ken Caillat, Richard Dashut / Sound Engineers: Ken Caillat, Richard Dashut / Assistant Sound Engineers: Rich Feldman, Hernán Rojas

Genesis and Lyrics

"The Ledge" is a very danceable number and spreads its optimism over just over two minutes. Yet it is impossible to ignore the bitterness in Lindsey Buckingham's lyrics, as he clearly teases his ex, Stevie Nicks, once again. "The Ledge" explores the idea of loyalty in love. "Six feet under" is not so much a reference to death as to the imminent end of a relationship. Clearly, the score had not been settled at the end of *Rumours*, and if he seems a little more detached, Lindsey still has a hard edge: "You're never gonna make it baby / Oohh, you're never gonna make me crazy." Referring to his partner's lies, he asks her to think about the consequences of her actions. The guitarist, however, denies any desire for revenge: "Lyrically, I didn't really have anything to say other than what I could put together that sounded musical," he explains. "There was probably something subconscious about the lyrics. You could say that about *Rumours* too. I don't think anyone in the band was in touch with the fact that we might have been writing dialogues with each other. It took the audience's point of view to help us understand that."[10]

Production

"The Ledge" and its unbridled arrangement are placed at the beginning of the track list, just after Christine McVie's gentle "Over and Over," to convince the listener from the outset that nothing will ever be the same again. Every means is deployed to try and stand out from *Rumours*, even if it means splitting hairs to find a new rhythm or an unconventional melody. For "The Ledge," Lindsey is in the thick of things, taking on drums, guitar, bass, and vocals, leaving John, Christine, and Mick out in the cold. He opts for a 2/4 rhythm signature (two quarter notes per bar) that reinforces the song's country tone. Both the guitar and drums are relatively raw, which also brings the track closer to the primitive post-punk that was very much in vogue at the time. "I was trying to find things that were off the radar," Lindsey explains. "I took a guitar and turned it way down, in the range of the higher notes of a bass, not like a baritone guitar, where it's correct, but where it's actually a little incorrect—the strings are flopping around and sharping when you hit them. I wrote a little figure with that, threw some teenage influences at it with the drums. It becomes a bit surreal—you throw a bunch of vocals on top that are communal, messy, a little bit punky even. [...] On this, that one guitar was covering everything. It was a concept piece on that level."[105] For the backing vocals, however, he needed the impetuous voices of his female colleagues, Christine McVie and Stevie Nicks, who joined in without forcing their talent onto this nervous and spontaneous, deceptively improvised atmosphere.

During recording, the band tried numerous attempts to use a 12-string guitar, a Chamberlin (ancestor of the mellotron), and a harmonium on "Think About Me," which achieved a creditable number 20 in the US charts.

THINK ABOUT ME

Christine McVie / 2:44

Musicians: Christine McVie: vocals, keyboards / Lindsey Buckingham: guitars, vocals, backing vocals / John McVie: bass / Mick Fleetwood: drums, vibraphone / Stevie Nicks: backing vocals / **Recorded:** Village Recorders, Los Angeles: May 1978–June 1979 / **Technical Team:** Producers: Fleetwood Mac, Ken Caillat, Richard Dashut / Sound Engineers: Ken Caillat, Richard Dashut / Assistant Sound Engineers: Rich Feldman, Hernán Rojas / **Single:** Side A: Think About Me / Side B: Honey Hi / **UK Release Date:** May 9, 1980, with Warner Bros. Records (ref. K 17614) / Best UK Chart Ranking: Did Not Chart / **Single:** Side A: Think About Me / Side B: Save Me a Place / **US Release Date:** February 20, 1980, with Warner Bros. Records (ref. WBS 49196) / Best US Chart Ranking: 20

Genesis and Lyrics

While Christine McVie had repeatedly explored the dense complexity of relationships and the obstacles to be overcome in order to keep her marriage afloat, she was less interested in describing the mechanisms leading to the birth of love. "Think About Me" explores this aspect: "All it took was a special look / And I felt I knew you before / I didn't mean to love you / Didn't think it would work out / But I knew we would be together." Subsequently, Christine, no doubt scalded by the difficult evolution of her relationship with John, which took a long time to settle down, moderates her expectations and lets her partner choose to come to her. She has no desire to control or possess him. She just confides in him that she will be by his side if he wishes to take things further. But this is clearly a posture,

as her inclination then dictates these words: "So let yourself go and let love begin." The refrains finally lift the veil on the nature of her feelings. She no longer hides her love: "Think about me."

Production

The sunny mood of "Think About Me," with its splendid vocal harmonies and perfectly calibrated arrangement, is reminiscent of the greatest hits of *Rumours*. However, this is an illusion when compared with the rest of the content of *Tusk*, which is often more experimental. Metaphorically speaking, the song is like a freeway from which one can exit and venture out onto small country roads. The path is clear, uncluttered, and straight. Lindsey and Christine handle the lead vocal parts with flair, amid finely chiseled backing vocals. Lindsey's guitar parts are once again brilliant, whether for his accompaniment, with a slightly crunchy sound reminiscent of the Beatles' famous "Day Tripper," or for his beautifully simple solo from 1:14 onward, just after a heartfelt and very cool "wow," which is impossible to attribute to anyone. For their part, Mick and John provide an efficient, warm rhythm section, the former with a snare drum that sounds both dull and slamming, and the latter with a bass that is as slick and babbling as it is solid on its feet when necessary. As for Christine, her warm keyboard sounds enhance the sumptuous production. "Think About Me" is the epitome of late-seventies California soft rock.

Stevie and Lindsey's relationship is once again the source of the guitarist's lyrics on "Save Me a Place."

SAVE ME A PLACE

Lindsey Buckingham / 2:40

Musicians: Lindsey Buckingham: vocals, guitar, bass, drums, keyboard / Stevie Nicks: backing vocals / Christine McVie: backing vocals / **Recorded:** Village Recorders, Los Angeles: May 1978–June 1979 / **Technical Team:** Producers: Fleetwood Mac, Ken Caillat, Richard Dashut / Sound Engineers: Ken Caillat, Richard Dashut / Assistant Sound Engineers: Rich Feldman, Hernán Rojas / **Single:** Side A: Not That Funny / Side B: Save Me a Place / **UK Release Date:** March 7, 1980, with Warner Bros. Records (ref. K 17577) / Best UK Chart Ranking: Did Not Chart / **Single:** Side A: Think About Me / Side B: Save Me a Place / **US Release Date:** February 20, 1980, with Warner Bros. Records (ref. WBS 49196) / Best US Chart Ranking: 20

Genesis and Lyrics

"Save Me A Place," probably the gentlest track Lindsey Buckingham ever composed for Fleetwood Mac, forms a bubble of tenderness obscured by pain and the need for solitude. Surprisingly vulnerable, the lyricist begs his loved one to "save a place" for him. This is undoubtedly the first step toward accepting a "different" relationship, a different kind of love. For a long time, Lindsey, like Stevie, Christine, and John, had compartmentalized his emotions; none of them really wanted to distance themselves to conclude their story, to the point of living in denial. Aggression and resentment often dominated their compositions, as on *Rumours*. Not so with "Save Me a Place." This time it is a question of appeasement, but also of the fear of losing something, whether it be love or

youth slipping away. This can be evoked by the word "play," which refers as much to children's games as to the musician's craft: "Don't know why I have to work / Don't know why I can't play."

Production

With its sophisticated arrangement by Lindsey Buckingham alone, "Save Me a Place" is one of the pleasant surprises on *Tusk*. Lindsey's painfully infectious voice is the foundation for emotions rarely shared by the guitarist. Overhung by magnificent, warm acoustic guitars, it is enriched by the precision of Christine and Stevie's backing vocals, whose vibratos are as complementary as they are moving. These tight harmonies, which never overuse effects to unnecessarily color a straightforward, heartfelt performance, instantly trigger goose bumps. The drums played by Lindsey, singularly lacking in subtlety, nevertheless manage to maintain a throbbing rhythm, while the musician makes the arrangement more swaying with his elastic bass playing. The piano, also played by Lindsey, is barely audible, but effectively fills the few spaces left by his guitars. The song starts gently and ends in a sea of benevolence, as if all the other musicians were closing their arms around Lindsey Buckingham in a tender gesture. But make no mistake, with Lindsey playing all the instruments, this is indeed a "self-cuddle," far from resolving the growing tension within the band.

SARA

Stevie Nicks / 6:26

In 1986, Stevie Nicks went to the Betty Ford Clinic to kick her cocaine habit. On arrival, she registered under the name Sara. This experience led to the writing of a new song, "Welcome to the Room…Sara," which appeared on the *Tango in the Night* album in 1987.

Musicians
Stevie Nicks: vocals, piano
Lindsey Buckingham: guitars, backing vocals
Christine McVie: keyboards, piano, backing vocals
John McVie: bass
Mick Fleetwood: drums

Recorded
Village Recorders, Los Angeles: May 1978–June 1979

Technical Team
Producers: Fleetwood Mac, Ken Caillat, Richard Dashut
Sound Engineers: Ken Caillat, Richard Dashut
Assistant Sound Engineers: Rich Feldman, Hernán Rojas

Single
Side A: Sara / **Side B:** That's Enough for Me
UK Release: December 14, 1979, with Warner Bros. Records (ref. K 17533)
Best UK Chart Ranking: 37

Single
Side A: Sara / **Side B:** That's Enough for Me
US Release: December 5, 1979, with Warner Bros. Records (ref. WBS 49150)
Best US Chart Ranking: 7

Single
Side A: Tusk / **Side B:** Sara
US Release: 1980 with Warner Bros. Records (ref. GWB 0388)
Best US Chart Ranking: Did Not Chart

FLEETWOOD MAC

Sara

Challenged in 1980 for plagiarism by a composer who claimed to have sent Warner lyrics called "Sara" in 1978, Stevie was able to demonstrate that her demo predated the claimant's submission.

Genesis and Lyrics

"Sara" is the first Stevie Nicks song to appear on the album. For years, speculation about the identity of Sara ran wild, fueled by the late revelation of the romantic relationship between Mick Fleetwood and Stevie Nicks that was playing out at the time of the composition of this iconic track. The mystery deepened with the arrival of a third protagonist, a woman named Sara Recor (coincidentally Stevie Nicks's best friend), who ended up winning the drummer's heart and officially uniting with him much later, between 1988 and 1992. Over the years, Stevie has said that the song was largely about Mick, revealing him to be that protective "great dark wing" evoked in the lyrics. In the first verse, Stevie addresses the musician, asking him to stay close to her. She then tells him that the light she expected from him has turned into an unexpected and devastating fire in her heart. Using the metaphor of the raging elements, she then speaks of drowning in a sea of love.

But nothing is ever simple and clear-cut when it comes to feelings in the world of Fleetwood Mac. Stevie Nicks has also said that some of the song's lyrics evoke Don Henley, the Eagles singer and drummer with whom she had an affair in 1977. In 1991, in an interview, Henley brought a new element of interpretation to this complex text, revealing that the romantic prism was not the only one to be taken into account, and that a personal drama was subtly evoked in the filigree. "I believe to the best of my knowledge [Stevie] became pregnant by me. And she named the [unborn] kid Sara, and she had an abortion" and then wrote the song of the same name to the spirit of the aborted baby. I was building my house at the time, and there's a line in the song that says, "But when you build your house / Oh, then call me home.")[101] Nicks, furious that Henley had made the story public, would only confirm her ex's claims in a 2014 interview with *Billboard* magazine. "[What Don says is] accurate, but not the entirety of it," she would confess, evoking at the same time her friend Sara: "Had I married Don and had that baby, and had she been a girl, I would have named her Sara. But there was another woman in my life named Sara, who shortly after that became Mick's wife, Sara Fleetwood."[101] "Sara" is therefore a very personal song for Stevie Nicks. The imaginary figure of Sara transcends the different faces that are linked to these passions and dramas, to become her alter ego and muse.

1979

Stevie Nicks's piano part, played on the demo, was retained because it could be heard on the selected vocal track.

Production

"Sara" emerged as a sixteen-minute extended demo. Then, with the help of the other band members, it was condensed into a nine-minute studio version (mixed for listening purposes, but not intended for broadcast). A further edit reduced it to six and a half minutes for the album. A final version was cut to 4:37 for the single and subsequent CD editions of the album.

Stevie composed "Sara" on a piano before presenting it to the others. Mick quickly understood the rhythmic complexity of the song: "I worked for days, sweating bullets to put the time to it," he explains. "The softness required was a drummer's nightmare, but a great challenge. In the end it took three days to get the brushwork to accompany that piano and vocal. The result was, in many ways, the ultimate Fleetwood Mac song of that era, the late 1970s: breathless, ethereal, almost ecclesiastical and somehow reverent, as Stevie pays tribute to her muse."[4] It was for this very reason that Stevie found it hard to let go of the very first version of the song, which was obviously too long at sixteen minutes to envisage a commercial destiny. But the young woman felt that it was in this form that it was most representative of what she really had in mind when celebrating "her" Sara. "My friend Sara was there when I wrote it," she says. "She kept the coffee going and kept the cassettes coming and made sure we didn't run out of drums, and it was a long, long night recording that demo. She was a great songwriter helper."[105] Stevie was so keen on this

sixteen-minute version that she played it to her exes J. D. Souther and Don Henley. The singer reports: "[They both said,] 'You know what, it's almost not too long. It's good in its full 16 minuteness—it's got all these great verses and it just kinda travels through the world of your relationships.' They were really complimentary to me and these are two great songwriters. I knew I had to edit it down, but I found it hard to get below seven minutes. As simple and pretty as the song was, it turned into a magical, rhythmic, tribal thing with all those 'oohs' and 'aahs.' It's a fun song to sing."[105] Beyond Stevie Nicks's spellbinding vocals, Lindsey Buckingham's involvement is once again decisive, in both arrangement and production. The guitarist devoted himself to making things smoother and smoother as the work on the song progressed, without really being interested in the meaning of the text: "Some of Stevie's songs were hard to rein in," he commented. "If you're very lyric driven and not overly worried about time and structure, if it's more freeform, which a lot of Stevie's things can be, six or more minutes is not hard to get to [...]." Then Lindsey added, "I wasn't delving into Stevie's private life at the time, so I was never told what it was actually about. I always assumed it was addressed to her friend, who was Mick's wife at the time."[105]

"Sara" was released as the second single from *Tusk*, with "That's Enough for Me" on Side B, on December 14, 1979, in the UK, and on December 5 in the US, where it peaked at number seven in the Billboard Hot 100 top 10.

Breaking all production rules, Lindsey Buckingham records Mick Fleetwood's drums (here on stage at the Los Angeles Forum in 1979) with a boombox as an overhead mic.

WHAT MAKES YOU THINK YOU'RE THE ONE

Lindsey Buckingham / 3:28

Musicians: Lindsey Buckingham: vocals, guitar, bass, piano / Mick Fleetwood: drums / **Recorded:** Home studio of Lindsey Buckingham, Hollywood: May 1978–June 1979 / Village Recorders, Los Angeles: May 1978–June 1979 / **Technical Team:** Producers: Fleetwood Mac, Ken Caillat, Richard Dashut / Sound Engineers: Ken Caillat, Richard Dashut / Assistant Sound Engineers: Rich Feldman, Hernán Rojas

Genesis and Lyrics

Lindsey Buckingham's longed-for isolation finally took its toll on his nerves. In the solitude of his home studio, the shadows of his partners parasitized his thoughts. He plunged back into memories of his tormented relationship with Stevie Nicks. Bile rose to the surface, dictating some raw lyrics. His verses are peppered with acerbic rhetorical questions, while the murderous phrase "What makes you think you're the one?" recurs. This is a reminder to his partner that their breakup means independence, and that he is no longer the one she can turn to in her hour of need.

Production

Lindsey Buckingham's *Tusk* is a new hallmark in the deconstruction of pop. The musician takes on all the roles—vocals, bass, guitar, piano—except the drums. And with good reason: In his mind, none other than Mick Fleetwood was capable of executing the pattern he had in mind. And yet, it did not require any amazing technique. Quite the

contrary, in fact. The rhythm is reduced to its simplest expression, the hit is straight, mechanical, almost robotic, as if executed by a beginner. An illusion, because Mick's playing is anything but instinctive, as he replaces with snare drum strokes what would otherwise be provided by bass drum strokes. To add to the impression of imperfection, Lindsey imagined a singular treatment for this instrument, the opposite of a traditional take. Normally, the drum kit is the instrument that requires the most pickups. The minimal set usually includes one for the bass drum, two for the snare (above and below), two overheads (above the kit) and two ambient mics a little way off. Bypassing this classic arrangement, Lindsey replaced one of the ambient mics and an overhead with an unexpected sensor. "We cut this with just me on piano and Mick on drums, on opposite sides of the room," he recalls. Lindsey placed another on top of the kit. "Aside from setting up the normal mics, we set up a cassette player, a boombox, in front of the drums and ran it into the desk. The mics in those devices have capacitors in them that act as really low-quality limiters," he added, "so you got this squash that's really explosive, a real garage, trashy sound that you could only get that way. A good-quality limiter couldn't replicate it."[105] Mick was convinced by the result. And for good reason: All you can hear is his drums, so to speak. With a metallic sound, they take precedence over the other instruments, notably the floating guitar and the silky groove of the bass.

The love triangle Stevie forms with Mick Fleetwood and Lindsey Buckingham fuels her guilt and the lyrics of "Storms."

STORMS

Stevie Nicks / 5:28

Musicians: Stevie Nicks: vocals / Lindsey Buckingham: guitars, backing vocals / Christine McVie: keyboards, backing vocals / John McVie: bass / Mick Fleetwood: drums / **Recorded:** Village Recorders, Los Angeles: May 1978–June 1979 / **Technical Team:** Producers: Fleetwood Mac, Ken Caillat, Richard Dashut / Sound Engineers: Ken Caillat, Richard Dashut / Assistant Sound Engineers: Rich Feldman, Hernán Rojas

Genesis and Lyrics

In this introspective song, Stevie Nicks confronts the guilt of her affair with Mick Fleetwood—then still married to Jenny—and the karmic vengeance she endured when her best friend, Sara, secretly moved in with him. "Another tragedy," Stevie explains. "[This song] was really about Mick. That's Stevie not happy with the way that relationship ended. That relationship destroyed Mick's marriage to Jenny, who was the sweetest person in the world. So did we really think that we were going to come out of it unscathed? So then what happened to me, my best friend falling in love with him and moving into his house and neither of them telling me? It could not have been worse. [...] Don't break up other people's marriages. It will never work and will haunt you for the rest of your miserable days."[105] The text carries many contradictory emotions. Nicks oscillates between the will to move on and the need to atone for her mistakes and express her sorrow: "Every night you do not come / Your softness fades away." The song reaches its emotional climax with the verse: "So I try to say goodbye, my friend." Stevie's use of the word "friend" is highly revealing. It ratifies both the end of their love and the return to a normalized situation. She promises him that their friendship will not be damaged by this experience. Despite the apparent gentleness of the confession, Stevie Nicks has a very harsh interpretation of her message: "'Oh, that one was a—excuse my language—fuck-you to Mick,' she said. [...] A song about independence, I say. 'Freedom,' she says. 'I am a totally free woman, and I am independent, and that's exactly what I always wanted to be.'"[106]

Production

Stevie composed "Storms" alone at the piano. Despite all its assets, the song was coolly received by Lindsey Buckingham, who was perhaps vexed by the care with which Stevie documented her relationship with Fleetwood. Lindsey's girlfriend at the time, Carol Ann Harris, recalled that Stevie Nicks took the demo to the studio to play it for the rest of the band, but in the face of Lindsey's venomous criticism, the listening session ended in verbal fisticuffs, insults and shouting included. "These fights left their bloody marks, over and over again," Harris remembered. "Added to the weight of the battle scars from Lindsey's and Stevie's past personal relationship, they made the atmosphere of the studio even uglier with each passing day."[70] However, that would not stop Lindsey, looking back, from admitting to loving the song. With good taste and delicacy, the band sublimated "Storms" in a folk and country setting, where everyone contributed without excess to one of Stevie's most finely balanced compositions. Mick limits himself to caresses on his bass drum and a tambourine, while Christine is very discreet behind her keyboard, content to color the song, just as John does on bass. Lindsey's restrained guitar work is again admirable, and the airy backing vocals frame Stevie's magnificent vibrato.

THE BEACH BOYS, reflected by their producer and founder BRIAN WILSON . . . .

Direction:
William Morris
151 El Camino
Beverly Hills

Press & Publicity:
Derek Taylor
9000 Sunset Blvd.
Los Angeles

International Fan Club:
P.O. Box 110
Hollywood
California

"That's All for Everyone" is perhaps the track on *Tusk* most influenced by Brian Wilson and his Beach Boys.

THAT'S ALL FOR EVERYONE

Lindsey Buckingham / 3:04

Musicians: Stevie Nicks: backing vocals / Lindsey Buckingham: vocals, guitars / Christine McVie: keyboards, backing vocals / Mick Fleetwood: drums / John McVie: bass / **Recorded:** Village Recorders, Los Angeles: May 1978–June 1979 / **Technical Team:** Producers: Fleetwood Mac, Ken Caillat, Richard Dashut / Sound Engineers: Ken Caillat, Richard Dashut / Assistant Sound Engineers: Rich Feldman, Hernán Rojas

Genesis and Lyrics

While *Tusk* is a melting pot of Lindsey Buckingham's recent influences such as new wave, punk, and other modern genres, "That's All for Everyone" looks to the lush pop of artists such as 10cc and the Beach Boys. The song reveals a different side of Fleetwood Mac, previously unexplored (or underexplored). "This was influenced by Brian Wilson," explains the singer-guitarist. "What I love about him is not just his music but his choices. He gave me the courage to flout success, showed me that what you need to do as an artist is take risks and find new avenues."[105] The result is a commercial folk ballad with an airy chorus. The melody is more Lindsey's focus than the lyrics on this song; the lyrics are used more for their musicality than for their meaning. But the repetition of phrases can also induce an obsession in the lyricist. The lyrics evoke his relationship with others, and the discrepancy between the altruism he feels he displays ("I call for everyone") and the way his behavior is perceived by the other members of the band. Faced with this discrepancy, his primary reaction is to isolate himself, to find "somewhere to go."

Production

Behind the drums, Mick Fleetwood imbues the track with a slow, reassuring rhythm, while his rhythm section side-kick John McVie provides a bass line that is elementary but deep enough to thicken the foundation. For her part, Christine adds some interesting keyboard colors, as if it were a xylophone or marimba, but always in the background. Lindsey's brilliant acoustic guitars coexist wonderfully with confident vocals, supported by celestial backing vocals. "That's All for Everyone" may seem harmless at first, but it is another underrated song on *Tusk*. It seems to have served as inspiration for many bands, from Radiohead to Tame Impala, who delivered an interesting reworking of the song in 2012 on *Just Tell Me That You Want Me: A Tribute to Fleetwood Mac*.

NOT THAT FUNNY

Lindsey Buckingham / 3:19

Musicians: Lindsey Buckingham: vocals, guitars, keyboards / Christine McVie: piano / John McVie: bass / Mick Fleetwood: drums / **Recorded:** Village Recorders, Los Angeles: May 1978–June 1979 / **Technical Team:** Producers: Fleetwood Mac, Ken Caillat, Richard Dashut / Sound Engineers: Ken Caillat, Richard Dashut / Assistant Sound Engineers: Rich Feldman, Hernán Rojas / **Single:** Side A: Not That Funny / Side B: Save Me a Place / **UK Release Date:** March 7, 1980, with Warner Bros. Records (ref. K 17577) / Best UK Chart Ranking: Did Not Chart

Genesis and Lyrics

The very name "Not That Funny" sounds like a hastily scribbled slogan on a T-shirt with holes in it, marking Lindsey's most legible attempt to follow the trail blazed by the young punk and new-wave guard. There's a touch of XTC, Buzzcocks, and Devo in this attempt to reproduce their rough and casual edge. With Phil Daniels–style diction—Daniels played Jimmy in the film *Quadrophenia* and narrated Blur's hit single "Parklife"—Lindsey throws his lyrics like darts. Like the music, they shed all poetic flourishes to focus on the essential, even if this means losing semantic depth. His short sentences are no more than the expression of a mood—in this case, a bad mood. For the narrator focuses his bile on his interlocutor, reproaching him for clinging on, complaining and wasting his time. The most damning sentence for the designated victim (Stevie Nicks, in all likelihood) comes in the second chorus: "You're here cause I say so." The implication is cruel: If I say otherwise, you don't belong. Reducing her to the role of accessory, Lindsey coldly finishes off his victim: "I didn't wanna be this late / So don't make me wait." Lindsey removes any remaining doubts about the identity of his interlocutor in the liner notes to the album's reissue: "This was directed at Stevie a little bit,"[105] he shyly concedes. In his view, it was also a question of the importance attached to the band's image, a hidden attack on Stevie and the attention, excessive for Lindsey's taste, that she pays to it. "There's something we are still having to deal with as a band: 'What's important here? People thinking you're cool or thinking you're cool yourself?' It's more how you feel about yourself, isn't it? This is a classic pitfall of the entertainment industry."[105]

Production

While onstage Lindsey would most often perform "Not That Funny" on the Rick Turner model designed for him by the luthier of the same name in 1979, the guitarist used a Fender Stratocaster for the recording. However, the natural sound of the instrument is greatly altered: It has undergone a VSO (variable sound oscillation, also known as vari-speed). This device allows the tape speed to be reduced or increased. "I just slow the machine down, come up with a picking part like that, double or triple it and tweak the VSO on either side so that it's slightly out of tune, and the whole thing comes out with all this phasing."[105] Once the track was structured, with a simple, round bass that played the fundamentals, Buckingham tackled the vocals. Inspired by the characteristically provocative punk accents, flirting with falsetto or spoken word—in the image of Johnny Rotten's mocking vocals in the Sex Pistols—he takes the complete opposite tack of what he demonstrated on *Rumours*.

The conditions for the vocal recordings defy all logic. Whereas a vocal take is (normally) done standing up, with the vocal air column well maintained, Lindsey decided to record on the floor, as if he were about to do push-ups. The microphone was taped to the floor by Ken Caillat. Lindsey recorded in a bathroom adjoining the studio—a replica of his own bathroom, which he demanded when the studio was fitted out. With his body under such tension, this limited his breathing capacity and prevented him from maintaining long phrase endings. On the other hand, the stiffness of his vocals and his nervous, raging side are enhanced. At around 2:00, you can hear variations in his sound, as if he were moving away from the microphone. These imperfections were retained to underline the spontaneity of the track—an apparent spontaneity only, since, like the other tracks, "Not That Funny" required many months of work before reaching its final version.

SISTERS OF THE MOON

Stevie Nicks / 4:36

Musicians
Stevie Nicks: vocals
Lindsey Buckingham: guitars, backing vocals
Christine McVie: keyboards, backing vocals
John McVie: bass
Mick Fleetwood: drums

Recorded
Village Recorders, Los Angeles: May 1978–June 1979

Technical Team
Producers: Fleetwood Mac, Ken Caillat, Richard Dashut
Sound Engineers: Ken Caillat, Richard Dashut
Assistant Sound Engineers: Rich Feldman, Hernán Rojas

Single
Side A: Sisters of the Moon / Side B: Walk a Thin Line
US Release: May 8, 1980, with Warner Bros. Records (ref. WBS 49500)
Best US Chart Ranking: 86

Enveloped in haunting melodies and poetic lyrics,
"Sisters of the Moon" celebrates sisterhood and magic.

Genesis and Lyrics

If Mick Fleetwood is to be believed, the genesis of "Sisters of the Moon" can be traced back to Fleetwood Mac's very first tour with its new Nicks/Buckingham duo. Not yet fully accepted by the critics, Stevie Nicks often isolated herself to blacken her notebooks and chase away the bad vibes that tended to get to her, to the point where she seriously considered leaving the band before enjoying the major successes we know about. "I have a strong image of Stevie during that first tour," explains the drummer, "sitting backstage and writing the lyrics to 'Sisters of the Moon' in her notebook, working into her art some of the torn and frayed feelings from those earliest days on the road."[4] A mystical, haunting song about sisterhood and the power of women, the lyrics in "Sisters of the Moon" evoke mystery and magic, as well as strength and resilience. But they also touch on themes of independence and finding one's own way in a male-dominated world ("She asked me: 'Be my sister / Sister, sister of the moon'"). Stevie Nicks's fascination with magic is fully expressed in this text, which blurs the boundaries between the real and the mystical. If the musician is to be believed, things seem much simpler: "I honestly don't know what the hell this song is about. I've been singing it on tour for the last two and a half years, and every time I'm thinking, What the hell is that? I think it was me putting up an alter ego or something, the dark lady in the corner, and there's a Gemini twin thing. It wasn't a love song; it wasn't written about a man, or anything precious. It was just about a feeling I might have had over a couple days, going inward in my gnarly trollness. Makes no sense. Perfect for this record!"[105]

Production

"Sisters of the Moon," unlike many of the songs on *Tusk*, is not the result of Lindsey Buckingham's solitary work in his home studio. In fact, it is one of the group's rare collective efforts, born of jam sessions at Village Recorders in Los Angeles. Its slow construction, giving the feeling that an explosion could occur at any bar, makes it one of the most intense tracks on the album. John's purring bass opens the ball, while Mick's powerful but haunting drums accompany Lindsey Buckingham's first arpeggios. The latter, with his almost aspirated notes, gives the

After the Mirage tour, "Sisters of the Moon" disappeared from the band's set list (here in Boston in 1979) and was not reinstated until 2013.

Transposed to the stage, "Sisters of the Moon" often extends far beyond its length on record, averaging 8:00 on the *Mirage* tour.

impression of using an EBow, the electronic device invented by Greg Heet in 1969. Created with guitarists in mind, this small object generates a magnetic field that vibrates a string. The resulting sound resembles that of a bowed note. Lindsey deftly plays his volume potentiometer to blend in and fade out of the arrangement. Before the vocals begin, the haunting backing vocals add a touch of mysticism to the song's opening. Christine provides meticulous background work, with keyboards that are sometimes soft and sometimes aggressive. This mystical hymn is fueled by one of the band's most brutal riffs since Peter Green's departure: chordal bursts take the song from muted verses to shattering choruses. But while often restrained, the track literally explodes from 3:42 onward with Lindsey Buckingham's screaming solo, reminiscent of his work on "The Chain." Like Stevie at the top of her game, the guitarist in turn seems totally possessed by the spirit of this enigmatic "sister of the moon." "Sisters of the Moon" was selected as the fifth single from *Tusk*, following "Think About Me." Released in the US on May 8, 1980, it failed to make better than eighty-sixth place on the Billboard charts.

The protecting angel sublimated by Stevie Nicks's lyrics has a face: that of Mick Fleetwood.

ANGEL
Stevie Nicks / 4:53

Musicians: Stevie Nicks: vocals / Lindsey Buckingham: guitar, backing vocals / Christine McVie: keyboards / John McVie: bass / Mick Fleetwood: drums / **Recorded:** Village Recorders, Los Angeles: May 1978–June 1979 / **Technical Team:** Producers: Fleetwood Mac, Ken Caillat, Richard Dashut / Sound Engineers: Ken Caillat, Richard Dashut / Assistant Sound Engineers: Rich Feldman, Hernán Rojas

Exploiting the potential of *Tusk* to the last breath, Warner Bros. decided to extract the "Angel" number as a sixth single, targeting the Dutch and French markets, which the label suspected would be sensitive to the ballad's soft-rock, slightly country flavor. But the song failed to make it onto the best-seller charts.

Genesis and Lyrics

While Lindsey Buckingham ruminated endlessly on his grievances with Stevie Nicks, the singer blossomed into a much more pleasant romantic present. Carried away by the budding love she secretly shared with Mick Fleetwood, she penned this tender, delicate song. "A song about Mick. Not so much my love affair with him. I was always taken with his style, and in those days he would walk in the room and I would just look up."[105] The nature of their relationship, secret and fueled by frustration, is clearly evoked: "I try not to reach out / When you turn 'round you say hello / And we both pretend." Stevie is well aware that the other members of the team are talking about it behind their backs: "Now they tell the story." Bathed in mysticism, the text conveys a great tenderness and an almost childlike admiration for the big guy: "It's all about him and his crazy fob watch and his really beautiful clothes. He's a very stylish individual and I was just this little California girl who'd never really known anybody like him."[105]

Production

Stevie not only flirts with Mick on this song, but also with country on the first section, before allowing herself to be swept away by hard-rock vibes on the finale. On this occasion, we discover the extent of her tessitura and the roughness of her timbre when she takes on more muscular terrain. Far removed from delicate, introspective ballads such as "Beautiful Child" and "Storms," two of Nicks's other contributions to the *Tusk* album, "Angel" develops a catchy, rhythmic melody. Despite the differences between Stevie and Lindsey, the latter was fully committed to the production of this song. He was involved in setting up the deeper counter-vocal that harmonizes with the main vocal: he is at the piano and she is standing at his side, they spent hours working on every intonation. Aware of the importance of this song to Stevie, Lindsey diplomatically offered advice. When Stevie lost herself in incidental vocalizations, he told her that it was too much, and put her back on the path to efficiency. Then, once the round, warm bass had been laid down, he took his Fender in hand and wove two parts that complement each other wonderfully, passing the baton like dance partners. On one side, he creates a feel-good country score, sprinkled with skillful playing effects, and on the other, a solo part, bursting with distortion, infuses a rock tension that electrifies the final minutes of "Angel."

Lindsey, flamboyant in his vermilion jacket with his sunburst-finished Gibson Les Paul, onstage at the Alpine Valley Music Theater in East Troy, Wisconsin, in 1978.

THAT'S ENOUGH FOR ME

Lindsey Buckingham / 1:48

Musicians: Lindsey Buckingham: vocals, guitar, banjo, drums /
Recorded: Village Recorders, Los Angeles: May 1978–June 1979 /
Technical Team: Producers: Fleetwood Mac, Ken Caillat, Richard Dashut / Sound Engineers: Ken Caillat, Richard Dashut / Assistant Sound Engineers: Rich Feldman, Hernán Rojas / **Single:** Side A: Sara / Side B: That's Enough for Me / **UK Release Date:** December 14, 1979, with Warner Bros. Records (ref. K 17533) / Best UK Chart Ranking: 37 / **Single:** Side A: Sara / Side B: That's Enough for Me / **US Release Date:** December 5, 1979, with Warner Bros. Records (ref. WBS 49150) / Best US Chart Ranking: 7

Genesis and Lyrics

"Every time you make me smile / It's the same old way it used to be […] Every time that sleep don't come / It's the same old pain that used to be." Even if he does not say much with this very short text, Lindsey Buckingham cracks the shell and exceptionally reveals his flaws. A simple smile is enough to revive the memory of a shared happiness, but it also awakens the memory of a painful breakup and causes insomnia in the narrator. Stuck in this emotional roller-coaster loop, he is doomed never to get out. At the heart of the song, Lindsey Buckingham includes vocals ("yeah, yeah, yeah, yeah, mmm, ah, oh") whose intonations reinforce the sense of nostalgia and suggest all that the narrator cannot express with words.

Production

With its frenetic feel—reminiscent of "Second Hand News" on *Rumours*, "That's Enough for Me" is one of three tracks on *Tusk* on which Lindsey Buckingham handled all the instruments, along with "The Ledge" and "Save Me a Place." The rendering is far less spectacular on this new track, with rudimentary drums that are, to say the least, rushed and singularly lacking in subtlety, as is the bass, whose presence is purely anecdotal. Lindsey Buckingham seems to devote all his energy to guitars and banjo, mixing rock and country. The song, whose working title was "Out on the Road," is sometimes played even faster live. Far from being the favorite of the other musicians, who chose not to contribute to it, it would have a hard time finding a lasting place in Fleetwood Mac's stage set. It was "rockabilly on acid," Lindsey explained. "An attempt to do something quite surreal, grounded in something recognizable. I was tapping into a general set of reference points on this album. But I never thought of it in terms of nostalgia. It was anti-nostalgia, if you will."[105]

Like the ghostly Syd Barrett, who suddenly appeared in the Pink Floyd studio after a few years' absence, Peter Green, physically transformed, made an anecdotal appearance on "Brown Eyes."

BROWN EYES

Christine McVie / 4:27

Musicians: Stevie Nicks: vocals, backing vocals / Lindsey Buckingham: guitars, backing vocals / Peter Green: guitar / Christine McVie: vocals, keyboards, backing vocals / John McVie: bass / Mick Fleetwood: drums, tambourine / **Recorded:** Village Recorders, Los Angeles: May 1978–June 1979 / **Technical Team:** Producers: Fleetwood Mac, Ken Caillat, Richard Dashut / Sound Engineers: Ken Caillat, Richard Dashut / Assistant Sound Engineers: Rich Feldman, Hernán Rojas

Genesis and Lyrics

A resolutely captivating song, "Brown Eyes" explores the emotions born of a simple exchange of glances. The lyrics may be simple and the refrain repetitive, but every second underscores the power and intensity of this fleeting moment. Several times, the narrator (Christine) questions this gaze: "What do you want to do?" The question suggests the hope of a deeper connection and reciprocity. The famous "sha-la-la-la-la-la-la-la," scattered throughout the track, expresses in a universal way what mere words cannot: the depth of the singer's desire. As if snapping out of her reverie, however, she worries about succumbing too easily to the charm of this "brown-eyed" person, regarding whose sincerity and honesty she asks: "Are you just another liar?" Despite this, she seems ready to follow him "all the way," providing further proof of the intensity of her desire.

Production

A deeply moving and introspective song, probably one of the most underrated on *Tusk*, "Brown Eyes" relies above all on evocative lyrics and repetitive refrains to capture those fleeting moments of intense attraction. John McVie's deep, venomous bass is supported by Mick Fleetwood's solid drums; his bass drum, conveying a penetrating sensuality, gives the impression of beating to the rhythm of a heart. Guitars and keyboards, set to a mysterious tremolo effect, carpet the arrangement effectively. They reinforce the intensity of the song, whose instrumental pause is a moment of catharsis, allowing the listener to reflect on the emotions conveyed in the lyrics. The intoxicating blend of vocals, guitars, and keyboards in this plaintive bridge leaves the listener with a lingering sense of melancholy, reflecting the bittersweet nature of unfulfilled desires. Fleetwood Mac founder Peter Green makes an uncredited appearance on this Christine McVie song. His solo is barely perceptible on the final fade-out but can be heard in its entirety on the 2015 reissue of *Tusk*.

"Peter was living in L.A. then and hanging out at my house a lot," Mick Fleetwood later explained. "He was still as he is now, changed, but he used to pop into the studio occasionally. I don't know if he was that interested or not, but he did play on this song, which I love. [...] The band's playing really shines. I can't recall why we only used Peter at the very end, but it's great that he's on here, because it's Peter and it's his band."[105] It did not, however, leave a lasting impression on Lindsey Buckingham: "I don't remember Peter Green coming in, so I don't think I made any judgement on whether to use it or not,"[105] he said later.

Christine McVie provides *Tusk* with one of its most accomplished ballads: "Never Make Me Cry."

NEVER MAKE ME CRY

Christine McVie / 2:14

Musicians: Christine McVie: vocals, piano / Lindsey Buckingham: guitars / John McVie: bass / Mick Fleetwood: drums / **Recorded:** Village Recorders, Los Angeles: May 1978–June 1979 / Technical Team / Producers: Fleetwood Mac, Ken Caillat, Richard Dashut / Sound Engineers: Ken Caillat, Richard Dashut / Assistant Sound Engineers: Rich Feldman, Hernán Rojas / **Single:** Side A: Tusk / Side B: Never Make Me Cry / **UK Release Date:** September 28, 1979, with Warner Bros. Records (ref. K 17468) / Best UK Chart Ranking: 6 / **Single:** Side A: Tusk / Side B: Never Make Me Cry / **US Release Date:** September 12, 1979, with Warner Bros. Records (ref. WBS 49077) / Best US Chart Ranking: 8

Genesis and Lyrics

Contrary to the musical direction set by Lindsey Buckingham, Christine McVie's "Tusk" is an ethereal, introspective pop number. Extending the gentle bubble of "Brown Eyes" with "Never Make Me Cry," Christine hunts in Joni Mitchell territory with this melancholy ballad imbued with disarming vulnerability. The narrator gives in to her love partner's "need" and allows him complete freedom in their relationship. She assures him that she will not cry if he wishes to go elsewhere—an antiphrasis that fools no one. The beginning of the second verse confirms this with a confession coupled with a terrible submission: "Now I may not mean everything / But I'm happy to have your love." In a final magnanimous gesture, Christine McVie, the first victim of this unbalanced love and wounded in her self-esteem, even assumes a maternal role. She tries to reassure her interlocutor in an unfair reversal of roles: "Don't worry baby, I'll be alright."

Production

Christine McVie's haunting alto voice reinforces the impact of the message. She carries a heavy emotional burden, without lapsing into pathos. Very quickly in the recording process, the vocal line stabilized and Christine found the right intensity in her interpretation. The orchestration raised more questions for the musicians. The keyboard parts, in particular, divided them. Although they are the foundation of the song, they covered Lindsey's subtle, mutated guitar playing, which sets a captivating folk scene when accompanied by a second guitar track providing the steamy slides. After various trials, it was decided to give priority to Buckingham's tracks, to the detriment of the keyboards, which found themselves placed further back in the mix.

I KNOW I'M NOT WRONG

Lindsey Buckingham / 2:59

Musicians: Lindsey Buckingham: vocals, guitars, keyboards, percussion, backing vocals / John McVie: bass / Mick Fleetwood: drums, percussion / **Recorded:** Village Recorders, Los Angeles, May 1978–June 1979 / Technical Team / Producers: Fleetwood Mac, Ken Caillat, Richard Dashut / Sound Engineers: Ken Caillat, Richard Dashut / Assistant Sound Engineers: Rich Feldman, Hernán Rojas

Genesis and Lyrics

Like "The Chain" on *Rumours*, "I Know I'm Not Wrong" was the first song to be worked on and the last to be finalized by the recording on *Tusk*. Its upbeat rhythm, compressed guitar sound, and incorporation of synthetic keyboards, heralding the musical decade to come, speak volumes about the sound Lindsey Buckingham wanted to project. He urged his comrades to jump onto the punk and new wave bandwagon. He mastered the codes both from a compositional and from a songwriting perspective. The latter is concise and incisive. Punk does not bother with verbiage and gets straight to the point to get its message across, usually a social one. The guitarist had not yet taken this last step, and remained attached to the theme that always drives his lyrics: love, and even more so, the relationship difficulties that stem from it. As is often the case, his songwriting exudes an unshakable assurance: "Don't blame me / Please be strong / I know I'm not wrong." The lyrics are directly linked to another Lindsey Buckingham track on this album: "Not That Funny." And for good reason—entire verses are common to both compositions: "Don't blame me," "Here comes the nighttime / Looking for a little more," and "Somebody outside the door." "I Know I'm Not Wrong" is therefore the thematic sequel to "Not That Funny" and is most likely addressed to Stevie Nicks.

Production

The change of musical formula brought about by "I Know I'm Not Wrong"—revolutionary even on the scale of a band that had gone from British blues boom reference to California rock standard-bearer—did not come without its difficulties. It required a great deal of trial and error. In fact, the song went through several iterations before taking on its final form after a year of hard work. The original demo, concocted by Lindsey in the privacy of his home studio, marked a real break with what he had been able to offer up to that point. Devoid of vocals at this early stage, it includes a childlike keyboard motif that lights up the intro, but quickly disappears in the recording process. The very new-wave keyboard arrangement at the end, on the other hand, was retained for its originality and the synthetic tinge it provides. Several guitar tracks were added over time, adding density to the melody. But the find that gives the track its singularity is the addition of an unlikely "instrument": a box of Kleenex. "I've often looked for alternatives for the function of things such as the snare and hi-hat—anything that would get away from the norm," Lindsey commented in 2009. "I'd think, 'What can I do on the two and four that doesn't sound like a snare?' Of course, in rock, you need the action and rhythm of that instrument, but why not subvert the norm and find other things? [...] Those aren't really big subversions—especially by today's standards—but, at the time, they were."[107]

1979

Despite their differences in character, John and Lindsey share a deep connection when playing their respective instruments.

HONEY HI

Christine McVie / 2:43

Musicians: Christine McVie: vocals, keyboards / Lindsey Buckingham: guitars, backing vocals / John McVie: bass / Mick Fleetwood: percussion / Stevie Nicks: backing vocals / **Recorded:** Village Recorders, Los Angeles: May 1978–June 1979 / **Technical Team:** Producers: Fleetwood Mac, Ken Caillat, Richard Dashut / Sound Engineers: Ken Caillat, Richard Dashut / Assistant Sound Engineers: Rich Feldman, Hernán Rojas / **Single:** Side A: Think About Me / Side B: Honey Hi / **UK Release Date:** May 9, 1980, with Warner Bros. Records (ref. K 17614) / Best UK Chart Ranking: Did Not Chart

Genesis and Lyrics

Love is once again the driving force behind Christine McVie's writing. "Honey Hi" expresses infinite tenderness for the loved one. The affectionate nickname "honey" is deliberate, since the other meaning of the word *honey* is also suggested by the term "sweet." In addition to reinforcing the mellowness of the musical setting conceived by Fleetwood Mac, this "honey" in the double sense of "darling/honey" provokes an unconscious connection between the feeling of well-being induced by love and the gustatory metaphor. "Who could be sweeter than you?" asks Christine, before adding, "Even sweeter than wine." The narrator's ecstasy is heightened when she introduces this religious exclamation: "Lord, it's good to talk to you."

Underlying all this, however, is the fear that the relationship will be weakened: "Don't take the love light away" and "Oh, I'm far from home." For McVie's writing is never monolithic, and always employs chiaroscuro. The threat comes from distance, as we understand that the two protagonists are far away from each other: "'Cause I'm far away from home." Christine McVie is weighed down by the constraints of an artist's life, and in particular her stage commitments.

Production

Christine's ballad, which combines elements of soft rock, pop, and folk, benefits from an arrangement that is as sober as it is effective. With its gentle melody and heartfelt lyrics, "Honey Hi" has an intimate feel. The musician's moving interpretation literally brings to life the lyrics, with which everyone can identify. Lindsey's gentle acoustic guitar, John's round, gently bouncing bass, Mick's benevolent percussion, Christine's melodic keyboard: All combine to create a soothing atmosphere that wonderfully complements the introspective themes explored in the song. The backing vocals on the chorus, from which Stevie Nicks's voice emerges, are an ideal complement to the singer's moving vocals.

"Beautiful Child" evokes Stevie Nicks's fond memories of Derek Taylor, one of her past lovers.

BEAUTIFUL CHILD

Stevie Nicks / 5:19

Musicians: Stevie Nicks: vocals, backing vocals / Lindsey Buckingham: guitars, backing vocals / Christine McVie: keyboards, backing vocals / Mick Fleetwood: drums / John McVie: bass / **Recorded:** Village Recorders, Los Angeles: May 1978–June 1979 / **Technical Team:** Producers: Fleetwood Mac, Ken Caillat, Richard Dashut / Sound Engineers: Ken Caillat, Richard Dashut / Assistant Sound Engineers: Rich Feldman, Hernán Rojas

Genesis and Lyrics

While Stevie Nicks has extensively documented her complicated relationships with men—foremost among them Lindsey Buckingham, Mick Fleetwood, and Don Henley—there is one who left her with wonderful memories, and to whom she dedicated "Beautiful Child." The song focuses on a brief affair the singer says she had with Derek Taylor, known for having been the Beatles' road manager and press attaché, but who also worked over the years with the Byrds, Harry Nilsson, the Monterey Pop Festival, the Beach Boys, and WEA Records. Brief (as Taylor was a married man at the time), but intense. In many ways, "Beautiful Child" resembles Stevie Nicks's coming-of-age song. "This is one of my very favorite ballads," the singer explains. "It's so from the heart. It was written about an English man (Beatles' late road manager Derek Taylor) I was crazy about who was quite a bit older than me—another one of my doomed relationships. He used to read poetry out loud to me in his beautiful English voice, and I would sit at his feet, just mesmerized, and he would say, 'You are a beautiful child,' and I'd say, 'I'm not a child anymore.'" This last phrase is repeated as it stands in the lyrics ("I'm not a child anymore"), supplemented by this phrase that can possibly be understood in a physical sense: "I'm tall enough to reach for the stars." "He was married, so we stopped, because it was going to hurt a lot of people. The song is like a straight retelling of the last night of that relationship. Every time I sing it I'm transported back to the Beverly Hills Hotel and walking across the grounds to get a cab after saying goodbye."[105]

Production

Wisdom and maturity are the key words in the arrangement of "Beautiful Child." As the song deals with a very complex theme for the author, and above all a no-win situation (that is, to give up on a love affair and suffer for it, or to keep it and make others suffer), a sober, effective accompaniment was needed to complement Stevie Nicks' bewitching voice. Christine McVie's piano is infinitely delicate, sparingly distilling notes in direct connection with her friend's heart, while the rhythm section seems to offer her a sympathetic shoulder to cry on. Even Lindsey's guitars show restraint and empathy, wandering through the song with a heart-rending tremolo. This fascinating tale, a veritable emotional outlet that delves into the complexities of a love relationship, would not be complete without the presence of the sublime, meticulously crafted vocal harmonies.

Mick Fleetwood in 1978.

A year after the release of "Walk a Thin Line," Mick Fleetwood reappropriated the song in 1981 on his first solo album, *The Visitor*, recorded in Accra, Ghana. The African band Adjo provided backing vocals alongside Sara Recor, his new love. George Harrison, Mick's ex-brother-in-law, added a twelve-string guitar and a slide part.

WALK A THIN LINE
Lindsey Buckingham / 3:44

Musicians: Lindsey Buckingham: vocals, guitars, backing vocals, piano, drums / Christine McVie: keyboards, backing vocals / John McVie: bass / **Recorded:** Village Recorders, Los Angeles: May 1978–June 1979 / **Technical Team:** Producers: Fleetwood Mac, Ken Caillat, Richard Dashut / Sound Engineers: Ken Caillat, Richard Dashut / Assistant Sound Engineers: Rich Feldman, Hernán Rojas / **Single:** Side A: Sisters of the Moon / Side B: Walk a Thin Line / **US Release Date:** May 8, 1980, with Warner Bros. Records (ref. WBS 49500) / Best US Chart Ranking: 86

Genesis and Lyrics
At the heart of Lindsey Buckingham's ebullient dismantling of Fleetwood Mac's musical formula on *Tusk*, "Walk a Thin Line" stands out from the guitarist's other compositions, most of which are edgy and abrasive, due to its ethereal character. Carried along by angelic backing vocals, its instrumentation blends perfectly with the sense of vulnerability suggested by the text. At least, this is what it sounds like on the surface. Scratch further and the isolation and lack of attention paid to the protagonist by those around him suggests otherwise. Lindsey's role within the group is that of a natural leader. He sets a course and dispenses advice and aphorisms to the other members: "Take your time," "Stay by my side," "Fate takes time." But he was not listened to. At least not enough for his taste: "But no one was listenin'." Annoyed by the dilettantism of his partners,

he knows that to be heard, he needs to be diplomatic to get his message across ("I walk a thin line"), and he knows that this is not his strongest point.

Production
Attentive to emerging British bands, Lindsey never lost sight of the "old guard." In his rare moments of distraction, the guitarist immersed himself in listening to classics from his record library, including *Sticky Fingers* (1971) by the Rolling Stones. He literally locked onto "Sway," Side B of "Wild Horses," a blues-rock classic whose originality lies in Charlie Watts's drumming. Just as the song is settling into the comfort of a moderate-tempo blues pattern, the Stones dandy breaks the ambient torpor with a military-inspired roll that turns the song on its head. Buckingham, decidedly obsessed with the rhythmic aspect on *Tusk*, wanted to include this same kind of break in "Walk a Thin Line." Here, too, the rhythm seems simple, obvious, and set to last throughout the song. It is the ideal base for a surprise attack on the listener. While the listener is comfortably lulled by Lindsey's whispering, caressing voice and the multiple backing vocals that envelop it, layers of superimposed snare drums launch an unexpected assault and make the melody jolt. Its musical qualities earned this track a place on Side B of the "Sisters of the Moon" single on May 8, 1980.

TUSK

Lindsey Buckingham / 3:36

Musicians
Lindsey Buckingham: vocals, guitars, percussion
Christine McVie: keyboards, backing vocals
John McVie: bass
Mick Fleetwood: drums, percussion
USC Trojan Marching Band: percussion, brass, woodwind
Stevie Nicks: backing vocals

Recorded
Village Recorders, Los Angeles: May 1978–June 1979
Dodger Stadium, Los Angeles: June 4, 1979

Technical Team
Producers: Fleetwood Mac, Ken Caillat, Richard Dashut
Sound Engineers: Ken Caillat, Richard Dashut
Assistant Sound Engineers: Rich Feldman, Hernán Rojas

Single
Side A: Tusk / Side B: Never Make Me Cry
UK Release: September 28, 1979, with Warner Bros. Records
   (ref. K 17468)
Best UK Chart Ranking: 6

Single
Side A: Tusk / Side B: Never Make Me Cry
US Release: September 12, 1979, with Warner Bros. Records
   (ref. WBS 49077)
Best US Chart Ranking: 8

FOR MAC-ADDICTS
During the Tusk tour in December 1979, Fleetwood Mac played five concerts at the Forum in Inglewood (near Los Angeles, California). The USC Trojan Marching Band appeared alongside the band at each of these shows, joining them on stage on a platform raised by hydraulic columns.

Genesis and Lyrics

Mick Fleetwood had long dreamed of a song that would reflect Fleetwood Mac's identity, combining a sense of grandeur with something more introspective. And so "Tusk" was born, based on a riff the band played when they took the stage, the lights went down, and it was announced, just before the first song, usually enabling Richard Dashut to set his levels behind the console. "It was just a little riff that Lindsey started playing one night, and I'm tapping my drums," Mick explained. "We used to play it in the dark for less than a minute every night. When we began the new album we tried doing something with it, but the idea was scrapped. Months and months went by, but that riff just would not leave my head."[4] Once in the studio, Mick placed a few drum overdubs on a song base consisting of a loop of this four-bar riff. In fact, this is what the band originally called the track: "The Riff."

Literally obsessed with this project, Mick then recalls his visit to Normandy the previous summer: "After my father's death, my sister Sally took my mother to Barfleur, a beautiful fishing village in the north of France that Mum always loved. We all missed Dad, and I was looking forward to joining them and spending time with Biddy; it was the first occasion I'd been able to do so since Dad's death."[2] A rockstar at the height of his fame, Mick did not shy away from any folly, and as soon as he disembarked from his Los Angeles–Paris trip, he got into a long white limousine hired for the occasion to drive him to this quiet village in the English Channel. The musician, who had already become quite drunk during the flight, continued to drink in the car and arrived in Barfleur with a raging hangover. As he tried to recuperate by sleeping, he was jolted awake by a local brass band touring the village. "I tried to get back to sleep after the band had passed, to no avail," he says, before adding, "Just when I thought they had stopped for half an hour, back they came roaring through the village again. It became clear there was to be no relief, so I got up and opened the shutters onto a wonderful scene by Bruegel: old peasants with bloodshot noses, young women garbed in colorful local costume, kids running around, drunks staggering after the band, the village all garlanded and festooned, everyone having a grand time *à la fête*."[4]

A creative anomaly, a whimsical idea, Mick's stroke of genius… *Tusk* closes the eponymous album with a fanfare.

The memory of this brass band, bringing young and old together in a festive atmosphere, gave Mick the idea of bringing a brass band on stage during Fleetwood Mac concerts. Why not the local brass bands of the towns where they performed? It could reinforce the closeness with the audience. The idea, though excellent, never came to fruition. Lindsey Buckingham began working on the project, devising a simple text that could be taken up by a chorus. The first lines, in the form of questions, seem to evoke the secret—which was no longer a secret—of the sentimental relationship between Mick and Stevie, their secrecy, the drummer's discreet visits to the singer after the sessions. ("Why don't you ask him if he's going to stay? / Why don't

you ask him if he's going away?") Then the lyrics take a more subversive turn, in keeping with the song's name, "Tusk," a slang word for a penis. So it is possible to read the rest of the text from a sexual angle: "Don't say that you love me / Just tell me that you want me." Not to mention the orgasmic "tusk" mantra, chanted repeatedly on the finale.

Production

Mick volunteered to put the finishing touches to the fanfare project: "In a typical burst of grandiosity, I said I wanted to go for an immense wall of sound, that I wanted to record the band in Dodger Stadium. Silence. They looked at me as if I were mad. Someone murmured that this idea was a little

The "Rumours Five" experienced a true consecration at the unveiling of their star on Hollywood's famous Walk of Fame on October 10, 1979.

off the wall."[4] Clearly not Judy Wong, a longtime friend of the band who had worked with them, as she was the first to say that she knew someone at the Dodger Stadium who could facilitate access. All that remained was to find a brass band: "I forget exactly how the University of Southern California's Trojan Marching Band was chosen to play the part of the village band on the album," explains Mick, "I went to one of the marching band's meetings, played them a tape of 'the riff,' and asked if they could manage an arrangement. The kids liked the idea."[4]

A few weeks later, on June 4, 1979, Fleetwood Mac, the 112 members of the Trojans, and a film crew gathered in a completely empty Dodger Stadium on a beautiful California afternoon for a recording, which went perfectly, with the help of a mobile studio. Everyone was ecstatic, including Stevie, who reminisced about her youth playing majorette. The only thing missing was John McVie, who, having finished recording all his parts for the album, was sailing to Hawaii, then on to the South Pacific aboard his boat. "In his place, we had a life-sized cardboard cut-out of him, and Christine and I took turns walking him around and placing him wherever we went,"[2] says Mick. "On some level this song was the embodiment of the spirit of the album," explained Lindsey Buckingham. "Riffs were a big thing for me, and Mick was always one to pick up on the potential of that. Christine helped me on this with some chords. The drum track is a loop. […] It was Mick's idea to include the marching band. It was a great thing for USC. Not a particularly hummable song in the normal sense, but it functioned as a commercial piece, and it's a killer moment in the live show."[105] Always willing to give of himself to push the boundaries of the studio, Lindsey Buckingham first

recorded part of his voice in a bathroom using a microphone he placed on the floor and which was connected to his home studio. Similarly, he added a few bits of percussion by banging on empty Kleenex boxes. Finally, with its chaotic ambience, tribal percussion, rumbling bass, and infectiously good-humored backing vocals, "Tusk" immediately won over the public, becoming one of the strangest singles ever to reach the top 10.

FOR MAC-ADDICTS

The marching band was captured on June 4, 1979, at Dodger Stadium, while the baseball franchise was on the road. The students of the USC Trojan Marching Band had finished their year and had taken their exams shortly before. Officially on vacation, almost all of them were present nonetheless, motivated by this historic event and delighted to receive a copy of the *Rumours* album as a gift on each of their dorm beds.

1979

John McVie, Mick Fleetwood, Lindsey Buckingham, and Stevie Nicks, onstage at the Boston Garden, November 17, 1979.

NEVER FORGET

Christine McVie / 3:40

Musicians: Christine McVie: vocals, piano, keyboard / Lindsey Buckingham: guitars, backing vocals / John McVie: bass / Mick Fleetwood: drums, percussion / Stevie Nicks: backing vocals
Recorded: Village Recorders, Los Angeles: May 1978–June 1979
Technical Team: Producers: Fleetwood Mac, Ken Caillat, Richard Dashut / Sound Engineers: Ken Caillat, Richard Dashut / Assistant Sound Engineers: Rich Feldman, Hernán Rojas

Genesis and Lyrics

The band's protean, experimental album concludes with a classically styled song by Christine McVie, who confirms, with this sweet melody, that she was not about to change her compositional style. A devoted partner when it comes to Buckingham's experiments on his songs, she remains true to her values and perfects her art with ever-greater care and delicacy when it comes to her own tracks. On "Never Forget," she sings of the complete happiness of being at the side of the loved one, without reserve (the adverb "never," marker of this absolute, unconditional love, is back, after "Never Make Me Cry," another of her tracks on this album). The lyricist marvels at simple moments like a walk under the stars on the arm of her companion, enjoy-ing the present moment while anticipating the future mem-ories they will create. This certainly explains why the album concludes with this track. After ten intense and cha-otic months spent breaking the mold of *Rumours* and redoubling the research for as many failures as successes, night fell on this incredible collective experience, and the team wished to retain only the best.

Production

Dominated by acoustic instrumentation, "Never Forget" places Lindsey Buckingham's guitar playing at the forefront, creating a rich, melodic texture by blending accompani-ment and solo ornamentation, and this is perfectly interwo-ven with Christine McVie's keyboard part. Over a metronomic rhythm, the bass's roundness reinforces the sense of well-being that emanates from the melody. Lindsey's and Stevie's soft, controlled vocal harmonies voluptuously envelop Christine McVie's deep, moving voice. A deft key change opens up an unexpected path at the fade-out, creating a slight frustration in the listener, who is left wanting more, even after an hour and fifteen minutes of music.

Previous spread: As part of the Tusk tour, Fleetwood Mac filled Wembley Stadium six nights in a row, from June 20 to 27, 1980. Quite a performance.

Above: A photograph of the band by Chris Callis, taken from behind, with them waving to the crowd, was chosen for the sleeve cover of the 1980 *Live* album.

Opposite: The mosaic of band photos adorning the inside of the *Live* album sleeve.

LIVE

Release Dates

United Kingdom: December 5, 1980
Reference: Warner Bros. Records—K 66097
Best UK Chart Ranking: 31
United States: December 5, 1980
Reference: Warner Bros. Records—2WB 3500
Best US Chart Ranking: 14

Disc 1

Monday Morning
Say You Love Me
Dreams
Oh Well
Over & Over
Sara
Not That Funny
Never Going Back Again
Landslide

Disc 2

Fireflies
Over My Head
Rhiannon
Don't Let Me Down Again
One More Night
Go Your Own Way
Don't Stop
I'm So Afraid
The Farmer's Daughter

A Toxic Atmosphere

The idea of releasing a live show had been floating around for two years already. But when Mick Fleetwood suggested that they go ahead with it at the end of the Rumours tour, he was met with reluctance from his partners, who preferred to concentrate on their work in the studio. When he came back at the end of the Tusk tour, the context was very different. The group was past the stage of mere fatigue. Life on the road and its complement of tense moments and excesses of all kinds had damaged the relationships between the musicians more than ever but had also gone backstage: consuming drugs and alcohol on stage, they provoked each other without restraint in front of the audience during concerts. Carol Ann Harris, Lindsey Buckingham's partner at the time, remembers the ritual before each concert, which spoke volumes about their conditioning and their need to maintain their enmities in order to retain the sincerity of their performances: "An hour and a half before the show, if there were any local press or VIP visitors roaming around the dressing room, they were kicked out of the backstage, leaving the inner circle of Fleetwood Mac free to do whatever it was they needed or wanted to do. The band members got dressed, snorted blow, made drinks, and threw sarcastic remarks at each other—remarks designed to wound and cut just enough to peel back the surface of old scars without, God willing, causing a full-scale war before the concert."[111]

Fleetwood Mac's famous "Rumours Five" lineup had existed for 13 years before they released *Live*, their first live recordings, on December 5, 1980.

The situation came to a head on March 22, 1980, in Auckland, New Zealand. Spotting Stevie Nicks on stage doing her usual arabesques with her shawl, Lindsey Buckingham put his jacket on his head and began to imitate her behind her back in a mocking way. Stevie Nicks said in 2013, "Well, that's not working for me. But I didn't do anything. This must have infuriated him, because he came over and kicked me. And I'd never had anyone be physical with me in my life. Then he picked up a black Les Paul guitar and he just frisbee'd it at me. He missed, I ducked—but he could have killed me."

"I'm not sure it happened,"[112] Lindsey insisted in 2013, but Christine McVie had a clear memory of that shocking moment: "Oh, it happened, all right. I threw a glass of wine in his face." At the end of the Tusk tour, on September 1, 1980, the band aspired to only one thing: Rest, far away from this toxic atmosphere.

Replenishing the Coffers

The publication of a live show therefore appeared to be a way to expand the discography and to quench the public's thirst for novelty while postponing the return to the studio, which would inevitably have generated new tensions. But above all, it would help to replenish the coffers. Despite the trilogy of hits (*Fleetwood Mac*, *Rumours*, and *Tusk* would accumulate over time the equivalent of 753 weeks on the charts, i.e., fourteen and a half years), the money was running out due to the musicians'

millionaire lifestyles and mismanagement by their team's financiers.

Indeed, three weeks after the end of the Tusk tour, the musicians met at Mick Fleetwood's home in Bel Air, each accompanied by a lawyer. The discussion quickly escalated because no one could understand how such a lucrative tour had brought them almost nothing in the end. Mick, as the manager, tried to make them understand that their expensive lifestyle was largely responsible for this shortfall, but the other members of the group did not listen to his arguments and dismissed him from his role as manager, even though they didn't doubt his honesty for a moment. The drummer thus paid for his lack of vigilance and lost his 10 percent commission on the band's income.

A Balanced Record

There was a plethora of material available to make up *Live*. The group, which had been fully aware since 1975 that it was going through a historic period, had indeed taken care to document all its performances—nearly four hundred—by recording each concert. When selecting the eighteen tracks that appear on this double live album, the musicians took great care to select a nice diversity of audiences and tracks, and not just the hits.

The United States was widely represented, including two recordings on November 5, 1979, in St. Louis, Missouri ("Oh Well" and "Sara"); three in Ohio on May 20 and 21, 1980 ("I'm So Afraid," "Not That Funny," and "Go Your Own

Brian Wilson and Lindsey Buckingham: Two studio workaholics driven by the desire to push back creative frontiers.

FOR MAC ADDICTS

In 1988, Lindsey Buckingham had the opportunity to work alongside his idol Brian Wilson on the album *Brian Wilson*, for which he composed and produced "He Couldn't Get His Poor Old Body to Move."

Way"); one in Oklahoma on August 22, 1980 ("Over & Over"); two again in Missouri, in Kansas City this time, on August 24 and 25, 1980 ("Over My Head" and "Say You Love Me"); one in Arizona on August 28, 1980 ("Never Going Back Again"); and three unreleased tracks—real plus-points of this album—played during private sets intended only for the technical team as a thank-you for their commitment, at the Santa Monica Civic Auditorium, California, on September 3 and 4, 1980 ("Fireflies," "One More Night," and "The Farmer's Daughter"). Europe was not to be outdone, with two London performances recorded at Wembley on June 25 and 26, 1980 ("Landslide" and "Rhiannon"), as well as "Dreams" and "Don't Stop," more unexpectedly, recorded during the sound checks before the band's appearance in Paris at the Palais des Sports on June 14, 1980. A surprising choice, which breaks the groove and the feel-good atmosphere instilled by the first tracks but gives a certain solemnity to these moments without an audience. This offered a new look at the professionalism of the group that was putting out these hits with aplomb despite that they were "only" sound checks. Asia also featured prominently, as the "Monday Morning" that opens this double album was recorded in Tokyo on February 3, 1980. The announcer's formal introduction inviting the audience to make some noise for Fleetwood Mac has even been retained: "Ladies and gentlemen, please give a warm welcome to Fleetwood Mac."

Most of the selected tracks were recorded during the Tusk tour. Strangely, the band included in the track list a song from the album *Buckingham Nicks*, "Don't Let Me Down Again," recorded live on November 17, 1975, in Passaic, New Jersey, during the Fleetwood Mac Tour, which was the first tour with this lineup. At the time, this song was usually played at the time of the encore, before "Hypnotized," which closed the set.

In terms of album representation, *Fleetwood Mac* has the largest delegation with "Monday Morning," "Say You Love Me," "Landslide," "Over My Head," "Rhiannon," and "I'm So Afraid." *Rumours* is also well represented, with the hits "Dreams," "Never Going Back Again," "Go Your Own Way," and "Don't Stop." "Over & Over," "Sara," and an epic, experimental, and wacky "Not That Funny" stretching over nearly nine minutes, are the standard-bearers of *Tusk*—only three titles. But it's not surprising for this album, which is not easy to reproduce on stage. "Oh Well," the oldest song performed live, is astonishing in more ways than one: Peter Green's bravura piece was released as a single in 1969, and it was perfectly mastered by Lindsey Buckingham. His voice didn't hold up to the blues grain of his predecessor, but the guitar playing of the playboy with brown curls, very different from that of Peter Green, shines with its precision and velocity in a register halfway between blues and heavy metal. Buckingham's guitar playing is undoubtedly one of the most beautiful assets of *Live*, with the vocal harmonies impeccably mastered on stage. He particularly shines acoustically on "Never Going Back" and with the electric guitar on "Sara" and "Rhiannon." The latter two tracks are probably the greatest successes of this record. The six-stringer's very rich ornamental playing coexists with the precious and meticulous choirs of his comrades and especially the voice of Stevie Nicks—in turn sensitive, powerful, authoritative, pop, and rock. In a word, dazzling with mastery.

Media coverage of *Live*, which arrived on December 8, 1980 (the day of John Lennon's assassination), suffered during its first weeks of release, with the music press logically prioritizing Lennon's tragic death. This is reflected in sales figures. After dominating the British charts with *Rumours* and *Tusk*, Fleetwood Mac had to settle for a modest thirty-first place and a "mere" gold record with *Live*, while their predecessors collected platinum certifications.

FIREFLIES
Stevie Nicks / 4:25

Musicians: Stevie Nicks: vocals / Lindsey Buckingham: guitar, backing vocals / Christine McVie: keyboards, backing vocals / John McVie: bass / Mick Fleetwood: drums / **Recorded:** Santa Monica Civic Auditorium, California: September 4, 1980 / **Technical Team:** Producers: Fleetwood Mac, Ken Caillat, Richard Dashut / Engineers: Ken Caillat, Richard Dashut, Trip Khalaf, Biff Dawes / **Single:** Side A: Fireflies / Side B: Over My Head / **US Release Date:** January 1981 by Warner Bros. Records (ref. WBS 49660) / Best US Chart Ranking: 60

Before Stevie Nicks on "Fireflies," no member of Fleetwood Mac had commented so clearly on life in the dysfunctional Fleetwood Mac family. During this slick rock piece with a very Californian sound, dominated by Lindsey Buckingham's fingerpicking—strongly reminiscent of Mark Knopfler's (Dire Straits)—the singer looks back on the tortuous but victorious journey of her band: "Long distance winners / Will we survive the flight? / Not one of us runs / From the firelight." The unwavering will and unwavering resistance of the members of Fleetwood Mac is the common thread running through this text. Perhaps the most moving passage is the one in which Stevie Nicks uses the personal pronoun "we" and the possessive "my." The first concentrates the idea of unity, and the second contains all the affection she can still feel for her comrades despite all the moments of tension: "We are dreamers in the night / Some call it my nightmare / My five fireflies / Oh, like a sailing ship / Not one of us runs."

ONE MORE NIGHT
Christine McVie / 3:43

Musicians: Christine McVie: vocals, keyboards / Lindsey Buckingham: guitar / John McVie: bass / Mick Fleetwood: drums / Stevie Nicks: backing vocals / Recorded / Santa Monica Civic Auditorium, California: September 3, 1980 / **Technical Team:** Producers: Fleetwood Mac, Ken Caillat, Richard Dashut / Engineers: Ken Caillat, Richard Dashut, Trip Khalaf, Biff Dawes

Endowed with a velvety melody, and caressed by seraphic choirs, "One More Night" bears the mark of romantic ballads by Christine McVie. For once, the lyricist doesn't use the first person. She's trying to take a bit of a step back. However, we find the narrative thread of her texts through the evocation of female desire, and the justification of adultery by the need for attention and intimacy. The title of the song, "One More Night," which was played the day after the end of the tour, could have suggested the singer's desire to extend the stage experience with one last date, but the story was ultimately much more personal for the singer, who was in a turbulent relationship with Dennis Wilson.

THE FARMER'S DAUGHTER
Brian Wilson / 2:25

Musicians: Lindsey Buckingham: vocals, guitar / Christine McVie: keyboards / John McVie: bass / Mick Fleetwood: drums / Stevie Nicks: backing vocals / **Recorded:** Santa Monica Civic Auditorium, California: September 4, 1980 / **Technical Team:** Producers: Fleetwood Mac, Ken Caillat, Richard Dashut / Engineers: Ken Caillat, Richard Dashut, Trip Khalaf, Biff Dawes / **Single:** Side A: The Farmer's Daughter / Side B: Dreams / **UK Release Date:** February 1981 by Warner Bros. Records (ref. K 17746) / Best UK Chart Ranking: Did Not Chart / **Single:** Side A: The Farmer's Daughter / Side B: Monday Morning / **US Release Date:** March 1981 by Warner Bros. Records (ref. WBS 49700) / Best US Chart Ranking: Did Not Chart

Fleetwood Mac had a close relationship with the Beach Boys. Not just because of Christine McVie's affair with Dennis Wilson at the time, but mostly because Lindsey Buckingham cultivated a boundless admiration for Dennis's brother, Brian Wilson. His work on *Pet Sounds* was, in the eyes of the guitarist, the yardstick of genius in terms of composition and production. Lindsey admired the spontaneity of their debut as much as he admired their 1966 pop cathedrals. For *Live*, he chose to cover the Beach Boys' "Farmer's Daughter" (which is adorned with a "The," by the way), which was originally recorded in 1963 for the Californians' second opus, *Surfin' U.S.A.*" While "Farmer's Daughter" went somewhat unnoticed at the time in the face of the Beach Boys' radio heavyweight, "Surfin' U.S.A.," this song stands out for being the first to be performed by Brian Wilson with a falsetto voice. A model of surf pop vocals, largely inspired by Dick Dale, this track already benefits from the gold standard work of the members in the development of the choirs. Lindsey Buckingham, who had a keen interest in harmonies, had the opportunity to establish himself as a worthy heir to this vocal technique.

The idea for this cover was born one evening at Village Recorders. Lindsey Buckingham and Stevie Nicks were working there when Dennis Wilson, Christine McVie, and photographer Ed Roach stopped by to greet them. They started talking about Brian Wilson, and Nicks and Buckingham began to talk about their admiration for the composer and their teenage memories related to the Beach Boys. Stevie and Lindsey then sang "Farmer's Daughter" a capella (a chaste love song about a young farm worker who flirts with the owner's daughter). Dennis told them how much he admired the quality of their performance, then left with Ed. When they returned in the early morning, Christine opened the door for them in tears. Dennis was worried that she was so upset, but she reassured him that she was just feeling emotional. She then made him listen to the fruit of their nocturnal work, a magnificent dreamlike cover of the aforementioned song that in turn brought tears to the eyes of the Beach Boys' drummer.

ALBUM

MIRAGE

Love in Store . Can't Go Back . That's Alright . Book of Love . Gypsy . Only Over You .
Empire State . Straight Back . Hold Me . Oh Diane . Eyes of the World . Wish You Were Here .
Outtakes: If You Were My Love . Smile at You . Goodbye Angel . Cool Water . Put a Candle in
the Window . Blue Monday . Teen Beat

RELEASE DATES
United Kingdom: June 18, 1982
Reference: Warner Bros. Records—K 56952
Best UK Chart Ranking: 5
United States: June 18, 1982
Reference: Warner Bros. Records—W1 23607
Best US Chart Ranking: 1

Mick Fleetwood's serenity in his Bel Air home was a façade as he had just been removed as the band's manager.

Once the Tusk world tour was over, the band expressed the need for a new creative era.

1982

A RETURN TO TRADITIONAL POP

After the September 1980 conciliation process involving musicians and lawyers that sealed the end of Mick Fleetwood's tenure as manager, everyone distanced themselves from the band. The idea was to give Mac members time to develop their solo projects. No one can say at this point whether this is a "see you again soon" or a proper goodbye.

Every Man for Himself

In January 1981, Mick traveled to Accra, Ghana, to finally bring to life a project he had been thinking about for three years: recording an album on the African continent. He recruited local musicians and developed *The Visitor*, an album that benefited from the support of Peter Green on guitar and vocals on a cover of "Rattlesnake Shake," George Harrison (on twelve-string guitar) on a reinterpretation of "Walk a Thin Line," and George Hawkins, who provided lead vocals on most of the tracks in the absence of Bob Welch, who had initially been approached but was in the end unavailable.

For her part, Stevie Nicks, supported by Jimmy Iovine and Tom Petty, drew on her cornucopia of work to create the album *Bella Donna*, made up of songs that she was unable to integrate into *Tusk*. While Mick Fleetwood's opus, released in June 1981, reached a respectable number forty-three on the Billboard charts on August 29, 1981, Stevie's opus (released on July 27, 1981) was much more successful, taking the top spot in the United States on September 5, 1981. Lindsey Buckingham, on the other hand, was slightly behind his peers at the start. His album *Law and Order*, which began recording in February 1981, was not released until October and reached the thirty-second position in the United States sales charts on November 7. Buckingham recorded it in the same way as he had approached *Tusk*, taking an experimental approach and in a do-it-yourself mode, with the equipment being just a simple multitrack tape, a few microphones, and a small console. He decided to make this album a space to enjoy some freedom since Mick Fleetwood, cooled by the relatively disappointing results of *Tusk*, made him understand that the next productions of Fleetwood Mac will have to be fundamentally different and reconnect with the luster of *Rumours*.

That leaves John and Christine McVie. The former has never shown any desire for a solo album and takes advantage of his free time to sail the seas aboard his yacht with his partner Julie. As for Christine, she hesitated to return to

The Château d'Hérouville in France provides Fleetwood Mac with a creative haven as well as an exceptional degree of comfort.

solo activity, traumatized by the failure of her first album, *Christine Perfect*, in 1970.

Life in the Castle

While each was busy with their respective projects, an article in the *New York Post* dated March 1981 caused a sensation by announcing that the band was on the verge of breaking up. The paper article was far from the truth, since the band planned to meet at the beginning of the following May to record new titles for a fourteenth studio opus at the castle of Hérouville, France. Located in a small village in the Vexin, one and a half hours away from Paris, this eighteenth-century mansion which was transformed into a recording studio at the end of the 1960s, is famous for having hosted the sessions of the trilogy *Honky Château* (1972), *Don't Shoot Me I'm Only the Piano Player* (1973) and *Goodbye Yellow Brick Road* (1973), by Elton John, Pink Floyd's *Obscured by Clouds* (1972), and David Bowie's *Pin Ups* (1973) and *Low* (1977).

McVie recalled in 2016: "It really was a rather beaten-up old castle. We were living in it, and then there was another area that was made to be a studio. And there were wine cellars underneath, which I believe we used as echo chambers. So it was unusual, but it also provided a "come-together" sort of moment. Because we really had no options to do anything else. In Sausalito, at least you were close to restaurants, clubs, whatever. But at the chateau, you were just there. We had the table tennis out, we had some radio-controlled helicopters, we had food cooked for us every night on the premises."

Recording outside the United States was a choice dictated by Mick Fleetwood, who moved to Monaco after selling his Bel Air home to evade US taxes. The last to land in Hérouville on his return from Ghana, he was pleased to note that the other musicians had not waited for him to get to work. Several pieces had already been sketched, and incidentally, the girls' rooms had been redecorated—notably with pink satin for Stevie. Obviously, the crisis meeting did not have the desired effect in reducing unnecessary expenditure. Regardless, the group fulfilled its fantasy and enjoyed a "French-style" castle lifestyle.

A Timid Album

Nevertheless, the band remained focused on its goal: to conquer the charts again. This would require a more accessible album than *Tusk*. The idea is therefore to reconnect with a traditional recording approach that is nevertheless ultra-demanding in terms of sound, as for *Rumours*.

In 2015, Buckingham recalled, "There was this kind of dictate that came down from the other four saying, 'Well, we're not going to do that process again, Lindsey, we're going to go back to something a little more straight ahead."

Freed from the demands and constraints imposed by the guitarist, the two sound engineers, Richard Dashut and Ken Caillat, regained a certain freedom of action. Each of the three composers arrived at the castle with a signature piece. For Christine, it was the pop ballad "Hold Me," inspired by her relationship with Dennis Wilson and destined to become the album's first single. But she also brought along

With *Mirage*, the band was keen to scale back on the experimental leniency granted to Buckingham and return to more conventional soft rock.

"Only Over You" (also inspired by Dennis), "Love in Store," and "Wish You Were Here." Stevie Nicks, on the other hand, had kept the track "Gypsy" from the sessions of her solo album *Bella Donna*, in preparation for Fleetwood Mac's new album, *Mirage*. She will dedicate this nostalgic pop-rock track with chiming guitar to her best friend, Robin Anderson, who died of leukemia. It was chosen as the second single, after "Hold Me." Lindsey also reserved for Fleetwood Mac a few "scraps" from his personal project, *Law and Order*. He arrived at the castle with "Can't Go Back" and "Eyes of the World." The guitarist would go on to compose three other songs on site: "Empire State," "Book of Love," and "Oh Diane," all co-written with Richard Dashut, whose duties now extended beyond production, to the point that he has become a true creative partner for Lindsey. Finally, the archives of the Buckingham/Nicks duo once again meet the needs of Fleetwood Mac, which emerges from behind the bundle of work on "That's Alright,"

composed in 1974. "Straight Back" was added later, as Stevie Nicks composed it in the winter of 1981 following her split from her producer, Jimmy Iovine.

The twelve songs of the track list exude a simplicity, a rediscovered spontaneity, such as "Oh Diane" and its apparent doo-wop naivety inspired by Neil Sedaka. Fleetwood Mac revives the pop feel and airy romanticism of the most popular compositions of their pre-*Tusk* repertoire. This will make some say that *Mirage* is *Rumours II*. And even if Buckingham would dismiss this assertion by declaring after his release of the record: "People say this is *Rumours II*. I don't see it that way, I certainly see it as a more conservative album, but there are a lot of albums coming out by artists who are sounding a little more pop and a little softer—Elvis Costello, Joe Jackson…" The guitarist will sometimes let his guard down, acknowledging a certain reluctance on the part of the band, mainly driven by the desire to make an album on the right track, and therefore

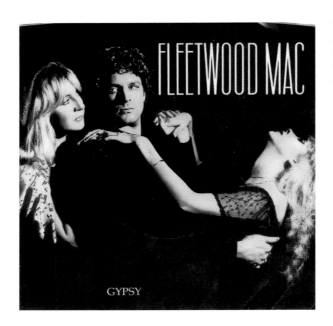

The cover of *Mirage*, featuring Christine, Lindsey, and Stevie in a sensual three-way waltz, was later used on the sleeve of the "Gypsy" single.

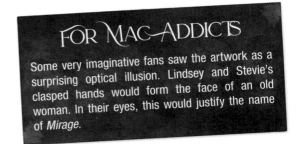

FOR MAC-ADDICTS

Some very imaginative fans saw the artwork as a surprising optical illusion. Lindsey and Stevie's clasped hands would form the face of an old woman. In their eyes, this would justify the name of *Mirage*.

not adventurous enough for his taste. He said: "We should have progressed but instead we just reacted against *Tusk*. It was pleasant but much too safe."

Laughter and Improv

While everyone brings their own personal touch to the album at the composition stage, Mick Fleetwood makes sure that the recording process is collective. Christine explains: "One common bond on *Mirage* is that the band is actually playing on everybody's songs the whole way through. Also there are no messages to one another on this album. This is not a diary like *Rumours*. It seems like a happy record to me. We all enjoyed making it. The tracks are self-explanatory in that way. *Mirage* is more cohesive than *Tusk*."

It is therefore no longer a question of pushing one of the band members aside or treading on each other's toes. The reproach is primarily directed at Lindsey Buckingham and his propensity to record the bass or drum parts himself under the pretext that it would be too complicated to convey his vision of the song. The sessions at the Château d'Hérouville, spread over the months of May and June 1981, consisted of a raw recording of the songs. The band started by refining "Gypsy," "Hold Me," and "Oh Diane." The first tests were encouraging; the musicians had found their groove. Within two months, most of the songs were canned. But the band was forced to take a break after eight weeks due to the successive releases of Stevie Nicks's *Bella Donna* (July 1981) and Lindsey Buckingham's *Law and Order* (October) and all the related obligations. The final recording—i.e., overdubs and mixing—took place in Los Angeles, at Larrabee Sound Studios and at the Record Plant. Only "Straight Back" was recorded late, in the middle of the winter of 1981. Once again, most of the work is done by Lindsey and, to a lesser extent, Christine and Mick. Stevie's contribution, caught up in her flourishing solo career and

the moral support she was giving to her friend Robin, is negligible on this album. As for John, who is not very committed, he distances himself from the studio and his ex-wife as soon as he has the opportunity. However, the musicians get along well when they are together to play. The atmosphere is relaxed, and conducive to creativity. "I don't know how spontaneous that was, when I look back," said Christine, remembering. "We might have pieced certain songs together. I just remember an awful lot of laughter, and quite a lot of sitting around noodling. I don't remember much frustration, or irritation. But at the same time I'm aware that this album feels more contrived." Despite good times shared, the finalization dragged on and ended up irritating everyone. While a good part of the recording was completed in eight weeks in Hérouville, the finalization of all the adjustments would take about ten months. Mainly because of Lindsey Buckingham, who was also working on his next solo album in addition to that of the band, and who kept coming back to the songs that were supposed to be finalized. He always finds fault with every track. So he re-records, edits, modifies the effects…And after a few weeks, he changes his mind again. Thus, if the conception of the titles was collective and spontaneous, their finalization was solitary and laborious.

A Successful Comeback

In March 1982, the record was finally ready. It was named *Mirage*. The group did not make any comment on the meaning of the name. So the audience let their imagination run wild: a reference to the (very relative) desert crossing of *Tusk* after the success of *Rumours* (since mirages appear in the desert)? A nod to *Rumours*? Because in the case of a rumor or a mirage, we believe in something that is not real…The final touch was the choice of the cover. The group called on photographer George Hurrell, renowned for his glamorous portraits of the great stars of Hollywood

Fleetwood Mac performing on stage at Wembley Stadium as part of the Tusk tour, June 1980.

during the 1930s and 1940s (Lauren Bacall, Humphrey Bogart, Bette Davis), when he worked for Metro-Goldwyn-Mayer, and who since the 1970s reconverted to photography of musicians and bands—for whom he has created covers (*Foreign Affairs* [1977] by Tom Waits, Queen's *The Works* [1984], Paul McCartney's *Press to Play* [1986]). For the first time, Christine and Lindsey find themselves in the spotlight. The two musicians stare at each other while the guitarist dances with Stevie, who throws her head back in a seductive manner. The scene induces a romantic three-some, creating from scratch a closeness between Lindsey and Christine (who seems to be waiting her turn) that never existed despite the many love combinations that existed in the group…The photo of the trio, selected for its perfect composition with the graceful movement of Stevie Nicks, is only partial, since the left part of the image showed Mick Fleetwood and John McVie, facing forward.

"Hold Me," as the first single (released in June 1982), paved the way for the album. It climbed to number four on the Billboard charts, giving an excellent indicator for the future. *Mirage* arrived on July 2, 1982. Fleetwood Mac returned to the top of the US album charts and in fact sat there comfortably for five weeks. At the same time, the UK's renewed interest in its expatriate children was confirmed, as *Mirage* entered the top five on this side of the Atlantic. *Mirage* is legitimately considered by the band—as well as by the record company—to be a commercial success. However,

the total sales of the two albums were quite close in the end: a little more than three million copies for *Mirage* and a little less than four million for *Tusk*, which was unfairly equated with a failure. "Gypsy" cemented the record's reputation with a twelfth place in the US in September. The third single, "Love in Store," peaked at number twenty-two in the US charts in November. In its wake, "Oh Diane" rebalanced the band's impact between the United States and the United Kingdom by achieving a strong performance in Fleetwood Mac's home country: ninth in the charts in the UK in December. The run ended with "Can't Go Back," but the soufflé had sunk: It could do no better than eighty-third in the United Kingdom. Regardless, the success of *Mirage* was already definitely confirmed.

The Mirage tour—Lindsey Buckingham's last before his departure—was limited to twenty-nine American dates, from September 1 to October 31, 1982. However, it led to a live video, released on VHS in 1983, documenting the last two shows performed in Los Angeles.

HÉROUVILLE, A FRENCH MYTH

Nestling in the countryside not far from Auvers-sur-Oise, some 25 miles from Paris, the Château d'Hérouville is home to the recording studio where Fleetwood Mac took refuge while putting the finishing touches to their thirteenth album, *Mirage*, in 1981. This ancient fifty-seven-room former courier relay station was built in 1740 and was famous for having allegedly been the love nest of Frédéric Chopin and Georges Sand, and a number of pop and rock classics had already resonated within the walls of its studios. Canned Heat, the Grateful Dead, Pink Floyd, David Bowie, and Elton John had all recorded on several occasions in this historic setting, isolated from the hustle and bustle of the city and offering a tranquility conducive to artistic creation.

The members of Fleetwood Mac did not all enjoy the experience in the same way. While Stevie Nicks, who had been fascinated by fairy tales since childhood, was captivated by the magic of the site, reputedly haunted by ghosts, Christine McVie lamented the lack of accessible activities in the area. Yet everything was designed to give artists a unique experience on-site, with cooks, sports facilities, a swimming pool, games rooms with table tennis, and pinball machines, lounges, and comfortable bedrooms. It was a true residential studio, an innovative idea at the time that would be emulated many times in the ensuing years. In addition to its personalized services and magical ambience, the château boasted state-of-the-art equipment for its time, which, combined with its special acoustics, delivered an inimitable sound.

Michel Magne's Visionary Dream

When he discovered the château in 1962, French film composer Michel Magne was won over by its unique atmosphere and bought it with his friend Jean-Claude Dragomir. Initially, he planned to use it as a home for his family and as a workspace for himself and his assistants. The attic in the north part of the building was converted to accommodate his instruments. In 1965, following Dragomir's accidental death, Magne bought his friend's shares from the Dragomir estate and became the sole owner of the premises. But a second tragedy struck four years later: a fierce fire ravaged the northern part of the building. The

39-year-old composer decided to take advantage of the renovation work to realize an old dream: to build a real recording studio. Magne spared no expense and invested in state-of-the-art equipment. The new 328-square-foot space, called the Chopin studio, sounded very different from the old Georges Sand studio, which also remained in use.

In 1971, Michel Magne hired a talented sound engineer, Dominique Blanc-Francard. Word of mouth spread like wildfire. In an impromptu appearance that same year by the Grateful Dead, playing to 200 people on LSD under the watchful eye of television cameras, Hérouville was soon circulating in the microcosm of show business. T. Rex recorded *The Slider* and *Tanx* there in 1972. Above all, Elton John recorded *Honky Château* in 1972, and *Don't Shoot Me I'm Only the Piano Player* and *Goodbye Yellow Brick Road* both in 1973. The Strawberry studio, as Magne called it, was born.

A Financial Black Hole

But from 1972 onward, financial issues began to plague Michel Magne's daily life. The luxury services offered by the château weighed dangerously on the accounts. The taxman latched onto the case and made life difficult for the composer, who handed over the commercial operation to Yves Chamberland (head of Davout Studios, France's most famous recording facility) in 1972. Despite the Chamerland's rigorous management, the business didn't go well. In 1974, the château was abandoned for many months before Laurent Thibault, co-founder of French prog-rock band Magma restored Hérouville to its former glory. In June 1974, he took over the running of the studio and gradually brought back the stars, notably David Bowie, who recorded *Low* in 1977 with Tony Visconti at his side. That same year, the Bee Gees and their *Saturday Night Fever* drew the spotlight to Hérouville. But the glitz hid a less glamorous reality. Michel Magne was financially ruined. Exhausted by the struggle, he sold the château to a property developer for a derisory sum. Laurent Thibault stayed on, however, to continue the studio's activities.

In 1979, Hérouville acquired France's first truly mobile 24-track studio, modeled on the Rolling Stones' studio. The

Michel Magne (second from left) had the control room fitted with a custom Diffona radio console by his electronics engineer friend Gérard Delassus (left).

French "Voyageur" equipment was mainly used for live recordings of French artists.

The Beginning of the End

In 1981, Fleetwood Mac went to Hérouville to record new tracks for the *Mirage* album. It was yet another addition to the château's prestigious roll of honor, and it was to be the château's last moment of glory for a long time to come. Four years later, the story turned dark again. Michel Magne, who had never recovered from the loss of his jewel, dragged on in his malaise and sank deeper and deeper into depression. On December 19, 1984, he died by suicide in a hotel room. In July 1985, Laurent Thibault left the château after twelve years of service. Then thirty years later, in 2015, Hérouville was given a new lease on life when two sound engineers and a financier (Jean Taxis, Thierry Garacino, and Stéphane Marchi) set about reviving the premises. The former Chopin studio was refurbished and housed a new training center for entertainment professionals. And the Georges Sand studio was fitted with high-performance analog equipment (Neve and API consoles, Studer tape recorders) as well as a 1901 Steinway B piano and an Avid Protools HD sequencer. Recordings resumed in 2016. *Le château d'Hérouville, une folie rock française* [The Château d'Hérouville, a French Rock Extravaganza], a documentary directed by Christophe Conte in 2023, traces the history of this mythical site.

FOR MAC-ADDICTS

It is said that Stevie Nicks demanded that paintings be hung on the walls of her room at Hérouville, covering over the graffiti left by David Bowie while he recorded *No Eldorado* in October 1974.

LOVE IN STORE

Christine McVie, Jim Recor / 3:17

Musicians
Christine McVie: vocals, keyboards, backing vocals
Lindsey Buckingham: guitars, backing vocals
John McVie: bass
Mick Fleetwood: drums, percussion
Stevie Nicks: backing vocals

Recorded
Le Château, Hérouville (France): May–July 1981

Technical Team
Producers: Fleetwood Mac, Ken Caillat, Richard Dashut
Sound Engineers: Ken Caillat, Richard Dashut
Assistant Sound Engineers: David Bianco, Carla Frederick

Single
Side A: Love in Store / Side B: Can't Go Back
US Release Date: November 3, 1982 with Warner Bros. Records (7-29848)
Best US Ranking: 22

John McVie's contributions on "Love in Store" are essential.

Genesis and Lyrics

With the exception of Lindsey Buckingham, who was beginning to find Richard Dashut a valuable writing partner, the musicians of Fleetwood Mac were not in the habit of sharing credits. Composing and writing were solitary exercises, so it might have been surprising that Christine McVie opened up this intimate space to someone outside the band and production team. It was Jim Recor, the ex-husband of Sara Jones Recor, one of Stevie's best friends and, incidentally, Mick Fleetwood's new partner and future wife... But the former manager of Loggins and Messina was on good terms with the whole band and was involved in the creation of "Love in Store." This song is presented as a declaration of love (as classic and direct as possible) to a partner in love: "You're the only one I ever felt / Could be special to me / You look at me and I just melt."

Production

An initial version of "Love in Store" was finalized at Château d'Hérouville. The song (which was chosen to open the album) was very coherent and set a new dynamic with drive and energy. Almost bouncy, it welcomes a xylophone, which Mick Fleetwood places on its opening, followed by a guitar which is played note by note and muffled.

But the result failed to satisfy Lindsey Buckingham who, at the overdub stage, went back to the drawing board in his usual fashion. Mick's percussion (woodblock, xylophone, guiro, and tambourine) was used more in the middle of the track and in the second part, to preserve the effectiveness of the first part, which was used to set up the melody. Lindsey also revisited the bass part in the introduction. The change was not spectacular, but the musician aimed for efficiency by choosing a simpler bass track from among those recorded. Already basic, the instrument's line was reduced to its simplest expression with only the single fundamental note retained: the *C*. Played using the fingerpicking technique, the bass repeats the bass drum pulses in a very academic-sounding way. But the impact is immediate, accentuating the rhythmic dimension of the track.

Lindsey did not stop there. He did not spare his own work either, pushing back the seductive Eastern-sounding

Mick Fleetwood's stay in Ghana for his solo album *The Visitor* in 1981 changed the drummer, who enriched his playing—particularly percussion—with new sounds.

guitar track on the second part and replacing it with simple guitar chords on the first, which he allowed to ring out.

Christine's deep, slightly detached vocals, contrasting with the playfulness of the melody, were retained. But Fleetwood Mac's signature vocal combinations were missing. And in this case, the collective work would result in a model of its kind in terms of harmonies. The producers installed a layered structure: Behind Christine's lead voice, a second voice, provided by Stevie Nicks, emerged, echoing the same line on the *F* chord, while extending the end of the phrase ("Instead of bringing me down" on the first verse) and ("Scared of feeling that way" on the second). The third stratum is Lindsey's, who provides fresh-sounding backing vocals, especially when supporting the end of the phrase.

On the other hand, Lindsey discarded the backing vocals provided by Stevie and himself, which they had added at the end of the track on the first version recorded at the château, considering that their nasal voices disrupted the lightness of the song.

Chosen as a single for the US market, the finalized track performed well, reaching number twenty-two on the

Billboard Hot 100. It also distinguished itself at eleventh place on *Billboard*'s specialized Adult Contemporary charts. This leading music magazine was won over by the song, which "exudes an almost nostalgic reminiscence of their work in the late 1960s. The harmonies are simply charming."

Mick Fleetwood rarely used the güiro, a percussion instrument common in the Caribbean, usually carved from a hollowed-out calabash. About 8 inches long and oblong in shape, it has transverse grooves on the surface over which the musician scrapes a stick or scraper back and forth, producing a stridulating sound. Slow friction produces low-pitched sounds, while fast friction produces high-pitched sounds.

CAN'T GO BACK

Lindsey Buckingham / 2:43

Musicians: Lindsey Buckingham: vocals, guitars, keyboards / Christine McVie: keyboards, backing vocals / John McVie: bass / Mick Fleetwood: drums, percussion / Stevie Nicks: backing vocals / **Recorded:** Le Château, Hérouville (France): May–July 1981 / **Technical Team:** Producers: Fleetwood Mac, Ken Caillat, Richard Dashut / Sound Engineers: Ken Caillat, Richard Dashut / Assistant Sound Engineers: David Bianco, Carla Frederick / **Single:** Side A: Can't Go Back / Side B: That's Alright / **UK Release Date:** April 1983 with Warner Bros. Records (ref. W 9848) / Best UK Ranking: 83 / **12" Single:** Side A1: Can't Go Back, face A2: Rhiannon / Side B1: Tusk, face B2: Over and Over / **UK Release Date:** April 1983 with Warner Bros. Records (ref. W 9848T) / Best UK Ranking: Did Not Chart / **Single:** Side A: Love in Store / Side B: Can't Go Back / **US Release Date:** November 3, 1982 with Warner Bros. Records (ref. 7-29848) / Best US Ranking: 22

Genesis and Lyrics

Lindsey Buckingham came to France reluctantly, as he did not appreciate the country very much, especially its gastronomy. He brought with him two new compositions: "Eyes of the World" and "Can't Go Back." "Can't Go Back" was, at this stage, a promising demo. It mobilizes two guitars in a seductive, refined interweaving pattern. It is accompanied by a rudimentary rhythm section reminiscent of Lindsey's approach on *Tusk*. The contributions of the other members transform the track from an intimate gem into a catchy, unifying retro pop song. But the guitarist's text retains the mood that dictated its composition: deep nostalgia. Like Stevie Nicks on "Gypsy," the lyricist delves into his memories, but the emotions that come to the surface are different from those of his partner. Where she evoked the past with a kind of tenderness and ingenuity, Lindsey lets out a desperate cry, imploring the intervention of a transcendent force: "I want to go back." But his cry is met with a compelling response from the backing vocals: "Can't go back."

Production

Mick Fleetwood is the first to take the plunge. Always open to Lindsey's rhythmic suggestions, which he knew to be innovative in this respect, the drummer set about reproducing the compact, mechanical, metronomic rhythm of the demo. To this end, he uses castanets to maintain a dull sound. He then doubles the tracks to add depth to the rhythm. He also adds a snare drum to give some punch. At the end of the song, Mick, always greedy for percussion, also adds a few maracas and bells. He adds just the right amount of discreet tintinnabulations to the finale. John, for his part, fleshes out the melodic line conceived by Lindsey, but the restrained grip loses some of the liquid sonority that was its charm. A childlike keyboard is added, on Lindsey's initiative, lending a kind of innocence and lightness to the melody. But he counterbalances this effect with his vocal performance, which is powerful, taut, and on the verge of breaking. His voice has never sounded so androgynous as on this track, where Stevie's and Christine's voices respond with passion.

"Can't Go Back" was chosen as the fourth single, in the wake of "Oh Diane." Despite its immediacy, it did not manage better than eighty-third place in the UK charts. The instrumental demo behind "Can't Go Back" was unveiled with the release of the deluxe edition of *Mirage* in 2016. Its working title was "Suma's Walk."

On YouTube, a fan of the band, amused by the melodic proximity of the 1982 demo and Stevie Nicks's solo track "Wild Heart," had fun isolating the singer's voice and placing it on "Suma's Walk," with convincing results.

The use of "That's Alright," a preexisting song from 1974, enabled the band to record collectively and without pressure, working on a tune they had already mastered.

THAT'S ALRIGHT
Stevie Nicks / 3:10

Musicians: Stevie Nicks: vocals, backing vocals / Lindsey Buckingham: guitars, backing vocals / John McVie: bass / Mick Fleetwood: drums, percussion / **Recorded:** Le Château, Hérouville (France): May–July 1981 / **Technical Team:** Producers: Fleetwood Mac, Ken Caillat, Richard Dashut / Sound Engineers: Ken Caillat, Richard Dashut / Assistant Sound Engineers: David Bianco, Carla Frederick / **Single:** Side A: Oh Diane / Side B: That's Alright / **US Release Date:** March 9, 1983 with Warner Bros. Records (ref. 7-29698) / Best US Ranking: Did Not Chart

Genesis and Lyrics
Following the successive departures of Danny Kirwan and Bob Welch, the residual fragments of country identity in Fleetwood Mac's DNA had gradually faded until they disappeared under the effect of the pop revolution fomented by Buckingham and Nicks. Yet the two newcomers were never averse to country. On the contrary, country music was an integral part of Stevie's training. She learned this kind of music from her grandfather, who was a connoisseur and familiarized her with the genre's standards from an early age. Then, as she moved around the country, the native of Phoenix traveled throughout the southwestern United States, particularly Texas, where country music is well established. She immersed herself in it, and it was only logical that this influence should one day find its way into her work. This came in the form of "Designs of Love." Recorded as a demo in 1974 (around the time of the first Buckingham Nicks album), it reappears on *Mirage* as a sumptuous ballad

packed with guitar arpeggios, sweet-sounding keyboard parts, and a banjo passage.

The lyrics remain unchanged, with a greater emphasis on instrumentation. The text reflects the turbulent times when Stevie Nicks and Lindsey Buckingham were still a couple but were already tearing each other apart. It tells of a sudden separation, initiated by the narrator. Her decision seems to be an impromptu one, if we are to believe the line: "Now I decided yesterday that I would leave you." But she quickly recovers, as if anticipating her partner's reproaches for her hasty decision: "Please, I've been takin' my time / You know, it's been on my mind."

Production
The recording of "That's Alright" goes far beyond the simple collective interpretation of an old demo. Important production choices were made. The drums, absent from the initial 1974 version, burst onto the scene in the band's new version. A little stiff on the snare drum, Mick Fleetwood's playing is more interesting and syncopated on the cymbals. The treatment of the guitars is also fundamentally different. Their sound is more polished than on the demo, which played on authenticity with takes captured by an ambient microphone. As for the banjo, it is relegated to ornamentation. But it is mainly Stevie Nicks's voice that takes the song to a new level, with a confident, technical performance, solidly supported by precision backing vocals.

BOOK OF LOVE
Lindsey Buckingham, Richard Dashut / 3:22

Musicians
Lindsey Buckingham: vocals, guitars
Christine McVie: keyboards, backing vocals
John McVie: bass
Mick Fleetwood: drums
Stevie Nicks: backing vocals

Recorded
Le Château, Hérouville (France): May–July 1981

Technical Team
Producers: Fleetwood Mac, Ken Caillat, Richard Dashut
Sound Engineers: Ken Caillat, Richard Dashut
Assistant Sound Engineers: David Bianco, Carla Frederick

1982

Stevie Nicks onstage at the Met Center in Bloomington, Minnesota, September 23, 1982.

Genesis and Lyrics

"Book of Love" is the song that best expresses Lindsey Buckingham's willing inflexion in Fleetwood Mac's musical direction. Thwarted in his experimental impulses by the other members of the band, the guitarist has clearly understood that he should henceforth reserve his creative whims for his personal projects. Indeed, even though he was no longer officially the band's manager, Mick Fleetwood did not want to risk another crash—narrowly avoided on the previous album—by leaving the controls to a kamikaze. Lindsey, surprisingly docile, therefore revised his material in depth, offering very simple pop songs in both writing and composition. Richard Dashut, now involved in the songwriting alongside the singer, was no stranger to this change of direction toward a lighter prose. Therefore, no abstruse images are used to describe the grief felt by the narrator of "Book of Love," whose girlfriend has just left him. Lindsey embraces his vulnerability. Rather than directing ire at his ex-girlfriend, he wonders about a transcendent, superior entity who, with a cruel pen, would reserve the worst outrages for him in the "book of love," a work in which everyone's love destiny would be written.

Production

Like "Empire State" and "Oh Diane," "Book of Love" was created at the Château d'Hérouville. Lindsey Buckingham and Richard Dashut put together a first demo of the song, based on a simple guitar chord progression and a mechanical drum machine pattern, severely lacking in vitality. This first draft nevertheless reveals the song's melodic potential, which is complemented by a little harpsichord-like keyboard motif, both childlike and heady, and then by a captivating, if still somewhat confused, combination of backing vocals. Ken Caillat takes charge of tidying up this promising sketch. He begins by bringing some life back into this robotic interpretation by asking Mick Fleetwood to reproduce the pattern chosen by his partner. Once he gets the hang of it, Fleetwood takes care of the execution with a slightly soft stroke to give bounce and resonance to his strokes. Lindsey then adds a crystalline acoustic guitar as an intro, discreetly accompanying this rhythm and bringing brilliance to the whole by occupying the high end of the

Lindsey Buckingham fingerpicking on his signature guitar, the Rick Turner Model 1.

spectrum to advantage, then an electric guitar during the song for the lead.

The keyboard, so characteristic of the demo, disappears, leaving more space for the dense vocal texture. Exemplary in its vocal harmonies, "Book of Love" combines angelic vocals with backing vocals supporting the end of phrases, responses to Lindsey's main vocals. Lindsey delivers a guitar part on the finale that is as inspired as his vocals, with a short solo whose tones evoke the playing of Toto's Steve Lukather.

FOR MAC ADDICTS

"Book of Love" was revisited by American indie rock band Papas Fritas as a depressive acoustic guitar ballad guided by a melancholy drawl. It appears on the *Pop Has Freed Us* compilation released in 2003.

GYPSY

Stevie Nicks / 4:27

Musicians
Stevie Nicks: vocals
Lindsey Buckingham: guitars, backing vocals
Christine McVie: piano, keyboard, backing vocals
John McVie: bass
Mick Fleetwood: drums, percussion

Recorded
Le Château, Hérouville (France): May–July 1981

Technical Team
Producers: Fleetwood Mac, Ken Caillat, Richard Dashut
Sound Engineers: Ken Caillat, Richard Dashut
Assistant Sound Engineers: David Bianco, Carla Frederick

Single
Side A: Gypsy / **Side B:** Cool Water
US Release Date: September 17, 1982 with Warner Bros. Records
  (ref. K 17997)
Best US Ranking: 46

Single
Side A: Gypsy (mono) / **Side B:** Gypsy (stereo)
US Release Date: August 18, 1982 with Warner Bros. Records
  (ref. 7-29918)
Best US Ranking: 12

FOR MAC-ADDICTS

Indirectly linked to "Gypsy" is Janis Joplin, Stevie Nicks's beloved icon, when the band Fritz was Joplin's opening act. One day, when the band lingered too long over their set, Joplin expressed her impatience from the side of the stage by yelling at Nicks and her bandmates to get out of the way and make way for her.

Genesis and Lyrics

When she began writing the lyrics in 1979, the singer, barely in her thirties, was swept up in a wave of nostalgia. She sketched her own portrait, in the guise of a freedom-loving "gypsy." She recalls her youth, her musical beginnings alongside Lindsey, the pure love that bound them together, and everything, including her dreams of success. In an interview with *Entertainment Weekly* in 2009, the musician revealed for the first time that this song is about her recurring desire to return to the days before she was famous. "Before Fleetwood Mac, Lindsey [Buckingham] and I didn't have any money, so we had a big mattress lying on the floor," Nicks recalled: "I'd laid out some old vintage blankets on it, and even though we didn't have any money, it was still very pretty.... Just that and a lamp on the floor, and that was it." She explained, "Today, when I feel cluttered, I take my mattress off my nice bed, wherever it is, and put it [on the floor] outside my room, with a table and a small lamp [next to it]." "Gypsy" evokes the difficulty of staying connected with the bohemian version of herself.

Stevie opened up to the audience at a Mac concert in Manchester, England, in 2015, when performing this song: "In 1968, Lindsey and I were living in San Francisco. We were in a very good band that opened for most of the bands on the local scene. Well-known bands at the time [...] We were living the dream, as it were. We were young, and it was just fantastic." She went on to clarify an element of the first line that intrigued the fans, the phrase "velvet underground." This was not a reference to the New York band founded by Lou Reed but about a San Francisco clothing store. "We'd heard about a boutique in downtown San Francisco where the rock'n'roll girls were clearing out their clothes, at least those who could afford them," recalls Stevie. "I thought, 'Well, I'll save up, I'll go over there and buy myself something from this fantastic store.' And that store was called the Velvet Underground. She continued: "So I went there. I walked into this beautiful store filled with beautiful things. I was pretty sure there'd be nothing within my reach. But I was in a place where I was sure Janis Joplin had been."

When Stevie returned to the lyrics around the time of the conception of *Mirage*, her life had undergone profound upheaval. First and foremost, there was the death of her

Stevie Nicks was strongly influenced by Janis Joplin's look and way of dominating the stage and audience.

Perhaps meeting Janis Joplin (shown here in 1969) was not to Stevie Nicks's taste, but it did not diminish her admiration for her.

best friend, Robin Anderson, from leukemia. Certain passages in the text then jumped out at her. While they were meant to depict the young Stevie at the dawn of her career, the singer realized that the words assumed a whole new meaning with the death of the young mother: "And the child was enough / Enough for me to love / Enough to love / She is dancing away from you now / She was just a wish / And her memory is all that is left for you now." Aware of the importance of this song and particularly won over by its musicality, Mick Fleetwood had no difficulty in promoting it as a single.

Production

When the Mac tackled "Gypsy," the track was still in demo form, as Stevie had recorded it with the help of Tom Moncrieff (former Buckingham Nicks bassist) in 1979, when it was first conceived. It features a long electric piano tremolo that creates a kind of vertigo for the listener as it navigates between the left and right channels of the stereo spectrum. The piano accompanies Stevie's melancholic, drawling voice, enveloped in a pronounced reverb that lends it an almost religious solemnity.

The band welcomed Stevie's creation with great interest. "I think 'Gypsy' is by far the best track on the album. Without a doubt," said Christine. "The whole song is very coherent. It's very musical. Very melodic. All the parts are relevant." Lindsey Buckingham's "Gypsy," however, was to be given more instrumentation. The tempo was accelerated to make it a midtempo ballad. As a sign of the new production direction, Mick Fleetwood develops a very classic, unimaginative rhythm section, in which the snare drum stands out. The low register is occupied by the bass, which also distinguishes itself by playing the fundamentals with clear purpose. In the middle register, Lindsey inserts the palm muting, typical of his precise, incisive guitar playing, which underpins the rhythmic dimension of the song. Widely used in funk, this style of playing also demonstrates its effectiveness in a soft-rock register such as this. But it is Christine's interventions that prove to be the most decisive in the realization of the track. She takes the gamble of inserting a honky-tonk piano, whose notes stand out perfectly as an elegant ornamentation within the meticulous production of the Dashut-Caillat duo. She also chose the Hammond and its warm tones to develop the

"Gypsy" was a significant success in the UK, where it sold 600,000 copies.

magical gimmick that characterizes the sound of this number.

A Stormy Video

As a single, "Gypsy" was endowed with an obligatory music video, as they became the new norm with the emergence of the MTV cable music channel, launched in August 1981, which broadcast music videos.

The video for "Gypsy" had its world premiere on the channel. Directed by Russell Mulcahy, the video mobilized numerous sets, extras, and costumed dancers. It was the most expensive music video ever shot at that time. As with "Hold Me," the shoot proved to be a stormy affair. Mulcahy discovered the heavy, sentimental pasts of all those involved, and the enmities that ensued. Furthermore, Stevie

Nicks, at the center of the arrangement as lead singer, was not at her best. Nicks, who'd entered rehab two weeks before filming began, was forced to interrupt her therapy in the midst of withdrawal and was very irritable. To make matters worse, the script gave her the unpleasant surprise of having to dance and be enveloped in Lindsey's arms when, in real life, they could no longer stand each other... "I'm pretty sure it shows on screen when you watch certain scenes," Christine McVie confirmed. "I'm the first to admit that none of us were sober. We were clearly under the influence of drugs and alcohol. But everyone was doing it. It was the norm." Ranking twelfth in the US charts on its release, the song became a staple of Fleetwood Mac's live set list. It ranks fifteenth among Fleetwood Mac's most frequently performed live tracks.

In 2017, Stevie Nicks recorded a new acoustic solo version of "Gypsy" for the Netflix show which had the same name. The show's creator, Lisa Rubin, listened to the song on repeat while working on the pilot.

There was a video of Stevie Nicks singing "Only Over You" and other songs taken during a 1981 shoot with Annie Leibovitz for the September 3, 1981 cover of *Rolling Stone*.

ONLY OVER YOU

Christine McVie / 4:09

Musicians: Christine McVie: vocals, keyboards / Lindsey Buckingham: guitar / John McVie: bass / Mick Fleetwood: drums / **Recorded:** Le Château, Hérouville (France): May–July 1981 / **Technical Team:** Producers: Fleetwood Mac, Ken Caillat, Richard Dashut / Sound Engineers: Ken Caillat, Richard Dashut / Assistant Sound Engineers: David Bianco, Carla Frederick / **Single:** Side A: Oh Diane / Side B: Only Over You / **UK Release Date:** November 19, 1982 with Warner Bros. Records (ref. 929824-7) / Best UK Ranking: 9

"Hold Me" and "Only Over You" were two musical testimonies to Christine's troubled and passionate relationship with Dennis Wilson.

Genesis and Lyrics

"Half of him was a little boy. The other half was crazy." In 1982, Christine McVie realized that Dennis Wilson—with whom she had an unstable relationship due to the alcoholic musician's fits of rage—could not be saved from himself. But two years earlier, when she put "Only Over You" down on paper, she charged herself with madness. "I'm out of my mind / But it's only over you / People think I'm crazy / But they don't know."

Christine was well aware that the people around her disapproved of the relationship and worried that she was once again under the influence of a man with the worst addictions. But her love for him ran deep, and although she knew this story would not have a happy ending, she wanted to believe that Dennis could rise above his problems.

Production

The beginnings of "Only Over You" date back to 1980, when Fleetwood Mac was on the Tusk tour. On the road, Christine began to sketch out a twilight ballad on the piano. An audio testimony attests to its existence in an embryonic piano-vocal version recorded during a jam session at a stopover on the tour.

Its slow rhythm and melancholy chord progressions evoke her beloved's compositions, such as "Time" and "Only with You." Lindsey Buckingham gave the track even

more drive when the band started working on it at the Château d'Hérouville. The tempo was quickened, and the sad dimension broken by Lindsey's delicate, soothing arpeggios and John McVie's reassuring bass. Christine McVie's vocals were tinged with a certain serenity, in keeping with the self-assurance she displays in her lyrics as she asserts herself, ignoring the opinions of others. The deluxe version of the album, released in 2016, contains an alternative take that bears witness to the multiple trials and tribulations of recording the track before it was finalized. Mick Fleetwood's drums are more present, especially on the intro where he rings out his ride cymbal. As for Lindsey Buckingham, he creates ethereal layers to great effect by playing with the volume.

FOR MAC-ADDICTS

Christine had this dedication written in small letters on the inside of the record sleeve: "With special thanks for the inspiration to Dennis Wilson."

"Empire State" served as an apology to New Yorkers after "The City" and "Miles Away," which had offended them.

The lap harp is a small harp with 16 to 22 strings, played on the knees.

EMPIRE STATE

Lindsey Buckingham, Richard Dashut / 2:52

1982

Musicians: Lindsey Buckingham: vocals, guitars, lap harp / Christine McVie: keyboards, backing vocals / John McVie: bass / Mick Fleetwood: drums / Stevie Nicks: backing vocals / **Recorded:** Le Château, Hérouville (France): May–July 1981 / **Technical Team:** Producers: Fleetwood Mac, Ken Caillat, Richard Dashut / Sound Engineers: Ken Caillat, Richard Dashut / Assistant Sound Engineers: David Bianco, Carla Frederick

Genesis and Lyrics

In 1973, Fleetwood Mac came close to a diplomatic incident when Bob Welch took a bite out of the Big Apple with his song "The City" on the album *Mystery to Me*. In it, the Californian saw New York as a dark and claustrophobic city, going so far as to describe it as a "prison without walls." Since then, the band had spared no effort to prove to their New York fans that they had no aversion to the city, performing there on eleven occasions. But perhaps the musicians felt the need to set their apology to music to make amends once and for all. It was Lindsey Buckingham, a West Coast native and not yet a member of the band at the time, who had taken up the pen to proclaim love for the Big Apple. In "Empire State," he speaks directly to the city in a way that is far removed from Welch's discourse: "New York, open your eyes to me / Let me be what I want to be."

Production

Perhaps "Empire State" is an affirmation of his attachment to New York and a way for Lindsey, an ex-Californian hippie, to emancipate himself from the West Coast folk scene and assert his modernity and open-mindedness. Musically, this track could not be further from folk, with its compressed bass and mutated electric guitar imposing a rock tension throughout the piece. With his high, almost androgynous voice, Buckingham seems to be paying homage to T. Rex. This closeness to glam rock was even more apparent on the first recording attempt made at Le Château (called the Early Version, available on the deluxe version of *Mirage* released in 2016), where the electric guitar was even more to the fore. On the finale, it launched into a frenzied blues-rock solo that ran out of steam until it deliberately ended in a dissonant spin. Urged on by the other members, Richard and Lindsey reduced the instrument's presence to a few sonic wisps on the finale, lost in the background of the mix. The guitar is muted in favor of a much more singular instrument, which is at the origin of the composition. It is Buckingham who plays the lap harp. The focus of attention throughout the track, the lap harp gives it a hypnotic, synthetic feel, like an electro sample before its time.

STRAIGHT BACK

Stevie Nicks / 4:11

Musicians: Stevie Nicks: vocals / Lindsey Buckingham: guitar, backing vocals / Ray Lindsey: guitar / Christine McVie: keyboards, backing vocals / John McVie: bass / Mick Fleetwood: drums /
Recorded: Le Château, Hérouville (France): December 1981 /
Technical Team: Producers: Fleetwood Mac, Ken Caillat, Richard Dashut / Sound Engineers: Ken Caillat, Richard Dashut / Assistant Sound Engineers: David Bianco, Carla Frederick

Genesis and Lyrics

"Straight Back" only appeared late in the recording process, when the band met for a few additional sessions at Château d'Hérouville, in December 1981. While Christine emphasized the happy, serene nature of the songs on *Mirage*, "Straight Back" is clearly an exception. It was born of Stevie's frustration when, due to her obligations with Fleetwood Mac, she had to make do with an eleven-date White Winged Dove tour to promote *Bella Donna* (between November 28 and December 13, 1981). On her return, she delivered this vengeful track to the other Mac members. Although she never explained herself, the lyrics are clear enough in evoking three things: her conflicted relationship with the other musicians in the group, her early days in music, which she describes as a "dream," and her solo work with Jimmy Iovine, with whom she has just broken up. Her complex relationship with the Mac, which she likens to a game of strategy, is captured in the opening lines of the song: "Which card shall I play?" Then, with a touch of nostalgia, she recalls her musical beginnings, when she was still full of dreams. But she pulls herself together, proclaiming that "the dream is not over." And with good reason: her solo career is taking off like a rocket. The second verse comes as an unexpected revelation and a thumbing of her nose at the band, as it seems to say that she was secretly composing for her next album, *The Wild Heart* (to be released in 1983) on the sidelines of the *Mirage* sessions: "Fingers find the ivory keys / And a song begins to begin /

Like a wolf on the run / And you will find while in the wind / Something that you lost." When the time comes to talk about her solo work away from Fleetwood Mac, she praises the complicity and exchanges she had with Jimmy Iovine, the producer of *Bella Donna*. In fact, their collaboration continued even after their breakup.

Production

"Straight Back" boasts a rich instrumentation, with particular attention paid to the acoustic guitar, which plays the accompaniment with admirable brilliance, with the meticulous sound recording work of the Dashut-Caillat duo. The guitar parts are shared between Lindsey Buckingham, who handles the lead guitar (and especially the final electric solo), and Ray Lindsey, who takes charge of the accompaniment. The latter was Fleetwood Mac's additional touring guitarist. He was recruited for the Tusk tour to assist Lindsey Buckingham and take over some of the rhythm parts. Because of this complementary role, he was asked to play on this track. His acoustic guitar accompaniment is sublimated by the ping-pong game set up by the producers, who alternately send the guitar to one side and the other of the stereo spectrum. The melody is completed by Christine's warm, retro-sounding keyboard. On this elegantly accomplished instrumentation, Stevie Nicks progressively allows her voice to build to a roar, starting from a low register and then gaining height as she pushes toward the high notes. Her expressive interpretation demonstrates exemplary breath control, with notes held throughout without ever faltering.

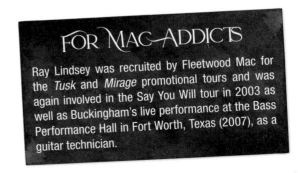

FOR MAC ADDICTS

Ray Lindsey was recruited by Fleetwood Mac for the *Tusk* and *Mirage* promotional tours and was again involved in the Say You Will tour in 2003 as well as Buckingham's live performance at the Bass Performance Hall in Fort Worth, Texas (2007), as a guitar technician.

HOLD ME

Christine McVie, Robbie Patton / 3:45

Musicians
Christine McVie: vocals, piano, keyboard, backing vocals
Lindsey Buckingham: vocals, guitars, backing vocals
John McVie: bass
Mick Fleetwood: drums, percussion
Recorded
Le Château, Hérouville (France): May–July 1981
Technical Team
Producers: Fleetwood Mac, Ken Caillat, Richard Dashut
Sound Engineers: Ken Caillat, Richard Dashut
Assistant Sound Engineers: David Bianco, Carla Frederick
Single
Side A: Hold Me / Side B: Eyes of the World
UK Release Date: June 25,1982 with Warner Bros. Records (ref. K 17965)
Best UK Ranking: Did Not Chart
Single
Side A: Hold Me / Side B: Eyes of the World
US Release Date: June 8, 1982 with Warner Bros. Records (ref. 7-29966)
Best US Ranking: 4
Single
Side A: Hold Me / Side B1: No Questions Asked, **Side B2:** I Loved Another Woman (Live)
UK Release Date: February 13, 1989 with Warner Bros. Records (ref. W 7528 T)
Best UK Ranking: 9

An unknown British musician, Robbie Patton was given the spotlight by Fleetwood Mac, who hired him to open for them on selected dates in 1979. A strong friendship developed between the singer and Christine McVie, who decided to produce his albums *Distant Shores* (1981) and *Orders from Headquarters* (1982). Lindsey, for his part, plays guitar on the single "Don't Give Up" (No. 26 in 1981). His contribution to "Hold Me" was a welcome returned favor.

Genesis and Lyrics

Christine McVie plays her strongest trump card right from the start of the Hérouville recording sessions: "Hold Me." Like "Only Over You," the track is dictated by the twists and turns of her passion for Dennis Wilson. Explains Mick Fleetwood in his autobiography, "Chris' songs, especially 'Hold Me,' convey her bittersweet reflections on her relationship with Dennis Wilson, which almost led to marriage. Instead, it ended in December, when Dennis moved out of her house and out of her life. Christine loved Dennis with all her heart (we all did). He embodied a fascinating but also trying episode in her life. I felt a certain responsibility because I was the one who introduced them. Dennis was completely crazy and Chris was like my sister. I could see the moment coming when Chris would go crazy trying to maintain her relationship with Dennis, who was already a guy with 20 thyroid glands, sucking down gargantuan amounts of coke, going on benders and swallowing endless pills. I was torn because Dennis was a friend and I could see him screwing up, chasing women. I didn't know if it was my place to tell Chris."[2] The songwriter, fully aware of her partner's vices, hides nothing of the difficulties that beset their daily lives: drugs ("Baby, don't you hand me a line"), Dennis's excesses for which she has to pay the piper ("But I'm the fool payin' the dues"), or the little time he gives to their relationship ("If you got a minute to spare"). As is often the case, McVie's writing plays on contrasts, blending reproach and seduction. The latter is expressed in the highly suggestive imagery of the lyrics "So slip your hand inside of my glove." Unexpectedly, this very intimate text was written four-handed with one of the singer's friends, musician Robbie Patton. This marks a major change in Christine's approach to songwriting, an exercise she had hitherto regarded as a solitary pursuit. On *Mirage*, not only does she not hesitate to ask for help in writing the lyrics but she also agrees to share the microphone with Lindsey Buckingham to sing her composition. How did she come to this decision, given that the initial demo, released on the album's deluxe edition in 2016, bears first witness to a solo interpretation?

"I think some things just happen instinctively," Christine reflected in 2016 in the columns of *Rolling Stone*. "I don't think it was planned. But I know that when I wrote the

With "Hold Me," Fleetwood Mac made a thunderous return to the top 5 of the 1982 Billboard Hot 100, five years after "Don't Stop."

song with Robbie, himself being a singer, he was singing the low part. At some point, it became obvious that Lindsey could do it."[113] Lindsey's flexible, androgynous voice made it easy for him to climb into the treble register, so in the end it was Lindsey who took the higher pitch.

Production

"When we recorded [the song], it was only half finished, really," Christine McVie told *Rolling Stone* in 2016. "But since everyone was apprehensive about it, we thought, 'Well, let's try and get something down on tape and that way, at least, we'll have the skeleton.' So we recorded it in a very basic form—there were huge parts with nothing on them. Then we built up the piece in sections." On the first recordings, the keyboard part dominated the rest of the instrumentation. Christine McVie soon opted for a contemporary-sounding Yamaha CP30 electric piano, to set the forthcoming single in its context of the period. The Hammond organ and the Fender Rhodes, which she usually favors, were put aside. The guitar is relatively absent at this stage, as Lindsey needed more time to create a suitable arrangement. Aside from a discreet accompaniment, he installed delicate arpeggio and clean ornamentation on the chorus. His best contribution comes in the middle section, at 2:00, where he combines a compressed motif with a sparing solo played on the upper end of the fretboard. He even adds a touch of refinement at the end of this musical segment with a twelve-string acoustic guitar that is richer in

harmonics (due to the resonance effect) than a traditional six-string guitar, since each string is doubled. The third key player is Mick Fleetwood. The former prince of shuffle blues was particularly at ease on this romantic soft-rock track. He is the one who gives all his originality to this classic instrumentation, with a bouncy, playful rhythm and delightful percussive elements (such as congas and tambourine).

The Video

"Hold Me" was released as a single in June 1982, accompanied by a music video. The video, directed by Steve Barron, is a real stage-setter, shot in the Mojave Desert. That was a choice that extended the theme suggested by the title *Mirage*. We see the band members dressed like archaeologists, digging up and dusting off fragments of their instruments with tweezers, as if trying to find and reconstitute their own past. But symbolically, it is also the hatchet they are digging up again, as their relationship during the shoot could not have been more strained. In fact, the five artists never appear together on film. Christine spent hours in make-up, and sometimes emerged from the dressing room so late that the shoot had to be postponed until the following day because the natural light had become too dim. Stevie, on the other hand, refused to walk in the sand in her platform shoes, which drove Mick mad. All this went over John's head, who was drunk most of the time. As for Lindsey, he was in a terrible mood.

OH DIANE

Lindsey Buckingham, Richard Dashut / 2:38

Musicians: Lindsey Buckingham: vocals, guitars, keyboards, backing vocals / John McVie: bass / Mick Fleetwood: drums, percussion / Christine McVie: backing vocals / **Recorded:** Le Château, Hérouville (France): May–July 1981 / **Technical Team:** Producers: Fleetwood Mac, Ken Caillat, Richard Dashut / Sound Engineers: Ken Caillat, Richard Dashut / Assistant Sound Engineers: David Bianco, Carla Frederick / **Single:** Side A: Oh Diane / Side B: Only Over You / **UK Release Date:** November 19, 1982 with Warner Bros. Records (ref. 929824-7) / Best UK Ranking: Did Not Chart / **12" Single:** Side A: Oh Diane / Side B1: Only Over You, Side B2: The Chain / **UK Release Date:** December 1982 with Warner Bros. Records (ref. 929823-0) / Best UK Ranking: 9 / **Single:** Side A: Oh Diane / Side B: That's Alright / **US Release Date:** March 9, 1983 with Warner Bros. Records (ref. 7-29698) / Best US Ranking: Did Not Chart

Genesis and Lyrics

Mick Fleetwood, the band's leader and historian, recalls his lieutenant's moods around the time of *Mirage*: "Lindsey was tired of being labeled the archetypal Northern Californian hippie. So he changed course, abandoning the new wave sound for a 1955 Eddie Cochran–style rock'n'roll vibe. I remember some tense conversations about the musical direction to take at the time. He always thought I resented him for the relatively disappointing sales of *Tusk*."[4] With the instrumental simplicity of this doo-wop influenced rock'n'roll, Lindsey combines lyrics in the same spirit as the light-hearted bluettes of the 1950s: "Oh no / Here I go again / Fallin' in love again / Love is like a grain of sand / Slowly slippin' through your hand." With this retro rock'n'roll, the antithesis of his previous work, the musician seems to be pursuing two objectives: to prove once again to the public that he is not subservient to folk—even though *Tusk* had already amply demonstrated his ability to project himself into experimental musical forms—and to prove to Mick that he could fall in line.

Production

"Oh Diane" was born under Lindsey's fingers as he worked with Richard Dashut on writing new material during the Hérouville sessions. They were aware of the song's anachronistic—even parodic—nature, but it proved devilishly catchy. The two men, similar in age, took a trip back in time to when they listened to the 45s of the pioneers of rock'n'roll: Buddy Holly, Elvis Presley, Little Richard, and Gene Vincent. Like Jeremy Spencer before him on *Kiln House*, Lindsey reconnected with the source of his art. He had no hesitation imitating the codes of the genre: He sings with an exaggerated tremolo à la Roy Orbison and encourages Christine to sing exaggeratedly ecstatic backing vocals. The other members play the game without restraint, also assuming a stereotyped style, such as John with his standard melodic motif with doubled notes, or Mick with a straight, unadorned rendition, barely emphasized by a tambourine. Chosen as the third single after "Hold Me" and "Gypsy," "Oh Diane" fared better than its predecessors in the UK. Though its progress was initially very slow as number sixty-nine on December 18, 1982, it finished ten weeks later at number nine in the country's singles charts. The proximity of the album to the wedding date of Prince Charles and Lady Diana, celebrated a year earlier on July 29, 1981, and the growing love of the British public for the princess, certainly contributed to its success.

EYES OF THE WORLD

Lindsey Buckingham / 3:44

Musicians
Lindsey Buckingham: vocals, guitars
Christine McVie: keyboards, backing vocals
John McVie: bass
Mick Fleetwood: drums
Stevie Nicks: backing vocals

Recorded
Le Château, Hérouville (France): May–July 1981

Technical Team
Producers: Fleetwood Mac, Ken Caillat, Richard Dashut
Sound Engineers: Ken Caillat, Richard Dashut
Assistant Sound Engineers: David Bianco, Carla Frederick

Single
Side A: Hold Me / Side B: Eyes of the World
US Release Date: June 8,1982 with Warner Bros. Records
 (ref. 7-29966)
Best US Ranking: 4
UK Release Date: June 25, 1982 with Warner Bros. Records
 (ref. K 17965)
Best UK Ranking: Did Not Chart

1982

Behind the apparent naïvete of the lyrics inspired by a children's nursery rhyme, Lindsey once again rails against Stevie.

Genesis and Lyrics

Lindsey Buckingham's creative momentum was interrupted while he was conceiving his solo album *Law and Order*, but he did not hold back creatively when he reunited with Fleetwood Mac in France for the *Mirage* sessions. He brought with him a new composition, "Eyes of the World." Except it was actually not so new. The songwriter said the acoustic guitar part on the song came from a Buckingham Nicks instrumental track. The song was "Stephanie," which was the second track of the duo's 1973 album.

"I've never had a problem taking an element from another song, as long as it's one of mine and I don't risk being attacked for it," the songwriter said, "and reusing it in a different way, as long as it's justified in this new context. It's like leaving little clues for listeners who are really paying attention. It's not a planned thing. I hate to admit it, but it's more a matter of opportunity. I think, 'Oh, this old thing would look good here.' Some people might think it's not a good idea to reuse elements like that, but my feeling is that, as long as you don't do it all the time, who cares?"

The borrowings don't stop there. Whether intentionally or not, Lindsey revisits the opening theme of Pachelbel's Canon, a piece of Baroque music composed in 1680 by the German organist Johann Pachelbel for three violins and basso continuo. A veritable standard that can easily be transposed to many instruments and had already been exploited by the Beatles on "I Wanna Hold Your Hand" and the Village People on "Go West." The chord progression was transposed to *B* flat. The harmonic sequence is therefore familiar, but the key change avoids an overly academic reproduction.

The lyrics, too, contain an unexpected borrowing. While the first verse is inspired by love resentments that we can easily imagine being addressed to Stevie Nicks, the second draws its first two lines from a traditional nineteenth-century English nursery rhyme to teach children the days of the week: "Monday's child is fair of face / Tuesday's child is full of grace."

Lindsey's version differs slightly from the original: "Monday's children are filled with face / Tuesday's children are filled with grace." Whether by chance or not, Lindsey was born on a Monday (October 3, 1949). But the trail ends

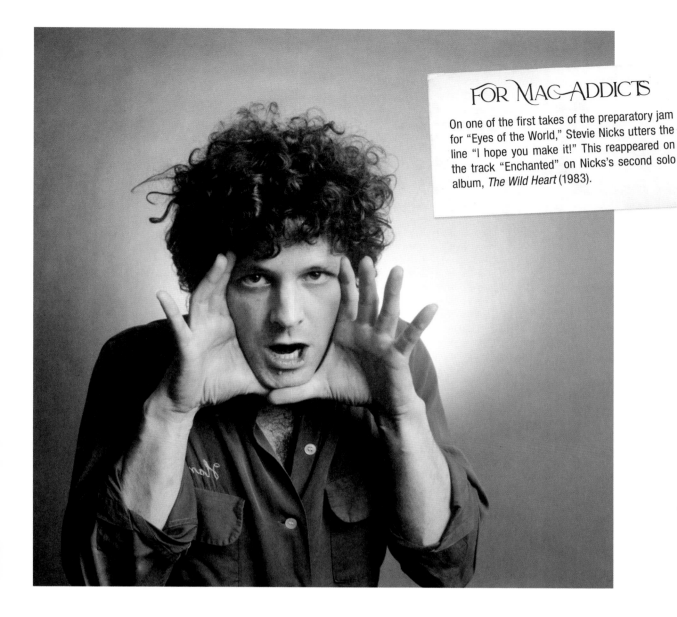

there, Stevie having been born on a Wednesday (May 26, 1948). The musician does not leave much room for interpretation, contenting himself with two very short verses. The emphasis is more on the musicality of the track than on the depth of its lyrics.

Production

To give everyone a chance to familiarize themselves with Lindsey's song, the musicians decided to jam, as they often did at Hérouville, during which they spin the melodic theme for several long minutes. This improvisation reinforces the group's cohesion, while accentuating the spontaneity of the song. At this stage, Lindsey and Stevie were content to accompany the melody with a few vocalizations, as the song had no lyrics as yet. Over the course of the sessions, this basic version was fleshed out with instrumentation that was as delicate as it was effective—including a penetrating drum set with a pleasant, subdued sound—and admirable vocal work, with backing vocals provided mainly by Christine that combined with the main vocal. The song also benefited from the crazy creativity of the producers. The intro, the fruit of fastidious and meticulous editing, with its short, whispered vocals appearing one after the other, as if the vocals were multiplying, is a perfect illustration. "Eyes of the World" proves once again Lindsey Buckingham's skill as a composer and his ability to synthesize the contributions of other musicians and to blend musical styles into a unique creation. This hybrid quality is very much in evidence on the final track, where we hear a classically inspired—even medieval—acoustic guitar mingling with the acidic, almost punk sounds of an electric guitar.

WISH YOU WERE HERE

Christine McVie, Colin Allen / 4:51

1982

Musicians
Christine McVie: vocals, piano
Lindsey Buckingham: guitar
John McVie: bass
Mick Fleetwood: drums

Recorded
Le Château, Hérouville (France): May–July 1981

Technical Team
Producers: Fleetwood Mac, Ken Caillat, Richard Dashut
Sound Engineers: Ken Caillat, Richard Dashut
Assistant Sound Engineers: David Bianco, Carla Frederick

Drummer Colin Allen, co-writer of "Wish You Were Here," also wrote the lyrics to "Alabama" on Mick Taylor's debut album.

Genesis and Lyrics

A gifted drummer, Colin Allen had been a fixture on the British jazz and blues scene since 1958. In 1963 he took part in Zoot Money's Big Roll Band (featuring future Police guitarist Andy Summers) and John Mayall's Bluesbreakers between 1968 and 1969. He was regularly called upon for recording sessions alongside artists such as John Lee Hooker, Mick Taylor, and Sonny Boy Williamson. Close to Fleetwood Mac because of his connection with John Mayall, Allen contributed lyrics to "Wish You Were Here" with Christine McVie. Unfortunately, it was not a success. The lyrics lapse into a syrupy romanticism of confounding mawkishness: "I wish you were here / 'Cause I feel like a child tonight / Each moment is a memory / Time's so unkind."

Production

"Wish You Were Here" shows just how far Christine McVie had come as a composer. Confined to a supporting role when she first joined the band, she gradually asserted herself as a composer, then, over the years, moved away from the boogie blues groove of her beginnings to focus on the melodic aspect of her art. She no longer hesitated to play emphatically, as evidenced by the intro to "Wish You Were Here."

Christine also delivers an impeccable vocal performance, with a drawling first phrase introducing a sense of melancholy before projecting her pure voice with conviction and emotion. She is supported by soft, distant backing vocals. In terms of breath management, the endings of the phrases are confidently mastered. John McVie sustains the melody with deep notes while Mick Fleetwood opts for a no-frills style of playing in which every stroke is skillfully

Christine and Lindsey at Hollywood's Hard Rock Hotel & Casino during their 2017 joint tour, during which they performed "Wish You Were Here" as a duet.

measured. His snare drum resonates in our hearts, magnificently served by a treatment that bears the hallmarks of Dashut and Caillat's signature sound production: a crystal-clear, precise sound, delivered to listeners as if they were present in the recording studio.

SMILE AT YOU

Stevie Nicks / 4:52

Musicians: Stevie Nicks: vocals / Christine McVie: vocals, piano, clavier, backing vocals / Lindsey Buckingham: guitar, backing vocals / John McVie: bass / Mick Fleetwood: drums / **Recorded:** Le Château, Hérouville (France): May–July 1981 / **Technical Team:** Producers: Fleetwood Mac, Ken Caillat, Richard Dashut / Sound Engineers: Ken Caillat, Richard Dashut / Assistant Sound Engineers: David Bianco, Carla Frederick

Another Stevie Nicks song is dogged over time by the musicians' procrastination, as they experiment, hesitate, and finally put off recording it until the tenth of never... Composed at the time of *Rumours*, sketched out during *Tusk*, then revisited during the *Mirage* sessions, it was re-recorded for "Say You Will" (2003). Two versions were recorded during the *Mirage* sessions in Hérouville. The first stands out for Nicks's faster, more visceral vocal interpretation, earning it the nickname "Angry Version." Lindsey tries to make his guitar growl, but it lacks attack and the bass is badly mixed, saturating the sound space. Despite these weaknesses, the track's potential is enormous. The second version (recorded at Le Château in early summer 1981 and released in the deluxe version of *Mirage* in 2016), offers a softer vision of the song, led by Christine's very prominent keyboards. Unfortunately, neither of these songs made it onto the track list of the Mac's thirteenth LP. Deemed too raucous by Lindsey Buckingham, "Smile At You" was passed over for "Straight Back." The guitarist was quick to get rid of a track with some unflattering passages depicting him as an egomaniac: "You needed someone to depend on you / I could not be her / I did not want to / My first mistake / Was to smile at you."

COOL WATER

Bob Nolan / 3:23

Musicians: Lindsey Buckingham: vocals, guitars, backing vocals / John McVie: bass, backing vocals / **Recorded:** Le Château, Hérouville (France): May–July 1981 / **Technical Team:** Producers: Fleetwood Mac, Ken Caillat, Richard Dashut / Sound Engineers: Ken Caillat, Richard Dashut / Assistant Sound Engineers: David Bianco, Carla Frederick / **Single:** Side A: Gypsy / Side B: Cool Water / **UK Release Date:** September 17, 1982 with Warner Bros. Records (ref. K 17997) / Best UK Ranking: 46

In 1980, a year before recording *Mirage*, Canadian country singer and actor Bob Nolan died of a heart attack. Founder of the popular group Sons of the Pioneers with Roy Rogers,

he was the interpreter of the country classic "Cool Water." Lindsey Buckingham, moved by his death, decided to cover this song, far removed from Fleetwood Mac's pop universe, as the Side B for "Gypsy." The recording was quickly rushed through, with the guitarist wishing to preserve the authentic atmosphere of this slow ballad. Only two acoustic guitars were required, one for rhythm and the other for ornamentation. The rest of the work consists of harmonizing several male voices (done by Lindsey himself and John McVie), giving the impression of a cowboy choir gathered around a campfire. Lindsey does not aim for the precision that is usually the charming feature of Fleetwood Mac's vocal harmonizations; it is more about recreating the collegiate atmosphere of the western vocal groups of the 1930s and 1940s. Like the other outtakes, "Cool Water" was unveiled to the public when the deluxe edition of *Mirage* was released in 2016.

PUT A CANDLE IN THE WINDOW

Christine McVie / 2:20

Musicians: Christine McVie: vocals, piano / Lindsey Buckingham: guitar / John McVie: bass / Mick Fleetwood: drums / **Recorded:** Le Château, Hérouville (France): May–July 1981 / **Technical Team:** Producers: Fleetwood Mac, Ken Caillat, Richard Dashut / Sound Engineers: Ken Caillat, Richard Dashut / Assistant Sound Engineers: David Bianco, Carla Frederick

For fans of Creedence Clearwater Revival, the song "Put a Candle in the Window" is bound to evoke the first line of "As Long as I Can See the Light." But Christine McVie's up-tempo rock has nothing in common with Creedence Clearwater Revival. Although pleasing for the pianist's velvety vocals and its syncopated rhythm underlined by Mick's nuance-free chops, it remains incomplete. In fact, the band recorded it with most of the lyrics missing. It is a safe bet that the song would also have benefited from additional arrangements to enhance its dynamics, if the band had gone through with the process. But it was unveiled "as is" on the deluxe edition of *Mirage* in 2016.

FOR MAC ADDICTS

The title chosen is "Put a Candle in the Window," but Christine clearly sings "in my window."

BLUE MONDAY

David Bartholomew, Antoine Domino / 1:32

Musicians: Lindsey Buckingham: vocals, guitar / Christine McVie: piano / John McVie: bass / Mick Fleetwood: drums / **Recorded:** Le Château, Hérouville (France): May–July 1981 / **Technical Team:** Producers: Fleetwood Mac, Ken Caillat, Richard Dashut / Sound Engineers: Ken Caillat, Richard Dashut / Assistant Sound Engineers: David Bianco, Carla Frederick

During one of the famous improvisation sessions organized at the chateau to improve cohesion, the group threw itself into a cover of a jubilant rhythm'n'blues track, Blue Monday. Written by Dave Bartholomew, it was first recorded in 1954, at the height of the rock'n'roll wave, by Smiley Lewis. But it was the version by Antoine Domino (aka Fats Domino) that history would remember, following his reworking of it two years later. In the process, he took a share of the songwriting credits alongside Bartholomew, his trumpeter and favored collaborator. The song recounts the week of a hardworking man, slaving away every day, with Saturday in sight to relieve the pressure, before embarking on another exhausting and unfulfilling week. This number, a treat for a pianist like Christine, who could hammer away at the keys at will, is slightly slowed down, but that does not stop Lindsey from singing at the top of his lungs with the energy of a belle époque rocker. This jubilant song found its place with the other outtakes on the six-CD/LP deluxe box set of Mirage (2016).

> A coincidence perhaps? The listing of the days of the week is common to the lyrics of three songs performed by Lindsey Buckingham with Fleetwood Mac: "Monday Morning" (which quotes Monday and Friday on Fleetwood Mac), "Eyes of the World" (Monday and Tuesday on Mirage), and then "Blue Monday" (which goes through the whole week).

GOODBYE ANGEL

Lindsey Buckingham / 3:12

Musicians: Lindsey Buckingham: vocals, guitars / Christine McVie: keyboards, backing vocals / John McVie: bass / Mick Fleetwood: drums / Stevie Nicks: backing vocals / **Recorded:** Le Château, Hérouville (France): May–July 1981 / **Technical Team:** Producers: Fleetwood Mac, Ken Caillat, Richard Dashut / Sound Engineers: Ken Caillat, Richard Dashut / Assistant Sound Engineers: David Bianco, Carla Frederick

Dominated by two beautifully interwoven acoustic guitars, Goodbye Angel reveals a more romantic, folk-oriented side to Lindsey Buckingham, who delivers a technically flawless vocal performance. The ends of the phrases shine with note-holding and unexpected highs (on "in" at 0:24) or lows (on "friend" at 1:11). The only lapse in taste is the overly ecstatic, syrupy female backing vocals. This outtake from Mirage was finally unveiled in 1992 as part of the compilation 25 Years—The Chain.

IF YOU WERE MY LOVE

Stevie Nicks / 5:42

Musicians: Stevie Nicks: vocals / Christine McVie: piano / Lindsey Buckingham: guitar / John McVie: bass / Mick Fleetwood: drums / **Recorded:** Le Château, Hérouville (France): May–July 1981 / **Technical Team:** Producers: Fleetwood Mac, Ken Caillat, Richard Dashut / Sound Engineers: Ken Caillat, Richard Dashut / Assistant sound engineers: David Bianco, Carla Frederick

No rational reason can justify the absence from the Mirage track list of "If You Were My Love," a captivating composition by Stevie Nicks. The musicians' culpable lack of interest in this song deprives it of possible Mac standard status. Stevie Nicks came up with the song as early as 1981, after working with Tom Petty and the Heartbreakers on "Stop Draggin' My Heart Around." Seduced by the cohesion and complicity of the band's musicians, she immediately decided to celebrate them in "If You Were My Love." "It sounds like a love song, but it's not," confirms Stevie in the columns of the Chicago Tribune in 1981, before explaining: "It's about getting out of your own life and getting attached to something that's not yours. It's like falling in love with another band for a minute. It's got nothing to do with [a love affair], let's be clear about that—there's absolutely nothing between me and anyone in this band. They're all married. They're all expecting babies. That's why I'm very comfortable with them, why I'm their friend and almost one of the 'guys' in the band."

Despite its qualities, "If You Were My Love" seems almost to be jinxed in some way. Although it should have been included in Bella Donna in 1981, it was dropped from the track list at the last minute. It resurfaced in 1982 during the Mirage sessions, also without success. In 1993, Stevie Nicks re-recorded it, this time completing the creative process. However, just as it was about to become part of Street Angel (Stevie's fifth opus), producer Thom Panunzio intervened and convinced the singer to withdraw the track. It was not until the 2014 compilation 24 Karat Gold: Songs from the Vault that "If You Were My Love" finally emerged from oblivion. But Stevie Nicks's version, with all due respect, falls far short of the timelessness of the one recorded by Fleetwood Mac in Hérouville, a delightful ballad illuminated by Christine's celestial piano and haunted by Stevie's melancholy voice. This version was finally unveiled in 2016 on the deluxe edition of Mirage.

ALBUM

TANGO IN THE NIGHT

Big Love . Seven Wonders . Everywhere . Caroline . Tango in the Night . Mystified .
Little Lies . Family Man . Welcome to the Room…Sara . Isn't It Midnight .
When I See You Again . You and I, Part II .
Outtakes: You and I, Part I . Book of Miracles . Ricky . Down Endless Street . Where We
Belong . Special Kind of Love .
What Has Rock & Roll Ever Done for You? . Ooh My Love . Juliet

RELEASE DATES
United Kingdom: April 13, 1987
Reference: Warner Bros. Records—WX65
Best UK Chart Ranking: 1
United States: April 13, 1987
Reference: Warner Bros. Records—1-25471
Best US Chart Ranking: 7

1987

SWAN SONG

Following an express two-month promotional tour for *Mirage* (September 1 to October 31, 1982), Fleetwood Mac took an indefinite break, which was to last several years, during which members had the opportunity to devote themselves to their own projects.

Headwinds

Initially, Christine McVie saw this break as a godsend, as she felt the need for a rest, to devote time to her dogs, her house, and her garden. But this kind of inactivity soon wearied the musician, and in 1983 she decided to follow up on *Christine Perfect*, her first solo album, released thirteen years earlier. When *Christine McVie* was released in January 1984, the keyboardist's first single, "Got a Hold on Me," reached number ten on the Billboard chart. However, she had no desire to go on tour, preferring to meet up with her Mac bandmates in the studio. Unfortunately for her, Lindsey Buckingham, the band's main creative force, was too busy putting the finishing touches to his second solo opus, *Go Insane*, to consider working on a new band album. In the absence of any prospects with Fleetwood Mac, Christine decided to hit the road in support of her album, which had meanwhile reached number twenty-six in the United States.

After indulging in a fun tour with Mick Taylor and John Mayall—who re-formed the Bluesbreakers for the occasion—in 1982, John McVie retired to the small Caribbean island of St. Thomas, where he spent the next three years nursing his alcoholism.

Mick's situation was not a happy one. The drummer had been spending lavishly for years, but reality—and the taxman—caught up with him at the end of the Mirage tour. As his musical activities outside the Mac were not paying off, he was forced to declare bankruptcy and sell everything he owned in the spring of 1984. Fortunately, there was a plan for his debts to be covered solely by royalties from existing recordings.

Stevie Nicks, meanwhile, completed her second album, *The Wild Heart*, shortly after the end of the Mirage tour. But the death of her best friend, Robin Anderson, on October 5, 1982, from leukemia, was a devastating loss that brought out raw emotion in Stevie. It translated to her recording, and *The Wild Heart* eclipsed the success of *Bella Donna*, released in the summer of 1981. As godmother to Robin's baby, Stevie felt she had a mission: to protect and provide the child with financial security and family stability. She took the surprising step of marrying Kim Anderson, her friend's widower, on January 29, 1983. A good but flawed idea that did not last long.

By 1985, John, Mick, Christine, and even Stevie were ready to reunite and start work on a new album, but Lindsey kept the band at arm's length. He shut himself away in the recording studio he had built for himself right across the street from his bedroom, in his luxurious Californian villa in Bel Air, where he spent his days working on his own projects: After the release of *Go Insane* (1984), which reached number twenty-three in the United States, he took part in the charity single "We Are the World" (1985) and the soundtrack to the film *Back to the Future*, while preparing his next solo album.

Unable to stand still, Christine took matters into her own hands and contacted Richard Dashut in 1985. She asked him to come and produce her cover of "Can't Help Falling in Love" for the soundtrack of the film *A Fine Mess*, and invited Lindsey, whom she knew to be an Elvis Presley fan, to the recording sessions as a lure. The latter accepted and soon saw Mick and John, who had joined Christine in the studio to persuade him to work on a new Mac album.

The *Tango in the Night* sessions got off on the wrong foot, Lindsey (here in his home studio) being the only one to show any interest in the project.

Lindsey reluctantly agreed, and an appointment was made to start the studio sessions.

Lindsey's Return

Nile Rodgers, Chic's virtuoso funk guitarist, was the first to be considered for a place behind the console. But the collaboration fell through. Reprise Records manager Mo Ostin put the band on the trail of Jason Corsaro, a sound engineer who had worked with the Cars, Debbie Harry, Chic, and Paul Simon, among others. The band held a few rehearsal sessions in November 1985, from which nothing usable came out. Lindsey realized that he would be satisfied only if he himself sat next to Richard Dashut in the producer's chair. The two men, who were due to collaborate on Lindsey's solo album, agreed to postpone the deadline and work on the Mac's fourteenth album.

For the recording, Lindsey set his sights on Rumbo Recorders. This studio, located in Los Angeles's Canoga Park district, was created in 1977 by Daryl Dragon, Captain in the popular pop duo Captain & Tennille. Initially designed for its creators, it was made available to other artists from 1982 onward, starting with Survivor and the recording of the *Eye of the Tiger* album. The main studio featured a sixty-square-meter control room—an exceptional amount of space—equipped with a sixty-input Neve V Series console and two Studer A827 24-track recorders. To assist him, Lindsey hired sound engineer Greg Droman,

whom he had met while working on the *Back to the Future* soundtrack, and with whom he was to collaborate on his next opus.

A Fastidious Recording

The first sessions began in November 1985. The recordings, which lasted seventeen long months until March 1987, soon proved to be tedious. This was mainly due to Lindsey's constant penchant for experimentation. Among the guitarist's innovative ideas was the recording of tracks at a slower speed, usually at midtempo, to allow the musicians, himself in particular, to take care of the execution of complex parts and to work serenely on ornamentation and ambience. The analog tape was then played back at normal speed. "We would do parts, and then double it and triple it and quadruple it," Droman recalled, "and each part would have maybe a little bit of a different tweak in the speed. That would give it a depth you wouldn't get normally, and a sort of chorusing effect." A five-minute track could stretch to ten minutes. Lindsey also innovated with the use of a Fairlight CMI, a synthesizer that could be utilized to sample parts of the recording, particularly the vocal parts. Despite the state-of-the-art equipment available at Rumbo Recorders, he decided to finalize the album at home, in his own studio. Most of the overdubs and all the mixing were done at home, using entirely analog equipment. "It wasn't a proper studio by any means, but it was where Lindsey felt at home,

Musical duo Captain & Tennille make their Canoga Park recording studio, Rumbo Recorders, available to the Mac.

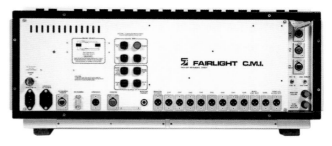

The Fairlight CMI CPU is equipped with floppy disk drives and a video control monitor.

and he was in charge," explained Mick in his autobiography. "There were no lounges and secluded corners to hang out in, because Lindsey's house was his home."[2] So a gigantic camper van was rented and parked in front of the guitarist's house as a place for the other musicians to relax.

Lindsey versus the World

The rest of the band did not seem to have much interest in the work, and Lindsey had the impression of working alone. He sensed no desire for unity, no feeling of camaraderie, and even less of a shared musical vision. He particularly resented Stevie, who was conspicuous through her frequent absences. Her solo Rock a Little tour ran from April 11 to October 6, 1986, after which she went into rehab. A regular user of narcotics for almost a decade, the young woman was in no fit state to record an album and needed serious medical assistance. In 2000, she explained her descent into hell: "I agreed to see this psychiatrist to make everybody happy. But if I had made a wrong turn and got lost and not arrived at that psychiatrist's office that day, the destiny of my life would have been so changed […] He gave me two little blue pills. One at morning and one at night. Within a couple of months that turned into four little blue pills. Then it became 15 blue pills […] he watched me grow heavier and the light went out in my eyes. […] I was sick and high and miserable and overweight. I knew I was going to die."[7]

Unfortunately, Lindsey's participation in *Tango in the Night* was to be short-lived—a fortnight at most. He found it hard to cope, between an absent Stevie and a Mick also consumed by his drug addiction, who fell asleep half the time he was in the studio. "There were a lot of drum machines and it was all a bit clinical and boring," recalls the drummer. "I always hung around during recording so I spent a lot of time with Lindsey but more often than not I'd find myself holed up in that trailer in his driveway, waiting for drug dealers to pay me a visit."[2] John was not to be outdone with his chronic alcoholism. His out-of-control drinking led to a long artistic block.

The album's greatest credit goes to Lindsey, who contributed five of his own compositions ("Big Love," "Caroline," "Tango in the Night," "Family Man," and "You and I, Part II"), which he was saving for his solo album. Without this contribution, there would simply have been no *Tango in the Night*; Stevie had contributed only two tracks ("Welcome to the Room…Sara" and "When I See You Again") and Christine four ("Everywhere," "Little Lies," "Isn't It Midnight," and "Mystified"). The last two songs had benefited from Lindsey's precious contribution.

Lindsey Buckingham ran the helm as best he could. A few weeks before the album's release, the disillusioned guitarist spoke to *Rolling Stone*. He had almost regretted having to put his solo work on hold: "I guess you could say the needs of the many outweighed the needs of the few […] I

The cover of *Tango in the Night* comes from a painting by artist Sir Brett-Livingstone Strong owned by Lindsey Buckingham.

FOR MAC-ADDICTS

Sir Brett-Livingstone Strong, the artist who created the cover painting for *Tango in the Night*, is also famous for having designed a life-size bronze statue of John Lennon, called *Imagine*.

decided, if we're going to do this, then let's really do this. This could very well be the last Fleetwood Mac album, so let's make it a killer."[62] In the same interview, he insisted: "I don't know if this is Fleetwood Mac's swan song, but if it is, then there's no doubt that it would be a more appropriate one than *Mirage*. Everyone is very happy to be done with [*Tango*], but they're also very happy with the end result." He added, "This album has some of the coherency of *Rumours*. It feels like a story, it works as a whole. And it has some of the charms of *Tusk*, with some of the rough edges polished up just a bit. On a production level, it's beyond anything we've done."[62] Lindsey provided an after-sales service, even if it meant overstating the case to keep up appearances: "That chemistry that made us what we were in the first place hasn't gone away. There was very little of a party atmosphere going on. I think that era is pretty much gone. Five years ago, the norm was to work from four in the afternoon to four in the morning or even later. This time around we'd start about two in the afternoon and finish by ten at night. It was a lot healthier."[62]

A few years later, Lindsey would be much more radical when recalling the recording period of *Tango in the Night*, refusing to take on alone the adverse role the others wanted to give him after his stormy departure in the summer of 1987. "It was a mess," he said. "For whatever reasons, there was no camaraderie left. Just getting people in the same room to create more semblance of a group became a huge hassle. Especially with Stevie, who was probably around for something like ten days for that whole record." The party thus accused, Stevie acknowledged her minimal contribution to *Tango*: "I started not being able to get to Lindsey Buckingham's house on time, and I would get there and everybody was drinking, so I'd have a glass of wine. Don't mix tranquilizers and wine. Then I'd sing horrific parts on his [Lindsey's] songs, and he would take the parts off. I was hardly on *Tango of the*

Night, which I happen to love." Indeed, Lindsey had a hard time editing Stevie's vocal parts. He had to cut out small pieces of tracks and put them together to give the illusion that they were complete takes.

In the face of adversity, Lindsey pulled through and saw the album through to the end, but the idea of leaving the band began to grow. "The way people were conducting their lives made it difficult to get serious work done. Mick was pretty nuts then. We all were. In terms of substance abuse, that was the worst it got," he recalled.

A Deceptive Success

Despite the difficulties and the noxious atmosphere, *Tango in the Night*, which took its name from the title track, hit the record stores on April 13, 1987. The cover featured a splendid painting by Australian artist Sir Brett-Livingstone Strong, depicting a lush jungle setting. An overt reinterpretation of Henri Rousseau's painting *La charmeuse de serpents*, the work conceals an element of unsolved mystery: We note the presence of what appears to be a UFO in the sky, while several pairs of eyes belonging to creatures unknown shine in the forest gloom.

This new album gave Fleetwood Mac the opportunity to make a resounding comeback. Its commercial success (15 million copies sold, number one in the UK and number seven in the US) made it one of the band's major albums, and the second best-selling after the unassailable *Rumours*. In the process, it laid the foundations for the soft-rock sound of the late 1980s, with sonorities that were extremely clean, even smooth at times, but imbued with a powerful sense of melody and a host of arrangements that blended synthetic and analog sounds.

The first single, "Big Love," quickly climbed into the US top 10 and received extensive airplay on radio stations across the country. Other hits followed, consolidating the success of *Tango in the Night*: Stevie's "Seven Wonders"

(co-written with Sandy Stewart), as well as two Christine tracks, "Everywhere" and "Little Lies."

For the general public, there was no doubt that the great Fleetwood Mac was about to hit the road for many months to crown this success. Except that in most of the interviews he gave, Lindsey implied that he was going back to his solo career, and that *Tango in the Night* had only come about because the band members did not want to end on a false note with *Mirage*.

All of a sudden, the album took on a new dimension, that of a musical farewell for the band's technical leader. The other members, however, were not taking the matter too seriously. In an interview with the *Los Angeles Times* on June 14, 1987, Stevie declared: "When Lindsey says, 'I think this will be the last record,' Mick and I and John kind of look at each other and go, 'Right, we have heard this before.' It is kind of like a love relationship when someone

is constantly saying, 'I am going to leave you' and never does." This underestimated Lindsey's bitterness, as he had been forced to "sacrifice" his best songs, which he had intended for his next solo album, to "save" this album, and thus Fleetwood Mac.

Mick, Stevie, Christine, and John worked Lindsey to the bone. At a meeting in July 1987, they finally got him to agree—albeit half-heartedly—to a tour to promote the album. In exchange, Lindsey had them agree that the tour would last no more than ten weeks.

The logistics were set in motion and numerous dates were quickly scheduled. But Lindsey suddenly went back on his word.

The Psychodrama of Lindsey's Departure

In a last-ditch effort to save Fleetwood Mac, Christine summoned everyone to her home in Coldwater Canyon

The volcanic and ambiguous relationship between Stevie Nicks and Lindsey Buckingham ends in an eruption, leading to the guitarist's departure.

Abrupt though Lindsey's departure may have been, his replacements were organized quickly. Rick Vito (far left) and Billy Burnette (second from right) were immediately enlisted. Fleetwood Mac's tenth lineup was born.

on August 7, 1987. No one wanted to face the humiliation of a canceled tour. Except Lindsey, who just wanted to leave. The argument quickly escalated: His bandmates' pleas accomplished nothing, as he categorically refused to go on tour. He felt that he had reached the peak of his creativity and should now devote himself entirely to his own career. He talked about the twelve years he had devoted to the band and explained that he was no longer prepared to continue doing everything: arranging, producing, playing guitar, singing…This comment deeply hurt Christine, whose singles had done particularly well on the radio, even more so than Lindsey's. Stevie finally lost her temper and broke the long silence, according to Mick's autobiography: "'Lindsey,' she said, 'you've broken my fucking heart on this.'" The outraged guitarist turned to her and angrily replied, "Hey, don't do this again. Don't start attacking me." He also said, "Get this bitch out of my way. And fuck the lot of you!" before leaving the room and heading for his car. Stevie ran after him. "It was a terribly sad moment," explained Mick, a helpless witness to this historic turning point in Fleetwood Mac's history, "because I could tell that even in her anger, a part of Stevie still loved Lindsey Buckingham and didn't want him to leave Fleetwood Mac." Outside, the two former lovers exchange a few words, but soon the full force of their feelings, repressed for years, rise to the surface. "Hey, man, you'll never be in love with anyone but yourself!"[4] Stevie finally blurted out. Slaps were exchanged, before Fleetwood Mac's new manager, Dennis Dunstan, and Stevie's manager, Tony Dimitriades, separated the two belligerents.

Once everyone was back inside, including Lindsey, the tension barely showed signs of subsiding. Christine lost her temper with Lindsey. John thought it was time to put an end to this ordeal and finally invited the guitarist to leave. Lindsey complied, but not without one last kind word for his now-former friends: "You're a bunch of selfish bastards!"[4] He returned to his car, settled behind the wheel, and sat in the driveway alone. No one went out after him. He stayed that way for about ten minutes, then finally turned on the ignition and drove off. This time, after twelve years of relative stability with the same lineup, Fleetwood Mac experienced a new existential crisis that would leave deep scars. "I want it clear that Lindsey Buckingham was not fired from Fleetwood Mac," said Mick. "He left the group on his own."[4]

After this latest clash, Lindsey issued a statement: "In 1985, I was working on my third solo album when the band came to me and asked me to produce the next Fleetwood Mac project. At that point, I put aside my solo work, which was half-finished, and committed myself for the next 17 months to produce *Tango in the Night*. It was always our understanding that upon completion of the *Tango* album I would return to my solo work. Of course I wish them all the success in the world on the road."

The rest of the band had no time to wallow in the gloom of Lindsey's departure. On the same evening of the altercation, Stevie and Mick gathered around a table at the chic Le Dome restaurant on Sunset Boulevard. They invited Billy Burnette, author of seven albums and son of rockabilly legend Dorsey Burnette; and Rick Vito, former lead guitarist for Bob Seger and Jackson Browne. The two men were invited to join Fleetwood Mac to save the upcoming tour. Without an audition, needless to say…As usual with Fleetwood Mac, there seemed to be only one motto: The show must go on. And only one goal: survival.

476 TANGO IN THE NIGHT

BIG LOVE

Lindsey Buckingham / 3:46

Musicians: Lindsey Buckingham: vocals, guitars, Fairlight CMI, synthesizer, drum programmer, percussion / John McVie: bass / Mick Fleetwood: drums / **Recorded:** Rumbo Recorders, Los Angeles: November 1985–March 1987 / The Slope, Los Angeles: November 1985–March 1987 / **Technical Team:** Producers: Lindsey Buckingham, Richard Dashut / Sound Engineer: Greg Droman / Assistant Sound Engineers: Ray Lindsey, Roy Hopper, Steve Matteucci / **Single:** Side A: Big Love / Side B: You & I, Part 1 / **UK Release Date:** March 13, 1987 / **Reference:** Warner Bros. Records (45 rpm ref.: W 8398) / Best UK Chart Ranking: 9 / **US Release Date:** March 23, 1987 / **Reference:** Warner Bros. Records (ref. 7-28398) / Best US Chart Ranking: 5 / **12" Single:** Side A1: Big Love (Extended Remix) / Side A2: Big Love (House on the Hill Dub) / Side B1: Big Love (Piano Dub) / Side B2: You and I, Part I / **US Release Date:** 1987 / **Reference:** Warner Bros. Records (12-inch single ref.: 0-20683) / Best US Chart Ranking: Did Not Chart

Genesis and Lyrics

Conceived by a Lindsey Buckingham more tortured than ever, "Big Love" deals with the loss of a sovereign, absolute love, and the emotional abyss that opens up beneath the narrator's feet when he has to confront his sudden solitude. The song, which traces the repeated failures of the guitarist's love affairs since his separation from Stevie Nicks, carries a host of feelings, between anguish, frustrated desire, and pure love. The opening lines "Looking out for love / In the night so still," which evoke this constant quest for love, set the action in the middle of the night, reinforcing the emotional intensity of the situation.

"Big Love" is a perfect illustration of Lindsey's ability to create complex and innovative compositions without ever losing sight of musical effectiveness. The song evolved from a demo he had recorded in the midst of some fifty other compositions, with a view to a new solo album. In the original version, he played mainly acoustic guitar and used his voice to create a distinctive rhythm. The song takes on a much more instrumentally laden pop-rock form after it is taken over by the Mac. It regained its original markers when, after leaving the band in 1987, Lindsey played it solo onstage in 1993, on a Gibson Chet Atkins SST with a capo on the fourth fret.

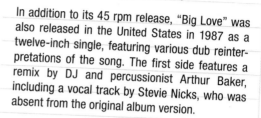

In addition to its 45 rpm release, "Big Love" was also released in the United States in 1987 as a twelve-inch single, featuring various dub reinterpretations of the song. The first side features a remix by DJ and percussionist Arthur Baker, including a vocal track by Stevie Nicks, who was absent from the original album version.

Production

"Big Love" has become a mainstay of Fleetwood Mac's repertoire, due to its distinctive fingerpicking guitar pattern, which creates a hypnotic rhythm throughout the song. Lindsey's virtuoso playing includes harmonics and percussive effects applied directly to the strings. The rhythm of Mick Fleetwood's drums is fast and syncopated, creating a constant tension, backed up by Lindsey's programming of drum loops on a drum machine. John McVie's bass adds depth to the track.

The song's structure is also interesting, with changes in dynamics reflecting the emotional variations expressed in the lyrics. The song starts gently, then builds in intensity as Lindsey expresses his need for love. The vocal harmonies—or rather, the overlapping, suggestive moans that make it sound like some kind of sexual encounter—create a sensual atmosphere that reinforces the emotional message. Rumors—quickly denied—first attributed them to Madonna, then to Stevie Nicks—which would have been rather edgy, considering the situation—but the singer does not appear in the credits. The reality is even more astonishing: This is the accelerated voice of Lindsey, who is responding in a slightly schizophrenic way to himself. The musician also provides convincing lead vocals and an infectiously urgent guitar solo.

"Big Love," the album opener, was chosen as the first single from *Tango in the Night* and provided with a big-budget, special-effects-packed music video. The musicians appear, instruments in hand, in different rooms of a mansion. All the sequences seem to flow seamlessly into one another, with a constant tracking shot. Audiences were receptive, with the song reaching number nine in the UK charts (where it was certified platinum) and number five in the United States.

Mick Fleetwood's drumming on "Seven Wonders" subtly blends power and finesse to create a spellbinding canvas of sound.

SEVEN WONDERS

Sandy Stewart, Stevie Nicks / 3:42

Musicians: Stevie Nicks: vocals, backing vocals / Lindsey Buckingham: guitars, Fairlight CMI, synthesizer, backing vocals / Christine McVie: synthesizer, backing vocals / Mick Fleetwood: drums, percussion / John McVie: bass / **Recorded:** Rumbo Recorders, Los Angeles: November 1985–March 1987 / The Slope, Los Angeles: November 1985–March 1987 / **Technical Team:** Producers: Lindsey Buckingham, Richard Dashut / Sound Engineer: Greg Droman / Assistant Sound Engineers: Ray Lindsey, Roy Hopper, Steve Matteucci / **Single:** Side A: Seven Wonders / Side B: Book of Miracles / **UK Release Date:** June 1987 / **Reference:** Warner Bros. Records (45 rpm ref.: W 8317) / Best UK Chart Ranking: 56 / **US Release Date:** June 1987 / **Reference:** Warner Bros. Records (45 rpm ref.: 7-28317) / Best US Chart Ranking: 19

Genesis and Lyrics

Once again, the band's microcosm, hitherto closed to outside intervention, opened up to other collaborations. For "Seven Wonders," Stevie Nicks called on Sandy Stewart. The twenty-nine-year-old Texas composer and lyricist had already worked with Stevie on three tracks from her 1983 solo album *The Wild Heart*: "If Anyone Falls," "Nightbird," and "Nothing Ever Changes." The experience was so conclusive that the two women continued to exchange songwriting ideas. Sandy sent Stevie a demo of "Seven Wonders"

in the hope that it would be used on the new Fleetwood Mac album. Her version included a line of vocals, but she had not bothered to include a lyrics sheet. When Stevie first listened to the song, she misunderstood one of the lines in the first verse. She heard "On the way down to Emmeline" instead of "All the way down, you held the line." When Sandy told her of the error, Stevie nevertheless chose to retain the word "Emmeline," which she liked the sound of, earning her credit as the song's co-writer.

The lyrics of "Seven Wonders" contrast the wonders the world has to offer with the wonders of love. And we soon realize that the narrator places the intensity of her past love affair, which nothing can match, far above the beauty of the Seven Wonders of the World. The video, shot to promote the release of the "Seven Wonders" single, is less scripted than previous Mac videos: It shows the band performing live on a stage, without an audience. The stage has a backdrop of thick red stage curtains, replicas of ancient columns, and, in the background, images of the Colosseum, the Taj Mahal, and even the Sphinx of Giza—none of which are on the canonical list of the Seven Wonders of the World. The American public responded well to "Seven Wonders", which reached number nineteen on the Billboard Hot 100.

EVERYWHERE

Christine McVie / 3:47

Musicians
Stevie Nicks: backing vocals
Lindsey Buckingham: guitars, Fairlight CMI, synthesizer, backing vocals
Christine McVie: vocals, synthesizer, backing vocals
Mick Fleetwood: drums, percussion
John McVie: bass

Recorded
Rumbo Recorders, Los Angeles: November 1985–March 1987
The Slope, Los Angeles: November 1985–March 1987

Technical Team
Producers: Lindsey Buckingham, Richard Dashut
Sound Engineer: Greg Droman
Assistant Sound Engineers: Ray Lindsey, Roy Hopper, Steve Matteucci

Single
Side A: Everywhere / Side B: When I See You Again
UK Release Date: November 1987
Reference: Warner Bros. Records (45 rpm ref.: W 8143)
Best UK Chart Ranking: 4
US Release Date: November 13, 1987
Reference: Warner Bros. Records (45 rpm ref.: 7-28143)
Best US Chart Ranking: 14

On its release, the single's music video was directed by Alex Proyas. While the lyrics abstractly express the feeling of love, the director visually translates a long narrative poem by Alfred Noyes (1880–1958), "The Highwayman," set in eighteenth-century rural England. It unites a highwayman with the daughter of an innkeeper. Two versions of the music video exist: one with sporadic appearances by the musicians, the other without.

Genesis and Lyrics
"I don't struggle over my songs," Christine explained regarding "Everywhere," in 1977. She added, "I write them quickly and I've never written a lot. I write what is required of me. I don't really write about myself, which puts me in a safe little cocoon...I'm a pretty basic love song writer." With "Everywhere," she effectively stays in her comfort zone: She depicts, with the gentleness and optimism that characterize her writing, the first stirrings, the birth of love. She wants to spend every minute with her lover, to follow him everywhere...But to get there, she has to confess her feelings, which she is incapable of doing. And even though she wants to cry out her love, she remains mute, as if paralyzed. The man she covets will have to decode her nonverbal communication: "You know that I'm falling and I don't know what to say / I'll speak a little louder, I'll even shout / You know that I'm proud and I can't get the words out." The idea for the song came to her during a meditation session, when she allowed herself to be overwhelmed by a wave of inspiring emotion.

Production
It is clear that Lindsey Buckingham is the man behind *Tango in the Night*, not only because he draws on his own repertoire of songs to help the band, but also because his ingenious ideas give the production a constantly renewed originality. "Everywhere" is a perfect example: Right from the intro, the listener is drawn in by what sounds like the haunting notes of a harp. In reality, this is a guitar processed at high speed. The various guitars take center stage, alongside the many synthesizer tracks recorded by Christine McVie, but without ever going overboard. The six-strings do more to consolidate the effectiveness of the melody, with the use of a very solid rhythm section that gives the song its catchy feel. The rhythm section remains highly disciplined and provides a solid foundation, even though Mick Fleetwood allows himself a few whimsical moments behind the drums. The synthesizer layers envelop brilliant vocal harmonies, helping to create the enchanting atmosphere of euphoric love in "Everywhere."

This track gave rise to a brief argument between Stevie and Christine. When the former discovered the recording in early 1987, she was deeply offended not to have been asked

to sing, as had been planned, and exclaimed: "I should be singing on 'Everywhere,' I should be heard on the vocal harmonies." When the latter learned of this, she was outraged: "I wanted you to sing on it too," Chris said in measured tones that signaled she was furious, "but you weren't here. In fact, we've been working for a year and you were only with us for a couple of days. Now why don't you just say you're sorry and we'll work it out?"[4] Put back in her place, Stevie eased back somewhat. The band members finally added their vocals in March 1987, in the home stretch of the recording process. Despite this stormy episode, Stevie held the song in high esteem. In her eyes, it simply "shows you that Christine is the hit songwriter in Fleetwood Mac."[70] The success of "Everywhere" proved her right: The song, chosen as a single, reached number four in the UK and number fourteen in the US on February 6, just more than a month after its release.

A little gem combining pop, rock, and synthpop, deceptively simple and shimmeringly beautiful, "Everywhere" stands out as one of the centerpieces of *Tango in the Night*.

Even for Lindsey Buckingham, a renowned studio perfectionist, *Tango in the Night* required courage and stamina.

CAROLINE
Lindsey Buckingham / 3:54

Musicians: Lindsey Buckingham: vocals, backing vocals, guitar, bass, keyboards, drum programmer / Christine McVie, Mick Fleetwood, John McVie, Stevie Nicks: (?) / **Recorded:** Rumbo Recorders, Los Angeles: November 1985–March 1987 / The Slope, Los Angeles: November 1985–March 1987 / **Technical Team:** Producers: Lindsey Buckingham, Richard Dashut / Sound Engineer: Greg Droman / Assistant Sound Engineers: Ray Lindsey, Roy Hopper, Steve Matteucci

"Caroline" joins the list of Fleetwood Mac songs featuring female first names, the majority of which are by Lindsey Buckingham and Stevie Nicks: "Jewel Eyed Judy" (*Kiln House*), "Rhiannon" (*Fleetwood Mac*), "Sara" (*Tusk*), "Oh Diane" (*Mirage*), "Welcome to the Room…Sara" (*Tango in the Night*), and "Miranda" (*Say You Will*).

Genesis and Lyrics
"Caroline" relies almost entirely on Lindsey Buckingham, who acts as lyricist, composer, singer, multi-instrumentalist, and producer. In this song, his writing is as concise, as is rarely the case. Lindsey depicts a demonic female figure in just a few character traits. The lyricist mercilessly lists the character's flaws: "so crazy," "lazy," "cagey," "stagey." His only objection is that she is "so attractive." On several occasions, he mentions a "fatal drop" or a "dusty fury on the mountaintop," suggesting through these dramatic images the terrible danger her suitors are in. Like a siren from Greek mythology, the female figure draws men to her, never to let them go again. The narrator acts as a guard, warning anyone who is seduced to "cut the cord if you can" while they are still able. The use of the first name Caroline is obviously not insignificant, since Lindsey had recently and acrimoniously separated from his partner, Carol Ann Harris, with whom he had been in a relationship since the end of the recording of *Rumours*.

Production
It is difficult to know who contributed to this track. Apart from the guitar parts, Lindsey wrote and programmed most of the drums and percussion. The dry sound, the unnatural reverb present on these rhythmic elements, and a very synthetic-sounding triangle seem to validate the fact that Lindsey recorded these instruments himself. However, it is not out of the question that Mick Fleetwood, who has already proved his ability to produce distinctive percussion in the past, might have added his own touch. The same goes for the bass, which Lindsey mastered sufficiently to record this minimalist line, although John McVie obviously could have done it, too. However, the notes seem very dry, which might lend credence to the theory that Lindsey plays synthetic bass on the keyboard. Neither Christine nor Stevie seems to be involved with "Caroline"; the few keyboards were provided by Lindsey himself, and the vocals were his too. In fact, he doubled his own voice on the chorus. A slight doubt remains as to the feminine and slightly Arabic-sounding vocals of the finale: Although Stevie and Christine could have sung this part, the effects-laden sequence does not enable us to discern the usual characteristics of their voices. With Lindsey having already performed this trick on the opening track, "Big Love," it is not impossible that he once again sped up his own voice until he achieved a satisfying, quasi-feminine-sounding result.

TANGO IN THE NIGHT

Lindsey Buckingham / 4:03

Musicians: Lindsey Buckingham: vocals, backing vocals, guitars, Fairlight CMI, synthesizer, programmer / Christine McVie: keyboards / John McVie: bass / Mick Fleetwood: drums, percussion / **Recorded:** Rumbo Recorders, Los Angeles: November 1985–March 1987 / The Slope, Los Angeles: November 1985–March 1987 / **Technical Team:** Producers: Lindsey Buckingham, Richard Dashut / Sound Engineer: Greg Droman / Assistant Sound Engineers: Ray Lindsey, Roy Hopper, Steve Matteucci

Genesis and Lyrics

Initially intended for Lindsey Buckingham's solo album, "Tango in the Night" was ultimately used to fill out the track list of Fleetwood Mac's fourteenth album, to which it gave its name. Highly representative of the album's spirit, the song has become one of the most emblematic in the band's repertoire. The lyrics evoke passion, seduction, and desire, sensations reinforced by the sophisticated musical arrangement. At the start of the song, Lindsey sketches a calm, peaceful scene by the sea ("Listen to the wind on the water / Listen to the waves upon the shore"). These relaxing sounds set a meditative mood. The narrator allows himself to be carried away by his thoughts until the aggressive electric guitar enters the scene. The surrounding elements take him back to a sweet memory: "Then I remember / When the moon was full and bright." He recalls an intense, passionate night spent with a young woman. The two characters are carried away by a fleeting nocturnal dance. The electric sensuality of the dance makes it impossible for them to sleep afterward. The famous "tango in the night" takes on its full meaning: a sensual dance and a passionate

Inspired by the passion of Argentinian tango, Lindsey Buckingham conceived "Tango in the Night" in chiaroscuro with a descending harmonic progression.

night, now long gone. The narrator explains that he treasures the memory of this magical night, as one keeps hold of a precious dream—in this case, in his pocket ("I keep the dream in my pocket").

Production

Like most of Lindsey Buckingham's productions for the album, the title track benefits from a complex and extensive arrangement. It was born out of a jam between the guitarist and Mick Fleetwood. The latter's massive strokes produce a devastatingly heavy and powerful sound, in tune with the heavy bass of his rhythm section accomplice, John McVie. The whole musical arrangement evokes the passion and urgency of the lyrics. The instruments interweave intelligently to create an intense atmosphere. Rarely have Lindsey's guitars sounded so sharp, from the heavy, driving riff of the verses through to the final solo, immersed in reverb but still revealing the high level of precision in the guitarist's playing. Lindsey also delivers a breathtaking, totally immersive vocal performance.

After "World Turning" in 1975, Christine McVie and Lindsey Buckingham again combined their compositional talents on "Mystified."

MYSTIFIED

Lindsey Buckingham, Christine McVie / 3:11

Musicians: Christine McVie: vocals, keyboards / Lindsey Buckingham: backing vocals, guitars, Fairlight CMI, synthesizer, programmer / Mick Fleetwood: drums, percussion / John McVie: bass / Stevie Nicks: (?) / **Recorded:** Rumbo Recorders, Los Angeles: November 1985–March 1987 / The Slope, Los Angeles: November 1985–March 1987 / **Technical Team:** Producers: Lindsey Buckingham, Richard Dashut / Sound Engineer: Greg Droman / Assistant Sound Engineers: Ray Lindsey, Roy Hopper, Steve Matteucci / **Single:** Side A: Isn't It Midnight / Side B: Mystified / **UK Release Date:** June 6, 1988 / **Reference:** Warner Bros. Records (45 rpm ref.: W7860) / Best UK Chart Ranking: 60

Genesis and Lyrics

Like Lindsey Buckingham, Christine has refined her writing, concentrating her efforts on a few punchy sentences rather than getting lost in redundant verbiage. Having discoursed so much in the past on all forms of love addiction, she is now able to be more economical. "Mystified" evokes a powerful desire and an emotional connection so deep and irrational that it borders on the mysterious. The attraction felt by the narrator is so irrepressible that it inundates the opening words: "Pretty baby / This feeling I just can't hide." Totally overwhelmed, the singer confesses to being "mystified," and even literally dazzled, in the following lines, as if under a spell: "The light that shines around you / It blinds my eyes / There's a magic surrounds you / Tell me where your secret lies."

Production

Christine McVie's song was composed with the help of Lindsey Buckingham. For all that, it is a perfect example of McVie's distinctive contribution to the band's sound—melodic, silky, and exuding romanticism. The Englishwoman's warm voice is supported by a meticulous musical arrangement, impeccable vocal harmonies, and rich, diverse instrumentation. The subtle, delicate pulse of the drums and percussion is essential to the development of the song's enchanting atmosphere. The soft, melodic keyboards are very discreet, while an acoustic guitar provides a distant accompaniment to Christine's soft, captivating voice. Lindsey adds a few refined notes on electric guitar at the end of the chorus, enhanced by a slight delay and a fine reverb. The bass part does not stand out for its originality, but it does provide a fundamental foundation, while the real harmonic richness of the song lies in the meticulous backing vocals.

LITTLE LIES

Christine McVie, Eddy Quintela / 3:41

Musicians: Christine McVie: vocals, keyboards, backing vocals / Lindsey Buckingham: backing vocals, guitars, Fairlight CMI, keyboards / John McVie: bass / Mick Fleetwood: drums, percussion / Stevie Nicks: backing vocals / **Recorded:** Rumbo Recorders, Los Angeles: November 1985–March 1987 / The Slope, Los Angeles: November 1985–March 1987 / Technical Team / Producers: Lindsey Buckingham, Richard Dashut / Sound Engineer: Greg Droman / Assistant Sound Engineers: Ray Lindsey, Roy Hopper, Steve Matteucci / **Single:** Side A: Little Lies / Side B: Ricky / **UK Release Date:** August 31, 1987 / **Reference:** Warner Bros. Records (45 rpm ref.: W 8291) / Best UK Chart Ranking: 5 / **US Release Date:** August 14, 1987 / **Reference:** Warner Bros. Records (45 rpm ref.: 7-28291) / Best US Chart Ranking: 4

Genesis and Lyrics

The lyrics of "Little Lies," a song co-written by Christine McVie and her husband at the time, Eddy Quintela, address the difficulty of coping with a relationship blighted by disillusionment. Even though she and Eddy are perfectly in love, the lyricist has accumulated so much experience from failed relationships that she is very familiar with them. From the very first words, the narrator speaks of a relationship that is coming to an end. Yet she wishes she could go back and rewrite history, erasing the mistakes she made ("If I could turn the page / In time then I'd rearrange just a day or two"). If only her partner had been able to tell her the comforting little lies that keep the illusion of happiness alive and prevent her from having to face up to an implacable reality…But he does not know how to lie: "You can't disguise / No, you can't disguise." And how she regrets it, because for her, lies are not signs of betrayal, but rather "little subversions" that safeguard passion. Now that she knows, she can no longer avoid ending a relationship that has become too painful: "No more broken hearts / We're better off apart, let's give it a try."

Production

"Little Lies" stands out as one of the catchiest songs on the album. The whole band mobilizes its energy, especially for the unstoppably melodic chorus, whose urgency is constantly revived by perfectly arranged vocal harmonies. The keyboards play a major role in the song's effectiveness, whether distilled into small notes or played as layers. Lindsey's production is once again impeccable, especially the harmonic balance: The occasional guitars are played in the background, and the emphasis is on the effect of the rhythm section during the chorus, with Mick and John delivering undoubtedly their best joint performance of the album, as well as on the vocal harmonies contributed by the discreet Stevie and Lindsey.

Christine's voice, meanwhile, comes across as very captivating, conveying a sense of both melancholy and optimism.

The Great Depression of the 1930s plunged thousands of families into poverty. A similarly critical situation informed Lindsey Buckingham's "Family Man," which explored the theme of responsibility, especially in the family.

FAMILY MAN

Lindsey Buckingham, Richard Dashut / 4:07

Musicians: Lindsey Buckingham: vocals, backing vocals, guitars, Fairlight CMI, keyboards, bass, drums and percussion programmer / Mick Fleetwood: percussion / Stevie Nicks: backing vocals / **Recorded:** Rumbo Recorders, Los Angeles: November 1985–March 1987 / The Slope, Los Angeles: November 1985–March 1987 / **Technical Team:** Producers: Lindsey Buckingham, Richard Dashut / Sound Engineer: Greg Droman / Assistant Sound Engineers: Ray Lindsey, Roy Hopper, Steve Matteucci / **Single:** Side A: Family Man / Side B: Down Endless Street / **UK Release Date:** December 7, 1987 / **Reference:** Warner Bros. Records (45 rpm ref.: W 8114) / Best UK Chart Ranking: 54 / **US Release Date:** January 29, 1988 / **Reference:** Warner Bros. Records (ref. 7-28114) / Best US Chart Ranking: 90

Genesis and Lyrics

Co-written by Lindsey Buckingham and co-producer Richard Dashut for Lindsey's solo album, which was to follow *Go Insane* (1984), "Family Man" eventually found its way into *Tango in the Night* as part of the guitarist's rescue operation. It focuses on the theme of family and highlights the narrator's efforts to assume his role within it, as well as the doubts that sometimes beset him when things get complicated, and choices have to be made. From the very first lines, the narrator insists that his responsibilities drive him to overcome difficulties without flinching. If he is so determined, it is because he is not alone on this journey. He probably has a wife and children to look after: "I am what I am / A family man." But he also refers to his mother, father, and brother, extending his responsibilities beyond his nuclear family.

As a single, "Family Man" performed disappointingly (fifty-fourth in the UK; ninetieth in the US). Its promotion may have been hampered by a somewhat makeshift video of black-and-white imagery of American families during the Great Depression with well-known images of the band from the "Seven Wonders" video.

Production

The instrumentation in "Family Man" is rhythmic and energetic. Lindsey wanted to give it a Hispanic feel and opted for a nylon-string guitar. The soft timbre of these strings is perfectly enhanced by a light reverb. But for once, Lindsey finds it hard to surprise and break away from clichés, offering a readable and relatively uninspired solo (with the exception of the last twenty seconds of the song). Similarly, the castanets offer little added value, other than another cliché about Spanish music. For the rest of the arrangement, Lindsey dispenses with Christine McVie's keyboards and provides the bass himself. Even Mick Fleetwood's contribution is limited to a few additional percussion elements—Lindsey provides the rhythmic backbone, using electronic drums. Stevie Nicks, relatively unassuming, contributes backing vocals to the chorus. If this forgettable track stands out at all, it is only because of the deep voice that intervenes a few times, almost comically. Again, the effect is achieved by slowing down Lindsey's vocal track.

WELCOME TO THE ROOM... SARA

Stevie Nicks / 3:41

Musicians: Stevie Nicks: vocals / Lindsey Buckingham: backing vocals, guitars, mandolin, programmer / John McVie: bass / Christine McVie: backing vocals, keyboards / Mick Fleetwood: drums, percussion / **Recorded:** Rumbo Recorders, Los Angeles: November 1985–March 1987 / The Slope, Los Angeles: November 1985–March 1987 / **Technical Team:** Producers: Lindsey Buckingham, Richard Dashut / Sound Engineer: Greg Droman / Assistant Sound Engineers: Ray Lindsey, Roy Hopper, Steve Matteucci

For eight months, Stevie was the wife of her best friend Robin's widower, Kim.

Genesis and Lyrics

"Welcome to the Room...Sara" responds to another Stevie Nicks song, the famous "Sara" from *Tusk*. Once again, the song refers to Sara (Recor), one of the singer's best friends, and to the baby Stevie never had, whom she wished she had named Sara. "[It's] very much a secret kind of song," Stevie explains. "Sara is from *Tusk*, that's the same Sara we're talking about—and she just has some experiences that she's talking about. I don't really want anyone to know whether I'm going into her room or she's coming into mine, or what's in the room. This room is an ominous room. I'm not Bob Dylan, but every once in a while I've gotta say something." This room, and more broadly the house in which the character lives, a "big old house," seems foreign to her. Disoriented, far from home, Sara, Stevie's double, loses herself in this maze. Stevie Nicks draws on the memory of her admission to a rehab center, the Betty Ford Center, where, lonely, lost, and in need, she felt she was losing part of her identity. It should be noted that it was under the name of Sara Anderson that the young woman (Anderson being her surname after marrying Kim Anderson) had registered at this clinic...At several points in the song, she evokes a desire for transformation and change, which seems to indicate a desire to start afresh and return in a new form or with new perspectives.

Constantly playing with identities, the lyricist adds another when she slips in allusions to Margaret Mitchell's 1936 novel *Gone with the Wind* into her song, referring to the Tara plantation ("It's not home and it's not Tara") and the novel's central character, Scarlett O'Hara ("Welcome to the room, Sara, Sara [for Scarlett]").

Production

The song begins with acoustic guitar and mandolin chords, then gradually incorporates small touches of electric guitar to densify the sonic texture. Percussion is also a mainstay of the musical arrangement, and it is difficult to tell whether it is played organically or programmed by Lindsey Buckingham. The foot-tapping rhythm section is very solid at this measured tempo. Mick Fleetwood's drums are lightly backed up by a drum machine, in keeping with the mood of 1980s pop tunes, while John McVie's bass delivers a simple but fundamental line to keep the track on the right footing. The synthesizers also play a major role in creating the song's atmosphere, producing layers of ethereal sounds that contribute to its haunting ambience. The song's structure follows a fairly classic verse-chorus pattern, but it evolves progressively, using ascending levels of intensity as the track progresses. Instrumental and vocal layers are superimposed to create a complex, captivating sound around Stevie's charismatic voice.

The band chose this neoclassical painting by Ingres to illustrate the cover of the single "Isn't It Midnight," whose chorus evokes the face of a pretty girl.

ISN'T IT MIDNIGHT

Christine McVie, Eddy Quintela, Lindsey Buckingham / 4:13

Musicians: Christine McVie: vocals, backing vocals, synthesizers / Lindsey Buckingham: backing vocals, guitars, Fairlight CMI / John McVie: bass / Mick Fleetwood: drums, percussion / **Recorded:** Rumbo Recorders, Los Angeles: November 1985–March 1987 / The Slope, Los Angeles: November 1985–March 1987 / **Technical Team:** Producers: Lindsey Buckingham, Richard Dashut / Sound Engineer: Greg Droman / Assistant Sound Engineers: Ray Lindsey, Roy Hopper, Steve Matteucci / **Single:** Side A: Isn't It Midnight / Side B: Mystified / **UK Release Date:** June 6, 1988 / **Reference:** Warner Bros. Records (45 rpm ref.: W 860) / Best UK Chart Ranking: 60

Genesis and Lyrics

Co-written by Christine McVie and Eddy Quintela, "Isn't It Midnight" is also credited to Lindsey Buckingham, to whom the song owes a great deal musically. Christine evokes her vain desire for a man. The line "Isn't it midnight on the other side of the world?" raises the question of distance, both physical and emotional. The narrator has been clearly seduced by the "so cool, calm and collected" side of the desired man. However, she confesses that she has never managed to establish any kind of emotional bond with him: "Well, my poor heart never connected" or "And I knew you'd never be mine." She must now rely on her memories to mitigate her own frustration, and she hopes he will remember her face when he looks back on his past.

Production

Christine McVie fans often remember her most "visible" tracks from *Tango in the Night*, namely "Everywhere" and "Little Lies." Yet "Isn't It Midnight" is by no means inferior in terms of quality, between Lindsey's searing guitars and Christine's shimmering pop keyboards. Somewhat underrated, this track is nonetheless a shining example of how modern recording technology and classic pop intelligence could feed off each other to create greatness in the midst of the 1980s. Lindsey's guitars, delivering catchy riffs and inspired, flowing solos, are the main attraction of the song, whose driving force remains Mick Fleetwood's intense drums, supported by a few synthetic sounds, and John McVie's throbbing bass. As for the keyboards, these are mainly used for the chorus sequences, to soften the sound environment for Christine McVie's deep, reverb-tinged voice. The song undergoes a number of dynamic variations, with guitars appearing and disappearing, but the rhythm is always very driving.

Sung in unison by Stevie and Lindsey, with Christine on backing vocals, "When I See You Again" was intended to close *Tango in the Night*. In the end, it was deemed too depressing to occupy this strategic position.

WHEN I SEE YOU AGAIN

Stevie Nicks / 3:49

Musicians: Stevie Nicks: vocals, backing vocals / Lindsey Buckingham: vocals, backing vocals, guitars / Christine McVie: backing vocals (?), keyboards / **Recorded:** Rumbo Recorders, Los Angeles: November 1985–March 1987 / The Slope, Los Angeles: November 1985–March 1987 / **Technical Team:** Producers: Lindsey Buckingham, Richard Dashut / Sound Engineer: Greg Droman / Assistant Sound Engineers: Ray Lindsey, Roy Hopper, Steve Matteucci / **Single:** Side A: Everywhere / Side B: When I See You Again / **UK Release Date:** February 27, 1988 / **Reference:** Warner Bros. Records (45 rpm ref.: W 8143) / Best UK Chart Ranking: 4 / **US Release Date:** November 13, 1987 / **Reference:** Warner Bros. Records (45 rpm ref.: 7-28143) / Best US Chart Ranking: 14

Genesis and Lyrics

The joint performance of Stevie Nicks and Lindsey Buckingham on "When I See You Again"—the only song in which they share the lead vocals—makes perfect sense when you consider that the two singers were once lovers. Indeed, it is "goodbye" that lies at the heart of this touching, melancholy acoustic ballad: Two lovers who are separating ponder the way to get out of the relationship while wondering what a possible reunion in the hypothetical future might look like. Would they mark the end (or renewal) of a chapter ("When I see you again / Will it be over?")? The two lovers do not seem quite ready for this final outcome, as indicated by the narrator's recurring question throughout the song, "What's the matter, baby?" which seems to convey the hope of support and comfort. The listener imagines her lost in thought, walking slowly, staring at the stairs…and beset by doubts. Perhaps staring at the stairs suggests deep reflection on a choice that must take her to another "floor" in her life. But does this staircase go up or down?

"When I See You Again" was originally intended to close *Tango in the Night*, but, according to Christine McVie, the song was a little too melancholy, so the band opted instead to add "You and I, Part II" at the end of the track list.

Production

Lindsey's acoustic guitars, whose arpeggios intertwine finely in the stereo spectrum, bring all the necessary sweetness to this song of love—doomed love, admittedly, but love nonetheless. Rare keyboards warmly envelop Stevie Nicks's moving voice, even if the singer's nasal vocals sometimes seem limited on this track. Lindsey's contribution, symbolic though it may be, adds further depth. Originally, though, it wasn't intended that the guitarist should sing alone, but rather in support of Stevie. "That's one of my favorite things," explains the singer. "I *made* him sing with me; I said, 'Lindsey, you're gonna sing on all my songs whether you like it or not—you *have* to sing this with me.'" Lindsey, making the best of a bad situation, complied, and sang "When I See You Again" in unison with Stevie, before Stevie played a final trick on him: "I snuck in and took my voice off. Otherwise, I'd have never gotten him to do it—see, Lindsey's pretty shy and he's singing differently there than he is on anything else on the record. He wouldn't think to do that: to sing on my song at the end. He would think to sing with me, but he wouldn't want to end it. But that's what I wanted, to leave people feeling they are really talking to each other."

YOU AND I, PART II

Lindsey Buckingham, Christine McVie / 2:40

Musicians: Christine McVie: vocals, synthesizers / Lindsey Buckingham: vocals, backing vocals, guitars, Fairlight CMI, drums and percussion programmer / John McVie: bass (?) / Mick Fleetwood: drums, percussion (?) / Stevie Nicks: backing vocals (?) / **Recorded:** Rumbo Recorders, Los Angeles: November 1985–March 1987 / The Slope, Los Angeles: November 1985–March 1987 / **Technical Team:** Producers: Lindsey Buckingham, Richard Dashut / Sound Engineer: Greg Droman / Assistant Sound Engineers: Ray Lindsey, Roy Hopper, Steve Matteucci

Genesis and Lyrics

The final track on *Tango in the Night*, "You and I, Part II" closes the album instead of "When I See You Again" because of the latter's dark atmosphere. The band wanted the album to end on an optimistic note, and this song's lyrics, written by Lindsey Buckingham and Christine McVie, bring a little lightness. At least at first, since the song is about idealized love. But then comes the specter of separation, symbolized by disturbing creatures: "Oh, the phantoms / Crawl out of the night." Whether or not this was intentional, the image seems to refer to the mysterious nocturnal figures hidden in the forest on the album cover. The song celebrates the desire for an eternal connection between two beings and the hope that time will stand still forever. In the opening lines ("I wake up with my eyes shut tight / Hoping tomorrow will never come for you and I"), the narrator is already dreading the end of her daydream. Her childlike reaction of keeping her eyes closed to ward off fate demonstrates her sensitivity and fragility. She tries to pull herself together, without being able to hold on to any certainty: "What will be, will be," she comments fatalistically, without giving up hope. In the end, anxiety triumphs over any form of rationality.

Production

"You and I, Part II," with its upbeat, catchy melody, somewhat mitigates the feeling of vulnerability that emanates from the lyrics, and perfectly symbolizes the complementarity between the demanding, fastidious Lindsey Buckingham and the more light-hearted Christine McVie. On the basis of an instrumental fine-tuned by Lindsey, the two voices intertwine seamlessly, particularly on the soft backing vocals. The synthesizers play a predominant role, mainly on the little gimmicks that take over from the acoustic guitars in the intro before they reappear with a steel drum–like sound after each chorus. Numerous percussion programs also flesh out the song, but it is hard to know whether Mick Fleetwood was asked to add more organic touches, which seems unlikely. The same applies to the minimalist bass part, which was originally mapped out by Lindsey, who probably did not need John McVie for an overdub. Stevie Nicks is conspicuously absent from the song. Far from being an essential Fleetwood Mac hit, the bouncy "You and I, Part II" is nonetheless the ideal good-humored song to conclude *Tango in the Night*.

YOU AND I, PART I

Lindsey Buckingham, Christine McVie / 3:46

Musicians: Christine McVie: vocals, synthesizers / Lindsey Buckingham: vocals, backing vocals, guitars, Fairlight CMI, drums and percussion programmer / John McVie: bass (?) / Mick Fleetwood: drums, percussion (?) / Stevie Nicks: backing vocals (?) / **Recorded:** Rumbo Recorders, Los Angeles: November 1985–March 1987 / The Slope, Los Angeles: November 1985–March 1987 / **Technical Team:** Producers: Lindsey Buckingham, Richard Dashut / Sound Engineer: Greg Droman / Assistant Sound Engineers: Ray Lindsey, Roy Hopper, Steve Matteucci / **Single:** Side A: Big Love / Side B: You & I, Part I / **UK Release Date:** March 23, 1987 / **Reference:** Warner Bros. Records (45 rpm ref.: W 8398) / Best UK Chart Ranking: 9 / **US Release Date:** March 23, 1987 / **Reference:** Warner Bros. Records (ref. 7-28398) / Best US Chart Ranking: 5

"You and I, Part I," originally only featured on Side B of the "Big Love" single, merged with "You and I, Part II," in a 6:26 version featured on the remastered reissue of *Tango in the Night*, released to mark the album's thirtieth anniversary in 2017. In its haunting intro, a few crystalline synthesizers mingle with guitar arpeggios. The short lyrics serve as a preamble to the second part, which is about a unique connection between two beings. Here, the theme of desire and love that we do not want to see disappear already surfaces ("You, under strange falling skies / You, with a love that would not die"). The mystery and fear of the unknown and the uncertain future of the relationship are then evoked: "You, where the strange wind blows / You, with the secrets no one knows."

DOWN ENDLESS STREET

Lindsey Buckingham / 4:28

Musicians: Lindsey Buckingham: vocals, backing vocals, guitars, Fairlight CMI, keyboards, bass, drums and percussion programmer / Christine McVie, John McVie, Mick Fleetwood, Stevie Nicks: (?) / **Recorded:** Rumbo Recorders, Los Angeles: November 1985–March 1987 / The Slope, Los Angeles: November 1985–March 1987 / **Technical Team:** Producers: Lindsey Buckingham, Richard Dashut / Sound Engineer: Greg Droman / Assistant Sound Engineers: Ray Lindsey, Roy Hopper, Steve Matteucci / **Single:** Side A: Family Man / Side B: Down Endless Street / **UK Release Date:** December 7, 1987 / **Reference:** Warner Bros. Records (45 rpm ref.: W-8114) / Best UK Chart Ranking: 54 / **US Release Date:** August 1987 / **Reference:** Warner Bros. Records (45 rpm ref.: 7-28114) / Best US Chart Ranking: 90

The omnipotent Lindsey Buckingham is involved in every section of "Down Endless Street." He recorded this song alone (although there is some doubt about some of the backing vocals) for Side B of "Family Man." With its rich, sophisticated production, this resolutely pop song evokes a separation. As his partner walks out the door, the narrator worries about his capacity for resilience.

SPECIAL KIND OF LOVE

Lindsey Buckingham / 2:53

Musicians: Lindsey Buckingham: vocals, backing vocals, guitars, Fairlight CMI, keyboards, bass, drums and percussion programmer / Christine McVie, John McVie, Mick Fleetwood, Stevie Nicks: (?) / **Recorded:** Rumbo Recorders, Los Angeles: November 1985–March 1987 / The Slope, Los Angeles: November 1985–March 1987 / **Technical Team:** Producers: Lindsey Buckingham, Richard Dashut / Sound Engineer: Greg Droman / Assistant Sound Engineers: Ray Lindsey, Roy Hopper, Steve Matteucci

Unfortunately still at the demo stage, "Special Kind of Love" features an excellent, clear-sounding electric guitar riff and a lovely, airy melody on the chorus. Lindsey Buckingham's backing vocals on his own lead add an extra touch of sweetness to the whole. Although it is unclear who Lindsey is referring to in this moderately paced ballad, it is about a relationship that deteriorated and ended, much to the narrator's regret. The words "We had a special kind of love," repeated over and over, underline the importance and singularity of the love the two partners shared.

BOOK OF MIRACLES

Lindsey Buckingham, Stevie Nicks / 4:30

Musicians: Lindsey Buckingham: guitars, keyboards (?), programmer (?) / Christine McVie: synthesizers (?) / John McVie: bass (?) / Mick Fleetwood: drums (?) / **Recorded:** Rumbo Recorders, Los Angeles: November 1985–March 1987 / The Slope, Los Angeles: November 1985–March 1987 / **Technical Team:** Producers: Lindsey Buckingham, Richard Dashut / Sound Engineer: Greg Droman / Assistant Sound Engineers: Ray Lindsey, Roy Hopper, Steve Matteucci / **Single:** Side A: Seven Wonders / Side B: Book of Miracles / **UK Release Date:** June 1987 / **Reference:** Warner Bros. Records (45 rpm ref.: W 8317) / Best UK Chart Ranking: 56 / **US Release Date:** June 5, 1987 / **Reference:** Warner Bros. Records (45 rpm ref.: 7-28317) / Best US Chart Ranking: 19

"Book of Miracles" is an instrumental that sounds rather too laid-back. It relies mainly on synthesizer strings and pretty melodic motifs, with a few guitars in the background, all backed by a very academic rhythm section. The song, credited to Lindsey Buckingham and Stevie Nicks (who was absent from the recording), ends up on Side B of "Seven Wonders." Stevie Nicks used some of the musical elements to create "Juliet"—on her solo album *The Other Side of the Mirror* (1989)—for which she retained full credit. However, a run-through version of "Juliet," with Stevie Nicks on vocals, was later unearthed for the remastered version of *Tango in the Night*, in 2017. It retraces the history: The song proposed by Stevie was reworked by Lindsey, when she was away, into "Book of Miracles," then reworked again by the singer two years later to make it her own.

RICKY

Christine McVie, Lindsey Buckingham / 4:25

Musicians: Christine McVie: vocals, backing vocals, keyboards / Lindsey Buckingham: backing vocals, guitars, Fairlight CMI, keyboards, bass, drums and percussion programmer / John McVie, Mick Fleetwood, Stevie Nicks: (?) / **Recorded:** Rumbo Recorders, Los Angeles: November 1985–March 1987 / The Slope, Los Angeles: November 1985–March 1987 / **Technical Team:** Producers: Lindsey Buckingham, Richard Dashut / Sound Engineer: Greg Droman / Assistant Sound Engineers: Ray Lindsey, Roy Hopper, Steve Matteucci / **Single:** Side A: Little Lies / Side B: Ricky / **UK Release Date:** August 31, 1987 / **Reference:** Warner Bros. Records (45 rpm ref.: W 8291) / Best UK Chart Ranking: 5 / **US Release Date:** August 14, 1987 / **Reference:** Warner Bros. Records (45 rpm ref.: 7-28291) / Best US Chart Ranking: 4

It is quite unusual to hear Christine McVie singing in a restrained way. Her lead vocals, sung essentially on breaths, are unusually unmelodic, leaving it to the backing vocals to animate the song. Lindsey Buckingham joins her to sing "Tell me, tell me, tell me," and "Please, please, please," with the rest of the vocals provided by Christine. Feelings of grief, nostalgia, and bitterness intersect in this message addressed to a mysterious Ricky (unlikely to be Richard Dashut), who left the narrator without so much as a goodbye.

JULIET

Stevie Nicks / 5:04

Musicians: Stevie Nicks: vocals / Lindsey Buckingham: guitars / Christine McVie: keyboards / John McVie: bass / Mick Fleetwood: drums / **Recorded:** Rumbo Recorders, Los Angeles: November 1985–March 1987 / The Slope, Los Angeles: November 1985–March 1987 / **Technical Team:** Producers: Lindsey Buckingham, Richard Dashut / Sound Engineer: Greg Droman / Assistant Sound Engineers: Ray Lindsey, Roy Hopper, Steve Matteucci

The run-through version of "Juliet" was finalized by Stevie Nicks alone on her fourth solo album, *The Other Side of the Mirror* (1989). But the singer retains a special affection for the band's first recording, made during the *Tango in the Night* sessions. However, the song, in the Mac's version, would not appear until thirty years later in the remastered edition of the album (2017). There is no doubt that this catchy, driving blues-rock would have been well suited to *Tango in the Night*.

OOH MY LOVE

Stevie Nicks, Rick Nowels / 3:52

Musicians: Stevie Nicks: vocals / Lindsey Buckingham: guitars / Christine McVie: keyboards / John McVie: bass / Mick Fleetwood: drums / Recorded / Rumbo Recorders, Los Angeles: November 1985–March 1987 / The Slope, Los Angeles: November 1985–March 1987 / **Technical Team:** Producers: Lindsey Buckingham, Richard Dashut / Sound Engineer: Greg Droman / Assistant Sound Engineers: Ray Lindsey, Roy Hopper, Steve Matteucci

In 1985, Stevie Nicks gave Rick Nowels his first major song-writer-producer credit, with the song "I Can't Wait" from her third solo album, *Rock a Little*. So she confidently shared a credit with him again, on the occasion of the creation of "Ooh My Love." However, with Fleetwood Mac, the song remained at the demo stage, which found its way onto the remastered version of *Tango in the Night* (2017). Disappointed by the song's rejection, Stevie reappropriated it for *The Other Side of the Mirror*, her fourth album, released in 1989. She has repeatedly claimed that it is one of her favorite songs: The lyrics evoke a princess cloistered in her castle, who dreams of the outside world but is held back by her fear of leaving a sanctuary where she knows she is safe.

WHERE WE BELONG

Lindsey Buckingham, Christine McVie / 2:52

Musicians: Lindsey Buckingham: vocals, bass, drums programmer / Christine McVie: vocals, keyboards / John McVie, Mick Fleetwood, Stevie Nicks: (?) / **Recorded:** Rumbo Recorders, Los Angeles: November 1985–March 1987 / The Slope, Los Angeles: November 1985–March 1987 / **Technical Team:** Producers: Lindsey Buckingham, Richard Dashut / Sound Engineer: Greg Droman / Assistant Sound Engineers: Ray Lindsey, Roy Hopper, Steve Matteucci

It is unfortunate that "Where We Belong" was not worked on beyond the demo. The song was weighed down by a lazy bass drum, an unwelcoming synthetic bass, and a very busy keyboard line. The Christine McVie–Lindsey Buckingham combination did, however, have an encouraging melodic motif and a very effective chorus. The song's message of optimism, hope, and confidence in the future might well have dissuaded Lindsey from slamming the door on the album's release…The lyrics "I believe, I believe, we need a little time" are a veritable invitation to patience, and "We are where we belong" seems to indicate that the current situation is the right one. Quite ironic, considering what would happen next.

In June 1980, the band received a series of awards for their latest recording exploits. *Rumours* achieved 15 platinum certifications in the UK, and *Tusk* one.

GREATEST HITS

Release Dates
United Kingdom: November 22, 1988
Reference: Warner Bros. Records—925 838-2
Best UK Chart Ranking: 3
United States: November 22, 1988
Reference: Warner Bros. Records—9 25801-2
Best US Chart Ranking: 14

Rhiannon
Don't Stop
Go Your Own Way
Hold Me
Everywhere
Gypsy
You Make Loving Fun
As Long As You Follow
Dreams
Say You Love Me
Tusk
Little Lies
Sara
Big Love
Over My Head
No Questions Asked

For The Final Count

A first *Greatest Hits*, released in 1971, showcased the best of Fleetwood Mac's Peter Green years, but no such record had yet celebrated the band's golden decade (1975–1987), which had just ended with the departure of Lindsey Buckingham. This separation was thus seen as the ideal moment for this musical inventory. As Christine pointed out in an interview with Bob Brunning on the release of the compilation on November 22, 1988: "It's the end of an era and the beginning of another. […] It's a collection from our Lindsey and Stevie period. There's no padding. There are also two introductory songs with Billy and Rick. It just seemed perfect timing to clean the slate and start the next chapter with these two guys."[5]

The idea was not only to represent each of the five albums released between 1975 and 1987 with at least two tracks each (even more for *Rumours* and *Tango in the Night*), most of them hits, but also to include two new unreleased tracks ("As Long As You Follow" and "No Questions Asked") in this collection of hits, to help generate two new single releases and gently introduce Rick Vito and Billy Burnette. A clever way of taking some of the pressure off the two new band members, before the release of a new album that would be judged by their contribution to the new lineup.

This compilation, which reached number fourteen in the US, is one of the band's biggest sellers, with 12 million records sold.

AS LONG AS YOU FOLLOW

Christine McVie, Eddy Quintela / 4:08

Musicians: Christine McVie: vocals, keyboards, synthesizers / Rick Vito: backing vocals, guitar / Billy Burnette: backing vocals, guitar / Stephen Croes: synclavier / John McVie: bass / Mick Fleetwood: drums, percussion / Stevie Nicks: backing vocals / **Recorded:** The Complex, Los Angeles: 1988 / **Technical Team:** Producers: Fleetwood Mac, Greg Ladanyi / Sound Engineer: Greg Ladanyi / **12" Single:** Side A: As Long As You Follow / Side B1: Oh Well (Live) / Side B2: Gold Dust Woman / **UK Release Date:** 1988 / **Reference:** Warner Bros. Records (12-inch single ref.: W7644T) / Best UK Chart Ranking: 66 / **Single:** Side A: As Long As You Follow (LP version) / Side B: Oh Well (Live) / **US Release Date:** 1988 / **Reference:** Warner Bros. Records (45 rpm ref.: 7-27644) / Best US Chart Ranking: 43

Genesis

"As Long As You Follow" is the first official recording of Rick Vito and Billy Burnette as members of Fleetwood Mac. The two men share the playing naturally: The former takes the lead guitar, while the latter feels more at home in a rhythmic role. They were not the only newcomers to the venture: Sound engineer Greg Ladanyi was recruited as producer to replace Richard Dashut, who had been dismissed because of his close relationship with Lindsey Buckingham. In the business, Greg Ladanyi has been on a roll ever since he won a Grammy Award for his sound engineering and mixing work on *Toto IV* (1982).

Lyrically, "As Long As You Follow" is a confession by Christine McVie to a man who has had the patience to wait for her. She knows she can trust him and feels ready to follow in his footsteps.

Production

This romantic message is set to music in the most suave manner, with a delicate, soft-rock instrumentation and sweet vocal harmonies. Rick Vito's deft arpeggios provided enough charm for this radio-friendly single to reach number sixty-six in the UK and number forty-three in the US.

FOR MAC-ADDICTS

Side B of "As Long As You Follow" features a live version of "Oh Well." This 1969 track, which links the band's past and future, was performed onstage at San Francisco's Cow Palace in 1987 with new Mac members Rick Vito and Billy Burnette.

NO QUESTIONS ASKED

Stevie Nicks, Kelly Johnston / 4:36

Musicians: Stevie Nicks: vocals / Rick Vito: backing vocals, guitar / Billy Burnette: backing vocals, guitar / Christine McVie: backing vocals, keyboards / John McVie: bass / Mick Fleetwood: drums, percussion / Dan Garfield: keyboard programmer / **Recorded:** The Complex, Los Angeles: 1988 / **Technical Team:** Producers: Fleetwood Mac, Greg Ladanyi / Sound Engineer: Greg Ladanyi / **Single:** Side A: Hold Me / Side B: No Questions Asked / **UK Release Date:** February 13, 1989 / **Reference:** Warner Bros. Records (45 rpm ref.: W 7528) / Best UK Chart Ranking: 94 / 12-inch **Single:** Side A: Hold Me / Side B1: No Questions Asked / Side B2: I Loved Another Woman (Live) / **UK Release Date:** February 13, 1989 / **Reference:** Warner Bros. Records (12-inch single ref.: W 7528 (T)) / Best UK Chart Ranking: 94

Genesis

Stevie Nicks was staying in a hotel when she had the idea for the melody and the beginning of the lyrics for "No Questions Asked." With no equipment to record this embryonic song, she was afraid of forgetting her promising first draft. Her friend Kelly Johnston came to her rescue with a tape recorder, which earned her a place in the credits as a thank-you. Without her, the song would probably never have seen the light of day, nor would it have been included on the *Greatest Hits* compilation. Fleetwood Mac would have otherwise lost out on a convincing Side B for the "Hold Me" single.

In "No Questions Asked," Stevie Nicks seems to be describing a love triangle. It is difficult to distinguish who is saying what because multiple pronouns are used. Unless she is referring to herself in the third person...The narrator sometimes addresses her lover directly or uses the third person, and when she says "She just seems to be missing," it is hard to determine whether she is talking about herself. But it is clear that she suffers from not being able to live her love in the open with the man she desires, painfully confessing at the end of the song: "I broke down like a little girl."

Production

Stevie Nicks's assertive, almost rocklike vocals contrast with the singer's confession of fragility in her lyrics. The roughness of her voice also contrasts with the soft-pop tone of the instrumentation, from which two main elements emerge: On the one hand are the highly synthetic guitars with their distinct roles—one assigned to gimmicks and the other to rhythm. On the other are the very full drums, with their exaggerated reverb. Very classical in construction, the track nevertheless features an original bridge at 1:41, introduced by a cymbal that Mick allows to ring out. This is followed by a melodic keyboard phrasing and a short, inspired solo by Rick Vito.

Billy Burnette provided Fleetwood Mac with an energy that he drew from his rockabilly background and created a fusion of lively riffs and driving rhythms.

BILLY BURNETTE AT THE SERVICE OF ROCK AND ROLL

Lindsey Buckingham's departure in the summer of 1987, shortly after the release of *Tango in the Night*, once again forced Fleetwood Mac to find a replacement on short notice, especially as the album's success called for a major tour. The band members chose guitarist Billy Burnette, who brought along the discreet Rick Vito. Both had long been familiar with the band they were about to join.

The Child of Rockabilly

Born on May 8, 1953, in Memphis, Tennessee, Billy is the son of Dorsey Burnette and the nephew of Johnny Burnette, two brothers who were members (with Paul Burlison) of the first Memphis rock band, the Rock 'n Roll Trio, considered a pioneer of rockabilly. He grew up in this musical world, where he rubbed shoulders with many artists, particularly after the Burnette family moved to Los Angeles. At the age of seven, his precocious guitar talent led to his first appearance on a Dot Records single, "Hey Daddy (I'm Gonna Tell Santa on You)," alongside star Ricky Nelson, a friend of his father and uncle.

In 1969, the young blues and rock enthusiast was a fan of Peter Green's Fleetwood Mac and was already touring with Brenda Lee and Roger Miller as rhythm guitarist. Three years later, he signed his first contract with Entrance Records and began his solo rock discography, with the album *Billy Burnette*, a title he also gave to two of his other albums, one released by Polydor in 1979 and the other by Columbia Records in 1981. He wrote for others and sometimes performed. In 1984, the guitarist took part in the *I'm Not Me* album by Mick Fleetwood, whom he had met a few months earlier on a TV show celebrating the birthday of *American Bandstand* host Dick Clark. This meeting, and his participation in Christine McVie's "So Excited" the same year, laid the foundations for a friendship that would influence the decision to integrate him into Fleetwood Mac in 1987. In the meantime, he put his songwriting skills to work for Ray Charles on "Do I Ever Cross Your Mind," in 1985.

The Providential Guitarist

Billy's career was going well when Fleetwood Mac approached him: He had just signed a contract with Curb/MCA and was nominated for the 1986 Academy of Country Music Awards as Best New Vocalist. Yet he had no hesitation in dropping everything overnight to join the band on tour. "That was like the circus taking off that day," he recounts in his biography. "There were I don't know how many trucks and trailers. We had our own private 727."

With his energetic style, the rockabilly-infused guitarist was to contribute effectively to Fleetwood Mac's survival from 1987 to 1995, while continuing to expand his own discography. In 1989, he took part in the *Behind the Mask* adventure and its promotional tour with the Mac. In 1991, when Rick Vito and Stevie Nicks left the band and Christine McVie asked for a break from touring, Billy helped John McVie record his first solo album. In 1994, he took part in the Mac's new album, *Time*, alongside Bekka Bramlett and Dave Mason, who had joined the band. The commercial failure of the album and tour led to the departure of Mason, Bramlett, and Billy. He would immediately form a duo with her—Bekka & Billy—and they released a self-titled album in 1997, just as Fleetwood Mac recalled the *Rumours* lineup to record *The Dance*.

Billy continued his career, regularly releasing solo albums and collaborating with numerous artists, including Christine McVie (with whom he co-wrote "Givin' It Back" for her album *In the Meantime*, released in 2004), Bob Dylan in 2003, and John Fogerty in 2005. In 2017, Billy Burnette released *Crazy Like Me*, an autobiographical book accompanied by an album of the same name, telling the story of rockabilly music and himself in his own way, from the time (1954) when the young Elvis Presley came to watch the Rock 'n Roll Trio rehearse in the laundry room of Lauderdale Courts, a postwar housing estate for the poor in Memphis.

RICK VITO, THE QUIET ONE

When Lindsey Buckingham left Fleetwood Mac with a bang in August 1987, Mick Fleetwood considered Billy Burnette as his replacement. Burnette suggested Rick Vito, whom he considered a better guitarist. Hiring both musicians to replace Buckingham alone, who had been so important to the band's sound for twelve years, did not seem out of place to Mick. Especially as the world of Fleetwood Mac already knew the guitarist...

A Fan from the Earliest Days

Born Richard Francis Vito on October 13, 1949, in Darby, Pennsylvania, Rick had been immersed in the world of Fleetwood Mac since his late teens. At the age of nineteen, he attended a Fleetwood Mac concert in Philadelphia, where he had the opportunity to admire his idol, Peter Green, on stage at the Electric Factory. "That experience made me really want to get into music professionally because they were so great and I related to what Peter was doing so much," he explained in 1999.

During the 1970s and early 1980s, Rick, who had become a professional guitarist, earned his stripes as a musician by accompanying artists such as Todd Rundgren, Bobby Whitlock, John Mayall, John Prine, Roger McGuinn, Bonnie Raitt, Rita Coolidge, and Jackson Browne. When Mick Fleetwood asked him to join the band, he was playing around Los Angeles with his own band, under his own name. Rick was reassured to learn that he would not be alone in the guitarist role vacated by Lindsey. "I felt honored to be asked to join Fleetwood Mac," Rick explains, "especially since I had seen them [...] with Peter Green. [...] When I did join, the band put zero pressure on me with regard to how I was supposed to play. They liked what I was doing, and as long as I captured the flavor of whatever song we were playing, they seemed happy with the results."

The Blues Touch

At work right from the Tango in the Night tour, Rick was fully aware that he was entering a new dimension by joining Fleetwood Mac, but he was determined to do his bit. He knew full well that it would be impossible for him to reproduce Lindsey's parts exactly: "I don't play remotely like Lindsey does and so I never attempted to," he explained

Rick Vito revived the band's blues pulse, drawing on the sonic intensity of Peter Green, one of his guitar role models.

in a 1999 interview. "Maybe I was thinking more in terms of adding back into the pot a little more of the blues flavorings that I loved when Peter was in the group, if anything. You cannot let yourself be intimidated by the accomplishments of others when opportunity knocks. You have to let loose with your own good stuff and go for it."

It was especially on *Behind the Mask* that Rick had the opportunity to show his full potential: "It was a very good record but it did not seem to have the big hit single that Warner Bros. was looking for. We were all hoping that it would have been more successful." Rick left Fleetwood Mac in 1991 and was replaced by Dave Mason, while Bekka Bramlett took over from Stevie Nicks, who also resigned. Rick has fond memories of this period: "I am still proud of everything I did with Fleetwood Mac. We worked very hard on each project. I wish that the band, as it was when I was there, would have done one more record together. We didn't give it enough time to really gel in my estimation."

During his three years with the Mac, Rick collaborated with Dolly Parton in 1987 and with Roy Orbison in 1989, then pursued a brilliant career as an accompanist, with artists such as Hank Williams Jr., Chuck E. Weiss, Boz Scaggs, and ex–Fleetwood Mac partners Stevie Nicks and Mick Fleetwood during his solo phase. He also launched his own discography in 1992, with *King of Hearts*, to which he added a dozen successors, up to *Soulshaker* in 2019.

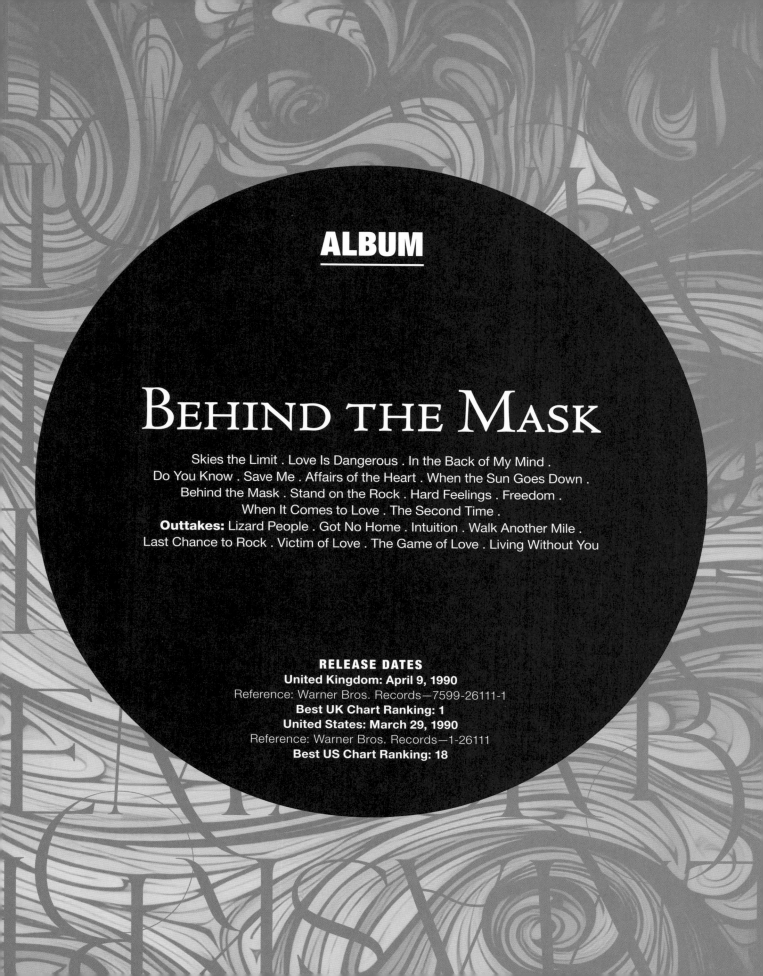

ALBUM

BEHIND THE MASK

Skies the Limit . Love Is Dangerous . In the Back of My Mind .
Do You Know . Save Me . Affairs of the Heart . When the Sun Goes Down .
Behind the Mask . Stand on the Rock . Hard Feelings . Freedom .
When It Comes to Love . The Second Time .
Outtakes: Lizard People . Got No Home . Intuition . Walk Another Mile .
Last Chance to Rock . Victim of Love . The Game of Love . Living Without You

RELEASE DATES
United Kingdom: April 9, 1990
Reference: Warner Bros. Records—7599-26111-1
Best UK Chart Ranking: 1
United States: March 29, 1990
Reference: Warner Bros. Records—1-26111
Best US Chart Ranking: 18

The integration of Billy Burnette (top left) and Rick Vito (bottom right) went smoothly. But musically, originality was lacking.

A BLAND ALBUM

Paradoxically, at a time when they had just lost Lindsey Buckingham, who had authoritatively taken over the creative reins, the members of Fleetwood Mac approached their new studio album with serenity. The specter of a potential commercial failure could not be more painful than the noxious, toxic period they had endured before his departure.

Back to the Collective

At the start of 1989, exhausted by the bloodletting and daily unpleasantnesses, Mick, John, Christine, and Stevie were longing for just one thing: peace of mind. The profiles of Rick Vito and Billy Burnette, well-versed in the thankless work of session musicians, were just what they needed. Accommodating and diplomatic, the two men, who had had the opportunity to get to know the Mac members and their public during the nine-month Shake the Cage tour (September 30, 1987 to June 28, 1988), ensured a smooth integration into a band they respected and admired. "I was always impressed with the original Fleetwood Mac," said Rick Vito humbly. "So my philosophy has been to keep it honest and to keep those guitars out there."

On January 15, 1989, the new Mac lineup began the sessions for their fifteenth studio album, from The Complex studio in Los Angeles to Vintage Recorders in Stevie Nicks's hometown of Phoenix. It would take eight months to complete. The new producer, Greg Ladanyi, co-founder of The Complex, was recruited on the advice of George Hawkins, who had worked on Mick Fleetwood's personal projects.

This Hungarian-born American sound engineer was not, however, the band's first choice. The members had initially selected Don Gehman, a former Criteria Studios engineer, producer of R.E.M.'s *Lifes Rich Pageant* (1986) and several John Mellencamp albums. But after Gehman's inconclusive trials, they changed their tune.

Greg Ladanyi was very engaged and brought a certain freshness to the table. Above all, he did not favor the opinion of one member over that of another, as Richard Dashut had done with Lindsey Buckingham. By Mick Fleetwood's own admission, Greg quickly established himself as the band's seventh member during the sessions. "This band has been fantastic about being here and being involved and letting me go and be part of the music in a way where I can help create some things with them," Greg testified in 1990. "The record was well arranged and well thought out despite the fact that Lindsey wasn't there," declared Christine shortly after the record's release. She not only expressed her gratitude to the producer, but above all she signified to Lindsey that the band was doing just fine without him, pointing out in passing the main flaw, in her eyes, of her ex–playing partner: "It doesn't sound like lots of little overdubs put on, you know, in excess […] on top of drum machine type things. […] It's not sort of constructed."

Clearly, Fleetwood Mac had chosen to reconstruct itself from a model in complete opposition to that imposed by Lindsey Buckingham: The time had come for everyone to have a say and for the band to work together.

For better or worse, the contribution of Greg Ladanyi (pictured here in 2007) to production is crucial on *Behind the Mask*, with its outrageously enhanced synthetic sounds.

FOR MAC-ADDICTS

Producer Greg Ladanyi was immortalized, much to his surprise, in "Cocaine," a song sung by Jackson Browne on *Running on Empty* (1977), an album on which Greg worked as sound engineer. One line mentions his name: "Late last night, about a quarter past four / Ladanyi come knockin' down my hotel room door."

A Fusion That Worked

For this process to work, the two newcomers did not need to start a war of egos or step on one another's toes. Thankfully, their personalities did not predispose them to this, and their roles were quickly defined: Rick Vito took over the solo parts and Billy Burnette the rhythm section. "[We] play well off one another," said Rick Vito in an interview, "[Burnette is] not some frustrated lead guitarist, but, rather, he's extremely inventive on rhythm guitar. He'll craft parts that are uniquely his own, as well as being complementary to what I'm doing. [...] We got to know each other musically by playing together and exciting the people. It was a real confidence booster that carried over when we headed into the studio."

Buckingham's absence would also lead to the awakening of old, dormant forces. Mick Fleetwood, Stevie Nicks, and, to a lesser extent, Christine McVie had settled into a kind of resignation—but also guilty comfort—in the face of Lindsey's authoritarianism. Over the course of the eight-month-long session, Christine and Stevie each contributed four compositions to the track list. The newcomers were not to be outdone, with Rick composing four tracks and Billy five. This was a far cry from the situation where Dave Walker and Bob Weston, had only crumbs to sink their teeth into on *Penguin* (1973). Rick Vito was honored by this level of trust: "Most of the songs I wrote were written in the studio. Blues rock is what I particularly like, and it was a matter of adapting some of the things I do to achieve a group sound. When I'd come up with something that the older members would say sounded 'Mac-ie,' I knew I had it."

A Singular Sound Identity

While the guitarist might have had the impression of fitting into the Fleetwood Mac mold, it was clear that there was not just one mold, but many. Since the band's beginnings, each newcomer had broken the previous mold to adapt it to his own playing. The one tailor-made by and for Lindsey Buckingham had nothing in common with that of Peter Green, Danny Kirwan, or Bob Welch. Blues tracks like "Stand on the Rock" or country songs like "When the Sun Goes Down" on the new album feature Vito's and Burnette's specific trademarks more than those of the band.

Such sonic signatures are achieved through unity in the equipment used. Rick Vito owned a number of Gibsons, including a Flying V, an Explorer, and a Les Paul, whose precision and warmth of sound he appreciated. However, he preferred another model: a guitar he designed and built himself. Distantly inspired by Reverend guitars, another of his favorite brands, this solid body featured an unusual S-shaped body with an underdeveloped horn (the upper part of the body farthest away from the guitarist), a small feature that facilitates access to the upper part of the neck and t herefore to the highest notes. With its blood-orange and black colors and white center, this eye-catching guitar sounded particularly well, with a fine balance in all registers. It was easy to handle, which enabled Vito to play precise, swift solos, such as the one on "Save Me."

Although he occasionally made use of his Gibson Les Paul, Billy Burnette showed a marked preference for his Fender Stratocaster, with which he demonstrates a welcome ease, as on the complex "In the Back of My Mind," which requires precision and a very pure sound, or the blues-rock "Stand on the Rock."

Burnette handled rhythm guitar while Vito found his place as lead guitarist.

The singular sonic identity of *Behind the Mask* is also defined by the sound of Christine McVie's synth, which, under the producer's direction, creates a multiplicity of bold, almost dated sounds, characteristic of the 1980s, just as a new decade is beginning...But it was above all the sound of Mick Fleetwood's drums that underwent a real upheaval. Pushed by Ladanyi, it was closer to the full, highly synthetic sound created by Phil Collins or Toto drummer Jeff Porcaro (Ladanyi was sound engineer on *Toto IV*). To achieve the snare drum's very metallic, slamming sound, the producer used a noise gate effect that cuts the sound signal above or below a certain threshold. The result is a very homogeneous sound, free of parasite noise, but with fewer dynamics and less variety. Ladanyi then added a healthy dose of reverb using an EMT 250 unit. A willing victim of this sonic revolution, Mick Fleetwood was even the instigator of certain innovations, proving to be a forerunner in the field of new technologies that were shaking up drumming. He incorporated Atari's Hotz MIDI Translator into his kit, a controller unique at the time for its ability to reproduce the dynamics of keystrokes using ultrasensitive pads to generate synthetic drum sounds.

Studious, Relaxed Sessions

For the historic members, these considerations of sound were important, but not overriding. The only thing that really counted for them was getting back to the pleasure of playing together. In this respect, the recording of *Behind the Mask* was a success. The thirteen songs involve a real collective effort. Everyone was fully committed to the project, respecting the schedule (arriving at the studio between 12 and 2 p.m., lights out around 10 p.m. or midnight). "We'd get there around noon, start working really hard," recalled Billy Burnette in 2022, "break for dinners, and then come back the next day, and then probably take everything off we did the previous day. They [the other band members] used to write songs in the studio. They'd bring in a couple of ideas and build on them. I came from the songwriter school where you demo first, and then finish them."

Another important change: The musicians were no longer there to party and indulge themselves. While the atmosphere was very relaxed, conducive to jokes and laughter, the musicians remained focused on the objective as soon as they picked up their instruments. A purgative event contributed to this relaxed atmosphere: Lindsey Buckingham, who had already reconnected with his former partners by

By the end of the Behind the Mask tour, Fleetwood Mac (here at the Met Center in Bloomington, Minnesota, on June 30, 1990) was once again on the verge of disintegration.

FOR MAC ADDICTS

In its CD version, the album is encoded in CD+G format, a novelty at the time, containing bonus material such as photos and song lyrics, as well as on-screen graphics synchronized with the music

1990

attending the wedding of Mick Fleetwood and Sara Recor on April 24, 1988, joined the band for a brief collaboration. He played acoustic guitar on the title track, "Behind the Mask." An act more symbolic than musically valuable, but one that had the merit of burying the hatchet two years after their separation.

A Neutral Album Cover

The break with the past and the desire to present themselves as a united collective motivated the decision not to feature any of the band members on the cover. Jeri Heiden, art director at Warner Bros., was asked to create a cover for their new album. Mick Fleetwood explained to her what he wanted: a photo that would spiritually represent the band without featuring them. Jeri Heiden called on photojournalist Dave Gorton to take the shot. Gorton had worked as director of photography at the *Philadelphia Inquirer*, was art director at the *Cincinnati Enquirer*, and also worked for the *New York Times* at the White House during the Carter and Reagan administrations. His collaboration with Fleetwood Mac was his first foray into the music business.

Gorton rose to the challenge with flying colors. The young girl in the foreground, with her tulle dress and wavy blond hair, recalls Stevie Nicks in her early days. With her face turned toward a radiant elsewhere, her eyes are closed, as if she were escaping reality and into her dreams. Behind her, in a setting reminiscent of the southwestern landscapes of the singer's childhood, a group of musicians are jamming around a small buffet. The African American guitarist, with his hollow body guitar and B. B. King looks, recalls the band's blues roots. A dog, its nose on the ground in search of food, is reminiscent of the one immortalized on the cover of *Peter Green's Fleetwood Mac*, the band's first

British album. The visual was a success. It even earned a 1991 Grammy Award nomination for best cover. But it failed to live up to Suzanne Vega's *Days of Open Hand*. Like *Tango in the Night*, *Behind the Mask* is named after one of the songs on the track list. And not just any song, as it is the one featuring Lindsey Buckingham.

A Glacial Reception

The package was ready, but was the public ready for the contents? Critics, still influential at the time, were quick to criticize the album as soon as it hit the stores. Although highly calibrated, lacking in inventiveness, and dated in its sound, the album had some elements to create some kind of impression, with three catchy singles released between

April and August 1990: "Save Me," "Skies the Limit," and "In the Back of My Mind." The first climbed to fifty-third in the UK and forty-third in the US, the second slipped completely under the radar, and the third managed only fifty-eighth place in the UK. The other two singles to be taken from this album during 1990, "Hard Feelings" and "Love Is Dangerous," were conspicuous by their complete absence from the charts.

Behind the Mask struggled. True, it topped the UK charts, but that was an illusion. *Tango in the Night*, also number one, went platinum there eight times. As for the band's eighteenth place in the US, it was their "worst" performance in America since 1974 and the album *Heroes Are Hard to Find*.

The media did not spare this new version of Fleetwood Mac, either. Apart from the *Los Angeles Times*, which raved about the collective effort—"without Buckingham's obsessively unique vision, the group has embraced an all-for-one, one-for-all attitude for what sounds like the most truly group effort since *Rumours*, or perhaps even since 1972's *Bare Trees*"[139]—opinions were lukewarm, even murderous. *Entertainment Weekly* reckoned that "most of *Behind the Mask* is pretty bland. The songs hardly add up to an album; the six musicians hardly add up to Fleetwood Mac"[140] But the sharpest attack was yet to come. Asked by *Rolling Stone* in 1992 how he felt about the album, Lindsey Buckingham unabashedly stoned it with a phrase as definitive as it was contemptuous: "Not an album I can say I took to heart."[62]

Belatedly chosen as a single, "Skies the Limit" fails to make Billboard's Hot 100 but earns a respectable tenth place on the Adult Contemporary chart.

The spelling of "Skies the Limit" is puzzling. Music history is full of such spelling anomalies, including "Odessey and Oracle" by the Zombies (instead of "Odyssey and Oracle") and "Cemetry Gates" by the Smiths (instead of "Cemetery Gates").

SKIES THE LIMIT

Christine McVie, Eddy Quintela / 3:45

Musicians: Christine McVie: vocals, keyboards / Billy Burnette: backing vocals, guitar / Rick Vito: backing vocals, guitar / Steve Croes: keyboards / John McVie: bass / Mick Fleetwood: drums, percussion / Stevie Nicks: backing vocals / **Recorded:** The Complex, Los Angeles: January–September 1989 / Vintage Recorders, Phoenix: January–September 1989 / **Technical Team:** Producers: Fleetwood Mac, Greg Ladanyi / Assistant Producer: Tim McCarthy / Sound Engineers: Bob Levy, Dennis Mays, Greg Ladanyi / Assistant Sound Engineers: Craig Porteils, Duane Seykora, Brett Swain, Paula Wolak / **Single:** Side A: Skies the Limit / Side B: The Second Time / **US Release Date:** July 1990 / **Reference:** Warner Bros. Records (45 rpm ref.: 7-19867) / Best US Chart Ranking: Did Not Chart

Genesis and Lyrics

A latecomer to the composition process, "Skies the Limit" is a compensatory song. In the summer of 1989, Christine McVie took a step back from the songs that had been piling up since the beginning of the sessions. She realized that the album was about to take a somewhat sinister direction. While satisfying from a musical point of view, this album featured rather slow tempos and a very dark tone, in her eyes. "Everything was getting to the point of where it was a downer album. It sounded like this was a potential suicide band, which it wasn't. I decided to write a song that was really up, it was a rally song." With the help of Eddy Quintela—her husband since 1986—the singer came up with resolutely positive lyrics. She evokes the presence of her partner by her side, a stabilizing element and source of optimism. With him, she can look to the future with serenity and climb mountains.

Production

The music is equally galvanizing, particularly due to its anthem-like, stadium-ready chorus. The introduction, with its occasional percussion, wispy keyboards, and rising guitar volume, does not augur well for such effectiveness, right up until the whiplash of the snare drum. Then the band really gets into the song, a direct, catchy, midtempo rock number that is not overflowing with fantasy. On this track, they rediscover their recipe for meticulously constructed vocal harmonies.

Like "Skies the Limit," "Love Is Dangerous," Rick Vito's composition, reaches number seven on the Mainstream Rock chart.

LOVE IS DANGEROUS

Stevie Nicks, Rick Vito / 3:18

Musicians: Stevie Nicks: vocals / Rick Vito: vocals, guitar / Billy Burnette: backing vocals, guitar / Christine McVie: backing vocals, keyboards / Steve Croes: keyboards / John McVie: bass / Mick Fleetwood: drums, percussion / **Recorded:** The Complex, Los Angeles: January–September 1989 / Vintage Recorders, Phoenix: January–September 1989 / **Technical Team:** Producers: Fleetwood Mac, Greg Ladanyi / Assistant Producer: Tim McCarthy / Sound Engineers: Bob Levy, Dennis Mays, Greg Ladanyi / Assistant Sound Engineers: Craig Porteils, Duane Seykora, Brett Swain, Paula Wolak / **Promo Single:** Love Is Dangerous / **US Release Date:** April 28, 1990 / **Reference:** Warner Bros Records (CD ref.: PRO-CD-4302) / Best US Chart Ranking: Did Not Chart

Genesis and Lyrics

Confronted frequently with disappointment in love, Stevie Nicks draws on her own experience to warn of the dangers of that sweet lark that is, in her eyes, love. The first verse's mention of a stranger lurking in the shadows personalizes this threat. The singer uses another explicit metaphor to reinforce her point: crystal hearts collapsing like sandcastles, referring to the ultrasensitive people much like herself. In the bridge, Stevie refers to a crossroads that symbolizes the decisive moment for those who choose to invest—or not—in a relationship. She urges the listener to exercise caution and reflect before making an emotional commitment.

Production

Rick Vito, the composer of this sophisticated up-tempo track, opens with an electric blues-rock guitar part executed with swift, precise, left-hand playing. Billy Burnette provides authoritative accompaniment, with a crunchy guitar sound that does what is required without overdoing it—Vito's guitar already takes up a lot of space. Vito, for his part, varies his playing a little more, adding slide parts with the bottleneck he wears on his little finger (enabling him to alternate picking and bottleneck playing without interruption). His explosive playing subtly led the band down a funky path when he began singing duets with Stevie Nicks. Mick Fleetwood's drums provide a steady pulse while adapting to the song's dramatic nuances. John McVie's bass adds a solid foundation, and Christine McVie's keyboards provide crucial melodic and harmonic elements. The careful construction of the track and the expressive vocal interpretation by Nicks and Vito, who display a beautiful complicity, make this one of the album's highlights.

IN THE BACK OF MY MIND

Billy Burnette, David Malloy / 7:02

Musicians
Billy Burnette: vocals, guitar
Christine McVie: vocals, keyboards
Rick Vito: guitar
John McVie: bass
Mick Fleetwood: spoken words, drums, percussion
Stevie Nicks: backing vocals

Recorded
The Complex, Los Angeles: January–September 1989
Vintage Recorders, Phoenix: January–September 1989

Technical Team
Producers: Fleetwood Mac, Greg Ladanyi
Assistant Producer: Tim McCarthy
Sound Engineers: Bob Levy, Dennis Mays, Greg Ladanyi
Assistant Sound Engineers: Craig Porteils, Duane Seykora, Brett Swain, Paula Wolak

Single
Side A: In the Back of My Mind / **Side B:** Lizard People
UK Release Date: August 13, 1990
Reference: Warner Bros Records (45 rpm ref.: W9739)
Best UK Chart Ranking: 58

12-Inch Single
Side A: In the Back of My Mind / **Side B1:** Little Lies (Live) / **Side B2:** The Chain (Live)
UK Release Date: August 13, 1990
Reference: Warner Bros. Records (12-inch single ref.: W9739T)
Best UK Chart Ranking: Did Not Chart

FOR MAC ADDICTS
During the Behind the Mask tour, which ran from March to December 1990, Fleetwood Mac opened their concerts with the imposing "In the Back of My Mind," followed by "The Chain," which, since its creation in 1977, has been played almost without fail at number one or two on the set list.

Genesis and Lyrics
Billy Burnette teamed up with Nashville-based producer, lyricist, and composer David Malloy to develop "In the Back of My Mind" ahead of the *Behind the Mask* recording sessions. Anxiously, he presented the result to Mick Fleetwood, who immediately expressed his enthusiasm for the track, with its inspiring lyrics. It depicts a man confronted with the absence of the one who loves him. In the narrator's tormented mind, the loved one lives on, fueling his lover's desire. Burnette takes advantage of the two female backing singers at his side to give them a full role in the story. They comment on his moods, addressing him directly in the second person: "You can't forget her," "And it drives you insane."

Production
According to Billy Burnette, who testified in a question-and-answer session with Fleetwood Mac fans in 2000, "In the Back of My Mind" almost made it into *The Guinness Book of Records* as the song with the most recording tracks at the time of its creation…It took three 48-track consoles to contain all the tracks selected for this titanic piece, which spans almost seven minutes in its album version. Given its complexity, "In the Back of My Mind" is logically the song that most mobilized the musicians during the *Behind the Mask* sessions.

The introduction alone required a colossal amount of work. Chilling keyboards, indistinct spoken words, sound effects of all kinds, and aggressive toms soon morph into a martial pattern. Rick Vito's guitar solo emerges, bursting with reverbs that split the sound space with authority, pure and airy as David Gilmour's could be. Then come the male vocals, backed by Stevie Nicks and Christine McVie. The song is set up, and the musicians unroll this epic track. At the three-minute mark, the band introduces a new twist to the structure with Christine McVie's lead vocals. This then gives way to an instrumental bridge that leads to a monumental, ad-libbed finale, with a veritable firework display of instruments stacked up track by track, over which Rick Vito's guitar flies. The latter then launches into a lamenting solo.

With Billy Burnette's successful integration, the guitarist is spurred to confidence, writing "In the Back of My Mind" and experimenting with new sounds.

Page 511: Christine McVie through the lens of Aaron Rapoport.

For its single version—the third from *Behind the Mask*—which was released only in the UK, "In the Back of My Mind" is shortened from 7:02 to 4:58. An illustration by artist Malcolm Tarlofsky adorns the sleeve. It depicts a person's head in profile, apparently taken from an ancient medical textbook. On the skull are drawn the areas supposed to represent the location of certain human qualities or feelings in the brain: self-esteem, combativeness, and so on. The song failed to convince the public, reaching number fifty-eight in the UK. Warner Bros. was due to release it as a single in the US, but it eventually opted for "Hard Feelings."

DO YOU KNOW

Christine McVie, Billy Burnette / 4:19

Musicians: Billy Burnette: vocals, guitar / Christine McVie: vocals, keyboards / Rick Vito: guitar / John McVie: bass / Mick Fleetwood: drums, percussion / **Recorded:** The Complex, Los Angeles: January–September 1989 / Vintage Recorders, Phoenix: January–September 1989 / **Technical Team:** Producers: Fleetwood Mac, Greg Ladanyi / Assistant Producer: Tim McCarthy / Sound Engineers: Bob Levy, Dennis Mays, Greg Ladanyi / Assistant Sound Engineers: Craig Porteils, Duane Seykora, Brett Swain, Paula Wolak

Genesis and Lyrics

Christine McVie and Billy Burnette had already worked hand in hand to create a song, "So Excited," for the singer's second solo album, *Christine McVie* (1984). But they were accompanied by composer Todd Sharp, a former Hall and Oates touring guitarist. This time, they wrote and composed what was to become an authentic duet, with the two artists sharing the lead vocals. The text lends itself to this, since it seems to feature former lovers, as suggested by the lines "If I have learned enough / To make it without you" and "If I ever fall in love again." They remain so close that one of them asks the other for advice on love. They fear their lack of expertise and knowledge on the subject. If they have indeed been lovers, then these fears express the failure of their relationship, because what they shared was not deep enough for them to grasp all there is to know about love. But the trust they have in each other counterbalances this sense of incompleteness, as they have managed to overcome their difficulties to achieve a form of wholeness that is far more fulfilling for them.

Production

The musicians opt for a very slow tempo on which to build "Do You Know," an endearing ballad blending folk and pop. On Billy Burnette's crystal-clear arpeggio with its detached notes, Rick Vito delicately adds an acoustic guitar, which appears only at the end of the other guitar's phrases. Mick Fleetwood takes a back seat, quietly sounding his cymbals and playing what seem to be congas.

Benefiting from ample space in the low register neglected by the guitars, John McVie makes his bass sound very smooth, producing an exceptional sound. The instrumental setup is rapid, with the bulk of the work concentrated on the vocals, which require very precise coordination not only between the two main voices but also with the skillfully harmonized backing vocals.

SAVE ME

Christine McVie, Eddy Quintela / 4:15

Musicians: Christine McVie: vocals, keyboards / Billy Burnette: backing vocals, guitar / Rick Vito: backing vocals, guitar / John McVie: bass / Mick Fleetwood: drums, percussion / Stevie Nicks: backing vocals / **Recorded:** The Complex, Los Angeles: January–September 1989 / Vintage Recorders, Phoenix: January–September 1989 / **Technical Team:** Producers: Fleetwood Mac, Greg Ladanyi / Assistant Producer: Tim McCarthy / Sound Engineers: Bob Levy, Dennis Mays, Greg Ladanyi / Assistant Sound Engineers: Craig Porteils, Duane Seykora, Brett Swain, Paula Wolak / **Single:** Side A: Save Me / Side B: Another Woman (Live) / **UK Release Date:** April 23, 1990 / **Reference:** Warner Bros. Records (45 rpm ref.: 5439-19866-7) / Best UK Chart Ranking: 53 / **12"** **Single:** Side A: Save Me / Side B1: Another Woman (Live) / Side B2: Everywhere (Live) / **UK Release Date:** 1990 with Warner Bros Records (12-inch single ref.: W 9866 (T) / Best UK Chart Ranking: Did Not Chart

Genesis and Lyrics

As much as the theme of rescue, induced by the oft-repeated phrase "Save me," the power of eye contact is at the heart of this song conceived by Christine McVie and her husband, Eddy Quintela. The eye is exploited throughout: "the laughing eyes," "the haunting stare," "hypnotize," "But you just won't look my way," "It's written in my eyes." The narrator attributes powers to her lover's gaze, which represents both danger and desire. But the difficulty for her is to capture it. So, to attract her partner's attention, she has no choice but to call on him for help.

Production

This highly effective FM rock number features a keyboard sound typical of the late 1980s, in the tradition of Toto. The guitars appear somewhat in the background in the first half of the track, leaving the spotlight to John McVie's five-string bass, whose ample sound envelops Christine's voice. But after a dreamy bridge on which Mick Fleetwood plays a wind chime (he also sprinkles the rest of the song with numerous percussion instruments more discreetly, such as a gong, finger cymbals, or a shaker), Rick Vito wakes up and makes his electric guitar sing on a precise, expressive solo.

Strangely enough, as if the band wanted to arrive on tiptoe, the album was released before any single. A cautious strategy that did not help the success of the singles. "Save Me," the first single to be released, performed well, particularly in Canada (number seven), but did no better than number fifty-three in the UK and number thirty-three in the US. Apart from the surprise revival of "Dreams" in 2020, this would be the last time a Fleetwood Mac single entered the top 40 in the US.

The track is the subject of an unscripted video, featuring only the musicians, instruments in hand, in a play of chiaroscuro. Only Mick Fleetwood's multiple facial expressions add variety to the video.

1990

Stevie Nicks and Billy Burnette complement each other perfectly on "Affairs of the Heart," which is articulated like a dialogue on the choruses.

AFFAIRS OF THE HEART
Stevie Nicks / 4:22

Musicians: Stevie Nicks: vocals / Billy Burnette: vocals, backing vocals, guitar / Rick Vito: backing vocals, guitar / Christine McVie: backing vocals, keyboards / John McVie: bass / Mick Fleetwood: drums, percussion / **Recorded:** The Complex, Los Angeles: January–September 1989 / Vintage Recorders, Phoenix: January–September 1989 / **Technical Team:** Producers: Fleetwood Mac, Greg Ladanyi / Assistant Producer: Tim McCarthy / Sound Engineers: Bob Levy, Dennis Mays, Greg Ladanyi / Assistant Sound Engineers: Craig Porteils, Duane Seykora, Brett Swain, Paula Wolak

Genesis and Lyrics

The only contribution to this album by Stevie Nicks, who wrote the music and lyrics, "Affairs of the Heart" should have appeared earlier in Fleetwood Mac's discography. The singer had in fact produced a first demo using a drum machine in 1988, with the idea of including it on the *Greatest Hits* compilation, released in November of that year. But the song was eventually dropped from the track list. In 1989, Stevie made a new, fairly accomplished demo, this time for inclusion on her solo album *The Other Side of the Mirror*. But once again, the song was shelved. It was during the recording of *Behind the Mask* that the composer finally took her song to the end of the creative process, giving shape to one of her most memorable songs, at least from a lyrical point of view. "It's better to have loved and lost / Than to never have loved at all." A statement inspired by a quatrain in *In Memoriam A.H.H.*, written in 1849 by Alfred, Lord Tennyson. The Victorian poet reflects on the sudden death of his friend Arthur Henry Hallam, victim of a cerebral hemorrhage: "I hold it true, whate'er befall; / I feel it when I sorrow most; / 'Tis better to have loved and lost / Than never to have loved at all." Stevie qualifies Tennyson's assertion, however, by having Billy Burnette, who provides second vocals, sing: "Ah but it's better not to lose."

Production

Mick Fleetwood takes matters into his own hands on the introduction to "Affairs of the Heart," unleashing a slamming attack on the toms before the guitar enters, then punctuating the end of the first phrase of the guitar's arpeggio with a castanet beat. This is the freshest part of this pop track. The song is built around the famous crystalline arpeggio, which is occasionally joined by a saturated but very discreet rhythm guitar. Christine adds some celestial keyboard notes that blend perfectly with the clean guitar. Stevie Nicks's dreamy vocals contribute a great deal to the track's melancholy mood. The track also features beautifully crafted backing vocals, reminiscent of the band's heyday in the second half of the 1970s.

WHEN THE SUN GOES DOWN

Rick Vito, Billy Burnette / 3:18

Musicians: Rick Vito: vocals, guitar / Billy Burnette: vocals, guitar / Christine McVie: backing vocals, accordion / John McVie: bass / Mick Fleetwood: drums, percussion / Stevie Nicks: backing vocals / **Recorded:** The Complex, Los Angeles: January–September 1989 / Vintage Recorders, Phoenix: January–September 1989 / **Technical Team:** Producers: Fleetwood Mac, Greg Ladanyi / Assistant Producer: Tim McCarthy / Sound Engineers: Bob Levy, Dennis Mays, Greg Ladanyi / Assistant Sound Engineers: Craig Porteils, Duane Seykora, Brett Swain, Paula Wolak

Genesis and Lyrics

A pretext for the enjoyment of playing, set to a high-tempo rockabilly rhythm, this light-hearted piece relies more on energy than on deep meaning. As the sun sets, the narrator begins a seductive parade, posing as the protective lover of a young woman who has been broken by another man. The narrator offers to comfort her, protect her, and help her rebuild her life. "Well he was just a fool, wonder why so cruel / But you'll forget him, when I come around." However, the singer's self-confidence and eagerness come up against a final obstacle: The lover must agree to open her door to him. But the text ends without the outcome being known.

Production

The band's two new recruits, Rick Vito and Billy Burnette, are at the helm on "When the Sun Goes Down." They demonstrate their complicity by sharing the solo vocals on the verses. Their timbres appear very close and blend ideally. The track exudes cohesion and the pleasure of playing as a group. For the first and perhaps only time on the record, the musicians seem to let themselves go: Billy Burnette decides to start the song alone, on a rockabilly rhythm that he loves. The sound-engineering team sets up a microphone as close to the strings as possible to capture all the friction of the plectrum on the strings. Unfortunately, the warmth and closeness of the guitar are immediately cooled when, for the sake of consistency with the other tracks, Greg Ladanyi chooses to maintain his very marked production ingredients: a metallic, synthetic sound and an omnipresent reverb. The magic instantly fades away under the effect of these production elements, thereby canceling out the effort at originality—in particular, Christine's initiative in abandoning her keyboard to play the accordion in a folk-sounding, Cajun style.

Mick Fleetwood's playing, with its deft accents and variations, is highlighted on the album's title track.

BEHIND THE MASK

Christine McVie / 4:18

Musicians: Christine McVie: vocals, keyboards / Rick Vito: backing vocals, guitar / Billy Burnette: backing vocals, guitar / Lindsey Buckingham: guitar / John McVie: bass / Mick Fleetwood: drums, percussion / Stevie Nicks: backing vocals / **Recorded:** The Complex, Los Angeles: January–September 1989 / Vintage Recorders, Phoenix: January–September 1989 / **Technical Team:** Producers: Fleetwood Mac, Greg Ladanyi / Assistant Producer: Tim McCarthy / Sound Engineers: Bob Levy, Dennis Mays, Greg Ladanyi / Assistant Sound Engineers: Craig Porteils, Duane Seykora, Brett Swain, Paula Wolak

Genesis and Lyrics

"Stevie and Lindsey had a rift at the band meeting when I joined the band. Something happened there," as Billy Burnette recalled with a neutral perspective. Since Lindsey's shock departure in 1987, water had flowed under the bridge and both parties had made numerous gestures of appeasement. The former member's participation in the title track put an end to the cold war period. It was all the easier because Lindsey was not emotionally involved in the song, since it was by Christine. And yet, if he had stopped to consider the lyrics, he might have taken umbrage with his ex-partner in music: "I don't know if I want you back," "There will never be a second chance for you," or "I recognize the shadows from your past" are all like stakes planted around the Fleetwood Mac fortress to ward off his return. Although the listener may read these words in a different way (Christine addressing a former lover), Lindsey Buckingham's face—appearing half-angelic, half-demonic in the lyrics—takes shape as the verses progress.

Production

Mick Fleetwood opens the song with a subtle interplay between snare drum and cymbals, between each powerful bass drum hit. The band then rolls out a carpet of notes skillfully woven between Christine's keyboards and Lindsey's acoustic guitar. Then Christine's deep, enveloping voice rises, floating, almost ethereal, as does John McVie's bass, letting its vibrant notes ring out and soar. The band regains its magic when it comes to the choruses, which bloom in the air like fireworks to the sound of Christine's and Stevie's passionate, high-pitched backing vocals. Rick Vito accompanies their verse endings with slide chords and very well-judged descending notes.

STAND ON THE ROCK

Rick Vito / 3:59

Musicians: Billy Burnette: vocals, guitar / Rick Vito: backing vocals, guitar / Christine McVie: backing vocals, keyboards / John McVie: bass / Mick Fleetwood: drums / Stevie Nicks: backing vocals / **Recorded:** The Complex, Los Angeles: January–September 1989 / Vintage Recorders, Phoenix: January–September 1989 / **Technical Team:** Producers: Fleetwood Mac, Greg Ladanyi / Assistant Producer: Tim McCarthy / Sound Engineers: Bob Levy, Dennis Mays, Greg Ladanyi / Assistant Sound Engineers: Craig Porteils, Duane Seykora, Brett Swain, Paula Wolak

Genesis and Lyrics

For his only contribution as composer and lyricist, Rick Vito delivers a vibrant declaration of love. At first glance, it seems to be addressed to a partner in love, to whom he confesses the strength of his unswerving feelings. Like an unshakable rock in the midst of a stormy sea, his love is and will remain immovable, even when subjected to the young woman's fickleness and energy, symbolized by the waves in perpetual motion. The narrator will not betray his vow of fidelity and love. This image of rock, through the double meaning of the word *rock*, allows Rick Vito to extend his metaphor to his attachment to the musical genre.

Production

"Stand on the Rock" is without doubt the song in which Rick Vito was most involved during his brief stint with Fleetwood Mac. It says a lot about the band's loss of identity with the arrival of Vito and Burnette. The markers of pop (of the Lindsey Buckingham period) have totally disappeared, and the new lineup is still searching for an identity. Witness the lackluster blues-rock FM attempt. Rick Vito's intention was laudable, however, in trying to revive the essence of the band's early days: its blues soul. But the Fleetwood Mac of the 1990s no longer bore an ounce of resemblance to Peter Green's, so reviving that memory was futile. All the more so since Greg Ladanyi's production, which creates a highly synthetic sound, distances him from the original authenticity Rick was pursuing. The result is a bland FM blues-rock number from which only John McVie's round, throbbing bass and Rick's guitar lead stand out, as he launches into unsurprising but clean, well-executed solos.

COVERS
"Stand on the Rock" inspired the Christian band the Imperials (active since 1964) to rework "Stand on the Rock" for their 1991 album *Big God*.

HARD FEELINGS

Billy Burnette, Jeff Silbar / 4:54

Musicians: Billy Burnette: vocals, guitar / Rick Vito: backing vocals, guitar / Christine McVie: backing vocals, keyboards / Stephen Croes: keyboards / John McVie: bass / Mick Fleetwood: drums / Stevie Nicks: backing vocals / **Recorded:** The Complex, Los Angeles: January–September 1989 / Vintage Recorders, Phoenix: January–September 1989 / **Technical Team:** Producers: Fleetwood Mac, Greg Ladanyi / Assistant Producer: Tim McCarthy / Sound Engineers: Bob Levy, Dennis Mays, Greg Ladanyi / Assistant Sound Engineers: Craig Porteils, Duane Seykora, Brett Swain, Paula Wolak / **Cassette Single:** Side A: Hard Feelings / Side B: Freedom / **US Release Date:** 1990 / **Reference:** Warner Bros. Records (cassette ref.: 9 19537-4) / Best US Chart Ranking: Did Not Chart

Genesis and Lyrics

Although Fleetwood Mac included numerous external collaborations on this album, it was the first time the band had called on a contributor that none of the members had known beforehand. The only element linking Jeff Silbar, co-composer of the song "Hard Feelings" with Billy Burnette, is Larry Henley. Henley, a regular collaborator with Billy Burnette, wrote "Wind Beneath My Wings" with Jeff Silbar in 1982, a song popularized by Bette Midler and included in the soundtrack of the film *Beaches* (1989). Fleetwood Mac could not ignore this song, such was its massive success (it topped the Billboard charts in June 1989, and won the Grammy Award for Song of the Year in February 1990).

The same sharp, scathing pen as Lindsey Buckingham's can be found in the lyrics written by Burnette, which he addresses to a former partner. "Don't you think you've hurt me enough?" declares the narrator, who rejects any gesture of reconciliation on the part of his partner. Friendship is not an option for him. A clean break is the only way to heal.

Production

Silbar enjoyed great credibility in country music circles, having spawned such hits as Kenny Rogers's "All My Life," Janie Fricke's "He's a Heartache (Looking for a Place to Happen)," J. C. Crowley's "I Know What I've Got," and Dolly Parton's "Tie Our Love (in a Double Knot)." However, "Hard Feelings" is far from the country genre and somewhere in the pop-rock environment between Wings and REO Speedwagon. Built on a simple verse-chorus structure, this song benefits from Billy Burnette's subtle rhythm playing. On the verses, the guitarist plays only backward and forward but accentuates certain chords, creating a growing tension before the melody is released on the choruses. Composer and arranger Stephen Croes (who has worked with Stevie Wonder, Kenny Loggins, and Alice Cooper) was asked to record some keyboards. He came up with the intro, featuring a synth played backward, distantly reminiscent of the Who.

FREEDOM

Stevie Nicks, Mike Campbell / 4:12

Guitarist Mike Campbell, inducted into the Rock and Roll Hall of Fame in 2002 as a member of Tom Petty and the Heartbreakers, would have had no idea when he co-wrote this Fleetwood Mac song that he would replace Lindsey Buckingham, alongside Neil Finn, for the 2018–2019 world tour.

More accustomed to writing mystical lyrics, with "Freedom" Stevie bluntly berates Lindsey Buckingham for his alleged "freedom" from the Mac.

Musicians

Stevie Nicks: vocals
Billy Burnette: backing vocals, guitar
Rick Vito: backing vocals, guitar
Christine McVie: backing vocals, keyboards
John McVie: bass
Mick Fleetwood: drums
Okyerema Asanté: percussion

Recorded

The Complex, Los Angeles: January–September 1989
Vintage Recorders, Phoenix: January–September 1989

Technical Team

Producers: Fleetwood Mac, Greg Ladanyi
Assistant Producer: Tim McCarthy
Sound Engineers: Bob Levy, Dennis Mays, Greg Ladanyi
Assistant Sound Engineers: Craig Porteils, Duane Seykora, Brett Swain, Paula Wolak

Cassette Single

Side A: Hard Feelings / **Side B:** Freedom
US Release Date: 1990
Reference: Warner Bros. Records (cassette ref.: 9 19537-4)
Best US Chart Ranking: Did Not Chart

Mike Campbell (left), here performing with Tom Petty, co-wrote "Freedom" with Stevie Nicks.

Genesis and Lyrics

Enchanted by her collaborative experience with Tom Petty and the Heartbreakers on "Stop Draggin' My Heart Around" from *Bella Donna* (1981), Stevie Nicks retained close ties with the band, especially guitarist Mike Campbell. Their friendship led to a long collaboration until 2014. Such was their chemistry that Stevie Nicks invited him to step into Fleetwood Mac territory to co-write "Freedom" with her for *Behind the Mask*. The lyrics of this song are about self-confidence. They depict a woman who, having finally broken free from the grip of a toxic man, takes undisguised pleasure in watching him fall: "Look at me with daggers / It won't do you any good / All the looks that you've used on me / Don't work now that you've fallen." In 1990, Stevie Nicks confessed on Channel 4's *Rock Steady* that she probably had Lindsey in mind when she wrote those lines.

Production

Stevie Nicks's vocals, which seem to contain a kind of satisfaction tinged with restrained, vengeful rage, are in the same register as the lyrics. They illustrate the belated victory of the oppressed over the oppressor (all things considered) and their satisfaction at enjoying a newfound freedom. Mick Fleetwood's willful drums and the abrasive guitars of Rick Vito and Billy Burnette do their job perfectly. But "Freedom" also leaves the listener frustrated, due to the artistic choices made during production by the musicians and Greg Ladanyi, notably that of drowning the track's most original elements in the mix, such as the African-flavored percussion played by Okyerema Asanté, a Ghanaian musician Mick encountered during the recording of his album *The Visitor*. No doubt a Lindsey Buckingham would have seized on this rhythmic element, as haunting as it is surprising in a pop-rock context like "Freedom," and built the instrumentation around it. To a lesser extent, Christine's original guttural backing vocals are not sufficiently highlighted, either.

WHEN IT COMES TO LOVE

Billy Burnette, Dennis Morgan, Simon Climie / 4:08

Musicians: Billy Burnette: vocals, backing vocals, guitar / Christine McVie: backing vocals, keyboards / Rick Vito: guitar / John McVie: bass / Mick Fleetwood: drums / **Recorded:** The Complex, Los Angeles: January–September 1989 / Vintage Recorders, Phoenix: January—September 1989 / **Technical Team:** Producers: Fleetwood Mac, Greg Ladanyi / Assistant Producer: Tim McCarthy / Sound Engineers: Bob Levy, Dennis Mays, Greg Ladanyi / Assistant Sound Engineers: Craig Porteils, Duane Seykora, Brett Swain, Paula Wolak

Genesis and Lyrics

As with "In the Back of My Mind" and "Hard Feelings," "When It Comes to Love" marks a major break in the Mac's repertoire, as the song features no contributions from historic band members and calls upon musicians from outside the band. Rockabilly guitarist Billy Burnette co-wrote the track with songwriting duo Dennis Morgan and Simon Climie. These two men have very different profiles. The former, a composer and session musician, has a predominantly country pedigree and repertoire. His hits include "Sleeping Single in a Double Bed" (1978) for Barbara Mandrell and "Smoky Mountain Rain" (1980) for Ronnie Milsap. Simon Climie, a member of the London duo Climie Fisher with Rob Fisher, favors pop and rock. We owe him "Invincible" for Pat Benatar. The two men had just conceived "I Knew You Were Waiting (for Me)" for George Michael and Aretha Franklin when Billy Burnette first heard of them in 1987. "That was Number One all over the world," Burnette recalled. "Dennis was a Nashville guy, but I met him in LA. We became really good friends. I got along with Simon, too. In fact, we just had a song on Rod Stewart's last album that we wrote back then. It was called 'Love in the Right Hands.'"

Unfortunately, this unprecedented collaboration resulted in lyrics as bland as its musical setting. The song could be summed up like this: You have to give love time to develop, and you have to nurture it patiently without plucking the fruits too quickly. "When it comes to love, got to take it easy / You can't be too careful, when it comes to love," sings Billy Burnette.

Production

Fleetwood Mac, who had been timidly moving in this direction for some years, now plunge headlong into soft rock under the influence of Billy Burnette and Rick Vito. Christine McVie also plays a major role in this changeover, with her keyboard parts sounding more and more like synthpop, almost anachronistic. Very much of the 1980s, these are already at odds with the grunge-rock alternative wave that swept the scene in the early 1990s. Burnette's vocals, with a timbre reminiscent of Toto or Don Henley, also play an important part in this FM sound. Last but not least, Greg Ladanyi's clean, smooth production contributes to this shift with its massive use of reverb, the erasing of the slightest country colorations present in the first part, and the absence of saturated guitars. With all rock flavor erased, the only interesting element left is the acoustic guitar part (at 2:29), which is skillfully and superbly executed.

FOR MAC ADDICTS

Dennis Morgan, co-composer of "When It Comes to Love," was inducted into the Nashville Songwriters Foundation's Songwriters Hall of Fame in 2004.

On the guitar-vocal ballad "The Second Time," Stevie Nicks tries to re-create with Billy Burnette the intimacy she enjoyed with Lindsey Buckingham on "Landslide" in 1975.

THE SECOND TIME

Stevie Nicks, Rick Vito / 2:31

Musicians: Stevie Nicks: vocals / Rick Vito: backing vocals, guitar / Christine McVie: keyboards / **Recorded:** The Complex, Los Angeles: January–September 1989 / Vintage Recorders, Phoenix: January–September 1989 / **Technical Team:** Producers: Fleetwood Mac, Greg Ladanyi / Assistant Producer: Tim McCarthy / Sound Engineers: Bob Levy, Dennis Mays, Greg Ladanyi / Assistant Sound Engineers: Craig Porteils, Duane Seykora, Brett Swain, Paula Wolak / **Single:** Side A: Skies the Limit / Side B: The Second Time / **US Release Date:** July 1990 / **Reference:** Warner Bros. Records (45 rpm ref.: 7-19867) / Best US Chart Ranking: Did Not Chart

Genesis and Lyrics

The name of this concluding ballad, "The Second Time," could not be more apt, as the lyrics seem to be a repetition of another Stevie Nicks song from his solo album *Bella Donna*: "After the Glitter Fades" (1981). Stevie recalls not only her arrival in Hollywood and her audacious, almost magical success, but also the other side of the celebrity coin: loneliness due to the absence of love. Both songs begin in the same way: "Well I never thought I'd make it / Here in Hollywood" in "After the Glitter Fades"; and "Was it my mind / Or was it true / That woman used to Hollywood living" in "The Second Time." The lyricist's questions to her listeners in the latter song (such as "Do you remember?") reinforce the link between the two tracks. "The Second Time" takes a fresh look at the failure described in the first song: The singer has finally managed to pull through, thanks to the friendship and support of those around her. The bitter verdict of "After the Glitter Fades" is thus partially softened by this touching ballad.

Production

The band might have expanded to six members and opened up to a few additional musicians, but only three of them are at work on "The Second Time": Stevie Nicks, as lyricist and singer; Rick Vito, as composer and guitarist; and Christine McVie, for the melodic support of her keyboard. In fact, this instrument was overpowered by the ultrasynthetic flute sound—which adds a shrill color to a ballad that stood on its own. Rick Vito draws a charming melody on acoustic guitar. This melody, played on two tracks, with magnificent passages in *A* minor chords, lends a melancholy tone to the whole. The acoustic guitar is an ideal accompaniment to Stevie Nicks's full, pure voice, whose gravity reflects the experience of a singer who has endured many trials since her early days in music.

Unlike many of its predecessors, the *Behind the Mask* album has not, to date, benefited from a deluxe reissue to highlight the outtakes that were left out. With the exception of "Lizard People," used as Side B of the single "In the Back of My Mind," all these tracks have remained unreleased. They weren't unearthed until 2022, when a bootleg, rare and unofficial by definition, was released: *The Other Side of the Mask*. But, through the magic of YouTube, these tracks are now available via the BehindtheMaskDemos page.

LIVING WITHOUT YOU
Rick Vito (?) / 4:01

Musicians: Christine McVie: vocals / Billy Burnette: guitar / Rick Vito: guitar / John McVie: bass / Mick Fleetwood: drums / **Recorded:** The Complex, Los Angeles: January–September 1989 / Vintage Recorders, Phoenix: January–September 1989 / **Technical Team:** Producers: Fleetwood Mac, Greg Ladanyi / Sound Engineer: Greg Ladanyi

Before its release, *Behind the Mask* was billed as a return to the band's blues roots. But, although that wasn't the case, "Living Without You" really does just that. This is the clearest attempt to reconnect with Peter Green's legacy. The sheer purity of Vito's lead guitar sound and his airy, precise playing could not be more explicit of the musician's desire to pay homage to his predecessor. As for Christine, she embraces this blues with an exceptionally warm, deep voice that plunges us into a dystopian reality, hinting at what Fleetwood Mac might have been like in its early days if the singer had taken over the lead vocals from Green or Spencer. Unfortunately, this track was never exploited, and it was only unveiled on the pirate release *The Other Side of the Mask*.

LAST CHANCE TO ROCK
Rick Vito / 3:38

Musicians: Rick Vito: vocals, guitar / Billy Burnette: backing vocals, guitar / Christine McVie: backing vocals, keyboards / John McVie: bass / Mick Fleetwood: drums / Stevie Nicks: backing vocals / **Recorded:** The Complex, Los Angeles: January–September 1989 / Vintage Recorders, Phoenix: January–September 1989 / **Technical Team:** Producers: Fleetwood Mac, Greg Ladanyi / Sound Engineer: Greg Ladanyi

The number of outtakes written by Rick Vito for *Behind the Mask* is a measure of the guitarist's commitment and desire to leave his mark on Fleetwood Mac. However,

"Last Chance to Rock" did not make much of an impression on his partners, since this retro rock'n'roll number, far too scholastic and steeped in Chuck Berry's style, was shelved after a single take and never exploited for official release. It was also included in the bootleg *The Other Side of the Mask*.

THE GAME OF LOVE
Billy Burnette / 4:09

Musicians: Billy Burnette: vocals, guitar / Rick Vito: guitar / Christine McVie: backing vocals, keyboards / John McVie: bass / Mick Fleetwood: drums / Stevie Nicks: backing vocals / **Recorded:** The Complex, Los Angeles: January–September 1989 / Vintage Recorders, Phoenix: January–September 1989 / **Technical Team:** Producers: Fleetwood Mac, Greg Ladanyi / Sound Engineer: Greg Ladanyi

The sound of "The Game of Love," recorded in a single take during the *Behind the Mask* sessions, does the track no favors, as it drowns in sonic mush. But the song's energy, dynamism, and catchy melodic phrase, which ends with a charming change of key, make a strong case for it. This song obviously deserved a better fate than ending up on the bootleg *The Other Side of the Mask*.

LIZARD PEOPLE
Mick Fleetwood, Peter Bardens / 4:48

Musicians: Mick Fleetwood: spoken words, drums, percussion / Christine McVie: backing vocals, keyboards / Billy Burnette: backing vocals, guitar / Rick Vito: backing vocals, guitar / John McVie: bass / Stevie Nicks: backing vocals / **Recorded:** The Complex, Los Angeles: January–September 1989 / Vintage Recorders, Phoenix: January–September 1989 / **Technical Team:** Producers: Mick Fleetwood, Dennis Mays / **Single:** Side A: In the Back of My Mind / Side B: Lizard People / **UK Release Date:** August 13, 1990 / **Reference:** Warner Bros. Records (45 rpm ref.: W9739) / Best UK Chart Ranking: 58

Genesis and Lyrics
Like Lindsey Buckingham, Mick Fleetwood is fond of experimentation. He was behind the inclusion of the poem "Thoughts on a Grey Day" on *Bare Trees* (1972). He also came up with the idea for the fanfare on *Tusk* (1979), as well as the spoken words he himself provides on "These Strange Times" (1995) and "Lizard People" (1989). "Lizard People" was developed by Mick himself with the help of Peter Bardens, one of the key figures of his musical youth, for whom Mick worked as drummer with the

Cheynes, Peter B's Looners, and Shotgun Express in the early 1960s. The keyboardist and drummer put on paper a surreal story about reptilians, lizard-men who had been spotted in a swamp and hunted down by rednecks armed to the teeth. But the creatures elude their gaze as they float through the air.

Production

Mick's delivery of this text is slow and sententious, almost robotic. His voice is occasionally sped up or slowed down by Dennis Mays, the sound engineer (promoted to producer in Greg Ladanyi's absence), who accompanies him in the fine-tuning of what started out as a joke before becoming a piece of music solid enough to be released. This vocal sleight-of-hand simulates the unstable mutation of the reptilian, which intermittently reverts to its original form and voice before changing to humanoid form. To support the unusual, surreal dimension of the discourse, Mick lays down a slow, hypnotic drum roll, accompanied by chimes. Christine, for her part, tirelessly repeats the same strange melodic motif on her keyboard. There is something of the primitive impulse that presided over the production of the Rolling Stones' "Sympathy for the Devil" behind the construction of this penetrating piece, which was chosen as Side B of the single "In the Back of My Mind."

WALK ANOTHER MILE

Rick Vito / 3:38

Musicians: Rick Vito: vocals, guitar / Billy Burnette: backing vocals, guitar / Christine McVie: backing vocals, keyboards / John McVie: bass / Mick Fleetwood: drums / Stevie Nicks: backing vocals / **Recorded:** The Complex, Los Angeles: January–September 1989 / Vintage Recorders, Phoenix: January–September 1989 / **Technical Team:** Producers: Fleetwood Mac, Greg Ladanyi / Sound Engineer: Greg Ladanyi

"Walk Another Mile" was tested as a group with Fleetwood Mac, but it was intended for Rick Vito's solo album, *King of Hearts*. A good, demonstrative blues-rock song, in which fellow musician Billy Burnette comes into his own, thanks to his rock'n'roll rhythmic foundation.

GOT NO HOME

Rick Vito / 3:15

Musicians: Rick Vito: vocals, guitar / Billy Burnette: backing vocals, guitar / Christine McVie: backing vocals, keyboards / John McVie: bass / Mick Fleetwood: drums / Stevie Nicks: backing vocals / **Recorded:** The Complex, Los Angeles: 1988 / **Technical Team:** Producers: Fleetwood Mac, Greg Ladanyi / Sound Engineer: Greg Ladanyi

Of the songs left off the track list, "Got No Home" is the one with the most obvious potential. It is built on a dynamic riff by Billy Burnette that is backed by John McVie's muscular bass line. As for Rick Vito, he has a field day with his copious, epic solos. This song, however, remains in the demo stage, as evidenced by the unfinished choruses, where the backing vocals are still too muddled to be fully effective. It was never officially released but appeared on the *The Other Side of the Mask* bootleg, which features a number of demos and alternative takes.

INTUITION

Rick Vito / 4:14

Musicians: Rick Vito: vocals, guitar / Billy Burnette: backing vocals, guitar / Christine McVie: backing vocals, keyboards / John McVie: bass / Mick Fleetwood: drums / Stevie Nicks: backing vocals / **Recorded:** The Complex, Los Angeles: January–September 1989 / Vintage Recorders, Phoenix: January–September 1989 / **Technical Team:** Producers: Fleetwood Mac, Greg Ladanyi / Sound Engineer: Greg Ladanyi

A sugary FM ballad, "Intuition" is best remembered for its floating choruses, with offbeat second-voice departures, but also suffers from the omnipresence of Rick Vito's overly demonstrative electric guitar, drowned in reverb. Although recorded with Fleetwood Mac (this version appears on the bootleg *The Other Side of the Mask*), it was first and foremost a solo composition by Rick Vito for his 1992 album *King of Hearts*.

VICTIM OF LOVE

Billy Burnette / 3:07

Musicians: Billy Burnette: vocals, guitar / Rick Vito: guitar / Christine McVie: backing vocals, keyboards / John McVie: bass / Mick Fleetwood: drums / Stevie Nicks: backing vocals / **Recorded:** The Complex, Los Angeles: January–September 1989 / Vintage Recorders, Phoenix: January–September 1989 / **Technical Team:** Producers: Fleetwood Mac, Greg Ladanyi / Sound Engineer: Greg Ladanyi

With a country-rock base that leaves no doubt as to the song's authorship (Billy Burnette), "Victim of Love" develops into a track with hidden dimensions, more complex than it first appears. Christine McVie includes an unexpected bridge over a descending scale on the keyboards, adding richness to a track that remained on the shelf. It was brought to the attention of fans only on the bootleg *The Other Side of the Mask*.

25 YEARS—THE CHAIN

Release Dates

United Kingdom: November 24, 1992
Reference: Warner Bros. Records—9362-45129-2
Best UK Chart Ranking: 9
United States: November 24, 1992
Reference: Warner Bros. Records—9 45129-2
Best US Chart Ranking: Did Not Chart

Disc 1

Paper Doll (New Song)
Love Shines (New Song)
Stand Back (Live) (Unreleased)
Crystal
Isn't It Midnight (Edited Alternate Version)
Big Love
Everywhere
Affairs of the Heart
Heart of Stone (New Song)
Sara
That's All for Everyone
Over My Head
Little Lies
Eyes of the World
Oh Diane
In the Back of My Mind
Make Me a Mask (New Song)

Disc 2

Save Me
Goodbye Angel
Silver Springs
What Makes You Think You're the One
Think About Me
Gypsy (Alternate Unreleased Version)
You Make Loving Fun
Second Hand News (Alternate Mix)
Love in Store (Alternate Mix)
The Chain (Alternate Mix)
Teen Beat
Dreams (Alternate Mix)
Only Over You
I'm So Afraid (Edited)
Love Is Dangerous
Gold Dust Woman (Alternate Mix)
Not That Funny (Live) (Unreleased)

Disc 3

Warm Ways
Say You Love Me

Don't Stop
Rhiannon
Walk a Thin Line
Storms
Go Your Own Way
Sisters of the Moon
Monday Morning
Landslide
Hypnotized
Lay It All Down (Unreleased Alternate Version)
Angel (Alternate Mix)
Beautiful Child (Alternate Mix)
Brown Eyes
Save Me a Place
Tusk
Never Going Back Again
Songbird

Disc 4

I Believe My Time Ain't Long
Need Your Love So Bad
Rattlesnake Shake
Oh Well, Part 1 (Original Mono Version—Rechanneled for Stereo)
Stop Messin' Around
Green Manalishi
Albatross
Man of the World
Love That Burns
Black Magic Woman
Watch Out
String-a-Long (Unreleased)
Station Man
Did You Ever Love Me
Sentimental Lady
Come a Little Bit Closer
Heroes Are Hard to Find
Trinity (Unreleased song from 1971)
Why

FOR MAC-ADDICTS

25 Years—The Chain immortalizes one of the emblematic instruments in John McVie's set: his Alembic bass, with a graphite neck designed by Jeff Gould (one of the first to benefit from it) and a sumptuous, straight-veined ebony body.

25 Years—The Chain is a four-disc sweep through a quarter-century of the band's history, tracing the journey from the British blues band (shown here in 1969) to purveyors of pop.

An Imbalanced Retrospective

Over the years, Fleetwood Mac's discography has been enriched by a number of compilations, some dispensable, some not. Reaching the quarter-century mark in 1992, the weather-beaten band, still standing despite the uninterrupted waltz of departures, celebrated this unexpected longevity with the release of a compilation. Warner designed a definitive object for the occasion: a supposedly complete panorama of the band's twenty-five years of existence, spread over four discs.

However, there is a glaring imbalance between the treatment of the Lindsey Buckingham period (*Fleetwood Mac*, *Rumours*, *Tusk*, *Mirage*), which takes up almost three discs, and the others, which are left with only crumbs—particularly those from the 1967–1974 phase, which covers the seminal contributions of Peter Green, Jeremy Spencer, Danny Kirwan, and Bob Welch. Despite the small amount of material on this earlier phase, Warner managed to include "String-a-Long," a solo track from Jeremy Spencer's eponymous album (1970). Apart from this misdeal, the offering does live up to the hype, with numerous surprises, from the full-length version of "Gypsy" (5:21) to the alternative version of "Isn't It Midnight," not forgetting "Lay It All Down" by Danny Kirwan, who is just as under-represented as Bob Welch. The compilation also includes five previously unreleased tracks, which in themselves justify the existence of *25 Years—The Chain*: four recent songs—"Paper Doll," "Love Shines," "Heart of Stone," and "Make Me a Mask"—recorded especially for the occasion.

The seventy-two tracks are housed in a neat box, stamped with gold lettering around a photo of John McVie's arm—recognizable by his penguin tattoo—ready to turn up the knob on his Alembic bass and do battle. Each member of the group has added a handwritten dedication to the booklet. Mick Fleetwood, for example, has crudely drawn a man behind a set of drums, accompanied by this quote from William Shakespeare: "If music be the food of love, then play on." Christine McVie has this to say: "There was always a piano in my house when I was growing up, and my father wanted me to become a concert pianist. […] Unfortunately for him, I discovered Fats Domino." Lindsey also takes part in the introspective exercise, writing: "Thanks for the memories—wouldn't have missed it for the world." Stevie Nicks, for her part, takes pride in her contribution: "The reason that 'Dreams' is so special to me is that it is the only number one single Fleetwood Mac has ever had. It's also the only one that I hang on my wall in Phoenix. I am very proud of that." John's thoughts turn more to the other members and to another song, the album's namesake, "The Chain": "I can still hear you saying, you would never break the chain!"

PAPER DOLL
Stevie Nicks, Rick Vito, John Herron / 3:56

Single: Side A: Paper Doll / Side B: The Chain / **US Release Date:** December 1992, Warner Bros. Records (ref. 7-18661) / Best US Chart Ranking: Did Not Chart / **Musicians:** Stevie Nicks: vocals / Billy Burnette: guitar, backing vocals / Rick Vito: guitar, backing vocals / Lindsey Buckingham: guitar, backing vocals / Christine McVie: keyboards / John McVie: bass / Mick Fleetwood: drums, percussion / **Recorded:** 1992 (?) / **Technical Team:** Producer: Richard Dashut

It had been some time since John Herron had been around Fleetwood Mac when he had the opportunity to put his name to one of the band's songs, "Paper Doll." This former furtive member of the Electric Prunes (1969) was a loyal collaborator with Rick Vito, whom he accompanies on keyboards on his solo opuses. He also co-wrote "It Ain't Over" with Billy Burnette on his 1985 album, *Try Me*. It was during the recording of this album that he met Christine McVie, who came to provide some backing vocals.

In 1988, Stevie Nicks wrote the melody and lyrics for "Paper Doll," while Rick Vito and John Herron worked out the chord progression for the track, which was to feature on their 1988 *Greatest Hits* compilation. The song was rejected by Mick Fleetwood, who was not entirely happy with the result, and was eventually replaced by another Nicks composition, "No Questions Asked." In 1992, "Paper Doll" came out of the box when the track list for *25 Years—The Chain* was put together and was rerecorded under the direction of Richard Dashut.

The song ventures into reggae territory, an unprecedented incursion for this pop rock band. Amid syncopated guitars and impressive chorus vocal lines executed in canon, the bass reigns with authority, John McVie proving particularly at ease in this register—devising a bouncy, rumbling line. Mick Fleetwood also takes pleasure in playing this reggae track, which lends itself to the use of multiple percussion instruments: timbales, congas, tambourine, güira. Stevie Nicks, for her part, takes hold of the text and, as she is so adept at doing, pours out her heart on a love story of the past and present. As for Lindsey, although no longer a member of the band, he contributes guitar and vocals, as well as production with Dashut.

Despite—or because of—its originality, this track, released as a single a month after the compilation (with "The Chain" on Side B), failed to make the singles chart. The group had to make do with its good performance in Canada, where it reached number nine on the singles chart in February 1993.

"Paper Doll" also featured in *The Very Best of Fleetwood Mac*, the band's nineteenth compilation, released in 2002 and 2009, as well as in all editions of *50 Years—Don't Stop*, the compilation released on November 16, 2018.

LOVE SHINES
Christine McVie, Eddy Quintela / 4:48

Single: Side A: Love Shines / Side B: The Chain (Previously Unreleased Alternative Mix) / **UK Release Date:** January 25, 1993, Warner Bros. Records (ref. W 0145) / Best UK Chart Ranking: Did Not Chart / **Musicians:** Christine McVie: vocals, keyboards / Billy Burnette: vocals, guitar, dobro, backing vocals / John McVie: bass / Mick Fleetwood: drums, percussion / **Recorded:** 1992 (?) / **Technical Team:** Producer: Patrick Leonard

In 1992, Fleetwood Mac in quartet configuration, without two of its members—Stevie Nicks and Rick Vito—tackled the recording of "Love Shines," an effective, solid pop-rock track written by Christine McVie. This affectionate declaration punctuated by catchy refrains, which could just as easily be addressed to a lover as to one of her bandmates, does not really suffer from the absence of lead guitarist Rick Vito. In fact, Billy Burnette, who plays dobro throughout, adds an electric guitar track, giving him the opportunity to perform a solo that compares favorably with his former partner. Chosen for release in Europe, the song struggled in the charts. It failed to chart in the UK and, in the space of four months, barely reached number fifty-one in Germany.

HEART OF STONE
Christine McVie, Eddy Quintela / 4:39

Musicians: Christine McVie: vocals, keyboards / Billy Burnette: guitar, backing vocals / John McVie: bass / Mick Fleetwood: drums / **Recorded:** 1992 (?) / **Technical Team:** Producer: Patrick Leonard

In the absence of Rick Vito and Stevie Nicks, Christine McVie takes the composition of "Heart of Stone" in her stride. In the introduction, the keyboardist chooses to return to the organ sounds that made her reputation before she switched to synthesizers in the 1980s. This slightly retro introduction quickly fades as the hard-hitting choruses assert themselves, as much in their musicality as in their lyrics. "So now you're saying you've been wrong / And you want to come back home." The rest of the song suggests that she's settling scores with one of her musical partners rather than a former lover: "And now you want to change your song." It could be that, through these allusions, Christine is drawing a portrait of Lindsey, back again as a guest on "Behind the Mask" (1990), "Paper Doll," and "Make a Mask" (1992). "Heart of Stone" was released only on this compilation.

The compilation gives pride of place to the luxurious years of the Rumours Five (here in 1975) and the songs of Lindsey Buckingham, presenting two previously unreleased relics: "Teen Beat" and "Make Me a Mask."

MAKE ME A MASK
Lindsey Buckingham / 4:02

Musicians: Lindsey Buckingham: vocals, synthesizer, mandolin, bass, guitar, percussion, backing vocals / **Recorded:** 1992(?) / **Technical Team:** Producer: Lindsey Buckingham

Once again, Fleetwood Mac benefits from the hyper-productive activity of Lindsey Buckingham. Even though he had not been a member of the band for several years, the composer, in the midst of producing his third solo opus, *Out of the Cradle*, donated "Make Me a Mask" to the Mac for the compilation. "Stevie wanted me to help with something of hers [on the box set *25 Years—The Chain*], so I spent some nights with her going through material and we came up with something. [...] I had recorded 'Make Me a Mask' during the sessions for *Cradle* [but] it really didn't fit on the rest of my album, so I gave it to [Fleetwood Mac]."

Lindsey parted with a real treasure here. Slow, bewitching, melancholy, and mystical, "Make Me a Mask" is inspired by traditional Japanese music, and even by the mask imagery of Noh, Kabuki, and kyōgen theaters, as evidenced by the title.

TEEN BEAT
Lindsey Buckingham, Richard Dashut / 2:43

Musicians: Lindsey Buckingham: vocals, guitar / John McVie: bass / Mick Fleetwood: drums / **Recorded:** Le Château, Hérouville (France): May–July 1981 / **Technical Team:** Producers: Fleetwood Mac, Ken Caillat, Richard Dashut / Sound Engineers: Ken Caillat, Richard Dashut / Assistant Sound Engineers: David Bianco, Carla Frederick

Recorded during the *Mirage* sessions in 1982, "Teen Beat" had never been unveiled to the public at the time of the release of *25 Years—The Chain*. It would only be presented in its original context in 2016, with the release of the deluxe edition of *Mirage*, in a longer version of around four minutes (compared to 2:43 on *25 Years—The Chain*). Recorded as a trio (Lindsey, John, and Mick), "Teen Beat" aspires to nothing more than enabling the musicians to let off steam on some jubilant rock'n'roll. The absence of lyrics (Lindsey screams and vocalizes) testifies to its embryonic state as just a jam session.

ALBUM

TIME

Talkin' to My Heart . Hollywood (Some Other Kind of Town) . Blow by Blow .
Winds of Change . I Do . Nothing Without You . Dreamin' the Dream .
Sooner or Later . I Wonder Why . Nights in Estoril . I Got It In for You .
All Over Again . These Strange Times

RELEASE DATES
United Kingdom: October 10, 1995
Reference: Warner Bros. Records—9362-45920-2
Best UK Chart Ranking: 47
United States: October 10, 1995
Reference: Warner Bros. Records—9 45920-2
Best US Chart Ranking: Did Not Chart

FOR MAC ADDICTS

The band did not take to the road to promote *Time* after its release, apart from a one-off performance on December 31, 1995. Only "Blow by Blow" and "Dreamin' the Dream" were played live in 1994.

The Five had reunited again for Bill Clinton's inaugural gala on January 20, 1993, but hopes of a band reunion were short-lived.

CHRONICLE OF A PREDICTED FIASCO

In early 1991, barely a month after the end of the Behind the Mask tour, Stevie Nicks and Rick Vito decided to leave Fleetwood Mac. This double departure was another blow for the band, because, while the guitarist had not had time to leave a significant mark on the group, the singer was its face and embodiment.

The Quest for a New Configuration

Mick Fleetwood could not just sit back and do nothing. While waiting to find a solution for Fleetwood Mac, he returned to his parallel band project, the Zoo. As part of this activity, he recruited a twenty-three-year-old singer, Bekka Bramlett, daughter of the Delaney & Bonnie duo. Though young in age, she combined charisma and vocal skills. Two years later, in 1993, when Fleetwood Mac reactivated, he invited her to join the band. Bekka already knew Billy Burnette and, incidentally, had grown up listening to Fleetwood Mac. The young woman, then aged twenty-six, did not hesitate for a second: 'Yes' was the only word that came out of my mouth," she recalls. Yet she was fully aware of the difficulty of the task ahead: replacing Stevie Nicks. "He already explained it before he offered it to me. And I knew that it was temporary. I was like, 'I'm going to have a

ball!' I love working with Mick. He's the best friggin' drummer I ever, ever, ever, ever worked with. [...] But when you're standing in front of the heat of Mick Fleetwood and then to your right is the power of John McVie. [...] You can go anywhere. They are definitely the net underneath your tight wire. You can literally fly and jump and twist and turn and flip and land like Simone Biles. You can do it. And then there's Billy Burnette, who is like family."

Mick Fleetwood also began looking for a guitarist to replace Rick Vito. Billy Burnette was still on board, but the experience of *Behind the Mask* had shown that two guitarists were not enough to fill Lindsey Buckingham's absence. Mick, unable to find such a rare pearl despite numerous auditions, finally asked one of his best friends, Traffic guitarist Dave Mason, if he would be interested. For the drummer, who imagined Mason was far too busy with his own activities, this was almost a joke. But Dave took the proposition very seriously and replied that he was extremely interested in the job. The deal was struck without even consulting the other members of the group. Unfortunately, the sum of individualities—however talented—does not necessarily make for a good team. Fleetwood Mac would learn this the hard way during the *Time* adventure.

Recording was hampered by the long Another Link in the Chain tour (July 4–December 31, 1994, and April 7–September 1, 1995), designed to showcase the new lineup in public. The tour was spread over more than a year, in a number of legs.

A Casting Error

The musicians began recording sessions at Ocean Way Recording, Hollywood, in September 1993, with the firm intention of not extending them beyond January 1994. This was not to be, however, as the sessions got off to a slow start and lasted well beyond January. Apart from the fact that they were interrupted several times by the interminable Another Link in The Chain world tour, during which the new Mac played no fewer than 110 concerts on several continents, the integration of the two new recruits proved to be much more complicated than expected.

In the case of Bekka Bramlett, this quickly became a problem. Indeed, fans and critics alike could not help comparing her to Stevie Nicks: "There is no replacing Stevie Nicks. Everybody knows that," Bekka conceded in an interview with *Rolling Stone* in 2023, before adding that she had deliberately chosen not to perform Stevie's signature songs: "That would have been weird. [...] I was like, 'I'm not doing "Rhiannon." I'm not doing "Dreams."' I fuckin' did 'Landslide' until I replaced it with 'Imagine.' I didn't want to fight too hard, man, but I definitely didn't want to do 'Rhiannon' and 'Dreams.'" It was a decision Christine McVie fully endorsed at the time. Shortly before the start of the tour, scheduled for July 4, 1994, she and Bekka sat down together over a few glasses of wine and Christine confided: "I do think it is quite honorable to not sing these particular songs of Stevie's." She also took the opportunity to give Bekka her blessing and to encourage her to "Give it some soul, girl. Give it" to this new stage version of Fleetwood Mac.

The integration of Dave Mason also posed a problem. Bekka Bramlett could not stand him. Nor could Christine, who, without questioning his talent, was simply not convinced by his arrival in the band. Later, she would confess about this new incarnation of Fleetwood Mac: "I find it a bizarre combination of people, but Mick chose Dave Mason...I don't think he is a bad guitar player, but I just don't know how he fits in with Fleetwood Mac...Great guitar player [though] he is, he would not have been my first choice. [...] Lindsey Buckingham, I think he was the most superlative guitar player this band will ever have. A true shining light. After Lindsey, everybody else seems a little pallid. I'm not talking talent, just chemistry for Fleetwood Mac."

The tour (July 4, 1994–December 31, 1995), which Christine decided not to take part in, exacerbated all these tensions. "Touring was never my favorite thing to do," the musician explained. "I get insomnia on the road. I can't sleep in strange beds night after night. Did not want to take sleeping pills, that is the beginning of the end. I would lie awake reading all night. This made me irritable. I had done it enough. Then I would drink a bottle of wine before bed... wake up with a hangover. It was a no win situation."

Mick Fleetwood and John McVie were never able to bring cohesion to this makeshift lineup. The former would later take full responsibility for this casting error and, by extension, for the disastrous commercial and artistic failure of *Time*: "I refused to give up [...]. In truth, my decision making was off; this is the one time I should not have soldiered on." The drummer readily admits to having felt his wings grow when the band reunited for Bill Clinton's inaugural ball in 1993: "Getting us all back on stage didn't spark a reunion as many, myself included, had thought it would, but it was inspiring enough for me to want to make new music."[2]

Everyone for Themselves

Recording, which had got off to a gentle start before leaving for the July 1994 tour, accelerated on their return. The

highly efficient band finished no fewer than twelve songs in the space of two weeks at the end of 1994, followed by seven more in the first few months of 1995. By the time they hit the road again on April 7, Fleetwood Mac had recorded nineteen uneven tracks, of which only twelve made it onto the final track list. This selection gave the album an atmosphere that oscillated between rock, country, and pop. A thirteenth song, "These Strange Times," was added at the last minute at the insistence of Mick Fleetwood, who composed it as a tribute to Peter Green. As if the drummer felt the need to turn to the "founding father" of a band that had lost its bearings. With the exception of Bramlett, the other members showed no interest in this composition, in which they refused to participate; the drummer was forced to call on an outside contributor, John Jones, for production, bass, guitars, and keyboards. This speaks volumes about the musicians' lack of involvement.

The songs, like the album credits, tell the story of this disjointed album. Everyone wrote, produced, or even performed tracks with the people of their choice: multi-instrumentalist John Jones, guitarist Michael Thompson, keyboardist Steve Thoma, and songwriters Franke Previte, Mark Holden, Deborah Allen, and Rafe Van Hoy.

Above all, the absence of Christine McVie on Dave Mason's tracks—and vice versa—says a great deal about the incompatibility of moods between the two. The singer preferred to call on studio musician Michael Thompson. This was a real affront to a disillusioned Dave Mason, who said: "I never did work on any of her stuff. She had somebody else play with her for that..." As Lindsey Buckingham had done before her on *Tango in the Night*, Christine on this album did much of the work without really putting her heart into it.

Mick Fleetwood, aware that things were not gelling and that the boat was taking on water on all sides, called on Billy Burnette, who returned during the recording. But Burnette was only involved in three compositions: "Talkin' to My Heart," "Dreamin' the Dream," and "I Got It in for You."

Richard Dashut, the magician-producer of *Rumours*, who had been called in by Mick to give the album some structure, was distraught by the recording methods used for this opus: Not only was everything composed on site, without a demo, but it was also done at a speed that disconcerted him: "We recorded it at Ocean Way," recalls Bekka Bramlett. "That was a super-familiar place for me. I'd been recording for so long. I've been at this since I was 15 [...]. I'd never met [producer] Richard Dashut, but it took me about two songs to recognize that he was the one that recorded *Rumours*. He was like, 'God, you're really quick.

During her brief stint with Fleetwood Mac (1993–1995), the talented Bekka Bramlett had to contend with critics who saw her only as a Stevie Nicks understudy.

Do you know how long it took to record *Rumours*? Four years!' He probably shouldn't have told me that. I was like, 'What? Oh no. Am I doing this too fast? Am I not caring enough?'"

Fleetwood Mac set off on tour again without taking the time to fine-tune the details: "Our new group undertook a world tour in support of *Time* over five months in 1994 and another five months in 1995, playing on bills with Crosby, Stills and Nash, REO Speedwagon, and Pat Benatar," recalls Mick Fleetwood. "We took the opportunity to revisit Fleetwood Mac's 1960s catalogue and in Tokyo we even got the chance to have Jeremy Spencer join us on stage for a few songs. We toured all over the world and it was hard, because when we weren't a support band, or playing mini-festivals, we headlined at small venues. We never should have done any of it. It was naive of me to do as I'd always done, to play on and immediately record an album and go back on the road [...]."[2]

An Inevitable Fiasco

When the *Time* album hit record stores in October 1995, the band was still on the road. In Christine's absence, and due to the growing disagreement between Bekka Bramlett and Dave Mason, Mick Fleetwood and John McVie formed the only link with the past.

Time, hampered by a lack of real promotion and a disappointing stage version, was harshly criticized. Its performance was catastrophic. In the United Kingdom, the album only reached number forty-seven in the album sales charts. In the United States, it was a train wreck: *Time* did not even make the charts.

The already fragile unity of the band cracked like the frail eggshell chosen to illustrate the album cover, from which emerges the head of a baby penguin—Mick Fleetwood's idea, brought to life by photographers Dale McRaven and Bonnie Nelson. A symbol of renewal, this baby penguin, which needs time (hence the album title) to grow up, was not to be given any time at all. The album's commercial failure sealed the fate of Dave Mason and Bekka Bramlett, while Billy Burnette decided to resume his solo activities. Behind the scenes, the *Rumours* lineup prepared their comeback, which materialized with *The Dance* in 1997, an album for which Christine McVie briefly came out of retirement.

BEKKA BRAMLETT, A BORN SINGER

Thanks to her parents, Delaney and Bonnie Bramlett, who formed the duo Delaney & Bonnie from 1967 to 1972, Rebekka Ruth Lazone Bramlett, known as Bekka Bramlett (born April 19, 1968), grew up alongside such stars as John Lennon, George Harrison, Gregg and Duane Allman, and Eric Clapton. Naturally, Bramlett showed an early interest in music, particularly vocals. Her first experience of backing vocals came at just four years of age, on her father's solo album *Mobius Strip*, released in 1973. Her contribution to the song "California Rain," although anecdotal, largely determined Bekka's destiny, and she began to dream of becoming a singer. When her parents divorced, they entrusted her to her maternal grandmother, who took her to church every Sunday. This change of environment ensured the young girl's stability while her parents struggled to find solo success and face up to serious addiction problems. But this estrangement did not impede her artistic dreams: "I briefly thought I'd be a lawyer, but I thought I'd be a singing lawyer," she says. "Then I wanted to be a jockey since I love horses, but I thought I'd be a singing jockey. Music is just what I'm good at."

From Backing Vocalist to Singer

She began her career as a backing vocalist for Belinda Carlisle, on the Good Heavens tour in 1988, then on the *Runaway Horses* album the following year. Her subsequent experiences revolved around the glam metal sphere, with contributions to projects by Richie Sambora (Bon Jovi's guitarist), Warrant, and Faster Pussycat. In 1992, she was asked by Mick Fleetwood to contribute to his band Zoo's album *Shakin' the Cage*. After collaborating with Joe Cocker in 1994, she finally received a call from Mick Fleetwood, who asked her to replace Stevie Nicks: "Young Bekka. It has come time where one of our family members is going to be away for a moment to embrace her health and well-being. You are the first of my choice to keep this beautiful band that we have nurtured for decades alive. If you are interested. There is no pressure. But would you be able to."[144] Bekka accepted without hesitation, and also without suspecting the artistic difficulties the band was about to go through.

In the summer of 1994, the Mac went on tour without the three most creative members of its history: Lindsey Buckingham, of course, Stevie Nicks, but also Christine McVie, who chose not to go on the road. "We ended up with a bunch of talented people playing good music," explains Mick Fleetwood, "but they should not have been touring as Fleetwood Mac. There were too many essential pieces missing from the machine this time. We were a totally different band, with only the original drummer and bass player, and our original name."[2]

Ejected when Stevie Nicks decided to return to the road for a lucrative tour with the *Rumours* lineup, Bekka Bramlett founded the duo Bekka & Billy, with Billy Burnette, who released a self-titled album in 1996. She then returned to her solo career. She released the albums *What's in It for Me* in 2002, and *I've Got News for You* in 2009. Over the years, she has added many prestigious names to her roster, including Bad Company, Jonny Lang, Billy Joel, Buddy Guy, Faith Hill, Kenny Rogers, 3 Doors Down, Bob Seger, John Oates, LeAnn Rimes, Robert Plant, and Lori McKenna.

Not a Stevie Part II

Concerning her short-lived stint with Fleetwood Mac, Bekka has never expressed any resentment: "I knew my job was to get Stevie back," she explained in an interview with *Rolling Stone* in 2023. "I wasn't a moron. I also knew this was a dangerous job when I took it. I knew I was facing tomatoes. But I didn't want to wear a top hat. I didn't want to twirl around. I wanted to be me. I even dyed my hair brown just so people in the cheap seats would know that Stevie wasn't going to be here."[144] Again to avoid comparison with Stevie, Bekka went so far as to refuse to sing the so-called signature songs, such as "Rhiannon" and "Dreams," on stage. The only thing the singer regrets about this experience is the harsh way in which she learned of her ousting. "That was heartbreaking. Mick fired me on a fax. [...] On my fax, he said, 'You wish you were in REO Speedwagon, so I'm going to go ahead and fire you now.' And then, of course, it was on CNN within 10 days. 'Stevie Nicks is back with Fleetwood Mac!'"[144] To her great credit, Bekka put aside this unkind treatment and ended up with nothing but positive memories of her time with one of the greatest bands of all time, saying, "It's always going to be an honor."

DAVE MASON,
THE MISUNDERSTOOD GENIUS

When he joined Fleetwood Mac in 1994, David Thomas Mason (born in Worcester on May 10, 1946) was the first Englishman to do so since 1972 and the Dave Walker–Bob Weston tandem. But it had been a long time since he left his homeland and adopted a Californian lifestyle.

In the Shadow of Masterpieces

His musical career began in England: As a teenager, he played in ambitious local bands such as the Jaguars and the Hellions, before becoming a roadie for the Spencer Davis Group. Then, in 1967, alongside guitarist Steve Winwood, he helped found the band that would make his name: Traffic. Around the time of the release of his first album, *Mr. Fantasy* (1967), he became friends with Jimi Hendrix, whose career was taking off in England. Hendrix invited him to record an electric version of Bob Dylan's hit, "All Along the Watchtower," at London's Olympic Studios. Dave Mason's contribution to twelve-string acoustic guitar became famous a year later on Hendrix's monumental *Electric Ladyland* album. Although uncredited, he also took part in the Rolling Stones' *Beggars Banquet* in 1968. After recording four albums with Traffic, Mason released his first solo album in 1970, *Alone Together*, featuring contributions from Leon Russell on keyboards, and Jim Keltner and Jim Gordon on drums, among others. He went on to contribute to other rock masterpieces in the new decade, including George Harrison's *All Things Must Pass*, *On Tour with Eric Clapton*, Delaney & Bonnie's *Motel Shot*, and Paul McCartney's *Venus and Mars* by Wings. In the late 1970s, he added a number of prestigious names to his list of collaborations, including David Crosby, Cass Elliot, Graham Nash, Joe Walsh, Stephen Stills, and Ron Wood. In the meantime, he had already delivered no fewer than eight albums under his own name, including *Dave Mason* in 1974, *Let It Flow* in 1977 (and its best-known single, "We Just Disagree"), and *Mariposa de Oro* in 1978. After his moderately successful album *Old Crest on a New Wave* in 1980, he left the Columbia label and struggled to attract the interest of another major label. He did, however, manage to release two albums in 1987: *Some Assembly Required* on Chumley Records and *Two Hearts* on MCA.

Too Heavy a Burden

Mick Fleetwood held the musician in high esteem. So he asked him to join Fleetwood Mac in the early 1990s. Lindsey Buckingham was a hard act to follow and, despite his virtuosity, Dave Mason found this an onerous responsibility. Furthermore, his disagreement with Bekka Bramlett, who was supposed to help people not think about Stevie Nicks, was notorious: "Oh God! I just couldn't stand him," she said, even though Dave Mason had worked with her parents, Delaney and Bonnie. "We couldn't get along at all." Like Bekka, he only recorded one album with Fleetwood Mac: *Time* in 1995, the band's biggest commercial flop. Much to Mason's dismay: "I could understand, from some people's point of view," he explains, "the *Rumours* album obviously sold so many copies. It was so huge that that sort of overshadowed everything else. We did the album, and Warner Bros. didn't really bother with it, frankly. So, it sort of just came out and died a death. And that was that. But we spent six or eight months making that record, on and off. It wasn't just slapped together. The problem was that [long-time Fleetwood Mac contributor] Christine [McVie] was on the album, but she wouldn't go on the road. That probably would have lent more credence to it. By the time we got on the road, all you had was [band founders] Mick [Fleetwood] and John McVie. So, it got to be classified as a Fleetwood Mac cover band."

Despite this disappointing experience, Dave Mason went on to pursue his solo career, releasing the albums *26 Letters—12 Notes* in 2008 and *Future's Past* in 2014. He was even inducted into the Rock and Roll Hall of Fame in 2004 as a founding member of Traffic.

Identified by the public as one of the pillars of the band Traffic, Dave Mason was considered by professionals to be a force to be reckoned with on the session circuit.

TALKIN' TO MY HEART

Billy Burnette, Deborah Allen, Rafe Van Hoy / 4:45

Musicians: Bekka Bramlett: vocals / Billy Burnette: guitar, vocals / Dave Mason: guitar, backing vocals / Christine McVie: keyboards, backing vocals / John McVie: bass / Mick Fleetwood: drums / **Recorded:** Ocean Way Recording, Hollywood / Sunset Sound Recorders, Hollywood: September 1993–May 1995 / **Technical Team:** Producers: Fleetwood Mac, Richard Dashut / Sound Engineer: Ken Allardyce / Assistant Sound Engineers: Charlie Brocco, Alan Sanderson, Allen Sides, David Eike, Richard Huredia, Tom Nellen, Dave Shiffman

Genesis and Lyrics

"Talkin' to My Heart" is the result of a collaboration between Billy Burnette and songwriter Rafe Van Hoy and country singer Deborah Allen. The pair had already written three songs for Billy Burnette's 1993 album *Coming Home*, an experience that led them to renew their partnership for the opening track of *Time*. This song explores the vulnerability we feel in the face of love. The lyrics emphasize the importance of not cheating and of being authentic. But the narrator, no doubt battle-hardened by some unfortunate experiences, calls for caution in the face of grand declarations of intent, and urges us not to give in to them too quickly.

Production

A song in typical pop rock format, "Talkin' to My Heart" relies essentially on the harmonious voices of Billy Burnette and Bekka Bramlett, which are perfectly compatible. Despite a predictable structure and fairly conventional arrangements, the guitars of Dave Mason and Billy Burnette blend ideally, between powerful chords and crystalline arpeggios. A few biting notes are deftly used to make the transition between the chorus and the reprise of the verses, while the lap steel guitar discreetly invites itself into the quieter part of the track. As for the rhythm section, it does not really sparkle, but provides an energetic groove. Melodically, it works, without showing any great originality.

In "Hollywood," Christine McVie expressed her weariness of touring, highlighting the sacrifices and challenges involved in a nomadic lifestyle.

HOLLYWOOD (SOME OTHER KIND OF TOWN)

Christine McVie, Eddy Quintela / 5:45

Musicians: Christine McVie: vocals, keyboards, backing vocals / Michael Thompson: guitars / John McVie: bass / Mick Fleetwood: drums, percussion / Bekka Bramlett: backing vocals / **Recorded:** Ocean Way Recording, Hollywood / Sunset Sound Recorders, Hollywood: September 1993–May 1995 / **Technical Team:** Producers: Christine McVie, Richard Dashut / Sound Engineer: Ken Allardyce / Assistant Sound Engineers: Charlie Brocco, Alan Sanderson, Allen Sides, David Eike, Richard Huredia, Tom Nellen, Dave Shiffman

Genesis and Lyrics

Christine McVie delivered five tracks co-written with her husband Eddy Quintela for *Time* with uneven outcomes. The lyrics of "Hollywood (Some Other Kind of Town)," tinged with a certain weariness, evoke the musician's desire to leave the artificial and often oppressive environment of Hollywood for a place better suited to her emotional and personal needs, a place that would allow her to lead a more authentic existence, in touch with nature. The song perfectly conveys Christine's state of mind at the time of recording *Time* and hints at the reasons for her refusal to take part in the album's promotional tour. The opening lines speak of her weariness of the city's blinding lights, incessant daytime noise, and endless nights. Christine is ready to leave it all behind, including the sunny weather ("I don't care for sunny weather"), for something more authentic and natural, and even rainier. Should we see this as a contrast between her native England and her adopted country, the United States?

Production

Christine McVie's gentle, slightly lazy keyboards are more than compensated for by her assured vocals, perfectly supported by Bekka Bramlett's steamy backing vocals. The rhythm section acquits itself honorably, but it is guitarist Michael Thompson's playing that really pulls the song together, especially his sharp, albeit very short, solo at 2:56. The chemistry between Christine McVie and Dave Mason was so bad that the keyboardist preferred to rely on the skills of session musician Michael Thompson for the recording of her *Time* tracks.

Although this predictable, unremarkable track is far from being one of Christine McVie's best contributions to Fleetwood Mac's repertoire, it does attest to the fact that the singer remains the band's best melody writer, especially in the absence of Stevie Nicks and Lindsey Buckingham.

BLOW BY BLOW

Dave Mason, John Cesario, Mark Holden / 4:24

Musicians: Dave Mason: vocals, guitar / Billy Burnette: guitar / John McVie: bass / Mick Fleetwood: drums, percussion / Steve Thoma: keyboards / Bekka Bramlett: backing vocals / **Recorded:** Ocean Way Recording, Hollywood / Sunset Sound Recorders, Hollywood: September 1993–May 1995 / **Technical Team:** Producers: Fleetwood Mac, Dave Mason / Sound Engineer: Ken Allardyce / Assistant Sound Engineers: Charlie Brocco, Alan Sanderson, Allen Sides, David Eike, Richard Huredia, Tom Nellen, Dave Shiffman

Dave Mason on stage with the Mac in July 1995. The first contribution to the group's repertoire, "Blow by Blow" bore witness to the unease between him and Christine McVie.

Genesis and Lyrics

Written by Dave Mason, John Cesario, and Mark Holden, "Blow by Blow" was the first song presented to the public by the new-look Fleetwood Mac, featuring Dave Mason and Bekka Bramlett, as it was featured—as a preview—on the multi-artist compilation *Soccer Rocks the Globe*, released in the spring of 1994 to coincide with the FIFA World Cup in the United States. From the very first verse, it is all about resilience and the determination to overcome life's trials and tribulations. The opening lines describe the constant dualities we face—all or nothing, ("It's always something / Or it ain't nothing at all"), feast or famine ("It's feast or famine"), too hot or out in the cold ("too hot or out in the cold")—while the phrase "Here we stand / Alone together" suggests that solidarity between beings does nothing to prevent feelings of loneliness. After this first verse, the narrator raises his head and decides to face up to the situation. One by one, as the expression "blow by blow" suggests, he faces up to his challenges ("I'm back on my feet again"), drawing on his inner resources.

Production

The guitars are front and center on this blues-rock tune with its fiery chorus, undoubtedly one of the album's catchiest tracks, albeit not its most original. Reluctant to collaborate with Dave Mason, Christine McVie was not willing to lay down keyboards on his composition, nor would she call upon his guitar skills on her own tracks. So it is session musician Steve Thoma who lurks in the background with thick layers of sound, while Bekka Bramlett takes center stage with vigorous backing vocals, responding to Dave Mason's virile vocals. Once again, the rhythm section, made up of Mick Fleetwood and John McVie, dispatches the day-to-day business with professionalism, but without any real magic, except perhaps on an ingenious bridge from 2:10 onward, right up to the guitar solo, which launches in at 2:30.

WINDS OF CHANGE

Kit Hain / 4:26

Musicians: Bekka Bramlett: vocals / Dave Mason: guitar, backing vocals / Billy Burnette: guitar, backing vocals / John McVie: bass / Mick Fleetwood: drums / Steve Thoma: keyboards / Christine McVie: backing vocals / **Recorded:** Ocean Way Recording, Hollywood / Sunset Sound Recorders, Hollywood: September 1993–May 1995 / **Technical Team:** Producers: Fleetwood Mac, Richard Dashut / Sound Engineer: Ken Allardyce / Assistant Sound Engineers: Charlie Brocco, Alan Sanderson, Allen Sides, David Eike, Richard Huredia, Tom Nellen, Dave Shiffman, John Courage / Mastering: Stephen Marcussen, assisted by Don Tyler

Genesis and Lyrics

British singer Kit Hain, a member of the pop rock duo Marshall Hain—still famous for their 1978 hit "Dancing in the City"—offers "Winds of Change" on a platter to Bekka Bramlett, who grabs it with gusto. This harmless ballad deals with the universal theme of the pain following a breakup in love, with a tone that oscillates between sadness and resignation. The winds of change are presented as an inescapable force that, over time, sweeps away the pain and enables the narrator to move forward. The whole piece is weighed down by meteorological metaphors that lack subtlety: lightning streaks across the sky to illustrate the moment of the breakup; rain to represent tears; or the wind that carries away everything in its path, the past and worries, to symbolize the force of change.

Production

Wrapped in mellow backing vocals, Bekka Bramlett's voice shines through on this tranquil ballad. The arrangement is fleshed out by warm acoustic guitars and meticulous electric guitars, both on the rhythm and on the few solo approaches. The rhythm section pulls no punches, while Steve Thoma's thick keyboards are reminiscent of 1980s pop. "Winds of Change" is an unremarkable piece, its only asset being Bekka's willing and refreshing vocals.

I DO

Christine McVie, Eddy Quintela / 4:28

Musicians: Christine McVie: vocals, keyboards / Billy Burnette: guitar, backing vocals / Michael Thompson: guitar / John McVie: bass / Mick Fleetwood: drums, tambourine / Bekka Bramlett: backing vocals / **Recorded:** Ocean Way Recording, Hollywood / Sunset Sound Recorders, Hollywood: September 1993–May 1995 / **Technical Team:** Producers: Christine McVie, Richard Dashut / Sound Engineer: Ken Allardyce / Assistant Sound Engineers: Charlie Brocco, Alan Sanderson, Allen Sides, David Eike, Richard Huredia, Tom Nellen, Dave Shiffman / **Maxi-Single:** Side A: I Do (Edit) / Side B: Talkin' to My Heart (Album Version)—Little Lies (Extended Version)—Little Lies (Dub) / **UK Release Date:** October 10, 1995, Warner Bros. Records (ref. 9362 43616-2) / Best UK Chart Ranking: Did Not Chart / **Single:** Side A: I Do (Edit) / Side B: I Do (Album Version) / **US Release Date:** October 10, 1995, Warner Bros. Records (ref. PRO-CD-7857) / Best US Chart Ranking: Did Not Chart

Genesis and Lyrics

The lyrics of "I Do," co-written by the couple Christine McVie and Eddy Quintela, express an enduring, unconditional love. The narrator explains that she seized her chance by offering her heart to her partner, convinced that their destinies were linked. Her commitment was deep and sincere from the outset, as was her willingness to invest herself emotionally. In Christine's words, the meeting was predestined: "We had a date with destiny." References to coming out of the darkness and the "long black night" suggest the lover's saving role, bringing light and hope after a painful period, metaphorically touched on by brief allusions to "stormy nights" and the experience of many full moons.

Production

The album's best track and only single, "I Do" is the song on *Time* that comes closest to the Fleetwood Mac repertoire of their heyday—not least due to the familiar presence of Christine McVie's warm voice. Mick Fleetwood and John McVie, relatively transparent on the other tracks of this sixteenth opus, seem at last to respond to the catchy melody, which they serve up effectively. Bekka Bramlett's backing vocals blend harmoniously with Christine's voice on a brilliant chorus, which first breaks tempo, as if to mark a suspended moment in the unconditional love evoked by the narrator, before starting up again on the optimistic "I do." Michael Thompson's guitar solo, though not flamboyant, delivers a catchy solo that makes one forget the band's official guitarist, Dave Mason, who is decidedly ostracized by Christine, the song's co-producer.

NOTHING WITHOUT YOU

Bekka Bramlett, Delaney Bramlett, Doug Gilmore / 3:06

Musicians: Bekka Bramlett: vocals / Dave Mason: guitar (?) / Billy Burnette: guitar, backing vocals / Christine McVie: keyboards, backing vocals / John McVie: bass / Mick Fleetwood: drums, percussion / Lindsey Buckingham: backing vocals / **Recorded:** Ocean Way Recording, Hollywood / Sunset Sound Recorders, Hollywood: September 1993–May 1995 / **Technical Team:** Producers: Christine McVie, Richard Dashut / Sound Engineer: Ken Allardyce / Assistant Sound Engineers: Charlie Brocco, Alan Sanderson, Allen Sides, David Eike, Richard Huredia, Tom Nellen, Dave Shiffman, John Courage / Mastering: Stephen Marcussen, assisted by Don Tyler

Genesis and Lyrics

Daughter of soul rock duo Delaney and Bonnie Bramlett, Bekka had been immersed in her parents' music since childhood. When her time came to make her contribution to Fleetwood Mac, she naturally drew on her father's work, presenting a song he recorded with Blue Diamond in 1975, "Nothing Without You," for which she adapted the lyrics, hence her presence in the author's credits. The first verses indicate a deep emotional connection between two beings that nothing can upset. The lines "Just lay down beside me / Let your love hide me" call for comfort and refuge in each other's love. In the depths of this intimacy, the narrator feels safe and loved. The repetition of the idea that "things don't mean a thing" without the presence of another underscores the centrality of the loved one in the singer's life: Love is the determining factor that gives meaning to everything. She acknowledges her emotional dependence and feels literally incomplete without the beloved, placing nothing above her love ("I love you more than love / And I put nothing above you").

Production

A catchy guitar riff launches this pop rock ballad awash with keyboards and warm backing vocals. While the melody remains relatively banal, the arrangement is highly elaborate. The guitars take center stage. Between 1:11 and 1:27, for example, the guitars come into their own, despite the lackluster score. The well-balanced mix enables each instrument to stand out, as do the omnipresent keyboards, which fill out the sound. Bekka Bramlett's vocals, particularly on the chorus, are lively, and the singer can count on some fine backing vocals to supplement the sound, provided in part by the returning Lindsey Buckingham, who, from album to album, maintained the link with his partners through his sporadic interventions. Unfortunately, while the song remains pleasant and benefits from an elaborate, precise production, the result is far from Fleetwood Mac's greatest standards.

Bekka Bramlett drew on her rich paternal heritage to revisit Delaney and Blue Diamond's "Nothing Without You" from 1975.

Bekka Bramlett and Billy Burnette had a brief romance, which is documented in *Dreamin' the Dream*.

DREAMIN' THE DREAM

Bekka Bramlett, Billy Burnette / 3:43

Musicians: Bekka Bramlett: vocals / Billy Burnette: guitar / Dave Mason: guitar / Christine McVie: keyboards (?) / **Recorded:** Ocean Way Recording, Hollywood / Sunset Sound Recorders, Hollywood: September 1993–May 1995 / **Technical Team:** Producers: Billy Burnette, Fleetwood Mac, Richard Dashut / Sound Engineer: Ken Allardyce / Assistant Sound Engineers: Charlie Brocco, Alan Sanderson, Allen Sides, David Eike, Richard Huredia, Tom Nellen, Dave Shiffman

Genesis and Lyrics

During the tour that preceded the recording of *Time*, Bekka Bramlett and Billy Burnette had an affair. "I had a crush on him since I was 12," Bekka recalls. "Then I had a crush on him while I was 15. I would listen to all his records. I was so proud of him, knowing that he was his father's little protégé. Billy learned a lot from his daddy and his uncle, of course, but he learned a lot from my dad, too. They used to write songs right outside my bedroom window." While they were finally reunited in Fleetwood Mac, Bekka waited for Billy to break up with his then girlfriend before declaring her love and kissing him in a bar. "Dreamin' the Dream" was written the day after that first kiss: "A couple of years ago, I said to

him, 'Dude, you wrote 80 percent of that song,'" explains Bekka, before adding: "He goes, 'I don't remember it that way.' I was like, 'I do.' That's because I was laying on the bed, trying to be sexy with my notepaper and pen instead of focusing on the song." Billy Burnette, meanwhile, also remembers a suspended moment: "I remember us writing that in a hotel room somewhere. I brought it back into the band. Dave, Christine, and Mick loved it, so it made the record. When you brought a new song in, everyone had to like it. It was something the band voted on."[133] Intended to celebrate the very real love affair between Bekka and Billy, this song features a woman who only enjoys this love in her dreams. In the morning, everything disappears. Waiting for her lover to come to her and make the romance a reality, she fantasizes about it night after night.

Production

Sublime arpeggios on an acoustic guitar, precise and crystal-line, a few discreet keyboards, and Bekka Bramlett's moving, emotionally engaged voice are enough to make "Dreamin' the Dream" one of the most refreshing moments on *Time*. For the singer, this is a chance to show off her vocal technique in a delicate register, where her vibrato works wonders.

SOONER OR LATER

Christine McVie, Eddy Quintela / 5:41

Musicians: Christine McVie: vocals, keyboards / Michael Thompson: guitar / John McVie: bass / Mick Fleetwood: drums, percussion / Fred Tackett: trumpet / Bekka Bramlett: backing vocals / **Recorded:** Ocean Way Recording, Hollywood / Sunset Sound Recorders, Hollywood: September 1993–May 1995 / **Technical Team:** Producers: Christine McVie, Richard Dashut / Sound Engineer: Ken Allardyce / Assistant Sound Engineers: Charlie Brocco, Alan Sanderson, Allen Sides, David Eike, Richard Huredia, Tom Nellen, Dave Shiffman

Genesis and Lyrics

The material Christine McVie brings to *Time* is of course not comparable to that which she composed for Fleetwood Mac in its heyday, with the exception of "Sooner or Later." At the heart of her text is an emotional waltz: resignation in the face of a past breakup, the desire to move on, and the realization that time will heal the wounds. In the opening lines, the narrator speaks of her initial intention to let go of her loved one, to look to the future and leave the past behind. However, the refrain reveals an inner conflict, born of the hope that this person might return to her side. In a somewhat caricatured way, the winter setting imposes a dark, melancholy atmosphere, while summer is associated with forgetfulness and lightness. The phrase "I am the lucky one" indicates that, despite the pain, the narrator considers herself lucky to have lived through this experience.

Production

"Sooner or Later" is an audaciously structured ballad, with guitars coloring a melancholy atmosphere. The backing vocals, particularly elaborate on the chorus, bring not only lightness, but also a dynamic that is well maintained by the rhythm section. From 2:46 onward, Fred Tackett's muted trumpet answers Michael Thompson's dark guitar chords, making the end of the song even more mysterious. However, this asset does not fully benefit the song, as the trumpet remains under-mixed and barely audible. Fortunately, Christine McVie's charismatic voice comes through perfectly.

I WONDER WHY

Dave Mason, Franke Previte, Tom Fuller / 4:28

Musicians: Bekka Bramlett: vocals / Dave Mason: vocals, guitar / Steve Thoma: keyboards / John McVie: bass / Mick Fleetwood: drums, percussion / **Recorded:** Ocean Way Recording, Hollywood / Sunset Sound Recorders, Hollywood: September 1993–May 1995 / **Technical Team:** Producers: Fleetwood Mac, Richard Dashut / Sound Engineer: Ken Allardyce / Assistant Sound Engineers: Charlie Brocco, Alan Sanderson, Allen Sides, David Eike, Richard Huredia, Tom Nellen, Dave Shiffman

Genesis and Lyrics

Dave Mason, teamed up for the occasion with songwriters Tom Fuller and Franke Previte (known for having been the lead singer of Franke and the Knockouts in the 1980s), composed "I Wonder Why," a track expressing the pain and confusion caused by the end of a romantic relationship. He opens up about his difficulties in overcoming this disappointment in love and his incomprehension of the reasons behind his partner's decision. "It's hard when a love goes wrong" sums up the song's central theme. The passage "Now I'm turning my back on confusion / I won't live in a world of illusion," however, shows his will and ability to overcome it all. He aspires to find inner peace and freedom from painful feelings.

Production

Dave Mason is probably the one who asked himself the fewest questions when it came to his partnership with Fleetwood Mac. Yet his versatile guitar playing and the tracks he offered the band work quite well, like "I Wonder Why." While its intense tempo and guitar attacks may initially bring to mind Chris Rea, the soaring chorus and Bekka Bramlett's beautiful Stevie Nicks–like interventions in the background reveal a certain originality on the part of the band's two newcomers. "I Wonder Why" is undoubtedly one of *Time*'s greatest successes, even though this song is artistically far removed from the hits that consolidated Fleetwood Mac's reputation.

NIGHTS IN ESTORIL

Christine McVie, Eddy Quintela / 4:47

Musicians: Christine McVie: vocals, keyboards / Michael Thompson: guitar / John McVie: bass / Mick Fleetwood: drums / **Recorded:** Ocean Way Recording, Hollywood / Sunset Sound Recorders, Hollywood: September 1993–May 1995 / **Technical Team:** Producers: Christine McVie, Richard Dashut / Sound Engineer: Ken Allardyce / Assistant Sound Engineers: Charlie Brocco, Alan Sanderson, Allen Sides, David Eike, Richard Huredia, Tom Nellen, Dave Shiffman

Genesis and Lyrics

The idyllic moments Christine McVie and her husband Eddy Quintela spent in his hometown of Estoril, Portugal, inspired the couple to write this song. References to their nights spent in Estoril revive their romantic memories. The dark clouds that gather, heralding the "coming storm," do not affect the comforting memories of their relationship: their kisses, the protective warmth of their love, and Christine's "never ending thrill."

Production

Fairly typical of Christine McVie's style, "Nights in Estoril" has that light, sweet fragrance of melancholy, sublimated by an airy chorus and a voice at once serious and empathetic. Michael Thompson's guitars take pride of place on this track, which is essentially driven by the singer's piano. John McVie delivers one of his best bass lines on the record, aided by a spirited and inspired Mick Fleetwood. One of the few truly satisfying numbers on *Time*.

I GOT IT IN FOR YOU

Billy Burnette, Deborah Allen / 4:08

Musicians: Billy Burnette: vocals, guitar / Dave Mason: guitar / Bekka Bramlett: backing vocals / John McVie: bass / Mick Fleetwood: drums, percussion / Christine McVie: backing vocals (?) / **Recorded:** Ocean Way Recording, Hollywood / Sunset Sound Recorders, Hollywood: September 1993–May 1995 / **Technical Team:** Producers: Fleetwood Mac, Richard Dashut / Sound Engineer: Ken Allardyce / Assistant Sound Engineers: Charlie Brocco, Alan Sanderson, Allen Sides, David Eike, Richard Huredia, Tom Nellen, Dave Shiffman

Genesis and Lyrics

"I Got It in for You" is the joint work of Billy Burnette and country singer Deborah Allen, who co-wrote "Talkin' to My Heart" at the start of the album. The confoundingly banal lyrics express a mixture of passion, obsession, and devotion to the person one loves. Mad with desire, the narrator sees himself as the shadow of his beloved, always close by, day and night—a confession as burning as it is unhealthy. The phrase "I've been watching every move you make" is reminiscent of the lines "And every move you make [...] I'll be watching you" from the Police's 1983 hit "Every Breath You Take." Further on, the narrator describes a physical closeness, without ever making contact: "I'm getting closer, inches away... / I've been running undercover in the darkness of the night."

Production

A rugged but uninteresting blues-rock track, "I Got It in for You" is best appreciated for its flamboyant guitar parts, well served by an intense rhythm section. Billy Burnette's vocals, accompanied by Bekka Bramlett's backing vocals, sound very clunky. As the melody can be considered relatively unremarkable, one still wonders how "I Got It in for You" managed to build consensus within the band and miraculously find a place on *Time*.

When she contributed to the *Time* album, Deborah Allen had written 14 out of 20 singles in Billboard's US Country chart.

ALL OVER AGAIN

Christine McVie, Eddy Quintela / 3:36

Musicians: Christine McVie: vocals, keyboards / Michael Thompson: guitar / John McVie: bass / Mick Fleetwood: drums, percussion / Bekka Bramlett: backing vocals / **Recorded:** Ocean Way Recording, Hollywood / Sunset Sound Recorders, Hollywood: September 1993–May 1995 / **Technical Team:** Producers: Christine McVie, Richard Dashut / Sound Engineer: Ken Allardyce / Assistant Sound Engineers: Charlie Brocco, Alan Sanderson, Allen Sides, David Eike, Richard Huredia, Tom Nellen, Dave Shiffman

Genesis and Lyrics

The fifth contribution to the album by the duo of Christine McVie and Eddy Quintela, "All Over Again" is certainly the most insipid, musically speaking. The lyrics are more interesting, however. Behind the apparent reflection on the end of a love relationship, the need to cut things short before tearing each other apart and ruining everything that came before, another reading emerges: that of a Christine McVie who has come to the end of the road with Fleetwood Mac, disappointed by the recruitment of new members, undermined by the successive departures of Lindsey, Stevie, and Rick, and exhausted by life on the road. When she speaks of "saying goodnight, turning out the light" ("Well it's time to say goodnight / And finally turn out the light"), she seems to be referring more to leaving the stage and turning off the spotlight than to letting go of the loved one. "But you can rely on a love that won't die" may be as much about the touring public as it is about the band. Her decision in no way alters her affection for either. The phrase "So let's stop before it's too late / And leave it all up to the fates" proves her integrity, her faith in her profession, which she cannot bury for the sake of money. She has no regrets and proclaims in the finale that she would do things exactly the same way again if she could.

Production

Melancholy is once again at the heart of "All Over Again." But the song seems to mark the creative limits of the McVie-Quintela duo having been reached. Indeed, the melody remains forgettable despite the infectious distress in Christine's voice. The synthesizer layers weigh the track down considerably, as does the clumsy, lackluster rhythm section. The backing vocals, though meticulous, can do nothing to save the track, and neither can Michael Thompson's hardworking but sterile guitars.

THESE STRANGE TIMES
Mick Fleetwood, Ray Kennedy / 7:07

Musicians
Mick Fleetwood: drums, percussion, guitar, spoken words
John Jones: keyboards, guitar, bass
Bekka Bramlett: backing vocals
Lucy Fleetwood: backing vocals

Recorded
Ocean Way Recording, Hollywood
Sunset Sound Recorders, Hollywood: September 1993–May 1995

Technical Team
Producers: John Jones, Mick Fleetwood, Ray Kennedy
Sound Engineer: Ken Allardyce
Assistant Sound Engineer: Jimmy Hotz

Her background as a backup singer made it easy for Bekka Bramlett to take on that role on a track like "These Strange Times."

Genesis and Lyrics

If Bekka Bramlett is to be believed, this long spoken-word track, composed by Mick Fleetwood and Ray Kennedy, did not impress many people within Fleetwood Mac: "Anyway, there was this one song that everyone fuckin' fought against him. Mick said to me, 'Nobody let me do any of my songs on any of these records. [...] They never let me do a song I did myself.' [...] I fought for it. Christine wouldn't do it. They wouldn't do it. Billy is always Switzerland. Dashut didn't know what to do. So we went literally across the street and cut this thing, and then we got Lucy to go 'Daddy, Daddy.'" Indeed, little Lucy Fleetwood, Mick's daughter, appears fleetingly alongside her father, with the versatile John Jones, and Bekka on backing vocals. The reason Mick was so keen to get this song on tape is that it is a tribute to Peter Green, Fleetwood Mac's early bandmate. The many references speak instantly to fans of the early band. Directing his thoughts to "a friend," he defines him as a "man of the world" (the title of one of Green's compositions). Then he recalls his inner struggle, "between the dark and the light," and above all his addiction, which appears in the guise of the devil, reducing his faith in life to nothing ("God is nowhere, God is nowhere"). The demonic shadow of "Green Manalishi" hovers over this passage. Reciting these words, Mick confides to his friend that he too has had to face his demons and go through this "hell." This confession is accompanied by a message of hope, like a hand extended to Peter Green, whom he knows to be in perdition since his departure from Fleetwood Mac, due to his brain having been fried by LSD.

Production

The vocal embodiment of a profound introspection on the meaning of existence, "These Strange Times" boldly closes the disappointing *Time*. Mick Fleetwood's stentorian vocals, aided by the presence of Bekka Bramlett, give this track a certain magnetism. Admittedly, its noncommercial format of over seven minutes, with no chorus, put many off, but the experience delighted the Mac drummer: "This is almost new age meets Burundi," he would say later. "It's a spoken word piece of mine, using a lot of drums I got in Ghana." For Mick, recording "These Strange Times" was almost a

On "These Strange Times," Mick's heart spoke through the drums and with spoken words that paid a vibrant tribute to Peter Green.

matter of vital necessity: "I haven't opened my gob in nearly 30 years, but I had this little philosophical, anecdotal thing I just had to get off my chest. It means a lot to me. The subject matter is inspired by Peter Green, but it's also about me. I nearly destroyed myself with drugs and alcohol and crazy behaviour, and this is a positive thought mode that you can get out of the dark, into the light. I was a functioning addict for a long time. It wasn't as bad as it sounds, because as long as I had my stuff, I functioned perfectly normally and looked just like anybody else, but I was dependent on drugs to maintain that state. So this song is about getting out of that mire."[8]

Fleetwood Mac reunited onstage at Warner Bros studios in Burbank, California, on May 23, 1997, for an audio and video recording that was published as the live album *The Dance*.

With *The Dance*, Fleetwood Mac returned to the top of the best-selling album charts in the United States for the first time since 1982. It sold almost 200,000 copies in its first week alone. The album then spent seven months in the top 40.

THE DANCE (1997)

The Chain
Dreams
Everywhere
Rhiannon
I'm So Afraid
Temporary One
Bleed to Love Her
Big Love
Landslide
Say You Love Me
My Little Demon
Silver Springs
You Make Loving Fun
Sweet Girl
Go Your Own Way
Tusk
Don't Stop

Release Dates
United Kingdom: August 19, 1997
Reference: Reprise Records—9362-46702-2
Best UK Chart Ranking: 15
United States: August 19, 1997
Reference: Reprise Records—9 46702-2
Best US Chart Ranking: 1

A Triumphant Return

Since the departure of Lindsey Buckingham in August 1987, the Mac had not been a success. Neither *Behind the Mask*, recorded in 1990 with guitarists Burnette and Vito, nor *Time*, recorded in 1995 with singer Bekka Bramlett and guitarist Dave Mason, managed to convince the public. Furthermore, sales declined from bad to worse.

A Bitter Failure

Faced with this acknowledgement of failure, the band decided to take a break. "I think the last band John and I put together with Dave Mason and Billy Burnette and Bekka Bramlett was in true Fleetwood Mac tradition," explained Mick Fleetwood in 2016, adding that "It was a long shot and it was totally reliant on whether the music would be accepted. It wasn't. And quite honestly, I don't think the record company heard the music either. We may as well not have made that album. It took its course, or didn't take its course, and it was nonexistent. This Fleetwood Mac had made its mark to such an extent that when Stevie left, in retrospect, it should have stopped."[8] This was a sentiment the drummer echoed on the tour that followed the album: "So there I was, the captain of a failing band with a volatile personnel situation, and it just wasn't worth saving. I have to say that we did go out and put on a great show each night, regardless of the feuding and shouting matches. We did a lot of Dave's stuff in our set and a lot of R&B classics that Bekka was great at performing. But that really wasn't what the thousands of people who came out to see Fleetwood Mac were after. As fun as it was, it just wasn't right historically. In the end, everybody got a letter of disengagement, which probably wasn't much fun for them but I didn't know how else to pull the plug, so I just pulled it,"[2] the drummer confessed in his autobiography.

The Famous Five Reunited

Fleetwood Mac's hiatus did not last: It was not long before the "*Rumours* Five" (the legendary *Rumours* lineup that had briefly re-formed on stage for president Bill Clinton's inauguration in 1993) were working together again. Even Mick Fleetwood, who dreamed of it, didn't dare believe it. Once again, it was Lindsey's solo album that became the starting point for a new adventure. "As Lindsey said, it was him doing an album and Mick got involved," confided John McVie. "They needed a bass player, so I got involved. They needed some vocals and keyboards and Stevie and Chris got involved."[8] When all five musicians were together in the same room, the chemistry was obvious, and there was never a hiccup to mar the sessions. This was not lost on Carl Stubner, Mick's manager and longtime friend of the band, who took it upon himself to find an official purpose for the reunion. When MTV offered to record a live show devoted to the band, Lindsey did not hesitate in putting his album to one side and jumping on board. Carl Stubner stepped into the breach. He landed a contract with the Reprise label (a division of Warner Bros.) and scheduled a tour.

An Immediate Success

During rehearsals for the MTV concert, three new songs were created: the edgy "My Little Demon" by Lindsey Buckingham, the harmonically rich pop-sounding "Temporary One" by Christine McVie, and the mid-tempo soft-rock "Sweet Girl" by Stevie Nicks. It was decided that these previously unreleased songs would take their place in a set list essentially made up of the Mac's greatest hits. The concert, recorded on May 23, 1997, at Warner Bros. studios in Burbank, California, became the live album *The Dance*. The name was inspired by Henri Matisse's 1910 painting *La Danse*, commissioned by Russian businessman and art collector Sergei Shchukin, who bequeathed it to the Hermitage Museum in Saint Petersburg. The album, the first in ten years recorded by this lineup, got off to a strong start in the United States, where it went straight to number one on the charts and stayed in the top 40 for over seven months. It should also be said that the timing was perfect, as *The Dance* arrived just in time to celebrate the twentieth anniversary of *Rumours*.

The band embarked on a forty-four-date tour of the United States, with a stopover in Canada. Begun on September 17, 1997, in Hartford, Connecticut, The Dance tour ended on November 30 of the same year. The band, looking fresh and rejuvenated, received excellent reviews and played to hundreds of thousands of fans every night, who were delighted to hear them perform their classics.

At the end of The Dance tour, Christine (shown here in October 1997) retired.

A flurry of awards crowns the end of The Dance tour. On January 12, 1998, Fleetwood Mac performed at the Waldorf Astoria Hotel in Manhattan to celebrate their induction into the Rock and Roll Hall of Fame.

FOR MAC ADDICTS

The live version of "Silver Springs," released as a single by Reprise in 1997, captured at Burbank Studios, went viral after the 2019 broadcast of the series *Daisy Jones and the Six*, inspired by the legendary rock band's turbulent history. In this moving performance, Stevie Nicks, who wrote the song about the end of her love affair with Lindsey, turned to her ex-lover, eyes misty with tears, powerfully hammering out the lyrics "You'll never get away from the sound of the woman that loves you."

Christine Leaves

At the end of this tour, despite its success, Christine McVie, tired of life on the road once again, decided to leave the band for good. She wanted to retire from the music business and move back to England. This time, her decision seemed irrevocable: "Throughout the tour we knew this was going to happen, but refused to admit it, because it was so great to be back together and on top of the world,"[2] recalls Mick, who added: "We hoped that she'd change her mind and I kept telling her not to be hasty about her decision. One night toward the end of the tour [...] I went to her hotel suite and I realised just how much her mind was made up. Before I could even steer the conversation towards asking her if she'd reconsider, Christine stopped me cold. 'Mick, don't ask me...Please don't ask me.' Christine knows me extremely well, like a sister knows her brother. With those few words, I knew she was done with Fleetwood Mac. 'You have my word,' I replied. And I never broached the subject again."[2]

Lindsey Buckingham also tried to hold Christine back until the last day of the tour, before they parted ways again, to no avail. Even Fleetwood Mac's induction into the Rock and Roll Hall of Fame in January 1998 did not convince her to give up her retirement.

For Stevie, the tour was a breath of fresh air and a timely return to the spotlight, at a time when her solo career was beginning to falter: "[The Dance tour] was very powerful and I think it really opened our eyes," the singer explained. "We'd been separated for a long time. I had absolutely no idea that Fleetwood Mac could reform at that point. And then all of a sudden, it was like all our plans had been thrown up into the air, everything had been turned upside down, and Fleetwood Mac was coming back [to life]."

The Dance spawned three singles in the United States ("Landslide," "The Chain," and "Silver Springs") and a fourth aimed at the European market, "Temporary One." But above all, the album earned the band three nominations at the 1998 Grammy Awards, in the categories Best Pop Album, Best Rock Performance by a Group or Duo for "The Chain," and Best Pop Performance by a Group or Duo for "Silver Springs." Although the band walked away from the ceremony empty-handed, that did not stop *The Dance* from consecrating Fleetwood Mac's return to the limelight. Even the president of the Reprise label, Howie Klein, admitted his surprise at the success: "Its performance exceeded our most optimistic projections, and what makes it even more remarkable is that, despite the UPS strike, few stores were able to get the album immediately." It now remained to be seen whether a "real" studio album would see the light of day again in the future—especially after the definitive departure of Christine McVie, one of the band's main creative pillars.

TEMPORARY ONE

Christine McVie, Eddy Quintela / 4:00

Musicians: Christine McVie: vocals, keyboards / Lindsey Buckingham: guitar, backing vocals / Brett Tuggle: guitar / Neale Heywood: guitar / John McVie: bass / Mick Fleetwood: drums / Lenny Castro: tambourine / Stevie Nicks: backing vocals / Sharon Celani: backing vocals / Mindy Stein: backing vocals / **Recorded:** Warner Bros. Studios, Burbank (California): May 23, 1997 / **Technical Team:** Producers: Lindsey Buckingham, Elliot Scheiner / Sound Engineer: Barry Goldberg / Assistant Sound Engineers: Guy Charbonneau, Charlie Bouis, John Nelson / Mastering: Ted Jensen

Like "Homeward Bound," featured on *Bare Trees* in 1972, this song written by Christine McVie (with the help of Eddy Quintela) deals with the musician's aversion to touring and her persistent homesickness when she was away from home for too long. The lyrics detail the suffering of two people physically estranged from each other, a theme that would recur in Christine's compositions until her departure from the band at the end of The Dance tour in 1998.

MY LITTLE DEMON

Lindsey Buckingham / 3:33

Musicians: Lindsey Buckingham: vocals, guitar / Brett Tuggle: guitar / Neale Heywood: guitar / Christine McVie: keyboards, backing vocals / Stevie Nicks: backing vocals / John McVie: bass / Mick Fleetwood: drums / Lenny Castro: tambourine / Sharon Celani: backing vocals / Mindy Stein: backing vocals / **Recorded:** Warner Bros. Studios, Burbank (California): May 23, 1997 / **Technical Team:** Producers: Lindsey Buckingham, Elliot Scheiner / Sound Engineer: Barry Goldberg / Assistant Sound Engineers: Guy Charbonneau, Charlie Bouis, John Nelson / Mastering: Ted Jensen

"My Little Demon" gave rise to a little stage ritual during concerts on The Dance tour. Lindsey Buckingham began by addressing the audience and explaining the song. The song is about the difficulty of not giving in to our inner darkness. The narrator struggles against this negative force, which he calls "my little demon." It alienates him from his

Fleetwood Mac in California, October 18, 1997. The Irvine Meadows venue was sold out.

friends and alters his personality. Buckingham takes up the theme of a pact with the devil, recalling the myth of bluesman Robert Johnson (who is said to have sold his soul in exchange for exceptional guitar skills), as he sings "My little demon, making me choose / Making me an offer I can't refuse." During Lindsey's speech, Mick Fleetwood entertained the audience by imitating the little devil, raising his drumsticks above his head to simulate a pair of horns. On this energetic rock number, Lindsey delivers a very fine solo, which is edgy and technical, between 1:53 and 2:05, but also on the finale, between 2:50 and 3:12.

SWEET GIRL

Stevie Nicks / 3:19

Musicians: Stevie Nicks: vocals / Lindsey Buckingham: guitar, backing vocals / Brett Tuggle: guitar / Neale Heywood: guitar / Christine McVie: keyboards, backing vocals / John McVie: bass / Mick Fleetwood: drums / Lenny Castro: tambourine / Sharon Celani: backing vocals / Mindy Stein: backing vocals / **Recorded:** Warner Bros. Studios, Burbank (California): May 23, 1997 / **Technical Team:** Producers: Lindsey Buckingham, Elliot Scheiner / Sound Engineer: Barry Goldberg / Assistant Sound Engineers: Guy Charbonneau, Charlie Bouis, John Nelson / Mastering: Ted Jensen

"Sweet Girl" tells the story of a woman who has made the choice to pursue an artistic career despite the fears of those closest to her, through a benevolent exchange, no doubt with her father, or at least a paternal figure. He imagines her alone in a world of which he knows nothing, and which he imagines to be pitiless. The young artist hears his concerns, but she has already made up her mind to follow her own path, even if it involves sacrifices and difficult times. Although not one of Stevie Nicks's most melodic songs, it still benefits from sumptuous vocal harmonies and fine guitar work.

ALBUM

Say You Will

What's the World Coming To . Murrow Turning Over in His Grave . Illume (9-11) .
Thrown Down . Miranda . Red Rover . Say You Will . Peacekeeper . Come . Smile at You .
Running Through the Garden . Silver Girl . Steal Your Heart Away . Bleed to Love Her .
Everybody Finds Out . Destiny Rules . Say Goodbye . Goodbye Baby .
Outtakes: Not Make Believe . Love Minus Zero / No Limit

RELEASE DATES
United Kingdom: April 15, 2003
Reference: Reprise Records—9362484792
Best UK Chart Ranking: 6
United States: April 15, 2003
Reference: Reprise Records—48394-2
Best US Chart Ranking: 3

2003

In the absence of Christine McVie, Stevie Nicks and Lindsey Buckingham share equal credit for *Say You Will*.

Now a quartet, the band redoubled its creativity, considering the possibility of a double album.

FOR MAC ADDICTS

Already full with its eighteen tracks, *Say You Will* could have accommodated more. Lindsey Buckingham had planned to work on four more of his solo tracks with Fleetwood Mac: "Gift of Screws," "Down on Rodeo," "Someone's Gotta Change Your Mind," and "The Right Place to Fade."

THE LATEST BOLT FROM THE BLUE

The shock was hard to take. But they had to get used to it. Christine McVie wouldn't be coming back for a new album. And even less so for a new tour. Fleetwood Mac without Christine: Was it still even possible? However, it would have to be, because, after the success of *The Dance*, it was clear that the Fleetwood Mac brand still had a bright future ahead of it and that no one from the band was really ready to stop. Lindsey Buckingham, who couldn't imagine recording his first album with Fleetwood Mac since 1987 without Christine, was convinced that she would resurface at some point. Just like Mick, who had never cut ties with her and still held out hope of hearing her say she was going to jump on the first plane to contribute to the next record every time she called to check in. This was not going to be the case.

The Return of Buckingham Nicks

After The Dance tour, which took place at the end of 1997, everyone resumed their activities. Stevie Nicks released the box set *Enchanted* and went on tour after celebrating her fiftieth birthday. Then she returned to the studio to develop *Trouble in Shangri-La*, the solo album she had started and had left on hold since 1995. It finally saw the light of day on May 1, 2001. During this time, Lindsey worked on his own project: *Gift of Screws*. He had also been working on that since 1995. He recorded a body of work at Ocean Way Recording as well as at home in his home studio, for which he called upon Mick Fleetwood and John McVie. The trio worked in isolation, sporadically supported by multitasking technicians, such as John Shanks, Stevie's collaborator on *Trouble in Shangri-La*, co-producer and musician, who provided keyboards on "What's the World Coming To" and guitar on "Peacekeeper." Lindsey also drew on the production

know-how of Rob Cavallo (who had collaborated with Green and would later become president of Warner Bros. Records). The good atmosphere that prevailed between Mick, John, and Lindsey led them, in 2001, to glimpse the possibility of making these songs the basis of the next Fleetwood Mac album. Lindsey had no regrets about sacrificing a solo album for the band. "There was a lot of bonding between the three of us," Lindsey recalled, "and it was a good place to start building a reconfigured dynamic between us. It was very difficult for me for years to have to work with Stevie when I didn't want to be around her."

Stevie Nicks was approached for the project. She sent five demos to her bandmates, before going on tour to promote *Trouble in Shangri-La* in July 2001. Her tour ended in the autumn in difficult conditions: In addition to recurrent bronchitis problems that forced her to cancel several concerts, she landed in New York City in the early hours of September 11, 2001, and learned of the attack when her assistant woke her after the second plane hit the World Trade Center. From her room at the Waldorf Astoria in Manhattan, Nicks spent the day following the events on television, while writing down her feelings in her diary. She performed a few remaining dates of her tour on the advice of her entourage. "When I went home to Phoenix for Christmas, I realized that I needed to say how I was feeling now; how I was feeling after that horrendous tour of mine. The way things stood, none of the songs on the new album were actually brand new, and as a writer that is not acceptable to me." On January 1, she went back to work and a flood of ideas burst into her head. "So, I went back to my journals, and I wrote 'Destiny Rules,' then 'Silver Girl,' then 'Illume,' then 'Say You Will.'"

Guardian of rhythm John McVie and his faithful Rick Turner Renaissance Electroline bass.

Say You Will was recorded in analog using a Sony 3348, a multitrack tape recorder. Lindsey did his edits the old-fashioned way, slicing the strips with a cutter. Mixing was still done digitally via the Pro Tools 64-track digital sequencer.

Finalization in Bel Air

In the summer of 2001, Stevie joined Mick, John, and Lindsey in Los Angeles at Bellagio House, a mansion in the Bel Air neighborhood that the band had rented to finalize the recording of the album in comfort. The lounge served both as a control booth (equipped with a Neotek Elite console and a 48-track tape set) and a recording room for instruments. A small adjoining room was reserved for vocals. Only the latter would really be fully used, since Lindsey's and Stevie's demos were already at an advanced stage and there were hardly any other vocal additions (Lindsey's on Stevie's tracks, and vice versa) that were needed. Lindsey recalls, "There really wasn't much to do because so much of it had John and Mick already [on it]. They were pretty much already there. The only thing we did was recall most of them and get Stevie's voice on them."

Stevie presented her four new demos, of which "Say You Will" and "Silver Girl" stood out. Lindsey and Stevie were sitting at the console, John and Mick were snuggled up on the couch. At the end of the listening session, the three men expressed their satisfaction and applauded Stevie, who gave them a little bow. Lindsey already realized that the album could well become a double. In the end, the two ex-lovers would count nine songs each on *Say You Will*. A fairness that could have been down to chance if it weren't for the fact that there were bitter negotiations in the background to preserve their respective egos.

A Natural Pursuit

This compromise satisfied the two songwriters, who were never better than when they challenged and inspired each other. Their complicated relationship continued to fuel their songs, as in the heyday of *Rumours*. Bittersweet, the lyrics oscillated between resentment and a desire for appeasement, depending on the mood of the moment. Fleetwood Mac has made this its business, as Stevie readily acknowledges: "If everybody's happy and everything's going along, then you have nothing to write about. So, Lindsey and I write about the chaos of our relationship, which is ongoing. We're both really selfish, and it's like, 'No, I want it to be this way!' It's like you have two serious bulls in a pen, and we argue all the time. There's continual trauma. But does it make for incredible works of music? Yeah, it does." It's funny to see how Lindsey and Stevie never stop answering each other in songs. Is it really a coincidence that *Say You Will* ends with "Say Goodbye," by the guitarist (in which he sings: "I let you slip away / There was nothing I could do / That was so long ago, yeah / Still I often think of you,"), and Stevie's "Goodbye Baby" (in which the singer replies: "Goodbye baby / I hope your heart's not broken / Don't forget me / Yes, I was outspoken")? There is, of course, room for doubt.

When journalists imagine their relationship is now peaceful and that their newfound friendship has probably never been stronger, Stevie immediately takes it upon herself to cool their ardor: "Um, Lindsey and I's relationship is sort of

With the release of *Say You Will*, Fleetwood Mac joined the exclusive circle of artists whose career sales were more than 50 million records in the United States.

the same. We work together and write together. We've been apart for gazillions of years now. And as I tell him: 'You have to understand that when I come in with a pretty-much finished demo, that's because you haven't been in my life. I had to go and learn how to make music without you.' And I did. And I learned it very well; I don't always need Lindsey to make my music come true." Lindsey echoed the same sentiment in the first interviews following the album's release in 2003: "Towards the end of the album we had some problems with the running order, and there were some issues with that which got Stevie and I into some over-the-phone conflicts. [...] You know, it's been hard for Stevie to feel good about what we've accomplished with this record. And I really hope she will at some point. She's yet to say: 'Good work on my songs, Lindsey,' even though that was basically what we were working on for the last year."

An Aborted Double Album

The track list also gave rise to bitter discussions between Lindsey and Mick. The former was clearly in favor of the double-album format, which, according to him, would allow them to present all the facets of their work, including the most adventurous, while the latter, who was not totally opposed at the beginning, finally expressed his fears of a new commercial failure, relaying the discourse of his manager and Warner. The documentary *Destiny Rules*, directed by Matt Baumann and Kyle Einhorn for VH1, which retraces some key moments in the making of *Say You Will*, testifies to their arguments. In it, Lindsey compares Fleetwood Mac to an independent director who would contribute to the history of cinema with his bold choices, as opposed to a Ridley Scott from whom we only expect blockbusters. At one point, the conversation gets tougher, and Lindsey, seeing that his arguments haven't hit their mark, introduces the

John McVie, Stevie Nicks, Mick Fleetwood, and Lindsey Buckingham during their concert at the Gwinnett Center Arena in Duluth, Minnesota, on September 7, 2003.

idea that, if he had known things would turn out this way, he would have reserved his songs for his own album, going so far as to utter a thinly disguised threat: "I own the masters." The same discussions took place between Lindsey and Stevie. The latter, even if she heard the guitarist's arguments, argued that fans are far removed from these considerations—that they think mainly about paying their rent and their bills, and are not ready to buy a double album just because it is important to Fleetwood Mac's artistic approach.

A Short-Lived Truce

Finally, after mixing and some overdubs by Lindsey at Cornerstone Studios in Chatsworth, California, eighteen songs (more than one hour and fifteen minutes) were packed into a single album, named *Say You Will* after one of the songs. The cover art was illustrated with a black-and-white photo featuring former couple Lindsey and Stevie, proving that their relationship was once again at the heart of Fleetwood Mac's work.

Say You Will was made to suffer a little for its length by the critics, but the album had a good reception from the public—despite the absence of Christine McVie, whose warm voice was missed by the fans. The alliance between Warner and the managers of each of the musicians—with the exception of Lindsey's Tony Dimitriades—resulted in the abandonment of the double-album format, which was considered too difficult to sell. Lindsey Buckingham's arrangement and production work was unanimously praised, and the album quickly climbed the charts, in its first week reaching number three on the charts in the United States. This figure confirmed the renewed interest in the band, six years after *The Dance*. In the end, some 1.6 million copies were sold.

Galvanized by the album's success, Lindsey Buckingham was so enthusiastic about its release that he confided, "Hopefully, if things go our way, next year we can make

another album." Lindsey didn't know it yet, but *Say You Will* would be the last album recorded by Fleetwood Mac, and it would be another decade before the band would expand their studio discography with a four-track EP. Indeed, behind all the good intentions in the world and the stated desire to bury the hatchet in the wake of *Say You Will*, Fleetwood Mac's life was just not programmed to be a long, quiet river. And Christine's absence, creatively and in terms of the band's unity, would only increase the simmering tensions in the band—especially between Lindsey and Stevie, as when the latter, just four years after

praising *Say You Will*, said, "It was a nightmare doing that record. It really was Lindsey's vision, and it wasn't very much about the other three of us. And of course, it was also the first record we had ever attempted to do without Christine [McVie, who left the band in the late 1990s]. Right there, the whole thing was completely insane. She is the magic mediator in that band and always was. She's the one who made light of everything and made everybody laugh and told us all that we were full of shit. She was the person who made it all work. So, when she wasn't there, that sunk the boat."

FOR MAC ADDICTS

A documentary entitled *Destiny Rules*, which recounts the highlights of the creation of the album *Say You Will*, was filmed by VH1 and broadcast in March 2004. Directors Matt Baumann and Kyle Einhorn followed the band for nearly a year and a half, from Stevie Nicks's arrival at Bellagio House to the tour that followed the album's release and accumulated nearly five hundred hours of footage.

All the Lindsey Buckingham tracks on *Say You Will* were originally intended for a solo album, except for "Peacekeeper" and "What's the World Coming To," created for the occasion.

WHAT'S THE WORLD COMING TO

Lindsey Buckingham, Julian Raymond / 3:47

Musicians: Lindsey Buckingham: vocals, guitar, keyboards, percussion / Stevie Nicks: backing vocals, keyboards / John Shanks: keyboards / John McVie: bass / Mick Fleetwood: drums, percussion / **Recorded:** Bellagio House, Los Angeles / Ocean Way Recording, Hollywood / Lindsey Buckingham's studio (California) / Cornerstone Studios, Chatsworth (California): 1995–1997; Summer 2001–Fall 2002 / **Technical Team:** Producers: John Shanks, Lindsey Buckingham / Sound Engineers: Ken Allardyce, Ken Koroshetz, Lindsey Buckingham, Mark Needham, Ray Lindsey

Genesis and Lyrics

Written by Lindsey Buckingham with the help of American songwriter and producer Julian Raymond, "What's the World Coming To" begins with rhetorical questions about the state of the world and questions the veracity of the information that is constantly being propagated. The lyricist does not specifically designate a person responsible, since he is content with "they," in which he probably includes the media and politics. "Everyone's gone to the moon" implies that people turn away from reality by seeking refuge in unattainable ideals or distant dreams. The phrases "house filled with shame," "there's no truth in my lies," and "there's no light in my eyes" suggest a loss of connection with others for the singer, who has given in to the darkness of his feelings in the solitude of his home. According to Buckingham, the world is slowly moving away from truth, mutual understanding, and authenticity, which leads to great frustration within him.

Realization

With a very simple structure, "What's the World Coming To" is divided into verses built on a sequence of chords (*F*, *A* minor, *D* minor, and *B* flat) and refrains in *F*, *C*, *F*, *B* flat, *F*, *C*, and *F*. Performed in a moderate pop-rock tempo, "What's the World Coming To" has a lavish production and gives pride of place to warm guitars. It features an addictive refrain that relies on beautiful vocal harmonies. The rhythm section is very comfortable, and Mick Fleetwood's playing behind his drums complements Lindsey Buckingham's lineup well. The latter's singing is not very confident at the end of the phrases. It is more controlled when Stevie Nicks's backing vocals intervene. The end of the song thus becomes more effective. A good opening track for *Say You Will*.

Journalist Edward R. Murrow preparing, with his wife Janet H. Brewster, for one of his radio broadcasts in January 1944. Lindsey Buckingham honored Murrow's memory and integrity in this song.

MURROW TURNING OVER IN HIS GRAVE

Lindsey Buckingham / 4:11

Musicians: Lindsey Buckingham: vocals, guitar, keyboards / John McVie: bass / Mick Fleetwood: drums, percussion / **Recorded:** Bellagio House, Los Angeles / Ocean Way Recording, Hollywood / Lindsey Buckingham's Studio (California) / Cornerstone Studios, Chatsworth (California): 1995–1997; Summer 2001–Fall 2002 / **Technical Team:** Producers: John Shanks, Lindsey Buckingham / Sound Engineers: Ken Allardyce, Ken Koroshetz, Lindsey Buckingham, Mark Needham, Ray Lindsey / Assistant Sound Engineer: Guy Charbonneau

Genesis and Lyrics

For once, Fleetwood Mac tackles a social issue with this song with the evocative title: "Murrow Turning Over in His Grave." Edward Roscoe Murrow was a figure in American journalism, a pioneer in television news broadcasting, considered one of the most courageous and honest in the history of the profession. Murrow made his mark during World War II with his radio news broadcasts listened to by millions of his countrymen. After that, he strongly opposed Senator Joseph McCarthy through a series of television reports that led to the downfall of that politician. It is this unavoidable media figure that Lindsey Buckingham refers to in "Murrow Turning Over in His Grave." The song deals with the themes of corruption, injustice, and the complacency of journalism.

"It was inspired by watching TV and seeing what it's become, how horrendous it's become as a tool to do exactly what Edward R. Murrow warned against when he gave his famous speech. He said if TV is allowed to distract and delude people, there will be a large, large price to pay down the line. And we're seeing that coming true on so many levels," explained Lindsey Buckingham, before adding, "Especially in the world today, where all the media is basically owned and controlled and edited to a certain point of view, in the name of objective news, by all the same people who are tied in with another company. A good example would be GE owning NBC. Murrow would be turning over in his grave if he were to see all of this. Not just the propaganda that passes for news, but the trivialization of so many things, and the intent to distract and delude that he was talking about."[152]

Realization

For "Murrow Turning Over in His Grave," Lindsey Buckingham did most of the production and arrangement. Starting with a blues-inspired acoustic riff, the guitarist is joined by Mick Fleetwood's dark drums, mostly played on toms. Further on, as the vocal tracks overlap, the refrain bursts out, letting the rhythm section have free rein, while Lindsey Buckingham launches into a long, extremely technical solo from 2:41, which reaches an emotional peak around 3:25, at the moment when the notes are at their highest. And when the listener prepares to abdicate in the face of this torrent of electricity, Buckingham puts a coin back in the machine and goes for even higher notes around 3:48 for a fiery finale.

Arriving in New York in the early hours of September 11, 2001, where she was due to perform two shows, Stevie considered suspending her tour. But her parents convinced her not to, arguing that her music could help people get through the crisis.

ILLUME (9-11)
Stevie Nicks / 4:50

Musicians
Lindsey Buckingham: vocals, guitar, keyboards, percussion
Stevie Nicks: vocals, keyboards
John McVie: bass
Mick Fleetwood: drums, percussion

Recorded
Bellagio House, Los Angeles / Lindsey Buckingham's studio (California) / Cornerstone Studios, Chatsworth (California): Summer 2001–Fall 2002

Technical Team
Producers: John Shanks, Lindsey Buckingham
Sound Engineers: Ken Allardyce, Ken Koroshetz, Lindsey Buckingham, Mark Needham, Ray Lindsey
Assistant Sound Engineer: Guy Charbonneau

The September 11 attacks in New York inspired in Stevie Nicks a poignantly serious hymn of resilience.

Genesis and Lyrics
In December 2001, Nicks returned home to Phoenix for the holidays, where she wrote several new songs. Back in Los Angeles, she presented the fruits of her labors to the other members of the group. She struggled to hide her nerves, worried that they wouldn't appreciate what she'd composed. "Illume (9-11)," inspired by the attacks on the Twin Towers on September 11, 2001, would move Lindsey to tears. Stevie, who was in New York at the time of the tragedy, found herself stranded in a devastated and traumatized city, a situation that immediately inspired her to write an intense text, into which introspective reflections and comments on the attacks were mixed. These are only hinted at through delicate images: "The candle that I burn" accompanies her prayer in tribute to the victims; "in a black sky" evokes the cloud of dust that darkened the city after the towers fell. "What we've been through" and "all of the trauma" touch with subtlety on the high emotion of living through an event of such magnitude ("I saw history go down").

Realization
Some percussion, rich acoustic guitars recorded with a piezo pickup, and a deep bass open "Illume (9-11)," immediately setting the scene for an intense track, in which Stevie Nicks's deep and expressive voice hits the listener right in the gut. While Stevie wasn't sure, Mick Fleetwood had strong words to reassure her: "This is classic Stevie Nicks; this is your modern-day 'Gold Dust Woman,'" he told her. "It's that Edith Piaf element of Stevie coming through on a lyric that's incredibly personal to her." At 3:24, Stevie sings more powerfully, making her lament irresistible until the finale, while the rhythm section sticks closely to the singer's emotions. The arrangement and production of Lindsey Buckingham and John Shanks are stunning, as are the colors brought by the former to his various guitar ornaments.

Lindsey Buckingham with Kristen Messner, his wife since 2000.

THROWN DOWN
Stevie Nicks / 4:08

Musicians: Lindsey Buckingham: vocals, guitar, keyboards, percussion / Stevie Nicks: vocals, keyboards / John McVie: bass / Mick Fleetwood: drums, percussion / **Recorded:** Bellagio House, Los Angeles / Lindsey Buckingham's studio (California) / Cornerstone Studios, Chatsworth (California): Summer 2001–Fall 2002 / **Technical Team:** Producers: John Shanks, Lindsey Buckingham / Sound Engineers: Ken Allardyce, Ken Koroshetz, Lindsey Buckingham, Mark Needham, Ray Lindsey / Assistant Sound Engineer: Guy Charbonneau

Genesis and Lyrics

Lindsey: "When you sing 'Now you're going home,' who are you talking about?"

Stevie: "I'm talking about you!"

Lindsey asks this during the documentary *Destiny Rules*, which traces the making of the album *Say You Will*. "Thrown Down" is a new dive into the complex and tumultuous relationship Stevie had had with Lindsey for more than two decades. The guitarist tried to suggest some adjustments in the text, such as changing the tense of the verbs to anchor the story in the past or opting for the third person to establish a little distance and universalize the subject. But Stevie wouldn't change her lines one iota. She even retorted that he wouldn't have allowed himself to make such suggestions if it had been Bob Dylan who stood in front of him, implying that she was on the same level of writing as Dylan. With considerable diplomacy, Lindsey explained that Bob Dylan might have treated this story in a more abstract way. But his arguments went unheard. These lyrics are intertwined with many feelings, all constitutive of what had bound the two of them together for years: resentment, love, desire, difficulties in communicating—which she mainly blames on Lindsey—and the desire to move on. The singer goes so far as to suggest that her partner has "fallen for her again," which was a fantasy, as Lindsey was in a relationship and had been a father for many years.

Realization

With this solo track that she didn't want to exploit for *Trouble in Shangri-La* because she couldn't get a mix that satisfied her (despite three different mixing attempts), Stevie Nicks proved once again that she was in great form. "It was just obvious to me it needed a guitar riff in the refrain [of 'Thrown Down']," recalls Lindsey. "It was a fairly simple thing, for some reason. There seems to be an understanding between us as to what to do." The song relies as much on Stevie's vocal performance as it does on Lindsey's inspired guitars or the solid performance of the rhythm section. Between the guitarist's haunting arpeggios and the airy choirs worthy of Fleetwood Mac's finest hours, subtle synthesizer touches slip in to enrich a brilliant arrangement. "Thrown Down" is one of the few tracks that show the band as able to perfectly manage Christine McVie's absence, both musically and vocally.

Mick Fleetwood behind his imposing Drum Workshop kit, complete with Zildjian gong, in London, November 30, 2003.

MIRANDA

Lindsey Buckingham / 4:17

Musicians: Lindsey Buckingham: vocals, guitar, keyboards, percussion / Stevie Nicks: vocals, keyboards / John McVie: bass / Mick Fleetwood: drums, percussion / **Recorded:** Bellagio House, Los Angeles / Ocean Way Recording, Hollywood / Lindsey Buckingham's studio (California) / Cornerstone Studios, Chatsworth (California): 1995–1997; Summer 2001–Fall 2002 / **Technical Team:** Producers: John Shanks, Lindsey Buckingham, Rob Cavallo / Sound Engineers: Ken Allardyce, Ken Koroshetz, Lindsey Buckingham, Mark Needham, Ray Lindsey

Genesis and Lyrics

Although Lindsey Buckingham has never confirmed it, "Miranda" may have been inspired by his short-lived companion, actress Anne Heche, to whom he dedicated another song on the *Say You Will* track list, "Come." But it could also be evoking Stevie Nicks. The lyrics, which describe a certain Miranda, an adored but desperately lonely media figure, are indeed appropriate for each of the two women. "Miranda" is a prisoner of the perverse relationship that binds her to fame, as the attention she receives and that she constantly seeks isolates her from others and slowly kills her. Her tragedy: "Can't stand to be loved / But she loves to be seen." She then behaves destructively. Addicted to drugs, she is also addicted to media exposure: "She sticks the camera right into her arm."

Realization

Lindsey Buckingham shows all his prowess with the guitar on "Miranda," randomly switching from a catchy gimmick on his National Resolectric to high-pitched electric notes that intertwine at the heart of the song in several river solos. The rhythm section is well placed—although a little behind the guitars—and features a solid Mick Fleetwood. He meticulously tortures a snare drum with a slamming sound, while his comrade John McVie offers a bass line that is as warm as it is deep. The other big draw is the catchy melody refrain, where the vocals of Lindsey Buckingham and Stevie Nicks strive to attain a captivating harmony.

Lindsey Buckingham and, in the background, Japanese percussionist Taku Hirano, who accompanied the Mac on the Say You Will tour.

RED ROVER
Lindsey Buckingham / 3:57

Musicians: Lindsey Buckingham: vocals, guitar / **Recorded:** Bellagio House, Los Angeles / Ocean Way Recording, Hollywood / Lindsey Buckingham's studio (California) / Cornerstone Studios, Chatsworth (California): 1995–1997; Summer 2001–Fall 2002 / **Technical Team:** Producers: John Shanks, Lindsey Buckingham, Rob Cavallo / Sound Engineers: Ken Allardyce, Ken Koroshetz, Lindsey Buckingham, Mark Needham, Ray Lindsey

Genesis and Lyrics

"Red Rover" appears to be the most enigmatic song on *Say You Will* and also the one that has given rise to the greatest number of interpretations, especially from Fleetwood Mac fans. Lindsey Buckingham gave the audience some keys to understanding it in a short speech given at a concert played in New York on June 6, 2004. He explained that this text was written from the point of view of the Greek gods who observe men from Olympus and despair at the evolution of their world. However, another theory is circulating among fans: It is actually about Christine McVie and the multiple attempts of the musicians to bring her back into the fold of the group—a credible hypothesis that would shed light on certain passages of the lyrics. Christine would address her partners through Lindsey's voice in the first verse: "Why do you come around / So very much?" to which his partners would respond in the refrain: "We come / To take you over." As if the tracks weren't blurred enough, Lindsey chose to name his song "Red Rover," after a common children's game in which a team of several participants faces off against one player. One at a time, the team members must reach the other side of the playing field getting past their opponent without being caught. According to Greek mythology, thus may men escape the divine punishment symbolized by the lone opponent, and in this case involving Christine, the group must continue without losing one of its members. Other interpretations, related to the death of a relative of Lindsey's, have also circulated.

Realization

"Red Rover" has an astonishing construction, which is essentially based on Lindsey Buckingham's versatile guitars, played with a capo. His precise and dazzling arpeggios demonstrate the guitarist's speed and technique. The ear thinks it picks up percussive elements, but it seems that this is the rhythmic work of the right-hand thumb on the low strings. No other element (keyboards, bass, backing vocals) seems to emerge from this strange composition, no doubt inspired by classical music: The bewitching "Red Rover" sounds very much like a piece recorded by Lindsey Buckingham alone, but it is impossible to categorically exclude any intervention by another member.

More than just his music, it was trumpeter Arturo Sandoval's troubled life experience that inspired Stevie Nicks to write "Say You Will."

The video shot for the release of "Say You Will" is only the recording of a live performance of the song. This video and the one of "Peacekeeper" (also a live performance) were only made available in 2019, when they were released on the band's official YouTube channel.

SAY YOU WILL
Stevie Nicks / 3:47

Musicians: Lindsey Buckingham: backing vocals, guitar, keyboards, percussion / Stevie Nicks: vocals, keyboards / John McVie: bass / Mick Fleetwood: drums, percussion / Sheryl Crow: Hammond organ and backing vocals / Madelyne Felsch, Molly McVie, and Jessica James Nicks—backing vocals / **Recorded:** Bellagio House, Los Angeles / Lindsey Buckingham's studio (California) / Cornerstone Studios, Chatsworth (California): Summer 2001–Fall 2002 / **Technical Team:** Producers: Lindsey Buckingham, Rob Cavallo, John Shanks / Sound Engineers: Ken Allardyce, Ken Koroshetz, Lindsey Buckingham, Mark Needham, Ray Lindsey / **Single:** Side A: Say You Will (Single Remix Fade) / Side B: Say You Will (Single Remix Cold) / **US Release Date:** June 16, 2003, Reprise Records (PRO-CDR–101137) / Best US Chart Ranking: Did Not Chart

Genesis and Lyrics
Two sources of inspiration fuel the song that gives its name to the album. One, unsurprisingly, is Lindsey Buckingham. "Everyone has experienced it," Stevie explained in a 2003 *Performing Songwriter* article: "Everybody's experienced it—when you like somebody, it makes you a different person. It changes you and it changes you in a minute. But that song is not just about Lindsey." Indeed, the singer links yet another intimate reflection on their tumultuous relationship to the story of the famous Cuban jazz trumpeter Arturo Sandoval. Stevie started writing "Say You Will" after seeing a movie about his journey. Exiled from his home country of Cuba, Arturo Sandoval had applied for political asylum in the United States, which he was denied for the first time in 1997, on the grounds that he had been a member of the Cuban Communist Party many years earlier. After President Bill Clinton intervened, he became a US citizen the following year. The connection between his relationship with Lindsey and the journey of a stateless musician is not obvious at first glance. But it is the breath of hope and the healing power of music and dance for wounds that she has mostly retained from the second story and applied to the first. "The refrain was written first, then I went back to write the verses…you have this great refrain that basically says, 'If you dance with me, you won't be mad at me anymore. We can be in a huge argument, but if we put on some music and start to dance, everything will be great.'"

Realization
Built on a moderate and catchy tempo, "Say You Will" relies on the plaintive voice of Stevie Nicks, surrounded by childlike backing vocals provided by Jessica Nicks (Stevie's niece), Maddy Felsch (Jessica's friend), and Molly McVie (John's daughter). The production is meticulous, highlighting the rhythm section and the versatile guitars of Lindsey Buckingham, who sings a very beautiful minimalist and melodic solo at 1:53. The song also benefited from the contribution of Sheryl Crow, who was invited for the first time to a Fleetwood Mac recording. She delivers a discreet Hammond organ part that is equally fundamental to lining the background of the song with warm layers, and offers, just like Lindsey Buckingham, some nice notes on the refrain.

PEACEKEEPER

Lindsey Buckingham / 4:10

Musicians: Lindsey Buckingham: vocals, guitar, keyboards, percussion / Stevie Nicks: backing vocals / John McVie: bass / Mick Fleetwood: drums, percussion / John Shanks: guitar / **Recorded:** Bellagio House, Los Angeles / Lindsey Buckingham's studio (California) / Cornerstone Studios, Chatsworth (California): Summer 2001–Fall 2002 / **Technical Team:** Producers: John Shanks, Lindsey Buckingham / Sound Engineers: Ken Allardyce, Ken Koroshetz, Lindsey Buckingham, Mark Needham, Ray Lindsey / **Single:** Side A: Peacekeeper (Single Mix) / Side B: Peacekeeper / Smile At You / **UK Release Date:** March 10, 2003, Reprise Records (9362 42631 2) / Best UK Chart Ranking: Did Not Chart / **Single:** Side A: Peacekeeper (Single Mix) / Side B: Peacekeeper (Single Mix Edit) / **US Release Date:** March 10, 2003, Reprise Records (PRO-CD–101067) / Best US Chart Ranking: 80

Genesis and Lyrics

Lindsey Buckingham's writing of "Peacekeeper" dates back to 2000, three years before the release of "Say You Will." When it was released as a single in the spring of 2003, the song tapped into a topic that would give it an unexpected dimension. Indeed, as the war in Iraq had just broken out, radio stations began to broadcast what they thought was a pacifist song. In reality, though the title is strangely prescient, the lyrics written by the guitarist evoke broader themes such as collective responsibility, the consequences of our individual actions, the complexity of love, and the need to make difficult decisions. "It was, in a very ironic way, looking at the kind of thinking that is matter of fact and desensitized with regard to certain actions that go on in the world, and the kind of blankness and conformity that goes along with that," Lindsey said of the song in 2003,

adding: "And then trying to look at what does that do for a married couple trying to work out their problems. How does it affect them? What is peace, really? The whole idea that there can be any static condition is obviously an illusion. So, can there ever really be peace? There can be moments of peace or long periods of peace, possibly, whether it's in the world or in a relationship. But it seems to me what peace really means is valuing the ideal of that and just being mindful of it—working towards the maintenance of it, even though you understand it will not always exist." While the verses symbolically evoke how destructive acts can impact everyone equally, in the collective and private spheres, the refrain encourages the peacekeeper to take his time, to wait for "the dark of night," to avoid impulsive decisions and allow time for things to evolve.

Realization

Both familiar and innovative, Peacekeeper evokes old hits such as "Dreams" or "Go Your Own Way," due to its gripping tempo and irresistible melody. The soft harmonies of the Buckingham-Nicks tandem are indeed extremely effective on the refrain. Lindsey Buckingham incorporates elements of country on the guitar and demonstrates an ever more precise playing on his fiendishly fast arpeggios. The presence of John Shanks as an additional guitarist brings additional color to the already rich panel of a perfectly produced song. For some parts, Lindsey Buckingham threaded his voice through an amplifier in an attempt to distort it ever so slightly. In the same way, he used an equalizer to cut off some of the high frequencies and accentuate the mid-frequencies, in order to get more warmth.

Co-composer of "Come," guitarist Neale Heywood supported Stevie Nicks on "New Orleans," on Stevie's solo album *In Your Dreams* (2011).

COME

Lindsey Buckingham, Neale Heywood / 5:59

Musicians: Lindsey Buckingham: vocals, guitar, keyboards, percussion / John McVie: bass / Mick Fleetwood: drums, percussion / Jamie Muhoberac: Hammond organ / **Recorded:** Bellagio House, Los Angeles / Ocean Way Recording, Hollywood / Lindsey Buckingham's studio (California), Cornerstone Studios, Chatsworth (California): 1995–1997; Summer 2001–Fall 2002 / **Technical Team:** Producers: Lindsey Buckingham, Rob Cavallo / Sound Engineers: Ken Allardyce, Ken Koroshetz, Lindsey Buckingham, Mark Needham, Ray Lindsey

Genesis and Lyrics

Lindsey Buckingham wrote "Come" with his ex-girlfriend Anne Heche in mind, when she left him to enter into a same-sex relationship with celebrity TV host Ellen DeGeneres. The song offers the point of view of a man who is cheated on and prefers to end the relationship before it falls apart. Did he make the right decision, or did he end it too early, before he realized the pain of lost love? That's why he gets a whiff of desire and hopes his partner will come back to him, if only for one last hug. In fact, it is more a question of desire and fever (the word "fever" comes up regularly) than of love. He is aware that there is nothing left to save on this side and that the damage has already been done: "Where's the harmony? Where's the humanity? / Love was a little too scarce."

Realization

The heavy theme of this track, co-written by Lindsey Buckingham and Neale Heywood, an English guitarist and composer who started touring with Fleetwood Mac in 1997, also generated a heavy arrangement. During the hushed and minimalist verses, Lindsey Buckingham's almost disembodied voice is accompanied by a guitar motif played with a unique fingering (the tremolo so clearly seen on the introductory arpeggios). On the other hand, the refrains appear unusually raging and metallic, full of distorted guitars and snare drums, which resonate as if they were metal trashcan lids. John McVie's bass is also heavy, while Lindsey Buckingham's voice seems to be possessed in places, to the point that we sometimes wonder if it's really him who is raging like this on the refrain, looking for unsuspecting notes. The presence of Jamie Muhoberac's Hammond organ is almost anecdotal, since the instrument essentially blends into the electric mayhem generated by the refrain.

Don Henley, founding member of the Eagles, with whom Stevie Nicks had a relationship between 1975 and 1977, and who inspired in her the songs "Sara" and "Smile at You."

SMILE AT YOU
Stevie Nicks / 4:32

Musicians: Lindsey Buckingham: guitar, keyboards, percussion / Stevie Nicks: vocals, keyboards / John McVie: bass / Mick Fleetwood: drums, percussion / **Recorded:** Bellagio House, Los Angeles / Lindsey Buckingham's studio (California) / Cornerstone Studios, Chatsworth (California): Summer 2001–Fall 2002 / **Technical Team:** Producer: Lindsey Buckingham / Sound Engineers: Ken Allardyce, Ken Koroshetz, Lindsey Buckingham, Mark Needham, Ray Lindsey

Genesis and Lyrics
Like Lindsey Buckingham, Stevie Nicks provided the album with old tracks that she had kept in reserve for a long time, such as the beautiful "Smile at You," which had been left out of other projects though she had tried several times to integrate it. Composed during the conception of the album *Rumours*, it was drafted for the first time for *Tusk*, then worked on more seriously during the recording of *Mirage*, in two versions, one calm and the other rather nervier. Left as an outtake, "Smile at You" is back for *Say You Will*, at a time when Stevie Nicks can express her creativity and impose her songs more than in the past. The song begins with an awareness of an unhealthy situation. The narrator addresses a man (Don Henley or Lindsey Buckingham) who is already in a relationship and refuses to leave his wife, contrary to his promises. The lover expresses her weariness of being the other woman forever. She is no longer fooled ("I have come to know / This world of changing faces") and wishes to regain her freedom because it is the only element on which she can act: If she "can't fight the world" (the lie is implied) and "can't change it," she can, on the other hand, leave and save herself ("Go on, save yourself").

Realization
Hypnotic vocal harmonies, sparse drums, and inspired guitars are at the heart of an almost perfect production. But to accompany Stevie Nicks's charismatic voice in her lament, it's John McVie's bass that proves to be the song's greatest asset. Slippery, this one is warm in sound and almost decadent with its descending notes that really pack a punch in the refrain. Lindsey Buckingham's sparse acoustic guitar notes on the finale are the perfect epilogue to a vibrant track—one of the fan favorites, and rightly so.

Lindsey's intense, flamboyant solo provides an epic, virtuoso finale to "Running Through the Garden."

RUNNING THROUGH THE GARDEN

Stevie Nicks, Ray Kennedy, Gary Nicholson / 4:33

Musicians: Stevie Nicks: vocals / Lindsey Buckingham: guitar, backing vocals / John McVie: bass / Mick Fleetwood: drums / **Recorded:** Bellagio House, Los Angeles / Lindsey Buckingham's studio (California) / Cornerstone Studios, Chatsworth (California): Summer 2001–Fall 2002 / **Technical Team:** Producer: Lindsey Buckingham / Sound Engineers: Ken Allardyce, Ken Koroshetz, Lindsey Buckingham, Mark Needham, Ray Lindsey

Genesis and Lyrics

Stevie Nicks co-wrote "Running Through the Garden" with Ray Kennedy and Gary Nicholson. The former had already collaborated with Fleetwood Mac, contributing to the setting to music of Mick Fleetwood's spoken poem "These Strange Times" in 1995. And the latter had participated in the song "Deal with It" from the album *Bekka & Billy*, which Billy Burnette had recorded with Bekka Bramlett in 1997, two years after leaving Fleetwood Mac. The idea for "Running Through the Garden" came to her while reading "Rappaccini's Daughter," an allegorical short story by American author Nathaniel Hawthorne (published in *The United States Magazine and Democratic Review* in 1844). In this story, Giovanni, a literature student, observes a young woman, Beatrice, walking in the lush neighboring garden of her father-in-law, an eccentric scientist who grows poisonous plants. Little by little, Giovanni understands that Beatrice is toxic to the organisms she approaches. Flowers and insects die when they come into contact with her. Giovanni eventually finds an antidote that would allow the two young people to live out their love. Alas, his find kills the girl. Touched by this dramatic love story, Stevie was directly inspired by it: "Until she herself / Became the deadliest poison […] Became just as fatal / As was her garden." At one point in the story, Stevie switches from the third person to the first person (a constant in her writing) to embody the beauty with deadly powers and warn her lover by giving him this order that tears his heart out but can save him: "Turn around."

Realization

Another meticulous production for Lindsey Buckingham, who perfectly masters the balance and dynamics of the instruments. The musician's warm acoustic guitars offer brilliance to a rhythm section that is once again very inspired. As for the electric guitars, they bring greater color to the space, without stealing the show from Stevie Nicks's haunting voice. On the pre-refrain, a few layers of keyboards bring more consistency to the melody, and the choirs bring intensity. The refrain is very effective, with a sustained bass and a very catchy melody. After a colorful first solo halfway through, Lindsey Buckingham sets the finale on fire from 3:50, with an incandescent solo. Another great contribution to *Say You Will* to be credited to Stevie Nicks.

Sheryl Crow made only a brief appearance, but it didn't take much at the time for the rumor of her permanent integration into the band to arise. Mick then declared to anyone who would listen that there was no question of replacing Christine with Sheryl, but that the latter would nevertheless be welcome if she wished to join the Mac on stage.

SILVER GIRL
Stevie Nicks / 3:59

Musicians: Lindsey Buckingham: vocals, guitar, keyboards, percussion / Stevie Nicks: vocals, keyboards / John McVie: bass / Mick Fleetwood: drums, percussion / Sheryl Crow: Hammond organ and backing vocals / **Recorded:** Bellagio House, Los Angeles / Lindsey Buckingham's studio (California) / Cornerstone Studios, Chatsworth (California): Summer 2001–Fall 2002 / **Technical Team:** Producer: Lindsey Buckingham / Sound Engineers: Ken Allardyce, Ken Koroshetz, Lindsey Buckingham, Mark Needham, Ray Lindsey

Stevie Nicks discovered a form of spiritual and artistic sisterhood with Sheryl Crow, who took part in the recording of "Silver Girl" and "Say You Will."

Genesis and Lyrics
In the absence of Christine McVie's support, Stevie Nicks invited her friend Sheryl Crow for two of her new songs, including the tender and soothing ballad "Silver Girl." The singer, who regretted that the group's feminine touch and girl power were diminished by Christine's absence—even if she understood the reasons for her withdrawal—hoped to restore a form of balance with Sheryl's presence at her side: "I penned 'Silver Girl' about Sheryl," she said. "It's an ode to a lady rock star who's always on the road and has a very hard time having relationships and settling down. So, it's also totally about me."

Stevie saw Sheryl Crow, who wrote "It's Only Love" for her on the album *Trouble in Shangri-La*, as a double of her younger self. "We all love her and try to take her along with us because we know that. It was very fun when she came to record with Fleetwood Mac. Lindsey likes her a lot and Mick loves her, and John loves her, and she's one of our little adoptees. So, the song is like an ode to the girl rock star, an ode to the question, 'Is it possible to find somebody to love?' When you're rich and famous, it's very hard to find somebody. That's not taking away the hope, but it is stating that it's difficult. When Sheryl asked me, 'Am I ever going to find anybody?' I say, 'Well, who knows? If you want to attain a certain amount of fame, then you have to work all the time, which is what you do. And you don't hang out very much, you are on the move. You're in New York, you're in L.A., you're in Switzerland, you're in Vietnam, you're never around for very long. You're like a willow wisp. So it kind of depends on what you want to do.' I kind

of made a choice when I was Sheryl's age, when I was 40, that I didn't really want to be tied down. There are many times during my life that I could've been married and I could've had children, and I made the decision to not do it." Indeed, the song's lyrics evoke a complex woman not unlike both Sheryl and Stevie, who is searching for her identity while facing challenges. The first few lines describe her as a "Silver girl / Lost in a high-tech world," then as a "Golden girl / Immersed in a hardcore world." "Shadows move across her face," symbolizing the trials and experiences that have left their mark on her. She is both a daring adventurer in a man's world and a vulnerable woman who sometimes feels lonely.

Realization
Mick Fleetwood's drums, including his snare drum with a sound that is both matte and slamming, imprints the quiet rhythm of this beautiful ballad, punctuated by beautiful ornamentations of guitars and mischievous keyboards. John McVie, too, provides his warm bass to serve up a catchy melody. But it's above all the stunning vocal harmonies that really make "Silver Girl," offering clear proof of Sheryl Crow's contribution right from the first listen.

STEAL YOUR HEART AWAY

Lindsey Buckingham / 3:33

Musicians: Stevie Nicks: vocals / Lindsey Buckingham: vocals, guitar, percussion / Christine McVie: keyboards, backing vocals / Dave Palmer: piano / John McVie: bass / John Pierce: bass / Mick Fleetwood: drums, percussion / **Recorded:** Bellagio House, Los Angeles / Ocean Way Recording, Hollywood / Lindsey Buckingham's studio (California) / Cornerstone Studios, Chatsworth (California): 1995–1997; Summer 2001–Fall 2002 / **Technical Team:** Producers: Lindsey Buckingham, Rob Cavallo / Sound Engineers: Ken Allardyce, Ken Koroshetz, Lindsey Buckingham, Mark Needham, Ray Lindsey

Genesis and Lyrics

Like many of the songs on this album, "Steal Your Heart Away" comes from Lindsey Buckingham's pool of compositions, on which he intended to draw to fuel a solo album. The charm of this acoustic ballad, both simple and refined, seems to fit perfectly with the repertoire of Fleetwood Mac, especially since the refrain calls for vocal harmonies that only the band knows how to produce. The text, as intimate as it is universal, depicts a man in the grip of loneliness, who suffers from the absence of love on a daily basis. He tries to extricate himself from his dreary daily life by thinking about the woman he secretly loves and hopes that one day he will be able to steal her heart and run away with her.

Realization

This undated personal composition—in which Christine had participated by recording a few backing vocals—offers a contemporary side of Fleetwood Mac with slick pop and modern, dynamic production, while preserving the essence of the band's defining musical formula: melody and care for vocals. It contains, moreover, all of Lindsey's skill and sensitivity when it comes to writing titles of absolute romanticism. This lover of rock'n'roll, an admirer of Roy Orbison, fashions an equivalent of his "You Got It," a standard classic that never becomes cheesy. As in his model, the incredibly elegant melody leads the whole composition toward a pop ideal. Particular care is taken with the vocal harmonies. Silky and precise, they benefit from one of Christine McVie's last interventions on record.

ON YOUR HEADPHONES

In "Bleed to Love Her," Lindsey Buckingham "self-quotes" at 1:51. He takes an entire verse from his own song "You Do or You Don't," which is on the album *Out of the Cradle* (1992): "Somebody's got to see this through / All the world is laughing at you / Somebody's got to sacrifice / If this whole thing's going to turn out right." The composer also uses the melody identically, which fits perfectly into the context.

BLEED TO LOVE HER

Lindsey Buckingham / 4:05

Musicians: Lindsey Buckingham: vocals, guitar, keyboards / John McVie: bass / Mick Fleetwood: drums, percussion / Stevie Nicks: backing vocals / Christine McVie: backing vocals / **Recorded:** Bellagio House, Los Angeles / Ocean Way Recording, Hollywood / Lindsey Buckingham's studio (California) / Cornerstone Studios, Chatsworth (California): 1995–1997; Summer 2001–Fall 2002 / **Technical Team:** Producers: Lindsey Buckingham, Rob Cavallo / Sound Engineers: Ken Allardyce, Ken Koroshetz, Lindsey Buckingham, Mark Needham, Ray Lindsey

Genesis and Lyrics

The presence of the studio version of "Bleed to Love Her," already unveiled during the 1997 reunion tour and in *The Dance*, sounds like a declaration of love from Lindsey to his band, as this song is of crucial importance, in hindsight, in the process that brought the members to find each other. Although he intended this track for his own discography, Lindsey had brought in John, Mick, and Christine to play in 1997. The pleasure they felt during the recording session led them to reconsider their future together and to play together again on stage. In this song, which has become highly symbolic, he presents an idealized but elusive female character who ignites the fire of desire in him before immediately extinguishing it.

Realization

With a simple guitar motif, played clearly, Lindsey Buckingham works the magic. His fingerpicking, with its vibrating high strings, draws a melody in its own right, which is complemented with great finesse by the vocal line. A fan of musical counterpoint, Lindsey imagines an unexpected, primal rhythmic for Mick's drums, with a snare drum whose sound is abnormally metallic and ultra-compressed. The combination of this rhythmic motif with the guitar and the almost tribal chorus notes tend to tip the song into an Afropop atmosphere.

In addition to his contribution to Stevie Nicks's "I Can't Wait" in 1985, songwriter Rick Nowels (pictured here in 2006) contributed to the success of nearly 90 hits and has been inducted into the Songwriters Hall of Fame.

Launched, so to speak, by Stevie Nicks in 1985, Rick Nowels went on to have successful collaborations ranging from Belinda Carlisle's "Heaven Is a Place on Earth" (number one in the United States in 1987) to Celine Dion's album *Falling into You* (awarded a Grammy in 1997). He has also collaborated with Madonna, Dido, Lana Del Rey, and Dua Lipa.

EVERYBODY FINDS OUT
Stevie Nicks, Rick Nowels / 4:28

Musicians: Stevie Nicks: vocals / Lindsey Buckingham: vocals, guitar, keyboards, percussion / Christine McVie: keyboards, backing vocals / John McVie: bass / Mick Fleetwood: drums, percussion / **Recorded:** Bellagio House, Los Angeles / Lindsey Buckingham's studio (California) / Cornerstone Studios, Chatsworth (California): 1995–1997; Summer 2001–Fall 2002 / **Technical Team:** Producer: Lindsey Buckingham / Sound Engineers: Ken Allardyce, Ken Koroshetz, Lindsey Buckingham, Mark Needham, Ray Lindsey

Genesis and Lyrics
To develop "Everybody Finds Out," Stevie Nicks turned to one of her favorite songwriters, Rick Nowels. The two artists knew each other well from having composed the singer's single "I Can't Wait," released in December 1985. At the time, she gave him his first major credit as a composer and producer. The track's number sixteen spot on the US charts encouraged Stevie to work with him again on *Rock a Little*, for which he was promoted to co-producer, and then on several tracks on her 1989 album *The Other Side of the Mirror*, including the hit "Rooms on Fire," which also reached number sixteen on the US singles chart. As the title of the song suggests, this text is about an extramarital affair the narrator is involved in. She confides in a friend and exposes the situation with little shame. All her entourage have noticed her amorous merry-go-round despite the thousands of precautions taken by the lovers, suggested by the themes of night and darkness. However, this love is strong, and it soon becomes clear that the narrator has no intention of ending the affair. Stevie Nicks has already tackled the theme of adultery in the songs "Kind of Woman" on *Bella Donna* (1981) and "Imperial Hotel" on *Rock a Little* (1985).

Realization
"Everybody Finds Out" is striking, from the very first seconds, in its originality. Stevie's voice is recessed, passed through a filter that reduces its clarity, as if it were going through a radio. Above all, it emerges in the middle of a percussion ensemble to the strains of pocket samba. The bass arrives, furtive, and inserts a pattern that is both groovy and heavy. The track then evolves into a Latin pop rock, where Lindsey's luminous acoustic guitar shines, appearing as light and delicate as Stevie's voice is dark and deep. When the guitarist intervenes vocally, he seems to pull his partner up by bringing a little optimism to the singer's desperate interpretation.

John McVie and Stevie Nicks rock Earl's Court, London, on November 29, 2003.

DESTINY RULES
Stevie Nicks / 4:26

Musicians: Lindsey Buckingham: vocals, guitar / Stevie Nicks: vocals / Christine McVie: keyboards, backing vocals / John McVie: bass / Mick Fleetwood: drums, percussion / **Recorded:** Bellagio House, Los Angeles / Lindsey Buckingham's studio (California) / Cornerstone Studios, Chatsworth (California): 1995–1997; Summer 2001–Fall 2002 / **Technical Team:** Producer: Lindsey Buckingham / Sound Engineers: Ken Allardyce, Ken Koroshetz, Lindsey Buckingham, Mark Needham, Ray Lindsey

Genesis and Lyrics

Stevie Nicks has often sung about the power of love and the impossibility of resisting it. In "Destiny Rules," she introduces the idea that this love is itself transcended by a greater force: fate. It is fate that prevents the narrator from living her love with the one she loves. This relationship is forbidden to her; it can only be a fantasy and exists only "in another life" or "in a parallel universe." However, it has already existed in this life, since the narrator asserts that

our "paths are not supposed to cross twice." The line "Maybe your arms are not supposed to go around me" reinforces this idea but is mostly reminiscent of another Nicks song, "No Questions Asked," from the Mac's *Greatest Hits* album (1988), in which she had already spoken about her grief at not being able to be with the man she loves: "And you miss those arms that used to go around you."

Realization

Lindsey Buckingham proves with this title his ease in the blues field. Armed with his National Resolectric, which combines the qualities of a dobro with its resonator and those of an electric guitar, he creates a harmonious marriage between tradition, striving to revive the legacy of the original Fleetwood Mac and the pop rock direction he himself had defined since his arrival. Stevie Nicks's textured, melancholy-tinged voice brings the lyrics to life with poignant intensity.

"Say Goodbye" was Lindsey's first step toward making amends and considerably softening his attitude toward his bandmate Stevie.

SAY GOODBYE
Lindsey Buckingham / 3:26

Musicians: Stevie Nicks: vocals / Lindsey Buckingham: vocals, guitar / **Recorded:** Bellagio House, Los Angeles / Ocean Way Recording, Hollywood / Lindsey Buckingham Studio (California) / Cornerstone Studios, Chatsworth (California): 1995–1997; Summer 2001–Fall 2002 / **Technical Team:** Producer: Lindsey Buckingham / Sound Engineers: Ken Allardyce, Ken Koroshetz, Lindsey Buckingham, Mark Needham, Ray Lindsey

Genesis and Lyrics

In a 2013 interview with *Rolling Stone* magazine about the song she wrote a decade earlier, Buckingham said, "As I said, Stevie and I have probably more of a connection now than we have in years. You can feel it. It's tangible on stage. In many ways, that song is the embodiment of that. When you look at 'Without You,' it's Stevie writing a song about me when everything was before us, and all those illusions were intact. 'Say Goodbye' was written 10 years ago, when most of our experience together was behind us. Part of those illusions had fallen away." He continues, "It was difficult for years to get complete closure. There was never any time to not be together. It was kind of like picking the scab off an open wound again and again. That's part of the legacy of the band. But 'Say Goodbye' is a very sweet song, and it's about her: 'Once you said goodbye to me / Now I say goodbye to you.' It took a long time. All those illusions have fallen away, but that doesn't mean that there isn't

resolve and hope and belief in the future in a different context. That's really what the song is about."[38]

Stevie and Lindsey perform this song together, symbolizing their entry into a new era—one of reconciliation, fragile but real. Steeped in good intentions, this composition is a beautiful statement from the singer, who has these tender words: "That was so long ago, yes / Still I often think of you."

Realization

"Say Goodbye" concentrates the essence of Lindsey Buckingham's guitar-playing qualities. It is based on his signature technique: Travis picking, a style of playing named after its pioneer, the legendary country musician Merle Travis. The quality and precision of his playing are not affected by the sustained tempo applied to this track. Quite the contrary: The musician maintains a precision at all times in his execution. He also ensures the melodic richness of the song by recording two guitar tracks that complement each other perfectly. In this already rich context, thanks to this guitar playing that is as melodic as it is percussive, there is no need for a rhythm section that would weigh the whole thing down. The singing, on the other hand, does not require a flamboyant interpretation. On the contrary, Stevie and Lindsey employ the tone of confession with a soft, fragile, almost whispered chant at the end of sentences.

With "Goodbye Baby," Stevie responds positively to Lindsey, who seems to want to enter a new, calming phase.

GOODBYE BABY
Stevie Nicks / 3:52

Musicians: Stevie Nicks: vocals / Lindsey Buckingham: guitar, keyboards, backing vocals / John McVie: bass / **Recorded:** Bellagio House, Los Angeles / Lindsey Buckingham's studio (California) / Cornerstone Studios, Chatsworth (California): Summer 2001–Fall 2002 / **Technical Team:** Producer: Lindsey Buckingham / Sound Engineers: Ken Allardyce, Ken Koroshetz, Lindsey Buckingham, Mark Needham, Ray Lindsey

Genesis and Lyrics

Adept at writing full of imagery, Stevie sometimes builds her texts by combining very different themes. She manages to unite them and form a narrative with drawers that can be opened up to various interpretations. In the case of "Goodbye Baby," there are three possible readings, which complement more than they oppose each other. The singer started with an old demo, "The Tower," named after her first line ("Don't take me to the tower"). That was all it took for fans to see it as a new evocation of the September 11 attacks, after the song "Illume (9-11)," also on *Say You Will*. The broken glass and tears cited in the text would agree with this theory; however, the demo, circa 1975, long predates 2001. That said, Stevie may have chosen to rework "The Tower" after September 11, 2001, because of its symbolic name. The second possible reading is that of a reply to Lindsey Buckingham, who had just written her "Say Goodbye." This hypothesis is all the more credible since the two songs are opportunely linked in the track list and their titles respond to each other: "Say Goodbye" / "Goodbye Baby." Finally, the third theory is that "Goodbye Baby" is an extension of "Sara," the 1979 song by Stevie Nicks, whose character evoked both the baby she aborted and her absent best friend, Robin Anderson. There is a link between two of these interpretations, of which Stevie is well aware: Robin's date of birth is September 11 (1948).

Realization

This sweet song is based on an interlacing of guitars played with infinite delicacy by Lindsey Buckingham. It's like a lullaby, a form that fits perfectly with Stevie Nicks's whispered *babies*. The sound recording of her voice is adapted to this atmosphere, since we hear the smallest details, right down to the singer's breath between each phrase. A performance to Lindsey's credit: Despite the spartan conditions for the voice recording, in a small room in Bellagio House, far from being as ideal as a professional recording booth, Lindsey managed to capture the emotion of the singer, who is on the edge, and to invite the listener into this bubble of intimacy.

NOT MAKE BELIEVE

Stevie Nicks / 4:28

Musicians: Stevie Nicks: vocals / Lindsey Buckingham: guitar, keyboards, backing vocals / John McVie: bass / Mick Fleetwood: drums / **Recorded:** Bellagio House, Los Angeles / Lindsey Buckingham's studio (California) / Cornerstone Studios, Chatsworth (California): Summer 2001–Fall 2002 / **Technical Team:** Producer: Lindsey Buckingham / Sound Engineers: Ken Allardyce, Ken Koroshetz, Lindsey Buckingham, Mark Needham, Ray Lindsey

In the process of being recorded, "Not Make Believe" was dropped at an advanced stage of its conception, well beyond demo status. Fortunately, a special edition of the album, released in April 2003 with four bonus tracks (a cover of "Love Minus Zero / No Limit" by Bob Dylan, "Not Make Believe," and live recordings of "Peacekeeper" and "Say You Will"), allows you to enjoy this outtake. Only a few imbalances persist in terms of mixing, with a bass and an electric guitar placed in front of the other instruments at 1:24, then a guitar with a violining effect whose volume could have been increased. But the whole thing offers a nice balance and an exceptional sound recording. Above all, this very catchy pop song is based on a superb melody, a multitude of small instrumental motifs that make it exciting to listen to, and a confident and powerful interpretation from Stevie Nicks, who pours out thoughts on the harshness of band life.

LOVE MINUS ZERO/ NO LIMIT

Bob Dylan / 4:11

Musicians: Lindsey Buckingham: vocals, guitar / John McVie: bass / Mick Fleetwood: drums, percussion / **Recorded:** Bellagio House, Los Angeles / Ocean Way Recording, Hollywood / Lindsey Buckingham's studio (California) / Cornerstone Studios, Chatsworth (California): 1995–1997; Summer 2001–Fall 2002 / **Technical Team:** Producer: Lindsey Buckingham

Lindsey Buckingham and Stevie Nicks have shared an unconditional love for folk music since their youth and their first musical experience together in the band Fritz. Bob Dylan, in particular, figures prominently in the personal pantheon of both artists. Lindsey offers a cover of Dylan that had been on his mind for some time: "Love Minus Zero / No Limit." For him, this song symbolizes the melodic timelessness of his musical hero as much as his artistic freedom. Anchored in folk, it was in fact on *Bringing It All Back Home*, the album that marks Dylan's break with his debut by integrating electric guitar. In his reinterpretation, Buckingham gives this instrument its rightful place. He keeps the series of three descending arrangements that form the skeleton of the song, while sculpting a delicate arrangement thanks to the addition of a new and beautiful guitar picking part at the end of the song.

THE 2003–2013 TOURS

In the decade following the release of *Say You Will*, Fleetwood Mac, now reduced to a quartet, reunited occasionally for tours and concerts, some of which resulted in live albums.

The Say You Will Tour (May 7, 2003–September 14, 2004)

Since the release of a new album has rarely been a guarantee of stability in Fleetwood Mac's history, there was no reason why *Say You Will* should be an exception to this rule. Tensions resurfaced between Lindsey and Stevie—both in the press and onstage. Incidents were to become more frequent during the Say You Will tour, which kicked off barely a month after the album's release. At the May 25 concert at the Continental Airlines Arena in East Rutherford, New Jersey, the guitarist loudly burst onto the stage, playing a few discordant notes just as the singer was about to unleash her legendary vibrato on "Dreams." Scorned by Lindsey, Stevie continued with the show as if nothing had happened. Later in the evening, Stevie took her revenge several times. In particular, she launched into the last verse of "Landslide," pretending to forget Lindsey's guitar solo.

Christine, far removed from these turpitudes, was finally enjoying her long-awaited retirement, and had no regrets about her choice. After seeing her bandmates perform in the UK in 2004, she said: "I saw them play on tour. It was quite fun, actually. Weird too. It was the first time in my musical career that I could observe the band from the audience's point of view. [...] They sounded great, but it was a strange feeling. I must say, when I went backstage and saw them, they all looked so tired that I thought I'd made the right decision. Stevie was really exhausted... She was still doing so much on stage. She's not as old as me, but she's not a teenager, either. I think they were fantastic, but I don't want to do that anymore."[79] However, Christine had not given up music altogether, and in 2004, with the help of producer Ken Caillat, she released a new solo album, *In the Meantime*, which she had no plans to promote onstage.

Parallel Destinies

In the years 2004–2013, Fleetwood Mac, although still touring, gave ground to Stevie's and Lindsey's personal ambitions. Stevie embarked on the Gold Dust tour in 2006, with Vanessa Carlton. Two years later, she toured with Chris Isaak on the Soundstage Sessions tour, which led to her first solo live album, *The Soundstage Sessions*, the following year. Lindsey Buckingham did not remain idle, either. He was highly productive, adding three new albums to his discography: *Under the Skin* (2006), *Gift of Screws* (2008), and *Seeds We Sow* (2011).

Lindsey Buckingham, however, always kept a close eye on Fleetwood Mac, not only giving the band a run for its money on tour, but also getting involved in the media whenever the band was in question, such as the time when rumors of Sheryl Crow's replacing Christine McVie had to be quashed in 2008. It was Sheryl herself who started it. "She announced she was going on tour with us. Stevie and Mick were understandably unhappy. It wasn't the right time

The band in concert at Madison Square Garden in May 2004.

Live in Boston, released in 2004, documents the September 23 and 24, 2003, concerts at Boston's Fleet Center (subsequently known as the TD Garden). The ten-track album is accompanied by two DVD videos of the concert. It reached number eighty-four on the Billboard 200.

and context for her to talk about it, because the matter hadn't been decided," Lindsey pointed out, adding: "After the friction this incident created between her and Stevie, I think Sheryl understood that she had to abandon the idea. Continuing as a four-piece may be a challenge, but I think it's better [for us]."

The Unleashed Tour (March 1–December 20, 2009)

On October 7, 2008, Mick Fleetwood announced on the BBC's *The One Show* that Fleetwood Mac would be touring the following year and hinted that a new album might follow. Although the band did indeed set off on the Unleashed tour on March 1, 2009, which included no fewer than eighty-one dates until December 20, the predicted album never saw the light of day. So, for the first time, the band would be touring without an album to promote.

Fleetwood Mac prepared to hit the road with a degree of optimism, touring the US, Canada, Germany, Ireland, the UK, Australia, and New Zealand. Relations between Stevie and Lindsey had become more peaceful in the preceding months, as the singer confided: "When Lindsey and I don't get along, nobody gets along. But we haven't had a single disagreement since we started rehearsing. And instead of treating me like his miserable old ex, he treats me like his difficult but beloved eldest daughter. He's been very kind." Unfortunately, after a few months, life on tour would rekindle the tensions, as the singer confessed much later: "My cousin John has seen Lindsey and me work since 1968. He said to me: 'When I saw you play in 2009 with Fleetwood Mac, there was nothing binding you together. It was as if you were concentrating on what you were going to ask room service for when you got home. Grilled cheese? Tomato soup?' In fact, between Lindsey and me, in 2009, everything was wrong."[72] But the bond was artificially maintained by the band's success: The Unleashed tour proved to be one of the most lucrative band tours of 2009, grossing nearly $85 million.

Time for forgiveness and the birth of a form of tenderness dawned in 2013.

EXTENDED PLAY

Release Dates
April 30, 2013
Reference: LMJS Productions (digital release)
Best UK Chart Ranking: Did Not Chart
Best US Chart Ranking: 48

Sad Angel
Without You
It Takes Time
Miss Fantasy

The Full Stop

The Mac's latest discographic chapter—and the last to date, released on April 30, 2013, amounts to an EP of just four songs, titled *Extended Play*. The spoils were meager for those who had been impatient for ten years, and the release was out of step with Mac practices, since the EP was available only in digital format. Since the release of his album *Seeds We Sow* in 2011, Lindsey Buckingham had perfectly understood that music consumption habits had profoundly changed, and that he had to adapt: "There's a gap between the preconceived ideas of people my age and what music has become," he explained to *Rolling Stone* in 2013. "I sent *EP* to Daniel Glass, the director of [the label] Glassnote, who loved it. But when he played it to his colleagues, guys in their twenties, they all wondered what the hell they were going to do with it." Stevie was not at all optimistic about the place of new Fleetwood Mac recordings in the contemporary music industry: "The

Internet has destroyed everything. I miss buying an album, lying on the floor for three days and examining it with a magnifying glass." At the end of December 2012, she confided again to *Rolling Stone*: "We have a new product, but I don't know what we're going to do with it. [...] The music business is very different right now. I just don't get it. [...] Nobody is really interested in buying albums with 14 songs anymore. It breaks my heart, but that's the way it is, and I have to accept it. Maybe the thing to do would be to release five or six songs at some point in the year."

2012: A Year of Gestation

At the beginning of 2012, with everyone back to business since the end of the Unleashed tour, Fleetwood Mac's recording future was still up in the air. Was the band still sufficiently commercially viable to release a new opus after a ten-year absence from the stores, or should they confine themselves to tours aimed at the more nostalgic? The question was still unresolved when the band decided to add a new chapter to their discography. Lindsey, Mick, and John met up in Hawaii to record new songs, as Stevie, too affected by the death of her mother, did not have the strength to take part in the sessions. The three men, with foresight, ensured that the new songs were recorded in a key that suited Stevie's voice, so that she could sing them later. "They did very well. I'm really proud of them." said the singer after

In 2013, Fleetwood Mac releases a digital EP, which they present live onstage, a domain where their self-assurance never fails them.

recording her vocal part in December of the same year. Back in Los Angeles, the band decided to produce this new album on their own, without the support of a record company, in Lindsey's studio, who recruited producer Mitchell Froom.

Using the Resources at Hand

Fleetwood Mac, who eventually abandoned the idea of an album in the face of Stevie's reluctance, opted for the EP. "She was defensive about recording an album," explains Mick, "then someone said, 'Let's just put out two tracks, they'll be downloadable when [tour] tickets go on sale.'" But Lindsey wanted a little more: "I said, 'Well, if Stevie won't do an album, let's at least do an EP. That's more concrete.'"

Between Lindsey's and Stevie's tours and albums, the four songs that make up the EP were not easy to get into the can, especially as they once again had to do without Christine McVie. At the end of 2012, things began to take shape, and the finishing touches were applied to *Extended Play* during a four-day session at Lindsey's house. The singer took advantage of a gap in her schedule to do some vocal takes. Between the work sessions, these four days would above all provide an opportunity for the two "terrible" ex-lovers to renew their dialogue: "It was great to spend time with Linds," Stevie explained to *Rolling Stone* on December 5, 2012. "We laid down our arms. [...] Now we see each other in a slightly different light. A favorable light."

Stevie and Lindsey managed to resolve their differences in a seminal discussion, known to fans as "The Talk." "I told him everything I'd wanted to tell him since 1968," Stevie confides. "Remember how cute we were? How we could fascinate people with our humor and intelligence just by walking into a room?"[72] After explaining to her ex that, if they were unable to become those people again, she seriously envisioned ending the Fleetwood Mac adventure: "I can work with other people who treat me with warmth and with respect. I want you to know that in my world, no one ever says a hurtful word," she said, before concluding in response to his silence: "The ball is in your court. The Lindsey of 2013 had better be great."[72]

After four days at Lindsey's place working on the music, Stevie declared herself ready for the forthcoming 2013 tour. "Fleetwood Mac Live 2013" (April 4, 2013–October 26, 2013), the band's first major tour since 2009, was organized to promote the release of the EP, but more importantly to commemorate the thirty-fifth anniversary of the release of their landmark album *Rumours*. With twenty-one sold-out concerts, the Live tour proved to be a phenomenal success, ranking seventeenth on *Billboard*'s top 25 highest-grossing tours of 2013.

On April 6, on stage at the Wells Fargo Center in Philadelphia, during the second concert of the tour, Lindsey Buckingham officially announced the release of *Extended Play* at the end of the month, when he introduced one of the new tracks, "Sad Angel," to the audience.

SAD ANGEL

Lindsey Buckingham / 4:03

Musicians: Lindsey Buckingham: vocals, guitar, keyboards, percussion / John McVie: bass / Mick Fleetwood: drums / Stevie Nicks: backing vocals / **Recorded:** Lindsey Buckingham's studio: 2012–2013 / **Technical Team:** Producers: Lindsey Buckingham, Mitchell Froom Digital / **Single:** Sad Angel / **UK/US Release Date:** April 2013 Best UK and US Chart Rankings: Did Not Chart

"Sad Angel" is one of Fleetwood Mac's countless discographic milestones dealing with the complex bond between Lindsey and Stevie. This time, the message is benevolent, a sign that the two artists had (perhaps) finally managed to heal their relationship. Lindsey's empathy is evident as she reflects on the struggles the singer has had to endure: "Hello, hello, sad angel / Have you come to fight the war?" I wrote the song for Stevie," Lindsey confirmed to Andy Greene in a 2013 interview. "She always had to fight for everything. She was coming off a solo album and was mentally re-joining the band. We're all warriors armed with a sword in a way."[38] When the song says "We fall to earth together" or "We fall on each other's sword," this is something of an understatement. The evocation of this memory is a tender gesture from the lyricist to Stevie, testifying that he has always been by her side, and that, whatever happens, he always will be, even in times of trial.

In this moderately paced pop-rock ballad, it is the rhythm section that takes center stage, with Mick Fleetwood and John McVie seemingly more involved than ever. Mick, in particular, plays a few rolls that serve the dynamics of the melody perfectly and give it plenty of energy. Lindsey's acoustic guitar adds warmth to the whole. The musician also adds a long solo from 1:41 onward, without showing off his technique. Melodically, the song works well, especially as Stevie's and Lindsey's voices always fit together admirably, even though Stevie's sometimes appears to be slightly behind.

WITHOUT YOU

Stevie Nicks / 4:39

Musicians: Stevie Nicks: vocals / Lindsey Buckingham: vocals, guitar, keyboards, percussion / John McVie: bass / Mick Fleetwood: drums, percussion **Recorded:** Lindsey Buckingham's studio: 2012–2013 **Technical Team:** Producers: Lindsey Buckingham, Stevie Nicks

"Without You" is a forty-year-old song, and although Lindsey and Stevie find it difficult to date its origins precisely, both agree that it predates their involvement with Fleetwood Mac. According to Lindsey, the song came from the composition sessions for the second Buckingham Nicks album, shortly before the duo were dropped by their record label, Polydor. But according to Stevie, it was written earlier. "I'm not so sure," said Lindsey, adding that: "It's a very sweet song that takes us back to a time when we were much more innocent. [Stevie] talks to me about our relationship, even though we'd only been together for a very short time. [...] I don't really know how it resurfaced."[38] Stevie claimed to have rediscovered it by chance on YouTube. Lindsay said, "She brought it to my house one day. John and Mick didn't really work on it. It makes sense to do this song that predates Fleetwood Mac because, at this stage, Stevie and I have more of a connection than we did at one time. It's a good thing."[38] On this track, Stevie expresses how important Lindsey's presence is to her and how much he enriches his life. Their connection is deep and exclusive: "Come to me now, and I'll never know another."

IT TAKES TIME

Lindsey Buckingham / 4:09

Musicians: Lindsey Buckingham: vocals, keyboards, piano / **Recorded:** Lindsey Buckingham's studio: 2012–2013 / **Technical Team:** Producers: Lindsey Buckingham, Mitchell Froom

Lindsey Buckingham finally laid down his arms at the feet of Stevie Nicks. The guitarist gives way to a poignant mea culpa in this introspective ballad, led by a dusky piano score, enhanced only by a few notes of keyboards simulating violins. Even though he introduces each of his mistakes with a "maybe" that is still a little reticent, he repents in the most disarming of ways. He admits that his apology comes late, that he has had difficulty admitting his wrongdoing, that he has lied to himself. He adds the line, perhaps the most striking in this confession, "and no one else," which completely exonerates Stevie Nicks. He alone bears the burden of his mistakes. He materializes the boundary that has often separated them, referring to a "line" ("that line"), and invites his partner to cross it in a gesture of appeasement. Through this invitation, he tells her that he accepts the idea of her saving him ("If you want to save me") and at the same time acknowledges that he needs to be saved. "I'm looking at some of my past actions and perhaps judging them more objectively,"[94] Lindsey explained. He added: "And maybe I am getting to a point in my life where I can look back and say, 'Hmm! Maybe I could have done things differently' and recognize that a lot of what drove certain creative actions and decisions came from this dialogue that seems to have been going on in slow motion over a number of years. We are still, in one way or another, in a process of evolution."[94]

Powerful and charismatic, Mick puts on a show in San José, California, on May 22, 2013.

MISS FANTASY

Lindsey Buckingham / 4:17

Musicians: Lindsey Buckingham: vocals, guitar, keyboards, percussion / John McVie: bass / Mick Fleetwood: drums, percussion / Stevie Nicks: backing vocals / **Recorded:** Lindsey Buckingham's studio, 2012–2013 / **Technical Team:** Producers: Lindsey Buckingham, Mitchell Froom

To coincide with the tour and the thirty-fifth anniversary of *Rumours*, a reissue of the album was released in Deluxe and Super Deluxe formats, which included previously unreleased demos and live tracks; it was accompanied *The Rosebud Film*, a documentary featuring concert excerpts. Both were released on January 28 and 29, 2013, by Warner-Rhino Records.

The cheerful "Miss Fantasy" offers an effective chorus and splendid vocal harmonies worthy of the greatest classics. Over a driving tempo provided by a rhythm section with a solid groove, a playful piano and a few notes of guitar enhance the meticulous arrangement. The lyrics mix dream and reality to evoke a one-way love affair. The narrator is in love with the woman to whom he is speaking, but her heart cries for someone else while his cries for her. An emotional distance separates the two protagonists. This is illustrated by the fact that her memory of the other is not the same as his: "Miss Fantasy / I can see you don't remember me / But I remember you." This difference adds to the pain of unrequited love. "I felt like I was drawing on the whole lexicon of memories and emotional connections from before Stevie and I were a couple,"[94] explained Lindsey.

THE END OF THE *"RUMOURS* FIVE"

A new dynamic was introduced into the band with the *Extended Play* EP. Now that it had been established that Christine would not be returning, Stevie and Lindsey were shedding the reserve that had prevented them from fully assuming leadership of the band as a duo. Their complementarity, which was still in evidence on *Say You Will* despite their control over the composition—that album was in fact more an assembly of two solo albums than a Fleetwood Mac album—is tangible on *Extended Play*. The chemistry of their early days, when they formed the Buckingham Nicks duo, is once again at work. "I was writing a lot of stuff. I thought about Stevie when I wrote these songs," said Lindsey. "Most of them are addressed to her. They were a dialogue with her." Lindsey also confessed in a 2013 interview that although he missed Christine, the four-handed format gave him the opportunity to be more himself onstage: "When you split the songs more or less in half, it gives you more opportunity to show yourself as you are and impose your presence and energy."[38]

Live 2013, a Gargantuan Tour

The band, which now thrived on the symbiosis of Lindsey and Stevie, showcased this aspect during Fleetwood Mac Live 2013, its first major tour since 2009, organized to mark the release of the EP, but above all to celebrate the thirty-fifth anniversary of the release of *Rumours*, the album that launched them into legend. It kicked off on April 4 in Columbus, Ohio. The schedule was gargantuan, with eighty-five dates taking them across three continents (North America, Europe, and Oceania), right up to the start of the following year (January 8, 2014, in Las Vegas). During a stopover in Tulsa, Lindsey Buckingham expressed his satisfaction to *Rolling Stone* journalist Andy Greene: "Our business is the best it's been in 20 years. There seems to be renewed interest. There are a lot more young people in the audience than there were three years ago."[38] But every time the band was interviewed, the same questions come up, dampening the enthusiasm of the remaining members: Will Christine make a comeback? Is her retirement definitive?

In September 2013, the prodigal band's return to England was underpinned by a triumphant three-concert series at London's O2 Arena. On the second and third nights, fans were in for a major surprise: Christine McVie joined the band onstage. The woman of whom Stevie had said on the radio, "There's no more chance [of her returning] than an asteroid hitting the earth," struck the hearts of fans on September 25 and 27, 2013. To thunderous applause encouraged by Mick Fleetwood, and after a few hugs with the other band members, she launched into an anthology version of "Don't Stop." The following month, while speculation was rife as to whether she would return to the band for good, some worrying news clouded the picture: John McVie had cancer. His treatment forced the band to cancel dates in New Zealand and Australia.

Christine's Return

In November 2013, Christine McVie, who granted an interview to the *Guardian*, lifted the veil on her intentions: "I love being with the band, I love the idea of playing music with them. I miss them all. If they asked me [to come back], I'd probably be delighted [...] But it hasn't worked out yet, so we'll have to wait and see." She then added: "I think I was simply starved for music. I suffered from a kind of delusion that I was an English country girl, good-looking, good-natured, or that sort of thing [...] And it took me 15 years to realize that wasn't really what I wanted." Furthermore, Christine overcame her fear of flying with the help of a therapist. Nothing now stood in the way of her return.

Stevie was the first person Christine turned to when she decided to return: "We were finishing up our Fleetwood Mac tour [Live 2013] when Christine called me and said, 'I'd like to come back to the band.' I said something like, 'Really? After 16 years.' And she replied, in her English accent [Stevie imitates the English accent by adopting a high-pitched voice]: 'Yes, I'd love to. I'd love to be back in the band.' I said, 'OK, well, you should come and see what we're doing. We'll be in London soon. You should come and stand on the side of the stage and see what you're getting back into, because it's been a long time since you left, Chris, and, now, it's like an athlete's show.' That's what she did, and she said, 'I can do this.'"

On January 13, 2014, Christine's return to the band was made official through Liz Rosenberg, her agent, who also announced the release of a new album and the programming of a tour. The On with the Show tour started on September 30, 2014, in Minneapolis and concluded on

Lindsey's and Christine's compositions, sketched out in Studio D at the Village Recorder, are used on a duo album, released in 2017.

November 22, 2015, in Auckland, New Zealand. The deal proved highly lucrative, generating nearly $200 million.

The Secession Album

The tour went according to plan. But as for the album, the band announced that such a project would not be forthcoming anytime soon, despite the constant involvement of Christine and Lindsey, who were accumulating unreleased material. Back in 2014, the two musicians found themselves in Studio D at the Village Recorders in Los Angeles, the very place where *Tusk* was conceived in 1979. They stayed there for two months and discovered a complicity they had never known before. The compositional work was fluid, each contributing to the other's tracks without any friction. "It evolved quite naturally, as I would send Lindsey my little rough demos, and he would refine and remix them into what turned out to be our best material to date, in my opinion." Mick Fleetwood and John McVie were also called upon to provide the rhythm section. Tracks such as "Red Sun," inspired by Christine's stay in Africa, and "Feel About You," were by four contributors and showed great promise. But there was one missing piece in the puzzle for these tracks to take the shape of a Fleetwood Mac album: Stevie Nicks. She was more than willing to participate in a new album, as she explained to *Billboard*: "Is it possible that Fleetwood Mac will make another record? I can't tell you yes or no, because I don't know. Honestly, I don't know... The question is: do you take the risk of going out there, setting yourself up in a room for a year [to record an album] and having everyone get in over their heads? And then not feel like going on tour because we've just spent a year arguing? Or do you just go on tour because you know you'll enjoy it and you love giving concerts? And Christine has only been back for [laughs] a year and a half."

With Stevie sticking to her guns, Christine and Lindsey, who refused to allow their compositions to be left on one side, opted to release their ten new tracks under their own names alone. The album, entitled *Lindsey Buckingham Christine McVie*, was released in June 2017 by Atlantic Records. Far from being some kind of ersatz production, the album is well structured and was supported by a forty-five-date US tour (June 21 to November 16, 2017). Buckingham and McVie put together a set list based on eight tracks from the album, supplemented by a few Fleetwood Mac songs and others from Buckingham in solo mode.

One Returns, the Other One Leaves

In January 2018, Fleetwood Mac was invited by MusiCares, a charity linked to the Grammy Awards, to be presented with an award. All the members were there. They entered to the sound of "Rhiannon," and Stevie Nicks headed to the lectern to deliver the acceptance speech. At the end of the ceremony, a new psychodrama unfolded backstage. Lindsey Buckingham did not like the fact that "Rhiannon" was chosen for their entrance, and Stevie did not like the smirk on the guitarist's face during her speech. The band's manager, Irving Azoff, informed Lindsey of Stevie's ultimatum: Either Lindsey left the band, or she would. In April 2018, the verdict was in: Buckingham was no longer part of Fleetwood Mac. The official reason given: artistic differences over the upcoming world tour, which had been presented as a possible farewell tour by Christine McVie, even before Lindsey's departure. Once again, two guitarists were recruited at short notice to fill Lindsey Buckingham's absence: Mike Campbell, the guitarist with Tom Petty and the Heartbreakers; and Neil Finn, the New Zealand singer and guitarist of Crowded House.

MIKE CAMPBELL, LOVE OF THE GUITAR

He was the lieutenant. The one Tom Petty, herald of American rock in the late 1970s, could always count on. In the spring of 2018, when the Heartbreakers, now orphaned of their leader, decided to call it a day, Mike Campbell chose to join Fleetwood Mac and his close friend Stevie Nicks.

The Band of a Lifetime

Michael Wayne Campbell (born February 1, 1950, in Panama City, Florida) first played guitar at the age of sixteen, when his mother bought him a Harmony acoustic from a pawnshop. The instrument was not a particularly good one and proved very difficult to play without callused fingers, but the sensations the instrument gave him encouraged him to persevere. He learned Bob Dylan's "Baby Let Me Follow You Down" by ear and repeated it tirelessly. As a rock fan, he quickly switched to electric with an entry-level Goya he found for $60. When he finally got his hands on a quality guitar, a Gibson SG lent to him by a friend, he realized that the guitar would be his instrument for life.

In 1968, he formed his first band, Dead or Alive, but the experience was cut short after two years. Just in time for him to audition in 1970 for Mudcrutch, a Gainesville-based band led by Tom Petty, who was looking for a guitarist. With a convincing version of Chuck Berry's "Johnny B. Goode," Mike was recruited. In 1975, just as they were about to take off with the release of their first single, Mudcrutch broke up. Tom Petty put together a new band, Tom Petty and the Heartbreakers, and once again put his faith in his guitarist. Keyboardist Benmont Tench, bassist Ron Blair (later replaced by Howie Epstein), and drummer Stan Lynch completed the team. Together, they would write an important page in American rock for four decades, producing a series of popular hits such as "American Girl," "Refugee," and "Learning to Fly." Affiliated with heartland rock alongside artists such as Bob Seger and John Mellencamp, the band, with its thirteen studio albums—the last of which, *Hypnotic Eye*, reached number one in the US sales charts in 2014—was inducted into the Rock and Roll Hall of Fame in 2002. Mike Campbell, for his part, is recognized as an exceptional guitarist, despite his individual approach to the guitar.

An Old-Style Sound

Endowed with exceptional skills, he has always avoided flaunting his technique, preferring to place it in the service of other people's songs. Attached to the warm, organic sound of his instruments, he has a conservative approach and always prefers vintage equipment to digital, and the raw sounds of his instruments to a string of all kinds of

His interlude with Fleetwood Mac was a form of gentle transition and therapy for Mike Campbell after the loss of his friend and bandmate Tom Petty.

effects. Ever since he first laid his hands on a Gibson SG in his youth, this distinctive instrument with its vermillion color and small horns has become a staple of his equipment. His favorite, a 1964 model, follows him everywhere. It cohabits with a 1954 Fender Telecaster, the one with which he immortalized "American Girl." He is also a fan of the sound and retro look of the Rickenbackers popularized by the Beatles. He owns, among others, a black 325 Capri, and a twelve-string version of the Hollowbody 360.

Although it was the band of his life, his commitment to the Heartbreakers was not exclusive. Mike Campbell took part in many recording sessions as a guest—most often for his idols, such as Bob Dylan, Aretha Franklin, Roy Orbison, and Roger McGuinn. But the one to whom he paid most attention was, of course, Stevie Nicks. He was involved on all her solo albums, from 1981's *Bella Donna* to 2014's *24 Karat Gold: Songs from the Vault*. So when it came to finding a replacement for Lindsey Buckingham on Fleetwood Mac's 2018–2019 tour, Stevie put his name forward. Mike had unfortunately been free of any engagements since the sudden death of Tom Petty, who died of a drug overdose on October 2, 2017. The commitment to the Mac was to be short-lived: At the end of the An Evening with Fleetwood Mac tour (October 3, 2018–November 16, 2019), Mike Campbell reactivated his 1960s rock-influenced band project the Dirty Knobs and recorded two albums, *Wreckless Abandon* in 2020 and *External Combustion* in 2022.

NEIL FINN, THE POP MELODY SPECIALIST

As leader of Split Enz and Crowded House, he is the man who put New Zealand on the rock map and enabled a generation of artists to dream beyond the Pacific Ocean. After joining Fleetwood Mac, he helped internationalize the band and save it from a breakup that had been announced in 2018.

A Family Affair

An outstanding sportsman in his teens, Neil Mullane Finn (born May 27, 1958, in Te Awamutu) devoted all his time to music. For as long as he can remember, his family was immersed in it. Dick, Mary, and their four children often gathered around the family piano and sang along together. Neil followed in the footsteps of his older brother Tim, whom he admired, when he began to learn guitar and piano. When, in 1972, his brother Tim formed his band Split Enz (initially called Split Ends), he watched with envy. Five years later, when the band's guitarist and vocalist, Phil Judd, left his post, Neil's dream became a reality and Split Enz became the Finn brothers' band, with them sharing the leadership. Under their influence, the band moved from the path of progressive rock to that of guitar-driven power pop. The metamorphosis paid off. In 1980, the album *True Colours* reached number one in New Zealand and Australia, but the band also made a big breakthrough in the United States (number forty). The same was true of *Waiata* the following year, and *Time and Tide* in 1982.

Two years later, spurred on by the success of his solo album, *Escapade* (1983), Tim Finn set out on his own. Feeling unable to continue without the two founding members, Phil Judd and his brother, Neil decided to end his involvement with Split Enz and form a new band, the Mullanes. This included ex–Split Enz drummer Paul Hester, bassist Nick Seymour, and the Reels guitarist Craig Hooper, who abandoned ship just before the recording of the first album.

An Unexpected Replacement

Neil took advantage of this change to rename his band, of which he was now the sole guitarist: Crowded House. The success of this pop-rock outfit, for which he fashioned magnificent melodic ballads, was immense: Their seven albums (from *Crowded House* in 1986 to *Dreamers Are Waiting* in 2021) fluctuated between first and second place in the Austrian charts. The first album even climbed to number twelve in the US record sales charts, propelled by the stunning single "Don't Dream It's Over" (number two in

In 2018, Fleetwood Mac became Neil Finn's third major band, following Split Enz and Crowded House.

the country). In 1996, it was the UK's turn to fall for Crowded House's addictive melodies, with the compilation *Recurring Dream: The Very Best of Crowded House* topping the charts. The history of Crowded House, peppered with breakups and re-formations, was not a smooth one. During one of these hiatuses, in 2018, Neil Finn was offered the chance to join Fleetwood Mac by just a phone call from Mick Fleetwood. The two men had known each other for two years, but nothing would have suggested such a proposition. The pop melodist therefore compensated for Lindsey Buckingham's departure during the An Evening with Fleetwood Mac tour—scheduled from October 2018 to November 2019—alongside Mike Campbell (Tom Petty and the Heartbreakers), the rock backup. Finn recalled: "It was something very inspiring and very surprising to be offered on the spur of the moment to join a band like Fleetwood Mac and to observe up close how human and unique this band is. This combination of talents is quite simply extraordinary. Their ability to reinvent themselves and survive line-up changes is now legendary."

THE END OF FLEETWOOD MAC

A New Tour for the New Lineup

In October 2018, the band embarked on the An Evening with Fleetwood Mac world tour (October 3, 2018–November 16, 2019) without Lindsey. This situation caused intense stress for the guitarist and also had a physical impact on him. During 2019, he underwent open heart surgery that damaged his vocal cords.

As for Fleetwood Mac, the new members, Mike Campbell and Neil Finn, had just a few months to prepare for this ambitious tour. The set list would include twenty-two songs each night and was assembled from the most eagerly-awaited titles: "The Chain," "Dreams," "Second Hand News," "Black Magic Woman," "Rhiannon," "Landslide," and "Go Your Own Way." The tour kicked off on October 3 in Tulsa, Oklahoma, and continued through the northern United States before reaching Canada in November. Then the band toured the US again until March 2019. After a three-month break, they played a handful of concerts in Europe in June, then headed off to Oceania to spend August and September there. After more dates in North America, the tour concluded with a final show in Las Vegas on November 16, 2019.

The graft had taken well with the two new members. The easy-going Neil Finn and Mike Campbell, who worked closely with Stevie Nicks, made a major contribution to the tour's success. A future with them seemed conceivable beyond this tour. At the beginning of 2020, Stevie had to take a period of enforced rest due to mononucleosis, which caused her to experience phases of extreme fatigue. As soon as she was back on her feet, she took part in the recording of Neil Finn's "Find Your Way Back Home," released on May 20, 2020, which also featured contributions from Mike Campbell and Christine McVie. The single was marketed as a benefit for the Auckland City Mission, a charity for the homeless. Although not officially released under the Fleetwood Mac label, this sumptuous, melancholy folk-pop ballad is a foretaste of what the new alliance might sound like on record. "I was honoured to be asked to write this song," says Neil Finn. "And I'm very grateful to have the support and talent of my Fleetwood Mac partners, Stevie, Christine, and Mike, as well as my son Elroy and my compatriot, singer Georgia Nott, who helped me with the recording."

An Evening with Fleetwood Mac tour marked the end of a rich and winding career after the death of Christine McVie in 2022.

The End for Mac

Two years passed without Fleetwood Mac resuming its activities. But no one in the band was worried. The musicians expressed their confidence in the press: The Mac would be back, and there was no question of separation. But time takes its toll, and years count double at the end of a career. On June 23, 2022, a *Rolling Stone* journalist asked Christine about her goals for the coming years. The musician, whose health was failing, lost none of her British phlegm and humor: "To stay alive, hopefully. I'm going to be 80 next year. So I'm just hoping for a few more years and then we'll see what happens." Unfortunately, however, she was not to be so lucky. On November 30, 2022, Christine McVie, who had been suffering from cancer, died of a stroke before reaching her eightieth birthday. The band's official press release testifies to the deep emotion that

gripped the musicians: "There are no words to describe our sadness at the passing of Christine McVie. She was truly unique, special and talented beyond measure. She was the best musician you could have in a band and the best friend you could have in your life. Individually and collectively, we cherish Christine deeply and are grateful for the incredible memories she leaves behind. We will miss her so much." But these words said little about the immense grief that overwhelmed her partners and best friends. Stevie, mourning her soulmate, said: "We'll meet on the other side, my love. Don't forget me." Mick declared, "Part of my heart is gone today."

In February 2023, at the Grammy Awards ceremony, when asked about Fleetwood Mac's future, the drummer cut short all speculation: "I sincerely believe that the loss of Chris spells the end." Stevie was on the same wavelength. On October 2, 2023, she reaffirmed this decision with this poignant image: "Who can I turn to on my right? There'll be no one left behind the Hammond organ."

In September 2023, less than a year after Christine McVie's death, *Rumours Live* was released, a musical snapshot of a band at the height of its creativity. The chosen recording, recorded by Ken Caillat using a mobile studio provided by Record Plant, dates from August 29, 1977, when the band played in Inglewood, California. The set list was fueled mostly by *Rumours*, with the exception of "Don't Stop" and "I Don't Want to Know." Their absence is largely offset by "Oh Well," "Say You Love Me," "Monday Morning," "Rhiannon," "Over My Head," "I'm So Afraid," "World Turning," "Blue Letter," and "Landslide."

THE DEATH OF PETER GREEN

Two years before Christine's death, Fleetwood Mac had already mourned the loss of one of the cardinal elements of its history: Peter Green. On July 25, 2020, Peter Green, the band's founding father, passed away in his sleep on Canvey Island, Essex, at the age of seventy-three. It had been half a century since the guitarist left the ranks of the band he helped create with Mick Fleetwood and John McVie, but neither his former partners nor the public has forgotten him. Tributes have been pouring in since his death, all praising the immense talent of a musician who never compromised and remained true to the blues. With his instinctive playing, he contributed to shaping British blues and helped it evolve beyond a mere ersatz version of American blues. He gave it personality through his wild, instinctive, and versatile playing, and he was also capable of the most graceful aerial flights. Although the Green God's talent waned over the years and his influence diminished, his integrity inspired many artists.

Journeys of No Return

Peter Green never recovered from the acid trips of his youth. In the years following his departure from Fleetwood Mac in May 1970, he was forced to undergo several stays in psychiatric hospitals, where doctors diagnosed schizophrenia. Green did not, however, break with music. In December 1970, he released his first solo album, recorded just one month after leaving the band. The album, mischievously dubbed *The End of the Game*, testifies to the artist's desire for freedom, as he felt stifled in his former band. The album consists of an improvised, experimental jam featuring Zoot Money on piano, Nick Buck on keyboards, Alex Dmochowski on bass, and Godfrey McLean on drums. His activity then continued on a dotted line, with a number of prestigious collaborations (*The Answer* by Peter Bardens, *Juju* by Gass, and *B. B. King in London* by B. B. King), because the electroconvulsive therapy he underwent to treat his schizophrenia only worsened his condition and adversely affected his musical abilities.

In 1979, Green's artistic breakthrough came with the release of his second LP, *In the Skies*, an album of personal compositions featuring guitarist Snowy White. It was followed by *Little Dreamer* (1980), *Whatcha Gonna Do?* (1981), *White Sky* (1982), and *Kolors* (1983), which was largely written by his brother Mike.

Lasting Ties

In 1982, Mick Fleetwood, pleased to see his friend's return to music, asked him to take part in the recording of "Rattlesnake Shake" and "Super Brains," two tracks from his solo album *The Visitor*. The drummer always kept a benevolent eye on his former partner, and tried on several occasions to lend him a hand with his projects. He even offered Peter Green and Jeremy Spencer a short-lived reunion of the original Fleetwood Mac lineup in the early 2000s, but the two former members declined the drummer's offer.

Peter Green preferred to focus on his own project, the Peter Green Splinter Group, with whom he released seven albums in the space of six years: *Peter Green Splinter Group* (1997), *The Robert Johnson Songbook* (1998), *Destiny Road* (1999), *Hot Foot Powder* (2000), *Time Traders* (2001), *Blues Don't Change* (2001), and *Reaching the Cold 100* (2003).

On February 25, 2020, Mick organized a concert in his friend's honor at the London Palladium, called Mick Fleetwood and Friends Tribute to Peter Green. It was attended by Billy Gibbons, David Gilmour, Jonny Lang, John Mayall, Christine McVie, and Steven Tyler. But Peter Green did not attend this final tribute.

Inducted into the Rock and Roll Hall of Fame in 1998 as one of the eight members of Fleetwood Mac, the blues guitarist was ranked fifty-eighth on *Rolling Stone*'s list of the one hundred greatest guitarists.

DISCOGRAPHY

LIVE ALBUMS

Live

Recorded between October 17, 1975 and September 4, 1980
UK Release: December 5, 1980 on Warner Bros. Records (ref. K 66097)
US Release: December 5, 1980 on Warner Bros. Records (ref. 2WB 3500)
Track Listing: Monday Morning • Say You Love Me • Dreams • Oh Well • Over and Over • Sara • Not That Funny • Never Going Back • Landslide • Fireflies • Over My Head • Rhiannon • Don't Let Me Down Again • One More Night • Go Your Own Way • Don't Stop • I'm So Afraid • The Farmer's Daughter

Live in Boston

Recorded between February 5 and 7, 1970 at the Boston Tea Party (Massachusetts)
UK Release: 1984 (ref. Shangai—HAI 107) and reissue 1998 (ref. Snapper Music Inc.—155552)
US Release: 1984 under the name "Jumping at Shadows" (ref. Varrick Records—VR020) and reissue 1998 (ref. Original Masters—155552)
Track Listing (1984): Oh Well • Like It This Way • World in Harmony• Only You • Black Magic Woman • Jumping at Shadows • Can't Hold On
Track Listing (1998): Vol. 1: Black Magic Woman • Jumping at Shadows • Like It This Way • Only You • Rattlesnake Shake • I Can't Hold Out • Got to Move • The Green Manalishi **Vol. 2:** World in Harmony• Oh Well • Rattlesnake Shake • Stranger Blues • Red Hot Mamma • Teenage Darling • Keep A-Knocking • Jenny Jenny • Encore Jam **Vol. 3:** Jumping at Shadows • Sandy Mary • If You Let Me Love You • Loving Kind • Coming Your Way • Madison Blues • Got to Move • The Sun Is Shining • Oh Baby • Tiger • Great Balls of Fire • Tutti Frutti • On We Jam

Live at the Marquee

Recorded December 29, 1967 at the Marquee Club, London
UK Release: March 1992 on Receiver Records Ltd. (ref. RRCD 157)
Track Listing: Talk to Me Baby • I Held My Baby Last Night • My Baby's Sweet • Looking for Somebody • Evil Woman Blues • Got to Move • No Place to Go • Watch Out for Me Woman • Mighty Long Time • Dust My Blues • I Need You, Come on Home to Me • Shake Your Moneymaker

Live at the BBC

Recorded between 1967 and 1971
UK Release: 1995 on Castle Communications (ref. EDF CD 297)
US Release: on Castle Communications (ref. CASTLE 114-2)
Track Listing: Disk 1: Rattlesnake Shake • Sandy Mary • I Believe My Time Ain't Long • Although The Sun Is Shining • Only You • You Never Know What You're Missing • Oh Well, Part 1 • Can't Believe You Wanna Leave • Jenny Lee • Heavenly • When Will I Be Loved • When I See My Baby • Buddy's Song • Honey Hush • Preachin' • Jumping at Shadows • Preachin' Blues • Need Your Love So Bad **Disk 2:** Long Grey Mare • Sweet Home Chicago • Baby Please Set a Date • Blues with a Feeling • Stop Messin' Round • Tallahassee Lassie • Hang On to a Dream • Linda • Mean Mistreatin' Mama • World Keeps Turning • I Can't Hold Out • Early Morning Come • Albatross • Looking for Somebody • A Fool No More • Got to Move • Like Crying Like Dying • Man of the World

The Dance

Recorded May 23, 1997 at the Warner Bros. Studios, Burbank (California)
UK Release: August 19, 1997 on Reprise Records (ref. 9362-46702-2)
US Release: August 19, 1997 on Reprise Records (ref. 9 46702-2)
Track Listing: The Chain • Dreams • Everywhere • Rhiannon • I'm So Afraid • Temporary One • Bleed to Love Her • Big Love • Landslide • Say You Love Me • My Little Demon • Silver Springs • You Make Loving Fun • Sweet Girl • Go Your Own Way • Tusk • Don't Stop

London Live '68

Recorded April 27, 1968 at the Polytechnic of Central London, London
UK Release: 1986 on Thunderbolt/The Magnum Music Group (ref. THBL 1.038)
US Release: 1994 on Magnum America/Thunderbolt (ref. MACD 003)
Track Listing: Got to Move • I Held My Baby Last Night • My Baby's Sweet • My Baby's A Good 'Un • Don't Know Which Way to Go • Buzz Me • The Dream • The World Keeps on Turning • How Blue Can You Get • Bleeding Heart

Shrine '69

Recorded January 25, 1969 at the Shrine Auditorium, Los Angeles
UK Release: 1999 on Rykodisc (ref. RCD 10424)
US Release: 1999 on Rykodisc (ref. RCD 10424)
Track Listing: Tune Up • If You'll Be My Baby • Something Inside of Me • My Sweet Baby • Albatross •Before the Beginning • Rollin' Man • Lemon Squeezer • Need Your Love So Bad • Great Balls of Fire

Fleetwood Mac: Live in Boston

Recorded September 23 and 24, 2003 at the Fleet Center, Boston (Massachusetts)
UK Release: June 15, 2004 on Reprise Records (ref. 7599 38607-2)
US Release: June 15, 2004 on Reprise Records (ref. 48726-2)
Track Listing: DVD The Chain • Dreams • Eyes of the World • Peacekeeper • Second Hand News • Say You Will • Never Going Back Again • Rhiannon • Come • Gypsy • Big Love • Landslide • Say Goodbye • What's the World Coming To • Beautiful Child • Gold Dust Woman • I'm So Afraid • Silver Springs • Tusk • Stand Back • Go Your Own Way • World Turning • Don't Stop • Goodbye Baby
Track Listing: CD Eyes of the World • Dreams • Rhiannon • Come • Big Love • Landslide • Silver Springs • I'm So Afraid • Stand Back • Go Your Own Way

In Concert

Recorded between November 5, 1979 and August 28, 1980
UK Release: March 4, 2016 on Warner Bros. Records (Ref. 081227947668)
US Release: March 4, 2016 on Warner Bros. Records (Ref. R1 553403)
Track Listing: Disk 1: Intro • Say You Love Me • The Chain • Don't Stop • Dreams **Disk 2:** Oh Well • Rhiannon • Over and Over • That's Enough for Me **Disk 3:** Sara • Not That Funny • Tusk • Save Me a Place **Disk 4:** Landslide • What Makes You Think You're the One • Angel • You Make Loving Fun **Disk 5:** I'm So Afraid • World Turning **Disk 6:** Go Your Own Way • Sisters of the Moon • Songbird

Rumours Live

Recorded August 29, 1977 at the Inglewood Forum (California)
UK Release: September 8, 2023 on Warner Bros. Records (ref. R2 567113)
US Release: September 8, 2023 on Warner Bros. Records (ref. R2 567113)
Track Listing: Say You Love Me • Monday Morning • Dreams • Oh Well • Rhiannon • Oh Daddy • Never Going Back Again • Landslide • Over My Head • Gold Dust Woman • You Make Loving Fun • I'm So Afraid • Go Your Own Way • World Turning • Blue Letter • The Chain • Second Hand News • Songbird

COMPILATIONS

English Rose

UK Release: 2007 on BGO Records (ref. BGOCD750)
US Release: December 1968 on Epic (ref. BN 26446)
Track Listing: Stop Messin' Around • Jigsaw Puzzle Blues • Doctor Brown • Track • Evenin' Boogie • Love That Burns • Black Magic Woman • I've Lost My Baby • One Sunny Day • Without You • Coming Home • Albatross

The Pious Bird of Good Omen

UK Release: August 15, 1969 on Blue Horizon (ref. 7-63215)
US Release: 2004 on Blue Horizon Remastered (ref. 90003-2)
Track Listing (UK Version): Need Your Love So Bad (Version #2 [Remake], Take 4) • Coming Home • Rambling Pony • The Big Boat • I Believe My Time Ain't Long • The Sun Is Shining • Albatross • Black Magic Woman • Just the Blues • Jigsaw Puzzle Blues • Looking for Somebody • Stop Messin' Round
Track Listing (US Version): Need Your Love So Bad • Rambling Pony • I Believe My Time Ain't Long • The Sun Is Shining • Albatross • Black Magic Woman • Jigsaw Puzzle Blues • Like Crying • Need Your Love So Bad (Version #1, Takes 1, 2 & 3) • Need Your Love So Bad (Version #2 [Remake], Takes 1 & 2) • Need Your Love So Bad (Version #2 [Remake], Take 3) • Need Your Love So Bad (US Version)

Black Magic Woman

UK and US Releases: 1971 on Epic (ref. EG 30632)
Track Listing: Disk 1: My Heart Beat Like a Hammer • Merry-Go-Round • Long Grey Mare • Hellhound on My Trail • Shake Your Moneymaker • Looking for Somebody • No Place to Go • My Baby's Good to Me • I Loved Another Woman • Cold Black Night • The World Keep on Turning • Got to Move **Disk 2:** Stop Messin' Round • Jigsaw Puzzle Blues • Doctor Brown • Something Inside of Me • Evenin' Boogie • Love That Burns • Black Magic Woman • I've Lost My Baby • One Sunny Day • Without You • Coming Home • Albatross

The Original Fleetwood Mac

UK Release: May 1971 on CBS (ref. CBS 63875)
US Release: 1977 on Sire (ref. SR 6045)
Track Listing: Disk 1: Drifting • Leaving Town Blues • Watch Out • A Fool No More • Mean Old Fireman • Can't Afford to Do It **Disk 2:** Fleetwood Mac • Worried Dream • Love That Woman • Allow Me One More Show • First Train Home • Rambling Pony No. 2

Greatest Hits

UK Release: November 22, 1988 on Warner Bros. Records (ref. 925 838-2)
US Release: November 22, 1988 on Warner Bros. Records (ref. 9 25801-2)
Track Listing (UK Version): Rhiannon • Go Your Own Way • Don't Stop • Gypsy • Everywhere • You Make Loving Fun • Big Love • As Long As You Follow • Say You Love Me • Dreams • Little Lies • Oh Diane • Sara • Tusk • Seven Wonders • Hold Me • No Questions Asked
Track Listing (US Version): Rhiannon • Don't Stop • Go Your Own Way • Hold Me • Everywhere • Gypsy • You Make Loving Fun • As Long As You Follow • Dreams • Say You Love Me • Tusk • Little Lies • Sara • Big Love • Over My Head • No Questions Asked

Vintage Years

UK Release: March 1975 on CBS (ref. 88227)
US Release: March 1975 on Sire (ref. SASH-3706)
Track Listing: Black Magic Woman • Coming Home • Rambling Pony • Something Inside of Me • Dust My Broom • The Sun Is Shining • Albatross • Just the Blues • Evening Boogie • The Big Boat • Jigsaw Puzzle Blues • I've Lost My Baby • Doctor Brown • Need Your Love So Bad • Looking for Somebody • Need Your Love Tonight • Shake Your Moneymaker • Man of the World • Stop Messin' Round • Rollin' Man • Love That Burns • If You Be My Baby • Lazy Poker Blues • Trying So Hard to Forget

Albatross

UK Release: 1977 on CBS / Embassy (ref. S CBS 31569)
Track Listing: Fleetwood Mac: Albatross • Rambling Pony • I Believe My Time Ain't Long • Doctor Brown • Stop Messin' Round • Love That Burns • Jigsaw Puzzle Blues • Need Your Love Tonight **Christine Perfect:** I'd Rather Go Blind • Crazy 'Bout You Baby • And That's Saying a Lot • I'm On My Way • No Road Is the Right Road • Let Me Go (Leave Me Alone) • I'm Too Far Gone (to Turn Around) • When You Say

Man of the World

UK Release: 1978 on CBS (ref. S 83110)
Track Listing: Disk 1: Man of the World • Black Magic Woman • Need Your Love Tonight • Oh Well (Part 1) • Watch Out • Love That Burns • I Can't Hold Out • Stop Messin' Round **Disk 2:** Albatross • Need Your Love So Bad • The Green Manalishi (with the Two Prong Crown) • Like It This Way • Looking for Somebody • Shake Your Moneymaker • Homework • I Believe My Time Ain't Long

The Collection

UK Release: 1987 on Castle Communications (ref. PLC—CCSLP 157)
Track Listing: Shake Your Moneymaker • Long Grey Mare • I Loved Another Woman • Got to Move • World Keep on Turning • Black Magic Woman • Need Your Love So Bad • Doctor Brown • Doctor Brown • Need Your Love Tonight • Love That Burns • Lazy Poker Blues • Dust My Broom • Drifting • Fleetwood Mac • Love That Woman • I've Lost My Baby • Man of the World • Someone's Gonna Get Their Head Kicked In Tonite • Watch Out • Homework • Rockin' Boogie • Jigsaw Puzzle Blues • Albatross

Greatest Hits

UK Release: November 1971 on CBS (ref. S 69011)
Track Listing: The Green Manalishi (with the Two Prong Crown) • Oh Well (Part 1) • Oh Well (Part 2) • Shake Your Moneymaker • Need Your Love So Bad • Rattlesnake Shake • Dragonfly • Black Magic Woman • Albatross • Man of the World • Stop Messin' Round • Love That Burns

The Original Fleetwood Mac: The Blues Years

UK Release: 1990 on Castle Communications/Essential Records (ref. ESBLP 138)

Track Listing: Disk 1: My Heart Beat Like a Hammer • Merry Go Round • Long Grey • Hell Hound On My Trail • Shake Your Money Maker • Looking for Somebody **Disk 2:** No Place to Go • My Baby's Good to Me • I Loved Another Woman • Cold Black Night • The World Keep on Turning • Got to Move **Disk 3:** Stop Messin' Round • Coming Home • Rollin' Man • Dust My Broom • Love That Burns **Disk 4:** Doctor Brown • Need Your Love Tonight • If You Be My Baby • Evenin' Boogie • Lazy Poker Blues **Disk 5:** I've Lost My Baby • Trying So Hard to Forget • Believe My Time Ain't Long • Ramblin' Pony • Black Magic Woman **Disk 6:** The Sun Is Shining • Need Your Love So Bad • Albatross • Jigsaw Puzzle Blues • Man of the World **Disk 7:** Watch Out • Worried Dream • Fleetwood Mac • First Train Home **Disk 8:** Drifting • Mean Old Fireman • Allow Me One More Show • Just the Blues **Disk 9:** The Big Boat • I'd Rather Go Blind • Watch Out • Homework • I Can't Hold Out **Disk 10:** Like It This Way • Last Night • I'm Worried • World's in a Tangle

25 Years—The Chain

UK Release: November 24, 1992 on Warner Bros. Records (ref. 9362-45129-2)

US Release: November 24, 1992 on Warner Bros. Records (ref. 9 45129-2)

Track Listing: Disk 1: Paper Doll • Stand Back (Live) • Crystal • Isn't It Midnight (Edited Alternate Version) • Big Love • Everywhere • Affairs of the Heart • Heart of Stone • Sara • That's All for Everyone • Over My Head • Little Lies • Eyes of the World • Oh Diane • In the Back of My Mind • Make Me a Mask **Disk 2:** Save Me • Goodbye Angel • Silver Springs • What Makes You Think You're the One • Think About Me • Gypsy (Alternate Unreleased Version) • You Make Loving Fun • Second Hand News (Alternate Mix) • Love in Store (Alternate Mix) • The Chain (Alternate Mix) • Teen Beat Dreams (Alternate Mix) • Only Over You • I'm So Afraid (Edited) • Love Is Dangerous • Gold Dust Woman (Alternate Mix) • Not That Funny (Live) **Disk 3:** Warm Ways • Say You Love Me • Don't Stop • Rhiannon • Walk a Thin Line • Storms • Go Your Own Way • Sisters of the Moon • Monday Morning • Landslide • HypnotizedcdLay It All Down (Unreleased Alternate Version) • Angel (Alternate Mix) • Beautiful Child (Alternate Mix) • Brown Eyes • Save Me a Place • Tusk • Never Going Back Again • Songbird **Disk 4:** I Believe My Time Ain't Long • Need Your Love So Bad • Rattlesnake Shake • Oh Well, Part 1 (Original Mono Version—Rechanneled for Stereo) • Stop Messin' Round • The Green Manalishi • Albatross • Man of the World • Love That Burns • Black Magic Woman • Watch Out • String-a-Long • Station Man • Did You Ever Love Me • Sentimental Lady • Come a Little Bit Closer • Heroes Are Hard to Find • Trinity • Why

The Best of Fleetwood Mac

UK Release: 1996 on Warner Bros. Records (ref. K 66097)

Track Listing: Albatross • No Place to Go • Merry Go Round • Long Grey Mare • Black Magic Woman • Rambling Pony • Watch Out • My Baby's Good to Me • The World Keep on Turning • Need Your Love So Bad • Doctor Brown • Love That Burns

The Vaudeville Years of Fleetwood Mac 1968–1970

UK Release: 1998 on Warner Bros. Records (ref. RDPCD 14 Z)

US Release: 2002 on Trojan Records (ref. 06076-80258-2)

Track Listing: Disk 1: Intro/Lazy Poker Blues • My Baby's Sweeter • Love That Burns • Talk to My Baby • Everyday I Have the Blues • Jeremy's Contribution to Doo-Wop • Everyday I Have the Blues • Bells • (Watch Out for Yourself) Mr. Jones • Man of Action • Do You Give a Damn for Me • Man of the World • Like This Way • Blues in B Flat Minor • Someone's Gonna Get Their Head Kicked In Tonight • Although the Sun Is Shining • Showbiz Blues **Disk 2:** Underway • The Madge Sessions—1 • The Madge Sessions—2 • (That's What) I Want to Know • Oh Well • Love It Seems • Mighty Cold • Fast Talking Woman Blues • Tell Me From the Start • October Jam • October Jam • The Green Manalishi (with the Two Prong Crown) • World in Harmony • Farewell

The Complete Blue Horizon Sessions 1967–1969

UK Release: 1999 on Columbia/Blue Horizon (ref. 494641 2)

US Release: 1999 on Sire/Blue Horizon (ref. 733003-2)

Track Listing: Disk 1 (Peter Green's Fleetwood Mac): My Heart Beat Like a Hammer (Take 2) • Merry Go Round (Take 2) • Long Grey Mare • Hellhound on My Trail (Take 1) • Shake Your Moneymaker • Looking for Somebody • No Place to Go • My Baby's Good to Me • I Loved Another Woman • Cold Black Night • The World Keep on Turning • Got to Move • My Heart Beat Like a Hammer (Take 1) • Merry Go Round (Take 1) • I Loved Another Woman (Take 1, Take 2, Take 3, Take 4) • I Loved Another Woman (Take 5, Take 6) • Cold Black Night (Take 1, Take 2, Take 3, Take 4, Take 5, Take 6) • You're So Evil • I'm Coming Home to Stay **Disk 2 (Mr. Wonderful):** Stop Messin' Round (Take 4) • I've Lost My Baby • Rollin' Man • Dust My Broom • Love That Burns • Doctor Brown • Need Your Love Tonight • If You Be My Baby • Evenin' Boogie • Lazy Poker Blues • Coming Home • Trying So Hard to Forget • Stop Messin' Round (Take 1, Take 2, Take 3) • Stop Messin' Round (Take 5) • I Held My Baby Last Night • Mystery Boogie **Disk 3 (The Pious Bird of Good Omen):** Need Your Love So Bad Version #2 (Remake) (Take 4) • Rambling Pony • I Believe My Time Ain't Long • The Sun Is Shining • Albatross • Black Magic Woman • Jigsaw Puzzle Blues • Like Crying • Need Your Love So Bad Version #1 (Take 1, Take 2, Take 3) • Need Your Love So Bad Version #2 (Remake) (Take 1, Take 2) • Need Your Love So Bad (Take 3) • Need Your Love So Bad (US Version) **Disk 4 (Blues Jam in Chicago— Volume One):** Watch Out • Ooh Baby • South Indiana—Take 1 • South Indiana—Take 2 • Last Night • Red Hot Jam (Take 1) • Red Hot Jam • I'm Worried • I Held My Baby Last Night • Madison Blues • I Can't Hold Out • Bobby's Rock • I Need Your Love (Take 2) • Horton's Boogie Woogie (Take 1) • I Got the Blues **Disk 5 (Blues Jam in Chicago—Volume Two):** World's in a Tangle • Talk with You • Like It This Way • Someday Soon Baby • Hungry Country Girl • Black Jack Blues • Everyday I Have the Blues • Rockin' Boogie • My Baby's Gone • Sugar Mama (Take 1) • Sugar Mama • Homework • Honey Boy Blues • I Need Your Love (Take 1) • Horton's Boogie Woogie (Take 2) • Have a Good Time • That's Wrong • Rock Me Baby **Disk 6 (The Original Fleetwood Mac):** The Original Fleetwood Mac Drifting • Leaving Town Blues (Take 5) • Watch Out (Take 2) • A Fool No More (Take 1, Take 2, Take 3, Take 4, Take 5, Take 6, Take 7, Take 8) • Mean Old Fireman (Take 1, Take 2) • Can't Afford to Do It • Fleetwood Mac • Worried Dream (Take 1) • Love That Woman • Allow Me One More Show • First Train Home • Rambling Pony No. 2 • Watch Out (Take 1) • Something Inside of Me • Something Inside of Me (Take 2) • Something Inside of Me (Take 3) • One Sunny Day • Without You • Coming Your Way (Take 6)

Showbiz Blues

UK Release: June 26, 2001 on Receiver Records (ref. RDPCD 15 Z)

US Release: June 26, 2001 on Castle Music (ref. 06076-81144-2)

Track Listing: Disk 1: Soul Dressing • If You Want to Be Happy • Outrage • The Sun Is Shining • Don't Be Cruel • I'm So Lonely and Blue • How Blue Can You Get? • My Baby's Sweeter • Long Grey Mare • Buzz Me Baby • Mind of My Own • I Have to Laugh • You're the One • Do You Give a Damn for Me (Alternative Take) • Him and Me • Show-Biz Blues (Alternative Take) • Fast Talkin' Woman Blues (Alternative Take) • World in Harmony (Alternative Take) • Leaving Town Blues **Disk 2:** Black Magic Woman • Jumpin' at Shadows • Rattlesnake Shake/ Underway • Stranger Blues • World in Harmony • Tiger • The Green Manalishi (with the Two Prong Crown) • Coming Your Way • Great Balls of Fire • Twist and Shout

Jumping at Shadows: The Blues Years

UK Release: April 22, 2002 on Indigo Records (ref. IGOXDCD 2507)
US Release: July 23, 2002 on Castle Music (ref. 06076 81181-2)
Track Listing: Disk 1: Black Magic Woman (Live) • Jumpin' at Shadows (Live) • Oh Well (Live) • Ride with Your Daddy Tonight • Do You Give a Damn for Me? • Love That Burns • World in Harmony • Long Grey Mare • Talk to Me Baby • Fast Talking Woman Blues • Man of the World (Early Version) • If You Let Me Love You • My Baby's Sweeter • Like It This Way • The Madge Sessions No. 2 • Lazy Poker Blues • I Have to Laugh • The Green Manalishi Disk 2: Man of the World (Single Version) • Showbiz Blues • Buzz Me Baby • Blues in B Flat Minor • It Takes Time • Leaving Town Blues • The Sun Is Shining • Uranus • Mind of My Own • How Blue Can You Get? • Trying So Hard to Forget • Two Harps • Thinking About a Woman • Kind Hearted Woman • Coming, I'm Coming • Stranger Blues (Live) • Coming Your Way (Live) • Rattlesnake Shake (Live)

The Very Best of Fleetwood Mac

UK Release: October 15, 2002 on Reprise Records (ref. 8122 73635 2)
US Release: 2002 on Reprise Records (ref. R2 73775)
Track Listing: Go Your Own Way • Don't Stop • Dreams • Little Lies • Everywhere • Albatross • You Make Loving Fun • Rhiannon (Single Version) • Black Magic Woman • Tusk • Say You Love Me • Man of the World • Seven Wonders • Family Man • Sara • Monday Morning • Gypsy • Over My Head (Single Version) • Landslide • The Chain • Big Love (Live, 1997)

The Best of Peter Green's Fleetwood Mac

UK Release: November 11, 2002 on Columbia (ref. S160004)
US Release: January 15, 2021 on Sony Music (ref. 19439813981)
Track Listing: Albatross • Black Magic Woman • Need Your Love So Bad • My Heart Beat Like a Hammer • Rollin' Man • The Green Manalishi (with the Two Prong Crown) • Man of the World • Something Inside of Me • Looking for Somebody • Oh Well—Part 1 • Oh Well—Part 2 • Rattlesnake Shake • Merry Go Round • I Loved Another Woman • Need Your Love Tonight • Worried Dream • Dragonfly • Stop Messin' Round • Shake Your Moneymaker • I'd Rather Go Blind • Albatross

Madison Blues

Recorded 24 November 24, 1969 (BBC Recording Studios, Maida Vale, London), November 10, 1970 (Paris Cinema, Lower Regent Street), November 24, 1970 (BBC Recording Studios, Maida Vale, London) and 1970–1971
UK Release: August 11, 2003 on Shakedown Records (ref. SHAKEBX110Z)
Track Listing: Disk 1: Hey Baby • It's You I Miss • Gone Into the Sun • Tell Me You Need Me • Crazy About You • Down at the Crown • Tell Me All the Things You Do • Station Man • The Purple Dancer • Station Man • Crazy About You • One Together • I Can't Stop Loving Her • Lonely Without You • Tell Me All the Things You Do • Jewel Eyed Judy Disk 2: Madison Blues • The Purple Dancer • Open the Door • Preaching Blues • Dust My Broom • Get Like You Used to Be • Don't Go Please Stay • Station Man • I'm on My Way • Jailhouse Rock • The King Speaks (Narrative) • Teenage Darling • Honey Hush

Green Shadows: Classics and Rarities Featuring Peter Green

UK Release: August 11, 2003 on Union Square Music/Metro (ref. METRCD111)
Track Listing: Man of the World • Long Grey Mare • Lazy Poker Blues • The Sun Is Shining • The Green Manalishi • Looking for Somebody (Live) • Dust My Blues (Live) • Showbiz Blues • Black Magic Woman • Love That Burns • Oh Well • Shake Your Moneymaker • No Place to Go • Got to Move (Live) • Jumping at Shadows • World in Harmony • Rattlesnake Shake (Live)

The Essential Fleetwood Mac

UK Release: June 2, 2007 on Columbia /Sony BMG Music (ref. 88697105392)
Track Listing: Disk 1: Black Magic Woman • Albatross • Long Grey Mare • No Place to Go • Merry-Go-Round • Watch Out • My Baby's Good to Me • Looking for Somebody • Coming Home • World's in a Tangle • If You Be My Baby • Worried Dream • Trying So Hard to Forget • Need Your Love Tonight • I Loved Another Woman • Love That Burns Disk 2: Dust My Broom • Rollin' Man • Lazy Poker Blues • I Believe My Time Ain't Long • Shake Your Moneymaker • Cold Black Night • Got to Move • Stop Messin' Round • Rockin' Boogie • Talk with You • Doctor Brown • Jigsaw Puzzle Blues • Like Crying • The World Keep on Turning • My Heart Beat Like a Hammer • Need Your Love So Bad

Opus Collection

US Release: 2013 on Rhino Custom Products (ref. OPCD-8755)
Track Listing: You Make Loving Fun • Go Your Own Way • Gypsy • Sara • World Turning • Tusk • Rhiannon • Dreams • Everywhere • Little Lies • Oh Diane • Never Going Back Again • Honey Hi • Landslide • Planets of the Universe (Demo)

50 Years—Don't Stop

UK Release: November 16, 2018 on Warner Bros. Records (ref. 603497855636)
US Release: November 13, 2018 on Warner Bros. Records (ref. R2 573692)
Track Listing: Disk 1: Shake Your Moneymaker • Black Magic Woman • Need Your Love So Bad • Albatross • Man of the World • Oh Well—Pt I • Rattlesnake Shake • The Green Manalishi (with the Two Prong Crown) • Tell Me All the Things You Do • Station Man (Single Version) • Sands of Time (Single Version) • Spare Me a Little of Your Love • Sentimental Lady (Single Version) • Did You Ever Love Me • Emerald Eyes • Hypnotized • Heroes Are Hard to Find (Single Version) Disk 2: Monday Morning • Over My Head (Single Version) • Rhiannon (Will You Ever Win) (Single Version) • Say You Love Me (Single Version) • Landslide • Go Your Own Way • Dreams • Second Hand News • Don't Stop • The Chain • You Make Loving Fun • Tusk • Sara (Single Version) • Think About Me (Single Version) • Fireflies (Single Version) • Never Going Back Again (Live 1980) Disk 3: Hold Me • Gypsy • Love in Store • Oh Diane • Big Love • Seven Wonders • Little Lies • Everywhere • As Long As You Follow • Save Me (Single Version) • Love Shines • Paper Doll • I Do (Edit) • Silver Springs (Live-Edit 1997) • Peacekeeper • Say You Will • Sad Angel

Before the Beginning: 1968–1970 Live & Demo Sessions

UK Release: November 15, 2019 on Sony Music (ref. 19075923252)
US Release: November 22, 2019 on Sony Music (ref. 19075923251)
Track Listing: Madison Blues • Something Inside of Me • The Woman That I Love • Worried Dream • Dust My Blues • Got to Move • Trying So Hard to Forget • Instrumental • Have You Ever Loved a Woman • Lazy Poker Blues • Stop Messin' Round • I Loved Another Woman • I Believe My Time Ain't Long (Version 1) • Sun Is Shining • Long Tall Sally • Willie and the Hand Jive • I Need Your Love So Bad • I Believe My Time Ain't Long (Version 2) • Shake Your Money Maker

EP

Extended Play

UK and US Release: April 30, 2013 on LMJS Productions (digital release)
Track Listing: Sad Angel • Without You • It Takes Time • Miss Fantasy

GLOSSARY

Backing track: An instrumental or vocal track, sometimes only rhythmic, recorded to accompany a singer or band.

Ballad: In twentieth-century popular music, a slow piece, usually below 95 beats per minute (bpm), conducive to daydreaming or slow dancing. Its structure is most often made up of verses alternating with a chorus.

Bend: A guitar technique that consists of pulling or pushing one or more strings parallel to the neck. It has the effect of raising the sound of a played note by a semitone or more.

Bottleneck: A glass or metal tube that the guitarist places on a finger and slides over the strings to obtain a metallic sound. Bluesmen developed this way of playing by using a bottleneck.

Bridge: The transition between two passages of a song. It most often refers to the sequence between the verse and the chorus.

Capo: A device that attaches to the neck of a guitar to change its key by pressing on the strings.

Charley: Diminutive of the high hat; drum element composed of two cymbals operated by a foot pedal.

Chorus: An effect achieved by adding an audio signal identical to the original signal, but with a very slight delay (about 20 ms) and an imperceptibly different pitch. This clever mixture has the effect of thickening the sound, comparable to the insertion of choirs, hence its name.

Click: Audio metronome sent by the sound engineer to the musicians' headphones during a recording session, which allows perfect synchronization with one another.

Cocotte: Whether it's "open," "closed," or "skank," a cocotte is a note-by-note guitar playing technique, used mostly in funk music.

Coda: A word of Italian origin that refers to the conclusion of a piece of music.

Cowbell: A small bell that serves as a percussion instrument. It takes its name from a bell worn around the neck of a farm cow to signal its location.

Crunchy: Describes a slight distortion of a sound or instrument to make it lose its clarity and give it a warm, powerful grain.

Delay: An audio effect that reproduces the acoustic phenomenon of an echo. Built into an effects pedal or mixer, it is applied to a voice or instrument to regularly repeat a sound by shifting its signal in time.

Detuning: A change in the pitch of a note or series of notes, achieved by intentionally detuning an instrument or the recorded signal.

Distortion: A sound effect created by degrading the quality of an audio signal by saturating the channel of an amplifier, by the distortion effect built into the device, or by means of a distortion pedal.

Dobro: A brand of guitar whose sound is amplified by a metal resonator. The word *dobro* comes from the name of its creators: the Dopyera Brothers, Americans of Slovak origin.

Doo-wop: A popular musical style during the 1950s. Inspired by gospel music, it is based on a precise harmonization of voices.

EBow: A case equipped with an electromagnet that, when brought close to the strings of a guitar, causes them to vibrate continuously.

Fade-out: A production technique that involves gradually decreasing the volume of an audio track until it becomes inaudible, creating a musical fade at the end of a song.

Fader: A vertical control knob on the mixer that is used to adjust the volume of each track in a recording.

Feedback: A physical phenomenon that occurs when the amplified transmitter (e.g., speaker) and receiver (e.g., singer's microphone or instruments) are placed too close together. It is similar to a shrill hiss or buzzing sound. Electric rock guitarists, such as Jimi Hendrix in the 1960s, have used this effect creatively in their songs.

Fiddle: Refers to the violin in country, mountain, bluegrass, and Anglo-Saxon folk music.

Fingerpicking: A technique of playing guitar, especially acoustic, specific to American folk music, blues, and bluegrass, in which the melody and rhythm are played at the same time.

Flanger: A phase-shifting effect achieved by mixing two similar signals, with one slightly delayed, creating an undulating sound.

Flattening: The first step in the post-production process that leads to an initial formatting.

Flight case: A sturdy storage case designed to protect an instrument or musical equipment when traveling.

Fret: A protruding metal bar built into the neck of some stringed instruments, especially guitars. They make it possible to vary the pitch of a note by controlling the length of the string that vibrates between the fulcrum and the bridge while ensuring harmonic accuracy.

Fretless: A type of musical instrument (guitar, bass, banjo) that does not have frets on the neck, unlike the standard model.

Fundamental: The base note on which a chord is built.

Fuzz: A sound effect that produces a saturated, thick, and fat sound. Popularized by artists such as the Rolling Stones and Jimi Hendrix, fuzz is applied mainly to electric guitars.

Gimmick: A short series of notes with an easily recognizable melody that catches the listener's attention and permeates the listener's memory. Originating in jazz, this process has gradually spread to other musical genres.

Glissando: Sliding between two notes.

Groove: A term that applies primarily to the rhythm of a song created by the bass and drums. Its usage beginning in the early twentieth century, the word frequently refers to Black American music genres.

Guitar hero: Unofficial title awarded to a guitarist who stands out as much for his virtuosity as for his creativity. Used to define the players of the electric six-string guitar in the hard rock and heavy metal styles of the 1980s, the term refers to the greatest guitarists of their genre.

Hammer-on: A guitar technique that involves playing a note by quickly tapping one's finger on a string that is already vibrating, creating a transition without using the pick.

Harmonics: Notes produced by the left hand (for right-handers) or by the right hand (for left-handers), by touching the string above frets 5, 7, or 12. They are so called because their frequencies are multiples of that of the open string.

Harmonization: A technique for multiplying a vocal line or instruments by completing it with its note in unison or in an octave. If the line that is complementary to the original line is played or sung on another note (e.g., a third, a fifth), this is called "polyphonic harmonization."

Hillbilly: A term for a person who lacks sophistication (colloquially sometimes called a "hick"), originally associated with the Appalachian region.

Hollow body: A type of guitar consisting of a partially hollowed-out body. This differs from a guitar with a solid body, also known as a full body.

Home studio: A space or the equipment used for recording and producing music at home that allows artists to create music independently.

Humbucker: A type of double-coil electric guitar pickup that provides a more powerful sound that is less prone to noise than a single-coil pickup.

Jam session: An improvisation session between several musicians gathered informally for the sole pleasure of playing together.

Laid-back: Literally meaning "casual." A way of playing slightly behind the rhythm to produce a relaxed effect.

Lap steel: A type of guitar similar to pedal steel but more rudimentary, played on the lap with the musician sliding a bottleneck or a steel bar over the strings.

Layering: A set of held notes.

Lineup: A list of musicians in a band.

Lo-fi: A recording method in which high frequencies are accentuated at the expense of low frequencies, deliberately giving the impression that the material used for the piece is of poor quality.

Mash-up: A song built up from several existing tracks.

Mastering: A step after mixing in the production of a song or album. It is intended to provide the recording with equal quality and optimized sound volume (regardless of the listening medium), as well as to homogenize all the songs on an album.

Mid-tempo: A song played at a moderate tempo.

Outtake: A piece of music recorded in the studio or on stage that was not selected for the official version of an album. It can be an unreleased track or an alternative version of an existing track, which can be unearthed for a compilation or a reissue.

Outro: The final section of a song (as opposed to the beginning, or "intro").

Overdub: A set of new sounds (vocals and/or instruments) added to an existing recording.

Palm muting: A guitar and bass technique that consists of muffling notes by placing the palm of the hand (right for right-handers, left for left-handers) on the strings near the bridge. The goal is to muffle the notes played with the pick.

Pattern: A rhythmic or melodic sequence that repeats in a song.

Phasing: A sound effect achieved by filtering a signal and creating a series of ups and downs in the frequency spectrum. Available as a pedal or rack, the effect often gives the feeling or a returning wave or breath.

Pick: See plectrum.

Picking: Technique of guitar playing, consisting of playing the rhythm with the thumb and the accompaniment and melody with the other fingers.

Piezo (piezoelectric): A sensor made of crystals that converts mechanical vibrations into electrical signals. Often used to electrify an acoustic instrument.

Pizzicato: A playing technique used on bowed string instruments that involves plucking the strings rather than using a bow.

Plectrum: A small, thin piece of plastic or metal used to pluck the strings of a stringed instrument.

Reverb: A natural or artificial echo effect applied to an instrument or voice during recording or mixing a song.

Reverse: The deliberate playing of a sound in reverse on an audio track.

Riff: A group of notes that repeats regularly during a song and accompanies the melody.

Scat: A vocal style specific to jazz, in which the use of syllables or incomprehensible sounds prevails over the singing of words.

Set list: A list of songs played by an artist or band at a show or concert.

Shuffle: A rhythmic figure that substitutes a ternary rhythm for a binary rhythm. Frequently used in the blues, it brings flexibility and movement to the song, which broadens the horizon of creativity.

Skiffle: In the United Kingdom, a style of folk music popular in the 1950s, inspired by jazz and blues, and in which the making of one's own instrument was a distinguishing feature.

Slap: An electric bass technique used mainly in funk and disco music, in which the strings are struck by the thumb and pulled by the other fingers of the right hand.

Slide: A technique used in guitar playing that refers to a continuous and rapid slide from one chord or note to another by sounding the intermediate notes.

Soft rock: A subgenre of rock characterized by soft and accessible melodic and harmonic elements.

Solid body: A type of guitar consisting of a fully solid body. This guitar is opposed to the hollow body, whose body has a cavity.

Storytelling: The art of telling a story in the writing of lyrics.

Strumming: A guitar technique that consists of sweeping all the strings of the instrument up and down with the right hand for right-handed people and with the left hand for left-handed people.

Sunburst: A type of finish for a guitar. The color distribution creates a gradient that mimics the effect of sunlight.

Synthpop: A musical style that emerged in the 1980s, in which the use of the synthesizer dominates.

Talk box: An effect that allows the musician to modulate the sound of his instrument through a plastic tube leading from the speaker to his mouth and to create synthetic sounds similar to the human voice.

Tom: A drum used mainly for breaks (drum rolls played to create breaks or restarts in a piece, often to make the transition between two parts, from verse to chorus for example, or between two cycles of the same part). In general, there are three types of toms: the alto, the mid, and the bass.

Tonic: Relating to the first, and therefore the most important, tone of a scale.

Track list: A list of songs on an album.

Transient: An element of sound that occurs at the beginning of a waveform (cracking, squealing, impact, etc.).

Twang: A snappy sound, close to the onomatopoeia that gives it its name, produced by some electric guitars, mainly by Fender's Telecaster model.

Vibraphone: An instrument in the percussion family made of metal plates. It is often confused with the xylophone, which is made of wood. It is often accompanied by an adjustable speed vibrato system, driven by a motor.

Vibrato: Also known as a "whammy bar," it's a lever accessory screwed onto the tailpiece of an electric guitar to adjust the pitch of a note emitted by the instrument.

Violining: An effect that consists of erasing the attacking notes of a guitar by playing the first chords at a volume before gradually increasing the sound via a potentiometer or a volume pedal. The sound produced, which gives the impression that it comes from afar, is reminiscent of the violin, hence the name violining.

Wah-wah: An audio effect produced by the oscillation of the sound frequency between the bass and the treble and which gives a sound reminiscent of a human voice repeating the onomatopoeia "wow" ("wah" in English). This effect, mainly used for electric guitars, is produced using the pedal of the same name.

BIBLIOGRAPHY

1—Harry Shapiro,"The Supernatural," *Mojo* (UK), May 1994.

2—Mick Fleetwood and Anthony Bozza, *Play On: Now, Then and Fleetwood Mac: The Autobiography*, London: Hodder & Stoughton, 2014.

3—Johnny Black, "Leader of the Mac," *Classic Rock Special Edition: The Blues Collection*, 2017.

4—Mick Fleetwood and Stephen Davis, *Fleetwood: My Life and Adventures in Fleetwood Mac*, New York: Avon Books, 1991.

5—Bob Brunning, *The Fleetwood Mac Story, Rumours and Lies*, 2nd ed., London: Omnibus Press, 2004.

6—"Q&A Sessions: John McVie," FleetwoodMac. net, September–October 2004, http://www. fleetwoodmac.net/fwm/index.php?option=com_ content&task=view&id=55&Itemid=69.

7—Leah Furman, *Rumours Exposed: The Unauthorized Biography of Fleetwood Mac*, New York: Citadel Press, 2000.

8—Bill Wasserzieher, "The Return of Jeremy Spencer," in Sean Egan, ed., *Fleetwood Mac on Fleetwood Mac: Interviews and Encounters*, Chicago: Chicago Review Press, 2016.

9—Alexis Sklarevski, "A Life with Fleetwood Mac—John McVie," *Bassplayer*, May–June 1995.

10—Norman Jopling, "Rock'n'Blues via Peter Green: The Big Beat Bug Bites Bluesman Peter," *Record Mirror* (UK), March 9, 1968.

11—Dick Weindling and Marianne Colloms, *Decca Studios and Klooks Kleek: West Hampstead's Musical Heritage Remembered*, London: The History Press, 2013.

12—Christopher Scapelliti, "The Key to Peter Green's 'Magic' 1959 Les Paul Tone," *Guitar Player*, November 2020, https://www.guitarplayer.com/players/ the-key-to-peter-greens-magic-1959-les-paul-tone.

13—Olivier Roubin, "Le blues dans la peau," interview with Gary Moore, *GuitarPart* (France), no. 85, April 2021.

14—Johnny Black, "Sound Your Funky Horn: Mick Fleetwood," *Mojo* (UK), December 1995.

15—Bill Wasserzieher, "Fleetwood Mac: The Return of Jeremy Spencer," *Blues Revue Magazine*, October–November 2006.

16—Matt Frost, "Mike Vernon: Producing British Blues," *Sound on Sound*, December 2010, https://www.soundonsound.com/people/ mike-vernon-producing-british-blues.

17—Ryan Reed, *Fleetwood Mac FAQ: All That's Left to Know About the Iconic Rock Survivors*, Lanham, MD: Backbeat, October 2018.

18—Norman Jopling, "Peter Green—The Guitarist Who Won't Forsake the Blues," *Record Mirror* (UK), August 19, 1967.

19—Dave Rybaczewski, "'Sun King' History," Beatles Music History, http:// www.beatlesebooks.com/sun-king.

20—"Fleetwood Mac to Put Christ on Wax," *Rolling Stone*, July 12, 1969, https:// www.rollingstone.com/music/music-news/ fleetwood-mac-to-put-christ-on-wax-236778/.

21—Martin Celmins, *Peter Green: The Biography*, Chessington, UK: Castle Communications, 1995.

22—Ian Middleton, "Fleetwood Mac from America…," *Record Mirror* (UK), January 4, 1969.

23—Henry Yates, "Then Play On: The Story of Fleetwood Mac Guitarist Danny Kirwan," *Guitarist*, October 24, 2018.

24—Ben Fisher, "Green God Breaks His Silence," *Guitar Player*, November 1994.

25—Steve Clarke, *Fleetwood Mac*, New York: Proteus Books, 1984.

26—Mat Snow, "Debauchery! How Fleetwood Mac Survived It," *Q* (May 1990), www.fleetwoodmac-uk. com/articles/archive/FMart_arc011.html.

27—Henry Yates, "Mick Fleetwood Interview: 50 Years of Fleetwood Mac," *Classic Rock*, March 18, 2021, www.loudersound.com/features/ mick-fleetwood-interview-50-years-of-fleetwood-mac.

28—Craig Rosen, "'Fleetwood Mac in Chicago': Just a Bunch of Kids from England Who Loved to Play the Blues," *Billboard*, May 14, 1994.

29—Steve Clark, "The Day God Saved Jeremy Spencer," *New Musical Express*, October 5, 1974.

30—Nick Logan, "Fleetwood Ready to Fight for Fame Again in America," *New Musical Express*, December 6, 1969.

31—Tom Taylor, "The Night That Fleetwood Mac Lost Peter Green and Danny Kirwan to Acid," *Far Out*, August 10, 2022, faroutmagazine.co.uk/fleetwood-mac-lost-peter-green-and-danny-kirwan-to-acid.

32—Andrew Darlington, *I Was Elvis Presley's Bastard Love-Child & Other Stories of Rock'n'Roll Excess*, Manchester, UK: Headpress, 2001.

33—Pander Green, "The Original Fleetwood Mac," 1971.

34—Samuel Graham, *Fleetwood Mac: The Authorized History*, New York: Warner Books, 1978.

35—Lloyd Grossman, "Future Games" album review, *Rolling Stone*, December 9, 1971, https://www.rollingstone.com/music/ music-album-reviews/future-games-197709/.

36—Nigel Williamson, "Fleetwood Mac: 'Everybody Was Pretty Weirded Out'—The Story of Rumours," *Uncut*, May 2003, https://www.uncut.co.uk/ features/fleetwood-mac-everybody-was-pretty-weirded-out-the-story-of-rumours-26395/.

37—Stephen Deusner, "Go Your Own Way," *Uncut*, May 2017.

38—Andy Greene, "Lindsey Buckingham Talks Fleetwood Mac Tour, New EP," *Rolling Stone*, May 7, 2013, https://www.rollingstone. com/music/music-news/lindsey-buckingham-talks-fleetwood-mac-tour-new-ep-92203/.

39—Brian Hiatt, "Stevie Nicks: A Rock Goddess Looks Back," *Rolling Stone*, January 29, 2015, https://www.rollingstone.com/music/music-news/ stevie-nicks-a-rock-goddess-looks-back-179984/.

40—Andy Greene, "Christine McVie on Her New Solo Collection 'Songbird,' Uncertain Future of Fleetwood Mac," *Rolling Stone*, June 16, 2022, https://www. rollingstone.com/music/music-news/christine-solo-collection-songbird-fleetwood-mac-1368670/.

41—"Stevie Nicks Remembers Former Fleetwood Mac Guitarist Bob Welch," *CBS This Morning*, July 11, 2012, https://www. youtube.com/watch?v=diXf-FuGzII.

42—"Pop Think In with Danny Kirwan of Fleetwood Mac," *Melody Maker*, 1969.

43—Garth Pearce, "Mum's the Word," *The Sun*, December 1, 2022, https://www. thesun.co.uk/tvandshowbiz/20620839/ fleetwood-mac-christine-mcvie-motherhood/.

44—Jenny Boyd, *Jennifer Juniper: A Journey Beyond the Muse*, Romsey, UK: Urbane Publications, 2020.

45—Chris Charlesworth, "There's No Reason Why We Shouldn't Stay Together for a Long While," *Melody Maker*, October 28, 1972.

46—"Q&A Sessions: Dave Walker: October 12–25, 2000," FleetwoodMac.net, http://www. fleetwoodmac.net/fwm/index.php?option=com_ content&task=view&id=119&Itemid=138.

47—"Q&A Sessions: Bob Welch: November 8–21, 1999," www.FleetwoodMac.net.

48—"Q&A Sessions: Bob Weston: August 4–17, 2003)," FleetwoodMac.net/fwm/index.php?option=com_ content&task=view&id=110&Itemid=127.

49—"Q&A Sessions: Bob Welch: August 2003," www.FleetwoodMac.net.

50—Gordon Fletcher, "Mystery to Me," *Rolling Stone*, January 3, 1974.

51—"Q&A Sessions: John McVie: January 2006," www.FleetwoodMac.net.

52—Joe Bosso, "Mick Fleetwood: My 11 Greatest Recordings of All Time," *Music Radar*, July 27, 2012.

53—Loraine Alterman, "Fleetwood Mac Flak: Manager Takes Name, Not Members, on Tour," *Rolling Stone*, February 28, 1974.

54—Cameron Crowe, "The Real Fleetwood Mac Stands Up," *Rolling Stone*, November 7, 1974.

55—Robert Christgau, "Fleetwood Mac: Consumer Guide Reviews," review of *Penguin*, https://www.robertchristgau.com/ get_artist.php?name=Fleetwood+Mac.

56—Tony Stewart, album review, *New Musical Express*, May 26, 1973.

57—Iron Maiden (ironmaiden), "RIP Martin Birch (1948–2020)…," Instagram, August 10, 2020, https://www.instagram.com/p/CDuDZ5OCXe-/.

58—Bud Scoppa, album review, "Fleetwood Mac," *Rolling Stone*, September 25, 1975, https://www.rollingstone.com/music/ music-album-reviews/fleetwood-mac-98110/.

59—Corey Irwin, "The Call Lindsey Buckingham Made Before Joining Fleetwood Mac," *Ultimate Classic Rock*, August 24 2021, https:// ultimateclassicrock.com/lindsey-buckingham-call-waddy-wachtel-fleetwood-mac/.

60—Michael Goldberg, "Lindsey Buckingham, Lonely Guy," *Rolling Stone*, October 25, 1984, https://www.rollingstone.com/music/music-news/ lindsey-buckingham-lonely-guy-2-186895/.

61—Mat Snow, "Debauchery! How Fleetwood Mac Survived It," *Q*, May 1990, Go Your Own Way (website), https://www.fleetwoodmac-uk. com/articles/archive/FMart_arc011.html.

62—David Wild, "Lindsey Buckingham: Post-Mac Attack," *Rolling Stone*, June 25, 1992.

63—Jancee Dunn, "Q&A: Stevie Nicks on Comedy, Fan Gifts, and 'Star Trek,'" *Rolling Stone*, September 22, 1994, https://www.rollingstone.com/music/music-news/qa-stevie-nicks-on-comedy-fan-gifts-and-star-trek-193127/.

64—Stephen Rodrick, "Lindsey Buckingham Won't Stop," *Rolling Stone*, September 9, 2021, https://www.rollingstone.com/music/music-features/lindsey-buckingham-fleetwood-mac-stevie-nicks-new-album-1221755/.

65— Lindsey Buckingham (lindseybuckingham), "Christine McVie's sudden passing is profoundly heartbreaking…," Instagram, December 1, 2022, https://www.instagram.com/p/ClpH8Beu3Ko/.

66—Sandra Halliburton, *Read Between My Lines: The Musical and Life Journey of Stevie Nicks*, Dallas: SK Halliburton Enterprises, 2006.

67—Stevie Nicks in *The Meldrum Tapes*, interview conducted by Ian "Molly" Meldrum, ABC Australia and MTV, 1986.

68—Vicky Greenleaf and Stan Hyman, "Stevie Nicks: She's Smiling Now," *Rock Magazine*, October 1983.

69—Gary Graff, "Stevie Nicks Calls New Album 'My Own Little Rumours,'" *Billboard*, April 27, 2011, https://www.billboard.com/music/music-news/stevie-nicks-calls-new-album-my-own-little-rumours-471854/.

70—Christopher R. Weingarten, et al., "Fleetwood Mac's 50 Greatest Songs," *Rolling Stone*, May 2, 2022, https://www.rollingstone.com/music/music-lists/fleetwood-macs-50-greatest-songs-192324/monday-morning-115538/.

71—Gary Graff, "Fleetwood Mac Shares Early Version of 1975 Classic 'Monday Morning': Exclusive," *Billboard*, November 1, 2018, https://www.billboard.com/music/rock/fleetwood-mac-monday-morning-early-take-8093899/.

72—James McNair, "The Mojo Interview: Stevie Nicks," *Mojo* (UK), December 2013.

73—Zoë Howe, *Stevie Nicks: Visions, Dreams & Rumours*, New York: Overlook Omnibus, 2015.

74—"Q&A Sessions: Keith Olsen: May 8–21, 2000," FleetwoodMac.Net, http://www.fleetwoodmac.net/fwm/index.php?option=com_content&task=view&id=145&Itemid=165.

75—Dave Simpson, "Fleetwood Mac's Christine McVie: 'Cocaine and Champagne Made Me Perform Better,'" *Guardian*, June 9, 2022, https://www.theguardian.com/music/2022/jun/09/fleetwood-macs-christine-mcvie-cocaine-and-champagne-made-me-perform-better.

76—Steve Pond, "The US Interview: Stevie Nicks," *US* magazine, July 9, 1990.

77—Mick Fleetwood, in *Sound City*, directed by Dave Grohl, documentary, Roswell Films, 2013, video, 25:30, https://watch.plex.tv/movie/sound-city.

78—Ken Caillat and Steven Stiefel, *Making Rumours: The Inside Story of the Classic Fleetwood Mac Album*, Hoboken, NJ: John Wiley & Sons, Inc, 2012.

79—Robin Eggar, "Christine McVie, 2004 (supplement in *Sunday Express*), 2004, cited in Sean Egan, *Fleetwood Mac on Fleetwood Mac: Interviews and Encounters*, Chicago: Review Press Incorporated, 2016.

80—Ken Caillat, "20 Questions with…," *Vintage King*, June 2023, https://vintageking.com/blog/2023/06/20-questions-ken-caillat.

81—Sylvain Siclier, *Fleetwood Mac un mythe réédité*, in *Le Monde* (France), January 31, 2013.

82—Rick Springfield (rickspringfield), "My amazing and talented friend Keith Olsen has passed away. Such a gifted producer…," Instagram, March 9, 2020, https://www.instagram.com/p/B9iJsmDB8Gz/?hl=fr&img_index=.

83—Johnny Black, "The Greatest Songs Ever! Dreams," *Blender*, May 2005, https://web.archive.org/web/20061019141247/http://www.blender.com/guide/articles.aspx?id=1989.

84—Angie Martoccio, "Flashback: Fleetwood Mac Play a Poignant 'Dreams' in 1977," *Rolling Stone*, February 4, 2019, https://www.rollingstone.com/music/music-news/fleetwood-mac-rumours-dreams-live-1977-stevie-nicks-787722/.

85—Brian Hiatt, "'She Sings to Me Every Night,' Christine McVie on Her Friendship with Stevie Nicks," *Rolling Stone*, December 1, 2022, https://www.rollingstone.com/music/music-features/christine-mcvie-stevie-nicks-friendship-lost-interview-1234638946/.

86—John Swenson, 'Rumours' album review, *Rolling Stone*, April 21, 1977, https://www.rollingstone.com/music/music-album-reviews/rumours-189491/.

87—Sally Rayl, "Nation Gripped in Massive Fleetwood Mac Attack," *Creem*, July 1, 1977.

88—Allison Rapp, "Fleetwood Mac's 'Rumours': A Track-by-Track Guide," *Ultimate Classic Rock*, February 4, 2022, https://ultimateclassicrock.com/fleetwood-mac-rumours-track-by-track/.

89—Fred Schruers, "Fleetwood Mac: Back on the Chain Gang," *Rolling Stone*, October 30, 1997.

90—Jordan Runtagh, "Lindsey Buckingham and Christine McVie Talk New Duets Album, and the First Time Playing Together in Fleetwood Mac," *People*, June 22, 2017.

91—Joe Bosso, "Fleetwood Mac Rumours Track-by-Track with Co-producer Ken Caillat," *Music Radar*, December 13, 2022.

92—Roisin O'Connor, "My Voice Will Haunt You: The Story Behind Fleetwood Mac's Blistering 1997 'Silver Springs' Performance," interview with Stevie Nicks on the BBC from 1991 via *Independent*, March 15, 2023.

93—Brittany Spanos, "'Silver Springs': Inside Fleetwood Mac's Great Lost Breakup Anthem," *Rolling Stone*, August 18, 2017.

94—Christopher Connelly, "The Second Life of Don Henley," *GQ*, August 1991, archive.ph/Gk6sp.

95—"Blonde on Blonde," interview between Stevie Nicks and Courtney Love, *Spin*, October 1997.

96—"'Rumours' DVD Transcript," The Lindsey Buckingham Resource: Still Going Insane (website), https://www.fleetwoodmac-uk.com/stillgoinginsane_old/articles/200100.html.

97—*Q* interview, 1977.

98—"Stevie Nicks: Through the Looking Glass." Documentary, 2013.

99—Cameron Crowe, "The True Life Confessions of Fleetwood Mac: The Long Hard Drive from British Blues to California Gold," *Rolling Stone*, March 24, 1977.

100—Phil Sutcliffe, "Take It to the Limit," *Mojo* (UK), December 2003.

101—Nigel Williamson, "Fleetwood Mac: 'Everybody Was Pretty Sold Out'—The Story of Rumours," *Uncut*, June 29, 2013.

102—Dylan Jones, "Was Fleetwood Mac's Tusk the Greatest Self-Sabotage in Rock'n'Roll History?," *GQ*, August 9, 2020.

103—Blair Jackson, "Stevie Nicks—Fleetwood Mac's Siren Soars with Her First Solo Album, Bella Donna," *BAM Magazine*, September 11, 1981.

104—Jim Irvin, interview with Stevie Nicks, "We Want to Be Together," *Mojo* (UK), July 2015.

105—Lindsey Buckingham, Mick Fleetwood, Stevie Nicks, liner notes, *Tusk* (reissue), Warner Bros. Records, December 4, 2015, stevienicks.info/tusk-track-by-track/.

106—Jenny Stevens, "Stevie Nicks on Art, Ageing and Attraction: 'Botox Makes It Look Like You're in a Satanic Cult!,'" *Guardian*, October 14, 2020, www.theguardian.com/music/2020/oct/14/stevie-nicks-on-art-ageing-and-attraction-botox-makes-it-look-like-youre-in-a-satanic-cult.

107—Will Romano, "Let the Right Sounds In: Fleetwood Mac's Studio Genius Opens Up About His Off-Kilter Production Techniques," *Electronic Musician*, April 1, 2009.

108—Richard Dashut, quoted in "The Recording of Fleetwood Mac's Rumours": Memories of the Making of 'Rumours,'" The Lindsey Buckingham Resource: Still Going Insane (website): https://www.fleetwoodmac-uk.com/stillgoinginsane_old/articles/197700.html.

109—Craig McLean, "Fleetwood Mac: The Superstars," *Q* magazine, June 2009, scans available in "Fleetwood Mac—June Q Magazine Interview (Scans)," Fleetwood Mac News, June 3, 2009, https://www.fleetwoodmacnews.com/search/label/Q%20Magazine.

110—Stevie Nicks, *The Making of Rumours* (VH1 video), 1997.

111—Carol Ann Harris, *Storms: My Life with Lindsey Buckingham and Fleetwood Mac*, Chicago: Chicago Review Press, 2007.

112—Adrian Deevoy, "You Make Fighting Fun," *Daily Mail*, December 28, 2013, stevienicks.info/2013/12/you-make-fighting-fun/.

113—Richard Bienstock, "Christine McVie on Fleetwood Mac's 'Peculiar' 'Mirage' Sessions," *Rolling Stone*, September 26, 2016.

114—Peter Blackstock, "Fleetwood Mac: Going Long with Lindsey Buckingham," *Austin American-Statesman*, October 12, 2016, https://www.statesman.com/story/entertainment/music/2016/10/12/fleetwood-mac-going-long-with-lindsey-buckingham/10208399007/.

115—Nick Hasted, "Drugs, Alcohol and Goofing Around: The Making of Fleetwood Mac's Mirage," *Classic Rock*, June 23, 2022, https://www.loudersound.com/features/fleetwood-macs-mirage-the-making-of.

116—Rob Tannenbaum, "Stevie Nicks Admits Past Pregnancy with Don Henley and More About Her Wild History," *Billboard*, September 26, 2014, www.billboard.com/music/music-news/stevie-nicks-interview-on-don-henley-fleetwood-mac-24-karat-gold-album-6266329/.

INDEX

Album and song titles are in bold.

PHOTO CREDITS

About the Authors

ROMUALD OLLIVIER is a musician, singer, radio host, broadcaster, journalist, and author. He was editor-in-chief of several French music magazines from 2003 to 2018, including *Guitar Part, Guitar Book,* and *Rock First,* and deputy editor-in-chief of *Rolling Stone*; he has conducted hundreds of interviews and written hundreds of articles. He has co-written numerous books on the guitar, various artists, and the history of rock, including *Elton John All the Songs* in 2022.

OLIVIER ROUBIN is a musician, record producer, radio host, broadcaster, journalist, and author. He was editorial director of several French music magazines from 1998 to 2018, including *Guitar Part* and *Rock First,* and deputy editor-in-chief of *Rolling Stone*. He has also conducted a large number of interviews and written many articles and artist biographies and has co-written books devoted to the guitar, music production, and the history of rock, including *Elton John All the Songs* in 2022.

Copyright © 2025, Éditions E/P/A—Hachette Livre
Translation copyright © 2025 by Black Dog and Leventhal Publishers

Translation by Caroline Higgitt and Paul Ratcliffe by arrangement with Jackie Dobbyne of Jacaranda Publishing Services Limited

Cover design by Katie Benezra
Cover copyright © 2025 by Hachette Book Group, Inc.

Original title: Fleetwood Mac, *La Totale*
Published by Éditions E/P/A—Hachette Livre, 2025

Black Dog & Leventhal Publishers
Hachette Book Group
1290 Avenue of the Americas
New York, NY 10104
www.blackdogandleventhal.com
BlackDogandLeventhal @BDLev

First English-Language Edition: April 2025
Black Dog & Leventhal Publishers is an imprint of Perseus Books, LLC, a subsidiary of Hachette Book Group, Inc. The Black Dog & Leventhal Publishers name and logo are trademarks of Hachette Book Group, Inc.

The publisher is not responsible for websites (or their content) that are not owned by the publisher. The Hachette Speakers Bureau provides a wide range of authors for speaking events. To find out more, go to www.HachetteSpeakersBureau.com or call (866) 376-6591.

The Hachette Speakers Bureau provides a wide range of authors for speaking events. To find out more, go to www.hachettespeakersbureau.com or email HachetteSpeakers@hbgusa.com.

Black Dog & Leventhal books may be purchased in bulk for business, educational, or promotional use. For more information, please contact your local bookseller or the Hachette Book Group Special Markets Department at Special.Markets@hbgusa.com.

LCCN: 2023945350

ISBNs: 978-0-7624-8630 4 (hardcover), 978-0-7624-8631-1 (ebook)

Printed in China

10 9 8 7 6 5 4 3 2 1